The Elgar Companion to the Chicago School of Economics

Edited by

Ross B. Emmett

James Madison College, Michigan State University, USA

Edward Elgar
Cheltenham, UK • Northampton, MA, USA

Published by
Edward Elgar Publishing Limited
The Lypiatts
15 Lansdown Road
Cheltenham
Glos GL50 2JA
UK

Edward Elgar Publishing, Inc.
William Pratt House
9 Dewey Court
Northampton
Massachusetts 01060
USA

A catalogue record for this book
is available from the British Library

Library of Congress Control Number: 2009941413

FSC
Mixed Sources
Product group from well-managed forests and other controlled sources
www.fsc.org Cert no. SA-COC-1565
© 1996 Forest Stewardship Council

ISBN 978 1 84064 874 4 (cased)

Printed and bound by MPG Books Group, UK

Contents

PART II SOME CHICAGO ECONOMISTS

Contributors

Orley Ashenfelter is the Joseph Douglas Green 1895 Professor of Economics at Princeton University. He is a recipient of the IZA Prize in Labor Economics, the Ragnar Frisch Medal of the Econometric Society, and the Jacob Mincer Lifetime Achievement award of the Society of Labor Economists. He has been President of the American Law and Economics Association and the Society of Labor Economics and he is currently President-elect of the American Economic Association.

H. Spencer Banzhaf is Associate Professor of Economics at the Andrew Young School of Policy Studies, Georgia State University. He is also a Faculty Research Fellow at the National Bureau of Economic Research (NBER) and a Senior Research Fellow at the Property and Environment Research Center (PERC). His research focuses on environmental economics and the history of applied economics.

William J. Barber is the Andrews Professor of Economics, Emeritus at Wesleyan University, Middletown, Connecticut. In three of his publications, he has made archival contact with members of the Chicago School: *From New to New Deal: Herbert Hoover, the Economists, and American Economic Policy, 1921–1933* (1985); *Designs Within Disorder: Franklin D. Roosevelt, the Economists, and the Shaping of Economic Policy, 1933–1945* (1996); and in *The Works of Irving Fisher* (1997), which he edited in 14 volumes.

Daniel K. Benjamin is the Alumni Distinguished Professor of Economics at Clemson University, and Senior Fellow at the Property and Environment Research Center in Bozeman, Montana.

Jeff E. Biddle is Professor of Economics at Michigan State University. He received his PhD from Duke University in 1985. His research in the history of economic thought has focused on twentieth-century American economics. He is also an editor of *Research in the History of Economic Thought and Methodology*.

Gordon L. Brady is a senior economist with the Joint Economic Committee of the US Senate. He received his PhD in economics from Virginia Tech in 1976 and has held numerous academic and government positions.

Glen G. Cain is Emeritus Professor of Economics at the University of Wisconsin. A labor economist, he received his PhD from the University of Chicago in 1964.

Ross B. Emmett is Professor of Political Economy and Political Theory and Constitutional Democracy at James Madison College, Michigan State University. He recently published a collection of his essays as *Frank Knight and the Chicago School in American Economics* (2009) and is currently working on a book about the history of Chicago economics. He is the lead editor for *Research in the History of Economic Thought and Methodology*, and has edited the two-volume *Selected Essays of Frank H. Knight* (1999) and the eight-volume *Chicago Tradition in Economics, 1892–1946* (2001).

Evelyn Forget is Professor of Economics in the Faculty of Medicine at the University of Manitoba, Canada. Recent publications include *Economists' Lives: Biography and Autobiography in the History of Economics* (edited with E. Roy Weintraub, 2008), *The Social Economics of Jean-Baptiste Say*, 1999 and *A Biographical Dictionary of Women Economists* (edited with M.A. Dimand and R.W. Dimand, 2000).

Morley Gunderson holds the CIBC Chair in Youth Employment at the University of Toronto and is a Fellow of the Royal Society of Canada. He is a Professor at the Centre for Industrial Relations and Human Resources (Director from 1985 to 1997) and the Department of Economics. In 2002, he was awarded the Industrial Relations Research Association Excellence in Education Award in Labor Economics and in 2003 the Gérard Dion Award for Outstanding Contributions to the Field of Industrial Relations.

J. Daniel Hammond is Hultquist Family Professor, Department of Economics, Wake Forest University. He was President of the History of Economics Society in 2001–02. His publications on the Chicago School include *Theory and Measurement: Causality Issues in Milton Friedman's Monetary Economics* (1996) and *Making Chicago Price Theory: Friedman–Stigler Correspondence, 1945–1957* (with Claire H. Hammond, 2006).

D. Wade Hands is Distinguished Professor of Economics at the University of Puget Sound in Tacoma, WA. He has written on a number of topics in the history and philosophy of economics. He is currently co-editor of *the Journal of Economic Methodology*. He is the author of *Reflection Without Rules: Economic Methodology and Contemporary Science Theory* (2001), and edited with Philip Mirowski *Agreement on Demand: Consumer Choice Theory in the 20th Century* (2006).

Sherryl D. Kasper is Professor of Economics at Maryville College, Maryville, Tennessee and the author of *The Revival of Laissez Faire: A Case Study of its Pioneers* (2002). She is currently researching the role of economists as public intellectuals.

Bruce E. Kaufman is Professor of Economics at Georgia State University. He publishes in labor economics, industrial relations, human resource management and the history of thought. His latest book is *Managing the Human Factor: The Early Years of Human Resource Management in American Industry* (2008).

David Laidler is Professor Emeritus of Economics at the University of Western Ontario, and a Fellow in Residence at the C.D. Howe Institute in Toronto. A specialist in monetary economics and its history, his most recent books include *Fabricating the Keynesian Revolution* (1999) and two volumes of his collected essays: *Money and Macroeconomics* (1999) and *Macroeconomics in Retrospect* (2004).

Hao Li is Professor of Economics at the University of Toronto. Li graduated from the University of Chicago in 1995 with Sherwin Rosen on his PhD dissertation committee. He continued to write joint papers with Rosen and visit him at Chicago and at Hoover until Rosen's untimely death in 2001. In 2006, the Canadian Economics Association awarded him the John Rae Prize for the best research record among Canadian economists over the previous five years.

Steven G. Medema is Professor of Economics and President's Teaching Scholar at the

University of Colorado Denver. He is the author of *The Hesitant Hand: Taming Self-Interest in the History of Economic Ideas* (2009), *Economics and the Law: From Posner to Post Modernism and Beyond* (with Nicholas Mercuro; 2nd edition, 2006), and *Ronald H. Coase* (1994). He served as editor of the *Journal of the History of Economic Thought* from 1999 to 2008.

Philip Mirowski is Carl Koch Chair of Economics and the History and Philosophy of Science, and Fellow of the Reilly Center, University of Notre Dame. He is author of, among others, *Machine Dreams* (2002), *The Effortless Economy of Science?* (2004), *More Heat than Light* (1989), and the forthcoming *ScienceMart™: A Primer on the New Economics of Science*. He has edited a book with Wade Hands on a history of the theory of demand theory in the twentieth century called *Agreement on Demand* (2006), and with Dieter Plehwe on the history of the rise of neoliberal doctrines, *The Road from Mont Pèlerin: The Making of the Neoliberal Thought Collective* (2009).

David Mitch is Professor of Economics at the University of Maryland, Baltimore County where he teaches economic history. He received his BA, MA, and PhD degrees, all in economics, from the University of Chicago.

Edward Nik-Khah is Associate Professor of Economics at Roanoke College, Virginia. He received his PhD from Notre Dame. 'A tale of two auctions' (*Journal of Institutional Economics*, 2008) won him the K. William Kapp prize for best article from the European Association for Evolutionary Political Economy. His current research focuses on George Stigler's role in building the foundations for Chicago economics.

John Pencavel is the Pauline K. Levin–Robert L. Levin and Pauline C. Levin–Abraham Levin Professor in the Department of Economics at Stanford University. He received his education at schools in London, at University College London, and at Princeton University. He served as editor of the *Journal of Economic Literature* from 1986 to 1998 and was President of the Society of Labor Economists in 2005–06.

Hugh Rockoff is Professor of Economics at Rutgers University, the State University of New Jersey, and a Research Associate of the National Bureau of Economic Research. His main academic interests are the financial and monetary history of the United States, especially during wartime.

Malcolm Rutherford is Professor of Economics at the University of Victoria, BC, Canada. He has published widely on the history of American institutional economics in the *History of Political Economy*, the *Journal of the History of Economic Thought*, the *Journal of Economic Perspectives* and the *European Journal of the History of Economic Thought*. He is the author of *Institutions in Economics: The Old and the New Institutionalism* (Cambridge University Press, 1994).

Eric Schliesser is BOF Research Professor in Philosophy and Moral Sciences at Ghent University. He publishes on Spinoza, Huygens, Newton, David Hume, Adam Smith, Milton Friedman, George Stigler, Warren Nutter, and Vernon Smith among others. He co-edited *New Voices on Adam Smith* (Routledge, 2006) and *Interpreting Newton* (Cambridge, in press). He will publish *Adam Smith* in the Routledge Philosophers series. He is currently working on a book, *The Rise and Fall of Chicago Economics, 1937–1976*.

Pedro Nuno Teixeira is Associate Professor in the Faculty of Economics, University of Porto and Director of CIPES – the Center for Higher Education Policy Studies (Portugal). His research interests focus on the economics of higher education and the history of economic thought, notably the historical development of human capital theory. He has published in several higher education and economic journals and is the author of *Jacob Mincer: A Founding Father of Modern Labour Economics* (2007), which won the prize of best book by the European Society of History of Economic Thought. He has also co-edited the volumes *Markets in Higher Education: Reality or Rhetoric?* (2004) and *Cost-Sharing and Accessibility in Higher Education: A Fairer Deal?* (2006).

Robert Van Horn is Assistant Professor of Economics at the University of Rhode Island. He is currently doing research on the history of the Chicago School of Antitrust. He received his PhD from Notre Dame in 2007 and was a postdoctoral fellow at the Duke University Center for the History of Political Economy (2008–09). He is editing, along with Philip Mirowski and Thomas Stapleford, a forthcoming book on the history of the Chicago School entitled *Building Chicago Economics*.

Stephen T. Ziliak is currently Trustee Professor of Economics at Roosevelt University. At the University of Iowa he earned a PhD Certificate in the Rhetoric of the Human Sciences simultaneous with his PhD in Economics (1996). He has co-authored three books and many articles with Deirdre N. McCloskey. Their most recent book is *The Cult of Statistical Significance* (2008) and they are currently working on *The Economic Conversation*, a textbook, co-authored with Arjo Klamer.

Preface

Edward Elgar proposed that I undertake a companion to the Chicago School several times in the late 1990s, and I finally took up the task almost ten years ago. The scope of the project, therefore, was framed in the early part of this decade. Given the recent renewed interest in the Chicago School, especially with regard to the role its ideas may have played in shaping the financial sectors' and the public's appreciation for financial market regulation, the volume will help to provide a historical perspective on the School's earlier incarnations.

The authors of the essays and biographies included here have been patient with my slow accumulation of materials and the delays resulting from my move from western Canada to Michigan in the last few years. I am glad that their work is finally appearing and thank them for their patience.

Several people have helped move this project to completion. First and foremost, my wife Kim encouraged me to stay with it and finish. Malcolm Rutherford, Steve Medema and Jeff Biddle played an early role in suggesting contributors. A couple of sessions organized by the History of Economics Society at the Society's annual meeting and the ASSA meetings included contributors to this volume. Phil Mirowski and Rob Van Horn organized a conference in 2007 at Notre Dame on the Chicago School, at which I met a couple of the more recent contributors to the volume. Finally, the text itself was proofread and rendered by several of my students: Brett Staron, Alan Bart, Laura Kovacek, Matt Stuart and Rachel Penn.

Ross B. Emmett

Introduction

Ross B. Emmett

The University of Chicago has been identified with a unique brand of economic thinking for at least half a century. The essays in this volume discuss various dimensions of the nature, development, and extensions of the Chicago brand, often known as the Chicago School of Economics. The term 'School' is used here in a 'positive' sense; to indicate that a common set of assumptions – methodological and theoretical – about the discipline was developed by the economists at the University of Chicago, who sought through their teaching and research to enrich, extend and promote their vision of economic science. In this sense, one could speak equally of a Chicago School, a Cambridge (UK) School, a Wisconsin School, perhaps even a Cambridge (MA) School, with each of these schools (perhaps at different times in the twentieth century) adopting different methodological and theoretical assumptions and promoting a different perspective of economic science.

In the popular literature, most discussion of the Chicago School is focused on its 'normative' or 'ideological' character. Chicago in this context is primarily known as a promoter of *laissez-faire*, of market-based solutions to public policy problems, and for its connections to the Reagan, Thatcher and even Pinochet governments (for a variety of views, see Klein 2007, Van Overtveldt 2007, Freedman 2008, Shleifer 2009). In contrast to some of the other schools of economics mentioned above, the Chicago School understood economics to be an applied policy science, and, with some exceptions, have not been afraid to suggest that their scientific findings had relevance to policy debate. The essays included here often show the interconnections between the Chicago School's methodology, its theory, and its policy advocacy and advice. However, the translation of economic science into public policy may yield surprises, and it is misleading to try to move from the normative or ideological back to the scientific in explaining a social scientific school of thought. For example, President Barack Obama has sometimes been identified as a 'Chicago School' Democrat (Leonhardt 2008). Ultimately, the question is whether the Chicago School's policy framework is driven by the effort to understand how the working of the price system in free markets may affect a particular policy situation, or whether the theoretical understanding of the price system in free markets is driven by the attempt to defend a particular policy framework. Evidence for both views is provided in the volume, although the balance is probably tipped toward the first answer to the question rather than the second.

What, then, is the approach to economics as a policy science that forms the positive foundation for the Chicago School? The approach can be examined from methodological, theoretical, and organizational points of view. Each of the three views reveals a different facet of Chicago economics. From a methodological perspective, the Chicago School is grounded in the combination of two assumptions found in its two most famous methodological articles. Milton Friedman's 'The methodology of positive economics' (Friedman 1953) claimed that progress in economics as a policy science can be significantly furthered by the use of a toolkit of basic models that require little additional theoretical work. Graduate study at Chicago became a process of immersion in those models so that they became so intuitive to one's work that, in combination with new empirical investigation, they opened the door to novel evaluations of market organization and government policy. The other methodological foundation for Chicago economics was codified twenty years later (although it had become standard practice at Chicago much earlier) in the article 'De gustibus non est disputandum' (Stigler and Becker 1977). Friedman's two colleagues pointed out that an economic policy science must assume that tastes and preferences are universally the same in order to usefully claim that economic phenomena can be explained in terms of changes in the cost sets that decision makers face. Science is not advanced by an explanation that ends with 'A's tastes are different from B's tastes', or that 'A's tastes changed'. The combination of the two assumptions has allowed Chicago economists not only to provide policy-relevant models for market phenomena, but also to expand the realm of social interaction that those models can be used to explain, often to areas previously considered outside the scope of economic theory (see, for examples, Becker 1996, Becker and Murphy 2000, Levitt and Dubner 2005). Frequently referred to even by insiders as 'economic imperialism' (Lazear 2000) this expansion is probably the most significant theoretical development in Chicago economics over the past thirty years, and was made possible by the methodological foundations built during the previous thirty years (see Medema 1998, 2000).

In terms of economic theory, Chicago economics in the post-war period was built on a firm foundation of Marshallian price theory. The Chicago 'canon', which students were often expected to become familiar with during their early price theory courses, was Marshall (1920), Knight (1921, 1933, 1936), Viner (1931), Friedman (1962), Stigler (1966), and Simons (2002). By the 1980s, students had added Alchian and Allen (1969), Becker (1971), and McCloskey (1985). With its clear focus on economics as an applied policy science, Marshallian price theory provided a small set of tools for use in a wide variety of policy areas to examine the outcomes of specific types of interventions. Because Chicago has largely avoided the analytical side trips that the rest of the discipline often engaged in during the post-war period, its economists were able to combine a rich understanding of the insights of price theory with a deepening understanding of empirical data to provide policy-relevant theoretical insights into many of the disciplinary subfields.

In fact, the combination of Chicago's theoretical and methodological insights redefined the nature of the disciplinary subfields. Prior to the 1940s, the fields differed substantively in their approaches to their study because they focused on the nature of the institutions and participants in the industries they studied. Economic theory, *per se*, was of little relevance, many argued, because it treated markets in the abstract, while most of the work of economists lay in the specifics of the markets in a particular industry or segment of the economy. Of what use, argued the institutionalists and others, was economic theory to, say, labor economics or transportation economics; fields in which the nature of the subject was far removed from the abstract model of perfect competition. While Chicago economists were not the only ones who challenged this argument, their work in showing the relevance of price theory to the empirical investigation of outcomes in labor markets and even transportation markets rewrote the discipline's approach to the relation of theory and actual societal outcomes. Rather than being a department in which a group of scholars all studied aspects of economic life, post-war Chicago economics became a scholarly group who used a common economic approach to analyze all aspects of life.

Central to the development of that common economic approach was the integration of the Chicago School's research and teaching missions. From the mid-1950s on, Chicago adopted an organizational framework that focused all members of the department – students, junior faculty and senior faculty alike – on the common mission of training economic scientists and advancing economics as an applied policy science. The framework created to meet this common mission is sometimes known as the 'workshop model' (Emmett 2007). Several of the essays mention the Chicago workshops in the process of discussing the development of the Chicago approach in particular subfields of economics: labor, money and banking, industrial organization, agricultural economics, public finance, international economics, economic history, law and economics, and the economic development of Latin America. By 1980, there were about 18 workshops functioning across the Economics Department, the Law School, the Business School, and the Committee on Public Policy Studies (which was to become in 1990 the Harris School of Public Policy Studies).

If the preceding identification of the Chicago School is correct, then the School is largely a post-war phenomenon. Melvin Reder (1982) and others (Bronfenbrenner 1962, Miller 1962) have argued that the post-war Chicago School is largely a continuation of the circle of scholars that gathered around Knight in the 1930s. Several essays in the volume examine the issue of continuity as they examine specific aspects of Chicago economics from the 1930s to the 1980s, and there are biographies of several key figures from the 1930s. However, while continuous elements are found (the 'Chicago' canon, after all, directs our attention to several pre-war contributions), the identification of economics as a policy science, and the creation of the workshop system that entrenched that understanding of economics in both teaching and research, make it clear that Chicago economics in the post-war period is a 'school of thought' in a way that the 'Knight circle' could only aspire to (for earlier versions of this argument, see Stigler 1962, Samuels 1976).

Not all the dimensions of the Chicago School are covered in this volume. While the lack of total coverage is unfortunate – efforts were made to obtain essays on international trade, household economics, and the role of the Cowles Commission at Chicago during the 1940s and early 1950s, for example – the essays included here provide ample evidence of the range and coherence of the Chicago approach. They also include some indication of the influence Chicago had on the broader discipline, not only in the essays on particular aspects of the Chicago tradition, but also through a couple of essays on people (Armen Alchian) or places (UCLA and the various Virginia universities at which James Buchanan and the Center for the Study of Public Choice have resided over the past 50 years) which interacted with Chicago in ways that both extended and challenged the Chicago perspective. Several of the essays also address the broader reach of Chicago economics as well as pointing toward new areas of research on the Chicago School: its relation to the development of neoliberalism and economic development in Latin America. Taken as a whole, the essays in the volume both survey the state of current knowledge about the Chicago School and suggest that much further research is required.

References

Alchian, A.A. and W.R. Allen (1969), *Exchange and Production: Theory in Use*, Belmont, CA: Wadsworth.
Becker, G.S. (1971), *Economic Theory*, New York: Alfred Knopf.
Becker, G.S. (1996), *Accounting for Tastes*, Cambridge, MA: Harvard University Press.
Becker, G.S. and K.M. Murphy (2000), *Social Economics: Market Behavior in a Social Environment*, Cambridge, MA: Belknap Press.
Bronfenbrenner, M. (1962), 'Observation on the "Chicago School(s)"', *Journal of Political Economy*, **70** (1), 72–5.
Emmett, R.B. (2007), 'Sharpening tools in the workshop: the workshop system and the Chicago School's success', paper presented at the Re-visiting the Chicago School of Economics conference, University of Notre Dame, September, available at: http://ssrn.com/abstract=1014015.
Freedman, C.F. (2008), *Chicago Fundamentalism: Ideology and Methodology in Economics*, Singapore: World Scientific.
Friedman, M. (1953), 'The methodology of positive economics', in *Essays in Positive Economics*, Chicago, IL: University of Chicago Press, pp. 3–43.
Friedman, M. (1962), *Price Theory: A Provisional Text*, Chicago, IL: Aldine.
Klein, N. (2007), *The Shock Doctrine: The Rise of Disaster Capitalism*, New York: Metropolitan Books.
Knight, F.H. (1921), *Risk, Uncertainty and Profit*, Boston, MA: Houghton Mifflin.
Knight, F.H. (1933), *The Economic Organization*, Chicago, IL: University of Chicago.
Knight, F.H. (1936), *Notes on Utility and Cost*, Chicago, IL: University of Chicago Press.
Lazear, E.P. (2000), 'Economic imperialism', *Quarterly Journal of Economics*, **115** (1), 99–146.
Leonhardt, D. (2008), 'Obamanomics', *New York Times Magazine*, August 24.
Levitt, S.D. and S.J. Dubner (2005), *Freakonomics: A Rogue Economist Explains Everything*, New York: William Morrow.
Marshall, A. (1920), *Principles of Economics*, 8th edn, London: Macmillan.
McCloskey, D.N. (1985), *The Applied Theory of Price*, 2nd edn, New York: Macmillan.
Medema, S.G. (1998), 'The trial of *homo economicus*: what law and economics tells us about the development of economic imperialism', in *New Economics and Its History*, Davis, J.B. (ed.), Durham, NC: Duke University Press, pp. 122–42.
Medema, S.G. (2000), "Related disciplines: the professionalization of public choice analysis', in *Toward a History of Applied Economics*, Backhouse, R.E. and J.E. Biddle (eds), Durham, NC: Duke University Press, pp. 289–323.
Miller, H.L., Jr. (1962), 'On the "Chicago School of Economics"', *Journal of Political Economy*, **70** (1), 64–9.
Reder, M.W. (1982), 'Chicago economics: permanence and change', *Journal of Economic Literature*, **20** (1), 1–38.
Samuels, W.J. (ed.) (1976), *The Chicago School of Political Economy*, East Lansing, MI: Association for Evolutionary Economics and Division of Research, Graduate School of Business Administration, Michigan State University.
Shleifer, A. (2009), 'The age of Friedman', *Journal of Economic Literature*, **47** (1), 123–35.
Simons, H.C. (2002), 'The Simons' syllabus', in *The Chicago Tradition in Economics, 1892–1945*, 8, Emmett, R.B. (ed.), London: Routledge, pp. 3–70.
Stigler, G.J. (1962), 'On the "Chicago School of Economics": comment', *Journal of Political Economy*, **70** (1), 70–71.
Stigler, G.J. (1966), *The Theory of Price*, 3rd edn, New York: Macmillan.
Stigler, G.J. and G.S. Becker (1977), 'De gustibus non est disputandum', *American Economic Review*, **67** (2), 76–90.
Van Overtveldt, J. (2007), *The Chicago School: How the University of Chicago Assembled the Thinkers Who Revolutionized Economics and Business*, Chicago, IL: Agate.
Viner, J. (1931), 'Cost curves and supply curves', *Zeitschrift für Nationalökonomie*, **3**, 23–46.

PART I

ESSAYS ON THE CHICAGO SCHOOL

1 The development of post-war Chicago price theory

J. Daniel Hammond

Introduction

Within a short time after the end of the Second World War the University of Chicago economics faculty was transformed. Jacob Viner, who along with Frank H. Knight personified Chicago price theory from the 1920s through the war years, decamped for Princeton. Though Knight remained at Chicago, he was less involved in the department's graduate program than he had been before the war. Henry Schultz, who brought his pioneering work on empirical estimation of demand to Chicago in 1926, died in an automobile accident in 1938. The native Pole, Oscar Lange, replaced Schultz teaching economic theory and mathematical economics, but in 1945 Lange was named Polish Ambassador to the United States and departed Chicago. Henry Simons died in June 1946. Paul Douglas, famous for the Cobb–Douglas production function, took leave from the university to join the Marine Corps during the war and afterwards withdrew from teaching and research to take up a political career.

These people were replaced by a cast of new faces. Theodore Schultz and D. Gale Johnson arrived from Iowa State in 1943 and 1944. Jacob Marschak came to Chicago when the Cowles Commission moved there from Colorado Springs in 1943. He recruited Tjalling Koopmans in 1944. Both had appointments in the Economics Department in addition to Cowles. Marschak was Director of the Cowles Commission from his arrival until 1948 when Koopmans replaced him.[1] H. Gregg Lewis was a graduate student when Henry Schultz died in 1938. When Lange was brought in to teach economic theory, Lewis was given the statistics and econometrics courses formerly taught by Schultz. After wartime interruptions to his teaching and dissertation research, Lewis received his PhD in 1947.

Among the new faces on the post-war Chicago economics faculty was Milton Friedman. In the spring of 1946 Friedman was hired to replace Jacob Viner as the department's price theorist. He began teaching in the next autumn quarter. The position came to Friedman after the department's choice as Viner's replacement, Friedman's officemate at the University of Minnesota, George J. Stigler, was vetoed by the university president.[2] Friedman and Stigler had both been at Chicago as graduate students, Friedman in 1932–33 and 1934–35. His training under Viner, Schultz and Knight provided a basis for the price theory courses he taught there from 1946 until 1964, and from 1972 until his retirement from classroom teaching in 1976.

Milton Friedman

When Friedman joined the faculty in 1946 there was a two-quarter price theory sequence, Economics 300A and 300B. Frank Knight still taught 301, the course Friedman took in 1932, but this no longer provided the instruction in price theory for PhD students. Economics 300A was devoted to the theory of price determination from a partial equilibrium approach. This theme continued into 300B, which also covered the theory of income and product distribution, capital theory, and general equilibrium.[3] Economics 300A and 300B, renumbered as 301 and 302 in 1959, were the locus of Chicago price theory for close to two decades. This chapter is a history of Chicago price theory through this locus. This will not be an account of all price theory at Chicago. For one thing, the Cowles Commission economists at Chicago developed their own type of price theory, with distinctive features unlike the price theory taught by Friedman. When the term 'Chicago price theory' is used, the reference is usually to price theory as taught by Friedman, and this is they way we shall use the term. Our history of Chicago price theory will be centered on the background, content and influence of Friedman's graduate price theory course.

That George Stigler and not Friedman was the Economics Department's first choice to replace Jacob Viner is not surprising in light of their prior scholarly achievements in the field. Stigler had published his PhD dissertation, *Production and Distribution Theories* (Stigler 1941) and two editions of a price theory textbook (Stigler 1942, 1946). Nine of his ten journal articles up to 1946 also were on price theory. Friedman did not have as substantial a record of scholarship in price theory. He had published an article in the *Quarterly Journal of Economics* that criticized A.C. Pigou's method for deriving demand elasticity information from budgetary data (Friedman 1935), and a rejoinder (Friedman 1936) to Pigou's brief and dismissive reply: 'I do not wish to comment on – indeed I have not studied – the constructive part of Mr. Friedman's article' (Pigou 1936, p. 532). He helped Schultz (1935) with his article 'Interrelations of demand, price, and income' and with his book *The Theory and Measurement of Demand* (Schultz 1938). But Friedman's contributions to Schultz's project were not sufficient for the latter to offer co-authorship. Friedman had co-authored with W. Allen Wallis 'The empirical derivation of indifference functions' (1942), and with Simon Kuznets, *Income from Independent Professional Practice* (1945).

Much of Friedman's work through the decade prior to his being hired at Chicago was in statistics. After graduate study at Chicago and Columbia from 1932 to 1935, his first job was as an economist with the National Resources Committee in Washington, DC. His group at NRC had the task of designing survey questionnaires and survey schedules, developing sampling techniques and performing data tabulation and analysis for use in setting weights on cost of living indices. The experience led to Friedman's second job, at the National Bureau of Economic Research (NBER) in New York City, working with Simon Kuznets on estimates of national income and its distribution. From this work came the professional incomes study which served as Friedman's Columbia PhD dissertation (Friedman and Kuznets 1945). The most important theoretical outcome was the concept of permanent income. While he was working for the NBER, Friedman gained his first experience teaching economic theory. This was in the Columbia University Extension. He taught elementary economics in 1937 and 1938, and from fall semester 1938 through spring semester 1940 a graduate course, 'Structure of neo-classical economics'. The material, readings and lectures from this course later became the core of his Chicago price theory course.

In 1940 Friedman left New York to join the faculty of the University of Wisconsin as Lecturer in Statistics. It is telling of his professional identity at this point in his career that he was hired to revamp the Wisconsin statistics program. When he applied for the position, Friedman listed his graduate school fields as economic theory, statistics and mathematics (at Chicago) and economics and statistics (at Columbia). He listed 14 publications other than book reviews, with five in analytical statistics and four in theory and estimation of demand. Of his three projects underway at the time, one was the professional incomes study with Kuznets and two were in statistics with W. Allen Wallis. He did not revamp the Wisconsin statistics program because of an internal struggle between the Wisconsin Economics Department and the School of Commerce, who shared the program. Those who favored the status quo in statistics instruction prevailed in the intramural struggle. In fact, Friedman did not even teach statistics. He taught economic theory, however, along with business cycles and a seminar on income and wealth. Friedman left Wisconsin after one year.

Friedman's next professional stop was at the Division of Tax Research of the US Treasury, after spending the summer of 1941 collaborating with Carl Shoup and Ruth Mack, whom he knew from Columbia, on a study (Shoup et al. 1943) on the use of taxes to avoid inflation. He spent two years at the Treasury working on tax reforms for war finance. Friedman moved from Washington back to New York in the spring of 1943, having been recruited by Wallis to the wartime statistics 'think-tank', the Statistical Research Group (SRG). Aside from internal reports for the US military, a book on statistics (Freeman et al. 1948) and three statistics articles resulted from Friedman's work at the SRG. When the SRG closed at the end of the war in 1945, Friedman returned to academic life at the University of Minnesota. There he and George Stigler shared an office and collaborated on *Roofs or Ceilings?* (1946). Friedman taught statistics and economics, mostly to undergraduates.

So Friedman arrived at Chicago in 1946 with work experience and publications in statistical theory, economic theory and applied quantitative analysis, and with experience teaching price theory, but without an established record of publishing on price theory. But then, the person he replaced, Jacob Viner, coupled teaching price theory with scholarship in other areas. Viner's specialties were international trade and finance and the history of economic thought. Viner's primary role at Chicago so far as price theory was concerned was the same as Friedman's, teaching the graduate price theory course, Economics 301. Knight, who had shared teaching 301 with Viner, was closer to a pure price theorist than either Viner or Friedman. But Knight's manner of pursuing price theory was out of step with that which Friedman brought to the department. Friedman coupled theoretical and data analysis. In his view, empirical facts were the very point of theory. Knight was a long way from being an empiricist. As Friedman later reflected on his approach, 'Knight never was influenced by any facts that he didn't observe casually himself. Knight was very funny that way. He was absolutely persuaded that inequality tended to increase. At least half a dozen times we talked him out of it. And half a dozen times he would come back' (Hammond 1992, p. 105).

It is one of the peculiarities of post-war Chicago price theory that the intellectual father's primary role was as teacher rather than author of books and articles. Throughout the period in which the Chicago approach to price theory was developing and spreading, Friedman's scholarly efforts were predominantly in monetary economics. Most of the PhD theses he supervised were in monetary theory and macroeconomics. However, from the fall quarter 1946 until winter quarter 1963, most Chicago graduate students took his price theory courses. So it was in his role as teacher especially that Friedman most contributed to the formation of Chicago price theory.

Chicago price theory: tools not theoretical puzzles

Perhaps more than any other feature, price theory of the post-war Chicago School is distinguished by being close to the ground. Compared with the other two post-war approaches to price theory identified by Hands and Mirowski (1998, see also Mirowski and Hands 1998), the Cowles version and the MIT revealed preference version, Chicago price theory tends to be more concrete, less abstract; more pragmatic, less speculative; a tool to solve problems rather than a set of problems to be solved, and derived to a greater extent from evidence rather than from abstractions. This characteristic of Chicago price theory is brought out in comparison with examples of the other two strands of post-war theory. In the Cowles tradition, for example, is Kenneth J. Arrow and Gerard Debreu's (1954) 'Existence of an equilibrium for a competitive economy'. An example of the MIT approach is Paul A. Samuelson's (1950) 'The problem of integrability in utility theory'. Both of these articles are exercises in pure mathematical economic theory. Samuelson concluded his paper on integrability of utility functions with the following tribute to empirical analysis, but did not pursue this himself:

> We have now completed our main task. We know what it is that integrability implies, and what non-integrability implies: we know the full empirical implications on the demand functions of being a Jeremy or a Gustav. Deductive analysis can carry us no farther. Observation of reality must be the decisive test as to which hypothesis is the more fruitful – or whether neither is very fruitful. (p. 376)

By way of contrast, an example of the Chicago approach is Friedman's permanent income hypothesis. He developed the idea, as we have seen, in the process of estimating incomes and their distributions empirically. In particular he and Kuznets (1945) were seeking an explanation of differences in incomes across five professional services markets. They decomposed income into permanent and transitory components. Friedman and others later used the permanent income hypothesis in different contexts, such as reconciling conflicting empirical evidence on what happens to propensities to consume as income changes (Friedman 1957) and explaining the demand for money (1956). Friedman made a 'close to the ground' claim for the permanent income hypothesis in *A Theory of the Consumption Function*: 'The hypothesis follows directly from the currently accepted pure theory of consumer behavior, seems consistent with existing empirical evidence, and has observable implications capable of being contradicted by additional evidence' (Friedman 1957, p. 6).

Another example of Chicago price theory is Gary Becker's *The Economics of Discrimination* (1957). Becker started with a social problem, racial discrimination, rather than with a theoretical problem. His presumption that racial discrimination was an economic phenomenon, subject to economic analysis, was novel at the time, and his analysis demonstrated the explanatory power of relatively simple price theory applied with imagination. Becker took graduate price theory from Friedman. He has written of what he found distinctive about Friedman's price theory course:

> The emphasis in his course on applications of theory to the real world set the tone for the department. It was considered necessary to have a strong working command of basic price theory, especially so-called partial-equilibrium supply and demand analysis. Yet the theory was not an end in itself or a way to display pyrotechnics. Rather, the theory became worthwhile only insofar as it helped explain different aspects of the real world. (Becker 1991, p. 142)

Numerous other examples of Chicago price theory were produced in the first twenty years after the war. They include, from Chicago faculty and students in Chicago journals: D. Gale Johnson (1950) 'Resource allocation under share contracts'; John S. McGee (1958) 'Predatory price cutting: the Standard Oil (N.J.) case'; Reuben A. Kessel (1958) 'Price discrimination in medicine'; Lester G. Telser (1960) 'Why should manufacturers want fair trade?'; Thomas G. Moore (1961) 'The purpose of licensing'; and Albert Rees (1963) 'The effects of unions on resource allocation'.

Chicago price theory: law school and beyond

Although our focus is on the price theory course that Friedman taught in the Economics Department, the Law School was also important to the development of Chicago price theory. Henry Simons taught economic theory in the Law School from 1939 until his death in 1946 (see Simons 2002), after which Aaron Director joined the Law School faculty. Director was Friedman's brother-in-law and the two shared ideas regularly. Price theory in the Law School had the same character as that in the Economics Department, theory in service of practical problems in the law. Initially Director brought price theory into Edward Levi's antitrust course, and then they extended the analysis to other parts of law. What is known today as Chicago law and economics is Chicago price theory applied to problems of the law (see the chapter on Chicago law and economics by Steven Medema in ch. 11, this volume). Several of the examples of Chicago price theory cited above are from the *Journal of Law & Economics*, which was founded and published by the Law School in 1958. Director was the journal's first editor.

Through the 1950s and 1960s, Chicago price theory spread to other institutions as graduate students took academic positions elsewhere and as economists outside Chicago were attracted by the novelty of the approach and its practical analytical power. So through time the Hyde Park campus of the University of Chicago diminished in importance as an identifier of Chicago price theory. Furthermore, with the passing of time the three distinct types of price theory circa 1950 that are identified by Hands and Mirowski (1998, see also Mirowski and Hands 1998) blended to a degree. However, despite some blurring of the borders of the Chicago heritage that was begun by Friedman, Director and others, Chicago price theory retains its identity to the present. It has recently been reinstitutionalized at the University of Chicago in the Initiative on Chicago Price Theory. This research center was founded by Gary Becker and Kevin M. Murphy in 2004 with the express purpose of sustaining and strengthening the tradition of Chicago price theory, 'which emphasizes the role of prices in the fundamental functions of an economic system and which values the development of testable hypotheses, efficient modeling, and rigorous applications'.[4] Steven D. Levitt, winner of the 2003 John Bates Clark Medal and co-author of the bestselling *Freakonomics* (Levitt and Dubner 2005) is currently director of the center.

Friedman's price theory course

As we have seen, Friedman's initial experience teaching price theory was at Columbia University in 1939–40. This experience is important background for his Chicago course, as was his experience in Jacob Viner's classroom. Another part of the Chicago background was his experience as Henry Schultz's student, assistant and collaborator. He distributed a handout to his Columbia students on income and substitution effects that included a diagram from Schultz's *The Theory and Measurement of Demand*. Also of importance, as we shall see in some detail, was the bond of friendship that Friedman and George J. Stigler formed when they were both on the faculty of the University of Minnesota in 1945–46.

The course Friedman taught at Columbia in 1939–40, 'Structure of neo-classical economics', formed the core of his price theory sequence at Chicago, and remained so as long as he taught the courses.[5] The Columbia reading list (Appendix 1A1) includes several items that he had read in Viner's course in 1932–33. The most important of these was the 8th edition of Alfred Marshall's (1920) *Principles of Economics*. Selections from Marshall's *Principles* were interspersed throughout both Friedman's and Viner's courses. Both their reading lists also included Henry Schultz's 'The meaning of statistical demand curves' (mimeographed English translation of Schultz 1930); Viner's (1931) 'Cost curves and supply curves'; J.B. Clark's (1899) *The Distribution of Wealth*; J.S. Mill's (1909) *Principles of Political Economy*; and Adam Smith's (1904) *Wealth of Nations*.

Friedman's course at Columbia was a two-semester sequence and at Chicago a two-quarter sequence. Viner taught price theory in one quarter in the 1930s. So Friedman had twice as much class time. In addition he developed the Columbia course seven years after he took price theory from Viner. With new ideas to be drawn from the literature, Friedman included readings on imperfect competition, such as Joan Robinson's (1933) *The Economics of Imperfect Competition*; Edward Chamberlin's (1933) *The Theory of Monopolistic Competition*; and Roy Harrod's (1934) 'Doctrines of imperfect competition'. He also included readings in mathematical economics that were not on Viner's list, such as R.G.D. Allen's (1938) *Mathematical Analysis for Economists* and (1934) 'The nature of indifference curves' and Oscar Lange's (1934) 'On the determinateness of the utility function'. Friedman also assigned selections from an older work, Frank Knight's (1921) *Risk, Uncertainty, and Profit*, that was not assigned by Viner, and more recent items such as J.R. Hicks's (1939) *Value and Capital* and (1932) *The Theory of Wages*, and J.M. Keynes's (1936) *General Theory*.

The reading lists for Economics 300a and 300b from fall quarter 1952 are in Appendix 1A2. As noted, Friedman retained a number of readings from the Columbia course. His students at Chicago, like his Columbia students, read extensively from Marshall's *Principles*. Along with Schultz's 'The meaning of statistical demand curves', they read E.J. Working's (1927) 'What do statistical "demand curves" show?'. In addition, for demand theory they read Allen (1934), portions of Hicks (1939) and chapter 3 of Knight (1921). And on supply theory they also read Robinson (1933); Chamberlin (1933); Harrod (1934); Viner (1931); and J.M. Clark's (1923) *Studies in the Economics of Overhead Costs*.

Alongside Marshall, Mill, J.B. Clark, Hicks and Smith for the theory of distribution, Friedman assigned to both his Columbia and Chicago students Knight's (1935) encyclopedia article on 'Interest' for capital theory and Gustav Cassel's (1925) *Fundamental Thoughts in Economics* for general equilibrium. He expanded the readings on capital and profit and on general equilibrium for his Chicago courses, with a number of readings that were published after Friedman taught the course at Columbia.

Friedman and Stigler on price theory

When Friedman left the University of Minnesota in the summer of 1946, George Stigler also departed. He had better luck with Brown University than he had had with Chicago and left Minneapolis for Providence. Stigler was at Brown for a year and then moved to Columbia University, where he remained until 1958, when he joined the Chicago faculty as the Charles R. Walgreen Distinguished Service Professor in the Department of Economics and the Graduate School of Business. Friedman's friendship with Stigler deepened during their year together at Minnesota, and Stigler had a substantial influence on the development of Chicago price theory even in his absence from the Chicago faculty and the Hyde Park campus.

During their year together at Minnesota, Stigler completed revisions of his price theory textbook, *The Theory of Competitive Price* (Stigler 1942). The revised and re-titled edition (Stigler 1946) came out just as Friedman began preparations for the course he was to teach at Chicago. After leaving Minneapolis, Milton and Rose Friedman drove to Oregon and spent the summer there with her family. Shortly after they arrived he wrote to Stigler:

> As you know, I have been reading Stigler [(1946)] to prepare for teaching; I have been also reading Marshall [(1920)]. And this noontime I was comparing what Marshall and Stigler had to say on the law of diminishing returns. Stigler, pp. 116–25; Marshall, Bk IV, ch. III, par. 1, pp. 150–3 in my edition. Marshall is very convincing; Stigler says, in effect, that Marshall is guilty of 'question-begging' [(Stigler 1946, p. 119)], that his 'and similar proofs are essentially tautological' [(ibid., p. 120)]; yet Marshall sounds anything but tautological, he sounds realistic and as if he were basing his results on sound observation. As nearly as I can figure it out, Stigler has a sound point; but with little trouble Marshall can be rehabilitated, and, when he is, is far more convincing than Stigler. I thought you might be interested in a brief discussion of the point, and it gives me an excuse to get it down on paper. (MF to GS, August 12, 1946, Hammond and Hammond 2006, p. 23)

This letter opened what became an extensive written conversation about price theory, a conversation that continued until Stigler joined Friedman on the Chicago faculty in 1958 (Hammond and Hammond 2006). Through this correspondence and through his textbook, Stigler joined Alfred Marshall and Ken Boulding (1941) as teachers in the shadows for Friedman's students.

Friedman's Economics 300A and 300B were split between price and distribution theory, with greater attention to the former. Rather than separating the theories of perfect and imperfect competition, as was the convention in other price theory courses, he intermingled the coverage according to which was relevant to the problem under discussion. This provides another example of how Chicago price theory is 'close to the ground'. Theory is used as a means of explaining real-world events rather than being studied for its own sake. Friedman began collecting applications of theory during the first quarter he taught the course. For example, he wrote to Stigler in November 1946:

> I am going to start picketing you long distance. 'Stigler is unfair to teachers of economic theory'. I wanted to assign some standard problems – dumping & price leadership & index no. – & lo & behold, they are all worked out in Stigler. I am enclosing a couple of problems which I finally worked out to get around Stigler's unfair competition. They are the same problems in somewhat disguised form. The first is a direct steal from Ed Shaw's article on inventories. (MF to GS, November 27, [1946], Hammond and Hammond 2006, p. 45)

Some of the problems he used in the early years became exemplars of Chicago price theory after they were included in Friedman's (1962) textbook, *Price Theory: A*

Provisional Text.[6] Friedman wrote on January 27, 1947 to thank Stigler for sending a question he had used on an exam. This is an example of Stigler contributing directly to Friedman's price theory course, and ultimately to his textbook (ibid., p. 268). The problem was related to the experience with Second World War price controls and product rationing. Stigler's statement of the problem was, 'prove that when there are 2 rationing systems, all consumers gain if one is convertible into the other – that is, if points may be purchased & sold' (MF to GS, January 27, [1947], Hammond and Hammond 2006, p. 52). Friedman complained that Stigler was wasting his time and improving his mind. He began to construct a proof of the proposition, then began to doubt its truth and worked for most of two days on a counter-example to disprove the 'speciously plausible' statement. At the end of the letter with the details of his counter-example, Friedman posed another problem for Stigler to ponder: 'Patent owners are reported in the literature as sometimes restricting output of licensees as well as charging a fee even though the patent owner himself produces nothing. How do you rationalize?' (ibid., p. 55).

The importance of Marshall, Knight, and Viner

Friedman believed that no work in price theory over the previous century surpassed Marshall's *Principles*. His very first statement to students in 300A was:

> Marshall's 'Principles' viewed contemporaneously, that is, as if he were writing today instead of a century ago, is still the best book available in economic theory. This is indeed a sad commentary on the economics of our time. Marshall's superiority is explained primarily by his approach to economics as contrasted with the modern approach. Marshall was interested in economics as a real problem rather than as a form of geometry. Economics was to him an engine of analysis, a tool to study the economic system as it actually works (Friedman, 'Lecture Notes "Price Theory"', undated, Milton Friedman Papers, Box 76).

Years later in an interview Friedman made a similar statement that reflects his opinion of what makes Chicago price theory distinctive. This comment was about Viner's price theory course rather than about Marshall:

> Interviewer (J.D. Hammond): Would you say that his [Viner's] 301 course had much of a methodological content?
> Friedman: That depends on what you mean by methodological. It had no explicit methodological content whatsoever. But there was a very strong implicit methodological content, since you came away very clearly with the feeling that you were talking about real problems. Part of the distinction is viewing economics as a branch of mathematics – as a game – as an intellectual game and exercise – as Debreu, Arrow, and so on – and it's a fine thing to do. There's nothing wrong with that. After all, mathematics is a perfectly respectable intellectual activity, and so is mathematization of economics or anything else. The other part of it is viewing it (using Marshall's phrase) as an engine of analysis. And there was no doubt that Viner viewed it as an engine of analysis, and no doubt when you were in his course that you came away with the feeling that economics really had something to say about real problems and real things. In that sense it had methodological content. (Hammond 1992, pp. 104–5)

The emphasis on making theory the servant of practical problems is also seen in Friedman's remark to students that his definition of economics was the study of the ways in which *a particular society* solves the economic problem: 'There are the methods in which our society solves its economic problem, other societies use different methods, and the relative importance of these methods is different for different societies. We shall restrict our study to the way in which the United States solves its economic problem; in particular the way it solves its problem through the free enterprise system'. He distinguished scientific positive economics from normative economics, suggesting that 'the ability to state the effects of particular changes is the only thing which gives economics the status of a science' (Friedman, 'Lecture Notes "Price Theory"', undated, Milton Friedman Papers, Box 76).

Friedman took portions of his opening lectures from Frank Knight's (1933) *The Economic Organization*. He spoke of the role of the economic system of any society to fix standards, that is, to set relative values of different ends in a community of different people. This is what sets economics apart from physics or engineering; efficiency and inefficiency are in the realm of economics, not of physics or engineering, where outputs always match inputs. He distinguished between different methods of fixing standards, dictation in the family, all or nothing voting plus dictation in the political sphere and proportional voting plus dictation in the commercial sphere.

Friedman stressed the importance of the price system in the five functions of any economic system, in addition to setting standards, organizing production, distributing the final product, economic maintenance and change, and reconciling short-run consumption and production. He stressed the importance of workable competition if one is to move from positive analysis of markets to normative approval of market outcomes. Friedman, who became known as a champion of freedom, distinguished between freedom to combine and freedom to compete. But he suggested that in the United States, combinations are not as prevalent as commonly presumed.[7]

Following his introductory remarks on the nature of economic analysis and the price system, Friedman gave the students an assignment that required use of Marshall's *Principles*. They were to define a demand curve with a list of 'other things' held constant, and to support their list with passages from Marshall. Friedman discussed in detail one of the other things held equal: wants. Friedman suggested that the appropriateness of treating wants as unchanged or subject to change depended on the problem at hand. In reality wants are always changing, so for instance, there is no such thing as satiety of wants. On this matter he cited Stigler's (1945) paper 'The cost of subsistence'. One can hear an echo of Frank Knight in Friedman's statement that 'real wants are for more wants. We see all around us the extent to which we live to work' (Friedman, 'Lecture Notes "Price Theory"', undated, Milton Friedman Papers, Box 76).

One can also see elements of Friedman's (1953) 'The methodology of positive economics' in his lectures for Economics 300A, when he makes the distinction between positive and normative economics, and also in discussion of the nature of theory as language, that is, theory as a set of filing boxes. Demand and supply are filing boxes for the various factors that influence willingness to buy and to sell. The appropriateness of the theoretical framework, that is, filing system, is determined by the extent to which the affecting factors can be sorted into one box or the other. The behavior of dealers in commodities, for example, does not sort cleanly into demand and supply, for dealers buy in order to sell. A second dimension of the filing boxes is separating short- from long-run phenomena, and this distinction is not one that can be made once and for all. Rather, sorting into the short- and long-run boxes depends on the problem at hand.

Friedman and Stigler revisited

Friedman and Stigler's deepening friendship left its mark not only on his price theory course but on revisions of Stigler's textbook and on the scholarship of both men. This can be seen in their correspondence. For example, we have already referred to the letter where Friedman contrasted Stigler's with Marshall's proofs of the Law of Diminishing Returns (or Law of Variable Proportions). Stigler's text discussed two types of proofs for the law. He labeled the first type a priori and defined it as 'attempt[s] to deduce the law from self-evident propositions' (Stigler 1946, p. 118). He labeled the second type of proof 'empirical: no one has discovered any important exceptions to the doctrine' (ibid., p. 120). He found a priori proofs unsatisfactory, and noted that they are 'essentially tautological'. In arguing in favor of the 'empirical' line of proof he referred readers to examples of 'quantitative verification' in numerous agricultural experiments, which, for example, showed that applying increasing amounts of fertilizer to a fixed plot of land leads to diminishing returns (ibid., p. 120).

Friedman considered these statements to be an attack on Marshall's method of proving the law. Paraphrasing Marshall:

> If the law of diminishing returns were not valid; that is, if the application of additional units of labor and capital to a piece of land yielded constant or increasing returns, then individuals would have no incentive to get additional land and we should observe in fact that individuals used and wanted very little. (MF to GS, August 12, 1946, Hammond and Hammond 2006, p. 23)

Friedman makes his point:

> Stigler says, in effect, that Marshall is guilty of 'question-begging', that his 'and similar proofs are essentially tautological'; yet Marshall sounds anything but tautological, he sounds realistic and as if he were basing his results on sound observation. As nearly as I can figure it out, Stigler has a sound point; but with little trouble Marshall can be rehabilitated, and, when he is, is far more convincing than Stigler. (Ibid., p. 23)

Friedman proceeded to 'rehabilitate Marshall' by setting up alternative hypotheses under different assumptions with respect to increasing and decreasing returns to variable proportions. He tested each hypothesis against observed fact, and drew his conclusions using the following method, 'Our hypothesis leads us to expect a certain result, we find that result, hence our hypothesis is not contradicted' (ibid., p. 23).

Friedman then posed a rhetorical question:

> You may ask, why all this fuss when Stigler accepts the law on other grounds, namely, technological experiments [which Stigler had labeled empirical proofs]. The reason is that *economic* empirical evidence of the kind given by Marshall [that farmers are willing to pay for more land] is intellectually far more satisfying to an economist than technological evidence. In addition, part of my purpose is to show that Marshall here as elsewhere, was proceeding on a truly scientific basis, not on that tautological, formal basis that enervates so much of modern theory. (Ibid., pp. 24–5, original italic)

Stigler replied:

> You say that *economic* empirical evidence is intellectually far more satisfying than technological evidence. I cannot claim even an intuitive understanding of this statement. Diminishing returns is technological, so you prefer an indirect to a direct proof:

1. Because you are freed of dependence on non-economic data? Perhaps, but this is clearly a move in the direction of a closed formal system – which you don't like.
2. Because it is more efficient? That depends on the case.
3. Because it is more elegant? No, this is pure formalism,
4. Because?

[Stigler then answers the question himself:]
As a matter of fact, I am coming to believe that you are more consistently abstract and a priori-ish than I. But it's cloaked over by your emphasis on realism, which I would like to have you define. I shall conjecture, if only to hasten the enlightenment, that you like a firm skeleton of rigorous theory well skinned with concrete illustrations, in the manner of Marshall and [Arthur F.] Burns, all oriented in accordance with your general view of how economic life runs. In any case, I do. (GS to MF, [August 19, 1946], Hammond and Hammond 2006, p. 26, original italic)

Stigler gave no ground to Friedman's argument in his letter. Yet, the 1952 revision of his textbook gives the impression that Friedman won the argument, and that Stigler came to believe that what he had labeled 'a priori' was after all an empirical test:

> The law of diminishing returns was first demonstrated with . . . the following argument. No one would resort to the cultivation of inferior lands if he did not 'run into' diminishing marginal returns on fertile land. Since inferior lands were in cultivation . . . diminishing returns must be present. . . .
> This early proof has been discussed because it is illustrative of the type of proof we shall give later. In essence we postulate diminishing marginal returns, deduce the consequences of this postulate for observable entrepreneurial behavior . . . and then test the consequences (predictions) against observation. (Stigler 1952, pp. 119–20)

Stigler no longer included a second type of proof, the 'empirical' proofs from agricultural experiments for which he stated a preference in the 1946 edition. Instead, he declared experimental evidence useful but for reassurance purposes only. 'Nevertheless is it reassuring to notice that diminishing marginal returns has been found in direct experiments in a considerable number of cases, and that continuously increasing marginal returns has not been found in such experiments' (ibid., pp. 121–2).

Another example of Friedman's influence on Stigler's thinking and revisions of *The Theory of Price* concerns the relationship between diminishing marginal utility and increasing marginal rates of substitution. Footnote 71 in the 1946 edition reads:

> The principle of an increasing S_{yx} [marginal rate of substitution] corresponds to the older theory of diminishing marginal utility of a commodity as its quantity increases. The two principles are equivalent in the special case where the marginal utility of *X* is independent of the quantity of *Y*; in general, however, neither necessarily implies the other. (Stigler 1946)

Friedman criticized Stigler for lack of rigor in this note, opening a debate over whether diminishing marginal utility is necessary or sufficient for increasing marginal rates of substitution (convex indifference curves) and stability of consumer equilibrium. Friedman came up with a utility function ($U = e^{2u} = x^2y^2$) that he claimed exhibited increasing rate of substitution along with increasing marginal utilities of x and y, contradicting Stigler's footnote (MF to GS, November 27, [1946], Hammond and Hammond 2006, pp. 44–5). Stigler conceded and replaced the footnote with Mathematical Note 8 in the next edition of his textbook. This note includes the statement, 'diminishing marginal utility does not imply convexity . . . nor does convexity imply diminishing marginal utility' (Stigler 1952, p. 301).

Stigler's suggestion in their exchange over proofs of the Law of Diminishing Returns that Friedman was becoming 'more abstract and a prior-ish than I' and that Friedman preferred 'a firm skeleton of rigorous theory well skinned with concrete illustrations, in the manner of Marshall and [Arthur F.] Burns, all oriented in accordance with your general view of how economic life runs' took the discussion into the methodology of price theory which was a frequent topic in their correspondence. Methodology, as much as the content of theory, distinguishes Chicago price theory. Friedman and Stigler had differences on methodology, but they were more alike than different. Stigler wrote of the way he organized his book, 'I wrote with a view of cleaning up technical details in print so I could spend my time in class on economics and that is what I do. But I do much more of this now than formerly and would undoubtedly approach things differently if I were to start anew' (GS to MF, [September 1946], Hammond and Hammond 2006, p. 39). Here we have evidence of Friedman encouraging Stigler to shift emphasis from theory for theory's sake to theory in the context of concrete problems.

Friedman also urged Stigler to develop the methodological content of his criticism of monopolistic competition. When Edward Chamberlin (1947) wrote an unfavorable review of *The Theory of Price*, Stigler asked for Friedman's advice on how to respond. He sent a copy of a letter to Chamberlin in which he wrote of monopolistic competition: 'I do not recall a single consistent application of it to a real problem, and this is the ultimate failure of a theory' (GS to EC, [August 1947], Hammond and Hammond 2006, pp. 62–3). Friedman replied to Stigler, 'the main additional point I would like to make is that you do not really go at all far enough'. Friedman then explained that he was engaged in an effort to distinguish description from scientific analysis and that he had come to the conclusion 'that every important scientific hypothesis almost inevitably must use assumptions that are descriptively erroneous' (MF to GS, November 19, 1947, Hammond and Hammond 2006, p. 65). As Friedman developed this argument, and the related historical thesis that his approach had been Alfred Marshall's also, in drafts of 'The methodology of positive economics' (1953) and 'The Marshallian demand curve' (1949) he came under Stigler's scrutiny. For instance:

> I think you are wrong in attributing to Marshall this meaning of his demand curve. Viz.
> You take the positions (1) he was realistic, and (2) he was a magnificent logician, and seek for an internally and externally consistent interpretation of what he says. In this I think you are too generous. If your interpretation is correct, you have convicted him of complete illiteracy; not even in his mathematical appendix does he give explicit support to you. (GS to MF, June 21, [1948], Hammond and Hammond 2006, p. 82)

Friedman and Stigler cross-fertilized on other price theory topics such as history of utility theory (Stigler 1950), base point pricing (Stigler 1949), welfare effects of income and excise taxes (Friedman 1952), economies of scale (Friedman 1955, Stigler 1958), the rationality of gambling (Friedman and Savage 1948, 1952) and the selections for Stigler and Boulding's *Readings in Price Theory* (1952). By the mid-1950s Friedman's research shifted away from price theory to monetary economics and in 1958 Stigler, who remained throughout his career first and foremost a price theorist, joined the Chicago faculty. So from the 1960s on, observers of Chicago economics tended to view Stigler and Friedman as, to borrow Gary Becker's moniker, Chicago's Mr. Micro and Mr. Macro (Becker 1991, p. 140). But as we have seen, there are two twists in the history of post-war Chicago price theory leading up to the 1960s. First, Friedman, Mr. Macro, was most responsible for the early post-war development of Chicago price theory. Second, Stigler, Mr. Micro, had a significant role in this development from the very beginning, despite the fact that he was not at Chicago.

Notes

1. In 1955, Marschak and Koopmans moved from Chicago to Yale with the Cowles Commission.
2. See Stigler (1988, p. 40). Stigler began his teaching career at Iowa State with Theodore W. Schultz as his department chair and D. Gale Johnson as one of his first students.
3. The description of Economics 300A and B in *Announcements: The College and the Division 1948–49 Session* reads: 'A systematic study of the pricing of final products and factors of production under essentially stationary conditions. Covers both perfect competition and such imperfectly competitive conditions as monopolistic competition, oligopoly, and monopoly. 300A deals primarily with the pricing of final products; 300B, with the pricing of factors of production'.
4. See http://research.chicagobooth.edu/pricetheory/about.
5. Friedman taught Econ 300 A & B (equivalent to Econ 301 & 302) regularly through the 1963–64 academic year. He then switched to teaching money and income courses until 1972 when he resumed teaching 301 and 302.
6. Friedman's textbook (1962) was the result of the initiative of two of Friedman's students – David I. Fand and Warren J. Gustus – who compiled notes from Friedman's lectures and persuaded him to edit them for publication. A revised version (Friedman 1976) was published without the 'provisional' subtitle.
7. One of the first PhD dissertations that Friedman supervised was G. Warren Nutter's empirical study of the extent of monopoly in the US economy from 1899 to 1939 (see Hammond 1999, ch. 5).

References

Milton Friedman Papers, Hoover Institution Archive, Stanford University.

Allen, R.G.D. (1934), 'The nature of indifference curves', *Review of Economic Studies*, **1** (2), 110–21.
Allen, R.G.D. (1938), *Mathematical Analysis for Economists*, London: Macmillan.
Arrow, K.J. and G. Debreu (1954), 'Existence of an equilibrium for a competitive economy', *Econometrica*, **22** (3), 265–90.
Becker, G.S. (1957), *The Economics of Discrimination*, Chicago, IL: University of Chicago Press.
Becker, G.S. (1991), 'Milton Friedman', in *Remembering the University of Chicago: Teachers, Scientists, and Scholars*, Shils, E. (ed.), Chicago, IL: University of Chicago Press, pp. 138–46.
Boulding, K.E. (1941), *Economic Analysis*, New York: Harper.
Cassel, G. (1925), *Fundamental Thoughts in Economics*, London: T.F. Unwin.
Chamberlin, E.H. (1933), *The Theory of Monopolistic Competition*, Cambridge, MA: Harvard University Press.
Chamberlin, E.H. (1947), 'Review of *The Theory of Price*', *American Economic Review*, **37** (3), 414–18.
Clark, J.B. (1899), *The Distribution of Wealth: A Theory of Wages, Interest and Profits*, New York: Macmillan.
Clark, J.M. (1923), *Studies in the Economics of Overhead Costs*, Chicago, IL: University of Chicago Press.
Freeman, H.A., M. Friedman, F. Mosteller and W.A. Wallis (1948), *Sampling Inspection*, New York: McGraw-Hill.
Friedman, M. (1935), 'Professor Pigou's method for measuring elasticities of demand from budgetary data', *Quarterly Journal of Economics*, **50** (1), 151–63.
Friedman, M. (1936), 'Marginal utility of money and elasticities of demand', *Quarterly Journal of Economics*, **50** (3), 532–3.
Friedman, M. (1949), 'The Marshallian demand curve', *Journal of Political Economy*, **57** (6), 463–95.
Friedman, M. (1952), 'The "welfare" effects of an income tax and an excise tax', *Journal of Political Economy*, **60** (1), 25–33.
Friedman, M. (1953), 'The methodology of positive economics', in *Essays in Positive Economics*, Chicago, IL: University of Chicago Press, pp. 3–43.
Friedman, M. (1955), 'Comment on "Survey of the Empirical Evidence on Economies of Scale" by Caleb

Smith', in *Business Concentration and Price Policy*, National Bureau of Economic Research, Princeton, NJ: Princeton University Press, pp. 230–38.
Friedman, M. (1956), 'The quantity theory of money – a restatement', in *Studies in the Quantity Theory of Money*, Friedman, M. (ed.), Chicago, IL: University of Chicago Press, pp. 3–21.
Friedman, M. (1957), *A Theory of the Consumption Function*, Princeton, NJ: Princeton University Press.
Friedman, M. (1962), *Price Theory: A Provisional Text*, Chicago, IL: Aldine.
Friedman, M. (1976), *Price Theory*, Chicago, IL: Aldine.
Friedman, M. and S. Kuznets (1945), *Income from Independent Professional Practice*, New York: National Bureau of Economic Research.
Friedman, M. and L.J. Savage (1948), 'The utility analysis of choices involving risk', *Journal of Political Economy*, **56** (4), 270–304.
Friedman, M. and L.J. Savage (1952), 'The expected utility hypothesis and the measurability of utility', *Journal of Political Economy*, **60** (6), 463–74.
Friedman, M. and G.J. Stigler (1946), *Roofs or Ceilings? The Current Housing Problem*, Irvington-on-Hudson, NY: Foundation for Economic Education.
Friedman, M. and W.A. Wallis (1942), 'The empirical derivation of indifference functions', in *Studies in Mathematical Economics and Econometrics: In Memory of Henry Schultz*, Lange, O., F. McIntyre and T.O. Yntema (eds), Chicago, IL: University of Chicago Press, pp. 175–89.
Hammond, J.D. (1992), 'An interview with Milton Friedman on methodology', in *Research in the History of Economic Thought and Methodology*, 10, Samuels, W.J. and J.E. Biddle (eds), Greenwich, CT: JAI Press, pp. 91–118.
Hammond, J.D. (ed.) (1999), *The Legacy of Milton Friedman as Teacher*, Cheltenham, UK and Northampton, MA, USA: Edward Elgar.
Hammond, J.D. and C.H. Hammond (eds) (2006), *Making Chicago Price Theory: Friedman–Stigler Correspondence, 1945–57*, London: Routledge.
Hands, D.W. and P. Mirowski (1998), 'Harold Hotelling and the neoclassical dream', in *Economics and Methodology: Crossing Boundaries*, Backhouse, R.E., D.M. Hausman, U. Mäki and A. Salanti (eds), New York: St. Martin's, pp. 322–97.
Harrod, R.F. (1934), 'Doctrines of imperfect competition', *Quarterly Journal of Economics*, **48** (3), 442–70.
Hicks, J.R. (1932), *The Theory of Wages*, London: Macmillan.
Hicks, J.R. (1939), *Value and Capital: An Inquiry into Some Fundamental Principles of Economic Theory*, Oxford: Clarendon Press.
Johnson, D.G. (1950), 'Resource allocation under share contracts', *Journal of Political Economy*, **58** (2), 111–23.
Kessel, R.A. (1958), 'Price discrimination in medicine', *Journal of Law & Economics*, **1**, 20–53.
Keynes, J.M. (1936), *The General Theory of Employment, Interest and Money*, New York: Harcourt, Brace.
Knight, F.H. (1921), *Risk, Uncertainty and Profit*, Boston, MA: Houghton Mifflin.
Knight, F.H. (1933), *The Economic Organization*, Chicago, IL: University of Chicago.
Knight, F.H. (1935), 'Interest', in *The Ethics of Competition*, New York: Harper & Bros., pp. 251–76.
Lange, O. (1934), 'On the determinateness of the utility function', *Review of Economic Studies*, **1** (3), 218–25.
Levitt, S.D. and S.J. Dubner (2005), *Freakonomics: A Rogue Economist Explains Everything*, New York: William Morrow.
Marshall, A. (1920), *Principles of Economics*, 8th edn, London: Macmillan.
McGee, J.S. (1958), 'Predatory price cutting: the Standard Oil (N.J.) case', *Journal of Law and Economics*, **1**, 137–69.
Mill, J.S. (1909), *Principles of Political Economy: With Some of Their Applications to Social Philosophy*, 7th edn, Ashley, W.J. (ed.), London: Longmans, Green.
Mirowski, P. and D.W. Hands (1998), 'A paradox of budgets: the postwar stabilization of American neoclassical demand theory', in *From Interwar Pluralism to Postwar Neoclassicism*, Morgan, M.S. and M. Rutherford (eds), Durham, NC: Duke University Press, pp. 260–92.
Moore, T.G. (1961), 'The purpose of licensing', *Journal of Law & Economics*, **4**, 93–117.
Pigou, A.C. (1936), 'Marginal utility of money and elasticities of demand', *Quarterly Journal of Economics*, **50** (3), 532.
Rees, A. (1963), 'The effects of unions on resource allocation', *Journal of Law & Economics*, **6** (October), 69–78.
Robinson, J. (1933), *The Economics of Imperfect Competition*, London: Macmillan.
Samuelson, P.A. (1950), 'The problem of integrability in utility theory', *Economica*, n.s. **17** (68), 355–85.
Schultz, H. (1930), *Der Sinn der statistischen Nachfragekurven* (The meaning of statistical demand curves), Bonn: Frankfurter Gesellschaft für Konjuncturforschung.
Schultz, H. (1935), 'Interrelations of demand, price, and income', *Journal of Political Economy*, **43** (4), 433–81.

Schultz, H. (1938), *The Theory and Measurement of Demand*, Chicago, IL: University of Chicago Press.
Shoup, C., M. Friedman and R.P. Mack (1943), *Taxing to Prevent Inflation: Techniques for Estimating Revenue Requirements*, New York: Columbia University Press.
Simons, H.C. (2002), 'The Simons' syllabus', in *The Chicago Tradition in Economics, 1892–1945*, 8, Emmett, R.B. (ed.), London: Routledge, pp. 3–70.
Smith, A. (1904), *An Inquiry into the Nature and Causes of the Wealth of Nations*, 5th edn, Cannan, E. (ed.), London: Methuen.
Stigler, G.J. (1941), *Production and Distribution Theories: The Formative Period*, New York: Macmillan.
Stigler, G.J. (1942), *The Theory of Competitive Price*, New York: Macmillan.
Stigler, G.J. (1945), 'The cost of subsistence', *Journal of Farm Economics*, **27** (2), 303–14.
Stigler, G.J. (1946), *The Theory of Price*, New York: Macmillan.
Stigler, G.J. (1949), 'A theory of delivered price systems', *American Economic Review*, **39** (6), 1144–59.
Stigler, G.J. (1950), 'The development of utility theory', *Journal of Political Economy*, **58** (4, 5), 307–27, 373–96.
Stigler, G.J. (1952), *The Theory of Price*, rev. edn, New York: Macmillan.
Stigler, G.J. (1958), 'The economies of scale', *Journal of Law & Economics*, **1**, 54–71.
Stigler, G.J. (1988), *Memoirs of an Unregulated Economist*, New York: Basic Books.
Stigler, G.J. and K.E. Boulding (eds) (1952), *Readings in Price Theory*, Chicago, IL: Richard D. Irwin.
Telser, L.G. (1960), 'Why should manufacturers want fair trade?', *Journal of Law & Economics*, **3**, 86–105.
Viner, J. (1931), 'Cost curves and supply curves', *Zeitschrift für Nationalökonomie*, **3**, 23–46.
Working, E.J. (1927), 'What do statistical "demand curves" show?', *Quarterly Journal of Economics*, **41** (2), 212–35.

Appendix 1A1

Assignments in course given at Columbia by M. Friedman entitled 'Structure of Neo-Classical Economics'

(Listed in order in which assigned)

First semester

Alfred Marshall, *Principles of Economics*, Book III, ch. 2, 3, 4; Book V, ch. 1, 2
Henry Schultz, 'The Meaning of Statistical Demand Curves,' pp. 1–10
E.J. Working, 'What do Statistical "Demand Curves" Show?,' *Q.J.E.*, Vol. XLI (1927), pp. 212–27
Frank H. Knight, *Risk, Uncertainty, and Profit*, ch. 3
Frederic Benham, *Economics*, pp. 89–100
J.R. Hicks, *Value and Capital*, pp. 11–37
Marshall, Book V, ch. 3, 4, 5, 12, Appendix H
A.L. Meyers, *Elements of Modern Economics*, ch. 5, 7, 8, 9
Joan Robinson, *Economics of Imperfect Competition*, ch. 2
J.M. Clark, *The Economics of Overhead Cost*, ch. 9
Jacob Viner, 'Cost Curves and Supply Curves,' *Zeitschrift für Nationaloekonomie*, Bd. III (Sept. 1931), pp. 23–46
Edward Chamberlin, *The Theory of Monopolistic Competition*, ch. 3, sec. 1, 4, 5, 6; ch. 5
M. Abramovitz, 'Monopolistic Selling in a Changing Economy,' *Q.J.E.*, Feb., 1938, pp. 191–214
R.F. Harrod, 'Doctrines of Imperfect Competition,' *Q.J.E.*, May, 1934, sec. 1, pp. 442–61

Suggested readings for mathematicians

O. Lange, 'On the Determinateness of the Utility Function,' *Review of Economic Studies*, Vol. 1 (1933–34), pp. 218ff.
R.G.D. Allen, 'The Nature of Indifference Curves,' *Review of Economic Studies*, Vol. I (1933–34), pp. 110ff.

Suggested reading in mathematics

R.G.D. Allen, *Mathematical Analysis for Economists*, ch. 2, pp. 28–30, 54–5; ch. 5, pp. 107–14; ch. 6; ch. 4

Second semester

Marshall, Book V, ch. 6
J.B. Clark, *The Distribution of Wealth*, Preface, ch. 1, 7, 8, 11, 12, 13, 23
John Stuart Mill, *Principles of Political Economy*, Book II, ch. 14
J.R. Hicks, *The Theory of Wages*, ch. 1–6
Adam Smith, *The Wealth of Nations*, Book I, ch. 10
Marshall, Book VI, ch. 1–5
Simon Kuznets and Milton Friedman, *Incomes from Independent Professional Practice*, Bulletin 72–3, National Bureau of Economic Research, section 5, appendix
F.H. Knight, 'Interest,' in *Encyclopedia of the Social Sciences*, also in *Ethics of Competition*
J.M. Keynes, *The General Theory of Employment, Interest and Money*, ch. 11–14
Gustav Cassel, *Fundamental Thoughts in Economics*, ch. 1, 2, 3

Appendix 1A2

October 1951
Economics 300A and B
Reading Assignments by M. Friedman

(Notes: 1. It is assumed students are familiar with material equivalent to that contained in George Stigler, *Theory of Price*, or Kenneth Boulding, *Economic Analysis*.
2. Reading marked with asterisk (*) are recommended, not required).

Knight, F.H., *The Economic Organization*, esp. pp. 1–37.
Keynes, J.N., *The Scope and Method of Political Economy*, Ch. I and II, pp. 1–83.
Hayek, F.A., 'The Use of Knowledge in Society,' *American Economic Review*, Sept., 1945; Reprinted in *Individualism and Economic Order*.
Marshall, Alfred, *Principles of Economics*, Bk. III, Ch. 2, 3, 4; Bk. V, Ch. 1, 2.
Friedman, Milton, 'The Marshallian Demand Curve,' *Journal of Political Economy*, December 1949.
Schultz, Henry, *The Meaning of Statistical Demand Curves*, pp. 1–10.
Working, E.J., 'What Do Statistical "Demand Curves" Show?' *Quarterly Journal of Economics*, XLI (1927), pp. 212–27.
Knight, F.H., *Risk, Uncertainty, and Profit*, Ch. 3.
*Lange, O., 'On the Determinateness of the Utility Function,' *Review of Economic Studies*, Vol. I (1933–34), pp. 218 ff.
*Allen, R.G.D., 'The Nature of Indifference Curves,' *Review of Economic Studies*, Vol. I (1933–34), pp. 110 ff.
Hicks, J.R., *Value and Capital*, Part I (pp. 11–52.)
Friedman, Milton, 'Income and Substitution Effects of a Change in Price' (mimeographed).
*Wallis, W.A. and Friedman, Milton, 'The Empirical Derivation of Indifference Functions,' in Lange et al., *Studies in Mathematical Economics and Econometrics*.
*Friedman, Milton and Savage, L.J., 'The Utility Analysis of Choices Involving Risk,' *Journal of Political Economy*, LVI (August 1948), pp. 279–304.
Marshall, Bk. V., Ch. 3, 4, 5, 12. Appendix II.
Robinson, Joan, *Economics of Imperfect Competition*, Ch. 2.
Clark, J.M., *The Economics of Overhead Costs*, Ch. 9.
Viner, Jacob, 'Cost Curves and Supply Curves,' *Zeitschrift fuer Nationaloekonomie*, Bk. III (Sept. 1931), pp. 23–46.
Friedman, Milton, 'The Relationships Between Supply Curves and Cost Curves' (dittoed).
Chamberlin, Edward, *The Theory of Monopolistic Competition*, Ch. 3, sec. 1, 4, 5, 6; Ch. 5.
Harrod, R.F., 'Doctrines of Imperfect Competition,' *Quarterly Journal of Economics*, May 1934, sec. 1, pp. 442–61.
Stigler, G.J., 'Monopolistic Competition in Retrospect,' Lecture 2 in *Five Lectures on Economic Problems*.

*Triffin, Robert, *Monopolistic Competition and General Equilibrium Theory*, esp. Part II, v. 67.
Robinson, E.A.G., *The Structure of Competitive Industry.*
* ________, *Monopoly.*
* Plant, Arnold, 'The Economic Theory Concerning Patents for Inventions,' *Economica*, Feb. 1934.
*Dennison, S.R., 'The Problem of Bigness,' *Cambridge Journal*, Nov. 1947.
Marshall, Bk. IV, Ch. 1, 2, 3; Bk. V, Ch. 6.
Clark, J.B., *The Distribution of Wealth*, Preface, Ch. 1, 7, 8, 11, 12, 13, 23.
Mill, John Stuart, *Principles of Political Economy*, Bk. II, Ch. 14.
Hicks, J.R., *The Theory of Wages*, Ch. 1–6.
Smith, Adam, *The Wealth of Nations*, Bk. 1, Ch. 10.
Marshall, Bk. VI, Ch. 1–5.
Friedman, Milton and Kuznets, Simon, *Income from Independent Professional Practice*, Preface, pp. v to x; Ch. 3, Sec. 3, pp. 81–95; Ch. 4, Sec. 2, pp. 118–37; App., Sec. 1 & 3, pp. 142–51, 155–61.
Knight, F.H., 'Interest' in *Encyclopedia of the Social Sciences*, also in *Ethics of Competition.*
Keynes, J.M., *The General Theory of Employment, Interest, and Money*, Ch. 11–14.
Weston, J.F., 'A Generalized Uncertainty Theory of Profit,' *American Economic Review*, March 1950, pp. 40–60.
Cassell, Gustav, *Fundamental Thoughts in Economics*, Ch. 1, 2, 3.
________, *The Theory of Social Economy*, Ch. 4.
Hicks, J.R., 'Mr. Keynes and the "Classics": A Suggested Interpretation,' *Econometrica*, Vol. 5, April 1937, pp. 147–59.
Modigliani, F., 'Liquidity Preference and the Theory of Interest and Money,' *Econometrica*, Vol. 12, no. 1 (Jan. 1944), esp. Part I, sec. 1 through 9, sec. 11 through 17; Part II, sec 21.
Pigou, A.C. 'The Classical Stationary State,' *Economic Journal*, Vol. 53, Dec. 1943, pp. 343–51.
________, 'Economic Progress in a Stable Environment,' *Economica*, 1947, pp. 189–90.
Patinkin, Don, 'Price Flexibility and Full Employment,' *American Economic Review*, XXXVIII, 4, Sept. 1948, pp. 543–64.

2 Chicago economics and institutionalism

*Malcolm Rutherford**

Introduction

For most economists the terms 'Chicago economics' and 'institutionalism' denote clearly antithetical approaches to the discipline. Members of the modern 'Chicago School' such as George Stigler and Ronald Coase have often made highly dismissive remarks concerning American institutionalism. Coase has commented that American institutionalists were anti-theoretical, and that 'without a theory they had nothing to pass on except a mass of descriptive material waiting for a theory, or a fire' (Coase 1984, p. 230). Stigler devoted himself to fierce attacks on the work of Gardiner Means, John Kenneth Galbraith, Richard Lester, and of anyone else who ventured to question either the virtues of the free market or the empirical superiority of competitive price theory. Some of these attitudes have their roots in the interwar period, most obviously in Frank Knight's views on the centrality of price theory to any properly 'scientific' economics (Knight 1924 [1999]), and in his bitingly critical attacks on the policy positions of institutionalist and other advocates of regulatory intervention and of the 'social control' of business (Knight 1932 [1999]). Nevertheless, what this chapter seeks to reveal is a much more complex interrelation between institutional and Chicago economics. To fully understand this relationship it is necessary to begin with the early years of the Chicago Department of Economics.

Chicago economics and institutionalism, 1892–1919

The Chicago Department of Political Economy was begun in 1892 with Laurence Laughlin as its head. While Laughlin was conservative in his economic and political views, and at odds with the historicist or 'new' school influence in American economics, he built a department that was diverse in its interests and had significant representation from those critical of 'orthodox' economics (Nef 1934). Most obviously, Laughlin brought Thorstein Veblen with him from Cornell, and shortly thereafter placed him in charge of editing the *Journal of Political Economy*. As Hodgson has argued (2004), Veblen's years at Chicago (from 1892 to 1906) were remarkably creative ones. During this time he published *The Theory of the Leisure Class* (1899), *The Theory of Business Enterprise* (1904), and developed much of the material that would appear later in *The Instinct of Workmanship* (1914). Veblen's presence on the faculty had a substantial impact on a number of students, particularly Wesley Mitchell and Robert Hoxie, but others as well. Mitchell's 1899 doctoral dissertation, 'History of the United States notes' – published as *A History of the Greenbacks* (Mitchell 1903) – was prepared under Laughlin's supervision, but Mitchell was deeply impressed with Veblen's analysis of pecuniary or 'business' institutions and their failings (including business cycles). In Mitchell's case these Veblenian ideas were combined with a strongly empirical bent, and John Dewey's instrumentalist philosophy (Dewey was a member of the Philosophy Department at Chicago from 1894 to 1902). Mitchell taught at Chicago as an instructor in 1901 and 1902 but, despite Laughlin's efforts to retain him, left for Berkeley in 1903.

Robert Hoxie completed his doctorate in 1905, and his earlier work, in particular, is full of Veblenian concepts. On the basis of his investigations of trade unions, Hoxie eventually came to reject the Veblenian notion of machine industry creating a radicalized trade union movement (Hoxie 1917), but Veblen also changed his views on that issue. Hoxie taught at Chicago from 1906 until his suicide in 1916. His teaching method was both empirical and focused on the actual functioning of institutions, and inspired many students. Clarence Ayres came to Chicago with the intention of studying with Hoxie, but Hoxie's death occurred very shortly afterward, and Ayres switched into philosophy.

On Hoxie's recommendation, Laughlin hired Walton Hamilton from Michigan to Chicago in 1913 (Dorfman 1974, p. 6). Hamilton only stayed at Chicago until 1915 when he moved to Amherst, but Hoxie and Hamilton became close friends. According to Hamilton, it was Hoxie who first used the term 'institutional economist' to describe himself (Hamilton 1916). Hamilton later introduced the term into the literature of economics in a paper presented at an American Economic Association (AEA) meeting in 1918 titled 'The institutional approach to economic theory' (Hamilton 1919). The paper is a manifesto for this 'institutional' approach to economics. Hamilton argued that anything that 'aspired to the name of economic theory' had to be (i) capable of giving unity to economic investigations of many different areas; (ii) relevant to the problem of control; (iii) related to institutions as both the 'changeable elements of economic life and the agencies through which they are to be directed'; (iv) concerned with 'process' in the form of institutional change and development; and (v) based on an acceptable theory of human behavior, one in harmony with the 'conclusions of modern social psychology'. According to Hamilton, among the 'leaders' of this move to develop an institutional economic theory were Thorstein Veblen and Wesley Mitchell.

Also involved in the same conference session was J.M. Clark, who had been hired to Chicago from Amherst by Laughlin in 1915. Clark's doctoral dissertation had been on railway regulation and Laughlin wanted a 'railway man' (J. Laurence Laughlin to H.C. Adams, 7 April 1915, H.C. Adams Papers, Box 10, Folder April 1915). At this point in his career, however, Clark was attempting to accommodate Veblen's critique of neoclassical economics, and was turning his interest to issues such as social value, economics and psychology, institutional reform and 'social control'. His paper at the 1918 conference session was titled 'Economic theory in an era of social readjustment' (Clark 1919), and complemented Hamilton's paper by arguing for an economics 'actively relevant to the issues of its time'.

Another member of this group was Harold Moulton. Moulton completed his PhD at Chicago in 1914 under Laughlin, but he also admired Veblen (Dorfman 1959). He became an assistant professor at Chicago in the same year. Clark, Hamilton, and Moulton co-authored *Readings in the Economics of War* (1918). Moulton developed interests in monetary and financial economics, and his work contained a clear underconsumptionist position. He was promoted rapidly and stayed at Chicago until 1922.

In the period up to 1918, the department at Chicago contained, at various times, virtually all of those individuals most closely associated with the founding of the institutionalist movement: Veblen, Hoxie, Mitchell, Hamilton, and Clark. Chicago, thus, has a strong claim to be seen as the birthplace of what became known as 'institutional economics'. Other Chicago graduates in economics from this time who would become associated with institutionalism include Edwin Nourse (PhD 1915) and Sumner Slichter (PhD

1918). Outside of economics, Clarence Ayres completed his dissertation in philosophy on economics and ethics (Ayres 1917) and remained at Chicago teaching philosophy until 1920 when he moved to Amherst and joined Walton Hamilton on the faculty. Later, in 1930 he was hired to Texas and became the leading figure in the institutionalist group there (Rutherford 2002, 2003).

It is also worth mentioning that Laughlin and his successor as department head, L.C. Marshall, encouraged women students, and that the Department of Political Economy had close connections with the then independent Chicago School of Civics and Philanthropy. Although not usually spoken of as a part of the institutionalist canon, much of the work done by these women was statistical and institutional in character. The first female PhD in economics was Katherine Bement Davis who came under the influence of Veblen and wrote her thesis on 'Causes affecting the standard of living and wages' (Davis 1900). Sophonisba Breckinridge obtained her PhD in 1901 in political science, but she also studied economics and her thesis was written under Laughlin on the topic of monetary history (Breckinridge 1903). She taught a course on 'The state in relation to labor' in the Department of Political Economy in 1902 (Hammond 2000b). She studied in the Law School, graduating in 1904, and then taught in Chicago's Department of Household Administration. In 1907 she began teaching in the Department of Social Investigation in the School of Civics and Philanthropy. She became Director of that Department in 1908, and Dean of the School in 1909. The second female PhD in economics was Edith Abbott, a student of Laughlin, Veblen, Mitchell, and Breckinridge (from whom she took courses in the Department of Household Administration). Her thesis was 'A statistical study of the wages of unskilled labor in the United States' (Abbott 1905). In 1908 she was hired by Breckinridge to teach statistics in the School of Civics and Philanthropy. She also taught in the Department of Political Economy in 1909–10 (Hammond 2000a).

Breckinridge and Abbott had a major impact on the School of Civics and Philanthropy. They encouraged their students to take graduate degrees in economics or political science and also worked to restructure the curriculum of the school itself, 'emphasizing statistics, empirical research and the scientific method, and making it increasingly like the graduate training in economics, political science and law that they themselves had received' (Hammond 2000b, p. 84). They produced a remarkable stream of empirical research and worked to make the school a part of the university, which they succeeded in doing in 1920 with the establishment of the Graduate School of Social Service Administration.

Chicago economics and institutionalism in the 1920s and 1930s

The interwar period is sometimes seen as a period in which the 'first Chicago School' was formed. The usual presentation of this first Chicago School tends to focus on Jacob Viner, Frank Knight, and Henry Simons (Miller 1962), seeing them as precursors to the modern Chicago School associated with Milton Friedman and Stigler. There is truth in this, particularly with respect to the 'affinity group' that formed around Frank Knight in the mid-1930s. In addition to Knight, Simons and Lloyd Mints, this group included Friedman, Rose Friedman Director, Aaron Director, Stigler and Allen Wallis (Reder 1982, pp. 6–7).

Nevertheless, throughout much of the interwar period the department remained very much a 'mixed bag' (ibid., pp. 2–3). Viner had been hired in 1916. He brought with him a commitment to neoclassical theory, but he was a scholar of considerable breadth and became close friends with J.M. Clark. Clark remained on the Chicago faculty until 1926 when he was hired away by Columbia (Viner was the other candidate seriously considered). At that point Clark had just completed his book *The Social Control of Business* (1926) which detailed numerous types of market failures and the need for regulation of business. The department also contained Leon C. Marshall in commerce, Chester Wright in economic history, Harry Millis in labor economics and James Field in population economics; all of whom were as much institutionalist as anything else. Millis was Commons's first graduate student at Indiana, and he always thought of Millis as one of 'his boys'. Field taught a course on standards of living, and in the early 1920s Marshall, Wright and Field all worked on an experiment to develop a 'case and problem presentation of economics' to supplement, and even substitute for, more traditional texts (Neill 1972, p. 27). Paul Douglas was hired in 1920, and combined neoclassical and institutional approaches. His work included important empirical applications of neoclassical theory, a broad interest in labor issues and a reform sensibility more in line with the institutionalists (Reder 1982, p. 3). Douglas also championed underconsumptionist ideas and led the effort to have Veblen nominated for the Presidency of the American Economic Association.

Graduates from the early 1920s included several individuals who took to institutionalist ideas and approaches. Harold Innis (PhD 1920) wrote under Wright's supervision but was much influenced by Veblen. He went on to have a major impact on economics and economic history in Canada. According to Innis, there was an informal group who met to discuss the work of Veblen. This group included Innis, Morris Copeland, Carter Goodrich and Frank Knight (then an instructor in statistics at Chicago), so it is clear that interest in Veblen's work at Chicago survived his departure by many years (Neill 1972, p. 12). Copeland graduated in 1921 under J.M. Clark's supervision (Copeland 1921). Copeland had been an undergraduate student at Amherst where Walton Hamilton was teaching. He went on to become a central member of the institutionalist movement in the interwar period (Rutherford 2002). Another Amherst student, Carter Goodrich, was awarded his doctorate from Chicago in 1921 for a thesis on British workshop politics (1920), prepared on the basis of work with Henry Clay in England, an opportunity arranged by Walton Hamilton. Goodrich later specialized in labor economics and American economic history, taught at Michigan and Columbia and was closely associated with the institutionalist movement (Rutherford 2004).

Other graduates with institutionalist credentials include Hazel Kyrk (PhD 1920) and Helen R. Wright (PhD 1922). Kyrk wrote on 'The consumer's guidance of economic activity' under Field, and won the prestigious Hart, Schaeffner and Marx prize, which led to her dissertation's publication as *A Theory of Consumption* (Kyrk 1923). In 1925 she was appointed to the Department of Home Economics at Chicago, and later held a joint appointment with the Department of Economics. She continued to work in the fields of consumption and household economics (Kyrk 1933). Kyrk was highly critical of marginal utility theory as a basis for a theory of consumption and emphasized the social nature of the formation of consumption values. She echoed Mitchell's view, expressed in his essay 'The backward art of spending money' (1912), that the 'business man's calculation of profit and loss cannot be transferred to a field not controlled by pecuniary standards' (Kyrk 1923, p. 144). Thus, consumption patterns relate to conventionally defined 'standards of living'. Kyrk undertook to measure and critically analyze existing standards of living, and to create policy to help achieve higher standards of living. In her later work, Kyrk discussed the household in both its producing and consuming roles, the division of labor between the sexes, employment and earnings of women, adequacy of family incomes, and issues of risks of disability, unemployment, provision for the future, social security and the protection and education of the consumer (Dorfman 1959, pp. 570–78, Hirschfeld 1997, Beller and Kiss 2001, 2003).

Helen Wright was encouraged to pursue her PhD in economics after studying with Breckinridge and Abbott in the School of Civics and Philanthropy; she wrote on the nineteenth-century British labor movement (Wright 1922). She and Edwin Nourse were then hired to the Institute of Economics by Harold Moulton, who had left Chicago to head up the Institute in 1922. She also taught in the Robert Brookings Graduate School founded in 1923 and headed by Walton Hamilton, and co-authored two books on the American bituminous coal industry with Hamilton (Hamilton and Wright 1925, 1928). The Brookings Graduate School had a strongly institutionalist orientation (Rutherford 2003). When the school disappeared in the merger that formed the Brookings Institution in 1928, Wright was invited to join the Graduate School of Social Service Administration by Abbott, and in 1941 she succeeded Abbott as Dean of the School.

In the later 1920s several important additions were made to the Chicago faculty in economics. Henry Schultz, a student of Henry Moore's at Columbia, came in 1926. Lloyd Mints took over the teaching of the money and banking courses in 1927. Frank Knight and his student, Henry Simons, arrived from the University of Iowa in 1927. Knight's relationship with the institutionalists is discussed in more detail below. Aaron Director initially joined the department to work with Paul Douglas but he soon became a leading member of the group that gathered around Frank Knight. On the other hand, Chicago also hired John Nef in 1929. Nef had completed a major work on the history of the British coal-mining industry (1932), had worked with Richard Tawney in England, and was a graduate of the Brookings Graduate School to which Hamilton had recruited him. Hamilton and Moulton helped him to obtain the position at Chicago (Nef 1973). Influenced by his Brookings experience, Nef was never happy with disciplinary divisions and (along with Knight, Robert Hutchins and others) was instrumental in founding the interdisciplinary Committee on Social Thought in the early 1940s.

Some criticisms of institutionalism did begin to emerge from Chicago from about the late 1920s onward, but these lines of attack did not come from a consistent point of view. In 1928 Henry Schultz complained:

> [S]ome economists, among whom are to be included not a few members of the institutional school, have, unfortunately, gotten the impression that any attempt to derive a law of demand must needs be based on no better psychology than that of James Mill. A few of them go so far as to deny the existence of the law of demand. (Schultz 1928, p. 95)

Schultz was to continue his critique of the institutionalists' approach to empirical work in a sharp rebuke to the work of the Wisconsin Tariff Research Committee, a Committee that included J.R. Commons and Walter Morton (Schultz 1935), and in a public lecture given in 1937 that was explicitly critical of Mitchell's quantitative methods (Schultz 1937 [2000]). In a 1928 AEA roundtable on quantitative methods, Viner (1928) defended qualitative neoclassical theory and expressed concerns about the applicability of natural science methods to economics. This contribution is clearly a response to Mitchell's view that quantitative work would lead to a very different kind of economics focused on quantitative measurement and empirically testable propositions (Mitchell 1925). Knight pursued a more radical line of attack, being altogether critical of the scientism of those who espoused quantitative and empirical methods. Knight also attacked the behaviorism of institutionalists such as Copeland, and the policy interventionism of those such as Sumner Slichter (Knight 1924 [1999], 1932 [1999]). Knight's criticisms were not limited to institutionalists, however, and he was hostile to both Schultz and Douglas (Reder 1982, p. 6). It is worth noting here that in 1935 the hostility between Knight and Douglas spilled over into the issue of the continued appointment of Simons and Director. Both had poor publication records and the department, with the sole exception of Knight, was opposed to reappointing them. Nevertheless Knight accused Douglas of conducting a personal vendetta against him and of being motivated by a 'thirst for blood' (Frank Knight to Paul Douglas, 5 January 1935, and Paul Douglas to Frank Knight, 5 January 1935, Frank H. Knight Papers, Box 59, Folder 16).

Despite the emerging criticism of institutionalist work, the idea of a Chicago Department dominated by a consistently neoclassical and conservative point of view does not hold for either the 1920s or 1930s. Viner and Knight had many differences, Knight was no orthodox neoclassical, Viner was not opposed to various types of intervention, and the socialist Oscar Lange joined the Chicago Department in 1938. Of course, Henry Simons had previously produced his *Positive Program for Laissez Faire* (Simons 1934) which is often seen as a highly free-market tract. It does propose strong enforcement of antitrust laws, a monetary rule to stabilize the price level, and a 100 percent reserve policy. All the same, Simons's monetary views were not unique to Chicago and were shared by some institutionalists, such as John R. Commons. Simons's further proposal that the regulation of natural monopolies should be replaced by public ownership was endorsed by institutionalists concerned with regulation issues, such as Columbia's James Bonbright.

Also, over much of this period one would be hard put to distinguish the doctoral dissertations being produced at Chicago from those at Columbia. Theodore Yntema (a Viner/Schultz student) stands out as having a theoretical dissertation, but many seem quite institutional. Hazel Kyrk passed on her anti-neoclassical views to her student Margaret Reid, whose thesis was entitled 'The economics of the household' (1931). In 1933 Ruth Allen graduated with a thesis on women's labor in cotton production (1933), supervised by Millis and with a committee that included Douglas, Knight and Mints. Allen went on to become an important member of the institutionalist group at the University of Texas (Bernasek and Kinnear 1996). One of the few students supervised to completion by Knight was Stigler, whose dissertation was in the history of economic theory (Stigler 1941). Friedman began under Schultz, but then went to Columbia to study with Harold Hotelling, and later (in 1937) joined the staff of the National Bureau of Economic Research, taking over Simon Kuznets's project on professional incomes. This project eventually became his 1945 doctoral dissertation (Friedman and Kuznets 1945).

Knight and institutional economics

In a recent article, Geoff Hodgson (2001) argues that Knight should be classified as an institutional economist, although a 'maverick' institutionalist (but see Emmett 1999,

2006b). Hodgson's argument is based largely on Knight's views on the limits to price theory, his deep interest in issues of institutional change and what he called 'historical sociology', his teaching of a course on 'Economics from an institutional standpoint', and his admiration for the work of Max Weber. Indeed, Knight had arrived in Chicago with the expectation of teaching in institutional economics and not in economic theory (Emmett 2006b). He knew the work of institutionalists such as Veblen, Commons, Mitchell, Copeland and Ayres well; indeed, he was friends with Ayres, and also corresponded frequently with Copeland and Max Handman on issues including valuation, behaviorism, economic history and the treatment of consumption. Knight's concern with valuation and consumption issues also led him to read and critique Hazel Kyrk's instrumental theory of valuation contained in her *Theory of Consumption* (Frank H. Knight Papers, Box 36, Folder 22). In addition, Knight encouraged Abram Harris's work on the interpretation of Veblen, Marx and institutional economics (Harris 1932, 1934). Nevertheless, Knight subjected the ideas of the institutionalists to sustained criticism, attacked all varieties of 'scientism', held a deeply distrustful view of political processes (and of those who sought political position or influence) and consistently maintained the central importance of standard price theory in any economic analysis, whether theoretical or historical in nature. These aspects of this thinking separate him from the members of the institutionalist movement in vital respects.

For Knight, economic theory deals with the problem of rational choice, of using given means to achieve given ends, or the sphere of 'economizing' behavior. Economic theory of this type is highly abstract and general: 'There are no laws regarding the *content* of economic behaviour, but there are laws universally valid as to its *form*. There is an abstract rationale of all conduct which is rational at all, and a rationale of all social relations arising through the organization of rational activity' (Knight 1924 [1999], p. 28). These general laws, in Knight's view, are *not* institutional or historically relative. Institutions 'supply much of their content and furnish the machinery by which they work themselves out, more or less quickly and completely, in different actual situations', but the 'general laws of choice among competing motives or goods are not institutional' (ibid., p. 30). For Knight, specific content came from the application of economic theory to particular historical situations, where resources, technology, institutions, social values and norms could be taken as given, but the theory itself was to be understood as an ideal type, both abstract and general.

The broader task of understanding the changing institutions, social values and norms was the subject matter of institutional economics or of historical sociology. These issues, and particularly the question of the development of capitalism and of its particular values, much concerned Knight. Knight made it clear that he did 'not take the American institutional economics very seriously', but he did 'take economics from an institutional standpoint very seriously' (Earl Hamilton, Economics 305 notes, Summer 1935, Frank H. Knight Papers, Box 38, Folder 8). What Knight wanted to do was to take up the institutionalist 'challenge' and 'make some real contribution toward an understanding of institutional development' (Frank Knight to Clarence Ayres, 16 February 1937, Clarence E. Ayres Papers, Box 3F290, Frank Knight folder). However, even in this context he argued that a proper understanding of the principles of the price theory was absolutely central. In his review of Sombart's *Modern Capitalism*, Knight complained that its 'most striking feature . . . is the author's failure to understand the elementary mechanics of the competitive economic organization' (Knight 1928 [1999, p. 134]), a complaint he extended to most historians and institutional economists. Of the American institutionalists, his most generous comments concerned Commons's work, work that he regarded as hopelessly unsystematic but highly 'suggestive and valuable' (Knight 1935). Kenneth Parsons's article 'John R. Commons' point of view' (Parsons 1942) originated as a paper for Knight's course; Knight being interested in the issue of whether Commons had 'a system' (Parsons 1976). Knight admired Weber on the grounds that 'he is the only one who really deals with the problem of causes or approaches the material from that angle that can alone yield an answer to such questions, that is, the angle of comparative history in the broad sense' (Knight 1928 [1999], p. 143).

In Knight's view both legal developments and the religious element stressed by Weber were major factors in the development of capitalism. In particular, he pointed to the 'change in the content of the property concept, its differentiation into numerous forms, and the liberation of both men and things from the prescription of authority and tradition', the development of rationality, science and of deliberative action, and the constructive rather than purely acquisitive nature that the 'spirit of enterprise' gained under capitalism (Knight 1928 [1999]). All the same, from the various outlines and course notes available it appears that while Knight provided an informed discussion of many episodes in economic history, and both presented and critiqued a wide variety of treatments of institutions and institutional change, he did not succeed in providing a complete or well-articulated treatment of his own views on institutional change.

Knight taught his course on 'Economics from an institutional standpoint' from the early 1930s through to at least 1942, but the course was not always offered. There is also mention of his teaching a seminar on Max Weber, a seminar attended by both Friedman and Stigler (Leeson 2000, p. 57). However, what most students took from Knight seems *not* to have been his concerns with issues of long-term institutional change, but his views of the central importance of price theory and of competitive markets. Knight's own work included both the 'as if' approach to the theory of rational choice, and the claim that the problem of monopoly and monopolistic competition was much overstated. Related to this was his generally positive appraisal of the competitive price system, at least as compared with any alternative political processes, and his classical liberal philosophy and set of values. These ideas became an important part of the later 'Chicago View' and were communicated to students through Knight's little book *The Economic Organization* (Knight 1933; see reading guide by Ross Emmett, ch. 4, this volume), as well as through his courses on theory and on the history of economic thought, the latter concentrating on Adam Smith. Among his students, Knight's concerns about the limits to price theory, and the problems created by changing social values, seem to have been largely ignored or dismissed (Stigler and Becker 1977, Emmett 2006a).

Chicago economics and institutionalism after 1940

Many changes occurred in the Chicago Department from the late 1930s onward. Henry Schultz died in a car accident in 1938, Douglas became increasingly involved in politics from 1939 on, the Cowles Commission arrived at Chicago in October 1939 (later resulting in appointments for Jacob Marschak and Tjalling Koopmans), Millis retired in 1940, T.W. Schultz joined the department from Iowa State in 1943 (soon to become head of the department), Lange left Chicago in 1945 and Viner in 1946. Simons, who had been teaching half time in the Law School, committed suicide in 1946, and Aaron Director was appointed to the Law School the same year. Milton Friedman was hired to the Economics Department and Allen Wallis to the Business School in 1946. Stigler was considered for the position filled by Friedman (he failed to impress the administration), but was eventually appointed in 1958 (in the School of Business with a joint appointment in economics). F.A. Hayek was also at Chicago from 1950, although his appointment was with Nef's Committee on Social Thought and he was never appointed to the Economics Department. It is worth noting that Nef made many efforts to have the department hire faculty in economic history and sought to maintain a degree of intellectual breadth in the department. At Nef's urging, offers were made to Harold Innis on more than one occasion, and Earl Hamilton was hired in 1947. Mention should also be made of the hiring of Margaret Reid in 1951 into a joint appointment in the departments of Economics and Home Economics. She had been a student of Hazel Kyrk's and a colleague of T.W. Schultz's at Iowa State, during which time she had written her *Economics of Household Production* (Reid 1934). Schultz also had an interest in the economics of the household and was keen to add her to the faculty to continue her empirical work on household and consumer behavior.

As indicated above, the mid-1930s saw the development of a small group of Knight's students who were beginning to function 'in a loosely coordinated fashion to advance their common ideas' (Reder 1982, p. 7). By 1945 the dominant position of Keynesian and imperfect competition theories in the profession led Simons to make proposals to preserve 'at least one place where some political economists of the future may be thoroughly and competently trained along traditional-liberal lines' (Coase 1993, pp. 244–5). Simons was pessimistic about the prospects, but the 'the key to the development and eventual dominance of the "Chicago View"' in the post-Second World War period was the uniting of Friedman, Stigler, and Wallis on the Chicago faculty (Reder 1982, p. 10). Friedman took the leadership in promoting the Chicago View, particularly in his price theory course, his work on macroeconomic and monetary economics and his methodological viewpoint. Friedman's main targets were Keynesian economics, the work of those associated with Cowles and the imperfect competition theories of Edward Chamberlin and Joan Robinson. Stigler also mounted many attacks, 'Demolition Derbies' to use Thomas Sowell's phrase (Sowell 1993), on monopolistic competition theory (Leeson 2000), on Paul Sweezy's kinked demand curve (Stigler 1947a), on Harvey Leibenstein's X-efficiency concept (Stigler 1976, Freedman 2002), on Richard Lester's challenge to marginalism based on a survey of business decision making (Stigler 1947b) and on institutionalist writing such as Gardiner Means's work on administered prices (Stigler and Kindahl 1970), J.K. Galbraith on countervailing power (Stigler 1954) and Berle and Means on corporate ownership and behavior (Stigler and Friedland 1983). Stigler was openly contemptuous of institutionalist work, saying: 'Institutional economics is dying out at a fantastic rate – though still not fast enough to suit me' (Sowell 1993, p. 788).

Chicago economics, however, became much more than a combination of traditional competitive price theory and monetarism, spreading itself into a variety of new areas. The Chicago View, with its strong pro-market, anti-regulatory, emphasis became the basis of Chicago law and economics. Simons's teaching in the Law School had begun this trend, but it was with Aaron Director and his contribution to teaching of the antitrust course with Edward Levi, and the founding of the *Journal of Law & Economics* in 1958, that brought Chicago law and economics to the fore (Duxbury 1995). Ronald Coase joined the Chicago Law School (from the University of Virginia) in 1964, and much work on the economics of property rights stemmed from Coase, Stigler and students such as Harold Demsetz. Others, such as James Buchanan and Warren Nutter developed Knight's concerns with classical liberal philosophy into the area of public choice theory; Buchanan by making the important distinction between the constitutional level of rules and the rules that emerge from the decision making within that constitution (Buchanan and Tullock 1962). In addition, Chicago became associated with the neoclassical approach to the economics of the household in the person of Gary Becker (1965, 1976). Becker spent 1954–57 at Chicago, then moved to Columbia, where he came into contact with Jacob Mincer, before returning in 1969. Mincer had also had exposure to Chicago as a post-doctoral student (Grossbard-Sheltman 2001). In these ways Chicago economics moved the analytics of price theory out of its traditional realm and into areas previously cultivated by American institutionalists. Thus, important elements of what has become known as the 'new' institutional economics – which often presents itself as diametrically opposed to the 'old' American institutionalism – also had their roots in Chicago.

Despite the obvious and substantial differences between old-style American institutional economics and modern Chicago School economics, there are a number of interesting links between them. Unlike Knight, both Friedman and Stigler undertook considerable amounts of empirical work. The empirical orientation of Friedman and Stigler can be seen especially strongly in their early connections with the National Bureau of Economic Research. Friedman's contact with the NBER began in 1937 when he took over Simon Kuznets's study of professional income. Later, at Arthur Burns's urging, he took on the study of the monetary aspects of the business cycle which resulted in Friedman and Schwartz's *Monetary History* (1963). These studies were very much in the traditional Mitchell–Burns NBER empirical mold. Friedman held both Mitchell and Burns in high regard (Burns had been his teacher at Rutgers), and the attack on Burns and Mitchell's *Measuring Business Cycles* (1946) by Koopmans of the Cowles Commission (Koopmans 1947) may have had something to do with Friedman's hostility to Cowles. Friedman's later methodological position, as expressed in his famous 'The methodology of positive economics' (1953), can be seen as a combination of NBER empiricism with various positivist notions of science and his own interpretation of Karl Popper's emphasis on the testing of predictions. Friedman's essay is clearly a criticism both of Cowles and of the various attacks then being made on the 'unrealism' of the standard neoclassical assumptions (Hirsch and De Marchi 1990, Hammond 1996). Stigler had also had an early association with the NBER, and he enthusiastically took up Friedman's emphasis on the testing of predictions, using it with great rhetorical force against the critics of competitive price theory.

Chicago, through the person of Robert Fogel, also has an association with cliometrics, but this too has some institutionalist connections. Fogel was a student of Carter Goodrich at Columbia, who was then working on questions relating to canals and American economic development, but given Fogel's empirical interests, Goodrich suggested he transfer to Johns Hopkins to work with Kuznets (Rutherford 2004).

Another line of connection runs from Margaret Reid to the 'new' economics of the household and consumption economics. Both Mincer and Becker were exposed to Reid's work on the household while at Chicago (Grossbard-Sheltman 2001). Moreover, the empirical work of Reid, along with others such as Dorothy Brady and Rose Friedman, on income and consumption was instrumental in prompting Milton Friedman's development of the permanent income hypothesis (Friedman 1957, p. ix, Forget 2000). Friedman himself had worked on professional income for the NBER, and a significant part of the work of Reid, Brady, and Rose Friedman was conducted through the NBER's Conference on Income and Wealth. A consistent interest in consumption and household economics, running from the institutional approaches of Veblen, Abbott, Kyrk and Reid to the neoclassicism of Theodore Schultz, Becker and Friedman, is a notable feature of the history of Chicago economics.

An additional, and fascinating, institutionalist–Chicago connection runs through Rutledge Vining. Vining graduated from Chicago in 1944 with a thesis on regional variation of short-run business cycles, but he had also been taught by Frank Knight. Vining became a research associate at the National Bureau, and it was Vining who wrote the reply to Koopmans defending the Burns/Mitchell approach to business cycles (Vining 1949). His NBER experience gave him an interest in the institutionalist conception of a 'price system' or 'economic system' that underlay much of the empirical work of institutionalists such as Mitchell and F.C. Mills, but which had never been made explicit (Rutledge Vining to Arthur Burns, June 10 and October 9, 1963, Arthur F. Burns Papers, Box 35, Folder Vining (2)). Vining sought to make a 'simple peace' between statistical economists and the methodological writings of Knight. For Vining, quantitative economics was not about solving social problems but about 'the behavior properties of population systems' (Vining 1950). Such systems can be thought of as consisting of individuals acting within a set of 'laws' or rules that are largely institutional in nature. Such laws he thought of as stochastic in nature, producing variations in outcomes. From this he developed a concern with the problem of 'diagnosing faultiness in the observed performance of an economic system' (Vining 1962) and an emphasis on ensuring that policy did not merely attack symptoms but operated on the level of the underlying rules or structure of the system. In Vining's view the policy maker's job was to choose the rules rather than to try to directly regulate outcomes. Vining spent his career at the University of Virginia (from 1945) and recruited Buchanan and Nutter there. For many years Buchanan and Vining were close, and Vining's emphasis on the underlying institutional rules was a vital factor in the development of Buchanan's own thinking, as Buchanan himself has often acknowledged (Buchanan and Tullock 1962, p. 210).

Finally, there are some connections between the Chicago law and economics movement, and the earlier legal realist movement. Legal scholars such as Karl Llewellyn were major figures in this movement, but it also involved institutional economists such as Commons, Walton Hamilton, and Robert Hale. Hamilton joined the Yale Law School in 1928 and Hale moved from economics to the Law School at Columbia in the same year. Hiring economists into law schools was thus very far from a Chicago invention; it was in fact the legal realists who 'initiated the interdisciplinary turn in American legal education' (Leiter 2001, p. 9001). Edward Levi was interested in the relationship between law and the social sciences, very much a realist theme, and entirely familiar with the work of Llewellyn and Hamilton. Llewellyn was hired from Columbia to Chicago in 1951, and it was while he was at Chicago that he made many of his major contributions to the formulation of the Uniform Commercial Code. Llewellyn's argument concerning commercial law is relevant in that he claimed that the courts tended to enforce the norms of prevailing commercial practice, including the obligation of 'good faith' or the observance of 'reasonable commercial standards of fair dealing in the trade' (ibid., p. 9000). A similar view was expressed by Commons. Schwartz (2001) has argued that this anticipated the more recent law and economics position concerning the efficiency of common law. Efficiency is 'an important norm of mercantile practice', thus if judges enforce these norms 'it will turn out that judges will try, among other things, to produce efficient outcomes' (Leiter 2001, p. 9001).

Posner and others have denied that Chicago law and economics owes anything directly to the legal realist movement, and this is a controversial topic (Posner 1995). Posner himself frequently cites Justice Holmes's sociological jurisprudence and refers often to John Dewey's pragmatism, both of which were sources for the more sociological end of the realist movement. On the other hand, it should not be surprising that Llewellyn himself did not entirely approve of the particular type of neoclassical law and economics being developed by Director and others at Chicago (Kitch 1983). As with other Chicago work, we find here an older institutionalist theme being reworked and modified through the application of neoclassical price theory.

Conclusion

If the term 'institutional economics' is defined broadly enough (to encompass any approach with a central concern with economic institutions) then there is a sense in which Chicago economics has always been institutional. The particular expression of this interest in institutions has, however, varied significantly. Initially, Chicago was the home of the American institutional economics of Veblen, Mitchell, Hoxie, Hamilton, Kyrk and others of similar viewpoint and this type of institutionalism persisted at Chicago much later than usually thought – well into the 1920s. Slightly later in the interwar period, Knight pursued his own attempt to develop the 'institutional standpoint' in order to deal with those factors taken as given by standard price theory. This attempt was explicitly in reaction to, and critical of, the previous work by those associated with American institutionalism, and Knight drew most inspiration from the work of Max Weber.

Knight's direct influence on later Chicago economics seems to have run more in terms of his commitment to the importance of price theory and his liberal philosophy than in terms of his particular treatment of institutions. Knight's students transformed this into a more general concern with the defence of the market and of liberal values, and related criticisms of government regulation and macro policy intervention. The work undertaken to develop these concerns, as well as the long Chicago tradition in consumption and household economics, seems to have led to a renewed interest in the functioning of various economic, social, legal and political institutions, but this time from an essentially neoclassical standpoint. This 'neoclassicalization' of older institutionalist themes was very much a trademark of the Chicago economics of the 1960s and 1970s.

Note

* Research for this chapter was supported by a research grant from the Social Science Research Council of Canada. My thanks to Claire Hammond and Ronnie J. Phillips for references and materials, to James M. Buchanan for sharing his knowledge of Chicago, Virginia, and of Rutledge Vining with me, and to my research assistant Cristobal Young.

References

H.C. Adams Papers, Bentley Historical Library, University of Michigan.
Clarence E. Ayres Papers, Center for American History, University of Texas, Austin.
Arthur F. Burns Papers, Dwight D. Eisenhower Library, Abilene, Kansas.
Frank H. Knight Papers, Special Collections Research Center, University of Chicago Library.
John U. Nef Papers, Special Collections Research Center, University of Chicago Library.
George J. Stigler Papers, Special Collections Research Center, University of Chicago Library.
University of Wisconsin-Madison Archives, Oral History Project.

Abbott, E. (1905), 'A statistical study of the wages of unskilled labor in the United States', PhD dissertation, Economics, University of Chicago, Chicago, IL.

Allen, R.A. (1933), 'The labor of women in the production of cotton', PhD dissertation, Economics, University of Chicago, Chicago, IL.

Ayres, C.E. (1917), 'On the nature of the relationship between economics and ethics', PhD dissertation, Philosophy, University of Chicago, Chicago, IL.

Becker, G.S. (1965), 'A theory of the allocation of time', *Economic Journal*, **75** (299), 493–515.

Becker, G.S. (1976), *The Economic Approach to Human Behavior*, Chicago, IL: University of Chicago Press.

Beller, A.H. and D.E. Kiss (2001), 'Hazel Kyrk', in *Women Building Chicago 1790–1990*, Schultz, R.L. and A. Hast (eds), Bloomington, IN: Indiana University Press, pp. 482–5.

Beller, A.H. and D.E. Kiss (2003), 'On the contribution of Hazel Kyrk to family economics', Paper presented at 'Institutional and Chicago economics', History of Economics Society session, Allied Social Science Association meeting, Washington, DC, January.

Bernasek, A. and D. Kinnear (1996), 'Ruth Allen: frontier labor economist', in *Political Economy and Public Policy*, vol. 9, *Economic Mavericks: The Texas Institutionalists*, Phillips, R.J. (ed.), Greenwich, CT: JAI Press, pp. 75–106.

Breckinridge, S.P. (1903), *Legal Tender: A Study in English and American Monetary History*, Chicago, IL: University of Chicago Press.

Buchanan, J.M. and G. Tullock (1962), *The Calculus of Consent: Logical Foundations of Constitutional Democracy*, Ann Arbor, MI: University of Michigan Press.

Burns, A.F. and W.C. Mitchell (1946), *Measuring Business Cycles*, New York: National Bureau of Economic Research.

Clark, J.M. (1919), 'Economic theory in an era of social readjustment', *American Economic Review*, **9** (1, Supplement), 280–90.

Clark, J.M. (1926), *The Social Control of Business*, Chicago, IL: University of Chicago Press.

Clark, J.M., W.H. Hamilton and H.G. Moulton (eds) (1918), *Readings in the Economics of War*, Chicago, IL: University of Chicago Press.

Coase, R.H. (1984), 'The new institutional economics', *Journal of Institutional and Theoretical Economics*, **140**, 229–31.

Coase, R.H. (1993), 'Law and economics at Chicago', *Journal of Law & Economics*, **36** (1, part 2), 239–54.

Copeland (1921), 'Some phases of institutional value theory', PhD dissertation, Economics, University of Chicago, Chicago, IL.

Davis, K.B. (1900), 'Causes affecting the standard of living and wages', PhD dissertation, Economics, University of Chicago, Chicago, IL.

Dorfman, J. (1959), *The Economic Mind in American Civilization*, vol. 4–5, 1918–1933, New York: Viking Press.

Dorfman, J. (1974), 'Walton Hale Hamilton and industrial policy', in *Industrial Policy and Institutionalism: Selected Essays*, Hamilton, W.H. (ed.), Clifton, NJ: A.M. Kelley, pp. 5–28.

Duxbury, N. (1995), *Patterns of American Jurisprudence*, Oxford: Clarendon Press.

Emmett, R.B. (1999), 'Introduction', in *Selected Essays by Frank H. Knight*, vol. 1, *'What is truth' in economics?*, Emmett, R.B. (ed.), Chicago, IL: University of Chicago Press, pp. vii–xxiv.

Emmett, R.B. (2006a), 'De gustibus *est* disputandum: Frank H. Knight's response to George Stigler and Gary Becker's De gustibus non est disputandum', *Journal of Economic Methodology*, **13** (1), 97–111.

Emmett, R.B. (2006b), 'Frank H. Knight, Max Weber, Chicago economics, and institutionalism', *Max Weber Studies*, Beiheft 1: *Weber and Economics*, 101–19.

Forget, E.L. (2000), 'Margaret Gilpin Reid (1896–1991)', in *A Biographical Dictionary of Women Economists*, Dimand, R.W., M.A. Dimand and E.L. Forget (eds), Cheltenham, UK and Northampton, MA, USA: Edward Elgar, pp. 357–61.

Freedman, C.F. (2002), 'The Xistence of definitional economics – Stigler's and Leibenstein's war of the words', *Cambridge Journal of Economics*, **26** (2), 161–78.

Friedman, M. (1953), 'The methodology of positive economics', in *Essays in Positive Economics*, Chicago, IL: University of Chicago Press, pp. 3–43.

Friedman, M. (1957), *A Theory of the Consumption Function*, Princeton, NJ: Princeton University Press.
Friedman, M. and S. Kuznets (1945), *Income from Independent Professional Practice*, New York: National Bureau of Economic Research.
Friedman, M. and A.J. Schwartz (1963), *A Monetary History of the United States, 1867–1960*, Princeton, NJ: Princeton University Press.
Goodrich, C.L. (1920), *The Frontier of Control: A Study of British Workshop Politics*, New York: Harcourt, Brace & Howe.
Grossbard-Sheltman, S. (2001), 'The new home economics at Columbia and Chicago', *Feminist Economics*, **7** (3), 103–30.
Hamilton, W.H. (1916), 'The development of Hoxie's economics', *Journal of Political Economy*, **24** (9), 855–83.
Hamilton, W.H. (1919), 'The institutional approach to economic theory', *American Economic Review*, **9** (1, Supplement), 309–18.
Hamilton, W.H. and H.R. Wright (1925), *The Case of Bituminous Coal*, New York: Macmillan.
Hamilton, W.H. and H.R. Wright (1928), *A Way of Order for Bituminous Coal*, New York: Macmillan.
Hammond, C.H. (2000a), 'Edith Abbott (1876–1957)', in *A Biographical Dictionary of Women Economists*, Dimand, R.W., M.A. Dimand and E.L. Forget (eds), Cheltenham, UK and Northampton, MA, USA: Edward Elgar, pp. 1–7.
Hammond, C.H. (2000b), 'Sophonisba Breckinridge (1866–1948)', in *A Biographical Dictionary of Women Economists*, Dimand, R.W., M.A. Dimand and E.L. Forget (eds), Cheltenham, UK and Northampton, MA, USA: Edward Elgar, pp. 81–8.
Hammond, J.D. (1996), *Theory and Measurement: Causality Issues in Milton Friedman's Monetary Economics*, Cambridge: Cambridge University Press.
Harris, A.L. (1932), 'Types of institutionalism', *Journal of Political Economy*, **40** (6), 721–49.
Harris, A.L. (1934), 'Economic evolution: dialectical and Darwinian', *Journal of Political Economy*, **42** (1), 34–79.
Hirsch, A. and N. De Marchi (1990), *Milton Friedman: Economics in Theory and Practice*, Ann Arbor, MI: University of Michigan Press.
Hirschfeld, M.L. (1997), 'Methodological stance and consumption theory: a lesson in feminist methodology', in *New Economics and Its History*, David, J.B. (ed.), Durham, NC: Duke University Press, 191–211.
Hodgson, G.M. (2001), 'Frank Knight as an institutional economist', in *Economics Broadly Considered: Essays in Honor of Warren J. Samuels*, Biddle, J.E., J.B. Davis and S.G. Medema (eds), London: Routledge, pp. 64–93.
Hodgson, G.M. (2004), 'Veblen in Chicago: the winds of creativity', in *Research in the History of Economic Thought and Methodology*, 22-A, Samuels, W.J. and J.E. Biddle (eds), Amsterdam: Elsevier Science, pp. 145–60.
Hoxie, R.F. (1917), *Trade Unionism in the United States*, New York: Appleton.
Kitch, E.W. (1983), 'The fire of truth: a remembrance of law and economics at Chicago, 1932–1970', *Journal of Law & Economics*, **26** (1), 163–234.
Knight, F.H. (1933), *The Economic Organization*, Chicago, IL: University of Chicago.
Knight, F.H. (1935), 'Review of *Institutional Economics*', *Columbia Law Review*, **35** (5), 803–05.
Knight, F.H. (1924 [1999]), 'The limitations of scientific method in economics', in *Selected Essays by Frank H. Knight*, vol. 1: *'What Is Truth' in Economics?*, Emmett, R.B. (ed.), Chicago, IL: University of Chicago Press, pp. 1–39.
Knight, F.H. (1928 [1999]), 'Historical and theoretical issues in the problem of modern capitalism', review of *Der Moderne Kapitalismus*, in *Selected Essays by Frank H. Knight*, vol. 1: *'What Is Truth' in Economics?*, Emmett, R.B. (ed.), Chicago, IL: University of Chicago Press, pp. 133–48.
Knight, F.H. (1932 [1999]), 'The newer economics and the control of economic activity', review of *Modern Economic Society*, in *Selected Essays by Frank H. Knight*, vol. 1: *'What Is Truth' in Economics?*, Emmett, R.B. (ed.), Chicago, IL: University of Chicago Press, pp. 172–210.
Koopmans, T.C. (1947), 'Measurement without theory', *Review of Economics and Statistics*, **29** (3), 161–72.
Kyrk, H. (1923), *A Theory of Consumption*, Boston, MA: Houghton Mifflin.
Kyrk, H. (1933), *Economic Problems of the Family*, New York: Harper & Bros.
Leeson, R. (2000), *The Eclipse of Keynesianism: The Political Economy of the Chicago Counter-revolution*, New York: Palgrave.
Leiter, B. (2001), 'Karl Nickerson Llewellyn (1893–1962)', in Smelser, N.J. and P.B. Baltes (eds), *International Encyclopedia of the Social and Behavioral Sciences*, New York: Elsevier Science, pp. 8999–9001.
Miller, H.L., Jr. (1962), 'On the "Chicago School of Economics"', *Journal of Political Economy*, **70** (1), 64–9.
Mitchell, W.C. (1903), *A History of the Greenbacks, with Special Reference to the Economic Consequences of Their Issue: 1862–65*, Chicago, IL: University of Chicago Press.
Mitchell, W.C. (1912), 'The backward art of spending money', *American Economic Review*, **2** (2), 269–81.

Mitchell, W.C. (1925), 'Quantitative analysis in economic theory', *American Economic Review*, **15** (1), 1–12.
Nef, J.U. (1932), *The Rise of the British Coal Industry*, 2 vols, London: Routledge.
Nef, J.U. (1934), 'James Laurence Laughlin (1850–1933)', *Journal of Political Economy*, **42** (1), 1–5.
Nef, J.U. (1973), *Search for Meaning: The Autobiography of a Nonconformist*, Washington, DC: Public Affairs Press.
Neill, R. (1972), *A New Theory of Value: The Canadian Economics of H.A. Innis*, Toronto: University of Toronto Press.
Parsons, K.H. (1942), 'John R. Commons' point of view', *Journal of Land and Public Utility Economics*, **18** (3), 245–66.
Parsons, K.H. (1976), Interview with Laura Small, University of Wisconsin-Madison Archives, Oral History Project, interview #081.
Posner, R.A. (1995), *Overcoming Law*, Cambridge, MA: Harvard University Press.
Reder, M.W. (1982), 'Chicago economics: permanence and change', *Journal of Economic Literature*, **20** (1), 1–38.
Reid, M.G. (1931), 'The economics of the household', dissertation, Economics, University of Chicago, Chicago, IL.
Reid, M.G. (1934), *The Economics of Household Production*, New York: Wiley.
Rutherford, M. (2002), 'Morris A. Copeland: a case study in the history of institutional economics', *Journal of the History of Economic Thought*, **24** (3), 261–90.
Rutherford, M. (2003), 'On the economic frontier: Walton Hamilton, institutional economics, and education', *History of Political Economy*, **35** (4), 611–53.
Rutherford, M. (2004), 'Institutional economics at Columbia University', *History of Political Economy*, **36** (1), 31–78.
Schultz, H. (1928), *Statistical Laws of Demand and Supply: With Special Application to Sugar*, Chicago, IL: University of Chicago Press.
Schultz, H. (1935), 'Correct and incorrect methods of determining the effectiveness of the tariff', *Journal of Farm Economics*, **17** (4), 625–41.
Schultz, H. (1937 [2000]), 'The quantitative method with special reference to economic inquiry', in *Research in the History of Economic Thought and Methodology*, vol. 18-C: *Twentieth Century Economics*, Fiorito, L. and W.J. Samuels (eds), Amsterdam: Elsevier Science, pp. 343–55.
Schwartz, A. (2001), 'Karl Llewellyn and the origins of contract theory', in *The Jurisprudential Foundations of Corporate and Commercial law*, Kraus, J.S. and S.D. Walt (eds), Cambridge: Cambridge University Press, pp. 12–53.
Simons, H.C. (1934), *A Positive Program for Laissez Faire: Some Proposals for a Liberal Economic Policy*, Chicago, IL: University of Chicago Press.
Sowell, T. (1993), 'A student's eye view of George Stigler', *Journal of Political Economy*, **101** (5), 784–92.
Stigler, G.J. (1941), *Production and Distribution Theories: The Formative Period*, New York: Macmillan.
Stigler, G.J. (1947a), 'The kinky oligopoly demand curve and rigid prices', *Journal of Political Economy*, **55** (5), 432–49.
Stigler, G.J. (1947b), 'Professor Lester and the marginalists', *American Economic Review*, **37** (1), 154–7.
Stigler, G.J. (1954), 'The economist plays with blocs', *American Economic Review*, **44** (2), 7–14.
Stigler, G.J. (1976), 'The Xistence of X-efficiency', *American Economic Review*, **66** (1), 213–16.
Stigler, G.J. and G.S. Becker (1977), 'De gustibus non est disputandum', *American Economic Review*, **67** (2), 76–90.
Stigler, G.J. and C. Friedland (1983), 'The literature of economics: the case of Berle and Means', *Journal of Law & Economics*, **26** (2), 237–68.
Stigler, G.J. and J.K. Kindahl (1970), *The Behavior of Industrial Prices*, New York: Columbia University Press.
Veblen, T. (1899), *The Theory of the Leisure Class*, New York: Macmillan.
Veblen, T. (1904), *The Theory of Business Enterprise*, New York: Charles Scribners.
Veblen, T. (1914), *The Instinct of Workmanship*, New York: Macmillan.
Viner, J. (1928), 'The present status and future prospects of quantitative economics', *American Economic Review*, **18** (1), 30–36.
Vining, D.R. (1949), 'Koopmans on the choice of variables to be studied and the methods of measurement', *Review of Economics and Statistics*, **31** (2), 77–91.
Vining, D.R. (1950), 'Methodological issues in quantitative economics: variations upon a theme by F.H. Knight', *American Economic Review*, **40** (3), 267–84.
Vining, D.R. (1962), 'On the problem of recognizing and diagnosing faultiness in the observed performance of an economic system', *Journal of Law & Economics*, **5**, 165–84.
Wright, H.R. (1922), 'The political labour movement in Great Britain, 1820–1914', PhD dissertation, Economics, University of Chicago, Chicago, IL.

3 Adam Smith and the Chicago School

*Steven G. Medema**

Introduction

Adam Smith's discussion of the system of natural liberty, its effects on the functioning of the market system, and the resultant implications for the economic role of the state has formed the basis for much of the subsequent economic literature analyzing the interplay of market and state. That there is no settled interpretation of this and any number of other aspects of Smith's work is clear; what is equally clear is that Smith's ideas have, via particular interpretive turns, been used to support the development of theories and frameworks for the analysis of economic policy. This is interesting for the interpretation given to Smith's ideas, the uses made of them in light of that, and how both of these factors influence the larger professional (and even popular) view of Smith. The present essay examines what may be the most fertile of these uses of Smith in the twentieth century: that associated with the Chicago School.

George Stigler opened his banquet speech at the Glasgow *Wealth of Nations* bicentennial conference by saying: 'I bring you greetings from Adam Smith, who is alive and well and living in Chicago' (Meek 1977, p. 3). This 'genial proprietary claim', as Ronald Meek calls it, was not pulled out of thin air. For, while Smith is shared by virtually all economists, it would be hard to argue that the association of his name with any subset of them since the classical period is as strong as that with the Chicago School. There is also no question that the Chicago School has both claimed and evidenced a close affinity with Smith – directly or indirectly – for three-quarters of a century. Frank Knight, who is rightly considered a central figure behind the establishment of the Chicago School, did a great deal to help cement the place of Smith within the Chicago tradition. While the Cambridge school and the American institutionalists, for example, were distancing themselves in important ways from Smith and the larger classical tradition,[1] Knight embraced Smith. He considered *The Wealth of Nations* 'a work in which wisdom, learning, and the power of analysis are joined to an extraordinary degree' (1951a, p. 8). The same can be said for Jacob Viner, another prominent member of the early Chicago School, who had a tremendous passion for the history of ideas, perhaps going beyond that of any other prominent member of the Chicago School.[2] Viner wrote extensively on Smith, and in very positive, although not hagiographic, terms.

This strong interest in Smith continued in the second generation of the Chicago School, where George Stigler, Milton Friedman and Ronald Coase figure so prominently. Coase, for example, held Smith in extremely high regard, saying that *The Wealth of Nations* is a book that he 'contemplates with awe', and that: 'In keenness of analysis and in its range it surpasses any other book on economics' (1977, p. 325). But it is George Stigler, Adam Smith's best friend in the estimation of some, who has probably done more than anyone else to cement the professional tendency to associate Smith with the Chicago tradition. Stigler calls Smith 'the premier economist of all time' and 'as great an economist as has ever lived' (1976a, p. 351; 1976b, p. 1200). A major reason for this is that, according to

Stigler: 'Perhaps no other economist has ever fully shared Smith's immense understanding of the forces that govern the structure and development of economies' (1952, p. 206). In surveying the broad contours of the history of economic thought in his essay on 'The Economist as Preacher', Stigler makes it very clear that Smith is one set apart when he says that:

> All but one of the economists I quote were highly intelligent, disciplined men whose views on subjects related to economics deserve your attention and thoughtful consideration, but no more. One, Adam Smith, is differently placed: if on first hearing a passage of his you are inclined to disagree, you are reacting inefficiently; the correct response is to say to yourself: I wonder where I went amiss? (1981 [1982], p. 4)

Beyond suggesting that Smith is more likely to be correct than any modern who disagrees with him (and Stigler may well be on solid footing here), Stigler is in one sense, at least, putting Ricardo, Mill, Marx, Jevons and Marshall on one plane, and Smith above them all – a fact perhaps as remarkable for the status Stigler gives to Marx as for that given to Smith.[3]

One gets a strong sense from Stigler's writings on Smith that he does associate Smith with economics 'properly done', and he repeatedly emphasizes the lessons that economists of the present day can draw from Smith's work.[4] Given the extent to which Smith's ideas, especially those regarding the efficacy of markets, were being called into question within the profession at large, Stigler's position on the perils of disagreeing with Smith is not innocuous. And in light of Stigler's view that the Chicago approach is superior to the neoclassical orthodoxy on a number of fronts, it would not be stretching things to suggest that Stigler's suggestion of particular affinity between Smith and Chicago was something more than tongue-in-cheek.

The standard depiction of the Chicago approach to economics is that it seizes on two aspects of Smith's thought – the efficacy of the system of natural liberty and the dim view of the abilities of the state to improve on the outcomes associated with natural liberty – and pushes them to the limit in its elaboration of a model of a competitive market system in which government is an impediment to, rather than a facilitator of, economic efficiency. And, like most caricatures, this one has elements of truth to it. The minimalist view of Smith has long pervaded the Chicago tradition, as well as the Virginia school tradition that in many ways sprang out of Chicago. However, the Chicago School's discussion and use of Smith is not homogeneous, and the differences are reflected in the distinctions one can see between what McCloskey has labeled 'the Good Old Chicago School' of, for example, Frank Knight, Jacob Viner and Ronald Coase, and the 'new' Chicago School of, for example, George Stigler, Gary Becker and Richard Posner. The latter group has given us the man Jerry Evensky (2005) has named 'Chicago Smith', a Smith read in Benthamite terms and whose work thus corresponds rather closely to their own rational choice-based analysis of competitive market structures in an a-institutional context. The former group, in contrast, paints a picture rather closer to what Evensky calls 'Kirkaldy Smith' – a Smith who is grounded in the Scottish Enlightenment mentality. This Smith is a bit harder to pin down and is more overtly attuned to the import of what Coase has called 'the institutional structure of production' and the role played by government within that structure.[5]

The purpose of this chapter is not to get into a lengthy debate over the merits of the different Chicago interpretations of Smith as against each other or against other interpretations of Smith extant in the literature. Rather, we want to draw out the features of these Chicago views of Smith and, resisting all but the most basic commentary, leave it to the reader of this *Companion* to contrast the Chicago views with each other and with other perspectives on Smith and his work.

George Stigler and the construction of 'Chicago Smith'

To understand the context for the 'new' Chicago School's view of Smith, it is useful to begin with Melvin Reder's (1987, p. 413) identification of the 'two main characteristics' of the Chicago School. The first of these characteristics is the 'belief in the power of neoclassical price theory to explain observed economic behavior'. The second characteristic is the 'belief in the efficacy of free markets to allocate resources and distribute income'. And, Reder says, correlative with the second is 'a tropism for minimizing the role of the state in economic activity'. It seems natural, then, that one finds two major threads in the political economy of 'Chicago Smith': (1) the construction of economic theory founded upon the principle of self-interest; and (2) a demonstration of the efficacy of a competitive market system and an elaboration of the resultant implications for the role of government vis-à-vis the market in economic activity.

It would surprise no one to hear the Chicago School's approach to economics described as 'a stupendous palace erected upon the granite of self-interest'. This phrase was not used to describe the Chicago School, however, but Smith's *Wealth of Nations*, and the person doing the describing was none other than George Stigler (1971 [1982], p. 136).[6] For Stigler, Smith's 'one overwhelmingly important triumph' was that 'he put into the center of economics the systematic analysis of the behavior of individuals pursuing their self-interest under conditions of competition' (1976b, p. 1201). Indeed, such is the primacy of the concept in Smith's system, on Stigler's reading, that he questions whether *The Theory of Moral Sentiments* (1976 [1759]) bears any relationship at all to Smith's economics (1960, p. 44). Self-interest is not only central here, it is almost miraculous in its impact on national wellbeing. In *The Wealth of Nations*, Stigler argues, Smith shows us that: 'The immensely powerful force of self-interest guides resources to their most efficient uses . . . in short, it orders and enriches the nation which gives it free rein. Indeed, if self-interest is given even a loose rein, it will perform prodigies' (Stigler 1971 [1982], p. 136).[7] So, on Stigler's reading, Smith considered the self-interested behavior that inevitably characterizes economic activity, channeled through a competitive system, as a recipe for efficient outcomes.

The centrality of self-interested behavior in the work of this 'Chicago Smith' led Stigler, circa 1971, to label Smith 'the premier scholar of self-interest' (1971 [1982], p. 139) and to call his aspect of Smith's work 'the crown jewel' of *The Wealth of Nations* (1976b, p. 1201). We do not know whether the maturation of Gary Becker caused Stigler to change his opinion on Smith's relative status among scholars of self-interest, but we do know that Stigler sees an essential continuity between what he considers Smith's model of self-interested behavior under competitive conditions and present-day economics. This continuity is evidenced in Stigler's view that Smith's approach 'remains to this day . . . the foundation of the theory of the allocation of resources' (1976b, p. 1201).[8]

In fact much of the reason for Smith's greatness seems to rest, for Stigler, in Smith's 'modern-ness'. Stigler sees the analytics that underpin and undergird Smith's positions carried through in modern economics, and this goes well beyond the basic notion of self-interested behavior in the economic realm. Stigler goes so far as to link up Smith's approach with contemporary economics imperialism, characterizing Smith as giving us 'a theorem of almost unlimited power on the behavior of man' that is 'Newtonian in its universality' (1976b, p. 1212). This 'always and everywhere' gravitational allusion is not accidental, but rather reflects what Stigler sees as the pervasiveness of self-interested behavior throughout human life.[9] Such is its generality, he says, that: 'we today are busily extending this construct into areas of economic and social behavior to which Smith himself gave only unsystematic study', and this, in turn, 'is tribute to both the grandeur and the durability of his achievement' (1976b, p. 1212).[10] There are other examples of modern-ness as well, such as when Stigler asserts that, for Smith, the 'negatively sloping demand curve was already axiomatic' (1950, p. 308).[11] He also points to Smith's argument that, '*as a matter of demonstrable economic analysis* . . . the individual in seeking his own betterment will put his resources where they yield the most to him, and that as a rule the resources then yield the most to society' (1965a, p. 2, emphasis added). In doing so here and elsewhere,[12] Stigler equates Smith's statements about increased national wealth with the much more modern (and precise) notion of 'efficiency'.

Stigler's portrait of a Smithian system in which self-interest reigns has a normative component, too. Stigler's Smith believed that self-interested behavior, channeled through the market, is likely to generate desirable social outcomes as long as government does not interfere with its operation. As Stigler noted in his 1964 Presidential Address to the American Economic Association, 'The main burden of Smith's advice . . . was that the conduct of economic affairs is best left to private citizens – that the state will be doing remarkably well if it succeeds in its unavoidable tasks of winning wars, preserving justice, and maintaining the various highways of commerce' (1965a, p. 1).[13] One would have to search hard to find a more apt depiction of what most would consider the Chicago view – of Smith or of the world.

Milton Friedman's (1978) bicentennial essay on 'Adam Smith's relevance for 1976', while exhibiting neither the breadth nor depth of Stigler's extensive Smith scholarship, evidences the same minimalist view we find in the above-quoted passage from Stigler's AEA Presidential Address. Friedman seems to espouse a spontaneous order view of Smith, noting that: 'The market, with each individual going his own way, with no central authority setting social priorities, avoiding duplication, and coordinating activities, looks like chaos to untutored eyes.' Yet, he says, 'through Smith's eyes we see that it is a finely ordered and effectively tuned system, one which arises out of men's individually motivated actions, yet is not deliberately created by men' (1978, p. 17).[14] The associated implications for the economic role of government are straightforward, says Friedman, consisting of 'those elementary functions' of government – defense, justice, and certain public works – 'that Smith regarded as alone compatible with the "obvious and simple system of natural liberty"' (1978, p. 7). In like manner, Edward Lazear (2000) – writing on economic imperialism, as it happens – tells us that Smith gave us 'a positive theory of the economy, with limited or no role for the state'.

Of course, Stigler did not go so far as to suggest that there is no role for the state in Smith's system. In fact, he says: 'When the individual does not know, or does not have the power to advance, his own interests, Smith feels remarkably free to have the state intervene' (1965a, p. 3). Yet, Stigler seems to think that, for Smith, such instances are rather limited, and he sees Smith's preference for 'private economic activity' deriving from two sources. The first was Smith's 'belief in the efficiency of the system of natural liberty' (1965a, p. 2). For example, Stigler says, *The Wealth of Nations* contains a great deal of preaching in its later pages, but Smith addresses little of it toward the private behavior of individuals (1981 [1982], pp. 4, 6). He cites Smith's attacks on protectionism as an illustration of the benefits of the system of natural liberty in that, in Stigler's view, they 'rested squarely on his theory of competitive prices'. That is, in Smith, according to Stigler, the 'crucial argument for unfettered individual choice in public policy was the efficiency property of competition' (1976b, p. 1201).[15]

The second source that Stigler finds for Smith's preference for private sector outcomes is that Smith 'deeply distrusted the state' – mostly because of its propensity to be captured by special interests (1965a, p. 3).[16] Smith's disparaging remarks about government officials are well known and need not be repeated here. What is worth noting, however, is Stigler's attitude toward Smith's discussion of political agents. Stigler contends that Smith 'implicitly locates the most numerous and consistent failures of self-interest in guiding people's behavior' in the political arena (1971 [1982], pp. 144–5).[17] Yet, he says, Smith's 'attitude toward political behavior was not dissimilar to that of a parent toward a child: the child was often mistaken and sometimes perverse, but normally it would improve in conduct if properly instructed' (1971 [1982], p. 142). The centrality of self-interest in Stigler's view of Smith comes through very clearly here, as he chastises Smith for failing to realize that political agents are self-interested in their behavior. In essence, Stigler is criticizing Smith for not being a prototype public choice economist. Nor is Stigler willing to allow that Smith's failure here could be explained by the fact that everyone else in that era, too, looked at political behavior in non-self-interested terms; Smith, he says, 'is a better man than everyone else' (1971 [1982], p. 143), and so should be above such slip-ups.

Recovering 'Kirkaldy Smith'? The 'Good Old Chicago School'

So far, the Chicago version of Adam Smith sounds pretty much as expected: his ideas correspond almost exactly to Reder's description of the Chicago approach. But there is a different Smith evidenced in the Chicago School literature – the Adam Smith of McCloskey's 'Good Old Chicago School' – and this Dr. Smith sounds a bit more eclectic and pragmatic than the 'Chicago Smith' of Stigler et al.

McCloskey has said that the 'Good Old Chicago School' is the legacy of Smith and the new Chicago School is that of Bentham – and thus the latter gives us a Smith read in Benthamite terms. We can see some evidence for McCloskey's position in that the part of 'Chicago Smith' that sees a world consisting of rational maximizers of self-interest promoting the general welfare within a framework of competition is somewhat difficult to find in the Smith portrayed by the Good Old Chicago School of Knight, Viner and Coase. For starters, Smith's man looks a lot less like *homo economicus* in the 'Good Old' depictions, and we certainly do not find the case for economics imperialism in this view of Smith. In fact, quite the opposite. In a market context, says Viner: 'The social sentiments are not aroused to action, and [Smith's] man behaves in response to calculating, rational self-interest' (1960, p. 60). However, things are rather different in other areas of life: 'For the social system as a whole, excluding its market aspects, the beneficial outcome of laissez faire, according to Smith, results from the social instincts embedded in human nature, as well as from the "moral sentiments"', including sympathy, desire for approval, conscience and benevolence (1960, p. 60). We find a similar perspective expressed by Coase, who argues that Smith's view of man is not economic man with his rational, single-minded pursuit of his self-interest. Indeed, he says:

> Adam Smith would not have thought it sensible to treat man as a rational utility-maximiser. He thinks of man as he is – dominated, it is true, by self-love but not without some concern for others, able to reason but not necessarily in such a way as to reach the right conclusion, seeing the outcomes of his actions but through a veil of self-delusion. (Coase 1976, pp. 545–6)[18]

The point, according to Coase, is that Smith saw that benevolence cannot serve as a coordinating force in a market context. It will work in certain small, close economic contexts – for example, within the family, or among certain business associates – but in modern society we must 'rely on the market, with its motive force, self-interest'.[19] Outside of this context though, behavior, for Smith, is rather more multifaceted.

This more complex characterization of Smith can be found in other areas as well. Consider, for example, the case of the invisible hand and private–social harmony. Viner does not reject the notion that Smith sees a correspondence between the pursuit of private interests and the promotion of the larger interests of society. He allows that both *The Theory of Moral Sentiments* and *The Wealth of Nations* find Smith postulating a harmonious order of nature within which man, in the course of pursuing his own interest, serves the larger interests of society (for example, 1927, pp. 208–10). But he is also convinced that 'the significance of the natural order in Smith's economic doctrines has been grossly exaggerated' (1927, pp. 219–20). In contrast to Stigler's portrait of a Smith who expresses virtually unlimited optimism regarding the working of self-interest, Viner argues that Smith saw the linkage between self-interest and societal interests as 'partial and imperfect' in the economic realm. Self-interest and competition, he says, were for Smith 'sometimes treacherous to the public interest they were supposed to serve' (1927, pp. 208, 231–2). Knight, too, dismisses the view that Smith 'believed in a universal harmony of interests among men', calling this 'merely one discouraging example of what passes widely in learned circles for history and discussion' (1951b, p. 267). To style Smith as 'the "apostle of self-interest"', he says, leaves out a great deal of the story, particularly given that Smith 'took no pains to conceal his dislike for some of the forms in which self-interest manifests itself in trade and industry' (1951a, p. 9).

Even if human nature does exhibit the sort of harmony that some read into Smith, Coase (1976, p. 543) says that this 'does not imply that no government action is required to achieve the appropriate institutional structure for economic activity'. This, of course, is more or less the explanation for Lionel Robbins's (1952) identification of the state as the invisible hand. But problems with the harmonization process carry the case for government action well beyond this. And, because self-interest works only imperfectly to promote the greater social interest, Smith was certainly not averse to what Viner calls 'government interference with private interests' if the effects of such interference were likely to be socially beneficial (Viner 1927, p. 217; Knight 1951a, p. 9).

One can see a significant break between the earlier and later Chicago views of Smith here, both in the extent of government action considered socially beneficial and in the rationale for perceived limits on state action. On the first of these subjects – the appropriate extent of government action – both Knight and Viner saw a basic preference for non-interference in Smith, but they were also clear about the extent to which exceptions to this principle can be found in *The Wealth of Nations*. Speaking of the classical period generally, Knight points out that: 'The laisser-faire economists of the straightest sect made exceptions of a sort which opened the way to much wider departures from the principle when and as changed conditions might seem to demand', and, he argues, this 'applies particularly to the great apostle of the movement, Adam Smith' (1947, p. 50). Viner makes a similar point when he says that: 'If Smith had adopted the term "laissez faire" as an appropriate label for his own policy views, he undoubtedly would not have interpreted it literally as a condemnation of all government interference with the activities of private individuals' (1968 [1991], p. 259).[20] In fact, says Viner, while Smith's 'one deliberate and comprehensive generalization' regarding the proper functions of the state would 'narrowly restrain' its activities, the actual range of activities pointed to by Smith was so extensive that, if Smith 'had been brought face to face with a complete list of the modifications to the principle of laissez faire to which he at one place or another had granted his approval, I have no doubt that he would have been astounded at his own moderation' (1927, pp. 218–19). So, it seems, would Stigler and Friedman.

As regards the rationale for the limits on state action, recall that, in making the case for a minimalist Smith, Stigler put the efficacy of private actions and the system of natural liberty on at least equal footing with the pitfalls of state actors and actions. Knight, in contrast, did not see Smith as one who advocated individual or private activity as inherently beneficial. For him, the case for the market in Smith rests largely on 'the stupidity of governments rather than the competence of individuals' (1947, p. 2). In that vein, Knight seems particularly fond of Smith's remark concerning 'that insidious and crafty animal vulgarly called a statesman or politician', to which he refers on multiple occasions (see, for example, 1951a, p. 23). In like manner, Viner views Smith's antipathy toward government intervention not as a commentary on government *per se*, but on the relative magnitude of the flaws associated with untrammeled private action on the one hand and with government incompetence and corruption on the other. Many of the activities required an assumption that government knew better than the individual what was in his interest, and that, says Viner, was something Smith could not concede (1927, p. 221). Coase sees the matter in virtually the same pragmatic way, suggesting that Smith was opposed to many forms of government action not just because he considered them unnecessary, but because he felt that 'government action would usually make matters worse' – an artifact of governments lacking 'both the knowledge and the motivation to do a satisfactory job in regulating an economic system' (1977, p. 319).

On Viner's reading, Smith saw government, even though inept, as the best option in some cases (1927, pp. 231–2), and Smith was willing to give government a wide berth 'where, by exception, good government made its appearance' (1927, p. 227).[21] While Stigler, as we have already seen, was quick to criticize Smith for seeming to assume that politicians were more or less immune from the self-interest that he ostensibly attributed to most other forms of human behavior, we see no such criticism from Viner. Viner, in fact, seems very pleased with the non-doctrinaire nature of Smith's belief that government could show that it was 'entitled to wider responsibilities' if it improved 'its standards of competence, honesty, and public spirit' (1927, p. 231).

Beyond the greater optimism about government in the Good Old Chicago interpretation, we also see here a Smith who claims less for market outcomes than does the Smith of the 'new' Chicago view. Against Stigler's efficiency-oriented view, Viner contends that: 'It is not clear that Adam Smith believed that laissez faire would carry the wealth of a nation to some kind of theoretically-conceivable maximum'. What is clear, according to Viner, is that Smith believed that, 'subject to a vague and in part logically inconsistent list of qualifications . . . economic society left to its autonomous operation would produce a higher level of economic welfare than would accrue if government, inefficient, ignorant, and profligate as in practice it was, should try to direct or regulate or operate it' (1960, p. 60).[22] This same 'it's better than the alternative' perspective can be found in Knight, who says that Smith showed how the 'apparent chaos of competition' is actually 'an orderly system of economic cooperation' where 'individual freedom' rather than 'central direction' leads not to some 'maximum', but simply to increased national wealth and want satisfaction as compared with the alternative (1951a, p. 9).

This last point is reflective of the fact that the tightly analytical, 'axiomatic', and even determinate aspect of 'Chicago Smith' is largely absent in the Good Old Chicago School interpretation. Knight saw Smith's approach evidencing 'hard common sense' – mixed with 'genial humanity' – rather than 'rigorous analysis' (1947, p. 3). This last sentiment is echoed by Viner, who notes that Smith extensively qualified his statements with words like 'perhaps', 'generally' and 'in most cases', as a result of which 'his models are not tight or rigorous' (1968 [1991], p. 257).[23] The Good Old Chicago Smith is more circumspect and provisional than the new Chicago Smith. Moreover, both Viner and Coase laud the lack of a priorism in Smith's analysis, and one of the things that Coase finds so important about Smith's analysis in *The Wealth of Nations* is 'its careful observations on economic life' (Coase, 1977, p. 309). Likewise, Viner points out on several occasions that Smith's analysis is 'built up by detailed inference from specific data and by examination of specific problems' (1927, p. 210).[24] This includes Smith's generalizations about the appropriate role for the state and even his assessment of which specific governmental functions are consistent with the natural order – the latter being that group of functions which promote the general welfare, as revealed empirically (1927, p. 220). What we have, in Viner and Coase, is an almost Marshallian Smith – a Smith in keeping with the affinity for Marshall so amply evident in their respective works.

Conclusion

In the Chicago School, then, we meet two contrasting views of Smith. One is rather straightforward and well defined, the other more nuanced. One sounds a great deal like a neoclassical economist, the other more pluralistic. One is something of a champion of laissez-faire, the other evidences a more broad-based role for government within the economic system. Neither of these distinctions should be surprising. In the first instance, Stigler, Becker and other members of the new Chicago School are rational-choice theorists, writing at the time of its ascendancy, whereas Knight and Viner were writing during a much more pluralistic period. The assumption of self-interested behavior meant something very different in the second half of the twentieth century than it did in the first half, and so is likely to have different content and meaning given to it across these epochs.

As for the market versus government question, it is true that both the Good Old Chicago School and the new Chicago School give us a fairly non-interventionist Smith, although a strong case can be made that the Smith of the Good Old Chicago School has a stronger interventionist streak. The new Chicago view offers us a Smith who believes in private cum market success and government failure, the combination of which leaves little room for useful intervention by the state. The Good Old Chicago School view is one where private cum market failure is somewhat more widespread, but where government failure is common, too. The choice, from this perspective, is between two imperfect options, and the implications for government action are less clear cut, a priori.

So we have elements of continuity over time, but also, and especially, significant differences of interpretation. This, of course, is to be expected in the literature on Smith. As Viner so accurately pointed out: 'Traces of every conceivable doctrine are to be found in that most catholic book, and an economist must have peculiar theories indeed who cannot quote from the *Wealth of Nations* to support his special purposes' (1927, p. 207). Of course, Viner's point here was not that Smith should be used for such purposes, but that there are lessons to be drawn from the eclectic, pragmatic and provisional nature of Smith's work. As he says in closing out his famous article, 'Adam Smith and laissez faire':

> In these days of contending schools, each of them with deep, though momentary, conviction that it, and it alone, knows the one and only path to economic truth, how refreshing it is to return to *The Wealth of Nations*, with its eclecticism, its good temper, its common sense, and its willingness to grant that those who saw things differently from itself were only partly wrong. (1927, p. 232)

Notes

* I would like to thank Jeffrey Young, Ross Emmett, Jerry Evensky, Dan Hammond, David Levy, Alain Marciano, Deirdre McCloskey, David Mitch, Leon Montes, Malcolm Rutherford, Amos Witztum, and participants in seminars at the University of Reims Champagne Ardenne, the 2006 meeting of the European Society for the History of Economic Thought, and the 2006 Summer Institute for the Preservation of the Study of the History of Economic Thought at George Mason University for their comments as this project unfolded.

1. On Cambridge, see, for example, Pigou (1932) and the discussion in Shackle (1967); within institutionalism, see, for example, Mitchell (1967, pp. 166–7), Clark (1926) and the discussion in Rutherford (2005).
2. The main challenger would be Stigler, but Stigler was much more of a historian of economic theory as against Viner's broader intellectual history perspective. See Stigler (1941, 1965b).
3. While Stigler certainly had an appreciation for Ricardo's analytical approach, he says that 'Ricardo had neither Smith's genius for isolating fundamental empirical relationships nor his supreme common sense' (1952, p. 205).
4. The same is true for Coase, who repeatedly laments how little economists have advanced upon Smith's work over the last two centuries. See, for example, Coase (1977).
5. This distinction is perhaps nowhere more evident than in the meanings attributed to 'The problem of social cost' by Coase and by Stigler, each of whom sees himself working squarely in the tradition of Smith. On this point see, for example, Medema (1996) and McCloskey (1998), who point out that Stigler's emphasis on the Coase theorem as the central message of 'The problem of social cost', is diametrically opposed to Coase's own view that: (a) the article is about the need for comparative institutional analysis (which the Coase theorem would render unnecessary); and that (b) the Coase theorem is merely a fiction to debunk Pigovian externality theory.

   One might be tempted to conclude that these differences between old and new Chicago are generational, but, as the subsequent discussion will make clear, it is methodological issues that are at the heart of many of the differences of interpretation, perhaps even including those related to the economic role of the state.
6. In support of this, Stigler cites Smith's statement that: 'though the principles of common prudence do not always govern the conduct of every individual, they always influence that of the majority of every class and order' (Smith 1976 [1776], II.2.36).
7. Citing Smith to the effect that: 'The natural effort of every individual to better his own condition, when suffered to exert itself with freedom and security, is so powerful a principle, that it is alone, and without any assistance, not only capable of carrying on the society to wealth and prosperity, but of surmounting a hundred impertinent obstructions with which the folly of human laws too often incumbers its operations;

though the effect of these obstructions is always more or less either to encroach upon its freedom, or to diminish its security' (Smith 1976 [1776], IV.5.82).

8. See also Becker (1976, 1981).
9. Both Stigler and Becker see evidenced in Smith the idea of fixed tastes and preferences that influence behavior across the spectrum of human behavior. See, for example, Stigler (1981 [1982], p. 6) and Becker (1976, p. 282).
10. Beyond Stigler's general reference to the origins of economics imperialism in Smith, Becker (1975) links his human capital theory very explicitly to Smith's discussion in *The Wealth of Nations*.
11. Citing Smith's statement that: 'A competition will immediately begin among [the buyers when an abnormally small supply is available], and the market price will rise more or less above the natural price' (Smith 1976 [1776], I.7.9).
12. See Stigler (1971 [1982], p. 136).
13. Elsewhere, Stigler (1976b, p. 1201) argues that: 'The crucial argument [of Smith's] for unfettered individual choice in public policy was the efficiency property of competition'.
14. Friedman says that 'Adam Smith's invisible hand' gives rise to 'the possibility of cooperation without coercion' (http://www.econlib.org/library/Essays/rdPncl1.html).
15. Stigler here quotes Smith's famous passage that: 'Every individual is continually exerting himself to find out the most advantageous employment for whatever capital he can command. It is his own advantage, indeed, and not that of the society which he has in view. But the study of his own advantage naturally, or rather necessarily leads him to prefer that employment which is most advantageous to the society' (Smith 1976 [1776], IV.2.4).
16. Citing Smith's remarks about legislatures being influenced by 'the clamorous importunity of partial interests' (Smith 1976 [1776], IV.2.44).
17. Stigler points to incomplete information, agency and public good problems mentioned by Smith as other instances of the failure of self-interest to comport with the social interest, but Stigler is of the mind that most of these were 'nonexistent or of negligible magnitude' for Smith (1971 [1982], pp. 144–5).
18. In discussing Smith's treatment of the American Revolution in *The Wealth of Nations*, Coase agrees that self-interested behavior likely explains at least some of the motivation of the revolutionary leaders, as Smith suggests. Yet, he says, it does not seem to be an adequate explanation for 'why the American leaders had followers' (Coase 1977, p. 324). Coase finds the explanation in *The Theory of Moral Sentiments* and the ideas, expressed by Smith, that: 'The great mob of mankind are the admirers and worshippers, and, what may seem more extraordinary, most frequently the disinterested admirers and worshippers of wealth and greatness' (Coase 1977, p. 324). This explanation of human motivation falls far closer to the Veblenian status emulation than to 'economic man'.
19. Coase goes on to opine that: 'If man were so constituted that he only responded to feelings of benevolence, we would still be living in caves with lives "nasty, brutish and short"' (Coase 1977, p. 315).

    Coase's perspective on the scope of benevolence vis-à-vis the market contains a particularly Coasean twist, as the following two quotations illustrate.

    'We just do not have the time to learn who the people are who gain from our labors or to learn their circumstances, and so we cannot feel benevolence towards them even if benevolence would be justified were we to be fully informed' (Coase 1977, p. 314).

    'Again, the observance of moral codes must very greatly reduce the cost of doing business with others and must therefore facilitate market transactions' (Coase, 1976, p. 545).

    What we see here is essentially a transaction cost explanation for the functioning of benevolence. In the former instance, the transaction costs associated with forming close relationships are sufficiently high to render the formation of such relationships either impossible or prohibitively costly. In the latter instance the observance of moral codes serves to reduce the transaction costs associated with market exchange. One might even say that, from this perspective, the impartial spectator, who regulates the interaction of benevolence and self-interest, is a transaction cost minimizer.
20. Viner goes on to list a string of activities that Smith sees as appropriate for the state.
21. Viner cites Smith's statement that: 'The ordinary, vigilant, and parsimonious administration of such aristocracies as those of Venice and Amsterdam, is extremely proper, it appears from experience, for the management of a mercantile project of this kind. But whether such a government as that of England; which, whatever may be its virtues, has never been famous for good oeconomy; which, in time of peace, has generally conducted itself with the slothful and negligent profusion that is perhaps natural to monarchies; and in time of war has constantly acted with all the thoughtless extravagance that democracies are apt to fall into; could safely be trusted with the management of such a project, must at least be a good deal more doubtful' (Smith 1976 [1776], V.2.5).
22. In a swipe at the circa-1920s mantra of 'social control' as against those who parroted 'demand and supply', Viner suggested that Smith's words regarding the 'impertinence and presumption . . . in kings and ministers, to pretend to watch over the oeconomy of private people' had present import: 'If the standards

of public administration are low, progress from a life regulated by the law of demand and supply to life under the realm of social control may be progress from the discomforts of the frying pan to the agonies of the fire' (1927, p. 221). See Smith (1976 [1776], II.3.36).
23. Here Viner cites the same passage that Stigler cites to justify his view of a more straight-on self-interest motive in Smith. See note 6 above, and Smith (1976 [1776], II.2.36).
24. This is not surprising, coming from Viner, who encouraged the development of quantitative analysis at Chicago, as against Knight's more purely theoretical approach and outright resistance to the quantitative turn in economic analysis. See, for example, Reder (1982, 1987). Stigler (1952, p. 205), too, appreciated Smith's empirical and commonsensical bent as against, say, Ricardo, but was far more taken with Smith's analytical efforts and what they ultimately gave us for the present.

References

Becker, Gary S. (1975), *Human Capital*, 2nd edn, New York: NBER and Columbia University Press.
Becker, Gary S. (1976), *The Economic Approach to Human Behavior*, Chicago, IL: University of Chicago Press.
Becker, Gary S. (1981), *A Treatise on the Family*, Cambridge, MA: Harvard University Press.
Clark, John M. (1926), *Social Control of Business*, Chicago, IL: University of Chicago Press.
Coase, Ronald H. (1976), 'Adam Smith's view of man', *Journal of Law and Economics*, **19** (October), 529–46.
Coase, Ronald H. (1977), '*The Wealth of Nations*', *Economic Inquiry*, **15** (3), 309–25.
Evensky, Jerry (2005), '"Chicago Smith" versus "Kirkaldy Smith"', *History of Political Economy*, **37** (Summer), 197–203.
Friedman, Milton (1978), 'Adam Smith's relevance for 1976', in Fred R. Glahe (ed.), *Adam Smith and The Wealth of Nations: 1776–1976 Bicentennial Essays*, Boulder, CO: Colorado Associated University Press, pp. 7–20.
Knight, Frank H. (1947), *Freedom and Reform*, New York: Harper & Brothers.
Knight, Frank H. (1951a), 'Economics', in *Encyclopaedia Britannica*, reprinted (1956) in *On the History and Method of Economics: Selected Essays*, Chicago, IL: University of Chicago Press, pp. 3–33.
Knight, Frank H. (1951b), 'The role of principles in economics and politics', *American Economic Review*, **41** (March), 1–29; reprinted in *On the History and Method of Economics: Selected Essays*, Chicago, IL: University of Chicago Press, 1956, pp. 251–81.
Lazear, Edward P. (2000), 'Economic imperialism', *Quarterly Journal of Economics*, **115** (February), 96–146.
McCloskey, Deirdre N. (1998), 'The good old Coase theorem and the Good Old Chicago School: a comment on Zerbe and Medema', in Steven G. Medema (ed.), *Coasean Economics: Law and Economics and the New Institutional Economics*, Boston, MA: Kluwer, pp. 239–48.
Medema, Steven G. (1996), 'Of Pangloss, Pigouvians, and pragmatism: Ronald Coase on social cost analysis', *Journal of the History of Economic Thought*, **18** (Spring), 96–114.
Meek, Ronald L. (1977), 'Smith and Marx', in *Smith, Marx, and After: Ten Essays in the Development of Economic Thought*, London: Chapman & Hall.
Mitchell, Wesley C. (1967), *Types of Economic Theory: From Mercantilism to Institutionalism*, Joseph Dorfman (ed.), New York: Augustus M. Kelley.
Pigou, A.C. (1932), *The Economics of Welfare*, 4th edn, London: Macmillan.
Reder, Melvin W. (1982), 'Chicago economics: permanence and change', *Journal of Economic Literature*, **20** (March), 1–38.
Reder, Melvin W. (1987), 'Chicago School', in Jon Eatwell, Murray Milgate and Peter Newman (eds), *The New Palgrave: A Dictionary of Economics*, Vol. 1, New York: Stockton Press, pp. 413–18.
Robbins, Lionel (1952), *The Theory of Economic Policy in English Classical Political Economy*, London: Macmillan.
Rutherford, Malcolm (2005), 'Walton H. Hamilton and the public control of business', in Steven G. Medema and Peter Boettke (eds), *The Role of Government in the History of Economic Thought*, Annual Supplement to Volume 37, *History of Political Economy*, Durham, NC: Duke University Press, pp. 234–73.
Shackle, G.L.S. (1967), *The Years of High Theory: Invention and Tradition in Economic Thought, 1926–39*, Cambridge: Cambridge University Press.
Smith, Adam (1976 [1759]), *The Theory of Moral Sentiments*, Oxford: Oxford University Press.
Smith, Adam (1976 [1776]), *An Inquiry into the Nature and Causes of The Wealth of Nations*, Oxford: Oxford University Press.
Stigler, George J. (1941), *Production and Distribution Theories*, New York: Macmillan.
Stigler, George J. (1950), 'The development of utility theory I', *Journal of Political Economy*, **58** (August), 307–27.
Stigler, George J. (1952), 'The Ricardian theory of value and distribution', *Journal of Political Economy*, **60** (June), 187–207.

Stigler, George J. (1960), 'The influence of events and policies on economic theory', *American Economic Review*, **50** (May), 36–45.
Stigler, George J. (1965a), 'The economist and the state', *American Economic Review*, **55** (March), 1–18.
Stigler, George J. (1965b), *Essays in the History of Economics*, Chicago, IL: University of Chicago Press.
Stigler, George J. (1971), 'Smith's travels on the ship of state', *History of Political Economy*, **3** (Fall), 265–77; reprinted (1982) in *The Economist as Preacher and Other Essays*, Chicago, IL: University of Chicago Press, pp. 136–45.
Stigler, George J. (1976a), 'Do economists matter?' *Southern Economic Journal*, **42** (January), 347–54.
Stigler, George J. (1976b), 'The successes and failures of Professor Smith', *Journal of Political Economy*, **84** (December), 1199–1213.
Stigler, George J. (1981), 'The economist as preacher', *The Tanner Lectures on Human Values*, Vol. 2, Salt Lake City, UT: University of Utah Press; reprinted (1982) in *The Economist as Preacher and Other Essays*, Chicago, IL: University of Chicago Press, pp. 3–13.
Viner, Jacob (1927), 'Adam Smith and laissez faire', *Journal of Political Economy*, **35** (April), 198–232.
Viner, Jacob (1960), 'The intellectual history of laissez faire', *Journal of Law and Economics*, **3** (October), 45–69.
Viner, Jacob (1968), 'Adam Smith', in David L. Sills (ed.), *The International Encyclopedia of the Social Sciences*, Vol. 14, New York: Macmillan and Free Press, pp. 322–9; reprinted in Douglas A. Irwin (ed.) (1991), *Essays on the Intellectual History of Economics*, Princeton, NJ: Princeton University Press, pp. 248–61.

This chapter was first published in Young, Jeffrey T. (ed.) (2009), *Elgar Companion to Adam Smith*, Cheltenham, UK and Northampton, MA, USA: Edward Elgar, pp. 346–57.

4 *The Economic Organization*, by Frank H. Knight: a reader's guide

Ross B. Emmett

Introduction

Generations of students at the University of Chicago during the 1930s and 1940s were introduced to economics by Frank H. Knight's little textbook, *The Economic Organization* (EO). Originally written for classroom use at the University of Iowa in the mid-1920s, the material in EO was intended as part of a larger textbook project.[1] Knight continued to work on an economics textbook throughout the 1930s and early 1940s, but no book was ever published. EO, therefore, contains the only textbook material of Knight's ever published.

In 1932, the four chapters Knight wrote in Iowa were included in the preliminary course reader for the newly formed general social sciences course in the College of the University of Chicago, at the suggestion of economist Harry Gideonese (Social Science Staff 1932). The publication of the four chapters as a booklet with the title *The Economic Organization* (Knight 1933) a year later made them available to students elsewhere in the university. Henry Simons required the booklet in conjunction with his course (Simons 2002), and it circulated widely among graduate students taking Economics 301. The booklet was reprinted as necessary for classroom use throughout the 1930s and 1940s, while the version included in the general social science course reader removed the third and fourth chapters in 1936. We do not know when the university discontinued publication of the booklet (copies continued to circulate among students long after publication ceased), but EO's publication by Augustus M. Kelley in 1951 made the book more widely available (Knight 1951).

EO, Jim Buchanan tells us, contains 'the elements of theory that helped to establish for Chicago its eminence in neoclassical economics' (Buchanan 1968, p. 425). In contrast with other textbooks of the time (for example, Ely et al. 1923), Knight's little book presented almost no historical or institutional details of the American (or any other) economy, spent only seven pages on monopoly and did not contain the words 'social control' anywhere in the text. Instead, it introduced the basic functions of an economy and the circular-flow diagram, highlighted the division of the 'market period' into four distinct periods (see Knight 1921a) and condensed the treatment of price theory Knight had provided in *Risk, Uncertainty and Profit* (RUP) (Knight 1921b) in a clear, straightforward manner amenable to undergraduate students. After reading the book, students understood how, in a free enterprise economy, the price system solved simultaneously the problems of valuation and imputation across all goods and factor markets. While this presentation is 'old hat' to the textbooks of today, the result was nothing less than revolutionary in the context of the 1930s and 1940s.

The four chapters of EO:

1. Social economic organization;
2. The price system and the economic process;

3. Demand and supply and price; and
4. Distribution: the pricing of productive products individually,

can be divided into two sections. However, the sections can be divided in two different ways. First, chapters 1 and 2 can be divided from chapters 3 and 4, on the basis of the observation that the last two chapters comprise the essence of price theory. Chapter 3 introduces the basics of demand and supply theory, elasticity and the problem of time in connection with the determination of price (the 'market period'). Chapter 4 examines the problem of imputation, and then addresses the determination of wages, interest, rent and profit from a price-theoretic framework. In a price-theoretic perspective, chapters 3 and 4 are the core of the book; the first two chapters are important, but introductory.[2] The price-theoretic perspective will be adopted in the discussion that follows, although more attention will be paid to the introductory chapters than the more familiar price theory chapters.

The other possible division of the four chapters comes with the adoption of a social organization perspective. In the first chapter, Knight argues that all economies perform the same functions, but that their forms of organization differ. The second, third and fourth chapters then go on to examine the functioning of the free-enterprise form of economic organization, which operates through the price system. Chapter 2 provides a bridge between the first chapter and the last two chapters, introducing the price system as the mechanism used in the free-enterprise form of economic organization. From the perspective of social organization, then, EO divides into two sections, with chapter 1 comprising the first section.[3]

Regardless of which perspective one approaches EO from, the booklet presents a general argument for a functional approach to the study of economics, identifies how the price system operating in a free-enterprise economy fulfills the basic functions of any economy, and then goes into detail regarding the operation of supply and demand in a free-enterprise economy, and the resultant distribution of income among wages, rents, profit and interest. All of this is accomplished in 119 pages.

Social organization, the price system, and the economic process

In 1932, Lionel Robbins declared economics 'the science of choice' (Robbins 1932). In the same year, when students at the University of Chicago opened their social sciences course reader, they read Knight's response: 'Such definitions come too near to saying that economics is the science of things generally, of everything that men are for practical reasons interested in. Such a definition is useless and misleading' (Knight 1951, p. 4).[4] While economists generally assume that people act rationally, much rational activity is not in the purview of economics: engineering, for example, or household management. Furthermore, Knight warned students against the inclination to analyze all life in terms of economics. 'Life is an art: and art is more than a matter of scientific technique, and the richness and value of life are largely bound up in the "more"' (p. 4).

What, then, is the proper subject of economics? 'Economics deals with the *social organization* of economic activity' (p. 6). Unorganized human activity exists, but there are significant advantages (and admittedly some disadvantages) which emerge from the differentiation of tasks through specialization. Because there are a limited number of ways to organize economic activity – Knight identifies six, ranging from the caste system to democratic socialism – and because modern society most often uses the free-enterprise system of social organization, economics practically reduces to the study of 'the structure and working of the system of free enterprise' (p. 6).

Any form of social organization, including free enterprise, has to fulfill five basic economic functions. First, the organization form must identify the 'relative importance of different uses of productive power' (p. 8) – the function of fixing standards. Second, decisions about the allocation and coordination of resources must be made – the function of organizing production. The third function is that of determining the mechanism for the distribution of the total product of the economy among its participants. Fourth, decisions must be made about the maintenance and progress of the economy; how will productive powers be used in the future, how will they be organized and allocated to enable future use and what will be the resulting distribution of total production among society's members? Finally, society must be prepared to adjust consumption to production in the very short run, when shortages and/or surpluses emerge.[5] Although these five functions have, through their adaptation by Paul Samuelson in his textbook, often been reduced to three – the decision about what to produce, how to produce it and how it will be distributed – Knight's conception of a functional approach is somewhat broader. The first and fourth functions both highlight the organizational need for a *scale of values*. Knight returns to this problem in the second chapter, when he points to one of the fundamental differences between social organization based on exchange and other forms: in the latter, decisions about the value scale are made outside the economy – by a decision of the dictator, some collective or tradition. Exchange forms of organization are the only ones that determine the value scale inside the economy; prices being set by the subjective valuations of individual participants in the market process.

The stage was now set for Knight's *pièce de résistance*: the introduction of the 'wheel of wealth' (p. 60) as an illustration of *micro*- (rather than macro-) economic issues. As Don Patinkin has shown (Patinkin 1981), Knight is the first to use the circular-flow diagram as a means of explaining the way in which the interaction of individuals and businesses in goods and factor markets simultaneously solve all the functions required for effective social organization (Knight 1951, pp. 61–6). Prices provide a measure of the social importance of goods and services (albeit 'not a true index of social importance according to any recognized ethical standard'), ensure that productive resources are allocated to the production of goods and services which place the highest value on them, and simultaneously distribute income across the productive resources accordingly. 'The principal connection between the price system and social progress', meanwhile, 'is mediated by the phenomenon of interest on capital' (pp. 63–5).

We arrive at the middle of EO with a theory of social organization, an examination of the characteristics of free enterprise economies and an explanation of how the price system fulfills the basic functions of social organization in hand. Knight's task in the two remaining chapters is to survey price theory.

Interlude: the inserted note at the end of the second chapter

In 1936, the staff of the general social sciences course at the University of Chicago decided to omit the third and fourth chapters of EO from their course reader. Shortly thereafter, in 1938, Knight wrote a note which he proposed to have added to the material in the reader (Knight 1938). The addendum outlined the problems he had, 13 years after writing EO, with the statement of the factors of production ('productive resources' or 'productive powers' in the text) contained in the second chapter (pp. 54–9). The note was never incorporated into the social sciences reader, but Knight was successful in inserting a shorter note in the blank space at the end of the second chapter in the booklet version. That note is important because it alerted the reader to the re-thinking of price theory that Knight had begun in 1930, shortly before EO had begun to be distributed at the university.

Central to Knight's rethinking of price theory was his rejection of the 'tripartite' division of the factors of production, which emerged from his reconsideration of both cost and capital theory. The note stated briefly what Knight had concluded: 'In a long-run view, both natural agents and laborers have the qualities of capital. The 'tripartite' classification is not a final analysis, as there are no 'ultimate' productive resources, not previously produced' (p. 66). For a longer version of the argument, students had to turn to Knight's other writings, especially 'Bemerkungen über Nutzen und Kosten' (Knight 1935a, 1935b) – the two-part article that Knight reprinted for his students in English as one essay 'Notes on utility and cost' (Knight 1936), and 'The Ricardian theory of production and distribution' (Knight 1935c). Reprints of the two were so frequently included with EO by students that Augustus M. Kelley simply included 'Notes on utility and cost' with EO when he reprinted it in 1951.

Demand, supply, price and distribution

The third and fourth chapters of EO are built upon the chapters in RUP which provide a comprehensive statement of price theory as a prelude to Knight's theory of profit based on uncertainty. The commonality of the material in the two books is quite natural: remember that EO was actually written only three years after RUP was published. About the time that EO was published by the university in booklet form, Lionel Robbins requested permission from Knight to republish RUP for use with graduate students at the London School of Economics (Knight 1921 [1933]). Graduate students at the University of Chicago who used EO were expected to know of the treatment in RUP, along with Jacob Viner's famous article on cost curves (Viner 1931).

There are, however, some differences between the treatment of price theory in EO and that in RUP. Some of these differences are stylistic; the result of Knight's adaptation of the same material to a different audience. More substantial differences between the two texts appear in Knight's treatment of the length of the market period and of monopoly in EO. In the same year that Knight published RUP, he also wrote an article (Knight 1921a) that corrected Alfred Marshall's treatment of the 'market period' in *Principles of Economics* (Marshall 1916). Knight's treatment of the theory of cost and production in EO is shaped around his revised Marshallian distinction between the momentary, short-run, and long-run prices provided in the earlier article.

At the end of the seventh chapter of RUP, which includes a summary of monopoly theory, Knight inserted a note which suggests the real need for a theory which falls between competition and monopoly. It was that note that started Edward Chamberlin, a student of Knight's at Iowa, on his journey toward a theory of monopolistic competition (Chamberlin 1933). EO includes no such note, nor does the text allow for such a theory: 'competition is universal' in the sense that all goods have substitutes (Knight 1951, p. 92).

Monopoly is then described solely in terms of 'the evils involved' (p. 92). While Knight's Chicago students would come to disagree with him on the nature of monopoly, their opposition to Chamberlin's theory finds its formative expression in EO.

***The Economic Organization* and Chicago economics**

One could argue that Chicago economists took the specifics of Knight's argument in EO away with them, but not the general argument. Where Knight warned against treating all of life as economics, and reminded readers that humans need to 'select the ends intelligently' (p. 4), Chicago economics became associated with the quest to explain all human action in terms of static and universal preferences (Stigler and Becker 1977). Where Knight argued that the operation of the price system in a free-enterprise economy established a value scale for human activity which required evaluation in terms of our ethical ideals and other forms of social organization, Chicago economics was eventually known for defending any economic practice that occurred through market processes. As George Stigler once said, Chicago economists came to be concerned first and foremost with the structure and working of a free-enterprise economy, while for Knight, what was at stake was the future of liberal democratic capitalism (Stigler 1987).

But adopting such a viewpoint would lead one to miss the point. EO is, ultimately, a clearly structured examination of the organization and working of a free-enterprise system. In a time-period when the operation of the price system in a free-enterprise economy was reviled first by progressives, second by institutionalists and historicists and finally by Keynesians, EO provided a 'scientific' – value-free, if you wish – statement of the price system's operation. Knight's opening ethical ruminations only reinforced the argument – if the skeptic Knight could provide such a clear articulation of the price system, certainly those less embroiled in debates over the future of liberalism could do the same. And subsequent generations of Chicago economists found that a clear understanding of economic relations governed by the price system provided an excellent basis for studying a wide range of new economic issues, ranging from the organization of industry to the organization of politics and the household (Becker 1976, Becker and Murphy 2000).

In fact, advocates of both capitalism and socialism found the exposition in EO beneficial. Milton Friedman and George Stigler built their price theory books on the base set by Knight (Stigler 1946, Friedman 1962), Paul Samuelson borrowed from EO in creating his famous textbook (1948),[6] and both the essays by Fred Taylor and Oskar Lange in *On the Economic Theory of Socialism* (Lange and Taylor 1938) adopt Knight's statement of the operation of the price system in free enterprise as the basis for their advocacy of market socialism. Thus, the legacy of EO runs deeply through the tradition of neoclassical economics in the twentieth century.

Notes

1. Minimally, the book was to include at least a concluding chapter on the social criticism of free enterprise (see Emmett 2008).
2. When the college staff teaching the social sciences courses revised their syllabus in 1936, they followed this division, removing the last two chapters and keeping the two introductory chapters.
3. The second division of chapters is reinforced by the fact that chapter 1 of EO has been the most popular excerpt, appearing (in its entirety or in part) in Knight (1953, 1958, 1965, 1967, 1968).
4. All page references in EO will be to the 1951 Kelly edition, which is most frequently available.

5. The fifth function is clearly a late addition. Only four functions are usually identified in the text (see Knight 1951, pp. 62–3 for an example), and the discussion of the fifth function in 'Social economic organization' bears a header which distinguishes it from the other four functions.
6. The second edition of *Economics* explicitly acknowledges Samuelson's debt to Knight (Samuelson 1951, Patinkin 1981).

References

Becker, G.S. (1976), *The Economic Approach to Human Behavior*, Chicago, IL: University of Chicago Press.

Becker, G.S. and K.M. Murphy (2000), *Social Economics: Market Behavior in a Social Environment*, Cambridge, MA: Belknap Press.

Buchanan, J.M. (1968), 'Frank H. Knight', in *The International Encyclopedia of the Social Sciences*, 3, Sills, D. (ed.), New York: Macmillan, pp. 424–8.

Chamberlin, E.H. (1933), *The Theory of Monopolistic Competition*, Cambridge, MA: Harvard University Press.

Ely, R.T., T.S. Adams, M.O. Lorenz and A.A. Young (1923), *Outlines of Economics*, 4th rev. edn, New York: Macmillan.

Emmett, R.B. (2008), 'Frank Knight and *The Economic Organization*', in *Archival Insights into the Evolution of Economics*, vol. 2, *The Anti-Keynesian Tradition*, Leeson, R. (ed.), New York: Palgrave Macmillan, pp. 21–46.

Friedman, M. (1962), *Price Theory: A Provisional Text*, Chicago, IL: Aldine.

Knight, F.H. (1921a), 'Costs of production and price over long and short periods', *Journal of Political Economy*, **29** (4), 304–35.

Knight, F.H. (1921b), *Risk, Uncertainty and Profit*, Boston, MA: Houghton Mifflin.

Knight, F.H. (1921 [1933]), *Risk, Uncertainty and Profit*, Series of Scarce Tracts in Economics and Political Science, no. 16, London: London School of Economics and Political Science.

Knight, F.H. (1933), *The Economic Organization*, Chicago, IL: University of Chicago.

Knight, F.H. (1935a), 'Bemerkungen über Nutzen und Kosten 1: Kritisches und Dogmengeschichtliches', *Zeitschrift für Nationalökonomie*, **6** (1), 28–52.

Knight, F.H. (1935b), 'Bemerkungen über Nutzen und Kosten 2: Versuch einer Neugestaltung der Kostentheorie', *Zeitschrift für Nationalökonomie*, **6** (3), 315–36.

Knight, F.H. (1935c), 'The Ricardian theory of production and distribution', *Canadian Journal of Economics and Political Science*, **1** (February, May), 3–25, 171–96.

Knight, F.H. (1936), *Notes on Utility and Cost*, Chicago, IL: University of Chicago Press.

Knight, F.H. (1938), 'Note on economic theory materials in syllabus for Social Science II', Frank H. Knight Papers, Box 30 Folder 24, University of Chicago Archives.

Knight, F.H. (1951), *The Economic Organization, with an Article 'Notes on Cost and Utility'*, New York: Augustus M. Kelley.

Knight, F.H. (1953), 'Social economic organization', in *Introduction to Social Science*, vol. 2: *Work*, Naftalin, A., B.N. Nelson, M.Q. Sibley, A.G. Papandreou and D.W. Calhoun (eds), Chicago, IL: J.B. Lippincott, pp. 57–71.

Knight, F.H. (1958), 'Social economic organization', in *Selections in Economics*, Epstein, R.C. and A.D. Butler (eds), Buffalo, NY: Smith, Keynes and Marshall, pp. 19–38.

Knight, F.H. (1965), 'The economic organization', in *Theories of Society: Foundations of Modern Sociological Theory*, Parsons, T., E. Shils, K.D. Naegela and J.R. Pitts (eds), New York: Free Press, pp. 454–7.

Knight, F.H. (1967), 'Social economic organization', in *The Business System: Readings in Ideas and Concepts*, vol. 1, Walton, C. and R. Eels (eds), New York: Macmillan, pp. 333–43.

Knight, F.H. (1968), 'Social economic organization', in *Readings in Microeconomics*, Breit, W. and H.H. Hochman (eds), New York: Holt, Rinehart & Winston, pp. 3–19.

Lange, O. and F.M. Taylor (1938), *On the Economic Theory of Socialism*, Minneapolis, MN: University of Minnesota Press.

Marshall, A. (1916), *Principles of Economics: An Introductory Volume*, 7th edn, London: Macmillan.

Patinkin, D. (1981), 'In search of the "wheel of wealth": on the origins of Frank Knight's circular-flow diagram', in *Essays on and in the Chicago Tradition*, Durham, NC: Duke University Press, pp. 53–72.

Robbins, L. (1932), *An Essay on the Nature and Significance of Economic Science*, London: Macmillan.

Samuelson, P.A. (1948), *Economics: An Introductory Analysis*, New York: McGraw-Hill.

Samuelson, P.A. (1951), *Economics: An Introductory Analysis*, 2nd edn, New York: McGraw-Hill.

Simons, H.C. (2002), 'The Simons' syllabus', in *The Chicago Tradition in Economics, 1892–1945*, vol. 8, Emmett, R.B. (ed.), London: Routledge, pp. 3–70.

Social Science Staff (1932), *Second-year Course in the Social Sciences (Social Science II)*, preliminary edn, Chicago, IL: University of Chicago.

Stigler, G.J. (1946), *The Theory of Price*, New York: Macmillan.
Stigler, G.J. (1987), 'Frank Hyneman Knight', in Eatwell, J., M. Milgate and P. Newman (eds), *The New Palgrave: A Dictionary of Economics*, vol. 3, New York: Stockton Press, pp. 55–9.
Stigler, G.J. and G.S. Becker (1977), 'De gustibus non est disputandum', *American Economic Review*, **67** (2), 76–90.
Viner, J. (1931), 'Cost curves and supply curves', *Zeitschrift für Nationalökonomie*, **3**, 23–46.

5 The Chicago School of welfare economics

*H. Spencer Banzhaf**

Introduction

Throughout the first half of the twentieth century, applied welfare economics of the type now used routinely in policy analysis was viewed by most Anglo-American economists to be a futile task. Even as government requirements for measures of the benefits of public projects grew in parallel with economists' skills in econometrically measuring demand, economists avoided even simple measures of welfare. But during the 1950s and 1960s, across a broad spectrum of schools, economists slowly began to lose their reluctance. Operations research, which met economics at such institutions as RAND, Cowles and the Harvard Water Program, formulated problems around an empirical pay-off function to be maximized, which in turn gave rise to welfare measures. Agricultural economics, with its tradition of empirical estimation of demand curves, began to estimate demand for public goods such as outdoor recreation for purposes of benefit–cost analysis (Banzhaf 2005). And, during the same period, key members of the Chicago School of Economics like Milton Friedman, George Stigler and especially Arnold Harberger began to turn to applied welfare economics as well.

Chicago, admittedly, seems an unlikely place for such a development. Representing the 'old Chicago', Frank Knight expressed the belief that on the one hand Marshallian demand curves, which do not hold utility constant, are not an appropriate tool for welfare measurement, while on the other hand Hicksian demands are a mere intellectual construct, unrelated to observable behavior and hence unmeasurable. Consequently, according to Knight, consumer surplus is a concept of 'extremely little practical significance' (Knight 1944 [1999], p. 268).

Representing the 'new Chicago', Milton Friedman (1953) famously articulated an instrumentalist approach to utility, in which utility maximization would be used only for formulating hypotheses and forming testable predictions.[1] This approach would certainly seem to rule out all welfare measurement. After all, if utility is only a posited 'as-if' mechanism for deriving testable predictions, and if demand has ontological precedence over utility, it is hard to see how normative prescriptions could be based upon it. Friedman himself seemed to say as much in his articles on expected utility with Leonard Savage (Friedman and Savage 1948, 1952):[2]

> The discovery – if such it be – that a class of individual behavior can be predicted by supposing individuals to act as if they were maximizing the expected value of a function unique except for origin and unit of scale has, in and of itself, no welfare implication at all; and none is added by adopting the convention of calling the expected value of that function 'utility'. As we remarked in our earlier paper, 'it is entirely unnecessary to identify the quantity that individuals are to be interpreted as maximizing with a quantity that should be given special importance in public policy'. (Friedman and Savage 1952, p. 473)

In other words, the role of utility in positive economics, as an engine for developing testable hypotheses, has no implications for welfare economics whatsoever.

Nevertheless, a second hallmark of the Chicago School has been a rigid focus on fundamentals that facilitates applied policy analysis (Miller 1962, Samuels 1976, Hirsch and De Marchi 1990, Levy 1999). And just as the old planners, represented by the agricultural economists, and the new planners, represented by the schools of operations research, were meeting the demands of a growing government, so too did the Chicago School (with direct connections to both) take note and respond in its own fashion. Chicago of course had its own agricultural economists in Theodore Schultz, Gale Johnson and George Tolley. More famously, Friedman, too, advanced a number of policy proposals, generally to limit government interference in the details of life. Among other policy prescriptions, he advocated simple monetary rules to govern the Federal Reserve (rather than a discretionary authority), the negative income tax and private vouchers for schooling.

Despite his methodological approach, in making some of these recommendations Friedman felt free to go so far as to use welfare arguments, as in his discussion of the supposed superiority of an income tax to an excise tax (Friedman 1952). Elsewhere, he even went so far as to measure welfare gains and losses. In 'The optimum quantity of money', Friedman (1969, p. 14) obtained 'a rough measure of the magnitude' of the welfare effects of inflation using consumer surplus, under various assumptions for the demand curve for cash balances.[3] While consumer surplus for a hypothetical economy might be viewed as only one more chimera in a fable already populated with helicopter drops of money, Friedman goes so far as to make actual empirical estimates of the welfare gains for his rule for the US economy (ibid., p. 44). As noted previously, this approach of integrating back from demand to a preference relation, and deriving normative conclusions from that relation, is surprising in light of his general view of preferences and utility maximization as instruments for deriving testable predictions. In other words, while in his earlier work and methodological writings he treated utility maximization 'as if' it were true, in this later work he seems to treat it as actually true.

George Stigler

While Friedman may have indulged in such exercises as an 'occasional hobby' (to use the words of Harberger 1964a), more important for this story is the work of George Stigler and Arnold Harberger. Stigler would appear to be every bit as unlikely a practitioner of welfare economics as Friedman. He concurred with Friedman's methodology and, through their extensive correspondence, helped contribute to its development (see Hammond and Hammond 2006). He also helped shape the Chicago view that demand takes precedence over utility, and indeed that demand theory did not require utility theory at all, for example in his survey of the history of utility theory (Stigler 1950, pp. 390, 396).

Stigler actually started as an unambiguous opponent of 'the New Welfare Economics'. In a 1943 article by that title, he criticized the new Hicks–Kaldor potential compensation criterion on three grounds. First, he pointed out that while benefit–cost tests might help to maximize national income, such was not the sole end of society or perhaps even the first. Second, as a matter of logic, the reference point for any actual compensation might be endogenous if stakeholders bargain for position or if the act of implementing a policy changes preferences. Finally, common principles of fairness and justice would prohibit actual compensation in many cases (Stigler 1943).

But even in this early article Stigler was also critical of the pretensions of economics to a science completely separate from ethics and policy, as advocated by Lionel Robbins. Advocating an alternative style of policy analysis from that of the new welfare economics, Stigler proposed that economists 'cultivate a second discipline', namely, observing the social aims of society broadly speaking. 'This discipline might be called, following J.N. Keynes, applied ethics' (ibid., p. 358). Turning back to their core discipline, economists could then help find the best way to achieve those aims.

Later, Stigler also began to question economists' seemingly blind acceptance of the efficacy of government solutions to achieve such social aims. In his 1965 Presidential Address to the American Economic Association, Stigler traced this blindness over time from Adam Smith, who seemed to think that government could effectively accomplish its aims, however ignorant or cynically determined they may be, to modern economists, with their more benign view of government (Stigler 1965, see also Stigler 1971). He suggested that there was in fact very little basis for taking government omniscience for granted, and advocated ascertaining the facts of the matter: 'The basic role of the scientist in public policy, therefore, is that of establishing the costs and benefits of alternative institutional arrangements' (Stigler 1965, p. 2).

By 'costs and benefits', Stigler did not mean formal cost–benefit analysis, with everything reduced to a dollar metric, but rather a Franklinian ledger of the general effects, good and bad, of policy. He suggested the following examples:

> The effect of regulation on public utility prices;
> The safety of production processes and final consumer goods under regulation versus free competition;
> The costs of preventing the failure of financial institutions through the restriction of competition, in comparison to using insurance;
> The effect of price supports on the distribution of income; and
> The effect of policies to preserve competition. (Ibid., p. 11)

What was needed, according to Stigler, was actual empirical study of the effects of regulation and other government policies.

Stigler began to remedy this perceived shortcoming by taking on the effect of regulation, concluding that regulation of electric utilities had produced no significant effect on rates (Stigler and Friedland 1962). Similarly, he argued that the Security and Exchange Commission had done little to protect shareholders (Stigler 1964). Perhaps his most sustained line of inquiry in this area was on the effect of policies to preserve competition. As he noted in his memoirs, he began his career as an enthusiastic trust-buster (Stigler 1988, pp. 97–9). Somewhat ironically, before returning to Chicago, he critiqued work by Harberger and others that had cast doubt on the benefits of government policies, Harberger (1954) having computed the deadweight loss of monopoly behaviors and estimating them to be small (Stigler 1956). Ten years later, Stigler came to the view that they had only minor effects on industry concentration and mergers (Stigler 1966a).

Stigler was thus eager to turn economics to the applied task of assessing government policy. Confident in the strength of markets and the ineffectualness of government, he and others at Chicago were ready to go on the offensive and put the matter to an empirical test. However, for Stigler, at least, the role of welfare economics in this contest is somewhat ambiguous, though it did grow over time.

The history of Stigler's textbook on price theory tracks his growing acceptance of welfare economics. At first (Stigler 1942, 1946), the closest he came to issues of welfare economics was to address 'the index-number problem' for determining a change in the cost of living and the standard of living. Neglecting an older average price or market basket perspective of W.C. Mitchell and Irving Fisher, he adopted the newer Konüs perspective on the problem, citing Frisch (1936) and Hicks (1940). This approach in fact is rooted in the new welfare economics, indexing the utility of an individual (or representative) consumer and modeled through expenditure functions (see Banzhaf 2004). However, Stigler did not delve into these technical details, and kept the discussion at a fairly intuitive level. That said, he did not limit the discussion to the empirical counterparts to such indices, like the Laspeyres index used for the US consumer price index (CPI). As actually computed, such an index resonates with the Chicago School's traditional emphasis on demand theory and marginal analysis (requiring no additional information beyond price interpreted as a marginal value) and on simple, robust measures. But Stigler also raised deeper interpretative issues, such as the meaning of such welfare indices when tastes change.

In his next edition, Stigler (1952) expanded this treatment, with separate sections on measuring national income and measuring the cost of living.[4] In the cost-of-living section, he mentions Konüs's utility-theoretic reasoning for why a Laspeyres index is an upper bound on a true cost-of-living index. Stigler further argues that

> in peacetime this upward bias is reinforced by the failure of the index compilers to make any real allowance for improvements in the qualities of goods, and during WW II this bias was more than offset by the failure to make adequate allowances for quality deterioration, disappearance of commodities, and non-price rationing. (Ibid., p. 91)

But as I discussed elsewhere (Banzhaf 2001, 2004), this position makes sense only in light of the new welfare economics' introduction of the utility-constant cost-of-living index; previous work by Irving Fisher and Wesley Clair Mitchell focused solely on the prices of things and not their utility, and did not necessarily perceive the same biases that appear so obvious from a utilitarian perspective.

In 1960, Stigler chaired an NBER panel charged with reviewing the US CPI, a review which emphasized the problem of quality change.[5] Indeed, the panel concluded: 'If a poll were taken of professional economists and statisticians, in all probability they would designate (and by a wide margin) the failure of the price indexes to take full account of quality changes as the most important defect of these indexes' (Price Statistics Review Committee 1961, p. 35).

Furthermore, the committee more fundamentally urged the Bureau of Labor Statistics (BLS) to make the welfare-constant Konüs cost-of-living index the operational concept for developing the CPI. Or more accurately, it *asserted* that that was in fact what the CPI intended to measure.[6] The Stigler committee did not limit itself to abstract discussion of the objective of price measurement, but made specific recommendations for addressing the shortcomings as it saw them. For example, it recommended calculating Paasche indexes to obtain an upper-bound measure of the substitution-bias inherent in the Laspeyres index (ibid., p. 52). To address the problem of new goods and quality change, it recommended that the BLS try to revise the basket of goods more often. Including new goods earlier would at least capture the usual decline in prices early in a product's life cycle, if not the benefits of the new good (pp. 31, 52). Among its suggestions for addressing more subtle quality changes, the committee introduced the work of Zvi Griliches (1961), a student of Harberger's at Chicago, on a 'hedonic' price index of automobiles that held quality constant (see Banzhaf 2001).[7]

In the final edition of his textbook, Stigler (1966b) maintained his discussion of the cost-of-living index while also highlighting Griliches's work. Moreover, Stigler for the first time brought the concept of consumer surplus into his discussion of demand theory. In doing so, he cited work by John Hicks and noted the limitation that ordinary consumer surplus is just an approximation unless the marginal utility of income is constant (ibid., p. 80). As an example of the application of consumer surplus, he cited the work of Hirshleifer et al. (1960), published by the University of Chicago.

Stigler's work thus represents, on one hand, a sustained agenda of policy analysis, and, on the other, a growing acceptance of monetary measures of welfare, as seen in the evolution of his price theory book and especially in his NBER review of the CPI. However, he never did have sufficient interest or confidence to bring these two sides together and empirically estimate consumer surplus or deadweight loss. That role at Chicago was played by Arnold Harberger.

Arnold Harberger

Harberger received his PhD from the University of Chicago in 1950, and was a professor there from 1953 to 1983. But he also had an eclectic background, receiving training during the brief time 'Chicago' and Cowles were together. He named Friedman, Jacob Marschak and Theodore Schultz as his most influential classroom teachers, and had a PhD committee consisting of Lloyd Metzler, Kenneth Arrow and Franco Modigliani (Levy 1999)!

Perhaps consistent with this background, Harberger is a more moderate Chicago figure. Politically, he has accepted the need for some income redistribution (for example, Harberger 1964b, p. 47) and even possibly the role of government as an employer of last resort (see Strassman 1976). Methodologically, he has certainly pursued welfare economics and even general equilibrium welfare effects, often employing more structuralist approaches (for example, Harberger 1959b). But lest his Chicago credentials be doubted, he is also a firm believer in market forces, and has advocated a government that would limit itself to simple proportionate taxes on all industries to avoid distortions (see Harberger 1964b, p. 56, and, on the activities of his heroes, Harberger 1993). His tendency to study the deadweight loss of taxation – in contrast to the benefits of policy provisions – is certainly suggestive of a more conservative take on policy analysis. While in some cases he found surprisingly small estimates of these losses and conceded that they might well be worth the benefits of policies or redistribution, he emphasized that the costs were unecessary and could be reduced by more even-handed treatments of the tax base (for example, Harberger 1964b, pp. 47, 56).

Harberger is also an advocate of the simple price-theory-with-real-world-applications approach to economics. In his mind, this was one of the most important elements of the Chicago School. As he put it in his 1999 interview,

> I think the entire atmosphere at Chicago for a long period there, in the 1960s and 1970s in particular, made it a cradle for the training of people in policy economics, always emphasizing fundamentals and always trying to give them a true sense of how economics links to the real world. (Levy 1999)

He went on to characterize his own style in the following way:

> Underneath it all is a certain element of modesty – a recognition that we're not going to be able to 'model' the world, that the world is not just going to accommodate itself to some little frame that we make up. On the other hand, there is almost no economic event where supply and demand does not enter. So if you really know how to handle supply and demand, put it into different contexts at different times, you're way ahead of the game. People coming from graduate school are going to fall flat on their face if they try to apply ultra-sophisticated models in tough real-world situations like the ex-Soviet empire. Those situations will be much better understood, diagnosed and acted upon by more fundamentals-oriented people who say, 'Well here we've got proto-markets that are just now being created; how do we see the forces of supply and demand working here?'. (Ibid.)

This interest in applying the forces of supply and demand to real-world situations also led him to some 43 consultant positions over the years with non-governmental organizations, US governmental agencies, and foreign governments. In his policy work Harberger found welfare measurement to be an indispensable tool, and could not understand economists' reluctance to participate. 'The measurement of deadweight losses is not new to economics by any means', he said, citing Jules Dupuit and more recent theoretical work by Harold Hotelling, Sir John R. Hicks, Gerard Debreu, James Meade and Harry Johnson.

> Nonetheless I feel that the profession as a whole has not given to the area the attention that I think it deserves. We do not live on the Pareto frontier, and we are not going to do so in the future. Yet policy decisions are constantly being made which can move us either toward or away from that frontier. What could be more relevant to a choice between policy A and policy B than a statement that policy A will move us toward the Pareto frontier in such a way as to gain for the economy as a whole, say, approximately $200 million per year, while policy B will produce a gain of, say, about $30 million per year? What could be more useful to us as a guide to priorities in tax reform than the knowledge that the deadweight losses stemming from the tax loopholes . . . open to explorers for oil and gas are probably greater in total magnitude than the deadweight losses associated with all the other inefficiencies induced by the corporate income tax? What could be more tantalizing than the possibility (which I believe to be a real one) that the U.S. tariff, whose indirect effect is to restrict the equilibrium value of U.S. exports, produces by this route a gain for the U.S. from a partial exploitation of U.S. monopoly power in world markets which nearly offsets (or perhaps more fully or more than fully offsets) the efficiency-losses produced by tariff-induced substitution of more expensive domestic products for cheaper imports? These and similar questions seem to me so interesting, so relevant, so central to our understanding of the economy we live in, that I find it hard to explain why the measurement of deadweight losses should be the province of only a handful of economists rather than at least the occasional hobby of a much larger group. (Harberger 1964a, pp. 58–9)

Harberger of course made it much more than an occasional hobby.

Harberger used the deadweight loss measure in three main applications during the 1950s and early 1960s. In his first application, one close to Stigler's own heart, Harberger estimated the deadweight loss from monopolists' output restrictions (Harberger 1954). Assuming that in long-run equilibrium distortion-free returns to capital would be equalized in all industries, Harberger estimated monopoly distortions as the diversion across industries of rates of return from economy-wide averages. Taking the simple expediency of assuming constant marginal costs in all industries and a constant unit-elastic demand for a representative consumer, he then estimated deadweight loss as the curvilinear triangles under this demand curve up to the point that would bring about the average rate of return (and likewise for competitive industries the area above the demand curve as resources are reallocated to the monopolized industries). This procedure yielded a surprisingly small welfare cost, on the order of $1.40 per capita. As noted previously, Stigler (1956) critiqued some of the assumptions of this analysis, but not the overall attempt at such a computation.[8]

Harberger's second application was to distortions in developing countries, part of his well-known consulting in Chile and elsewhere in Latin America (Harberger 1959b). Here, he estimated similar simple measures of deadweight loss from trade barriers, again using a stylized demand curve and assuming the shadow price of all trade barriers was equivalent to a tariff of 50 percent. To estimate the effect of labor and capital distortions, he employed a simple analytical general equilibrium model, assuming Cobb–Douglas utility of a representative consumer and Cobb–Douglas production for 10 industries using labor and capital and inputs. He then analyzed a few 'what-if' distortions across sectors to compute the share of income lost. Again, the take-home message of this work is that the distortions appear small, on the order of 5 to 10 percent of GDP.

His third application was to a set of domestic tax issues. In a study for the US House of Representatives Ways and Means Committee, he estimated deadweight loss from unequal taxation on corporations across industries, relative to an even-handed tax (Harberger 1959a). In other work, he estimated the losses from special treatment of just the minerals and energy sectors (Harberger 1955 [1974], 1961 [1974]). He later summarized this work and added the distortions to labor–leisure choice (Harberger 1964b). He estimated the distortion to labor supply to be on the order of $1 billion; the distortion of the corporate income tax to be $0.5 billion to $1.5 billion; and the distortion from special depletion rules in the minerals industry to be $0.5 billion to $1 billion; and he cited work by David Laidler (eventually published in Laidler 1969) putting the distortion from special treatments of owner-occupied housing at $0.5 billion to $1 billion.

In Harberger's earliest work, he felt little need to justify his use of consumer surplus as a welfare measure. To a large extent, he simply stated his measure, often without using the term 'consumer surplus' or deadweight loss, but often with at least a passing reference to Hotelling (1938) for support. On some occasions, he justified using a Marshallian measure on the grounds that income effects would be small (Harberger 1959b); on others he simply assumed Hotelling's integrability conditions without explanation (Harberger 1964a, p. 62).

Later, Harberger began to defend consumer surplus more vigorously. He first offered four reasons 'for the apparent unpopularity of the loss-measurement game' (ibid., p. 59):

> Welfare measures are so approximate that economists must accept offering estimates with a precision no better than a factor of 2 to 3;
> General equilibrium effects may be important but are difficult to account for;
> Welfare measures do not address the important issue of the allocation of money; and
> Consumer surplus, 'in spite of its many rehabilitations, is still looked upon with suspicion by many economists'. (Ibid., p. 60)

In his well-known article 'Three basic postulates for applied welfare economics', Harberger (1971) elaborated on these points. He also added the concern that an analysis based on consumer surplus is only valid if the marginal utility of income is constant.

Harberger addressed these concerns in several ways. As to the first objection, he argued that estimates within factors of 2 or 3 can in many cases substantially reduce the uncertainty about policies, a perspective that perhaps emboldened him to conduct the what-if exercises discussed above. As to the second, he noted that Hotelling (1938) had in fact lent support to a generalized consumer surplus measure. He also agreed that general equilibrium effects could be important, but offered a more positive strategy for addressing them. He suggested that one first begin with partial equilibrium effects, then incrementally identify the most important secondary markets and compute welfare effects there as well. The key secondary markets would be those with strong substitution or complementarity relationships to the first *and* with large distortions (otherwise effects would only be pecuniary). As to the third objection, he simply conceded that distributional issues were also important, but could be considered separately.

He further defended consumer surplus by now developing it along the lines of Hotelling (ibid.), as merely a second-order approximation to a welfare change. This had the advantage of dodging the tricky issues of the marginal utility of income and integrability conditions, and maintained a simple intuitive appeal. Harberger himself called it 'a more "pragmatic" approach', that could be taken 'as a matter of convention', in contrast to a 'strictly theoretical' level at which would require the Hicks–Slutsky properties (Harberger 1971, p. 792). The pragmatic approach had the advantage of being simple, 'robust' (in the sense of handling a number of first-order policy questions, such as whether (a) will help or hurt, or if (a) or (b) is better, in contrast to finding an optimum), and was part of a long tradition (p. 795). Harberger added that consumer surplus could be thought of as being generated by a line integral over continuously updated marginal utilities of money. He then seized upon the further rhetorical point that most economists accepted net GDP as a pragmatic gauge of welfare, but that such measures of national income were only a first-order approximation, and subject to all the other critiques of consumer surplus as well. Thus, consumer surplus had the advantage of being more acceptable than simple index numbers.

Finally, as noted previously, Harberger emphasized the important need for welfare measures to guide policy. In the US, 'in an era where literally thousands of studies involving cost–benefit analysis or other types of applied welfare economics are underway at any given moment', a set of protocols was badly needed (ibid., p. 785). In developing countries, he further suggested that the need was so great that the first order of business when preparing to give aid should be to train project evaluators to rationally use any assistance (Strassman 1976, p. 286).

Conclusions

In the early 1950s, the University of Chicago's Department of Economics would not have seemed like fertile ground for the sprouting of welfare measurement. Frank Knight had criticized both the coherence of Marshallian consumer surplus and the relevance of the Hicksian variety; Milton Friedman privileged the positive role of theory in yielding testable predictions over any normative role, and George Stigler was on record opposing potential compensation criteria and privileging demand over any preferences from which they may (or may not) be derived. And yet, Chicago did so become. As Friedman and Stigler became more engaged in policy (and political) debates, they permitted normative conclusions to flow from consumer theory. In the case of the Stigler committee's review of the CPI, they also advocated that such an approach be embodied in official statistics.

Nevertheless, the key figure sprouting in this environment was Arnold Harberger, who was influenced as much by Cowles as by Friedman and T. Schultz. In this fact alone we can see the importance of respecting the diversity and tensions within that group we call 'the Chicago School of Economics'.

Notes

* For helpful comments, I thank William Coleman, Daniel Hammond, Arnold Harberger, David Levy, Phillip Mirowski, and participants of the History of Economics Society Meetings and George Mason Workshop for the Preservation of the History of Economics.

1. Boland (1979) explains Friedman's methodology in these terms. Hirsch and De Marchi (1990) offer an interpretation of Friedman's instrumentalism with greater nuance, in light of the context of his historical connections and actual practice. Nevertheless, there remains the fundamental tension between justifying the use of implausible (and possibly inaccurate) premises on the grounds of their predictive power, on the one hand, and, on the other, deriving *normative* deductions from them.
2. See also Friedman (1953) and Robertson (1954) for discussion and amplification of the point.
3. Although Friedman does not cite him, this approach was introduced by his Chicago colleague Martin Bailey (1956), who in turn drew on discussions with Harberger.
4. Interestingly, it is not until this edition of the book that Stigler moves the chapter of demand prior to the chapter on utility theory, stating in the preface that he wanted to make the book more empirically grounded.
5. The Price Statistics Review Committee also included Dorothy Brady, Edward Denison, Irving Kravis, Philip McCarthy, Albert Rees, Richard Ruggles and Boris Swerling.
6. It is worth quoting this curious-sounding passage at length. The Committee begins its section on the CPI with the following:

   > It is often stated that the Consumer Price Index measures the price changes of a fixed standard of living based on a fixed market basket of goods and services. . . . But in the presence of the introduction of new products, and changes in product quality, consumer tastes, and relative prices, it is no longer true that the rigidly fixed market basket approach yields a realistic measure of how consumers are affected by prices. . . .
   >
   > In periods of wartime, when specific goods in the fixed market basket are no longer freely available to the consumer, the divergence of such an index from practical reality becomes obvious. . . . Few economists or consumers come to the defense of the rigidly fixed market basket approach under these circumstances. This suggests strongly that what is in fact being measured is not the cost of a fixed set of consumer goods and services, but rather the cost of maintaining a constant level of utility.
   >
   > The present logic of revision of weights and the methods of introduction of new products into the index and adjustments for quality change are de facto recognition that at a practical level the index must reflect the impact which prices are having on the consumer's standard of living. At the same time many individuals involved in producing and using the index shy away from recognizing the underlying principles which guide the construction of the index and its application in the major analytic uses. There is often a tendency to try to adhere to the more comforting position of having an index of a fixed market basket of goods since acceptance of such a position avoids the difficult decisions required to approximate a utility-based price index. (1961, p. 51, see also p. 52)

   In other words, those in charge of computing the index do not *really* understand the concept they are measuring; their own actions in updating weights and splicing in new goods necessarily belie their statements that they are measuring a fixed basket.
7. Griliches himself could be added as a key figure in the trend of the Chicago School to welfare economics. He of course maintained a lifelong interest in price index problems, and addressed other applied welfare economic issues as well, such as the spillovers from technological change. Like Harberger, Griliches was somewhat of an eclectic figure. He received his Master's degree in agricultural economics from Berkeley, where he would have been surrounded by the agricultural economists' policy activism. He also learned Cowles-style econometrics from George Kuznets, and came to Chicago in part because of Cowles. Cowles decamping just as he arrived, he turned to work with its former student Arnold Harberger.
8. The relationship between Stigler and Harberger is open to speculation. In all his discussion of welfare economics in his textbook, Stigler never cited Harberger, and gave him only passing mention in his memoirs (Stigler 1988). But Harberger denies any strained relations in a recent interview (Emmett 2007).

References

Bailey, M.J. (1956), 'The welfare cost of inflationary finance', *Journal of Political Economy*, **64** (2), 93–110.

Banzhaf, H.S. (2001), 'Quantifying the qualitative: quality-adjusted price indexes, 1915–1961', in *The Age of Economic Measurement*, Klein, J.L. and M.S. Morgan (eds), Durham, NC: Duke University Press, pp. 345–70.

Banzhaf, H.S. (2004), 'The form and function of price indexes: an historical accounting', *History of Political Economy*, **36** (4), 589–616.

Banzhaf, H.S. (2005), 'Consumer surplus with and without apology', unpublished manuscript.

Boland, L.A. (1979), 'A critique of Friedman's critics', *Journal of Economic Literature*, **17** (2), 503–22.

Emmett, R.B. (2007), 'Oral history and the historical reconstruction of Chicago economics', in *Economists' Lives: Biography and Autobiography in the History of Economics*, Weintraub, E.R. and E.L. Forget (eds), Durham, NC: Duke University Press, pp. 172–92.

Friedman, M. (1952), 'The "welfare" effects of an income tax and an excise tax', *Journal of Political Economy*, **60** (1), 25–33.

Friedman, M. (1953), 'The methodology of positive economics', in *Essays in Positive Economics*, Chicago, IL: University of Chicago Press, pp. 3–43.

Friedman, M. (1969), 'The optimum quantity of money', in *The Optimum Quantity of Money, and Other Essays*, Chicago, IL: Aldine, pp. 1–50.

Friedman, M. and L.J. Savage (1948), 'The utility analysis of choices involving risk', *Journal of Political Economy*, **56** (4), 270–304.

Friedman, M. and L.J. Savage (1952), 'The expected utility hypothesis and the measurability of utility', *Journal of Political Economy*, **60** (6), 463–74.

Frisch, R. (1936), 'Annual survey of general economic theory: the problem of index numbers', *Econometrica*, **4** (1), 1–38.

Griliches, Z. (1961), 'Hedonic price indexes for automobiles: an econometric analysis of quality change', in *Price Statistics of the Federal Government*, New York: National Bureau of Economic Research, pp. 173–6.

Hammond, J.D. and C.H. Hammond (eds) (2006), *Making Chicago Price Theory: Friedman–Stigler correspondence, 1945–57*, London: Routledge.

Harberger, A.C. (1954), 'Monopoly and resource allocation', *American Economic Review*, **44** (2), 77–87.

Harberger, A.C. (1955 [1974]), 'The taxation of mineral industries', in *Taxation and Welfare*, Harberger, A.C. (ed.), Chicago, IL: University of Chicago Press, pp. 208–17.

Harberger, A.C. (1959a), 'The corporation income tax: an empirical appraisal', in *Tax Revision Compendium: Compendium of Papers on Broadening the Tax Base*, vol. 1, US Senate, Committee of Ways and Means (ed.), Washington, DC: US Government Printing Office, pp. 231–50.

Harberger, A.C. (1959b), 'Using the resources at hand more effectively', *American Economic Review*, **49** (2), 134–46.

Harberger, A.C. (1961 [1974]), 'The tax treatment of oil exploration', in *Taxation and Welfare*, Harberger, A.C. (ed.), Chicago, IL: University of Chicago Press, pp. 218–28.

Harberger, A.C. (1964a), 'The measurement of waste', *American Economic Review*, **54** (3), 58–76.

Harberger, A.C. (1964b), 'Taxation, resource allocation, and welfare', in *The Role of Direct and Indirect Taxes in the Federal Revenue System*, Due, J.F. (ed.), Princeton, NJ: Princeton University Press, pp. 25–70.

Harberger, A.C. (1971), 'Three basic postulates for applied welfare economics: an interpretive essay', *Journal of Economic Literature*, **9** (3), 785–97.

Harberger, A.C. (1993), 'Secrets of success: a handful of heroes', *American Economic Review*, **83** (2), 343–50.

Hicks, J.R. (1940), 'The valuation of social income', *Economica*, n.s. **7** (26), 105–24.

Hirsch, A. and N. De Marchi (1990), *Milton Friedman: Economics in Theory and Practice*, Ann Arbor, MI: University of Michigan Press.

Hirshleifer, J., J.C. De Haven and J.W. Milliman (1960), *Water Supply: Economics, Technology, and Policy*, Chicago, IL: University of Chicago Press.

Hotelling, H. (1938), 'The general welfare in relation to problems of taxation and of railway and utility rates', *Econometrica*, **6** (3), 242–69.

Knight, F.H. (1944 [1999]), 'Realism and relevance in the theory of demand', in *Selected Essays by Frank H. Knight*, vol. 2: *Laissez-faire: Pro and Con*, Emmett, R.B. (ed.), Chicago, IL: University of Chicago Press, pp. 243–83.

Laidler, D. (1969), 'Income tax incentives for owner occupied housing', in *Taxation of Income from Capital*, Harberger, A. and M.J. Bailey (eds), Washington, DC: Brookings Institution, pp. 50–76.

Levy, D.M. (1999), 'Interview with Arnold Harberger', available at minneapolisfed.org/pubs/region/99-03/harberger.cfm (accessed July 17, 2007).

Price Statistics Review Committee (1961), *The Price Statistics of the Federal Government*, New York: National Bureau of Economic Research.

Miller, H.L., Jr. (1962), 'On the "Chicago School of economics"', *Journal of Political Economy*, **70** (1), 64–9.
Robertson, D.H. (1954), 'Utility and all what?', *Economic Journal*, **64** (256), 665–78.
Samuels, W.J. (ed.) (1976), *The Chicago School of Political Economy*, East Lansing, MI: Association for Evolutionary Economics and Division of Research, Graduate School of Business Administration, Michigan State University.
Stigler, G.J. (1942), *The Theory of Competitive Price*, New York: Macmillan.
Stigler, G.J. (1943), 'The new welfare economics', *American Economic Review*, **33** (2), 355–9.
Stigler, G.J. (1946), *The Theory of Price*, New York: Macmillan.
Stigler, G.J. (1950), 'The development of utility theory', *Journal of Political Economy*, **58** (4, 5), 307–27, 373–96.
Stigler, G.J. (1952), *The Theory of Price*, rev. edn, New York: Macmillan.
Stigler, G.J. (1956), 'The statistics of monopoly and merger', *Journal of Political Economy*, **64** (1), 33–40.
Stigler, G.J. (1964), 'Public regulation of the securities markets', *Journal of Business*, **37** (2), 117–42.
Stigler, G.J. (1965), 'The economist and the state', *American Economic Review*, **55** (1/2), 1–18.
Stigler, G.J. (1966a), 'The economic effects of the antitrust laws', *Journal of Law & Economics*, **9**, 225–58.
Stigler, G.J. (1966b), *The Theory of Price*, 3rd edn, New York: Macmillan.
Stigler, G.J. (1971), 'Smith's travels on the ship of state', *History of Political Economy*, **3** (2), 265–77.
Stigler, G.J. (1988), *Memoirs of an Unregulated Economist*, New York: Basic Books.
Stigler, G.J. and C. Friedland (1962), 'What can regulators regulate? The case of electricity', *Journal of Law & Economics*, **5**, 1–16.
Strassman, W.P. (1976), 'Development economics from a Chicago perspective', in *The Chicago School of Political Economy*, Samuels, W.J. (ed.), East Lansing, MI: Association for Evolutionary Economics and Division of Research, Graduate School of Business Administration, Michigan State University, pp. 277–94.

6 Chicago monetary traditions

David Laidler

Introduction

In popular understanding, the University of Chicago monetary tradition is inextricably linked to the ideas of Milton Friedman, which extend well beyond that area to encompass a general belief in the efficacy of market mechanisms as regulators of economic life, and an equally general scepticism about the desirability of government intervention therein (Reder 1987). Chicago 'monetarism' is seen as having challenged (more or less successfully, depending on the commentator) a previously dominant 'Keynesian' consensus on these matters. Though Chicago monetary economics can, and should, be judged on its theoretical and empirical merits, I shall also pay some attention to its broader political connections in this chapter, because such considerations are important in locating its position in the broader history of American economic thought.

The first Chicago tradition

The history of Chicago monetary economics long antedates the outbreak of the monetarist controversy of the 1950s. The first chairman of the Chicago Economics Department, James Laurence Laughlin, was one of America's most influential monetary economists between the 1880s and the foundation of the Federal Reserve System in 1913 (Friedman 1987, Dimand 2003). Along with his student Henry Parker Willis, eventually a professor at Columbia Business School, he continued to expound his ideas in the debates about monetary policy of the 1920s and 1930s, though another important student, Wesley Clair Mitchell, had by then largely broken free of his influence.

Laughlin was conservative in both his politics and his economics throughout his long life, as his writings (Laughlin 1885, 1903, 1933) attest. He was a staunch defender of the gold standard during the debates about bimetallism, and his close association with the Republican Party, forged during that debate, prevented him playing a direct role in the creation of the Federal Reserve system, though he exerted considerable indirect influence on that process, both through the force of his ideas and through Willis who played a direct role as counsel to Congressman Carter Glass's Banking sub-committee. Here, Laughlin and Willis represented what Dimand (2003) has termed the 'Lasalle Street Tradition', which sought to prevent any American central bank being dominated either by the Federal government or private interests centered on New York. The division of the system into 12 districts, each served by what was initially supposed to be its own central bank, reflected this viewpoint.

But Laughlin's conservatism does not link him to any later Chicago monetary tradition, because, in the monetary area, and in the first of several strokes of irony that mark that tradition's development, he was a leading opponent of the quantity theory of money. Long after marginalist ideas permeated microeconomics, Laughlin remained a devotee of the classical cost-of-production theory of value, and of the related idea that gold was the 'natural' standard of value. These ideas led him to treat price-level variations under the gold standard as originating in changes in the cost of production of individual goods. They also led him to oppose proposals for countering the deflation that marked the 1873–96 period by monetary expansion based on reintroducing silver into the monetary system, and hence restoring bimetallism to the US monetary system.

For Laughlin these ideas, which were supported by the progressive wing of the Democratic Party, and notably by William Jennings Bryan, were ill-conceived and dangerous (Laidler 2004). There was indeed a strong inflationist element among the bimetallists, but Laughlin rejected not just that, but the quantity theory of money upon which even responsible bimetallists, such as Francis Walker, (ironically) of MIT, based their case. He and his fellow defenders of gold monometallism were so successful in discrediting the quantity theory in popular thought that Irving Fisher's *Purchasing Power of Money* was written explicitly to reinstate it as a scientifically respectable doctrine, and is best read as a rebuttal of Laughlin's ideas (Fisher 1911).

When it came to banking, Laughlin expounded a version of what Lloyd Mints (1945), a contributor to the interwar Chicago tradition to be discussed below, would later call the 'real bills doctrine'. Laughlin took over from the mid-nineteenth century British 'Banking School' the view that the banking system should grant short-term credit in sufficient amounts to meet the 'needs of trade', which were themselves conditioned by real factors. This goal would be best accomplished by a banking system configured to provide an 'elastic currency'. Neither Laughlin (nor the Banking School before him) made a careful and consistent distinction between money and credit, but in practice their prescription was that a banking system should confine itself to providing short-term loans to finance inventories and goods in process in whatever amounts were demanded, and they were sometimes unfortunately vague about the role of the rate of interest in conditioning that demand. Such behavior, they believed, would make the banking system a passive agent in an economy that could otherwise be trusted to run smoothly, and prevent it from contributing to monetary instability.

These views, which were also held by Willis, had a considerable influence both on the design of the Federal Reserve system, and on its policies in the 1920s and early 1930s, when, it is now widely agreed, the Fed's passivity permitted an ordinary cyclical downturn to get out of hand and develop into what Friedman and Schwartz (1963) would call 'the Great Contraction'. Laughlin and Willis were prominent among those who took a fatalistic attitude towards the economy's collapse in the early 1930s, defended the Fed's passive stance and opposed any policies actively designed to promote recovery. By that time, however, such ideas were no longer represented among active members of the Chicago department.

The interwar Chicago tradition

No proposition is more closely associated with Friedman's monetary economics than that the Federal Reserve system was largely responsible for the severity of the Great Contraction, and Lloyd Mints had developed a version of this argument as early as the late 1940s (Mints 1950). The contrast between early Chicago monetary economics as represented by Laughlin and Friedman's version could, therefore, hardly be starker. Friedman argued (1956a, 1974) that even in the early 1930s, Chicago was distinct in being already the home of a body of ideas, built around the quantity theory of money, that took an optimistic view of what monetary policy could have achieved in fighting the

Contraction. And, he claimed, the strength of the intellectual tradition in question had rendered Chicago essentially immune to the influence of Keynes's ideas after 1936, and hence had laid the intellectual basis for his own work of the 1950s and 1960s.

Now in the economic thought of the interwar United States, the quantity theory of money is most closely associated with Irving Fisher, whose academic home was (another irony) Yale, not Chicago; but to understand just what is right and what is wrong with Friedman's account of the Chicago monetary tradition during the Great Contraction, it must first be appreciated that the debates of that time were considerably more than a simple matter of 'quantity theory versus real-bills doctrine' with Fisher and his followers on one side and Laughlin and his heirs on the other. In the 1920s, Fisher was beginning to display some of that intellectual rigidity that would in due course earn him the reputation of a monetary crank, and he spent a good deal of time campaigning, first for a monetary policy based upon his 'compensated dollar' scheme, and then, less specifically, for the imposition by law of a price-level stability mandate on the Federal Reserve system.

Fisher's extremism left open a considerable middle ground in the debate between him and the real-bills camp that was occupied by a variety of proponents of what was then called 'credit control', the deployment by the Federal Reserve of discretionary monetary policy to help stabilize cyclical fluctuations (Mehrling 1997). These middle-ground ideas were heavily influenced by the British economists Ralph Hawtrey (1919) and the Keynes (1923) of the *Tract on Monetary Reform.* Prominent, though by no means alone, among their exponents was Allyn Young, who had been Frank H. Knight's PhD supervisor at Cornell. Young was at Harvard in the 1920s, and, prior to his departure for the London School of Economics in 1927, an occasional advisor to Governor Benjamin Strong of the Federal Reserve Bank of New York. He was, however, evidently well known and admired at Chicago, and not just by Knight. The influenza which was to cause his premature death in 1929 was in fact contracted during a visit to the university to discuss and decline an offer of the chairmanship of the Economics Department (Blitch 1996).

A good part of the Chicago monetary tradition of the interwar years is properly located in the above-mentioned middle ground. Before the onset of the Contraction it offered cautious support for the deployment of discretionary monetary policy and more urgent support thereafter. Charles Oliver Hardy, a lecturer at Chicago between 1918 and 1922, and later closely associated with the Brookings Institution, and Jacob Viner, at Chicago from 1919 until 1946, come to mind here as cautious proponents of monetary stabilization policies. But the heretical underconsumptionism of William Truffant Foster and Wadill Catchings was also vigorously represented in the Chicago department by Paul Douglas, better remembered nowadays for his work in labor economics and his later accomplishments as a US senator, who had joined the department in 1920 and would remain an active member until his entry into politics in the late 1930s. At the other end of the political spectrum, Henry Simons, who joined the department in 1927, combined the quantity theory with a rule-based approach to monetary policy similar in many essentials to Fisher's, and with a broader commitment to *laissez-faire*, while mention should also be made of Aaron Director and Lloyd Mints, who came to share his views.

Director, later Friedman's brother-in-law, initially joined the department to work with Douglas, and produced with him a rather conventional survey volume on *The Problem of Unemployment* (Douglas and Director 1931) in which Douglas's underconsumptionism was temporarily replaced by monetary analysis that owed a good deal to Keynes's *Tract*. Soon afterwards, however, Director became, along with his sister Rose Director and Simons, a leading member of the conservative group that gathered around Frank Knight. At this time, relations between Knight and Douglas were so bad that they communicated only in writing, and Douglas, having failed to prevent Simons obtaining tenure, was rewarded by Director's banishment to the Chicago Law School. Mints wrote nothing of interest before 1945 but nevertheless taught a brand of monetary economics throughout the 1930s and into the early 1950s that seems to have been heavily influenced by the ideas of Simons and owed essentially nothing to the Keynes of the *General Theory* (Mints 1946, 1950).

Evidently, then, monetary economics at Chicago was anything but scientifically or politically homogeneous during the Great Contraction, but the economic problems of the time meant that economists with very different understandings of how the economy functioned, and of very different political persuasions too, could sometimes agree about policy, and so it was at Chicago for a while. In the early 1930s it was natural for an underconsumptionist of Douglas's stripe to support with renewed vigor the continuous fiscal and monetary expansion that he had been recommending even during the boom of the 1920s. And it was equally natural for a quantity theorist such as Viner (1932, 1933) to deplore the influence of the real-bills doctrine on Federal Reserve policy and to join Simons and others among his colleagues in supporting immediate monetary expansion as a palliative for the contraction, though Viner was troubled that such policies might require the US to abandon the gold standard, of which he was a supporter.

As banking problems in the United States became more and more acute in 1932–33, it was also natural to look for ways of ensuring that monetary expansion could in fact be engineered. And, it is not surprising that 'fiscal inflationism', the use of money-financed budget deficits to bring about monetary expansion, should find support from a group that had Douglas at one theoretical and political extreme and Simons at the other, and included Viner for a while too. Nor was it surprising that a proposal for backing demand deposits with a 100 percent reserve requirement in order to give the authorities firm control over the behavior of the money supply, and to prevent any future collapses of the market for bank credit generating monetary contractions – the central feature of which A.G. Hart (1935) would term the 'Chicago Plan for banking reform' – would also emerge from and find support among this diverse group.

Friedman's story, recently revived by Tavlas (1998), of a unique 'Chicago tradition' based on the quantity theory, that advocated tackling the Depression by fiscal and monetary expansion long before the ideas of Keynes began to sweep the United States from a beach-head established at Harvard in 1936, is nevertheless over-simple. To begin with, even the policy proposals emanating from Chicago itself were not uniquely related to the quantity theory of money. Douglas's version of them was, as we have seen, based not on the quantity theory, but on an underconsumptionist theory. By 1933, furthermore, he was also beginning to cite Keynes's multiplier analysis as set out in *The Means to Prosperity* (1933) in support of his policy recommendations. More generally, monetary explanations of the contraction, proposals for monetary expansion in general and fiscal inflationism and 100 percent reserve requirements in particular were neither unique to Chicago economists, nor originated among them (see Reeve 1943, Humphrey 1971, Phillips 1995, Laidler 1999, chs 8 and 9). Such ideas are to be found independently and more or less fully articulated in the writings of a number of non-Chicagoans in the early 1930s, in some cases before they appear in Chicago sources.

This is not to deny that such ideas were discussed and promoted at Chicago. Over and above the contributions made by members of the Chicago Department of Economics, two conferences held there in 1931 and 1932 under the auspices of the Harris Foundation also attest to this (Wright 1931, 1932). At the first of these, Keynes himself spoke, and following his recently published *Treatise on Money,* proposed a monetary cure for the gathering downturn based on driving down the long rate of interest. According to Davis (1971) he disappointed his audience, Chicagoans and others alike, by his timid attitude towards expansionary fiscal policy. From the second conference, there emerged a nowadays well-known petition to President Herbert Hoover advocating vigorous monetary and fiscal expansion, signed by 12 members of the Chicago department (though not by Douglas), but also by 12 non-Chicagoans, among whom were Irving Fisher, Alvin Hansen (Minnesota), Carl Snyder (Federal Reserve Bank of New York) and John H. Williams (Harvard).

The picture that emerges from all this is not of Chicago as a unique institution where ideas that had difficulty maintaining more than a foothold elsewhere were developed and promoted during the 1930s, but rather as a department that was one important and vigorous participant in a much more widespread tradition in monetary economics, many (but not all) of whose adherents deployed the quantity theory of money in a critique of economic policies based on the real-bills doctrine and in proposals to supplant those policies with vigorous monetary and fiscal expansion.

To the extent that Chicago made a unique contribution to this tradition, it was the approach to economic policy that we associate with the writings of Henry Simons, but to which Aaron Director almost surely significantly contributed as well, not to mention Lloyd Mints. Most advocates of a monetary explanation of the Great Contraction, fiscal inflationism and 100 percent money combined these ideas with support for the more general policy activism of the New Deal – Lauchlin Currie whom Viner took with him to Washington from Harvard in 1934 is a case in point – but these Chicago economists linked them instead with Fisher's case for rule-guided monetary policy and made the resulting package a central component of what Simons termed *A Positive Program for Laissez-faire* (Simons 1934). Within the context of the Chicago department, it is natural to contrast Simons's program with Paul Douglas's democratic socialist agenda, as set out in *The Coming of a New Party* (Douglas 1932), but including, as Simons did, proposals for vigorous antitrust policies and serious income redistribution, it was (another irony) in some ways closer to the progressive populism against which Laughlin had fought in the 1890s, than to the conservative agenda associated with Chicago from the 1950s onwards.

The indisputable continuity between the specifically monetary component of Simons's program and Friedman's later work is not, however, the result of Chicago's being free of Keynesian economics in the interim. Chicago reviewers of the *General Theory,* who included Viner, Knight and Simons were critical of the book, the last two being downright hostile, and Knight does seem to have managed to prevent Chicago awarding Keynes an honorary degree in 1941. Beginning in the 1940s, Chicago was nevertheless home to such Keynesians as Oscar Lange, Jacob Marshak and Lloyd Metzler, not to mention the staff of the Cowles Commission, and to graduate students such as Don Patinkin whose work provided a key foundation of what came to be called the 'neoclassical synthesis' (see Patinkin 1981). This Keynesian influence would not be dominant for long, but that too was not because of the resilience of any local tradition. After Simons's untimely death in 1946, only Mints remained at Chicago to teach the monetary ideas of the mid-1930s, and it is notable that among the accomplishments with which George Stigler credits Friedman after his arrival at Chicago in 1946 is the revival there of 'the study of monetary economics, which had become moribund' (Stigler 1988, p. 151).

Friedman and the monetarist tradition

Friedman had been a graduate student at Chicago for a while in the 1930s, but the links between his work and that of Simons are not straightforward. His PhD was from Columbia, and his empiricism, not to mention his frequently displayed preference for the NBER techniques of Arthur Burns and Wesley Clair Mitchell over the more conventional econometric methods of the Cowles Commission, also display a Columbian influence (see the chapter on *A Monetary History* by Hugh Rockoff, ch.7, this volume). Furthermore, Friedman's early macroeconomic work was conventionally Keynesian, in the tradition of the inflationary gap analysis of Keynes (1940), and paid little explicit attention to the role of money.

Before the early 1950s, Friedman was, in any event, mainly visible as a statistician and micro-theorist with strong mathematical skills. Two things established him as a critic of the then dominant American economic orthodoxy inherited from the late 1930s, which viewed the economy as dominated by large firms, who were fit objects for regulation because their administered prices had more to do with the exercise of monopoly power than the efficient allocation of resources, and held faith in fiscal rather than monetary tools for activist macro-stabilization. First, in his famous essay 'The methodology of positive economics', Friedman (1953) defended the empirical relevance of the theory of the profit-maximizing firm, particularly in its perfectly competition version, on the basis of its capacity to make useful predictions – we learned much later that his approach was influenced by contacts made with Karl Popper through the Mont Pèlerin Society (Friedman and Director Friedman 1998). Second, he restated and defended the quantity theory of money (Friedman 1956a).

Friedman's restatement made the quantity theory a theory of the demand for money that bore a strong resemblance to Keynes's (1936) version of liquidity preference theory, albeit without the 'liquidity trap' which was then a prominent feature of textbook expositions of the latter, but that hardly made his work 'Keynesian'. Keynes's theory had roots of its own in the work of Alfred Marshall, Arthur Pigou and Frederick Lavington, who had developed a version of the quantity theory based on the interaction of the stock supply and demand for money (in contrast to Fisher's more traditional money times velocity flow approach), and this approach had also influenced the middle ground of American monetary economics discussed earlier, where much earlier Chicago work had been located. Even though, before Friedman, the quantity theory had been understood to deal with the influence of the quantity of money on prices and not just the demand for money, it is a necessary condition for such influence to be systematic and predictable that the demand for money be a stable function of but a few arguments, and this was the central proposition of his essay. Furthermore, empirical studies of the influence of money on inflation played a central role in the work of his colleagues and students (see Friedman 1956b, Meiselman 1970), so overall, Friedman was quite right to claim a place for his work in a quantity theory-based tradition.

The claim that a particular macroeconomic relationship was both simple and empirically stable was not new in 1956. Keynes had made it on behalf of the consumption function twenty years earlier, and by the 1950s, a stable marginal propensity to save out of current income, and hence a stable multiplier, was seen as the *sine qua non* for successful fiscal policy. Friedman's *Theory of the Consumption Function* (for which he received his Nobel Prize) showed that the, by then numerous and well-known, anomalies in observed income consumption relationships could be resolved by postulating that consumption (of non-durable goods) was a stable function of *permanent* income, so that saving would be an unstable sum of the fraction of permanent income saved and transitory fluctuations around it (Friedman 1957). Thus, Friedman's work in the 1950s replaced a supposedly empirically stable savings function with a stable demand for money function, thereby undermining conventional policy wisdom, which emphasized the efficacy of fiscal rather than monetary tools. And to this he added a keen appreciation of the possibility that policy in general, but monetary policy in particular, worked with long and variable time lags that made its use for active stabilization purposes problematic.

By the end of the 1950s, then, Friedman (1959) was suggesting that monetary policy be used to create a background of macroeconomic stability by being tied down to a constant rate of growth for the money supply and suggesting that, in such a regime, there was no place for stabilization by fiscal means. Small wonder that he recognized the relationship between his views and those espoused by Henry Simons (1936) two decades earlier, though Simons had favored a price stability rule. Small wonder also that, with the links between his policy proposals and a conservative political agenda being so evident, his work was greeted with skepticism and sometime outright ridicule in more orthodox circles.

But, we should note, Friedman's policy conclusions followed from well-specified economic theory. And he soon extended the latter by showing that the then widely held belief that inflation and unemployment varied inversely with each other along a Phillips curve that might be exploited by policy makers, rested on the hidden postulate that economic agents suffered from permanent money illusion (Friedman 1968). Friedman also developed a considerable body of empirical evidence, not least that presented in Friedman and Schwartz's (1963) *A Monetary History of the United States*, and particularly its chapters arguing for an essentially monetary explanation of the Great Contraction along lines that a number of middle-ground American economists of the early 1930s had adopted at the time. Politically unpalatable or not, then, the economics profession in due course had to take Friedman's views seriously. Because they involved economics that had political implications, rather than economics distorted by preconceived ideology, Friedman's views invited theoretical and empirical criticism, and ultimately received it, in the course of the so-called 'monetarist controversy'.

The style of monetary thought that Friedman had established at Chicago by about 1970 had antecedents, of course. In addition to Simons, his analysis of money in the Great Contraction had important predecessors such as Clark Warburton (1966) and Lauchlin Currie (1934 [1968]) (whom he did not acknowledge until much later). And

Friedman had ideas in common with economists working elsewhere too. Karl Brunner and Allan Meltzer, first at UCLA and later at Ohio State, Rochester and Carnegie-Mellon universities, respectively, had begun to publish the first of their own significant contributions to the development of 'monetarism' in the early 1960s (surveyed retrospectively in Brunner and Meltzer 1993). Franco Modigliani's life-cycle model of consumption was close to Friedman's. A.W. Phillips had analyzed the problems raised by lags in the effect of policy, and Edmund Phelps's debunking of the idea of a long-run inflation unemployment trade-off had even appeared a little earlier than Friedman's. Moreover, Friedman was anything but a lone wolf in his own university. His theoretical and policy ideas were buttressed by a series of empirical studies, mainly carried out by students, many of whom would in due course go on to make considerable reputations of their own. It was also at about this time (1960) that the formidable Harry Johnson was appointed at Chicago as a 'Keynesian' counterweight to Friedman, and undertook the task of ensuring that students were exposed to the whole literature of monetary economics, and not just Chicago's contribution to it.

But, when all is said and done, the Chicago monetary tradition of the late 1960s was more homogeneous, more distinctive and more the product of the ideas and energy of one man than anything that had been seen in the interwar years. And yet at that time it was also a tradition in search of an important policy problem (Johnson 1971). The quantity theory was primarily a theory of price-level behavior. Friedman and his associates had demonstrated its relevance to important inflationary episodes of the past, and to Latin America too, where Arnold Harberger's (1963) paper on inflation in Chile made an important contribution to the 'monetarist' side of the highly ideologically charged 'monetarist–structuralist' debate that was then in progress. But even if monetary factors had played a major role in US monetary history, not least the 1930s, the relevance of all this to the current US and European experience was not quite clear, not least because, no matter what theory said, contemporary economies did seem to be characterized by an inflation–unemployment trade-off.

All this changed in the 1970s, as the inflation which in hindsight can be seen to have begun developing from the early 1960s onwards took hold, not just in the United States but in the whole Western world. The Chicago monetary tradition not only had its problem, but it was simultaneously presented with extra empirical support as the inflation–unemployment trade-off vanished. At this time too, it went through a further important theoretical extension, as the idea of a stable demand for money function was used by Harry Johnson, Robert Mundell (appointed to Chicago in 1964) and their students as the foundation of what came to be known as the 'monetary approach' to balance of payments and exchange rate analysis (see Frenkel and Johnson 1976).

By the end of the 1970s, 'monetarism' had also found strong political supporters, notably among what would become the Reagan administration in the United States and the Thatcher government in the United Kingdom; though we should note that the first efforts to bring inflation down by way of monetary contraction started, albeit tentatively, in both countries before the accession of either to office. But it was under them that a monetary cure for inflation was vigorously applied, alongside a more general shift to *laissez-faire* economic policies. As a result, the political association between the Chicago monetary tradition and conservative politics, which had already received an unfortunate boost in Chile where, under the Pinochet regime, such policies had already become associated with military dictatorship, became firmly cemented in public perceptions.

After monetarism

Space does not allow a full discussion of why the quantity theory of money, which had been associated with progressive politics when the University of Chicago was founded, migrated to the right by the late 1970s (see Laidler 2004). It is, however, important to the story of monetary economics at that university to note that problems with the definition and measurement of money, long the Achilles' heel of that doctrine, reasserted their significance with a vengeance at that time. Financial innovations, some but not all of which were themselves responses to inflation, began to undermine the empirical stability of the demand for money function. On the policy front, this contributed to the difficulties that central banks encountered in ensuring a smooth end to inflation, and within academic monetary economics it contributed to an intellectual vacuum, which was soon to be filled, not least at the University of Chicago, by new classical economics.

Tobin's (1981) characterization of new classical economics as 'Monetarism Mark 2', notwithstanding, the latter doctrine's connection to Chicago was not as strong as that of Monetarism Mark 1. Three of its leading proponents in its early days, Robert E. Lucas, Jr., Thomas Sargent and Robert J. Barro, held faculty positions at Chicago, but the last two, both Harvard PhDs, did not settle there. And while Lucas and Neil Wallace were Chicago graduates, neither had written PhD theses on monetary topics, while Lucas's earliest work on rational expectations and the cycle was done at Carnegie Mellon University, where he was certainly influenced by Allan Meltzer. It is too early to assess the place of new classical economics in the history of monetary economics. In its earliest form, which had the Lucas (1972)–Sargent and Wallace (1976) 'money supply surprise' model of the cycle as its centerpiece, it had seemed to have a great deal in common with Friedman's work: hence the 'Monetarism Mark 2' label. It attributed economic fluctuations to monetary shocks, denied the existence of a long-run inflation unemployment trade-off and in ruling out the effectiveness of discretionary stabilization policy as a theoretical, rather than merely empirical, matter, it affirmed its conservative political links. But crucially, the model's logical structure required that prices move simultaneously with, or even ahead of quantities after a monetary shock, and this was quite contrary to one of the most basic stylized facts of the cycle that Friedman had long stressed.

In the face of the money supply surprise model's inevitable empirical failure, new classical economists clung not to their model's monetarist characteristics, but to the market-clearing and rational expectations postulates, the two features that they had added to Friedman's analysis, and took them in a number of directions – into real business cycle theory, monetary models based on Samuelson's overlapping generations model of money, models of the origins of money and even into endogenous growth theory. And at the same time, so called 'new Keynesian economics', which emphasizes the role of market failures and nominal stickiness in the monetary economy began to look a lot like the 'old monetarist economics' of Friedman and Brunner and Meltzer. In short, though old debates in monetary economics carry on in new forms, and economists based at Chicago still contribute to them, it is hard indeed to identify a distinctively 'Chicago tradition' within the literature they are generating.

References

Blitch, C.P. (1996), *Allyn Young: The Peripatetic Economist*, Basingstoke: Macmillan.

Brunner, K. and A.H. Meltzer (1993), *Money in the Economy: Issues in Monetary Analysis*, Cambridge: Cambridge University Press.

Currie, L.B. (1934 [1968]), *The Supply and Control of Money in the United States*, New York: Russell & Russell.

Davis, J.R. (1971), *The New Economics and the Old Economists*, Ames, IA: Iowa State University Press.

Dimand, R.W. (2003), 'Competing visions for the US monetary system, 1907–1913: the quest for an elastic currency and the rejection of Fisher's compensated dollar rule for price stability', *Cahiers d'économie politique*, **45**, 101–21.

Douglas, P.H. (1932), *The Coming of a New Party*, New York: McGraw-Hill.

Douglas, P.H. and A. Director (1931), *The Problem of Unemployment*, New York: Macmillan.

Fisher, I. (1911), *The Purchasing Power of Money*, New York: Macmillan.

Frenkel, J.A. and H.G. Johnson (eds) (1976), *The Monetary Approach to the Balance of Payments*, Toronto: University of Toronto Press.

Friedman, M. (1953), 'The methodology of positive economics', in *Essays in Positive Economics*, Chicago, IL: University of Chicago Press, pp. 3–43.

Friedman, M. (1956a), 'The quantity theory of money – a restatement', in *Studies in the Quantity Theory of Money*, Friedman, M. (ed.), Chicago, IL: University of Chicago Press, pp. 3–21.

Friedman, M. (ed.) (1956b), *Studies in the Quantity Theory of Money*, Chicago, IL: University of Chicago Press.

Friedman, M. (1957), *A Theory of the Consumption Function*, Princeton, NJ: Princeton University Press.

Friedman, M. (1959), *A Program for Monetary Stability*, New York: Fordham University Press.

Friedman, M. (1968), 'The role of monetary policy', *American Economic Review*, **58** (1), 1–19.

Friedman, M. (1974), *Milton Friedman's Monetary Framework*, Gordon, R.J. (ed.), Chicago, IL: University of Chicago Press.

Friedman, M. (1987), 'J. Laurence Laughlin', in *The New Palgrave: A Dictionary of Economics* (vol. 3), Eatwell, J., M. Milgate and P. Newman (eds), London: Macmillan, pp. 139–40.

Friedman, M. and R. Director Friedman (1998), *Two Lucky People: Memoirs*, Chicago, IL: University of Chicago Press.

Friedman, M. and A.J. Schwartz (1963), *A Monetary History of the United States, 1867–1960*, Princeton, NJ: Princeton University Press.

Harberger, A.C. (1963), 'The dynamics of inflation in Chile', in *Measurement in Economics: Studies in Mathematical Economics and Econometrics in Memory of Yehuda Grunfeld*, Christ, C. (ed.), Stanford, CA: Stanford University Press, pp. 219–50.

Hart, A.G. (1935), 'The "Chicago plan" for banking reform: a proposal for making monetary management effective in the United States', *Review of Economic Studies*, **2** (2), 104–16.

Hawtrey, R.G. (1919), *Currency and Credit*, London: Longmans, Green.

Humphrey, T.M. (1971), 'The role of non-Chicago economists in the evolution of the quantity theory in America, 1930–1950', *Southern Economic Journal*, **38** (1), 12–18.

Johnson, H.G. (1971), 'The Keynesian revolution and the monetarist counter-revolution', *American Economic Review*, **61** (2), 1–14.

Keynes, J.M. (1923), *A Tract on Monetary Reform*, London: Macmillan.

Keynes, J.M. (1933), *The Means to Prosperity*, New York: Harcourt, Brace.

Keynes, J.M. (1936), *The General Theory of Employment, Interest and Money*, New York: Harcourt, Brace.

Keynes, J.M. (1940), *How to Pay for the War: A Radical Plan for the Chancellor of the Exchequer*, London: Macmillan.

Laidler, D.E.W. (1999), *Fabricating the Keynesian Revolution: Studies of the Interwar Literature on Money, the Cycle, and Unemployment*, Cambridge: Cambridge University Press.

Laidler, D. (2004), 'From bimetallism to monetarism: the shifting political affiliation of the quantity theory', in *Political Events and Economic Ideas*, Barens, I., V. Caspari and B. Schefold (eds), Cheltenham, UK and Northampton, MA, USA: Edward Elgar, pp. 9–36.

Laughlin, J.L. (1885), *The History of Bimetallism in the United States*, New York: Appleton.

Laughlin, J.L. (1903), *The Principles of Money*, New York: Charles Scribner's Sons.

Laughlin, J.L. (1933), *The Federal Reserve Act: Its Origins and Problems*, New York: Macmillan.

Lucas, R.E., Jr. (1972), 'Expectations and the neutrality of money', *Journal of Economic Theory*, **4** (2), 115–38.

Mehrling, P. (1997), *The Money Interest and the Public Interest: American Monetary Thought 1920–1970*, Cambridge, MA: Harvard University Press.

Meiselman, D. (ed.) (1970), *The Varieties of Monetary Experience*, Chicago, IL: University of Chicago Press.

Mints, L.W. (1945), *A History of Banking Theory in Great Britain and the United States*, Chicago, IL: University of Chicago Press.
Mints, L.W. (1946), 'Monetary policy', *Review of Economics and Statistics*, **28** (2), 60–69.
Mints, L.W. (1950), *Monetary Policy for a Competitive Society*, New York: McGraw-Hill.
Patinkin, D. (1981), *Essays on and in the Chicago Tradition*, Durham, NC: Duke University Press.
Phillips, R.J. (1995), *The Chicago Plan and New Deal Banking Reform*, Armonk, NY: M.E. Sharpe.
Reder, M.W. (1987), 'Chicago School', in *The New Palgrave: A Dictionary of Economics*, vol. 1, Eatwell, J., M. Milgate and P. Newman (eds), New York: Stockton Press, pp. 413–18.
Reeve, J.E. (1943), *Monetary Reform Movements: A Survey of Recent Plans and Panaceas*, Washington, DC: American Council on Public Affairs.
Sargent, T.J. and N. Wallace (1976), 'Rational expectations and the theory of economic policy', *Journal of Monetary Economics*, **2** (2), 169–83.
Simons, H.C. (1934), *A Positive Program for Laissez Faire: Some Proposals for a Liberal Economic Policy*, Chicago, IL: University of Chicago Press.
Simons, H.C. (1936), 'Rules versus authorities in monetary policy', *Journal of Political Economy*, **44** (1), 1–30.
Stigler, G.J. (1988), *Memoirs of an Unregulated Economist*, New York: Basic Books.
Tavlas, G. (1998), 'Was the monetarist tradition invented?', *Journal of Economic Perspectives*, **12** (4), 211–22.
Tobin, J. (1981), 'The monetarist counter-revolution today – an appraisal', *Economic Journal*, **91** (361), 29–42.
Viner, J. (1932), 'International aspects of the gold standard', in *Gold and Monetary Stabilization*, Wright, Q. (ed.), Chicago, IL: University of Chicago Press, pp. 3–39.
Viner, J. (1933), *Balanced Deflation, Inflation or More Depression?*, Minneapolis, MN: University of Minnesota Press.
Warburton, C. (1966), *Depression, Inflation, and Monetary Policy: Selected Papers, 1945–1953*, Baltimore, MD: Johns Hopkins University Press.
Wright, Q. (ed.) (1931), *Unemployment as a World Problem*, Chicago, IL: University of Chicago Press.
Wright, Q. (ed.) (1932), *Gold and Monetary Stabilization*, Chicago, IL: University of Chicago Press.

7 On the origins of *A Monetary History*

*Hugh Rockoff**

Introduction

Milton Friedman and Anna J. Schwartz's *A Monetary History of the United States* (1963a) is arguably the most important book in economics since *The General Theory* (Keynes 1936).[1] It has inspired and informed an enormous amount of research. Even footnotes have produced voluminous and contentious literatures.[2] This chapter explores some of the work that influenced the *Monetary History*.[3] It shows that the ideas of several Chicago economists – Henry Schultz, Henry Simons, Lloyd Mints and Jacob Viner – left clear marks. However, it argues that the most important influence may have been Wesley Clair Mitchell and his classic book *Business Cycles* (1913). Mitchell, and the National Bureau of Economic Research (NBER or the Bureau), provided the methodology, in particular the emphasis on long accurate time series of monthly data and the analysis of the effects of specific variables on the business cycle. Mitchell's book, as I try to show below, contained a preliminary exploration of the issues examined in more detail, and for a longer historical period, in the *Monetary History*. Mitchell concluded that money played an independent, predictable and important role in shaping the business cycle. Friedman and Schwartz's work, although it differed on several particulars, most importantly on the role of bank-lending policies in the transmission of monetary impulses, strongly reinforced Mitchell's basic conclusions.

Perhaps the most important reason for exploring the origins of the *Monetary History* is that it facilitates understanding. Although the *Monetary History* is enormously influential, and although its analyses of particular events are often taken to be authoritative, its basic findings are often misunderstood because the book arose from a methodological tradition that differs markedly from the tradition underlying modern macroeconomics. Young economists often find the book especially challenging because they have not been trained in, perhaps not even exposed to, the historical methods used by Friedman and Schwartz.

The influences on the *Monetary History* that I stress have largely been ignored in the literature on the origins of the *Monetary History*. The initial reviews ignored Mitchell and the Chicago economists and viewed it as a response to Keynesian economics. Harry Johnson in his review (1965), for example, does not mention Mitchell or other earlier work on business cycles. Johnson briefly summarizes Friedman and Schwartz's basic findings, indeed he accepts them, but he concentrates his attention on the absence of a formal theoretical model, and on the implicit assumption that he sees in Friedman and Schwartz that the demand for money was not a function of the rate of interest.[4] Johnson's (1971) evaluation of monetarism as a whole does not even mention the *Monetary History*. Don Patinkin in a series of papers (1969, 1972, 1979), although more directly concerned with other aspects of Friedman's work, downplayed the contribution of the Chicago economists, ignored Mitchell and the NBER and stressed Friedman's unacknowledged debt to Keynes.

Much of the subsequent literature focused on whether Friedman and Schwartz had properly acknowledged their debt to previous analysts of the Great Depression. David Laidler (1993), for example, showed that important elements of the work of the British economist Ralph Hawtrey and the Harvard economists Allyn Young and Laughlin Currie can be found in the *Monetary History* and related work by Friedman and by Friedman and Schwartz. Indeed, at various times Friedman and Schwartz have conceded that they did not give due recognition to the work of one or another previous scholars. I shall consider one case, Jacob Viner, below. On the other hand, Friedman and Schwartz's treatment of previous scholars has its defenders. Frank G. Steindl (1995), notably, argued that while a number of economists in the 1930s, such as Currie, had produced elements of the Friedman–Schwartz interpretation of the Depression, none produced a detailed analysis of the way decisions by banks and the public influenced the supply of money, and none produced an interpretation that integrated supply and demand.

Historians of economic thought interested in Mitchell, for example Howard Sherman (2001), have downplayed Mitchell's views about the role of money in the business cycle, or emphasized the differences between Mitchell, and Friedman and Schwartz. Mitchell expressed doubts about the usefulness of monetary aggregates and about the quantity theory; Friedman and Schwartz embraced both. There is, of course, some truth in the initial reaction to the *Monetary History* and the more recent writings of historians of economic thought. Friedman and Schwartz were critics of the Keynesian orthodoxy of the day, and they did compute monetary aggregates and use the quantity theory. However, ignoring Mitchell's *Business Cycles* or focusing on the differences between Mitchell, and Friedman and Schwartz misses the agreement on the most important issues: on methodology and on conclusions about the role of money in the business cycle.

The institutional history of how the *Monetary History* came to be is relatively well known. Indeed, Friedman and Schwartz (1963a, p. xxi) provide the essentials in the *Monetary History*. And J. Daniel Hammond (1996) provides a carefully organized account of the origins of the Bureau's monetary project and a description of how the book uses the Bureau's methodology. The project was one of many started at the Bureau to expand on issues that Mitchell had initially surveyed in *Business Cycles*. It had started before Friedman and Schwartz took over. Originally James W. Angell and Caroline Whitney, a student of Angell at Columbia who completed her degree at Columbia in 1935, were assigned to the project. Schwartz replaced Whitney, possibly because Whitney was experiencing health problems. And when Angell later left the project, Arthur Burns, who had replaced Mitchell as director of the NBER, asked Friedman to take over.[5] The choice of Friedman made sense. Friedman had successfully completed several projects at the Bureau. He had already, moreover, developed an interest in the problem of inflation while working at the Treasury during the Second World War, although Friedman's work at that time was Keynesian in the sense that it emphasized taxes and spending rather than the stock of money (Friedman 1943, Shoup et al. 1943). Most important, as it would turn out, Friedman's skills as a theorist perfectly complemented those of Anna Schwartz, a superb economic historian. Burns also suggested that Friedman talk to Walter W. Stewart at Princeton about the project, and it was Stewart who suggested an 'analytical narrative' as a background for the statistical study.[6]

Work on the *Monetary History* went on in two places. The statistical work was carried out in New York under Anna Schwartz's direction, while Friedman remained at

Chicago. There, Friedman recruited graduate students who participated in his workshop and who wrote dissertations related to issues being explored in the *Monetary History*. Much of the joint work of writing the book took place in correspondence between Friedman in Chicago and Schwartz in New York. Although its institutional origins have been documented before, there is more to be said about the basic conclusions about the role of money in the business cycle reached in the *Monetary History* and the relationship between those conclusions and the earlier work by Mitchell and by economists at Chicago.

The rest of the chapter is arranged as follows. The next section describes Mitchell's career and his interest in money. The third section develops five conclusions about the role of money in the business cycle that summarize Mitchell's views as expressed in *Business Cycles*. Then, I describe how Friedman and Schwartz's work reinforced, modified and in one case rejected Mitchell's conclusions. The chapter then turns to the exploration of the Chicago influences on the *Monetary History*. While Mitchell's work provided the methodology, it was the Chicago economists who provided much of the analytic framework. This lays the groundwork for a restatement of Friedman's (1950) mathematical model of Mitchell's views. The parallels between this model and Friedman's subsequent mathematical models strengthen the case for seeing a close connection between *Business Cycles* and the *Monetary History*. I then look at some of the influential criticisms of the *Monetary History*, arguing that by time it appeared, Mitchell's work, indeed the Bureau's approach in general, was unfamiliar to many economists, and that this partly explains the failure of many economists to understand what Friedman and Schwartz had accomplished. The penultimate section defines more precisely the 'clinical methodology' that underlies the work of Mitchell and of Friedman and Schwartz. And the final section attempts an explanation of why Mitchell's conclusions about the role of money are so similar on so many fronts to the conclusions reached by Friedman and Schwartz.

Wesley Clair Mitchell

Wesley C. Mitchell is usually remembered today for his non-monetary contributions: his founding of the NBER and the stimulus it provided for research such as the early studies of national income. But Mitchell had a deep and continuing interest in monetary phenomena. Mitchell studied at the University of Chicago as both undergraduate and graduate student during the 1890s, an exciting period in American monetary history that included several financial panics and the famous 'Battle of the Standards' (gold or bimetallism?).[7] J. Laurence Laughlin, the professor at Chicago who supervised Mitchell's dissertation and encouraged Mitchell's career, was a prominent defender of the gold standard. Mitchell's dissertation, 'A history of the United States' notes' (1899), discussed the issue of fiat paper money by the North during the Civil War; the published version also addressed the effects of the greenbacks on interest rates, prices, wages and related variables (Mitchell 1903).

Mitchell's teaching career began at Chicago in 1900. In 1903 he moved to the University of California at Berkeley where he would spend a remarkably productive decade, including publication of *Gold, Prices, and Wages under the Greenback Standard* (1908). Here Mitchell covered the years 1862 to 1878, the entire period when the United States was on the 'Greenback standard' – the currency was not convertible into gold. Theory played a role in the shaping of this volume – Mitchell examined the relationship between the gold premium and prices, an item Friedman and Schwartz would take up in the *Monetary History*, and he discussed the patterns of lags among economic variables – but on the whole the emphasis was on data rather than analysis. Mitchell described the book as the 'statistical apparatus of a book still to be written' (quoted in Burns 1949, pp. 17–18).

In 1907 Mitchell lectured at Harvard on money and business cycles. In 1908 he returned to California and began to work on his third classic: *Business Cycles*. Mitchell's enormous capacity for work served him well. Despite the huge scope of Mitchell's vision, and the length of the manuscript (600 pages), it was completed in record time. Burns (1949, p. 23) put it this way: 'In the amazingly short time of three years, Mitchell had worked out and written one of the masterpieces in the world's economic literature'.

Business Cycles consisted of three parts. The first was a review of existing theories of the business cycle. The second was a compendium and analysis of time series (prices, currency, profits, the condition of the banks and so on) covering the United States, Britain, France and Germany from 1890 to 1911. The third was a description and explanation of the typical business cycle combined with a comparison of the United States and Britain during the crisis of 1907. This final chapter, although cast as a description, comes closer than anything else Mitchell wrote to representing his 'model' of the business cycle.

Here Mitchell described something approaching a true *cycle*: expansion was followed by contraction and contraction by expansion, with some regularity. The expansion, which would diffuse widely through the economy, automatically produced forces – pressures of costs on prices and tensions in the money market – that inevitably reduced profits and produced a contraction. The contraction, which would also diffuse widely, then produced changes in relative prices, such as a fall in costs relative to final product prices, which produced expansion. Friedman and Schwartz agreed that adjustments in relative prices would reverse contractions, so that in the end the economy would return to full employment, but they viewed the forces depressing the economy as random shocks, rather than as the inevitable products of expansions. A long-term statistical portrait of the economy, to put it somewhat differently, had the appearance of a cycle, and the language of cycles could be used to describe the economy, but only the forces making for recovery were truly inherent in the system.[8]

Mitchell did not argue that money was the central element in the business cycle. The cycle, according to Mitchell, was a complex and recurring phenomenon dependent on a wide range of factors, especially the interaction of wages, prices and profits. However, he did accord money an independent and important role in the cycle, and he cited historical events such as the increase in the world stock of gold after 1896 and the banking crisis of 1907 to make his point.

In future years Mitchell served as the first director of the NBER and became a major public economist. He also remained a highly productive scholar. *Business Cycles: The Problem and Its Setting* (Mitchell 1927) provided a much richer empirical description of the business cycle than the 1913 volume, but did not attempt to push the analysis of the causes of the cycle further. With Burns he published *Measuring Business Cycles* (Burns and Mitchell 1946), and the NBER also published posthumously an unfinished manuscript that Mitchell was working on at his death in 1948, *What Happens During Business Cycles: A Progress Report* (1951). Each of the studies completed after 1913 contained new empirical data, and new discussions of the timing of the business cycle. However,

Mitchell never produced an explicit analysis of the causes of the cycle to replace his 1913 effort.

Each topic that Mitchell addressed in his 1913 volume – prices, wages, employment, national income, money, interest rates and so on – became a project at the NBER. A researcher was assigned the task of accumulating data – the Bureau had a strong preference for monthly data – and turning points (from contraction to expansion and expansion to contraction) were identified in the economy as a whole (reference cycles) and in individual series (specific cycles). The specialists then analyzed the relationships between specific cycles and reference cycles. Friedman and Schwartz (1963b) completed some work of this kind, and they had intended to do an entire volume on money and business cycles. This goal, however, was never reached. In the end they completed three volumes: the *Monetary History* (1963a), *Monetary Statistics of the United States* (1970), and *Monetary Trends in the United States and the United Kingdom* (1982).

In the *Monetary History*, episodes were treated chronologically, and the focus in each discussion was on whether there was a relationship between changes in monetary policy and changes in the economy. Differences from one episode to another in the time between changes in monetary policy and responses were, for the most part, not addressed in detail. This issue was addressed in some of the related work and surely would have been addressed in the volume on cycles.

The reasons for Mitchell's decision not to revise his 1913 description of the cycle are unclear. Perhaps he was simply waiting for the full flowering of the empirical work at the Bureau that he had set in motion. Money is a good example. Given the prominent role played by money in his 1913 account of the cycle, it made sense to wait until the Bureau's money project had clarified the role of money before revising his description. In the end, Mitchell's failure to produce a revised description of the business cycle, and his concentration on data led to a telling criticism of Mitchell and the Bureau. *Measuring Business Cycles* (Burns and Mitchell 1946) was criticized by Tjalling Koopmans (1947) as 'Measurement without theory', a label that would trouble the Bureau and its workers for years to come. Friedman's (1950) essay 'Wesley C. Mitchell as an economic theorist', which I shall discuss below, was written partly to reverse the negative image of Mitchell that had developed from Koopmans's criticism.

In 1941, in lieu of a new theoretical treatment of the business cycle, Mitchell republished the third part of his 1913 book with 'betterments in wording and correction of an arithmetical blunder' (1913 [1959], p. vii). Therefore, the third part of this early volume contains the fullest available description of how Mitchell viewed the cycle and the role he assigned to money.

Friedman clearly held *Business Cycles*, if not all of Mitchell's later work, in high regard.[9] In a response to a letter from mathematician Edwin B. Wilson for a list of works Friedman considered 'thoroughly good' in the sense that they used theory as a way of organizing facts, and facts as a way of modifying theory, Friedman composed a list of five. *Business Cycles* was at the top of the list, although Friedman did not indicate that his choices were listed in order (Stigler 1994, p. 1200). The list also included Burns and Mitchell's *Measuring Business Cycles* in second place. Much later Friedman would say that the 1913 volume 'was a book', but the 1927 volume was not, referring to the lack of a theoretical framework in the later volume (Friedman 2002).

Friedman's understanding of Mitchell's approach recognized both strengths and

Table 7.1 Sources cited in the Monetary History

Author	Book or article	Citations
	The top six authors	
Friedman, Milton	Various articles and books	29
Mitchell, Wesley C.	On Civil War era (10), on business cycles (7)	17
Sprague, Oliver M.W.	*History of Crises under the National Banking Act*	14
Cagan, Phillip	*Determinants and Effects* (9) and 'The demand for currency' (3)	12
Warburton, Clark	Various journal articles	11
Fisher, Irving	Various articles and books	4
	Other	
Hayek, Friedrich A.	*Prices and Production*, etc.	0
Keynes, John Maynard	*The Treatise on Money*, *The General Theory*, etc.	0
Schumpeter, Joseph A.	*Business Cycles*, etc.	0

Note: I have excluded responses to criticisms or comments on earlier drafts. I have also excluded references to the diaries of Charles S. Hamlin and George L. Harrison that Friedman and Schwartz cited repeatedly in their analysis of monetary policy making during the Great Depression.

Source: Friedman and Schwartz (1963a).

weaknesses. In a letter to Burns offering comments on his (Burns 1949) description of Mitchell's career, Friedman described Mitchell's approach as follows.

> In truth, Mitchell's great and overwhelming genius was in his unparalleled capacity for bringing together an enormous mass of material, putting it into systematic form, and giving an orderly, lucid, and meaningful account of it. This capacity is demonstrated no less in his expositions of empirical material – The History, Gold etc. – than in his expositions of theoretical literature – part I of both business cycle volumes, *The Role of Money in Economic Theory*, *Types of Economic Theory*. But this virtue inevitably carried with it a vice. He did such a masterful job – both intellectually and in literary form and style – that he misled both himself and his readers into taking his descriptions as explanations. I cannot emphasize too strongly that this vice (surely too strong a word) was an inescapable corollary of the virtue. Nor need I emphasize that this comment is a very different from saying that analysis or theory were absent. They played a crucial role. They provided the organizing principle for the descriptions; and the descriptions themselves were analytical descriptions. (Milton Friedman to Arthur Burns, 12 April 1949, Milton Friedman Papers, uncatalogued)[10]

One quantitative index of the influence of particular authors on the *Monetary History* is the number of times they are cited in the text. Table 7.1 shows the top six authors, and by way of contrast, some prominent authors who were not cited. By this criterion Mitchell, the most frequently cited author (next to Milton Friedman) was the most influential. Citations to Mitchell significantly outdistance those to Irving Fisher and other monetarists. Friedrich Hayek, John Keynes and Maynard Joseph Schumpeter were not cited. Citations, of course, are a crude index of influence. Ideas may be so widely accepted that no citation is necessary; a source of data may be cited repeatedly. A book in one's own library may be cited often; a book in the university library may be cited once. To go deeper I develop five propositions that summarize Mitchell's main conclusions about the role of money in the business cycle and show that these propositions also encompass the main findings of Friedman and Schwartz.

From Mitchell to Friedman and Schwartz

Briefly these propositions can be described as follows: (1) there are changes in money that are independent of the business cycle, (2) these changes are regularly associated with changes in economic activity, (3) money therefore causes changes in economic activity, (4) while money influences the business cycle, so do many other things, and (5) changes in bank-lending rates are an important part of the transmission mechanism. Below I have placed my summary of Mitchell's conclusions in italics, and my summary of how Friedman and Schwartz extended Mitchell's conclusions underneath. I show that Friedman and Schwartz strongly reinforced Mitchell's conclusions on the first three issues with new data and arguments. Friedman and Schwartz did not break new ground on the fourth issue, the role of non-monetary forces, which was outside their assignment, although they discussed a wide range of non-monetary forces. On the last issue, the role of bank lending, Friedman and Schwartz reached a different conclusion from Mitchell. Friedman and Schwartz emphasized a direct channel running from changes in money to changes in national income, while Mitchell emphasized a channel that ran through bank lending and credit markets. It is interesting in this respect that one of the main differences of Friedman and Schwartz with their close allies Allan Meltzer and Karl Brunner was over whether credit market effects should be ignored, and that the most widely accepted addition to the Friedman and Schwartz interpretation of the Great Depression, the influential work of Ben Bernanke (1983), restores the role of bank lending to the central role in the monetary transmission process.

My propositions, although designed for the purpose of comparing Mitchell with Friedman and Schwartz, are closely related to the propositions Friedman and Schwartz used to summarize their findings. In their concluding chapter, Friedman and Schwartz (1963a, p. 676) identified four principal findings: (1) 'changes in the behavior of the money stock have been closely associated with changes in economic activity', (2) 'the interrelation between monetary and economic change has been highly stable', (3) 'monetary changes have often had an independent origin', and (4) 'in monetary matters, appearances are deceiving'. My propositions (1)–(3) cover Friedman and Schwartz's (1)–(3). Their fourth proposition was also adumbrated by Mitchell (1913 [1959], pp. 1–2) who noted that observers usually attributed the revival of business from a contraction to 'happy accidents' and missed the underlying forces that tended to make for recovery.

Here then are what I believe to be Mitchell's main conclusions about the role of money in the business cycle.

1. *There are different types of money – gold, paper money issued by the government, paper money issued by banks, and bank deposits. The amounts of gold and paper money issued by the government are relatively independent of the business cycle, while the amount of deposits is highly dependent on the business cycle. Paper money issued by banks is an intermediate case* (ibid., pp. 50–52).

Mitchell was content to look at each component of the stock of money separately and was skeptical about the wisdom of adding them up. Friedman and Schwartz, on the other hand, were determined to add up assets and produce an estimate of the total quantity of money. Friedman and Schwartz, however, preserved the most important aspect of Mitchell's analysis of the supply of money by introducing the distinction between high- and low-powered money. This distinction preserved Mitchell's main point and clarified how gold and paper money issued by the government (high-powered money) differed from bank deposits (low-powered money). Friedman and Schwartz set out their formal analysis of the supply of money in Appendix B of the *Monetary History* (1963a, pp. 780–89), and included sections on the supply of money in most chapters, typically labeled 'factors accounting for changes in the money stock'.[11] I shall consider their analysis in more detail later in the chapter.

Phillip Cagan carried out much of the analysis of the supply of money in *Determinants and Effects of Changes in the Stock of Money, 1875–1960* (1965). Although published two years after the *Monetary History*, Cagan's manuscript was at hand when Friedman and Schwartz were writing the *Monetary History*. Friedman and Schwartz cite this unpublished study nine times (see Table 7.1) and an earlier study by Cagan (1958), 'The demand for currency relative to the total money supply', three times. Clearly, Cagan deserves much of the credit for pushing forward this aspect of Mitchell's analysis.

2. *Changes in the stock of money have been associated with predictable changes in economic activity. Increases in money have been associated with economic expansions and inflation; decreases with contractions and deflation.*

Mitchell based his findings in *Business Cycles* mainly on his reading of the period 1890 to 1911, although his earlier work on the Civil War and post-bellum periods must have played a role as well. The events of most interest to monetary historians during the period from 1890 to 1911 were the inflation from 1896 to 1911 and the financial panics in the United States in 1893 and 1907. His interpretations of these events were one of the main sources of his conclusions about the role of money in the business cycle.

Mitchell argued, for example, that increases in the supply of gold influences the business cycle. In Mitchell's words,

> An abundant supply of gold favors a revival of business activity by giving the banks liberal reserves and thereby increasing their ability to lend credit at moderate rates of interest. This feature of the situation grows more important as the revival ripens into full prosperity. . . . That is, an increasing supply of gold favors the continuance of prosperity by retarding the accumulation of one of the stresses characteristic of one of its later stages – namely, tension in the money market. (Mitchell 1913 [1959], p. 52)

At a later point in his discussion Mitchell was more explicit in referring to the period after 1896, and in pointing to an effect on prices:[12]

> Hence such an increase in the world's production of gold as has been going on in recent years tends to cut short and to mitigate depressions as well as to prolong and to intensify prosperity. By thus altering somewhat both the intensity and the relative duration of these two phases of business cycles, it tends to an upward direction to those long-period movements of the price curve in which the years of depression and of prosperity are averaged. (Ibid., pp. 138–9)

Friedman and Schwartz also analyzed the effect of the increase in world gold production at the turn of the century. They agreed with Mitchell that the gold discoveries increased long-term inflation:

> The proximate cause of the world price rise [from 1897 to 1914] was clearly the tremendous outpourings of gold after 1890 that resulted from discoveries in South Africa, Alaska, and Colorado, and from the development of improved methods of mining and refining. (Friedman and Schwartz 1963a, p. 137)

They were skeptical, however, that rapid growth of the stock of gold had increased the rate of growth of real income over a period of several business cycles, a claim that might be read into Mitchell's claim that economic expansions had been lengthened and contractions shortened. One piece of evidence was their comparison of the 1903–13 period, which was one of 'moderately stable growth', with 1882–92 (ibid., pp. 186–7). There was a substantial difference in inflation: the national income deflator fell at a rate of 2.0 percent per year from 1882 to 1892, but rose at a rate of 2.0 percent per year from 1903 to 1913. There was not, however, a dramatic difference in the growth of the real economy: real income rose 3.5 percent per year from 1882 to 1892 and 3.3 percent per year from 1903 to 1913 (ibid., p. 185).[13]

Mitchell also stressed that banking panics could disrupt economic activity, and he included a detailed comparison of the panic of 1907 in the United States with the crisis – it never degenerated to the point where it could be called a panic – in Britain (1913 [1959], pp. 74–122).[14] A banking panic, Mitchell argued, produced disarray in the normal means of settlement, and discouraged banks from making loans available in the normal way. Both developments produced the contraction in economic activity.

The close association of banking panics with severe economic declines was also important to Friedman and Schwartz. In the concluding chapter to the *Monetary History* they noted that there had been six severe economic contractions in the period they examined: 1873–79, 1893–94, 1907–08, 1920–21, 1929–1933 and 1937–38. Each was marked by a decline in the stock of money, and four – 1873–79, 1893–94, 1907–08 and 1929–33 – 'by major banking and monetary disturbances' (Friedman and Schwartz 1963a, pp. 677–8).

3. *History provides persuasive evidence that the direction of causation can run from money to economic activity: History proves that money matters. This conclusion follows from proposition (1), that some monetary changes are independent of current or future changes in the economy, and proposition (2) that significant changes in economic activity are associated in a predictable way with changes in money.*

Mitchell, as far as I am aware, never developed this point explicitly. However, it is implicit in his description of the business cycle. His treatment of the supply of gold in the 1890s is a good example. As we saw above, Mitchell (1913 [1959], pp. 138–9) concluded 'that an increase in the world's production of gold as has been going on in recent years tends to cut short and to mitigate depressions as well as to prolong and to intensify prosperity'. Mitchell also noted that the increase in the gold supply was independent of the increase in prosperity. Mitchell (ibid., pp. 50–51) listed a number of ways that an economic expansion would decrease gold production, for example by raising costs of production while the final product price remained fixed, and a number of ways that an expansion would increase gold production, for example by encouraging people to buy risky stocks in gold mines. He concluded, however, that 'in recent times' the net effect of cycle-related factors had 'certainly been overshadowed by the influence of other factors not directly dependent upon the condition of business – the progress of the mining and metallurgical technique, the discovery of new gold deposits, and the maintenance of order in the chief producing districts'. Clearly it followed that causation had run from the independent increase in the supply of gold to the mitigation of depressions.

Mitchell's contrast between the United States in 1907 and Britain in 1907 also points to a causative role for money. The United States suffered a severe banking panic and a severe contraction in economic activity. Britain suffered a milder monetary stringency and a milder decline in economic activity, mainly because of timely actions by the Bank of England. The Bank owed its commanding presence to a long historical process that was largely independent of business conditions in 1907. It followed that monetary policy was an independent influence on the economy.

In his concluding chapter Mitchell gave forceful expression to the importance of a lender of last resort, and the need for one in the United States:

> That occasionally crises still degenerate into panics in America, but not in Great Britain, France, or Germany, arises primarily from differences in banking organization and practice. In each of the three European countries the prevalence of branch banking and existence of a central bank so organizes the banking system as a whole that reserves can be applied when and where needed although they constitute only a small percentage of aggregate demand liabilities of all the branches. In marked contrast to the policy of American banks, the central bank not only carries a reserve far in excess of immediate requirements in ordinary times, but also uses it boldly in times of stress.[15] (Ibid., p. 159)

Friedman and Schwartz further developed the argument that historical details about monetary institutions and the origin of monetary changes would illuminate the direction of causation between money and economic activity. What is needed to show persuasively that money matters are natural experiments, crucial experiments as Friedman and Schwartz style them, occasions when the stock of money changed for reasons that were clearly independent of contemporaneous or future economic changes in real income or prices.

The gold-based inflation from 1897 to 1914, stressed by Mitchell, also appears as a major case study in the *Monetary History*. In fact, Friedman and Schwartz argue that this episode provides the best evidence from their array of episodes on the direction of causation:

> The *clearest example* [that the direction of causation may run from money to income; emphasis added] is perhaps the monetary expansion from 1897 to 1914, which was worldwide and reflected an increased output of gold. The increased output of gold was partly a consequence of earlier decades of declining prices, which encouraged gold production, and so speaks also for the mutual interaction between monetary and economic changes. But clearly the monetary expansion cannot be attributed to the contemporary rise in money income and prices. By itself, the rise in money income and prices made for a reduced output of gold in the world at large and for an outflow of gold from any single country in a gold standard world. If the common movement of money and income was not purely coincidental, the direction of influence must run from money to income. (Friedman and Schwartz 1963a, p. 686)

Although natural experiments are the best evidence that history can provide, it is not the only evidence. Even in the absence of a natural experiment, historical episodes can be compared and contrasted, as Mitchell did when comparing the United States and Britain in 1907. In the *Monetary History* Friedman and Schwartz confined themselves to the United States, so for the most part this kind of comparison could not be made.[16] However, they could and did make comparisons across time as when they compared the contraction of 1907–08 with the contraction of 1929–33.[17] They were also able to compare experiences during major wars, something Mitchell writing in 1913 could not do. Here Friedman and Schwartz (ibid., p. ch. 10, *passim*) noted that prices rose more in the First World War than in the Second World War, a fact consistent with the degree of monetary expansion in the two wars, but not consistent with the degree of mobilization.

Although Friedman and Schwartz pressed the case for using history to prove causality running from money to income, it was Cagan (1965) who developed the argument in greatest detail, especially in the penultimate chapter, 'The cause-and-effect relations between money, prices, and output'. In his forward to Cagan's book, Friedman (1965) summarizes Cagan's conclusions about the causal role of money, and reports that 'originally, we did not expect the examination of the supply of money to provide evidence on such general issues as the causal relation between money and prices' (pp. xxvii–xxviii). Perhaps because Cagan's monograph was published two years after the *Monetary History*, Cagan's detailed development of the case for using history to prove that money influences the business cycle was frequently missed by the critics of Friedman and Schwartz. Friedman's remark in the introduction to the Cagan volume also suggests that Mitchell's recognition that some apparently important monetary changes were the result of forces independent of the business cycle was not the direct inspiration for Cagan's analysis, although Cagan (1965, pp. 143–5) does discuss some of Mitchell's ideas about the money supply.

4. *The business cycle is the result of both monetary and non-monetary forces. Money matters, but so do many other things.*[18]

Mitchell's list of important influences on the business cycle was long. Money was merely one actor on a crowded stage. Friedman and Schwartz also assumed that there were many factors affecting the business cycle. This statement may seem to contradict a commonly accepted view that Friedman and Schwartz claimed that money explains everything. The common wisdom, however, is simply mistaken. Like Mitchell, Friedman and Schwartz assumed that even in the absence of mistakes in monetary policy there would be a business cycle, sometimes a very volatile business cycle, caused by other factors.

Friedman and Schwartz frequently describe the non-monetary forces influencing the business cycle explicitly. Agriculture provides one example. Mitchell (1913 [1959], p. 2), noted that in 1891, 'Unusually large American crops of grain, sold at exceptionally high prices, cut short what was promising to be an extended period of liquidation after the crisis of 1890, and suddenly set the tide of business rising'.[19] And Friedman and Schwartz noted three cases in which a 'fortuitous combination' of favorable harvests in the United States and unfavorable harvests in Europe boosted economic activity in the United States: 1879–82, 1891 and 1896 (Friedman and Schwartz 1963a, pp. 97–8, 107, 140).[20]

The stock market is another source of non-monetary forces addressed by both Mitchell and by Friedman and Schwartz. Mitchell (1913 [1959], pp. 69–70) argued that a decline in stock prices during the last phase of an economic expansion would set in motion forces that contributed to the following recession. Costs would rise more rapidly than prices during the expansion, squeezing profits and putting downward pressure on stock prices. Reduced valuations for firms, especially smaller firms, in turn would reduce the availability of credit, and force cutbacks in production. Similarly, Friedman and Schwartz argued that the Crash of 1929 had depressed economic activity by reducing the willingness of consumers and business enterprises to spend because the Crash 'spread uncertainty where dazzling hopes of a new era had prevailed' (1963a, pp. 306–7).

In most cases, however, Friedman and Schwartz simplified their task by assuming a non-monetary cycle that would continue even in the absence of monetary disturbances. The non-monetary disturbances that often drove the economy off its full-employment trend, and the underlying tendency of a market economy to fight its way back to full employment, in other words, were often assumed rather than described in detail. The decision to abstract from non-monetary forces was justified by the division of labor at the Bureau. Friedman and Schwartz's assignment was to clarify the role of money in the business cycle; other forces were the province of other investigators. Friedman and Schwartz's basic formula then was to describe how monetary forces pushed or pulled a cycle determined by non-monetary forces.

In their discussion of the 1920–21 recession, for example, they write as follows:

> The extraordinary disturbances of the First World War period certainly induced national and international adjustments in the use of real resources on a far larger scale than is usual, and were unquestionably a source of uncertainty. Those disturbances might well have made it impossible to avoid a more than usually severe cyclical movement in this country, though our experience after Second World War demonstrated that this result need not follow. But there can be little doubt that Federal Reserve policy [very large increases in the discount rate] was a further and not unimportant factor contributing to the severity of the movement. (Ibid., p. 237)

In their discussion of the effects of monetary contraction in the early 1930s they write as follows:

> All in all, the figures for the first four or five months of 1931, if examined without reference to what actually followed, have many of the earmarks of the bottom of a cycle and the beginning of revival.
>
> Perhaps if those tentative stirrings of revival had been reinforced by a vigorous expansion on the stock of money, they could have been converted into sustained recovery. But that was not to be. (p. 313)

The obvious implication is that there are other forces that make for recovery besides money, but those forces are abstracted from the discussion. Part of the story was simply the inherent tendency of a free market economy to right itself after a recession.

Another example of their treatment of the non-monetary cycle occurs in the discussion of the 1937–38 recession. Friedman and Schwartz attributed a great deal of damage to the decision made by the Federal Reserve prior to the recession to double the required reserve ratios of banks and to sterilize the inflow of gold. Nevertheless, they do not claim that there would have been continued expansion in the absence of the change in monetary policy. Their statement is far more circumspect, and assumes a business cycle that is independent of monetary policy:

> Consideration of the effects of monetary policy on the stock of money certainly strengthens the case for attributing an important role to monetary changes as a factor that significantly intensified the severity of the decline and also probably caused it to occur earlier than otherwise. (p. 544)

And in discussing the recovery from this recession, they write:

> Recovery came after the money stock had started to rise. . . . Munich and the outbreak of war in Europe were the main factors determining the US money stock in those years, as Hitler and the gold miners had been in 1934 to 1936. Doubtless, other factors helped to account for the onset of recovery and for its pace, but the rapid increase in the money stock certainly at the very least facilitated their operation. (p. 545)

Again, Friedman and Schwartz assume that 'other factors', left unnamed, influenced the business cycle. Indeed, in this quotation the possibility that money was merely 'facilitating' other forces, Mitchell's way of putting things, is acknowledged.

The continuity with Mitchell's views cannot be allowed, of course, to obscure the difference in emphasis. It is probably a fair conjecture that if Friedman and Schwartz and Mitchell had been asked for a summary figure indicating the amount of business fluctuations accounted for by independent changes in money Friedman and Schwartz would have produced a higher figure than Mitchell.[21] Mitchell, moreover, was not directly concerned in his work at the Bureau with focusing on policy variables because in his day adherence to the gold standard and the absence of a central bank eliminated the potential for short-term monetary policies. Much of Friedman's later writings focus on money, not because other factors don't affect the business cycle, but rather because of his belief that of the policy instruments available to the government, money is by far the most important.

5. *Bank lending plays a central role in the transmission mechanism. When banks are flush with reserves they extend loans, lowering interest rates and encouraging economic activity.*

Recall again the statement quoted from Mitchell above about the impact of gold during the period after 1897. In it, Mitchell claimed that the way that an abundant supply of gold had ameliorated fluctuations was 'by giving the banks liberal reserves and thereby increasing their ability to lend credit at moderate rates of interest'. Friedman and Schwartz ignored the bank-lending channel emphasized by Mitchell. Instead, they emphasized a direct channel running from a temporary excess of money holdings to increased spending.

Friedman and Schwartz do not explain why they rejected the bank-lending channel stressed by Mitchell and other early theorists. Part of the explanation may be that concurrent work on investment suggested that interest rate changes had little effect on investment spending. Another part of the explanation may be that Friedman and Schwartz had already begun to work out a description of the transmission mechanism from money to economic activity that relied on a more direct channel connecting changes in money with changes in income. The report on their statistical findings published in the *Review of Economics and Statistics* (Friedman and Schwartz 1963b) contained a description of how an increase in money produced by an open market purchase would gradually produce changes in portfolio holdings and affect economic activity. Interest rates would be affected, but only as part of a larger process.

Friedman's famous essay 'The optimum quantity of money' (Friedman 1969) carried this sketch a step further. Here he began with a simple, and now famous, thought experiment: a helicopter flies over an economy that relies on fiat paper money and drops more. Friedman concludes that in this simplified economy spending will increase, producing an increase in nominal income. If the economy is at full employment, the result will be higher prices. He argues, moreover, that this conclusion holds even as more sophisticated institutional arrangements are added to the model.[22]

Another reason why Friedman and Schwartz may have deemphasized the bank-lending channel was empirical. In 1893 and 1907, the banking crises that most concerned Mitchell, the crises were associated with high nominal interest rates, but in the early 1930s, a crisis of major importance to Friedman and Schwartz, the crisis was associated with low nominal rates. In 1893 the stock market crash came in May and the banking panic in June (Friedman and Schwartz 1963a, p. 108). The monthly commercial paper rate also reached its peak of 15 percent in June, after averaging about 4 percent in 1892.[23] In 1907 the stock market slide began in March and the first major bank failure occurred in October. The monthly commercial paper rate hit its peak of 10 percent, nearly twice the 1906 rate, in November and December. In the 1930s, however, events unfolded differently. The stock market crash occurred in October 1929 when the commercial paper rate also peaked at a little over 6 percent. The onset of the first banking panic, however, did not occur until a year later. And the commercial paper rate, which then stood at about 3 percent, was in the midst of a long decline that seemed to be unaffected by the banking crisis.

To account for events in the early 1930s, therefore, Friedman and Schwartz were forced to broaden their interpretation of the determinants of nominal interest rates. First, the rate of interest was determined in the market for credit and therefore influenced by factors outside the banking sector. The recession that began in the late 1920s (and was perhaps intensified by the stock market crash) reduced the demand for loanable funds and the rate of interest. Moreover, the channels running from changes in the stock of money to interest rates were complex. The supply of bank loans declined because of the runs on the banks and the associated increase in bank reserve ratios, but the decline in economic activity produced by the decline in the stock of money working directly on spending, reduced the demand for loans even more and contributed to the fall in economic activity.

For Friedman and Schwartz, the complexity of the relationships between money and interest rates argued against seeing interest rates as a simple indicator of the lending capacity of the banks and against using interest rates as a guide to monetary policy. In the crucial period from 1929 to 1932, nominal rates had given the misleading signal that monetary policy was 'easy'. Avoiding the worst–case scenario, a repeat of the Great Depression, was a good reason for focusing on the stock of money rather than nominal interest rates.

There were, it is true, other ways that interest rates could have been used as indicators of monetary policy. Although not stressed in the *Monetary History*, the decline in the price level, the result in part of the decline in the stock of money, lowered nominal rates while disguising the increase in real rates. This argument suggests that real interest rates would have worked better than nominal rates as an indicator of monetary policy in the Depression. Anna J. Schwartz (1981) later drew attention to the rise in real rates, as Meltzer (2003, p. 730) did more recently. Meltzer also pointed to the rising spread between high- and low-risk assets, a development that was also noted by Friedman and Schwartz (1963a, p. 312), as an indication of the need for monetary expansion.

Mitchell was not breaking new ground in emphasizing the bank-lending channel. The debate between monetary economists who emphasized the channel and those who emphasized the quantity theory and a direct connection between increases in money and increases in economic activity was heated throughout the nineteenth century (Laidler 1999 [2004]). Mitchell, of course, was well aware of this debate. Laughlin, his thesis advisor at Chicago, supported the banking school, and Mitchell had, as Friedman pointed out, an unprecedented command of the economic literature as a whole.

The neglect of the bank-lending channel proved to be one of the many controversial aspects of the *Monetary History*. Allan Meltzer and Karl Brunner, the most formidable allies of Friedman and Schwartz when it came to monetary policy – it was Brunner who coined the term 'monetarism' – consistently argued that the credit channel had to be included in models of how monetary policy influenced the economy (Brunner and Meltzer 1988, see Laidler 1991 for a good retrospective account of Brunner's work).

One of the few modifications of the Friedman–Schwartz view of the Great Depression that has become widely accepted by economic historians, moreover, is the argument developed by Bernanke (1983) that the banking crises in the early 1930s produced changes in the lending practices of banks that made the depression deeper and longer than it otherwise would have been. Bernanke did not reject the possibility of the direct channel from money to income stressed by Friedman and Schwartz, but he argued that the failure of banks and the destruction of the value of collateral raised the cost of credit intermediation and depressed economic activity. Bernanke (ibid., p. 258) could find no 'exact antecedents' for his work. While he is undoubtedly right that there are no exact antecedents, one can point to a strong family resemblance between Bernanke's bank-centric description of the causes of the Great Contraction and Mitchell's bank-centric descriptions of earlier panics such as that in 1907. Of course, by the time Bernanke wrote, Mitchell's work had ceased to have any direct influence on the profession.

The Chicago connection

The *Monetary History* was an NBER book, but also a Chicago book. Friedman had studied at Chicago, although his PhD was awarded by Columbia, and he was a professor at Chicago during the time he was working on the *Monetary History*. In Friedman's time as a student at Chicago there were four professors whose work appears to have influenced the *Monetary History*: (1) Henry Simons and (2) Lloyd Mints, both monetary theorists; (3) Jacob Viner, an expert on international trade, history of economic thought and other areas including money; and (4) Henry Schultz, a pioneer in the estimation of demand curves.

In his NBER interview, Friedman (2002) remembered that he had taken courses with both Mints and Viner, but not with Simons, although Friedman recalled that he knew Simons and had read his work. All three were quantity theorists and in that sense, Friedman remembered, their ideas provided the framework for the *Monetary History*. In Friedman's memory, the key figure was Viner, whose one-quarter course opened Friedman's mind to the power of economic theory. In the interview, Friedman (2002) did not see much of a connection between his work with Schultz and his work for the Bureau, although Friedman again emphasized his lack of introspection.

We can, however, conjecture influences of all four. One has to use the qualified phrase 'conjecture influences' because we do not have, for the most part, a trail of footnotes that leads from the work of these scholars to the *Monetary History*, and because Friedman, who as noted above describes himself as not very introspective, has not attempted to construct the links in retrospect.

Simons's most important contribution to monetary economics was his famous distinction between 'rules' and 'authority' in the conduct of monetary policy (Simons 1936). Simons argued that it was better to bind the Federal Reserve with a specific rule, rather than follow the undemocratic course of allowing it to use its discretion in setting monetary policy. Simons's preferred rule was stabilizing the price level. He considered the rule of stabilizing the stock of money or its growth rate, but thought that this rule would not work as long as close substitutes for money were ubiquitous. Substantial institutional reforms would need to be undertaken, such as his proposal for 100 percent reserve banking, before a monetary rule would be preferable to a price rule. Friedman (1959), on the other hand, rejected a price rule, because it would be hard to hold the Federal Reserve responsible for prices when they were influenced by so many non-monetary variables, and preferred a monetary rule, discounting the problem posed by close substitutes for money.

The *Monetary History* supported the case for a 'Friedman Rule' by showing that a single, consistently defined monetary aggregate, basically currency held by the public plus all deposits held by the public in commercial banks, could explain over 90 years of monetary history in the United States. The evidence on this issue was augmented in the companion volume, *Monetary Statistics* (Friedman and Schwartz 1970). Over six hundred pages in length, this volume not only described the methods by which Friedman and Schwartz estimated the stock of money, fulfilling the Bureau mandate for a detailed report on how numbers were estimated, but also presented detailed arguments and statistical evidence to show that their simple sum monetary aggregate worked well throughout the period they examined. Thus, the *Monetary History* and *Monetary Statistics* showed that Simons's concern that variations in the volume of close substitutes for money, or variations in their degree of 'moneyness', would undermine the effectiveness of a rule based on a monetary aggregate was unwarranted.[24]

I am only aware, however, of one passage in the *Monetary History* that speaks explicitly to the value of a monetary rule. In looking back at the Great Depression, Friedman and Schwartz note that the stock of money rose at an unusually rapid rate during the expansions from 1934 to 1936 and from 1938 to 1941. Those unusually rapid increases, however, were justified by the unusually rapid decline from 1929 to 1933. They conclude their analysis of the Great Depression with the following passage:

> How different the history of that fateful dozen years might have been if the money stock had grown steadily at its average rate of 2½ per cent per year, let alone at the higher long-term his-

> torical rate, instead of first falling by one-third from 1929 to 1933 and then doubling from 1933 to 1941. (Friedman and Schwartz 1963a, p. 545)

A monetary rule whatever its failings, in other words, would avoid the worst-case scenario: a repeat of the Great Depression.

Lloyd Mints, whom Friedman did study with at Chicago, is remembered mainly for his analysis of the 'real bills doctrine' (Mints 1945).[25] This doctrine held that the goal of monetary policy should be to increase or decrease the money supply in response to changes in the 'needs of trade'. Moreover, the doctrine held that this goal could be realized by making sure that banks confined their lending to the discounting of 'real bills' – loans arising from the purchase of grain, not loans arising from the purchase of land for speculation. One of the main problems with the real-bills doctrine, according to Mints, is that the nominal values of real bills will rise during inflations and fall during deflations. Hence a monetary policy built on the real-bills doctrine will simply ratify inflation or deflation, rather than stabilizing the price level. Friedman and Schwartz (1963a, p. 169) refer to Mints's critique of the real-bills doctrine when they criticize the Federal Reserve Act for partially incorporating ideas arising from the real-bills doctrine. Overall, Friedman and Schwartz cite Mints's book three times for various purposes.

Mints criticized the Federal Reserve for its handling of the Great Depression (Mints et al. 1946, pp. 62–3, Mints 1950). He pointed out that the Federal Reserve had permitted a massive decline in the stock of money during 1929–31 and argued that this decline had contributed to the severity of the Depression. This point became a major conclusion in Friedman and Schwartz's interpretation of the Great Depression, and one of the key points that generations of economists have taken from the *Monetary History*. It is possible that Mints's views on the role of the Federal Reserve in the Great Depression formed part of the background that shaped the narrative in the *Monetary History*, but his views about the Federal Reserve's behavior in the early 1930s are not cited explicitly.

Jacob Viner was also a sharp critic of the Federal Reserve's policy in the early 1930s. In a symposium on Friedman's work, Friedman (1972, pp. 939–40) expressed his admiration for Viner's criticism of the Federal Reserve in the Depression and quoted extensively from Viner's public lectures in the early years of the Depression. He notes, for example, that in a talk given in Minneapolis on 20 February 1933, Viner strongly criticized the Federal Reserve:

> It is often said that the federal government and the Federal Reserve system have practiced inflation [an increase in monetary assets in Viner's lexicon] during this Depression and that no beneficial effects resulted from it. What in fact happened is that they made mild motions in the direction of inflation, which did not succeed in achieving it, did not succeed even in accomplishing 'reflation'; but which probably did slow up somewhat the rate of price decline . . . At no time . . . since the beginning of the Depression has there been for so long as four months a net increase in the volume of bank credit outstanding. On the contrary, the government and Federal Reserve bank operations have not nearly sufficed to countervail the contraction of credit on the part of member and non-member [of the Federal Reserve system] banks. (Viner quoted in Friedman 1972, pp. 939–40)

Friedman (1972, p. 940) went on to point out the connection with the *Monetary History*.

> Can anyone who knows my work read Viner's comments and not see the direct links between them and Anna Schwartz's and my *Monetary History* (1963a) or between them and the empirical *Studies in the Quantity Theory of Money* (1956b)? Indeed as I have read Viner's talk for the purposes of this paper, I have myself been amazed to discover how precisely it foreshadows the main thesis of our *Monetary History* for the depression period, and have been embarrassed that we made no reference to it on that account.

Friedman's remarks seem to document the influence of Viner, and the other Chicago monetarists, on the *Monetary History*. They also suggest that there may be links between other works and the *Monetary History*, such as between *Business Cycles* and the *Monetary History*, which cannot be established simply by reading footnotes, especially when the role of the earlier work was not to provide specific facts but to set the stage for the latter work.

In addition to the monetary theorists at Chicago (Simons, Mints and Viner) one can also point to another figure as a possible influence on the *Monetary History* and the related work by Friedman and Schwartz on money: Henry Schultz. To be sure, Schultz, whose magnum opus *The Theory and Measurement of Demand* (1938) consisted of a series of studies of the demand for agricultural products, may seem a strange choice as a major influence on monetary economics. Nevertheless, Friedman did work closely with Schultz. Friedman served as Schultz's research assistant in 1934, and at several points in his book Schultz acknowledges Friedman's contribution. More importantly, one can detect a number of parallels between Friedman's work and Schultz's, especially in Friedman's famous essay 'The quantity theory of money – a restatement' (Friedman 1956a).

Schultz took the theoretical ideas of Alfred Marshall and other theorists of demand and restated them so that they could be tested using then current statistical tools. Friedman's essay can be read as a similar effort to take the ideas developed by Simons and Mints at Chicago, and by Irving Fisher and other quantity theorists, and restate them so that they could be tested using statistical methods.[26]

Perhaps the most important argument in Schultz's book was that ordinary least squares could be used to identify the demand curve for an agricultural product. The supply of an agricultural product, say corn, Schultz argued, varied a lot compared with demand because of the weather, so an ordinary least squares regression of quantity of corn on the price of corn would identify the demand curve.[27] Friedman's strictly analogous argument was that the supply of money varied a lot compared with demand, because, for example, governments frequently resort to inflationary finance, and that therefore one can identify the demand for money with ordinary least squares.

Schultz's decision to include only the price of corn and the prices of a few close substitutes in his demand function is strictly analogous to Friedman and Schwartz's decision to include only a few variables including the own rate of return on money (for currency, the rate inflation) and the rates of return on bonds and equities in the demand function for money.

When faced with plausible alternative estimates of the supply of corn, Schultz solved the problem by choosing the estimate that was most highly correlated with the price of corn. Friedman and Schwartz applied the same empirical approach to choosing the best estimate of money. They constructed a series of plausible alternatives – M_1 which included currency and demand deposits, M_2 which included currency and all deposits at commercial banks, M_3 which included additional money-like assets and so on – and chose the estimate M that was most highly correlated with income. This approach is spelled out in *Monetary Statistics*, and provides the basis for using M_2 in the *Monetary History*.

Finally, just as Schultz's ultimate purpose was to use his estimates to evaluate the effects of New Deal agricultural policies, such as output restrictions, Friedman and Schwartz's ultimate purpose was to use his estimates to evaluate the effect of alternative monetary policies.

The issue of what influence non-Chicago economists, especially Keynes, had on Friedman and Schwartz became extremely contentious. In the opening section, Friedman claimed in his 1956 paper that he was merely developing Chicago's 'oral tradition'; Keynes was not mentioned. This contention was attacked by Don Patinkin (1969, 1972, 1979) and Harry Johnson (1971) who saw the reference to an oral tradition that apparently included interest rates in the demand for money as a way of bringing in Keynesian ideas without mentioning Keynes. It would take us too far afield to go into the details of this debate. However, we should note that Friedman had his defenders as well as detractors. Frank Steindl (1990) pointed out that Simons had referred to the oral tradition at Chicago in a review of a book on monetary conditions in the early 1930s by Currie (Simons 1935). And George Tavlas (1998) showed that Friedman's approach was anticipated in the work of Knight and Mints.

Friedman's mathematical restatement of Mitchell's theory

Further evidence of Friedman's deep understanding of Mitchell, and of the way that the Chicago emphasis on economic theory shaped that understanding, is to be found in Friedman's (1950) essay 'Wesley C. Mitchell as an economic theorist'. In this essay, Friedman provided a mathematical model of Mitchell's theory of the business cycle. If we look closely at this model, the starting point of the *Monetary History* is clear. In what follows I have used the symbols that Friedman and Schwartz used in later work because these are likely to be more familiar, rather than the symbols Friedman used in his original essay. I have also suppressed some of the non-monetary equations in the Mitchell–Friedman model.[28] Friedman, for example, modeled Mitchell's conclusions about the important role of final product prices and costs in determining profits and the level of investment spending. Here, however, I shall concentrate on Friedman's attempt to model Mitchell's conclusions about the relationships between the monetary variables and other sectors of the economy. I shall, however, consider three equations Friedman included that describe a simple Keynesian multiplier model. The inclusion of these equations was a precursor to Friedman's (1970) attempt to find a simple 'common model' that could be specialized as a Keynesian or Monetarist model.

Define the following terms:

Y = total national income;
C = consumption (induced expenditures);
I = investment (autonomous expenditures);
H = high-powered money (gold or paper money issued by the government) = $C_p + R$;
C_p = currency in the hands of the public;
D = deposits in the hands of the public;
M = money = $C_p + D$;

M^d = money demanded;
M^s = money supplied;
R = bank reserves = currency held by banks;
b = the bank's ratio of deposits to reserves = D/R;
b^* = the bank's desired ratio of deposits to reserves;
p = the public's ratio of deposits to currency = D/C_p;
λ = a shift term for a financial panic; and
i = the rate of interest.

Let us start with the banks. By definition the actual ratio of deposits to reserves is:

$$b = D/R. \tag{7.1}$$

Based on Mitchell's empirical observations, Friedman assumed the desired amount of deposits created by banks per dollar of reserves, b^*, to be a function of the current level of income, and the presence or absence of a banking panic:

$$b^* = f_1(Y, \lambda). \tag{7.2}$$

The variable λ is my addition, a shift term introduced to clarify how a banking panic would affect the economy. The partial derivative of b^* with respect to income, $f_1^{\,1}$, is assumed to be positive. When income increases in a cyclical expansion, lending opportunities improve, and so banks reduce the amount of reserves they wish to keep behind each dollar of deposits. The partial derivative of b^* with respect to a panic, $f_1^{\,2}$, is assumed to be negative: in a panic banks want higher reserves to protect themselves against runs, so they reduce lending.

The interest rate, i, is assumed to be dependent on the relationship between the actual and desired ratios of the banking system:

$$i = f_2(b^* - b). \tag{7.3}$$

The derivative $f_2^{\,1}$ is assumed to be negative. If the desired bank ratio exceeds the actual bank ratio, banks will increase lending, and increased lending will lower interest rates. Equation (7.3) is part of the bank-lending channel that Mitchell stressed, Friedman and Schwartz downplayed and recent research has again brought forward.

There is also a demand for money equation. This relationship became central to Freidman and Schwartz's thinking about the role of money:

$$M^d = f_3(Y, i). \tag{7.4}$$

Friedman adopts the standard assumptions that $f_3^{\,1}$ is positive, because money is a normal good, and $f_3^{\,2}$ is negative, because the interest rate is the cost of holding money. In later work (for example, Friedman 1956a and Friedman and Schwartz 1982), Friedman and Schwartz (1963a) elaborated on this simple equation, and took into account wealth, the interest paid on deposits, inflation and other variables. The estimation of demand for money equations for a time was a major cottage industry for economists.

The ratio of deposits to currency is a function of the level of income, and the panic shift term:

$$p = f_4(Y, \lambda). \tag{7.5}$$

The partial derivative of p with respect to income, $f_4^{\,1}$, is assumed to be positive – as income increases the demand for deposits grows relative to currency because deposits require more sophistication, but are capable of handling larger and more complex transactions. And the partial of derivative of b with respect to the panic shift, $f_4^{\,2}$, is negative – in a panic people want high-powered money.

Finally if we combine the definitions of M^s, H, b and p, from the initial list of variables we can derive an equation explaining the stock of money in terms of its 'determinants':

$$M^s = H{*}b(1 + p)/(b + p). \tag{7.6}$$

This is, with some changes in symbols, equation (12) of Appendix B of the *Monetary History* (ibid., p. 791).

On one level this equation is merely an identity derived by manipulating the definitions of M^s, H, b and p.[29] However, equation (7.6) can also be viewed as an equation that explains the relationship between the stock of money and the business cycle. It elegantly separated the determinants of the stock of money during Mitchell's era into elements he identified as independent of the business cycle from elements he identified as dependent. H includes gold, greenbacks and national banknotes. The amount of gold, although influenced by economic conditions, was also subject to important influences that were independent of the business cycle such as the discovery of new goldfields and the discovery of new technologies for securing gold from gold ore. The government determined the amount of greenbacks outstanding. The third component of high-powered money, national banknotes, is a more complex case.

Mitchell, as we noted above, thought that bank-issued currency was an intermediate case because at the time he was writing national banknotes were backed by Federal government bonds. Friedman and Schwartz wrestled with this issue as well. Ultimately they decided to include bank-issued currency in their definition of high-powered money. They pointed out that national banknotes had to be backed by Federal government bonds, were guaranteed by the Federal government and that after 1874 the Treasury had 'control over the amount outstanding, through its decisions that determined the volume of bonds bearing the circulation privilege and the interest coupon on them' (Friedman and Schwartz 1963a, pp. 780–81).[30] The last consideration echoes Mitchell's emphasis on supply independence.

If we take the total derivative of (7.6) we get the following:

$$dM^s/M^s = dH/H + [p/(b + p)]db/b + [p(b - 1)/(1 + p)(b + p)]dp/p. \tag{7.6$'$}$$

This equation – equivalent to equation (22) in Appendix B of the *Monetary History* (ibid., p. 794) – shows that the stock of money will increase if the amount of high-powered money increases, the amount of deposits banks create with each dollar of reserves increases or the amount of deposits that the public wants to hold relative to each dollar of currency it holds increases.[31]

Suppose that we also take the total derivatives of equations (7.4) and (7.5), and combine with (7.6′). To keep things simple, suppose that we also assume that λ is zero (there is no panic), and that the interest rate *i*, the bank money ratio *b* and the public's money ratio *p* are fixed. Then we have a quantity theory model specialized to show the effect of an increase in high-powered money:

$$dY/dH = [b(1 + b)/(b + p)](1/f_3^{\,1}). \tag{7.7}$$

A change in high-powered money, *H*, is multiplied by the money multiplier, $[b(1 + b)/(b + p)]$, to become a change in the total stock of money, and that amount in turn is multiplied by velocity, $1/f_3^{\,1}$, to become a change in income. An influx of gold, for example, would increase *H* and raise nominal incomes.

Similarly, we can derive the effect of a financial panic on the level of economic activity through its effects on the stock of money. To keep things simple, in this case we can hold the amount of high-powered money *H*, the bank ratio *b* and the interest rate *i* constant. With those assumptions we have a simple quantity theory simplified to show the effect of a financial panic:

$$dY/d\lambda = f_4^{\,2}/(f_3^{\,1} - f_4^{\,1}[H(b - 1)b/(b + p)^2]). \tag{7.8}$$

This expression is more complex than (7.7). The sign of the numerator is negative because $f_4^{\,2}$, the effect of a banking panic on the demand for deposits relative to currency, is negative. The sign of the denominator, however, is in principle ambiguous because the effect of income on the demand for money $f_3^{\,1}$ and the effect of the fall in income on the demand for bank money $f_4^{\,1}$ are both positive. If $f_3^{\,1}$ is sufficiently large compared with $f_4^{\,1}$, $dY/d\lambda$, the effect of the banking panic on income will be negative. Equations (7.6), (7.7) and (7.8) are the workhorses of the *Monetary History,* although only (7.6) is developed explicitly. Most of the discussions in the *Monetary History* are, in other words, descriptions of why the stock of money changed, and of how the changes in the stock of money produced changes in the economy.

To see the bank-lending channel that Mitchell stressed, we can combine equations (7.2) and (7.3) with the 'Keynesian' part of the Mitchell–Friedman model. First we have a simple definition of income as a sum of consumption and investment:

$$Y = C + I. \tag{7.9}$$

Consumption is assumed to be a simple function of the level of income:

$$C = f_5(Y), \tag{7.10}$$

where, of course, $f_5^{\,1} > 0$. And investment is assumed to be a function of the rate of interest:

$$I = f_6(i), \tag{7.11}$$

where, $f_6^{\,1} < 0$.

Combining equations (7.2) and (7.3) with (7.9), (7.10) and (7.11) yields a simple Mitchell–Friedman–Keynes model that emphasizes the bank lending channel. Perhaps the most interesting case is a financial panic. Taking the total differentials of equations (7.2), (7.3), (7.9), (7.10) and (7.11) and rearranging terms yields:

$$dY/d\lambda = (f_1^{\,2} f_2^{\,1} f_6^{\,1})/(1 - f_5^{\,1} - f_1^{\,1} f_2^{\,1} f_6^{\,1}). \tag{7.12}$$

This expression is clearly negative; a panic reduces income. The numerator is negative because it is the product of the negative effect of the panic on the banking system's desired ratio deposits to reserves ($f_1^{\,2}$), the negative effect of lower desired deposit–reserve ratios on interest rates ($f_2^{\,1}$), and the negative effect of higher interest rates on investment ($f_6^{\,1}$). All this is multiplied by $1/(1 - f_5^{\,1} - f_6^{\,1} f_2^{\,1} f_1^{\,1})$, which is simply an augmented form of the simplest Keynesian multiplier $1/(1 - f_5^{\,1})$.

The next step would be to derive the full impact of a financial panic on economic activity by combining the direct channel, emphasized by Friedman and Schwartz and modeled in equation (7.8), and the bank-lending channel, emphasized by Mitchell and modeled in equation (7.12). The resulting equation, however, is quite complex and does not suggest new insights.

To sum up, the elements that Friedman included in his later efforts to develop a formal model of the role of money – a supply of money function that distinguishes between high- and low-powered money, a set of general equations that can be specialized as a Keynesian or quantity theory model, and the direct connection between money and income – can be found in his 1950 model of Mitchell's theory of the business cycle. Mitchell's emphasis on a bank-lending channel, although modeled in the 1950 paper, however, never played a role in the *Monetary History* or related work.

The critics of monetarism

When looking at the early reception of the *Monetary History* it is hard to escape the realization that much of the difference between Friedman and Schwartz and their critics resulted from the willingness of Friedman and Schwartz to follow Mitchell in placing great weight on historical evidence; while their critics were looking for mathematical models and statistical tests. The critics were sure that Friedman and Schwartz had failed to understand that correlating changes in money and changes in economic activity proved nothing about causation. Money might be correlated with national income because changes in money caused changes in national income, because changes in national income caused changes in money or because money and changes in national income were produced by some third factor, say changes in fiscal policy. In short, Friedman and Schwartz had confused correlation with causation. Their critics recognized that at some points Friedman and Schwartz had noted the hazards involved in attempting to read causation from charts of economic variables, but the critics insisted that Friedman and Schwartz had nevertheless fallen into this trap.

Perhaps the best-known attack on the work of Friedman and Schwartz along these lines was James Tobin's (1970) paper, 'Money and income: post hoc ergo propter hoc?' Tobin presented an 'ultra Keynesian' model, in which money didn't matter, that fit Friedman and Schwartz's findings regarding the relationship between money and income better, according to Tobin, than did a 'Friedman model'. Tobin (p. 301) mentioned the

Monetary History as a source of evidence, but focused his firepower on the timing evidence. In his reply, Friedman (1970) stressed the important role that the historical evidence played in his conclusion that money mattered.

Peter Temin in his book *Did Monetary Forces Cause the Great Depression*? (1976) made a point similar to Tobin's. Temin's criticism has been especially influential among economic historians. Temin (p. 3) argued that chapter 7, 'The Great Contraction, 1929–33', of the *Monetary History* could be discussed independently from other chapters. After a close reading, Temin found that the chapter was merely a detailed description of how the supply of money and other variables had changed during the contraction. He then draws the following conclusion from this finding:

> Friedman and Schwartz's main conclusions are that the level of income fell as sharply as it did in the early 1930s because of a massive fall in the stock of money. This stock in turn fell because of sustained effects of multiple banking crises, that is because of a restriction in the supply of money. But an account of the supply of money cannot be taken for an account of the stock of money unless it is known that demand plays no role. The *Monetary History* appears to have been designed to show just this – but it turns out to be a narrative based on such an assumption, not an argument for it. Friedman and Schwartz referred elsewhere [in other articles and books] to The *Monetary History* to show that the stock of money was historically determined independently of income and that the correlation between money and income therefore must be interpreted to mean that movements in the stock of money determine movements of income. The *Monetary History*, however, does not provide independent evidence for this proposition. It follows that the hypothesis about the cause of the Depression must be regarded as unproven as well. (Ibid., pp. 30–31)

Temin's preferred methodology for determining causative relationships is to look for the contrasting predictions of different hypotheses. What he terms 'the money hypothesis' (the Friedman and Schwartz hypothesis), he argues, predicts a rise in short-term interest rates during 1929–33, and what he terms 'the spending hypothesis' (the Keynesian hypothesis) predicts a fall in short-term rates. Since short-term rates fell, he concludes that monetary forces did not cause the Depression. The emptiness that Temin finds in the Friedman and Schwartz narrative of 1929–33 is the result, partly, I believe, of a decision to reject the Mitchell–Friedman–Schwartz method for determining causation. Friedman and Schwartz's chapter 7 is indeed essentially a narrative constructed on the assumption that money matters. It contributes to the case for believing that money matters only to the extent that it provides another data point. For Friedman and Schwartz the conclusion that the decline in the stock of money aggravated the contraction, and that it could have been prevented by appropriate policy measures, follows from the whole body of evidence.[32]

The independence of monetary change from the cycle that Temin is looking for is clearly useful for establishing that monetary change has an effect on the economy. Natural experiments such as the increase in gold at the turn of the century are more informative than the more endogenous movements in the stock of money in the Great Contraction. However, every case adds or subtracts something from the persuasiveness of the overall generalization. The claim, to put it somewhat differently, that the patient would have perked up if given 'Buck-You-Up-O' (from P.G. Wodehouse) cannot be proven by looking at one case. This claim can only be demonstrated by looking at a 'large' number of cases.

Monetary clinicians

Both Mitchell, and Friedman and Schwartz can be likened, to push the analogy further, to medical researchers undertaking a clinical study. Case histories are written up and compared, and reasonable inferences are made. Patients who were treated with Buck-You-Up-O recovered more quickly from the influenza than patients who were not treated. A natural experiment may increase the persuasiveness of the argument. A pair of identical twins came down with the flu. The twin who was given Buck-You-Up-O recovered more rapidly than the twin who was not treated. Still, a clinical study cannot have the authority of a large-scale double-blind scientific experiment. Even twins may differ because of life experiences, because they contracted different versions of the flu or for other reasons.

Each episode that Mitchell, or Friedman and Schwartz investigate is a separate case study. The Great Contraction taken as a whole, as we noted above, is essentially a single case history.[33] By itself it proves little, as Temin and others have noted. The patient was suffering from a severe case of the flu, the doctor failed to give the patient Buck-You-Up-O, and the patient took a long time to recover. This case is consistent with the idea that Buck-You-Up-O reduces the severity of the flu, but not much evidence in itself.

The natural point at which to draw conclusions about causation from case studies is at the point when cases can be compared and contrasted. This is what Friedman and Schwartz do in their final chapter, 'A summing up', although comparisons that bear on causation are scattered throughout their narrative. In the final chapter Friedman and Schwartz compare the 1929–33 contraction with the 1907 crisis:

> Comparison of the 1907 banking panic under the earlier system [before the Federal Reserve] and the closely similar liquidity crisis which began in late 1930 offers strong evidence for this judgment [that the 1930 crisis was handled badly]. If the earlier system had been in operation, and if everything else had proceeded as it did up to December 1930, the experience of 1907 strongly suggests that there would have been a more severe initial reaction to the bank failures than there was in 1930, probably involving concerted restriction by banks of the convertibility of deposits into currency. The restriction might have had more severe initial effects toward deepening the economic contraction than the persistent pressure on the banking system that characterized late 1930 and early 1931 had. But it would have cut short the spread of the crisis, would have prevented cumulation of bank failures, and would have made possible as it did in 1908 recovery after a few months. (Friedman and Schwartz 1963a, pp. 693–4)

This, it seems to me, is a reasonable way for a clinician to proceed. The two patients, patient number 1907 and patient number 1930, appear to have been suffering from the same condition, a severe case of the flu. Patient number 1907 was given Buck-You-Up-O; patient number 1930 was not. Patient number 1907 suffered a sharp intensification of his condition, but then recovered quickly; patient number 1930 suffered a prolonged decline and slow recovery. Therefore, this comparison suggests that Buck-You-Up-O is effective. A reasonable argument, of course, is not a foolproof argument. Another clinician might conclude that patient 1907 was suffering from a less severe case of the flu. And the constitution of the two patients was not identical: patient number 1930 may have been weaker. When looking at the Great Depression we can easily create reasons why the 1930 case may have been different from the 1907 case. For one thing, the 1930 case occurred after the First World War had shaken confidence in the gold standard and other fundamental economic institutions (a point well made by Hirsch and De Marchi 1990, pp. 236–7).

The next step in a clinical study is to summarize the weight of the evidence suggested by the individual cases. It is interesting that here Friedman and Schwartz turn explicitly to a medical analogy:

> The strength of the evidence furnished by those three quasi-controlled experiments [the adoption of restrictive monetary policies in 1920, 1931, and 1936] can be made clearer by an analogy. Suppose we had the medical records of 42 married couples (to match the 42 years of Federal Reserve history from 1919 to 1942 . . .). Suppose 3 men and 4 women were found to have a specified illness; suppose 3 of the 4 women turn out to be the wives of the 3 men with the same illness. The presumption that the illness was contagious would certainly be very strong. (Friedman and Schwartz 1963a, pp. 689–90)

In fact the probability of this result by chance according to them would be 1 in 2,870.[34]

Although Friedman and Schwartz were more systematic and self-conscious than Mitchell about using historical case studies as raw materials for drawing conclusions about the effectiveness of monetary policy, their inductive methodology is clearly an extension of the practices of Mitchell and the other business-cycle researchers at the Bureau.

Explaining the continuity

The institutional origins of the *Monetary History* explain the similarities in methodology, the clinical methodology. Mitchell sketched the forces producing a typical business cycle in *Business Cycles* (1913). At the Bureau, researchers then explored in detail each area that Mitchell had subjected to a preliminary investigation. These studies followed the 'Bureau Methodology'. Long time series of monthly data (where possible) were constructed, the behavior of the time series during the Bureau-defined business cycles was computed and an explanatory narrative was constructed. Although the *Monetary History* is the best known of these studies, many became classics. Friedman and Schwartz themselves made use of Frederic Macaulay's (1938) study of interest rates, Burns's (1934) study of production, John Kendrick's (1961) study of productivity and of course, Simon Kuznets's studies of national income, such as Kuznets (1961).

The similarity in methodology between *Business Cycles* and the *Monetary History*, however, does not explain the similarity in conclusions. What, then, explains it? Could the similarity in conclusions have been the result of some sort of subtle pressure to reinforce the founder's conclusions? This seems unlikely. The atmosphere at the Bureau was one in which researchers were free to pursue their research wherever it led. Some of Friedman and Schwartz's early decisions, moreover, went against Bureau tradition. Friedman and Schwartz, as we noted, rejected Mitchell's bank-centric view of the transmission mechanism. Moreover, they emphasized the growth rate of the stock of money in some of their work, and linked changes in the growth rate of money with turns in the business cycle. Anna Schwartz (2001) recalled that this decision did not receive a warm reception from Burns, the President of the Bureau, or Geoffrey Moore, the research director. Finally, in response to an earlier draft of this chapter that had suggested a direct influence, Anna J. Schwartz wrote that any influence 'must have been subliminal. I am unaware of any discussion I had with Milton linking Mitchell's work with ours' (Personal communication with the author, email, March 2006).

Friedman and Schwartz, moreover, were familiar with many ideas besides those produced by the National Bureau. Frank Steindl (2004) has shown, based on lecture notes from a course that Friedman gave at the University of Wisconsin, that from his earliest days in academic life, Friedman was familiar with a remarkably wide range of literature on the business cycle. It seems unlikely then that a lack of the awareness of alternatives to Mitchell's vision prevented Friedman and Schwartz from moving away from his position. Indeed, as we showed above, Friedman and Schwartz rejected Mitchell's emphasis on the credit channel, and incorporated ideas drawn from the Chicago economists of the 1930s.

It was probably simply the findings uncovered in the course of their research that in the end reinforced the conclusions Mitchell had reached based on his exploration of the 1890–1911 period. The underlying stability of monetary relations, in other words, explains the continuities between *Business Cycles* and the *Monetary History*. If a small clinical study showed that taking aspirin reduced the frequency of heart attacks, and if a larger longer study of the effects of taking aspirin on the frequency of heart attacks confirmed the results of the earlier study, the explanation for the similarity in findings would simply be that taking aspirin did in fact reduce the frequency of heart attacks.

Conclusions

One of the best ways to understand what Friedman and Schwartz accomplished in the *Monetary History* is to compare it with (what I argue is) its closest predecessor in methodology and in many of its most important conclusions: Mitchell's *Business Cycles* (1913). Five propositions, I have argued, summarize the key similarities and differences:

1. Like Mitchell, Friedman and Schwartz concluded that some changes in the stock of money could occur for reasons independent of current and future changes in economic activity. The increase in the supply of money beginning in the late 1890s that resulted from the discovery of new goldfields in South Africa and other countries and new methods of extracting gold from ore was cited both by Mitchell and by Friedman and Schwartz as a clear example of an independent change in the stock of money.
2. Like Mitchell, Friedman and Schwartz found that changes in the stock of money had important effects on the economy. They agreed with Mitchell, for example, that the expansion of the stock of gold from 1897 to 1914 had raised prices.
3. Like Mitchell, Friedman and Schwartz argued that the combination of independent changes in money, which could be observed by looking closely at the historical circumstances in which changes in money occurred, and the resulting changes in the economy provided persuasive evidence that money mattered. Friedman and Schwartz, building on important work by Phillip Cagan, however, were more systematic and self-conscious about this inference.
4. Like Mitchell, Friedman and Schwartz worked on the assumption that money was merely one of many factors producing business cycles. Although Friedman and Schwartz did not attempt to provide a comprehensive discussion of the non-monetary factors that affected the business cycle, they discussed non-monetary forces when they believed them to be important. For example, they discussed the coincidence of good harvests in the United States with poor harvests in Europe

on a number of occasions in the nineteenth century, the stock market crash of 1929, wartime mobilizations and demobilizations, and the rise of labor unions in the 1930s. Most importantly, they assumed that there was an inherent tendency for the economy to recover from recessions. In many cases, however, they simply assumed the existence of a non-monetary cycle and described how it was affected by changes in monetary policy. The role of monetary policy during a recession, for example, might be described, as was the effect of the decrease in the stock of money in the 1937–38 recession, as 'a factor that significantly intensified the severity of the decline' (Friedman and Schwartz 1963a, p. 544).

5. Unlike Mitchell, Friedman and Schwartz ignored the bank-lending (credit) channel. Mitchell thought that changes in bank-lending policies were the most important part of the transmission mechanism linking changes in money with changes in economic activity. An unexpected increase in bank reserves would produce an increase in bank lending, a fall in interest rates and an increase in investment that would generate increased economic activity. Friedman and Schwartz, on the other hand, stressed a direct channel from increased money to increased economic activity and downplayed the bank-lending channel. It is interesting to note that one of the major developments in monetary economics in the decades after Friedman and Schwartz wrote was a partial return to the bank-centric view of the role of money.

Both Mitchell in 1913 and Friedman and Schwartz in 1963, to sum up, can be described as monetary clinicians. They summarized cases in which the economic patient was given more or less money, and described the reasons for the change in the dosage and the consequences. They understood that one case study taken separately – the increase in the gold supply after 1896, the panic of 1907, or even the Great Contraction from 1929 to 1932 – could prove little by itself. They argued, however, that taken together the case studies suggested persuasive generalizations about the role of money in the business cycle.

The *Monetary History*, of course, was not simply an extension of *Business Cycles*. Friedman and Schwartz employed their own ideas, and those of other economists including major figures at Chicago in the 1930s – Henry Schultz, Jacob Viner, Lloyd Mints and Henry Simons – to sharpen the analysis. The influence of Schultz can be seen mainly in the statistical analysis that was not reported in the *Monetary History*, but rather in other places, such as *Monetary Statistics* (1970) and *Monetary Trends* (1982). However, the other Chicago economists left an imprint on the *Monetary History* itself. From Viner and Mints came, among other things, the sharp criticism of the Federal Reserve for failing to stop the contraction of the stock of money in the early 1930s – monetary policy had failed not because it was not effective, but because it was not tried. From Simons came the important distinction between 'rules versus authorities' in the conduct of the monetary policy. Friedman and Schwartz did not follow Simons in opting for a price stability rule over a money supply rule. However, they addressed his concerns when they considered alternative policies in the Depression. 'How different the history of that fateful dozen years might have been if the money stock had grown steadily at its average rate of 2½ per cent per year, let alone at the higher long-term historical rate, instead of first falling by one-third from 1929 to 1933 and then doubling from 1933 to 1941' (Friedman and Schwartz 1963a, p. 545).

Although the ideas came from many sources, the methodology of the *Monetary History*, to reiterate, came from Mitchell and the NBER. As Bordo and Schwartz (2004) show, Friedman usually summed up the methodological differences between himself and his many critics by explaining that he was a Marshallian while his critics were Walrasians. He, like Marshall, preferred using simple abstract theories to explain facts, rather than complex general equilibrium models. The term 'Marshallian' is undoubtedly the best simple description of the methodology underlying his work as a whole. When it comes to characterizing the methodology of the *Monetary History* taken separately, however, the best one-word term may be 'Mitchellian'.

Notes

* The ideas developed here were first broached in Rockoff (2000). I am grateful to Michael Bordo, Ross Emmett, Daniel Hammond, David Laidler, Malcolm Rutherford, Anna J. Schwartz and the participants in a seminar at Rutgers University in October 2006 for detailed comments on previous drafts. I am also grateful to Claudia Goldin for making available tapes of interviews that she conducted with Anna J. Schwartz and that she and Larry Katz conducted with Milton Friedman for the NBER, and to Daniel Hammond for alerting me to and making available documents from the Milton Friedman papers. I am responsible for any of the errors and mistaken judgments that remain.

1. A JSTOR search over all journals and years for the combination of Friedman and 'Monetary History' produced 718 hits, while Keynes and 'General Theory' produced 3,380. Since 1990 the figures are 255 and 615 (all counts in August 2007). A search of the Social Science Citation Index for the period from 1997 to 2005 revealed 349 citations to the *Monetary History* and 960 to the *General Theory*.
2. Robert E. Lucas (1994), Jeffrey Miron (1994) and Anna J. Schwartz (2004) discuss the continuing influence of the *Monetary History* on monetary economics.
3. Although Friedman and Schwartz modestly styled their work 'A monetary history', most commentators, friend and foe alike, refer to *the Monetary History*, a usage I shall follow.
4. Reviews by C.A.E. Goodhart (1964) and Harold T. Shapiro (1965) struck similar notes.
5. Burns had been an influential teacher of Friedman at Rutgers University where Friedman had done his undergraduate work. It was Burns who initially brought Friedman into the Bureau (Friedman 2002).
6. Stewart, an influential economist at the Federal Reserve Board and a director of the National Bureau, had many connections to Mitchell. Before the First World War he had taught a course at Amherst on business cycles based on Mitchell's work, shortly afterwards he had worked with Mitchell on a project on wartime prices, and in 1922 he became Director of the Division of Research and Statistics at the Federal Reserve Board on Mitchell's recommendation (Rutherford 2003).
7. My summary of Mitchell's career is based on Burns (1949).
8. Friedman developed this idea further in his 'plucking' model – the economy was like a string on a musical instrument that could be plucked but would return to its normal shape (Friedman 1993, 1964 [1969]).
9. Friedman took Mitchell's course on business cycles at Columbia but remembered it as dull (Friedman 2002).
10. Daniel Hammond located this important letter and shared it with me. It is suggestive that the term 'analytical description' that Friedman used here to describe Mitchell's work is similar to the term 'analytical narrative' that Friedman and Schwartz used to describe the suggestion made by Walter Stewart that led to the *Monetary History*.
11. Friedman and Schwartz reserved the term 'money supply' for the change in the stock of money.
12. Here Mitchell was reaching a conclusion his advisor at Chicago, Laughlin, who was a critic of the quantity theory, had firmly rejected – the notion that the increase in the stock of gold had produced the increase in prices (Laughlin 1911). Laughlin preferred to attribute the increase in prices to increases in costs and increases in monopoly.
13. A recent estimate of GDP preserves the contrast. Real GDP rose 3.6 percent per year from 1882 to 1892, but only 2.6 percent per year from 1903 to 1913. The GDP deflator fell 0.8 percent per year from 1882 to 1892, but rose 1.7 percent per year from 1903 to 1913 (Johnson and Williamson 2006).
14. In Mitchell's view, the crisis in Britain never degenerated into a panic.
15. Mitchell's claim that the Bank of England carried reserves far in excess of its immediate requirements was an exaggeration. In some cases, such as the Barings Crisis (1890), the Bank had to rely on the cooperation of private British banks or foreign central banks to make adequate reserves available.
16. In *Monetary Trends*, Friedman and Schwartz (1982) compared American and British experiences, although in that volume the emphasis was more on statistical than historical analysis. In the *Monetary*

History, Friedman and Schwartz did not systematically examine events in other countries although they did, occasionally, refer to experiences in other countries. For example, they (1963a, p. 352) used a comparison of the US and Canada in the Great Contraction to analyze the effects of bank failures. (There were many in the US and none in Canada.)

17. The conclusions in this case are somewhat different. Comparing the mildness of 1907–08 in England, which had a central bank, with the severity of 1907–08 in the United States, which lacked a central bank, supports the case for central banking. Comparing 1907–08 in the United States with 1929–33 in the United States raises doubts about central banking.
18. One is tempted to write 'real and monetary forces' and to describe a 'real cycle' that would exist even in the presence of an optimal monetary policy. The term 'real business cycle', however, has come to identify a line of thinking that would exclude some of the mechanisms that Mitchell included in his list of non-monetary forces.
19. Mitchell (1913 [1959], p. 115) also thought that a large harvest sold at high prices had mitigated the effects of the 1907 crisis in England.
20. Two qualifications: (a) although the combination may have been fortuitous from the point of view of the American economy, there may be, of course, an underlying meteorological explanation; and (b) Friedman and Schwartz were looking at the balance of payments, so the effect on the economy they had in mind may have run from exports to the balance of payments to the supply of gold to economic activity; in other words, through a monetary channel.
21. Sherman (2001) discusses many of the non-monetary components of Mitchell's analysis of the business cycle.
22. Students from my generation at Chicago – I started in 1967 – may remember Professor Friedman asking his graduate class in monetary economics, where the *Optimum Quantity* was a basic text, why people who collected the cash dropped from the helicopter would immediately spend it rather than hoard it. The answer that I was contemplating: 'that's what I would do', although not completely irrelevant, was not the correct answer. The correct answer was that since by assumption the economy had already reached its long-run equilibrium, each person separately had already achieved their desired ratio of money to income and therefore would choose to restore that equilibrium by gradually reducing their excess cash balances.
23. There was a run-up in the fall of 1892, with the monthly rate peaking at 10 percent in December. The rate is the end-of-month 3-year commercial paper rate, available at http://www.globalfinancialdata.com.
24. In the post-war era there were changes in the banking system – the introduction of deposit insurance and the heavy investment by commercial banks in government bonds during the war – that moved the system in the direction that Simons thought was necessary to make a money rule workable.
25. In my time at Chicago, as I remember, the doctrine was always referred to as the 'Fallacious Real Bills Doctrine'.
26. While working with Schultz, Friedman evidently read widely in the literature on the measurement of demand curves. It was this literature, I believe, that is brought to bear in the 1956 paper. I am grateful to Dan Hammond for making the need to be careful at this point clear to me.
27. Alternatively, one could regress price on quantity. Schultz paid close attention to measurement error and how measurement error would affect the elasticity estimates derived from regressions of quantity on price compared with regressions of price on quantity. Friedman and Schwartz also paid close attention to this distinction in their subsequent empirical research.
28. Five of the eleven equations in Friedman's model concern the monetary sector.
29. By definition $M = Cp + D$ and $H = S + R$. Dividing M by H, rearranging terms and substituting b for D/R and p for D/Cp yields equation (7.6).
30. Most of the bonds carrying the circulation privilege were held by banks.
31. Normally b will exceed 1 because normally banks lend out part of their deposits and hold only fractional reserves.
32. Friedman and Schwartz, as David Laidler pointed out to me, may have encouraged the idea that their discussion was intended as proof by itself that monetary forces had caused the Great Depression by publishing chapter 7 as a separate book, *The Great Contraction, 1929–1933* (Friedman and Schwartz 1965).
33. In monetary history one can have cases within cases. In 1932 there was a brief time in which the Federal Reserve deliberately switched to an expansionary policy of open market purchases of bonds. Friedman and Schwartz drew attention to this case as a natural experiment on the effectiveness of an expansionary policy within the confines of the Great Contraction.
34. The probability of the first sick husband being paired with a sick wife if the pairing is random is 4/42. The probability of the second sick husband being paired with a sick wife if the pairing is random and if the first sick husband was paired with a sick wife is 3/41. The probability for the third sick husband being paired is 2/40. The probability of all three sick husbands being paired with sick wives is therefore $(4/42)*(3/41)*(2/40) = 1/2870$.

References

Milton Friedman Papers, Hoover Institution Archives, Stanford University, CA.

Bernanke, B.S. (1983), 'Nonmonetary effects of the financial crisis in propagation of the Great Depression', *American Economic Review*, **73** (3), 257–76.

Bordo, M.D. and A.J. Schwartz (2004), 'IS–LM and monetarism', in *The IS–LM Model: Its Rise, Fall, and Strange Persistence*, De Vroedy, M. and K.D. Hoover (eds), Durham, NC: Duke University Press, pp. 217–39.

Brunner, K. and A.H. Meltzer (1988), 'Money and credit in the monetary transmission process', *American Economic Review*, **78** (2), 446–51.

Burns, A.F. (1934), *Production Trends in the United States since 1870*, New York: National Bureau of Economic Research.

Burns, A.F. (1949), 'Wesley Mitchell and the National Bureau', in *The Twenty-ninth Annual Report, National Bureau of Economic Research*, New York: National Bureau of Economic Research, pp. 3–55.

Burns, A.F. and W.C. Mitchell (1946), *Measuring Business Cycles*, New York: National Bureau of Economic Research.

Cagan, P. (1958), 'The demand for currency relative to the total money supply', *Journal of Political Economy*, **66** (4), 303–28.

Cagan, P. (1965), *Determinants and Effects of Changes in the Stock of Money, 1875–1960*, New York: Columbia University Press.

Friedman, M. (1943), 'The spending tax as a wartime fiscal measure', *American Economic Review*, **33** (1, part 1), 50–62.

Friedman, M. (1950), 'Wesley C. Mitchell as an economic theorist', *Journal of Political Economy*, **58** (6), 465–93.

Friedman, M. (1956a), 'The quantity theory of money – a restatement', in *Studies in the Quantity Theory of Money*, Friedman, M. (ed.), Chicago, IL: University of Chicago Press, pp. 3–21.

Friedman, M. (ed.) (1956b), *Studies in the Quantity Theory of Money*, Chicago, IL: University of Chicago Press.

Friedman, M. (1959), *A Program for Monetary Stability*, New York: Fordham University Press.

Friedman, M. (1964 [1969]), 'Monetary studies of the National Bureau', in *The Optimum Quantity of Money, and Other Essays*, Chicago, IL: Aldine, pp. 261–84.

Friedman, M. (1965), 'Foreword', *Determinants and Effects of Changes in the Stock of Money, 1875–1960*, Cagan, P. (ed.), National Bureau of Economic Research, Studies in Business Cycles, no. 13. New York: Columbia University Press, pp. xxiii–xxviii.

Friedman, M. (1969), 'The optimum quantity of money', in *The Optimum Quantity of Money, and Other Essays*, Chicago, IL: Aldine, pp. 1–50.

Friedman, M. (1970), 'Comment on Tobin', *Quarterly Journal of Economics*, **84** (2), 318–27.

Friedman, M. (1972), 'Comments on the critics', *Journal of Political Economy*, **80** (5), 906–50.

Friedman, M. (1993), 'The "plucking model" of business fluctuations revisited', *Economic Inquiry*, **31** (2), 171–7.

Friedman, M. (2002), Interview with Claudia Goldin and Larry Katz, National Bureau of Economic Research, August 16.

Friedman, M. and A.J. Schwartz (1963a), *A Monetary History of the United States, 1867–1960*, Princeton, NJ: Princeton University Press.

Friedman, M. and A.J. Schwartz (1963b), 'Money and business cycles', *Review of Economics and Statistics*, **45** (1, part 2, supplement), 32–64.

Friedman, M. and A.J. Schwartz (1965), *The Great Contraction, 1929–1933*, National Bureau of Economic Research, Princeton, NJ: Princeton University Press.

Friedman, M. and A.J. Schwartz (1970), *Monetary Statistics of the United States: Estimates, Sources, Methods*, New York: National Bureau of Economic Research.

Friedman, M. and A.J. Schwartz (1982), *Monetary Trends in the United States and the United Kingdom, Their Relation to Income, Prices, and Interest Rates, 1867–1975*, National Bureau of Economic Research, Chicago, IL: University of Chicago Press.

Goodhart, C.A.E. (1964), 'Review of *A Monetary History of the United States, 1867–1960*', *Economica*, n.s. **31** (123), 314–18.

Hammond, J.D. (1996), *Theory and Measurement: Causality Issues in Milton Friedman's Monetary Economics*, Cambridge: Cambridge University Press.

Hirsch, A. and N. De Marchi (1990), *Milton Friedman: Economics in Theory and Practice*, Ann Arbor, MI: University of Michigan Press.

Johnson, H.G. (1965), 'A quantity theorist's monetary history of the United States', *Economic Journal*, **75** (298), 288–96.

Johnson, H.G. (1971), 'The Keynesian revolution and the monetarist counter-revolution', *American Economic Review*, **61** (2), 1–14.
Johnson, L.D. and S.H. Williamson, (2006) *The Annual Real and Nominal GDP for the United States, 1790–present*, Economic History Services, available at: http://www.eh.net/hmit/gdp (accessed July 12, 2007).
Kendrick, J.W. (1961), *Productivity Trends in the United States*, New York: National Bureau of Economic Research.
Keynes, J.M. (1936), *The General Theory of Employment, Interest and Money*, New York: Harcourt, Brace.
Koopmans, T.C. (1947), 'Measurement without theory', *Review of Economics and Statistics*, **29** (3), 161–72.
Kuznets, S. (1961), *Capital in the American Economy: Its Formation and Financing*, National Bureau of Economic Research, Princeton, NJ: Princeton University Press.
Laidler, D.E.W. (1991), 'Karl Brunner's monetary economics – an appreciation', *Journal of Money, Credit and Banking*, **23** (4), 633–58.
Laidler, D.E.W. (1993), 'Hawtrey, Harvard, and the origins of the Chicago tradition', *Journal of Political Economy*, **101** (6), 1068–103.
Laidler, D.E.W. (1999 [2004]), 'Variations on a two-interest-rate theme', in *Macroeconomics in Retrospect: The Selected Essays of David Laidler*, Cheltenham, UK and Northampton, MA, USA: Edward Elgar, pp. 161–79.
Laughlin, J.L. (1911), 'Causes of the changes in prices since 1896', *American Economic Review*, **1** (2), 26–36.
Lucas, R.E., Jr. (1994), 'Review of *A Monetary History of the United States, 1867–1960*', *Journal of Monetary Economics*, **34** (1), 5–16.
Macaulay, F.R. (1938), *Some Theoretical Problems Suggested by the Movements of Interest Rates, Bond Yields and Stock Prices in the United States*, New York: National Bureau of Economic Research.
Meltzer, A.H. (2003), *A History of the Federal Reserve*, vol. 1, 1913–1951, Chicago, IL: University of Chicago Press.
Mints, L.W. (1945), *A History of Banking Theory in Great Britain and the United States*, Chicago, IL: University of Chicago Press.
Mints, L.W. (1950), *Monetary Policy for a Competitive Society*, New York: McGraw-Hill.
Mints, L.W., A.H. Hansen, H.S. Ellis, A.P. Lerner and M. Kalecki (1946), 'A symposium on fiscal and monetary policy', *Review of Economics and Statistics*, **28** (2), 60–69.
Miron, J.A. (1994), 'Empirical methodology in macroeconomics: explaining the success of Friedman and Schwartz's *A Monetary History of the United States, 1867–1960*', *Journal of Monetary Economics*, **34** (1), 17–25.
Mitchell, W.C. (1899), 'A history of the United States notes', dissertation, Economics, University of Chicago, Chicago.
Mitchell, W.C. (1903), *A History of the Greenbacks, with Special Reference to the Economic Consequences of Their Issue: 1862–65*, Chicago, IL: University of Chicago Press.
Mitchell, W.C. (1908), *Gold, Prices, and Wages under the Greenback Standard*, Berkeley, CA: University of California Press.
Mitchell, W.C. (1913), *Business Cycles*, Berkeley, CA: University of California Press.
Mitchell, W.C. (1913 [1959]), *Business Cycles and Their Causes*, Berkeley, CA: University of California Press.
Mitchell, W.C. (1927), *Business Cycles: The Problem and Its Setting*, New York: National Bureau of Economic Research.
Mitchell, W.C. (1951), *What Happens During Business Cycles: A Progress Report*, New York: National Bureau of Economic Research.
Patinkin, D. (1969), 'The Chicago tradition, the quantity theory, and Friedman', *Journal of Money, Credit and Banking*, **1** (1), 46–70.
Patinkin, D. (1972), 'Friedman on the quantity theory and Keynesian economics', *Journal of Political Economy*, **80** (5), 883–905.
Patinkin, D. (1979), 'Keynes and Chicago', *Journal of Law & Economics*, **22** (2), 213–32.
Rockoff, H. (2000), 'Review of *A Monetary History of the United States, 1867–1960*', EH.Net Economic History Services, available from: http://eh.net/bookreviews/library/rockoff (accessed August, 2007).
Rutherford, M. (2003), 'On the economic frontier: Walton Hamilton, institutional economics, and education', *History of Political Economy*, **35** (4), 611–53.
Schultz, H. (1938), *The Theory and Measurement of Demand*, Chicago, IL: University of Chicago Press.
Schwartz, A.J. (1981), 'Understanding 1929–1933', in *The Great Depression Revisited*, Brunner, K. (ed.), Boston, MA: Martinus Nijhoff, pp. 5–48.
Schwartz, A.J., (2001), Interview with Claudia Goldin, National Bureau of Economic Research, November 19.
Schwartz, A.J. (2004), 'Why *A Monetary History* has had a long life', *Cato Journal*, **23** (3), 353–5.
Shapiro, H.T. (1965), 'Review of *A Monetary History of the United States, 1867–1960*', *Canadian Journal of Economics and Political Science*, **31** (4), 606–08.

Sherman, H. (2001), 'The business cycle theory of Wesley Mitchell', *Journal of Economic Issues*, **35** (1), 85–97.
Shoup, C., M. Friedman and R.P. Mack (1943), *Taxing to Prevent Inflation: Techniques for Estimating Revenue Requirements*, New York: Columbia University Press.
Simons, H.C. (1935), 'Review of *The Supply and Control of Money in the United States*', *Journal of Political Economy*, **43** (4), 555–8.
Simons, H.C. (1936), 'Rules versus authorities in monetary policy', *Journal of Political Economy*, **44** (1), 1–30.
Steindl, F.G. (1990), 'The "oral tradition" at Chicago in the 1930s', *Journal of Political Economy*, **98** (2), 430–32.
Steindl, F.G. (1995), *Monetary Interpretations of the Great Depression*, Ann Arbor, MI: University of Michigan Press.
Steindl, F.G. (2004), 'Friedman and money in the 1930s', *History of Political Economy*, **36** (3), 521–31.
Stigler, S.M. (1994), 'Some correspondence on methodology between Milton Friedman and Edwin B. Wilson; November–December 1946', *Journal of Economic Literature*, **32** (3), 1197–203.
Tavlas, G. (1998), 'Was the monetarist tradition invented?', *Journal of Economic Perspectives*, **12** (4), 211–22.
Temin, P. (1976), *Did Monetary Forces Cause the Great Depression?*, New York: Norton.
Tobin, J. (1970), 'Money and income: post hoc ergo propter hoc?', *Quarterly Journal of Economics*, **84** (2), 301–17.

8 Chicago and economic history

*David Mitch**

Introduction

On first consideration, economic history would seem at best peripheral to standard depictions of the Chicago School of Economics. The Chicago School can be seen as emphasizing the universality of *homo economicus*: responding to incentives, the presence of scarcity, and the influence of market forces. This would seem to accord little scope for historical perspective or specificity. Yet the University of Chicago Economics Department (which should be distinguished from a 'Chicago School of Economics') has had a long tradition of economic history in its curricula and economic historians on its faculty from its founding in the 1890s. During what some would identify as the zenith of the Chicago School (for example, Stigler 1988), from the late 1940s to the 1970s under the aegis of Milton Friedman, George Stigler, and Gary Becker, Chicago hired some particularly prominent economic historians. The first was Earl Hamilton in 1947, followed by Robert Fogel and Donald McCloskey during the 1960s and then David Galenson in the 1970s. Fogel and McCloskey were at the vanguard of the cliometric movement in economic history in the 1960s. And Fogel's contributions were recognized with his receipt of the Nobel Prize in Economics in 1993. How did the Chicago department come to acquire such prominent researchers in the field during a period in which one might think that the rise of a coherent Chicago School would lower the priority accorded to economic history? Throughout, this chapter is informed by two central questions. First, what conception of the relationship between economic history and economics more generally has prevailed at Chicago at various times? Second what has been distinctive about how Chicago economic historians, especially during the cliometric era of the 1960s and 1970s, have pursued economic history?

Courses in economic and business history were offered from the very founding of the Economics Department at the University of Chicago in 1892. Thus Chicago like other American departments avoided the *methodenstreit* between historical and theoretical economics that characterized the English, German, and Austrian academic traditions in economics, finding a common home for economic history and economic theory in the same departments (de Rouvray 2004, pp. 226–7). One can attribute this both to a native American institutionalism which featured historical perspective and to German academic influences, including interest in the German Historical School.

The first identifiable specialist economic historian in the Chicago department is Chester Whitney Wright who joined the department in 1907 and taught there until 1944. Wright received all his degrees including his PhD from Harvard, completing his thesis *Wool-growing and the Tariff* under the supervision of Frank Taussig (Wright 1910). For many years, Wright offered a course on the economic history of the United States; lecture material from this course was eventually published in his comprehensive textbook (Wright 1941). Wright took up the study of economic history because of the light it could shed on general issues in economics. Wright labels his approach as 'the functional approach to economic history' – that is, the use of economic history to address a significant issue in economics (ibid., p. ix). However, a contrasting thread is Wright's emphasis on the diversity and complexity of forces at work in long-run economic trends which in turn seems to imply for Wright the importance of taking a historical approach rather than a theoretical one (Wright 1938 [1965]). Wright also emphasized the importance of non-economic factors in influencing economic trends.

In 1929, John Ulrich Nef, Jr. was appointed to the Economics Department at Chicago.[1] Nef's father was a prominent chemist, who had founded the Chemistry Department at Chicago. Nef's doctoral thesis, subsequently published as a major two-volume study, was on the economic causes and consequences of the rise of the British coal industry (Nef 1932). This study and Nef's (1941, 1952) subsequent work on mining and metallurgy in Central Europe suggested that industrialization had origins in the sixteenth and seventeenth centuries rather than the more orthodox view locating its origins in the eighteenth and nineteenth centuries.

Nef continued to publish on the causes and consequences of industrialization in early modern France and England (Nef 1940 [1957]). However, his attention was increasingly drawn to the interrelations between economic affairs and other dimensions of human life (see Nef 1973). By the 1940s, he shifted his attention increasingly away from economic history and departmental affairs to pursue the development of his pet project, the Committee on Social Thought.

It is doubtful whether Frank Knight should be classified as an economic historian. However, Knight had translated Max Weber's lectures, *General Economic History* (1927 [1981]), just before arriving at Chicago and taught, at least once, a seminar on Weber and the German Historical School. He was also listed to teach a course on European Economic History as well as a course on 'Economic Institutions and their History'.[2] The differences between Nef and Knight regarding the nature and contribution of economic history became evident in the 1940s when the issue arose of finding a replacement for the retiring Chester Wright. Exchanges between Nef and Knight centered around the issue of whether economic history should be broadly integrative, which was Nef's vision, or should be fundamentally grounded in economic analysis, which was Knight's preferred approach.

Nef's preferred candidate to replace Wright was Harold Innis. Offers were made to Innis both in 1944 and in 1947. In contrast, Knight favored hiring an economic historian who grounded his work in perspectives from economic theory and who would pursue the subject in a more narrowly defined, traditional way. Knight's view prevailed with the recruitment of Earl Hamilton to the department in 1947 to fill the position vacated by Wright.

Hamilton studied with Edwin Gay at Harvard and began his teaching career at Duke in the mid-1920s, moving to Northwestern in 1947 (for biographical details, see Emmett 1999). Hamilton wrote three major books based on extended periods of archival research in Spain involving the collection of large amounts of price and wage data covering periods of a few centuries (Hamilton 1934, 1936a, 1947). Hamilton can be seen as part of a broader movement in the 1930s and 1940s towards a more quantitatively and empirically based economic history and economics (de Rouvray 2004). His work was also distinctive for its efforts to go beyond simply the accumulation of data to consider issues of general 'cause and consequence' (Cole and Crandall 1964, p. 383). In particular, his

Spanish project led him inductively to quantity theories of the money supply to price-level relationship and also suggested implications for the distributional consequences of inflation. Hamilton had clearly established himself as one of the world's leading economic historians by the time that he was recruited to Chicago in 1947. He had an impact on the Chicago department in a number of ways. He served as editor of the *Journal of Political Economy* between 1948 and 1954,[3] and a number of his students went on to prominent careers in their own right, including Rondo Cameron and Richard Timberlake.

But in a number of respects Hamilton's years at Chicago were not fruitful ones. While at Chicago, he did not develop his research on monetary history much beyond his earlier work on the Spanish price revolution. Much of his scholarly efforts during his Chicago years were spent researching the career and economic system of John Law, which produced the accumulation of a considerable body of primary source material, but no major study of Law's system was ever completed (partial efforts include Hamilton 1936b, 1969).

In addition to monetary issues, there was growing interest in the department during the 1950s in economic development, and this appears to have spurred an associated interest in economic history. T.W. Schultz as department chair was active in cultivating the department's workshop system during the 1950s. There are some indications that Schultz was trying during this period to stimulate activity in economic history in Chicago workshops and in student training more generally. In the late 1950s and early 1960s, the university's *Announcements* listed Hamilton as running a 'Research Group in the History of Growth and Development' for which he submitted a proposal which appears to have been funded by the Ford Foundation (1956, p. 146). Hamilton did not run an actual seminar with periodic speakers or presenters; instead, his research group was primarily a way of providing funding for graduate students.

Arcadius Kahan came to Chicago in 1955 to work on Soviet agriculture with D. Gale Johnson. By the early 1960s, much of his research focused on Russian economic history and he was an active participant in the Workshop in Economic History, founded by Robert Fogel in 1964. He continued to teach in the Economics Department until his death in 1982.

Kahan's presence in the department during the 1960s and 1970s is of interest because his approach to economic history was primary source based at the same time as cliometricians were employing tools from economic theory, econometrics and statistics. Nevertheless, much of Kahan's work was based on developing quantitative series for key aspects of the Russian economy. His landmark and posthumously prepared work *The Plow, the Hammer, and the Knout* (1985) suggested a buoyant performance of the Russian economy in the eighteenth century including that of the agricultural sector in contrast with a tradition emphasizing its backwardness. His work on both the eighteenth- and-nineteenth-century Russian economies emphasized the value of market forces in shaping progress, in contrast with the view of Alexander Gerschenkron and others that emphasized the importance of government policy in bringing about change (Weiss 1989, pp. x–xi).

Schultz's tenure as chair of the Economics Department between 1947 and 1960 was thus one in which substantial attention was given to economic history. Earl Hamilton was recruited as a high-profile senior replacement for Chester Wright. Schultz assisted with efforts to fund a research group in economic history. And Bert Hoselitz and

Arcadius Kahan, scholars with serious interests in economic history, were also teaching on the faculty.

Robert Fogel and the new economic history at Chicago

Recruitment and early career

The department continued to give priority to economic history in the 1960s. However, by the early 1960s, Hamilton was no longer active in the intellectual life of the department. A number of prominent members of the department shared the view that economic history was a legitimate field within economics and sought to recruit someone who would provide it with an active presence. Milton Friedman, for example, said

> I believe some knowledge of economic history is indispensable for a student of economics. It is only from a knowledge of the past that we can make judgements about the future. Only by studying economic history can we know what economic problems have arisen in the past, what kind of measures have been taken to deal with them and how these measures have worked out. (Personal communication with author, email, July 21, 2005)

Thus, Chicago began looking for an economic historian to replace Hamilton. Robert Fogel was invited to visit Chicago as Ford Foundation Visiting Research Professor for the 1963–64 academic year and in the Fall of 1963 he was offered a tenured appointment. Fogel began graduate study in economic history in the late 1950s after a stint as a communist party organizer and exposure to accompanying Marxist intellectual influences. After completing his master's thesis at Columbia on the Union Pacific Railroad under the supervision of Carter Goodrich, he moved to Johns Hopkins to work with Simon Kuznets on his doctoral dissertation on railroads and economic growth (Fogel 1960).

The new economic history

Robert Fogel is commonly regarded as one of the pioneers of 'cliometrics', alternatively labeled the 'new economic history' (also sometimes labeled 'econometric history' and, as will be noted further below, 'historical economics'). One general definition of cliometrics is the study of history using quantitative methods and social science perspectives. In the late 1950s and early 1960s, the use of quantitative methods and social science models was becoming more widespread not only in economic history and but also in other fields of history.

Fogel conceived of the application of quantitative methods to history as entailing not only statistical analysis of empirical data but also the use of formal mathematics. In considering what is distinctive about the use of quantification and perspectives from economic theory in the cliometric approach, Fogel emphasized the interrelationship between theory and measurement. Theory, he argued, was an aid to more effective measurement (Fogel 1966).

One tool of the cliometric approach that has been distinctively associated with Fogel is the employment of counterfactual analysis (see Fogel 1970, including the discussion). The basic principle of counterfactual analysis is that in order to determine the impact of some factor, one must consider what would have occurred in the absence of that factor. Applying this principle to historical economic development, Fogel states:

> one cannot determine the economic effects – negative or positive – of the tariff, slavery, the corporation, railroads, the Bessemer converter, the reaper, the telegraph, the Homestead Act, or interregional trade without considering how the economy would have developed in the absence of such institutions, processes, and artifacts. (Fogel 1967, p. 285)

Fogel did not originate the application of counterfactual analysis to economic history. This was proposed in Conrad and Meyer's methodological essay (1957 [1964], pp. 23–4). And Fogel was also influenced by Fritz Machlup's (1952, pp. 448–54) discussion of counterfactual reasoning. The employment of counterfactual analysis by Fogel in his study of the impact of the railroad on American economic growth provoked accusations by the traditional economic historian, Fritz Redlich, that Fogel's work was 'fictitious' and 'quasi history' (Redlich 1965, p. 486). While Redlich acknowledged the value of counterfactual analysis, he thought that it should be classified as social science research rather than historical analysis.

Part of the reason why Fogel's use of counterfactual analysis in his work on the impact of the railroads was singled out for attention and criticism was not just his explicit methodological employment of counterfactuals – other economic historians frequently employed them – but the degree to which he pursued it. Albert Fishlow's (1965) counterfactual analysis of transport in the absence of railways was based on the existing canal system in 1859. Fogel argued in his analysis of the 1890 situation that in the absence of the railroad there would have been a considerable expansion of the nation's canal system. He then proceeded to propose a hypothetical canal system that might have been constructed by 1890 in the absence of the railway, finding that such an extended canal system substantially lowered his estimate of the social saving attributable to the railway. In reply to his critics, Fogel (1979, pp. 6–7) argued that Fishlow's employment of the existing canal system for his counterfactual analysis was also hypothetical. But it is likely that developing such an elaborate counterfactual canal system earned Fogel's work the title of 'figments' from Redlich (1965, 1970).

Fogel's subsequent work displayed his indefatigable efforts at data collection and measurement. His Nobel citation described him as an 'empiricist, who never leaves any sources unexplored' (Royal Swedish Academy of Sciences 1993). In this regard, Fogel shares much in common with his immediate predecessor at Chicago, Earl Hamilton.[4] Indeed, Fogel emphasized the continuity between the old and new economic history in his reply to Kuznets's concern that cliometrics showed insufficient respect for the work of traditional economic historians:

> I do not view the increasing emphasis being put on the more rigorous use of theory and statistics by younger economic historians as a break with the past; I consider it a further development of a long existing trend in the discipline. At the same time I do not want to weaken my criticism of what I believe has been a serious underestimation of the opportunity that exists for extending quantitative methods worked out in other fields of economics to the domain of history. (Robert W. Fogel Papers, Box 157, Folder: Simon Kuznets)

Economic history as the study of economic growth

Although the economic history workshop at Chicago was broadly conceived, Fogel's own research agenda in the mid-1960s placed the primary focus of research in economic history on the determinants of economic growth. Fogel's work on the economic impact of the railroads had been motivated by an interest in the contribution of a generally perceived key innovation to economic growth.

In the early 1960s, the study of economic growth was a common focus of cliometric activity (Drukker 2006). Fogel had begun graduate work in economic history with an interest in the determinants of economic growth.[5] Kuznets had been working for some time on comparative studies of economic growth at the national level. Fogel saw his own work on the railroads and US economic growth as following in the footsteps of Kuznets, but at the industry level rather than at the aggregate national level (Fogel 2005).

While in the midst of work on his dissertation on the railroads in the early 1960s, Fogel had projected both a textbook on American economic history 'within the framework of growth economics' and a research monograph entitled *Strategic Factors in American Economic Growth*. Fogel appears to have had a definite conception behind the phrase 'strategic factors' and for many years subsequently he offered courses alternatively entitled 'Strategic Factors in American Economic Development' and 'Strategic Factors in American Economic Growth'. In a memo to Lionel McKenzie, then chair of the Economics Department at the University of Rochester, Fogel distinguished between 'major factors' and 'strategic factors' in economic growth. In Fogel's view, major 'connotes only an ordering of importance. A major event need not be one which is capable of altering the design of a given pattern; it can have limited consequences'. In contrast, a strategic factor in Fogel's view is one 'whose absence would have fundamentally altered the record of development'. He cites the development of cheap inland water transportation as an example of a strategic factor while the decision not to renew the charter of the Second Bank of the United States he regards as a major event but without strategic consequences (Robert Fogel to Lionel McKenzie, February 1, 1961, Robert W. Fogel Papers, Box 159, Folder: Lionel McKenzie).

While Fogel emphasized the value of using cliometric tools, he thought that their fruitfulness should ultimately be evaluated on whether they led to and supported new interpretations to traditional questions (Fogel 1966). In other words, he did not think that the cliometric revolution had reformulated the questions that economic history should address. And, he argued that the traditional questions of economic history had focused on the determinants of economic growth (Fogel 1965, p. 92). Fogel (ibid., p. 94) explicitly conflates economic change with economic growth, a view that he again affirmed recently (Fogel 2005).

However, Fogel's teacher at Columbia, Carter Goodrich (1960, p. 536) noted that 'there remain certain points to be considered before economic historians can agree to abdicate in favor of the new discipline of Economic Growth'. He argued that 'economic historians cannot accept its limitations as to time or to subject matter'. He goes on to state that economic life in primitive societies and 'issues involving human values and other effects of economic changes' have also been 'central themes for economic historians in the past'.[6] In a later evaluation of quantitative economic history, Fogel acknowledges that the new economic history had emphasized issues of growth and development at the expense of distributional and welfare issues (Fishlow and Fogel 1971).

The economic history of slavery

A prominent application of cliometric methods by Fogel in which the original aim had been to understand issues related to economic growth was the study of the economics of antebellum slavery. As his research on this topic progressed, it went well beyond consideration of the determinants of economic growth to a wide array of other issues. Fogel (1975a, p. 667) suggests that, having been struck by the anomalous result that preliminary calculations showed slave agriculture was more efficient than free agriculture, he and Engerman made the decision in 1968 'to throw our full energies into the study of slavery'. Their research effort can be situated in both a longstanding historiography on slavery as such and a longstanding historiography on the determinants of economic growth in the US South concerning the extent to which slavery contributed to Southern economic stagnation. With the latter issue, there was continuity with Fogel's previous focus on economic growth.[7]

Nevertheless, it can be argued that much of the impetus for interest in slavery in the late 1960s in the US stemmed from the civil rights movement of the 1960s (Fogel and Engerman 1974a, p. 17). The implicit shift in Fogel's research to a historical topic that resonated with current events may have been of some consequence for the subsequent direction of cliometric work. It implied a shift away from studying the determinants of long-run growth, a topic that would seem to provide strong grounds for incorporating historical analysis into economics. Furthermore, in his work on slavery, Fogel also sought to reach a much broader public audience than just that of professional economic historians.

Both the aim of reaching a general public and the tensions of reconciling that with the rigor of research aimed at professional scholars came to the fore in the two volumes of *Time on the Cross* (Fogel and Engerman 1974b, 1974a). The first volume contained the basic text of the work and can be viewed as aimed primarily at the general reader. The second volume contained technical appendices which provided supporting detail for the conclusions and interpretations reported in the first volume. In their prologue to the primary volume, Fogel and Engerman note the decade and a half of work by cliometricians beginning with the work of Conrad and Meyer (1957 [1964]) based on the 'processing of large quantities of numerical data' (Fogel and Engerman 1974b, p. 4) to challenge previous historical interpretations of slavery. They go on to explain their decision to present this new interpretation to a general audience:

> The review based on these new techniques and hitherto neglected sources has contradicted many of the most important propositions in the traditional portrayal of the slave system. As significant as the correction of past errors is the new information brought to light on the conditions of black bondage. Though the investigations are still in progress, enough have been completed so that the main features of the actual operation of the slave economy are now clear. The reconstruction which has emerged is so much at variance with common beliefs *and its implications are so central to the understanding of contemporary issues*, that we believe the new findings should no longer be restricted to the pages of esoteric scholarly journals. (p. 4; emphasis added)

In the Prologue to *Time on the Cross*, Fogel and Engerman (ibid., p. 10) already note that interpretation of cliometric findings entailed going beyond the findings themselves. A year after the book's publication, Fogel (1975b, 1975c, 1975a) wrote a number of pieces in which he acknowledges the limits of quantitative methods and that history was a humanistic not a scientific discipline and that his work on slavery had forced him to confront this issue.

Publication of *Time on the Cross* set off intense debate with warring factions as much within the fold of cliometricians as without (see Bogue 1990, Atack and Passell 1994).

By the later 1970s the intensity of the debate had lessened and Fogel had moved on to research the demographic issues considered further below. However, he continued to consider the issues raised in the debate, culminating in the publication of *Without Consent or Contract* (Fogel 1989) 15 years after *Time on the Cross*. In a concluding afterword – entitled 'The moral problem of slavery', Fogel acknowledges moral considerations which transcend and shape the interpretation of his economic findings. Similar issues eventually come to the fore in *The Fourth Great Awakening and the Future of Egalitarianism* (Fogel 2000). Thus, in an epiphany reminiscent of John Nef, Fogel came to appreciate that work on the relatively restricted topic of the economics of American slavery had led him to pursue wide-ranging cultural, ethical, and political issues.[8]

Fogel and the Kuznets tradition of long-run economic change

In 1975, Fogel departed Chicago, first to assume the Pitt Professorship at Cambridge University and then to teach in the Economics Department at Harvard before returning to Chicago in 1981 to succeed George Stigler as holder of the Charles R. Walgreen Chair of American Institutions in the Graduate School of Business. During his stay at Harvard, he also became involved with the reorganization of the National Bureau of Economic Research and was involved with establishing the NBER's Development of the American Economy (DAE) project. Both the DAE project and his work on demography and nutrition implied a focus on long-run change, arguably the basis for integrating economics and economic history. Fogel's own subsequent work has focused more on long-run trends in demography than economic history as such. He currently describes his research areas as the bio-demography of aging and health economics rather than economic history (Fogel 2005); all the same, his influence on economic history through his students working on related projects continues and his demographic work has been a major impetus behind the rise of the field of historical anthropometrics (Eichengreen 1994, pp. 175–7, Goldin 1995, pp. 203–5, Mokyr 2005, Miesel and Vega 2006).

Although Fogel has achieved renown for his application of economics and quantitative methods to the study of history, his research throughout his career has been informed by the view that economic history is indispensable for understanding economic processes and current economic issues. He believes (Fogel 2005), to quote Schumpeter (1954, p. 12), that 'the subject matter of economics is essentially a unique process in historic time'. His work on the railroads was intended to address a key issue regarding economic growth. His work on slavery was motivated by a desire to use an understanding of the past to inform contemporary social issues. His more recent work on nutrition and mortality has focused on the centrality of long-run change (Fogel 2004). And his presidential address to the American Economic Association argued that the discipline of economics requires historical perspective to come to grips with the problem of accelerating technological change (Fogel 1999).

Historical economics

After trying unsuccessfully to recruit Albert Fishlow at the senior level, Chicago in the late 1960s decided to recruit a new or recent PhD working in economic history. While the department had a slight preference for someone working on European economic history, field of research was not a priority. However, Fogel did put priority on someone who combined acute historical sensibilities with strong analytical skills; that is, on a cliometrician.

As a junior hire, Deirdre McCloskey joined the Chicago department in 1968. Her dissertation was completed at Harvard under the direction of Alexander Gerschenkron. At Harvard she also worked with John Meyer, who as noted above, had co-authored the pioneering cliometric study of slavery. Meyer's main field of research was transportation economics. McCloskey has attributed to Meyer her initial mastery of applied economics, her acquisition of 'an engineering approach to economics', and thus her subsequent penchant for asking 'how big/quantitative oomph' questions in both economic and historical research (Combs 2001, pp. 3–4). As an economic historian, McCloskey has specialized in British economic history. Her dissertation and subsequent book (McCloskey 1973) focused on the issue of Victorian entrepreneurial decline. Her analysis of productivity trends in the British iron and steel industry argued against claims of British entrepreneurial failure. She proceeded to apply cliometric methods to a variety of topics in British economic history including tariff policy and the poor laws and the workings of the gold standard . Her attention then turned to an extended effort at developing economic models to understand the scattering of plots in English medieval agriculture and the causes and consequences of the subsequent enclosure movement. Unlike traditional approaches which focused on institutional aspects of English landholding such as partible inheritance, she applied models of risk diversification. She has also been associated more generally with the promotion of cliometric methods to the study of British economic history.

McCloskey has written extensively on the significance of economic history and on the methodological approaches the field has employed. While acknowledging such names as cliometrics, the new economic history, and econometric history, McCloskey's preferred term, or as she puts it, the 'best of a bad lot', is 'historical economics'. Unfortunately, William Ashley used 'historical economics' in the sense opposite to her use – McCloskey says his usage bears 'irrelevant echoes of the so-called "historical school"' (McCloskey 1987, p. 13) – because he aimed to use history as a basis for developing economics. But McCloskey prefers the term because a historical economist is one who 'applies economic methods (usually simple) to historical facts (not always quantitative)' (McCloskey and Hersh 1990, p. ix).

In contrast with Fogel's view of the distinctive features of the new economic history, McCloskey's historical economics puts more emphasis on the use of economic theory and rather less on the systematic collection of data or on putting economic history on a firmer quantitative footing. But this is a matter of emphasis rather than a categorical distinction (McCloskey 1978, pp. 15, 19).

One recurring theme in both McCloskey's substantive work in economic history and in her surveys and assessments of work in the field is the pervasiveness of maximizing behavior and the presence of market forces in past economic activity. In her survey, 'The achievements of the Cliometrics School', she reports 'the conclusions have often been variations on the theme, "The Market, God Bless It, Works"' (ibid., p. 21). This is clearly a theme with which McCloskey has considerable sympathy. And, it is one with considerable resonance with usual depictions of the Chicago School of Economics. Indeed after noting the intellectual imperialism in the 1960s of economics into fields such as law, marriage, politics, and anthropology, McCloskey argues that:

> the economics of history was merely the first of these aggressive extensions of economics into new fields. Like a Victorian imperialist imbued with evangelical Christianity, the economist

> fancies himself possessed of Scientific Method, hard-headedness, vision, and a unique spiritual gift – the maximising model of man – which suits him to an imperium over lesser breeds. So too he reckons, in history. (McCloskey 1987, p. 14)

McCloskey's emphasis on the use of economic theory in historical explanation is a theme of David Galenson's work as well. Galenson was recruited to Chicago in 1978. His work has focused on the efficiency of the market for indentured servants in colonial North America and the role of markets in other historical settings (Galenson 1981, 1989).

Regarding why economists should study economic history, McCloskey argues 'economics needs what historical economics has gotten from its association with history: seriousness about facts, an interest in the long run, and habits of scholarship that make for a cumulative science' (McCloskey and Hersh 1990, p. x). And she urges a number of practical reasons why 'economists should read and write economic history' which can be loosely summarized as the value of history in providing a laboratory for the economist and the resulting improvements in economic theory that result as the discipline of economics attempts to come to terms with the findings of history (McCloskey 1976, pp. 439–55).

While arguing forcibly for the value of economic history, these formulations do not appeal to Schumpeter's strong claim of the centrality of historical processes to economics and hence of the centrality of economic history to the same. In McCloskey's formulation of the aims of historical economics cited above, she explicitly emphasizes in both her 1978 and her 1987 statements that it is economics in the service of history rather than history in the service of economics (McCloskey 1978, p. 15, 1987, p. 14). In one of her early uses of the term 'historical economics', she (1976, p. 437) acknowledges Schumpeter's formulation, suggesting that it was shared by 'the postwar officers of the American Economic Association'. Yet in making her case, McCloskey backs off from emphasizing the centrality of historical processes to economics in favor of the arguments above.[9] Indeed, at the end of her article, she acknowledges that 'An economist, least of all a cliometrician cannot argue that there are no substitutes for history in the production of important economics, no more than he can argue that there was no substitute for the railway in American economic growth' (ibid., p. 454).

McCloskey and Galenson in their practice of historical economics were, to quote George Stigler, 'influenced by the tradition of rigorous, realistic, imaginative use of price theory' (Stigler n.d., p. 8). McCloskey (1976, 1978, 1987) has argued persuasively that the application of price theory to history has yielded many insights. Such applications have often supported a Chicago view of the world regarding the pervasiveness of market forces and maximizing behavior. However, the Chicago price theory tradition could also be seen as arguing against the view, to cite McCloskey again, 'that there are no substitutes for history in the production of important economics' (McCloskey 1976, p. 454).

Economic history at Chicago since 1980

The arrival of David Galenson in the department in 1978 and the return of Robert Fogel to Chicago in 1981 saw the development of some influential strands of research in economic history. Historical anthropometrics blossomed as a field of research, furthered by the efforts of a number of Fogel's students including John Komlos and Richard Steckel.

By the mid-1980s, there were perceptions both within and outside the department, that economic history in practice had diminished in vitality, a diminution some attributed to the cliometric movement itself.

Critics asked if economic history is nothing more than economics applied to old datasets, why should the economics profession devote substantial resources to the study of economic history (Stigler 1984, Solow 1986)? Historical issues have not been completely abandoned by Chicago economists. James Heckman has done extensive historical work on twentieth-century trends in the economic status of African-Americans while Robert Lucas has taken up the study of economic growth including a piece, albeit chiefly theoretical, on the industrial revolution (Lucas 2002, pp. 109–89). Nevertheless, economic history by the turn of the twenty-first century, no longer had the presence in the department that it did in the 1960s.

In a book suggestively entitled *How Economics Forgot History*, Geoffrey Hodgson (2001b, p. 232) states that 'postwar economic history dwindled in independence and stature to the point where it felt necessary to prove its virility by adopting mainstream econometric techniques'. While Hodgson does not single out the Chicago department for historical amnesia, he does view such prominent post-war Chicago luminaries as Milton Friedman and Gary Becker as contributing to the 'triumph of barren universality' (ibid., pp. 232, 241) at the expense of enriching the discipline with historical specificity. When discussing Knight's putative institutionalism, Hodgson (2001a) argues that Knight's legacy was lost with the ascendancy of the post-war Chicago School under the aegis of Friedman.[10]

The evidence reviewed here indicates a more complex picture. Since 1945, such prominent economic historians as Hamilton, Kahan, Fogel, McCloskey, and Galenson all joined the Chicago faculty. Moreover, if a broad definition of economic history is employed, including dissertations completed in other departments, the percentage of dissertations completed in the field was no lower during the 2001–06 period than it was during the 1940s.[11] Throughout its history, prominent members of the department who have not been specialists in economic history have nevertheless taken a serious interest in the subject on the grounds that it could provide fundamental insights into economic behavior. These include J. Laurence Laughlin, Knight, T.W. Schultz, Friedman, and James Heckman. And the cliometricians – Fogel, McCloskey, and Galenson – have employed econometrics and applied price theory not for the sake of displaying technical prowess but as tools that could provide substantive insights into economic behavior in the past and long-run economic change.

Notes

* The author wishes to thank the Special Collections Research Center at the University of Chicago Library, and Duke's Economists' Paper Project for permission to quote from materials in their collections. He also thanks Robert Fogel for generous permission to use material from his papers at the University of Chicago and the interview conducted in August 2005, and for answering questions related to the chapter. Steve Stigler gave permission to quote from his father's unpublished essay on the Chicago School, for which the author thanks him. Deirdre McCloskey, Ross Emmett, and Milton Friedman were also generous with responses to questions, and the author thanks them for permission to use material used here. Stanley Engerman and Gavin Wright among many other scholars also provided helpful comments.

1. Biographical material provided in the finding aid for the John U. Nef, Jr. Papers.
2. Based on a list of courses offered by Frank Knight compiled by Ross Emmett.
3. The editorial leadership Hamilton provided for the journal is suggested by the appeal by then chair T.W. Schultz and accompanying signed petition signed by all economics faculty for Hamilton to reconsider

when he indicated his intent in early 1953 to step down as editor (see T.W. Schultz to Earl J. Hamilton, February 9, 1953, with accompanying signed petition, Earl J. Hamilton Papers, Box 4).

4. Fogel indicated that in the 1960s, he saw the differences between himself and Earl Hamilton as being much sharper, with Fogel using much more theory and econometrics, whereas he has come to see much more commonality with regard to their emphasis on quantification and empiricism (Fogel 2005).
5. Fogel stated that he became interested in issues of long-run change and economic growth with 'the great Marxian issues in the back of my mind' (Fogel 2005).
6. For similar concerns, see Paul David to Robert Fogel, December 4, 1964, Robert W. Fogel Papers, Box 149, Folder: Paul David.
7. Fogel recently said that the long-run change has always been the focus of his work, and he turned to the issue of slavery in order to understand how institutions affect economic growth (Fogel 2005).
8. One of Fogel's current faculty appointments at the University of Chicago is with the Committee on Social Thought, established by, and recently renamed after, John Nef.
9. However, she does assert, 'The biggest question in economics, of course, is what explains modern economic growth' (McCloskey and Hersh 1990, p. xii), a question that could be viewed as either fundamentally historical or at least one that calls for extensive use of historical perspective. Earlier she had also acknowledged the importance of work on economic growth to economic history, noting that the initial focus of cliometrics for its first 15 years was 'the history of economic growth in nineteenth century America' (McCloskey 1978, p. 23). And in her 2001 interview, she responded to the question of what important questions she would suggest young economic historians study by saying, 'the biggest and most important one: Why Modern Economic Growth?' (Combs 2001, p. 11).
10. For alternative views on Knight's institutionalism, see Malcolm Rutherford's (ch. 2, this volume) as well as Emmett (2006, 2009).
11. If only dissertations completed within the Department of Economics are considered, then there was a substantial drop between the two time periods in the percentage completed in economic history. More information regarding economic history dissertations completed at the University of Chicago is available from the author upon request.

References

Department of Economics Records, Special Collections Research Center, University of Chicago Library.

Earl J. Hamilton Papers, Economists' Papers Project, Book, Manuscript, and Special Collections Library, Duke University, Durham, NC.

Robert W. Fogel Papers, Special Collections Research Center, University of Chicago Library.

John U. Nef, Jr. Papers, Special Collections Research Center, University of Chicago Library.

Atack, J. and P. Passell (1994), *A New Economic View of American History from Colonial Times to 1940*, 2nd edn, New York: Norton.

Bogue, A.G. (1990), 'Fogel's journey through the slave states', *Journal of Economic History*, **50** (3), 699–710.

Cole, A.H. and R. Crandall (1964), 'The International Scientific Committee on price history', *Journal of Economic History*, **24** (3), 381–8.

Combs, M.B. (2001), 'An interview with Deirdre McCloskey', *Newsletter of the Cliometrics Society*, **16** (2), 3–13.

Conrad, A.H. and J.R. Meyer (1957 [1964]), 'Economic theory, statistical inference, and economic history', in *The Economics of Slavery and Other Studies in Econometric History*, Chicago, IL: Aldine, pp. 3–30.

de Rouvray, C. (2004), '"Old" economic history in the United States: 1939–1954', *Journal of the History of Economic Thought*, **26** (2), 221–39.

Drukker, J.W. (2006), *The Revolution that Bit Its Own Tail: How Economic History Changed Our Ideas on Economic Growth*, Amsterdam: Aksant Academic.

Eichengreen, B. (1994), 'The contributions of Robert W. Fogel to economics and economic history', *Scandinavian Journal of Economics*, **96** (2), 167–79.

Emmett, R.B. (1999), 'Earl J. Hamilton', *American National Biography*, vol. 9, New York: Oxford University Press, pp. 917–18.

Emmett, R.B. (2006), 'Frank H. Knight, Max Weber, Chicago economics, and institutionalism', *Max Weber Studies*, Beiheft 1: *Weber and Economics*, 101–19.

Emmett, R.B. (2009), 'Did the Chicago School reject Frank Knight?', in *Frank Knight and the Chicago School in American Economics*, London: Routledge, pp. 145–55.

Fishlow, A. (1965), *American Railroads and the Transformation of the Antebellum Economy*, Cambridge, MA: Harvard University Press.

Fishlow, A. and R.W. Fogel (1971), 'Quantitative economic history: an interim evaluation, past trends and present tendencies', *Journal of Economic History*, **31** (1), 15–42.

Fogel, R.W. (1960), *The Union Pacific Railroad: A Case in Premature Enterprise*, Baltimore, MD: Johns Hopkins University Press.
Fogel, R.W. (1965), 'The reunification of economic history with economic theory', *American Economic Review*, **55** (1/2), 92–8.
Fogel, R.W. (1966), 'The new economic history: its findings and methods', *Economic History Review*, new series, **19** (3), 642–56.
Fogel, R.W. (1967), 'The specification problem in economic history', *Journal of Economic History*, **27** (3), 283–308.
Fogel, R.W. (1970), 'Historiography and retrospective econometrics', *History and Theory*, **9** (3), 245–64.
Fogel, R.W. (1975a), 'From the Marxists to the Mormons', *Times Literary Supplement*, New York, 13 June, pp. 667–70.
Fogel, R.W. (1975b), 'The limits of quantitative methods in history', *American Historical Review*, **80** (2), 329–50.
Fogel, R.W. (1975c), 'Three phases of cliometric research on slavery and its aftermath', *American Economic Review*, **65** (2), 37–46.
Fogel, R.W. (1979), 'Notes on the social savings controversy', *Journal of Economic History*, **39** (1), 1–54.
Fogel, R.W. (1989), *Without Consent or Contract: The Rise and Fall of American Slavery*, New York: Norton.
Fogel, R.W. (1999), 'Catching up with the economy', *American Economic Review*, **89** (1), 1–21.
Fogel, R.W. (2000), *The Fourth Great Awakening and the Future of Egalitarianism*, Chicago, IL: University of Chicago Press.
Fogel, R.W. (2004), *The Escape from Hunger and Premature Death, 1700–2100: Europe, America and the Third World*, Cambridge: Cambridge University Press.
Fogel, R.W. (2005), Interview with David Mitch, Chicago, August.
Fogel, R.W. and S.L. Engerman (1974a), *Time on the Cross: Evidence and Methods – a Supplement*, Boston, MA: Little Brown.
Fogel, R.W. and S.L. Engerman (1974b), *Time on the Cross: The Economics of American Negro Slavery*, Boston, MA: Little Brown.
Ford Foundation (1956), *Annual Report 1956*, New York: Ford Foundation.
Galenson, D. (1981), *White Servitude in Colonial America*, Cambridge: Cambridge University Press.
Galenson, D. (1989), 'Preface', in *Markets in History: Economic Studies of the Past*, Cambridge: Cambridge University Press.
Goldin, C. (1995), 'Cliometrics and the Nobel', *Journal of Economic Perspectives*, **9** (2), 191–208.
Goodrich, C.L. (1960), 'Economic history: one field or two?', *Journal of Economic History*, **20** (4), 531–8.
Hamilton, E.J. (1934), *American Treasure and the Price Revolution in Spain, 1501–1650*, Cambridge, MA: Harvard University Press.
Hamilton, E.J. (1936a), *Money, Prices, and Wages in Valencia, Aragon, and Navarre, 1351–1500*, Cambridge, MA: Harvard University Press.
Hamilton, E.J. (1936b), 'Prices and wages under John Law's system', *Quarterly Journal of Economics*, **51** (1), 42–70.
Hamilton, E.J. (1947), *War and Prices in Spain, 1651–1800*, Cambridge, MA: Harvard University Press.
Hamilton, E.J. (1969), 'The political economy of France at the time of John Law', *History of Political Economy*, **1** (1), 123–49.
Hodgson, G.M. (2001a), 'Frank Knight as an institutional economist', in *Economics Broadly Considered: Essays in Honor of Warren J. Samuels*, Biddle, J.E., J.B. Davis and S.G. Medema (eds), London: Routledge, pp. 64–93.
Hodgson, G.M. (2001b), *How Economics Forgot History: The Problem of Historical Specificity in Social Science*, London: Routledge.
Kahan, A. (1985), *The Plow, the Hammer, and the Knout: An Economic History of Eighteenth-century Russia*, Chicago, IL: University of Chicago Press.
Lucas, R.E., Jr. (2002), *Lectures on Economic Growth*, Cambridge, MA: Harvard University Press.
Machlup, F. (1952), *The Political Economy of Monopoly: Business, Labor and Government Policies*, Baltimore, MD: Johns Hopkins University Press.
McCloskey, D.N. (1973), *Economic Maturity and Entrepreneurial Decline: British Iron and Steel, 1870–1913*, Cambridge, MA: Harvard University Press.
McCloskey, D.N. (1976), 'Does the past have useful economics?', *Journal of Economic Literature*, **14** (2), 434–61.
McCloskey, D.N. (1978), 'The achievements of the Cliometric School', *Journal of Economic History*, **38** (1), 13–28.
McCloskey, D.N. (1987), *Econometric History*, London: Macmillan.

McCloskey, D.N. and G.K. Hersh, Jr. (1990), *A Bibliography of Historical Economics to 1980*, Cambridge: Cambridge University Press.
Miesel, A. and M. Vega (2006), 'Los origenes de la antropometrica historica y su estado actual' (The origins of anthropometric history and its present state), *Cuadernos de historia economica y empresarial*, no. 18, Cartegena, Columbia: Banco de la República.
Mokyr, J. (2005), 'Hockey-stick economics: review of *The Escape from Hunger and Premature Death, 1700–2100*, by Robert Fogel', *Technology and Culture*, **46** (3), 613–17.
Nef, J.U. (1932), *The Rise of the British Coal Industry*, 2 vols, London: Routledge.
Nef, J.U. (1940 [1957]), *Industry and Government in France and England, 1540–1640*, Ithaca, NY: Cornell University Press.
Nef, J.U. (1941), 'Silver production in Central Europe, 1450–1618', *Journal of Political Economy*, **49** (4), 575–91.
Nef, J.U. (1952), 'Mining and metallurgy in medieval civilization', in *Cambridge Economic History of Europe*, vol. 2, Postan, M. and E.E. Rich (eds), Cambridge: Cambridge University Press, pp. 696–734.
Nef, J.U. (1973), *Search for Meaning: The Autobiography of a Nonconformist*, Washington, DC: Public Affairs Press.
Redlich, F. (1965), '"New" and traditional approaches to economic history and their interdependence', *Journal of Economic History*, **25** (4), 480–95.
Redlich, F. (1970), 'Potentialities and pitfalls in economic history', in *The New Economic History: Recent Papers on Methodology*, Andreano, R.L. (ed.), New York: John Wiley, pp. 85–99.
Royal Swedish Academy of Sciences (1993), Press release, October, available at: http://nobelprize.org/nobel_prizes/economics/laureates/1993/press.html (accessed 28 January, 2010).
Schumpeter, J.A. (1954), *History of Economic Analysis*, New York: Oxford University Press.
Solow, R.E. (1986), 'Economics: is something missing?', in *Economic History and the Modern Economist*, Parker, W.N. (ed.), Oxford: Blackwell, pp. 21–9.
Stigler, G.J. (1984), 'Economics – the imperial science?', *Scandinavian Journal of Economics*, **86** (3), 301–13.
Stigler, G.J. (1988), *Memoirs of an Unregulated Economist*, New York: Basic Books.
Stigler, G.J. (n.d.), 'The Chicago School of economics', Robert W. Fogel Papers, Box 166, Folder: George Stigler, Chicago, IL: Special Collections Research Center.
Weber, M. (1927 [1981]), *General Economic History*, Knight, F.H. (trans.), New Brunswick, NJ: Transaction Books.
Weiss, R. (1989), 'Introduction', in *Russian Economic History: The Nineteenth Century*, Kahan, A. (ed.), Chicago, IL: University of Chicago Press, pp. ix–xii.
Wright, C. (1910), *Wool-growing and the Tariff: A Study in the Economic History of the United States*, Cambridge, MA: Harvard University Press.
Wright, C. (1938 [1965]), 'The nature and objectives of economic history', in *New Views on American Economic Development: A Selective Anthology of Recent Work*, Andreano, R.L. (ed.), Cambridge, MA: Schenkman, pp. 27–38.
Wright, C. (1941), *Economic History of the United States*, New York: McGraw-Hill.

9 Chicago and the development of twentieth-century labor economics

*Bruce E. Kaufman**

Introduction

The two universities in America that exercised the largest influence on the economic study of labor during the twentieth century are Chicago and Wisconsin. They are also the home of the two major rival paradigms that have vied back and forth over the years for dominance: the institutional/industrial relations approach (Wisconsin) and the neoclassical/price theory approach (Chicago). During the first half of the century the Wisconsin paradigm was ascendant and, even at Chicago, labor economics was heavily colored by this tradition; in the last half of the century, however, the pendulum swung decisively toward Chicago, and the neoclassical/price theory approach came to rule the field. In other places I have described the major principles and historical evolution of the Wisconsin School in labor (Kaufman 2004a, 2006); in this chapter I do the same for the Chicago School. By the end, one readily appreciates why Chicago has been the most influential force shaping modern labor economics and why economists at Chicago have won more Nobel prizes than any other university in the world.

Labor at Chicago: the early years

The study of labor as a separate field in American economics did not begin until the first decade of the twentieth century, although recognizable work in the field goes back at least to Richard Ely's *The Labor Movement in America* (1886, see Kaufman 2004a). The beginning point of the field is marked by the publication of the first collegiate labor text, *Labor Problems* by Thomas Adams and Helen Sumner of Wisconsin (1905, see McNulty 1980). The tenor and format of the book, and the focus on labor 'problems', typified the Wisconsin institutional approach. That is, the book first examined a series of maladies or 'evils' arising from the capitalist market system, such as low wages, long hours and child labor, and then in the latter part of the book surveyed a variety of institutional solutions to these problems, such as trade unionism, protective labor legislation and progressive management. Revealingly, no chapter was devoted to the labor market and the issue of wage determination received only a few pages of discussion, in part because the Marshallian demand/supply model of wage determination had not yet been formalized (Marshall in *Principles of Economics* (1890) stated in words that wages were determined by supply and demand but did not draw the diagram or derive the curves), and in part because the institutionalists thought that most labor markets diverged significantly from Marshall's competitive model (and hence caused numerous labor problems). The labor 'problems' approach remained quite popular into the 1950s and 1960s.

Only a small number of universities had any discernible specialization in labor up to the Second World War, and the total number of labor economists (broadly defined) was probably less than one hundred (Kerr 1994). Wisconsin was the leading center for labor studies, having five labor faculty led by John R. Commons who was widely recognized as the nation's foremost labor authority (Lampman 1993). Other universities that had some specialization and recognition in labor were Berkeley, Chicago, Columbia, Harvard, Johns Hopkins, MIT, Princeton and Stanford. A number of these programs were oriented toward industrial relations (that is, the institutional study of labor problems) and none was neoclassical or 'analytical' in the modern sense, for a price theory approach to the subject simply did not exist. Illustratively, no labor textbook of the 1920s and 1930s, as far as I am aware, featured a demand–supply diagram of wage determination; indeed, not even John Hicks's *Theory of Wages* (1932) did so.

According to McNulty (1980, p. 149), the first labor dissertation written at Chicago was in 1900 by Katherine Bement Davis on causes affecting the standard of living and wages. The faculty did not contain a recognized writer on labor subjects, however, until Robert Hoxie returned to the Chicago faculty in 1906 after a two-year stint at Cornell.

Hoxie grew into an institutionalist and labor expert, but did not start out this way. For a decade his theoretical approach was largely orthodox and the subjects investigated centered on the tariff, bimetallism and the demand/supply concepts (Hamilton 1916). Slowly, however, Hoxie came under the influence of Thorstein Veblen's institutionalism, as well as fellow Chicagoan Frank Fetter's 'psychological economics'. As a result, Hoxie grew disenchanted with the idea that economic behavior is well explained by deductively derived universal laws operating through competitive markets, and increasingly looked at economics as a contingent, evolutionary process conditioned by history, institutions and social arrangements. Convinced of the need to inductively develop generalizations and theory from hands-on empirical investigation of concrete cases, Hoxie shifted to the study of labor.

Using the 'go and see' approach of Ely and Commons, Hoxie attended union conventions, did field interviews with workers and toured manufacturing plants to observe methods of labor management. Out of this research came several works that received national recognition and established Chicago as a locus for labor research. Perhaps best known today and still occasionally cited is Hoxie's work on trade unionism, including an article in the Chicago-published *Journal of Political Economy* (*JPE*), 'The trade-union point of view' (1907) and a book *Trade Unionism in the United States* (1917). In the book, Hoxie developed a famous fivefold taxonomy of union types: business, uplift, revolutionary, predatory and dependent unionism. Another book Hoxie published actually received greater attention at the time. Hoxie was commissioned by the presidential-appointed Commission on Industrial Relations to investigate the impact of Frederick Taylor's newly developed practice of scientific management on labor. His findings and conclusions, dispassionately presented but tending toward the critical, were published in *Scientific Management and Labor* (1915) and stirred considerable debate and discussion.

Hoxie was succeeded at Chicago by Harry Millis. In 1920, Millis was joined by Paul Douglas. The two men formed the core of the labor field at Chicago until the late-1930s/early 1940s when Millis took a leave to chair the National Labor Relations Board and Douglas became increasingly involved in city politics and later volunteered to serve with the Marine Corps in the Pacific during the Second World War. Millis returned to the faculty in 1945 but died in 1948; Douglas also returned to Chicago but left in 1948 when he won election to the US Senate as a liberal Democrat. Both Millis and Douglas were elected presidents of the American Economic Association (Millis in 1934; Douglas in 1947).

Like Hoxie, Millis's initial area of research and teaching interest was outside of labor (public finance). In 1911, however, he served as a staff researcher for the US Immigration Commission and subsequently published several journal articles on the economic consequences of immigration. At the same time, Millis (1914) also published a lengthy and relatively favorable analysis of the minimum wage in the *JPE*. In the 1920s Millis became extensively involved in labor arbitration and developed a national reputation in this area. 'Millis was in his time perhaps the country's greatest arbitrator', his Chicago colleagues and students claimed upon his death (Brown et al. 1949, p. 747). They went on to say that the skill served him well as department chair. His output of scholarly research dwindled through the mid-1930s as he became increasingly involved in public service. In 1938, however, Millis was co-author and editor of two major and much-cited books. The first was the first two volumes of a three-volume set, *The Economics of Labor*, co-authored with Royal Montgomery of Cornell and written as a labor problems text (1938a, 1938b); the second was the series of industry case studies in the edited volume *How Collective Bargaining Works* (Twentieth Century Fund 1942). His last major publication was *From the Wagner Act to Taft–Hartley* with Emily Clark Brown (1950).

In 1920, Douglas was hired as an assistant professor of economics at Chicago. He states in his autobiography, 'with the coming of Jacob Viner, Frank Knight, Henry Schultz, John Nef, and others, by the end of the 1920s the department was second to none in the nation'. He goes on to add, 'Best of all, men were encouraged at Chicago to think, study, and produce for themselves. There was complete academic freedom . . . no wonder I fell in love with the university' (Douglas 1971, pp. 43–4).

Glen Cain has called Douglas 'the greatest labor economist in the first 50 years of the century' (see also Cain 1979, quoted in Samuelson 1979, p. 923). He brought to the study of labor a superior intellect, advanced (for that period) skills in theory and statistics, a large degree of doctrinal open-mindedness, meticulous attention to detail and strong commitment to keeping theory closely grounded in empirical facts. Early in his career Douglas was one of the leading authorities on the newly developed practice of personnel management, illustrated by his second *JPE* article 'Plant administration of labor' (Douglas 1919, see Kaufman 2000). He also wrote on apprenticeship programs, shop committees and co-edited a massive and well-received volume of articles for college labor problems courses (Atkins et al. 1923).[1]

From the mid-1920s onward, Douglas turned his attention to several subjects central to modern-day labor economics but which at that time were virtually unexplored. The one he is best known for is co-development of the Cobb–Douglas production function and the statistical estimation of marginal productivity curves. This work was first presented at the American Economic Association (AEA) meetings in 1927, was presented in far more detail in his magnum opus *The Theory of Wages* (Douglas 1934), and was again extended in his AEA presidential address 'Are there laws of production?' (Douglas 1948). His conclusion to this question was 'Yes', at least as a long-run tendency. Complementing his work on labor demand, Douglas in *The Theory of Wages* also estimated cross-sectional labor supply curves, regressing labor force participation rates for a number of age–sex groups on real wages for a number of large cities. He found that the labor supply curves for both men and women were negatively sloped.[2] Douglas's work on labor supply curves was later extended in a *JPE* article with Erika Schoenberg (Schoenberg and Douglas 1937). Also deserving mention is Douglas's laborious work in constructing time-series estimates of real wages in America from 1890 to 1926 (Douglas 1930), two books on unemployment and combating economic depression (Douglas and Director 1931, Douglas 1935), and articles on unemployment insurance (for example, Douglas 1931).

Millis and Douglas shared similar views on issues of labor theory and policy. Both saw value in neoclassical theory as a general framework for modeling the economy and guiding economic analysis. They also thought that the theory explained certain basic features of wages and employment, albeit more often as long-run tendencies. Douglas (1934, p. 95) states, for example, 'The method of the marginal productivity school, as indeed of the entire school of orthodox economists, has described a portion of reality', while Millis concludes 'We have in the productivity analysis at least an explanation of tendencies striving to work themselves out' (Millis and Montgomery 1938a, p. 206). But both men also agreed that orthodox theory was a poor and somewhat biased account of wage determination in the short run. The problem, they thought, is that some of the assumptions of orthodox theory substantially depart from real-world conditions, especially those that operate to protect the workers' interests. Thus, Douglas states:

> It will be seen . . . that the assumptions which depart most from reality are those which ascribe more power to the workers than they actually possess. . . . It can thus be said that up until the summer of 1933 the forces which operated against labor's receiving its marginal product were stronger that those which tend to prevent capital from securing its margin. (Douglas 1934, p. 94)

He goes on to conclude, 'An increased activity by the state in behalf of labor, or further unionization on the part of the wage-earners, would have helped to redress this balance' (p. 95). In a similar vein, Millis argues that the linchpin assumption of orthodox theory is that labor markets are competitive but he concludes, 'The only truthful statement that can be made . . . is that in many cases such competition simply does not obtain' (Millis and Montgomery 1938a, pp. 192–3). For this reason, Millis testified before Congress in favor of enactment of the National Labor Relations Act:

> The great majority of wage-earners are employed under such conditions that they must act in concert with reference to wage scales, hours, and working conditions if they are to have a reasonably effective voice as to the terms on which they shall work. Without organization there is in most of modern industry unequal bargaining power. (Millis 1949, p. 1553)

Although Douglas and Millis questioned the short-run accuracy of competitive theory due to the unreality of some of its assumptions, this type of reasoning was later strongly criticized by Milton Friedman (1953) in his famous methodological essay.

Three other Chicago economists of the interwar period require mention. They are Frank Knight, Jacob Viner and Henry Simons. None were labor economists, but Knight and Simons occasionally wrote on labor subjects. More importantly, all had a significant influence in forming and shaping what in the post-Second World War period became recognized as 'the Chicago School' (Miller 1962, Reder 1982).

Many people consider Knight and Viner the father figures of the modern Chicago School, in part because they made seminal contributions to price theory and in part because both were strong advocates of free markets and economic liberty. But Knight also contributed an important idea in labor theory. He argued that the traditional distinction between the three factors of production, land, capital and labor, is fallacious and in reality there is only one generic input, capital (Knight 1933). His reasoning is that the greatest portion of the value of any factor input comes from prior investment in upgrading its quality, such as draining and fertilizing land and educating and training labor. This idea, earlier discussed in embryonic form by Adam Smith, W.S. Jevons and Alfred Marshall, was later taken by Theodore Schultz and Gary Becker and developed into the theory of human capital.

Henry Simons also deserves mention, partly for his writings on labor and also for the influence of his libertarian free market views on Friedman, Stigler and other Chicago graduate students of that period. Simons was a student and protégé of Knight. He published relatively little and a good portion of what he wrote was in the nature of policy tracts promoting economic liberalism. He was also an acerbic critic of labor institutionalism, calling it 'social work twaddle' (quoted in Bronfenbrenner 2004, p. 97). Despite his modest publication record, testimony from students suggests that Simons's views had significant influence (Wallis 1993, Rosen 1994). Simons also had a joint appointment with the Law School and he and colleague Aaron Director laid the early foundation for what was later to become the world famous program at Chicago on law and economics.

In what would appear to be singularly inauspicious timing, Simons in 1934 published a tract entitled 'A positive program for *laissez-faire*'. He lays out his position with these words:

> the great enemy of democracy is monopoly, in all forms: gigantic corporations, trade associations, and other agencies for price control, trade-unions – or, in general, organization and concentration of power within functional classes. . . . The existence of competition within such groups, on the other hand, serves to protect the community as a whole and to give an essential flexibility to the economy. (Simons 1948, p. 43)

Later, Simons focused his critique of collectivism specifically on labor unions. In doing so, he directly attacked the idea promoted by Douglas and Millis that labor and product markets are seriously imperfect and individual workers suffer from an inequality of bargaining power. Regarding labor and product markets, for example, Simons (ibid., p. 129) states 'monopsony in the labor market is, I think, very unsubstantial or transitory' and 'enterprise monopoly is also a skin disease, easy to correct when and if we will, and usually moderate in its abuse'. The trade union, on the other hand, 'enables an aristocracy of labor to build fences around its occupations, restricting entry, raising arbitrarily the costs and prices of its products, and lowering the wages and incomes of those outside, and of the poor especially' (p. 138). He concludes, 'For my part, I simply cannot conceive of any tolerable or enduring order in which there exists widespread organization of workers along occupational, industrial, functional lines' (pp. 121–2).

The beginning of the modern Chicago School in labor

Through the Second World War the Economics Department at Chicago remained relatively diverse and pluralistic. Thereafter, the departure or death of men such as Lange, Douglas and Millis, combined with the hiring of Milton Friedman in 1947 and the arrival at Chicago of Friedrich Hayek in 1950, greatly changed the complexion and tenor of the faculty. Out of this new mix grew the modern Chicago School, firmly set in place in 1958 when George Stigler was recruited to the faculty of the Graduate School of Business (with a joint appointment in economics).

The defining characteristics of the modern Chicago School are a matter of some debate (see Miller 1962, Samuels 1976, Reder 1982) and are covered in more detail elsewhere in this volume. In a sentence, I would characterize them as a deep commitment to rigorous scholarship and open academic debate, an uncompromising belief in the usefulness and insight of neoclassical price theory, and a normative position that favors and promotes economic liberalism and free markets. With regard to labor, Walter Oi (2004, p. 336) recalled of his graduate student days in the late 1950s: 'The Chicago approach to labor economics put price theory in a prominent place and relegated the importance of institutions'. Also downgraded, with only a few exceptions, were macroeconomic aspects of labor markets.

The transformation from the interwar pluralistic and somewhat institutional approach of Douglas and Millis to the thoroughly neoclassical and unabashedly imperialistic approach developed by Becker and colleagues in the 1960s and 1970s did not happen overnight but unfolded in a gradual process spanning two decades (Emmett 1998). The beginning point of the transformation is with Friedman, Stigler and H. Gregg Lewis in the early 1940s. I focus on the work of Friedman and Stigler largely as it pertains to labor.

Friedman and Stigler were in the top rank of neoclassical price theorists and were arguably the two most ardent and skilled defenders/developers of Marshallian microeconomic theory, particularly in its competitive market version. One must recall that when Friedman and Stigler began their careers, competitive market theory – widely perceived as the core of the neoclassical paradigm – traded at a deep intellectual discount due to the imperfect competition revolution pioneered by Edward Chamberlin and Joan Robinson and the macroeconomic revolution pioneered by John Maynard Keynes. Both revolutions suggested that competitive demand/supply analysis was largely inapplicable to modern economies populated with large price/wage-setting corporations and trade unions and prices and wages were neither very flexible nor able to clear most product and labor markets. The obvious implications were that economics needed a new (or substantially revised) corpus of theory and the market economy needed regulation and guidance by the visible hand of government. Of all markets, the common view (for example, Lester 1941) was that labor markets were the ones that most seriously diverged both structurally and behaviorally from the competitive ideal.

The modern Chicago School started out, in effect, as a counter-revolution aimed at restoring competitive price theory as the foundational mode of theorizing in economics. This agenda was clearly signaled in Stigler's (1942) second book, a price theory textbook entitled *The Theory of Competitive Price* – the revised second edition was retitled simply *The Theory of Price* (Stigler 1946b). Notably, the last chapter is devoted to the demand and supply of labor and both are explicated without any mention made of imperfect competition in either product or labor markets, despite the fact that Robinson (1933) only a few years earlier had developed the theory of monopsony.

Stigler's uncompromising commitment to competitive theory, and penchant to define the debate in ways that favored his position (Freedman 1998), was also illustrated a few years later in his *American Economic Review* (*AER*) article, 'The economics of minimum wage legislation' (Stigler 1946a). Paul Douglas had several years earlier published an article 'The economic theory of wage regulation' (1938). In it he reviews four rationales for a minimum wage: to prevent competition from ratcheting down labor standards (a 'race to the bottom'), to raise the efficiency of labor, to prevent wage disputes and strikes and to increase purchasing power and aggregate demand. After a review of the pros and cons of minimum wages, he concludes:

> There is sufficient evidence that competition fails to work perfectly, and that there is a considerable degree of monopoly or imperfect competition in the purchase of labor, as to make one skeptical about wages being fixed solely by natural law. To the degree that these noncompetitive forces are at work, there is a strong case for governmental participation in the fixing of at least some wage rates. (Ibid., p. 214)

Stigler's article is a study in contrasts. Perhaps believing the past literature on the minimum wage was irredeemably flawed, Stigler proceeds *de novo* and cites neither Douglas nor any other previously published theoretical or empirical work on the minimum wage. He begins by defining (or redefining) the objective of the minimum wage as 'the elimination of extreme poverty' (Stigler 1946a, p. 358). Given this goal, the first section of the paper analyzes the theoretical impact of a minimum wage. Revealingly, the heading is entitled 'Competitive wage determination' and the first sentence declares 'Each worker receives the value of his marginal product under competition'. Stigler reviews the implication of competitive theory and concludes that the minimum wage is likely to cause reduced employment, a misallocation of resources, reduced earnings for workers in the non-covered sector and a reduction in national output. He briefly notes two objections to competitive theory but dismisses the relevance of either, stating that employer control of wages is 'not very relevant to the question of a national minimum wage' (ibid., p. 360) and the 'shock effect' often cited by institutional economists (the positive effect a minimum wage has on spurring managerial efficiency) is 'particularly inappropriate to the industries paying low wages' (p. 359). Because of the numerous negative repercussions of a minimum wage, Stigler concludes 'the manipulation of individual prices is neither an efficient nor an equitable device for changing the distribution of personal income' (p. 362). He ends by observing that the problem with manipulating prices to achieve social goals is that it harms incentives and the better approach, particularly with regard to raising the income of the family unit, is to provide a lump-sum transfer to the poor, such as by 'extend[ing] the personal income tax to the lowest income brackets with negative rates in these brackets' (p. 365). This idea was later popularized by Friedman as the 'Negative Income Tax'.

Friedman espoused the same position on labor markets and competitive theory. For example, in response to critical comments by Paul Samuelson about the applicability of competitive theory to labor markets, Friedman (quoted in Wright 1951, p. 254) responded: 'The question is whether it [competitive theory] gives you the right answer, and I would argue that it substantially does'. He goes on to say 'The important point is that forces [noncompetitive elements] which bulk large when you look under the microscope at the individual case, but which vary from firm to firm and industry to industry, are likely to bulk small when you look at the aggregate'. In another place, Friedman largely dismisses the institutionalists' claim that labor markets are rife with imperfections and workers bargain at a disadvantage. Friedman (1962, p. 190) says, for example, that the demonstration a minimum wage can increase employment in a monopsony labor market is 'little more than a theoretical curiosum', the claim that employer-mandated work schedules prevent workers from securing their desired work hours is 'almost entirely specious' (p. 205), and that a more detailed examination reveals 'the bargaining disadvantage [in wage determination] is by no means always on the side of labor' (p. 201).

Friedman and Stigler's competitive price theory counter-revolution was greatly advanced by two other lines of argument. The first was their methodological attack on realism in economic theory. The opening shot was fired by Stigler (1949) in a lecture 'Monopolistic competition in retrospect', was most famously and persuasively made by Friedman (1953) in his chapter 'The methodology of positive economics', and was then carried forward into labor economics *per se* by Simon Rottenberg (1956) in an article 'On choice in labor markets'.

During the 1930s–50s, competitive price theory was widely attacked as of dubious value because its predictions were thought to be frequently in error, such as the 'law of one price', the ability of prices and wages to self-equilibrate markets and the equality of wages and marginal revenue product. Critics, in turn, attributed this problem to the fact that the structure and assumptions of price theory either omitted crucial aspects of behavior or modeled them in a way that departed too far from reality.

One of the most famous attacks was by Richard Lester (1946) in his *AER* article 'Shortcomings of marginal analysis for wage-employment problems'. His central charge was that the neoclassical theory of the firm provides a very inaccurate account of how firms set and change employment in response to variations in product demand and other such factors. Based on survey evidence and findings of other studies, he noted that employment is principally a function of effective demand and has at best a very weak relationship to wage rates, while in reaction to an exogenous rise in wages firms typically respond not by reducing the scale of production (the textbook neoclassical prediction) but by endeavoring to lower cost by increasing sales effort (to expand output and lower cost by moving along downward-sloping marginal and average variable cost curves) and managerial efficiency (the shock effect). He concluded that the predictive errors of neoclassical theory were caused by certain assumptions that were (allegedly) contradicted by empirical evidence and the fact employers could not make the marginal calculations depicted in the theory. He concluded 'this paper raises grave doubts as to the validity of conventional marginal theory and the assumptions upon which it rests' (ibid., p. 81).

Friedman's essay on positive economics was a direct response to Lester, as well as Chamberlin and the other critics of competitive neoclassical price theory. His counterattack proceeded along three lines. First, he contended that the critics had misconstrued the purpose and test of a theory. The critics rejected neoclassical theory, Friedman asserted, because they claimed that its assumptions are unrealistic. But assumptions must by their very nature be unrealistic in a descriptive sense. Therefore, the only valid test of a theory is its ability to predict. Even if businessmen cannot actually make marginal calculations, as long as their behavior accords 'as if' they do, the theory is a useful scientific device. Friedman's second line of argument was to claim that competitive price theory in fact had a good record of prediction. As Reder (1958) later noted, however, this point was more asserted than demonstrated. His third and perhaps most persuasive argument was to point out that the critics either had no alternative theory or had a theory that was largely empty of additional predictive content. Whether Friedman's essay effectively won the argument on substantive grounds is still a matter of debate (Boland 2003, Reder 2003); what is far less questionable is that in the minds of most economists he triumphed. Evidence suggests that this is most certainly true in labor economics (Boyer and Smith 2001), with the long-run effect of restoring competitive price theory as the base-line paradigm used in the field (Manning 2003).

The competitive price theory counter-revolution also moved ahead due to a second contribution of Friedman and Stigler. This was to use the tools of price theory to explain the market imperfections and deviant observations that the critics kept holding up as evidence against the theory. A very influential example related to labor is Stigler's (1962) article 'Information in the labor market'. One of the chief anomalies that institutional critics cited to impugn competitive theory was the existence in local labor markets of substantial wage dispersion among workers within finely detailed occupational groups (suggesting refutation of the 'law of one wage'). This dispersion was, in turn, attributed to various market imperfections that seemed to contradict the assumptions of competitive theory, such as the existence of imperfect information and costs of mobility. Stigler accepted the existence of wage dispersion but then turned the tables on the critics by demonstrating that price theory could not only explain why wage dispersion exists but could also show that the alleged anomaly was in fact a product of rational economizing behavior. He argues that labor market information is like any other good – efficiency is promoted if workers invest in additional job searching only as long as the marginal gain in earnings outweighs the marginal cost. Since information is scarce and can only be produced and acquired at positive cost, the implication is that workers should engage in only a finite and possibly quite limited amount of job search, thus permitting the existence of wage dispersion even in an otherwise competitive labor market. The virtues of Stigler's article are several-fold: it not only explains a deviant observation but also shows that the alleged anomaly is in fact an efficient outcome produced by rational economizing behavior; demonstrates the explanatory power and insight of orthodox price theory; greatly strengthened and energized the research program on job search theory and behavior; and generated a number of new hypotheses and insights amenable to empirical testing. A number of doctoral students at Chicago and other universities (for example, John McCall, Dale Mortensen) took up Stigler's ideas and created a rapidly expanding theoretical and empirical literature on job search.

Although Friedman and Stigler established the broad approach and agenda that came to define Chicago labor economics, they were general theorists and were not actively involved in the labor field as either researchers or teachers. Creating and leading modern labor economics at Chicago thus fell to someone else more directly involved in labor studies. By unanimous agreement, the person who filled this role is H. Gregg Lewis.

Lewis has been called the 'founder of the "Chicago School" of labor economics' (Becker 1976b), the 'father of modern labor economics' (Ashenfelter 1994), and the 'father of analytical labor economics' (American Economic Association 1982). Biddle (1996, p. 184) describes Lewis as representing 'uncompromising neoclassicism'.

Lewis did not have an extensive set of publications, a fact his students and colleagues ascribe to excessive perfectionism (Biddle 1996). In several cases he wrote influential papers that circulated widely but were never published, or that were published in relatively obscure places – for example, an article in Spanish in a Chilean journal (Lewis 1969). His major influence, as will be described shortly, came through his teaching, mentoring, dissertation supervision, running the Labor Economics Workshop and collaboration with colleagues. But the publications he produced were, nonetheless, influential both as scholarly works and markers of a unique 'Chicago' approach to labor.

The labor field in the 1945–60 period was heavily dominated by economists with a neo-institutional/Keynesian orientation, and industrial relations was the big subject. Many industrial relations programs were established around the country, including an Industrial Relations Center at Chicago in 1945. Major names in the field included John Dunlop, Frederick Harbison (at Chicago), Clark Kerr, Charles Myers, Richard Lester, Arthur Ross and Lloyd Reynolds (Kaufman 1988). These economists sought to integrate the study of labor markets and labor institutions; espoused a multidisciplinary approach combining economics with insights from related fields such as psychology, sociology and management; largely eschewed mathematics and theoretical formalism for a literary and case-study type of research (augmented by the occasional diagram); and gave considerable research emphasis and normative sympathy to collective bargaining. As typified by Lester's attack on marginal analysis, they also felt deep skepticism about the theoretical integrity and empirical relevance of neoclassical price theory, most particularly the competitive labor market model. Reynolds's (1949) popular labor text *Labor Economics and Labor Relations* did not contain a single demand/supply diagram, while a survey article on wage theory concluded that 'competitive theory is useful in explaining general, long-term trends in wage relationships' but for analysis in the short- to medium-term 'competitive theory seems completely out of touch with the world of actuality' (Pierson 1957, pp. 18–19). In addition to feeling antipathy toward competitive theory, these labor economists perceived that the reigning 'theorists' in the economics discipline were hostile to both labor unions and a social science 'realist' style of research, leading them in 1947 to break away from the AEA and form the Industrial Relations Research Association (IRRA) (Kerr 1994, Kaufman 2004a). Most certainly, Chicago-style price theory, and Stigler and Friedman in particular, represented this group's *bête noir* (Dunlop 1984).

Lewis's first article on labor appeared in the *JPE* in 1951 and was titled 'The labor-monopoly problem: a positive program'. It was the only publication Lewis wrote in which he espoused a normative policy position and it clearly put him in the camp of Simons, Friedman and Stigler. Indeed, Biddle (1996) concludes that Lewis most likely moved into the labor area to push forward and flesh out Simon's critique of monopoly unionism, a fact suggested by the title Lewis gave the article and his statement on the first page: 'Labor monopoly is private economic protectionism of essentially the same type as private enterprise monopoly and has the same consequences' (Lewis 1951, p. 277).

The next significant labor article by Lewis is 'Hours of work and hours of leisure' (Lewis 1956). It is an exemplar of the Chicago approach to labor economics and, in my opinion, signals the beginning point of what today is called modern labor economics. Perhaps with some irony, the article was presented at the annual meeting of the IRRA! Lewis first lays out the neoclassical labor/leisure theory of work hours, describes how the secular increase in real wages in the economy leads to countervailing income and substitution effects, and explains that the long-run decline in average work hours over the twentieth century implies that the former was larger in size than the latter.[3] Lewis then fits this result into a competitive demand/supply framework and explains the secular decline in work hours as the result of an upward-shifting perfectly elastic labor demand curve along a stable negatively inclined labor supply curve. Foreshadowing a methodological proposition later advanced by Becker, Lewis (ibid., p. 206) argues that 'the relative cost and taste factors . . . I believe, tend to be quite stable'. Lewis then moves from theory to empirical evidence where he examines the relationship between real wage rates and changes in hours of work among a cross-section of industries. Finally, he considers the influence of institutional factors on the decline in work hours, such as employer work schedules, unions and government legislation, but largely dismisses their importance on the grounds that they either 'complicate the theory . . . without substantial gain', or 'play only a minor role' (p. 198).

No doubt the work Lewis is best remembered for is his empirical studies of the union relative wage effect, which first appeared in *Unionism and Relative Wages in the United States* (Lewis 1963). The book illustrates two of the hallmarks of Lewis's research method: painstaking attention to detail and rigorous specification of empirical relationships. His *JPE* paper (1951), and a later book chapter 'Competitive and monopoly unionism' (1959), argued that unions use monopoly power to raise wages. Given his empirical bent, it was a natural step for Lewis to then try to measure the size of the union monopoly effect. Also steering him in this direction was the fact that he supervised several dissertations at Chicago in the 1950s (for example, Albert Rees, Stephen Sobotka, Leonard Rapping) that investigated the effect of unions on wages. These studies, and others that were published during this period, reported large variations in the union relative wage effect depending on the industry, time period and empirical methodology. To narrow this dispersion, Lewis took twenty of these studies and meticulously reexamined and re-adjusted their data and findings. He also provided evidence on union wage effects from time-series and cross-section regression equations. His conclusion was that unions on average raise wages 10–15 percent, although the size of the union effect varies with factors such as macroeconomic climate, industry concentration and extent of unionization in the market (Lewis 1963).

Lewis's book became the standard reference work on union relative wage effects for several decades and inspired a large and still growing literature; it was also a pioneering application of multiple regression analysis to labor market data. Among the best-known follow-up works is *What Do Unions Do?* (Freeman and Medoff 1984); one of the co-authors (Freeman) had been an assistant professor at Chicago in the early 1970s. Lewis (1986) also published a follow-up book, *Union Relative Wage Effects: A Survey*, that reviewed and synthesized the findings of two hundred studies. Again, he found the average union effect to be approximately 15 percent.

As influential as Lewis's publications were, they were by common agreement not in and of themselves his most important contribution to the labor field. Ashenfelter (1994) argues that it was Lewis's 'research style' that was his greatest legacy, passed on principally through teaching, dissertation supervision and personal correspondence. In a similar vein, Rees (1976, pp. S3–4) argues that 'no one can rival Lewis in being responsible for this transition [from the institutional to analytical approach]. The overwhelming majority of analytical labor economists have been his colleagues, his students, or students of his students'. He goes on to observe 'This influence has been achieved more through teaching and criticism than through publication'.

The flowering of modern labor economics at Chicago

Friedman, Stigler and Lewis set the stage in the 1940s–50s for the development and growth of neoclassical labor economics at Chicago. The real flowering and rise to dominance in the academic world of what is now known as 'modern labor economics' did not, however, take place until later, spanning roughly the 25 years from 1960 to 1985. After 1985, Chicago-style labor economics became so widely accepted and imitated that the approach became largely synonymous with labor economics itself. The people who carried forward this transition were, in turn, the graduate students and younger colleagues of these men. The list reads like a 'who's who' in modern labor economics, but certainly the towering name is Gary Becker.

Production of doctoral students accelerated at Chicago after 1940 and in the next three decades Chicago produced more PhDs in labor than any other university (Teixeira 2007). In terms of quality, according to Rees (1976) Chicago also had the highest minimum standards for dissertations (and, he states, Lewis had the highest minimum standards in the department). In the labor area, Columbia University was another important training ground for doctoral students and in effect served as a second home for Chicago-style labor economics (Grossbard 2006).

In the 1940s and early 1950s, Chicago graduated a number of general economic theorists who later also published well-recognized works in the labor area. Examples include Herbert Simon, Martin Bronfenbrenner and Melvin Reder. In this early time period, Chicago also produced numerous labor economists, such as G. Warren Nutter, Albert Rees and Ethel Jones. As a generalization, both these theorists and labor economists represented the 'soft' or 'decaffeinated' version of Chicago economics, meaning a strong commitment to theory and analytical methods but more willingness to incorporate or countenance imperfect competition, institutional factors and 'heterodoxy'. Two examples from the theorists include Simon's (1951) theory of the employment relationship and Bronfenbrenner's (1956) theory of potential monopsony.

Playing a particularly important role in this era were Reder and Rees, both of whom served as important intellectual bridges between the 'hard' Chicago group (Friedman/Stigler/Lewis) and the neo-institutional/industrial relations group that then dominated the labor field. Rees, a Chicago graduate and faculty member, wrote numerous well-received articles on unions, wages, inflation, unemployment and manpower programs. Two books, *The Economics of Trade Unions* (Rees 1962) and *Workers and Wages in an Urban Labor Market* (Rees and Schultz 1970), exemplify his ability to use neoclassical theory as the framework but also open up room for market imperfections and non-economic considerations. The latter book was co-authored with George Schultz, dean of the Chicago Graduate School of Business in the 1960s and professor of industrial relations. The publication of Rees's labor textbook, *The Economics of Work and Pay* (1973), along with Belton Fleischer's (1970) *Labor Economics*, effectively demarcate the inflection point in the labor field where it transitioned from the neo-institutional era to the neoclassical era. Fleischer had been on the Chicago faculty in the early 1960s.

Reder did two years of graduate work at Chicago in the 1940s and then came back from Stanford to serve on the Chicago faculty in 1974. He published a number of articles and books on topics in microeconomic theory and welfare economics, but the largest proportion was on labor topics related to wages, work hours, income distribution, unions and unemployment. Also noteworthy is his 1982 article 'Chicago economics: permanence and change', arguably the authoritative statement on the development and doctrines of the Chicago School. Reder also showed greater willingness and ability to use price theory in labor economics than was true of the neo-institutionalists, but far more than Friedman, Stigler or Lewis he wove in qualifications and highlighted shortcomings. For example, a year after Lester's critique of marginal productivity theory, Reder (1947) published his own analysis. The gist of his argument was that the theory may be accepted as a good approximation in a situation of pure competition since corporate managers are forced to maximize profit, but in cases of imperfect competition the predictions of the theory are less reliable because managers have discretion to pursue other goals. From a 'hard' Chicago perspective, this position uncomfortably skirts heterodoxy.

Likewise, in his comprehensive survey of the wage determination literature, Reder notes: 'There are two general approaches to the theory of wage structure. One is the market theory, or the competitive hypothesis, the other is what we might roughly term institutional' (Reder 1958, p. 84). Explicit in this statement is the position that the institutional analysis represents an alternative economic theory of wages, a claim that Lewis and the other hard neoclassicists deny (Becker 1971, Biddle 1996, p. viii). Reder goes on to conclude:

> [T]he wage and related data we possess refer primarily to a period in which short-run forces operated with unusual violence [the 1930s–40s], and the competitive hypothesis was therefore unusually ineffective. . . . However, for longer periods (for example, a half-century), or for making inter-area comparisons, there may be more to the competitive hypothesis, *for the purpose of* explaining relative wage rates, than most labor economists think. (Reder 1958, p. 85, emphasis in original)

Again, Reder makes a qualified case for the usefulness of competitive price theory but, at the same time, limits its applicability in the short run far more than Friedman or Stigler would accept.

Soft neoclassicism is not the hallmark of the next Chicago labor economist on our list; indeed, he made his reputation and earned his Nobel award for applying and extending price theory to the farthest reaches of economic behavior. I refer of course to Gary Becker. It seems fair to say that Becker has not only had the greatest impact on labor economics of any single economist in the post-Second World War period but also did the most to make the Chicago approach the dominant paradigm in the field and a highly successful invader of other disciplines *a là* 'economic imperialism'.

Becker received his PhD degree at Chicago in 1955 and taught on the faculty until 1957. He then left for a position at Columbia, returning to Chicago in 1969. He recounts that Friedman's graduate price theory course was by far his most influential classroom learning experience (Becker 1991). Becker wrote his dissertation under Lewis on the subject of discrimination and had it published as his first book, *The Economics of Discrimination* (Becker 1957). Becker looked at a competitive labor market with majority and minority workers, introduced a 'taste for discrimination' into the utility function of employers, employees and customers, and worked out the implications for relative wages and employment of the two groups. The book exemplified several themes that remained constants in Becker's subsequent half-century of high-profile publications: consideration of a topic then viewed as largely outside the domain of economic analysis; a corollary amount of criticism/antagonism from traditionalists and skeptics; a creative and sophisticated use of neoclassical price theory to model the problem and derive hypotheses; a check of the hypotheses with empirical data; and conclusions and implications favorable to free markets.

Becker's contributions to labor economics, and economics in general, span a wide range of subjects and could easily be the subject of an entire essay (see Sandmo 1993, Febrero and Schwartz 1995, see also the biography of Becker by Pedro Teixeira, ch. 16, this volume). Among them are union restrictions on entry, fertility, labor supply, human capital investment, marriage, time allocation, social interactions and crime, as well as a larger research program on rational choice.

Probably most fundamental and influential is Becker's theory of the allocation of time and his incorporation of production (and investment) into household behavior (Becker 1965). Traditional microeconomic theory postulates that individuals and households maximize a utility function made up of various market goods. Becker generalized this model by arguing that market goods are not the final determinants of satisfaction but are inputs that are combined with time in a household production function to create the final goods and services. Thus, a lobster dinner is not the determinant of satisfaction in the consumer's utility function; rather, it is the dining experience that is produced with the lobster dinner and the consumer's time.

The time allocation model has had a substantial influence in several areas of labor economics. One is labor supply. Becker's theory provides the basis for a significant generalization of the traditional labor/leisure model. For example, it provides a framework for considering joint household decision making, thus allowing for interaction between the labor supply decisions of husbands, wives and children (pursued in early dissertation work by Chicago students such as Glen Cain and Marvin Kosters). A second dimension opened up for analysis is the interaction between household fertility decisions and labor supply, while a third is modeling the life-cycle pattern of labor supply (Becker and Ghez 1975). The Becker model also suggests that the relevant income variable is not the observed income but 'full income' (non-labor income plus maximum attainable full-time earnings); leisure is not a final good in the utility function but an input of time with market goods to produce consumption experiences; the relevant prices affecting decision making are no longer observed market prices but also shadow prices that incorporate the opportunity costs of time; a change in the market wage yields a broader array of substitution effects, such as by changing input proportions in household production; and a change in labor supply that might appear to stem from a change in tastes becomes explicable as a reaction to a relative change in shadow prices. In keeping with Chicago tradition, Becker insists that these theoretical extensions are not to be viewed as ends in themselves but acquire significance to the degree that they help illuminate real-world behavior.

A second area of labor economics (broadly defined) that Becker has also pioneered is the economics of the family. One of his early and more controversial papers (at least then) developed an economic model of fertility choice (Becker 1960). Becker reasoned that the number of children couples have is to a significant degree a choice variable and thus presumably influenced by rational considerations of benefit and cost. He thus posited a demand function for children and showed that desired fertility should vary in a systematic way with the price of children (composed of both direct and opportunity costs), parents' potential earnings and various taste factors. This way of looking at fertility has since been widely used in the empirical literature of demography and population economics. Over the next two decades Becker carried forward this line of work and developed theories of marriage, divorce, household division of labor and the influence of family background on children's economic success, brought together in his book *A Treatise on the Family* (Becker 1981).

A third area of fundamental importance in labor economics in which Becker played a leading role is human capital. The concept of human capital, and its importance in economic growth, was highlighted in the late 1950s by (among others) Theodore Schultz, a specialist in economic development and agricultural economics at Chicago and a subsequent Nobel winner. Likewise, 15 years earlier, Friedman and Kuznets in a path-breaking book, *Income from Independent Professional Practice* (1945), had calculated the capitalized value of lifetime earnings, while Jacob Mincer at Columbia published an article on human capital and the distribution of income (1958). But it was Becker in his book *Human Capital* (1964) who really popularized the concept, analytically developed it and applied it in a broad-based way to labor markets. Becker showed that any use of resources that increases future human productivity at a cost today can be considered a form of human capital investment, and that the greater the investment the greater must be the future income in order to provide a competitive rate of return. This framework helped explain many observed features of labor markets, such as the positive correlation between education and income and the shape of age–earnings profiles. Also famous and oft-used is Becker's distinction between general and specific on-the-job training. Many Chicago and Columbia labor graduates (for example, Barry Chiswick, Giora Hanoch, Walter Oi, Solomon Polachek and Sherwin Rosen) made reputations by extending the theory and empirical analysis of human capital, while others took the human capital concept and applied it to related labor market phenomena, such as migration, health and occupational attainment.

Two more general points about Becker's work also deserve brief comment as they pertain to the larger evolution of labor economics and the Chicago School. During the 1950s the neo-institutional view of labor markets was ascendant and, as earlier described, these economists largely rejected a competitive explanation for wage determination, at least in the short-to-medium run. One line of criticism was directed at various (alleged) lacunas in marginal productivity theory, calling into question the existence of a well-defined downward-sloping labor demand curve. A second line of criticism suggested that there also exists no well-defined labor supply curve due to various imperfections and institutional constraints (for example, attenuated mobility, fixed employer work schedules, union contracts). Dunlop (1957) concluded that of the two the lack of an adequate labor supply theory was the most damaging, leading him to comment 'the pivotal task of wage theory is to formulate an acceptable theory on the supply side' (p. 128). Historically viewed, the Chicago neoclassical restoration in labor economics was built, first, by beating back the institutional criticism of the labor demand curve and, second, by providing the 'acceptable theory' of labor supply that Dunlop claimed was missing. Most certainly, both lines of attack were spearheaded by Chicago economists, and on the labor supply side Becker, Mincer and Lewis were guiding lights.

Becker's work has also led to an interesting evolution in the basic tenets of the Chicago School (or his branch). In the Friedman/Stigler era, 'Chicago economics' meant a commitment to neoclassical price theory, a competitive market model of the economy, and the efficient allocation of resources through market forces and the Invisible Hand. Not coincidentally, the titles of Friedman's and Stigler's economic textbooks were *Price Theory* (Friedman 1962) and *The Theory of Price* (Stigler 1946b) while one admirer labeled Stigler 'Adam Smith's best friend' (Rosenberg 1993). The focus of price theory is on markets and supply and demand, yet Becker's agenda is to extend economics into areas of human behavior (for example, marriage, the family) where resources are allocated and coordinated by *non-market* means. To accomplish this task, he has broadened traditional *price theory* into what might be called *choice theory* (Kaufman 2004b), where the linchpin of choice theory is the model of rational choice and, more specifically, the model of constrained utility maximization. Prices still play a fundamental role in guiding and coordinating human behavior, but now prices often take the form of shadow prices and operate in non-market institutions. Thus, Becker's 'economic approach' subsumes the competitive model but makes the central analytical construct the theory of rational behavior, thereby permitting economic analysis to be extended to virtually all forms of human behavior (Becker 1976a). Similarly, as a fortuitous byproduct, the domain of heterodox economics appears to be narrowed from various theories of imperfect competition to theories of non-choice or irrational choice (if such is possible), further marginalizing heterodox challengers and allowing Becker to assert 'there is only one kind of economic theory' (Becker 1971, p. viii).[4] A potential downside is worth noting, however. While Chicago economists still take as a null hypothesis the principle that market economies generate Invisible Hand outcomes (Lazear 2000), it is less obvious how a theory of rational choice generates this conclusion, particularly when this theory is used by many labor economists to explain the existence of rigid wages, unemployment, internal labor markets and a host of other seemingly non-competitive elements (Boyer and Smith 2001).

I now want to fill in the picture and bring it up to the present time with the contributions of a number of other Chicago economists. The list is quite large, so the space for each is limited.

First on the list is Jacob Mincer. Mincer did graduate work at Chicago and then finished at Columbia (Heckman 2003, Teixeira 2007). He relates in an oral history interview that he considered being called a labor economist 'an insult' (said in some jest) until he took Lewis's graduate labor course and saw that price theory could be applied to labor issues (Teixeira 2006, p. 10). After Becker joined the faculty at Columbia, he and Mincer began to collaborate, particularly through the auspices of the National Bureau of Economic Research (NBER). The two also jointly ran a Chicago-style Labor Economics Workshop at Columbia that was a fountainhead for the development of modern labor economics (Grossbard, 2006). In 2004 the Society of Labor Economists awarded Mincer its first lifetime achievement award in recognition of his role as 'the father of modern empirical labor economics'.

Among Mincer's many contributions to labor economics, two stand out for particular attention (Rosen 1992, Heckman 2003). The first was to formally model and empirically examine the determinants of married women's labor supply. In his first paper on the subject, presented at a conference organized by Lewis, Mincer (1962) reconciled two apparently conflicting trends: over time higher real wages and incomes were associated with rising female labor force participation, but at a point in time women with spouses with higher incomes participated less. At a conceptual level, Mincer's innovations were to cast the labor/leisure choice in a family context, broaden the income variable to include permanent and transitory components, and introduce the correlation between husband's and wife's earnings abilities; at an empirical level he was able to separately estimate income and substitution effects on married women's labor supply. He found that the latter was larger than the former and reconciled the time-series and cross-section trends by observing that higher female wages over time led to an expansion of female participation through the dominant substitution effect, while the negative income effect from the husband's earnings explains the cross-section result. Mincer's second major contribution was to develop the human capital earnings function and provide a theoretical explanation for the parabolic shape of the life-cycle age/earnings profile (Mincer 1974). The human capital earnings function (the log of earnings as a function of years of schooling, experience and other variables) quickly became one of the most widely used empirical tools in labor economics.

Next on the list is Sherwin Rosen. Rosen wrote his dissertation at Chicago, served on the economics faculty for many years, and died in his year (2001) as AEA president. Like fellow Chicago graduate Walter Oi, Rosen went against the tide and wrote his thesis on labor demand. Both Oi and Rosen examined the consequences of fixed costs for employment determination, in Rosen's case with regard to speed of adjustment to a demand shock. Rosen, like a number of Chicago faculty, also wrote on aspects of unions (Rosen 1969). Rosen's two most significant contributions to labor economics were his *JPE* paper on hedonic prices and implicit markets and his paper with Edward Lazear on tournament theories of compensation (Rosen 1974, Lazear and Rosen 1981). The former paper, although developed in terms of prices in product markets, has had wide application in labor economics. What Rosen showed was how competitive markets attach implicit prices to the N characteristics of indivisible goods, thereby achieving an efficient allocation of resources. The model has been widely used in labor economics as a generalization and formalization of Adam Smith's theory of compensating wage differentials and has been applied to topics such as employee benefits and occupational safety and health (see Hartog 2002).

I now come to another Nobel winner, James Heckman. Heckman has made major contributions to both economics and micro-econometrics, many of which were done in studies of labor markets. Heckman wrote his dissertation under Orley Ashenfelter at Princeton and then joined the Chicago Economics Department in 1973. His earliest work was on models of labor supply (frequently co-authored with graduate students and colleagues, such as Thomas MaCurdy, Christopher Flinn and Robert Willis). Among his contributions were to integrate the theories of consumption and labor supply, develop an empirical lifetime setting for labor supply and statistically analyze labor force participation, hours of work and wages. In all of this work he focused particularly on the identification and estimation of structural economic parameters from micro data (Blundell 2001). A central motivation for doing so, in turn, was to use these parameter estimates to simulate the effect on labor supply and other outcomes of existing or prospective policy programs (for example, the effect of introducing daycare vouchers on the labor supply of low-educated mothers).

A contribution Heckman is particularly renowned for is his work on sample selection bias. Selection bias arises in estimating structural models with causes of outcomes that are partially unobservable. A classic case is estimating the parameters of a labor supply function for married women, many of whom do not participate in the market and thus have an unobservable shadow wage. Building on earlier work by Lewis (1974) and others, Heckman in a long series of papers developed techniques to correct for selection bias, such as his famous two-step 'Heckit estimator' (Heckman 1979). Another area pioneered by Heckman is the separation of state dependence and heterogeneity in panel data. A labor example concerns unemployment: if we observe that people who were unemployed in the past are also more likely to be unemployed in the current period, can we infer a causal relation or does it arise from a stable but unobservable personal trait (for example, laziness)? Heckman's work in this area led to a long series of papers on fixed effects, discrete choice models, duration analysis, hazard models and event history methodology (Heckman 2001). Heckman's contributions are so wide and substantial that they form part of the toolkit of every current-day doctoral student in labor economics.

In the labor area, another Chicago economist deserving highlight is Edward Lazear. Although Lazear did his doctoral work at Harvard, he was greatly influenced by the Chicago approach and joined the Chicago faculty in 1974 (he is now at Stanford). Lazear has written articles and books on a variety of labor economics subjects, including earnings differentials, schooling, retirement and labor unions. His best-known contribution and source of recognition, however, is as the progenitor of the new labor subfield 'the economics of personnel'.[5] The economics of personnel is a classic case study of the Chicago approach in action. Before Lazear and other neoclassical economists came into the area, personnel/human resource management (HRM) was largely the province of management and industrial relations scholars and featured a research stream that was heavily descriptive and lacking either theoretical content or rigorous empirical analysis. Following Becker's lead, Lazear took numerous personnel topics, such as alternative methods of compensation, pensions, executive compensation and performance effects of incentive pay, and modeled them using the tools of price theory. The result was numerous hypotheses and implications that were new, insightful and a fertile area for empirical testing (Lazear 1999). As a result, the literature in the economics of personnel has boomed over the last two decades, leading by most accounts to a substantial invigoration of the HRM field (Gunderson 2001).

Lazear also served as founding editor of the *Journal of Labor Economics* (*JOLE*), established in1983 and published by the University of Chicago Press. Prior to the creation of *JOLE* most of the labor journals in the US catered to industrial relations and union topics (*Industrial and Labor Relations Review*, *Industrial Relations*, *Journal of Labor Research*), with the *Journal of Human Resources* (published at Wisconsin) being the major exception. As Chicago-style analytical labor economics blossomed over the 1970s, Lazear and others saw a need to create a new journal that would both welcome neoclassical research and serve as a forum for advancement of modern labor economics. *JOLE* was not only successful but quickly became the leading labor journal in the country and, arguably, the world. Through symposiums and special issues, *JOLE* also promoted and highlighted Chicago-related labor economists, such as special issues commemorating the contributions of Reder (1984), Rees (1990), Mincer (1993), Lewis (1994) and Ben-Porath (1997).

Overlapping with the economics of personnel is another rapidly growing collection of subfields in economics that is also having a major impact in labor, variously called contract and property rights economics, law and economics, and new institutional economics (NIE). Much of this literature traces its origins back to another Chicago Nobel winner, Ronald Coase, with significant contributions also coming from Chicago law professor (and judge) Richard Posner (Schwab 1997). (See biography of Posner, and essay on Chicago law and economics, both by Steven Medema, chs 26 and 11, respectively, in this volume.) In early neoclassical price theory, the institutional structure of the economy was typically taken as a 'given'. In another example of generalization and imperialism, Coase (1937, 1992) endogenized the economy's institutional structure by introducing a new cost concept (transaction cost) and using simple marginal reasoning to deduce conditions under which exchange would take place through markets or within formal organizations. This line of research has evolved in numerous directions with many applications to labor. Examples include the choice of employees versus independent contractors, team forms of production and large literatures on principal–agent, adverse selection and moral hazard problems in employment. While some of this research program is complementary to and supportive of orthodox price theory (for example, Alchian and Demsetz 1972), another portion, particularly in the NIE, opens the door in 'hard' Chicago circles to what may be an uncomfortable degree of heterodoxy (for example, Williamson 1985). Indeed, Coasean reasoning may call into question the theoretical integrity of the very model that has formed the core of traditional Chicago labor economics – the competitive labor market model. That is, if, as Coase claims, multi-person firms dissolve into single person proprietorships with zero transaction cost, then a perfectly competitive labor market seemingly cannot exist since firms have no employees and instead obtain labor services from independent contractors in product markets (Kaufman 2007). Here would be a large irony for Chicago!

In closing this review, discussion must be given to one other Chicago Nobel winner: Robert Lucas. Lucas is best known for his work in macroeconomics and monetary theory. But Lucas wrote his dissertation at Chicago in the early 1960s on a labor-related topic (substitution between capital and labor in US manufacturing) and in later years contributed a number of other articles dealing with labor markets, including real wages and inflation, unemployment in the Great Depression, and adjustment of labor markets to demand and supply shocks (Hall 1996). The modeling of labor markets by Lucas is 'classic Chicago' in that the theory is built on rational behavior and competitive equilibrium.

Conclusion

Viewed over the course of the twentieth century, the University of Chicago has had a larger influence on the development of labor economics than any other institution. This is surely a major achievement. The ingredients for success appear several-fold: a century-long commitment to the highest standards of scholarship and academic debate; a remarkable record of recruiting and developing creative, high-quality graduate students and faculty; prescient foresight that Marshallian partial equilibrium price theory would prove to be the most productive and insightful engine of analysis in economics; an unexcelled record of marrying innovative theory with empirical applications to real-world behavior; and a well-articulated normative commitment to and defense of individualism and free markets that has greatly influenced public policy and meshed well with the shift of world opinion toward market solutions to social problems.

Whether Chicago remains the preeminent intellectual force in labor economics in the twenty-first century is an interesting question that only time will tell. Without question, however, what we know as modern labor economics today springs first and foremost from Chicago. One only need look at the 53 chapters of the multi-volume *Handbook of Labor Economics* (Ashenfelter and Layard 1986, Ashenfelter and Card 1999) to see the imprint of Chicago everywhere. Success has its price, however, and Chicago now faces a field increasingly built in its own image and crowded with imitators, increasing the challenge of staying on top and maintaining a distinctive identity. But such are the rigors and challenges of competitive markets!

Notes

* The author acknowledges with appreciation the helpful information and comments provided by Gary Becker, Jeff Biddle, Glen Cain, Shoshana Grossbard, Lee Hansen, Edward Lazear, John Pencavel and Melvin Reder.

1. Douglas is identified on the title page of *The Worker in Modern Society* as Professor of Industrial Relations.
2. Jacob Mincer later showed that Douglas's finding for women was in error because he did not adequately separate income and substitution effects.
3. Derobert (2001) claims that Scitovsky (1951) first presented the modern labor–leisure diagram, but Stigler presented it earlier in *The Theory of Competitive Price* (1942).
4. The last quote comes from Becker's (1971) textbook which, revealingly, substitutes in the title the more general term 'economic theory' for the term 'price theory' used by Friedman and Stigler.
5. Lazear credits the name to Reder.

References

Adams, T.S. and H. Sumner (1905), *Labor Problems*, New York: Macmillan.

Alchian, A.A. and H. Demsetz (1972), 'Production, information costs, and economic organization', *American Economic Review*, **62** (5), 777–95.

American Economic Association (1982), 'H. Gregg Lewis: Distinguished Fellow', *American Economic Review*, **72** (4), frontispiece.

Ashenfelter, O. (1994), 'H. Gregg Lewis memorial comments', *Journal of Labor Economics*, **12** (1), 138–43.

Ashenfelter, O. and D. Card (1999), *Handbook of Labor Economics*, vol. 3, A–C, New York: Elsevier.

Ashenfelter, O. and R. Layard (1986), *Handbook of Labor Economics*, vols 1 and 2, Amsterdam: North-Holland.

Atkins, W.E., P.H. Douglas and C.N. Hitchcock (1923), *The Worker in Modern Economic Society*, Chicago, IL: University of Chicago Press.

Becker, G.S. (1957), *The Economics of Discrimination*, Chicago, IL: University of Chicago Press.

Becker, G.S. (1960), 'An economic analysis of fertility', in *Demographic and Economic Change in Developed Countries*, Princeton, NJ: Princeton University Press, pp. 209–31.

Becker, G.S. (1964), *Human Capital: A Theoretical and Empirical Analysis, with Special Reference to Education*, New York: Columbia University Press.

Becker, G.S. (1965), 'A theory of the allocation of time', *Economic Journal*, **75** (299), 493–515.

Becker, G.S. (1971), *Economic Theory*, New York: Alfred Knopf.

Becker, G.S. (1976a), *The Economic Approach to Human Behavior*, Chicago, IL: University of Chicago Press.

Becker, G.S. (1976b), 'Prefatory note', *Journal of Political Economy*, **84** (4, part 2: Essays in labor economics in honor of H. Gregg Lewis), S1.

Becker, G.S. (1981), *A Treatise on the Family*, Cambridge, MA: Harvard University Press.

Becker, G.S. (1991), 'Milton Friedman', in *Remembering the University of Chicago: Teachers, Scientists, and Scholars*, Shils, E. (ed.), Chicago, IL: University of Chicago Press, pp. 138–46.

Becker, G.S. and G. Ghez (1975), *The Allocation of Time and Goods over the Life Cycle*, New York: Columbia University Press.

Biddle, J.E. (1996), 'H. Gregg Lewis', in *American Economists of the Late 20th Century*, Samuels, W.J. (ed.), Cheltenham, UK and Brookfield, VT, USA: Edward Elgar, pp. 174–93.

Blundell, R. (2001), 'James Heckman's contributions to economics and econometrics', *Scandinavian Journal of Economics*, **103** (2), 191–203.

Boland, L.A. (2003), 'Methodological criticism vs. ideology and hypocrisy', *Journal of Economic Methodology*, **10** (4), 521–6.

Boyer, G.R. and R.S. Smith (2001), 'The development of the neoclassical tradition in labor economics', *Industrial and Labor Relations Review*, **54** (2), 199–223.

Bronfenbrenner, M. (1956), 'Potential monopsony in labor markets', *Industrial and Labor Relations Review*, **9** (4), 577–88.
Bronfenbrenner, M. (2004), 'Instead of a philosophy of life', in *Reflections of Eminent Economists*, Szenberg, M. and L. Ramrattan (eds), Cheltenham, UK and Northampton, MA, USA: Edward Elgar, pp. 95–107.
Brown, E.C., P.H. Douglas, F.H. Harbison, L. Lazaroff, W.M. Leiserson and S. Leland (1949), 'Harry Alvin Millis, 1873–1948', *American Economic Review*, **39** (3), 742–50.
Cain, G. (1979), 'Paul H. Douglas', in Sills, D. (ed.), *International Encyclopedia of the Social Sciences*, vol. 18, *Biographical Supplement*, New York: Free Press, pp. 153–6.
Coase, R.H. (1937), 'The nature of the firm', *Economica*, n.s. **4** (16), 386–405.
Coase, R.H. (1992), 'The institutional structure of production', *American Economic Review*, **82** (4), 713–19.
Derobert, L. (2001), 'On the genesis of the canonical labor supply model', *Journal of the History of Economic Thought*, **23** (2), 197–215.
Douglas, P.H. (1919), 'Plant administration of labor', *Journal of Political Economy*, **27** (7), 544–60.
Douglas, P.H. (1930), *Real Wages in the United States, 1890–1926*, Boston, MA: Houghton Mifflin.
Douglas, P.H. (1931), 'The partial stabilization of workers' incomes through unemployment insurance', *Annals of the American Academy of Political and Social Science*, **154**, 94–103.
Douglas, P.H. (1934), *The Theory of Wages*, New York: Macmillan.
Douglas, P.H. (1935), *Controlling Depressions*, New York: W.W. Norton.
Douglas, P.H. (1938), 'The economic theory of wage regulation', *University of Chicago Law Review*, **5** (2), 184–218.
Douglas, P.H. (1948), 'Are there laws of production?', *American Economic Review*, **38** (1), 1–41.
Douglas, P.H. (1971), *In the Fullness of Time: The Memoirs of Paul H. Douglas*, New York: Harcourt, Brace Jovanovich.
Douglas, P.H. and A. Director (1931), *The Problem of Unemployment*, New York: Macmillan.
Dunlop, J. (1957), 'The task of contemporary wage theory', in *New Concepts in Wage Determination*, Taylor, G.W. and F.C. Pierson (eds), New York: McGraw-Hill, pp. 117–39.
Dunlop, J. (1984), 'Industrial relations and economics: the common frontier of wage determination', in *Proceedings of the Thirty-ninth Annual Meeting*, Madison, WI: Industrial Relations Research Association, pp. 9–23.
Ely, R.T. (1886), *The Labor Movement in America*, New York: Thomas Crowell.
Emmett, R.B. (1998), 'Entrenching disciplinary competence: the role of general education and graduate study in Chicago economics', in *From Interwar Pluralism to Postwar Neoclassicism*, Morgan, M.S. and M. Rutherford (eds), Durham, NC: Duke University Press, pp. 134–50.
Febrero, R. and P.S. Schwartz (eds) (1995), *The Essence of Becker*, Stanford, CA: Stanford University Press.
Fleischer, B. (1970), *Labor Economics: Theory and Evidence*, Englewood Cliffs, NJ: Prentice-Hall.
Freedman, C.F. (1998), 'No ends to means: George Stigler's profit motive', *Journal of Post Keynesian Economics*, **20** (4), 621–48.
Freeman, R. and J. Medoff (1984), *What Do Unions Do?*, New York: Basic Books.
Friedman, M. (1951), 'Some comments on the significance of labor unions for economic policy', in *The Impact of the Union*, Wright, D.M. (ed.), New York: Harcourt Brace, pp. 204–34.
Friedman, M. (1953), 'The methodology of positive economics', in *Essays in Positive Economics*, Chicago, IL: University of Chicago Press, pp. 3–43.
Friedman, M. (1962), *Price Theory: A Provisional Text*, Chicago, IL: Aldine.
Friedman, M. and S. Kuznets (1945), *Income from Independent Professional Practice*, New York: National Bureau of Economic Research.
Grossbard, S. (ed.) (2006), *Jacob Mincer: A Pioneer of Modern Labor Economics*, New York: Springer.
Gunderson, M. (2001), 'Economics of personnel and human resource management', *Human Resource Management Review*, **11** (4), 431–52.
Hall, R.E. (1996), 'Robert Lucas, recipient of the 1995 Nobel Memorial Prize in Economics', *Scandinavian Journal of Economics*, **98** (1), 33–48.
Hamilton, W.H. (1916), 'The development of Hoxie's economics', *Journal of Political Economy*, **24** (9), 855–83.
Hartog, J. (2002), 'Desperately seeking structure: Sherwin Rosen (1938–2001)', *Economic Journal*, **112** (483), F519–31.
Heckman, J.J. (1979), 'Sample selection bias as a specification error', *Econometrica*, **47** (1), 153–61.
Heckman, J.J. (2001), 'Micro data, heterogeneity, and the evaluation of public policy: Nobel lecture', *Journal of Political Economy*, **109** (4), 673–748.
Heckman, J.J. (2003), 'Some brief remarks on the life and work of Jacob Mincer', *Review of Economics of the Household*, **1** (4), 245–7.
Hicks, J.R. (1932), *The Theory of Wages*, London: Macmillan.
Hoxie, R.F. (1907), 'The trade-union point of view', *Journal of Political Economy*, **15** (6), 345–63.

Hoxie, R.F. (1915), *Scientific Management and Labor*, New York: Appleton.

Hoxie, R.F. (1917), *Trade Unionism in the United States*, New York: Appleton.

Kaufman, B.E. (1988), *How Labor Markets Work: Reflections on Theory and Practice by John Dunlop, Clark Kerr, Richard Lester, and Lloyd Reynolds*, Lexington, MA: DC Heath.

Kaufman, B.E. (2000), 'Personnel/human resource management: its roots as applied economics', in *Toward a History of Applied Economics*, Backhouse, R.E. and J.E. Biddle (eds), Durham, NC: Duke University Press, pp. 229–56.

Kaufman, B.E. (2004a), *Global Evolution of Industrial Relations: Events, Ideas, and the IIRA*, Geneva: International Labor Organization.

Kaufman, B.E. (2004b), 'The institutional and neoclassical schools in labor economics', in *The Institutionalist Tradition in Labor Economics*, Champlin, D.P. and J.T. Knoedler (eds), Armonk, NY: M.E. Sharpe, pp. 13–38.

Kaufman, B.E. (2006), 'Industrial relations and labor institutionalism: a century of boom and bust', *Labor History*, **47** (3), 295–318.

Kaufman, B.E. (2007), 'The impossibility of a perfectly competitive labor market', *Cambridge Journal of Economics*, **31** (5), 775–87.

Kerr, C. (1994), 'Social economics revisionists: the "real world" study of labor markets and institutions', in *Labor Economics and Industrial Relations: Markets and Institutions*, Kerr, C. and P.D. Staudoher (eds), Cambridge, MA: Harvard University Press, pp. 66–108.

Knight, F.H. (1933), 'Capitalistic production, time and the rate of return', in *Economic Essays in Honour of Gustav Cassel*, London: George Allen & Unwin, pp. 327–42.

Lampman, R.J. (1993), *Economists at Wisconsin, 1892–1992*, Madison, WI: Department of Economics, University of Wisconsin.

Lazear, E.P. (1999), 'Personnel economics: past lessons and future directions', *Journal of Labor Economics*, **17** (2), 199–236.

Lazear, E.P. (2000), 'Economic imperialism', *Quarterly Journal of Economics*, **115** (1), 99–146.

Lazear, E.P. and S. Rosen (1981), 'Rank-order tournaments as optimal labor contracts', *Journal of Political Economy*, **89** (5), 841–64.

Lester, R.A. (1941), *The Economics of Labor*, New York: Macmillan.

Lester, R.A. (1946), 'Shortcomings of marginal analysis for wage-employment problems', *American Economic Review*, **36** (1), 63–82.

Lewis, H.G. (1951), 'The labor-monopoly problem: a positive program', *Journal of Political Economy*, **59** (4), 277–87.

Lewis, H.G. (1956), 'Hours of work and hours of leisure', in *Proceedings of the Ninth Annual Meetings*, Champaign, IL: Industrial Relations Research Association, pp. 196–206.

Lewis, H.G. (1959), 'Competitive and monopoly unionism', in *The Public Stake in Union Power*, Bradley, P. (ed.), Charlottesville, VA: University of Virginia Press, pp. 181–208.

Lewis, H.G. (1963), *Unionism and Relative Wages in the United States: An Empirical Inquiry*, Chicago, IL: University of Chicago Press.

Lewis, H.G. (1969), 'Interes del Empleador en las Horas de Trabajo del Empleado' (Employer interest in employee work hours), *Cuadernos de Economia*, **18**, 38–54.

Lewis, H.G. (1974), 'Comments on selectivity biases in wage comparisons', *Journal of Political Economy*, **82** (6), 1145–55.

Lewis, H.G. (1986), *Union Relative Wage Effects: A Survey*, Chicago, IL: University of Chicago Press.

Manning, A. (2003), *Monopsony in Motion: Imperfect Competition in Labor Markets*, Princeton, NJ: Princeton University Press.

Marshall, A. (1890), *Principles of Economics*, London: Macmillan.

McNulty, P.J. (1980), *The Origins and Development of Labor Economics: A Chapter in the History of Social Thought*, Cambridge, MA: MIT Press.

Miller, H.L., Jr. (1962), 'On the "Chicago School of Economics"', *Journal of Political Economy*, **70** (1), 64–9.

Millis, H.A. (1914), 'Some aspects of the minimum wage', *Journal of Political Economy*, **22** (2), 132–59.

Millis, H.A. (1949), 'Testimony', in *Legislative History of the National Labor Relations Act, 1935*, US National Labor Relations Board (ed.), Washington, DC: US Government Printing Office, pp. 1553–6.

Millis, H.A. and E.C. Brown (1950), *From the Wagner Act to Taft–Hartley: A Study of National Labor Policy and Labor Relations*, Chicago, IL: University of Chicago Press.

Millis, H.A. and R.E. Montgomery (1938a), *Labor's Progress and Some Basic Labor Problems*, New York: McGraw-Hill.

Millis, H.A. and R.E. Montgomery (1938b), *Labor's Risks and Social Insurance*, New York: McGraw-Hill.

Mincer, J.A. (1958), 'Investment in human capital and personal income distribution', *Journal of Political Economy*, **66** (4), 281–302.

Mincer, J.A. (1962), 'Labor force participation of married women', in *Aspects of Labor Economics*, National Bureau of Economic Research (ed.), Princeton, NJ: Princeton University Press, pp. 63–106.
Mincer, J.A. (1974), *Schooling, Experience, and Earnings*, New York: Columbia University Press.
Oi, W. (2004), 'A view from the Midway', in *Reflections of Eminent Economists*, Szenberg, M. and L. Ramrattan (eds), Cheltenham, UK and Northampton, MA, USA: Edward Elgar, pp. 332–41.
Pierson, F.C. (1957), 'An evaluation of wage theory', in *New Concepts in Wage Determination*, Taylor, G.W. and F.C. Pierson (eds), New York: McGraw-Hill, pp. 3–31.
Reder, M.W. (1947), 'A reconsideration of the marginal productivity theory', *Journal of Political Economy*, **55** (5), 450–58.
Reder, M.W. (1958), 'Wage determination in theory and practice', in *A Decade of Industrial Relations Research, 1946–1956*, Chamberlin, N.W., F.C. Pierson and T. Wolfson (eds), New York: Harper & Bros., pp. 64–97.
Reder, M.W. (1982), 'Chicago economics: permanence and change', *Journal of Economic Literature*, **20** (1), 1–38.
Reder, M.W. (2003), 'Remarks on "The methodology of positive economics"', *Journal of Economic Methodology*, **10** (4), 527–30.
Rees, A. (1962), *The Economics of Trade Unions*, Chicago, IL: University of Chicago Press.
Rees, A. (1973), *The Economics of Work and Pay*, New York: Harper & Row.
Rees, A. (1976), 'H. Gregg Lewis and the development of analytical labor economics', *Journal of Political Economy*, **84** (4, part 2: Essays in labor economics in honor of H. Gregg Lewis), S3–8.
Rees, A. and G.P. Schultz (1970), *Workers and Wages in an Urban Labor Market*, Chicago, IL: University of Chicago Press.
Reynolds, L.G. (1949), *Labor Economics and Labor Relations*, Englewood Cliffs, NJ: Prentice-Hall.
Robinson, J. (1933), *The Economics of Imperfect Competition*, London: Macmillan.
Rosen, S. (1969), 'Trade union power, threat effects and the extent of organization', *Review of Economic Studies*, **36** (2), 185–96.
Rosen, S. (1974), 'Hedonic prices and implicit markets: product differentiation in pure competition', *Journal of Political Economy*, **82** (1), 34–55.
Rosen, S. (1992), 'Mincering labor economics', *Journal of Economic Perspectives*, **6** (2), 157–70.
Rosen, S. (1994), 'H. Gregg Lewis and modern labor economics', *Journal of Labor Economics*, **12** (1), 139–43.
Rosenberg, N. (1993), 'George Stigler: Adam Smith's best friend', *Journal of Political Economy*, **101** (5), 833–48.
Rottenberg, S. (1956), 'On choice in labor markets', *Industrial and Labor Relations Review*, **9** (2), 183–99.
Samuels, W.J. (ed.) (1976), *The Chicago School of Political Economy*, East Lansing, MI: Association for Evolutionary Economics and Division of Research, Graduate School of Business Administration, Michigan State University.
Samuelson, P.A. (1979), 'Paul Douglas's measurement of production functions and marginal productivities', *Journal of Political Economy*, **87** (5, part 1), 923–39.
Sandmo, A. (1993), 'Gary Becker's contributions to economics', *Scandinavian Journal of Economics*, **91** (1), 7–23.
Schoenberg, E.H. and P.H. Douglas (1937), 'Studies in the supply curve of labor: the relation in 1929 between average earnings in American cities and the proportions seeking employment', *Journal of Political Economy*, **45** (1), 45–79.
Schwab, S. (1997), 'The law and economics approach to workplace regulation', in *Government Regulation of the Employment Relationship*, Kaufman, B.E. (ed.), Madison, WI: Industrial Relations Research Institute, pp. 91–123.
Scitovsky, T. (1951), *Welfare and Competition: The Economics of a Fully Employed Economy*, Chicago, IL: R.D. Irwin.
Simon, H.A. (1951), 'A formal theory of the employment relationship', *Econometrica*, **19** (3), 293–305.
Simons, H.C. (1948), *Economic Policy for a Free Society*, Chicago, IL: University of Chicago Press.
Stigler, G.J. (1942), *The Theory of Competitive Price*, New York: Macmillan.
Stigler, G.J. (1946a), 'The economics of minimum wage legislation', *American Economic Review*, **36** (3), 358–65.
Stigler, G.J. (1946b), *The Theory of Price*, New York: Macmillan.
Stigler, G.J. (1949), 'Monopolistic competition in retrospect', in *Five lectures on Economic Problems*, London: Longmans, Green, pp. 12–34.
Stigler, G.J. (1962), 'Information in the labor market', *Journal of Political Economy*, **70** (5, part 2: Investment in human beings), 94–105.
Teixeira, P. (2006), 'An interview with Jacob Mincer', in *Jacob Mincer: A Pioneer of Modern Labor Economics*, Grossbard, S. (ed.), New York: Springer, pp. 7–18.
Teixeira, P.N. (2007), *Jacob Mincer: A Founding Father of Modern Labour Economics*, Oxford: Oxford University Press.

Twentieth Century Fund, Labor Committee (1942), *How Collective Bargaining Works: A Survey of Experience in Leading American Industries*, New York: Twentieth Century Fund.
Wallis, W.A. (1993), 'George J. Stigler: in memoriam', *Journal of Political Economy*, **101** (5), 774–9.
Williamson, O.E. (1985), *The Economic Institutions of Capitalism: Firms, Markets, Relational Contracting*, New York: Free Press.
Wright, D.M. (1951), 'Selections from the discussion of Friedman's paper', in *The Impact of the Union*, D.M. Wright (ed.), New York: Harcourt Brace, pp. 235–59.

10 *Human Capital*, by Gary S. Becker: a reading guide

Pedro Nuno Teixeira

Introduction

The metaphor of skilled people as a costly type of capital has faced troubled times since its first appearance. Until the mid-twentieth century most economists paid little attention to the economic analysis of education and hesitated in using 'human capital' as an analogy for skilled labor. Resistance came from a belief that education gave access to nice and well-paid jobs without enhancing people's productivity, and because it seemed problematic and not realistic to regard qualified labor as a type of capital. The belief in education's irrelevant role in labor market outcomes was strengthened by the fact that the economic study of labor markets was unconnected to the analysis of education. Accordingly, human capital research did not develop much during the first 150 years or so of the existence of economics as an independent subject of scientific inquiry.

In the aftermath of the Second World War this situation changed, prompted by several developments that converged to give increasing prominence to the economic effects of education. One of those changes was the changing possibilities and interests in the research on personal income, namely the belief that it was possible to provide causal explanations for the distribution of income, and that education was a good candidate to be included among those potential explanatory factors. The second aspect was the post-war revival of growth debates that, alongside the expansion of educational systems in most Western countries, led to an increasing emphasis on the qualification of the labor forces as a key factor in explaining differentiated growth performances. Lastly, the neoclassical ascendancy in economics in general and labor in particular challenged the notion that the labor market required unique treatment, paving the way to the systematic application of the tools of neoclassical analysis to this area of research.

From metaphor to research program

Seizing the moment, a group of economists frequently connected with Chicago, namely T.W. Schultz, Jacob Mincer and Gary Becker, managed to turn the metaphor of human 'capital' into a research program that would spread across the discipline's subfields. The human capital theorists regarded the metaphor as a potent explanation for various aspects of economic research. The discipline became fully aware of the metaphor's use through Schultz, especially with his Presidential Address to the American Economic Association (Schultz 1961), and he had a prominent role in disseminating the concept in its early years among economists and policy makers. However, since the 1960s, human capital has become progressively associated with Becker.

Becker has long been interested in applying economic theory to new topics or areas of human behavior that were not normally analyzed from a price-theoretic perspective. In the late 1950s (1957) when Becker started worked at the National Bureau of Economic

Research (NBER), he decided to analyze the monetary rates of return to different levels of education, especially college. The stimulus of one of his mentors, T.W. Schultz, as well as the interest and discussions raised in the activities of the Columbia Labor Workshop, especially his increasingly close relationship with Mincer, made him enlarge the scope of the project. Accordingly, in 1964 Gary Becker published his monograph *Human Capital*,[1] extending the theoretical framework outlined in papers he had already published to provide an extensive picture of what was already becoming known as 'human capital theory' (Becker 1960, 1962). He defined human capital as 'activities that influence future monetary and psychic income by increasing resources in people' (Becker 1993, p. 11). Its main forms were schooling and on-the-job training, although he also considered medical care, migration and searching for information about prices and incomes.

As Becker explains in the preface to the first edition, the work grew in terms of theory and empirical evidence. On the one hand, Becker became increasingly focused on developing a general theory of human capital investment, and not merely on assessing the profitability of those investments. That included an explanatory framework for the shape of age–earning profiles, the concentration of human capital investment at earlier ages and the personal distribution of income, on the basis of the process of accumulation of human capital, and extending Mincer's work on personal distribution of earnings by relating the distribution of earnings explicitly to rates of return and investment costs (Teixeira 2007). On the other hand, the empirical analysis, initially focused on the Census reports on the incomes of persons with different amounts of education and reports from the Office of Education on the costs of education, enlarged its coverage to different groups and periods.

Becker begins his analysis by focusing on the hitherto largely overlooked on-the-job training (ch. III). Emphasis on this type of capital is justified for its importance among types of human capital, and the transferability of the analysis for other types of human capital. The fact that workers increase their skills while on the job has not only an impact on future productivity but also a cost, namely the time used in training activities that could have been used in productive efforts. He therefore tries to investigate the economic decision-making process regulating the quantity and time spent in training.

Becker starts from the equilibrium conditions of the competitive firm, including the costs and returns to the firm providing training, and then introduces the henceforth-classic distinction between specific and general human capital, the former being 'that type useful in many firms besides those providing it' (p. 33). Since this type of training increases the marginal product of the worker in other firms, the firm will have no incentive to bear any of its cost, but rather pass it to the worker. The latter is willing to take it, because this training increases future earnings, regardless of the firm he/she is working with, hence, workers accept wages below their current opportunity level in order to cover the costs of their training. This will produce a steeper curve of earnings, since at earlier ages workers will bear the costs of training and at later ages will benefit from this investment. Then, Becker analyzes specific training, which increases the productivity of the worker more to the firm providing it. Since in this case the worker loses most of the benefit by moving to another firm, he/she will not be willing to support its costs. By contrast, the firm will be willing to support most of its cost, since it will collect the returns in the form of higher productivity. Firms will tend to pay a premium to workers benefiting from specific training in order to reduce turnover and therefore avoid losing the investment made (which becomes a sort of sunk cost).[2] Becker acknowledges that most training actually is neither completely specific nor general, and therefore the cost will tend to be shared between the worker and the firm. The way this will be shared will depend on other attitudes such as attitudes towards risk, desires for liquidity and especially patterns of labor turnover. He then makes a brief analysis of the case of schooling, using an analogy with on-the-job training. Schools are regarded as firms specialized in the production of training, in which case the costs are largely supported by the individual, namely in the form of lower earnings (forgone earnings of full-time students).

In the following chapter (IV) Becker discusses the assessment of the rate of return to the investment in human capital. He focuses on the case of general training, assuming that specific training can be analyzed on similar grounds. He analyzes the way in which human capital (costs and returns) can be introduced into an equation representing the present value of lifetime net earnings. The approach nevertheless faces two problems: a priori knowledge and specification of the investment period is not straightforward, and the investment period does not correlate perfectly with the forgone earnings. Thus, Becker decides to adopt an approach that assumes the cost of an investment in human capital as the earnings forgone and the rate of capitalization as a weighted average of the rates of return on the individual investments. By doing this one does not need to know the period of investment, since this, and the costs and returns, can simultaneously be estimated from information on net earnings.

Becker's solution allows him to explore the evolution of the incentive to invest in human capital in different periods, notably the relation between life span and the rate of return (pp. 86ff). This has the advantage of providing a unified explanation for an array of behavior related to human capital. First, he can explain the longer periods of schooling demanded by younger generations, not so much as a result of a different mentality as of different incentives, that is, longer periods of life allowed longer periods for collecting the returns to these investments (thus raising their profitability). Second, he can help us to understand why individuals switch between activities; those with a preference for more general training and less specific training depress their prospects in terms of earnings. The obvious candidates here are females. Third, he can argue that the spread of education was largely induced by technological progress; the demand for skilled labor rising changed the relative rates of return (as measured by wage differences and costs). Finally, the lifetime perspective helps to place into perspective the difficulties in financing investments in human capital and the risk of underinvestment due to shortsighted behavior by youngsters. Becker believed these difficulties to be exaggerated if one took into account what happened with other types of capital and the stronger incentives to invest at earlier ages.

Expanding the research program's research

After publication of the first edition of *Human Capital*, the decision to place human capital choices within a lifetime framework allowed Becker to reformulate consumer theory by adjusting it to encompass the allocation of time and goods within the household (Becker 1965). In the book, the model is extended, by introducing a third sector (investments in human capital) to a framework of decisions over time and to investment in human capital (pp. 70ff). This approach aimed to include the interaction between changes in wage rates over the life cycle resulting from the accumulation of human capital, the allocation of time between market and non-market sectors, and the impact of human capital on the productivity of household behavior at a time when Becker was largely focused on his economic analysis of family behavior.[3] This framework explains the decline of investment in human capital with age, due to reduced profitability (smaller time-spans and rising forgone earnings). This approach also underlines the effect of human capital on non-market efficiency, leading for instance to different patterns of consumption.

By the late 1960s, Becker also devoted significant attention to income distribution and the development of a theory determining the amount of investment in human capital by a 'representative' person and the relationship between earnings, investments and rates of return, as shown in his Woytinsky Lecture (Becker 1967, see Becker 1993, pp. 108ff).[4] In his model, Becker starts by analyzing the demand and supply curves for human capital. The demand curves are assumed to be downward sloping due to diminishing marginal returns to investment in human capital, based on intellectual and physical limitations. Moreover, later investments present lower returns since these benefit the worker during shorter periods. Supply curves are assumed as upward sloping due to the fact that funds available for each individual are not only limited but also increasingly costly, hence the return has to compensate the rising cost.

Becker then analyzes the differences in investments in human capital as the result of differences in the supply or demand conditions (pp. 119ff). In the former case, what he calls the 'egalitarian view', the differences in human capital are seen as the result of different opportunities due to differences in environment, luck or family wealth. In the case of differences in the demand, what he calls the 'elite view', inequality is the result of individual differences in the capacity to benefit from investments in human capital. In this case some people are assumed as more able than others, achieving higher returns for the same investment, thus having an additional incentive to invest more in human capital. The level of opportunities is assumed in this case as generally similar. He considers that to explain the same level of inequality, the egalitarian approach has to presume a higher inequality of opportunities than the elite approach about capacities. He then explores the possibility of varying both the demand and supply curves per individual, though he thinks they tend to be related (p. 131).

For Becker it was the interacting effect between ability and schooling that helped to clarify Pigou's paradox, that is, the skewness of the income distribution curve. More able students would have a higher incentive to invest in human capital, thus accentuating the inequality in the distribution of each aspect individually considered (p. 97). In this context he considers as well the effect of family background and its importance by affecting both the supply and demand conditions for the individual, giving some attention to the distribution of property income (p. 144). Overall he suggests some overstatement of the effect of schooling on earnings, and understatement of the effect of background. He finishes this section by discussing the possible effects in terms of efficiency and equity of certain public policies aiming to change the differences in the level of investments in human capital. This includes policies promoting equality of opportunities, objective selection, compulsory minimum levels of investment in human capital and improvements in the capital market.

In the second part of the book, Becker develops his empirical analysis, which he finds generally supportive of the human capital approach. The main group analyzed is that of white male college graduates, by using cross-section samples for 1939 and 1949 (ch. V). In the analysis Becker emphasizes the relevance of forgone earnings in terms of costs, rather than direct costs, and thus the impact of good economic conditions and the lack of information and motivation as the main reasons limiting poorer students' investment in human capital. He also considers, though less extensively, other groups of college students, such as college dropouts, non-whites, women and rural workers (pp. 183ff). Overall, these groups present smaller though not negligible returns. This analysis indicates significant variability between and within groups (p. 195), something that would occupy a lot of subsequent research on human capital. Rates of return were also calculated for high-school graduates for several years of the first half of the twentieth century (ch. VII), which seem to decline less than those of college education during the same period.

Becker acknowledges several empirical limitations, such as the fact that the data are cross-sectional (hence, more vulnerable to the effects of business cycles), and the concentration on formal education. However, the main problem is the possible effect of other factors, namely ability, leading to an overestimation of the effect of schooling (pp. 171ff). He makes some adjustments trying to standardize the returns for ability, namely by comparing the case of college students with that of high-school graduates. The results for the separate adjustments for rank in high school, IQ, and father's occupation, suggest to Becker that the rate to college education for a typical graduate is still consistently higher than that of the typical high-school graduate. He also analyzes college dropouts, and his results indicate that these have rates of return (and IQs) slightly higher than high-school graduates and lower than college graduates, which is interpreted as further support of the human capital interpretation. Finally, he analyzes the sample of brothers assembled by Donald Gorseline (1932) in his pioneering work, underlining the effect of education even when attempting to standardize for other factors. The subsequent research on the economic effects of education would devote significant attention to this interaction, namely to the possible correlation between IQ levels and educational demand.

In his empirical work, Becker clearly privileges the study of the private monetary returns to human capital, due to the difficulties associated with the measurement of externalities and social benefits (ch. VI). The topic is rather complex since the limitations in terms of measurement made the results very vulnerable to criticisms. His stance is illustrated by the fact that Becker diminished the emphasis on the social benefits from his earlier estimates of the returns to human capital, and by the time he finished the book, these were significantly underplayed. It suggests that the more he delved into it the less convinced he became that at the time he could make a strong empirical case for the existence of these benefits. The analysis of these social and non-pecuniary benefits would require specific empirical work that would be done some years later at the NBER and by some of his doctoral students.

Becker also explores empirically the effects of earnings and wealth at different lifetime stages (ch. VIII). He concludes that the average incomes at each class age are strongly related to education. Incomes tend to be relatively low at the beginning of labor force participation, then rise, peak at middle ages (45–54) and decline later. However, both the rise in income and the peak age seem to be clearly (and positively) related to levels of education and other investments in human capital. Moreover, the rates of return do not seem to be affected either by additional years of schooling (when adjusted for ability), or by the rapid growth in the number of high-school and college graduates. According to Becker, the rise of mass education instead of bringing a strong decrease in returns, as implied by the scarcity hypothesis and the idea of quasi-rents for educated workers, had shown some stability, and by this endorsed productivity effects of investments in human capital, and of a skill-biased technological progress that demanded increasing levels of qualified labor.

Criticisms

From its early days, human capital research faced significant resistance. Initially, the problems mostly concerned the label 'human capital' sounding like exploitation, making the concept a problematic one not immediately well accepted either within or beyond the disciplinary boundaries. Becker was initially dubious about using the expression due to the potential controversy it could and would cause, though he eventually decided to stick with it and face the critics. Moreover, the fact that this approach came to epitomize the attempts of applying (neoclassical) economics to a growing array of social issues created additional resistances within and outside economics. The criticisms to human capital research echoed earlier debates about the best approach to labor economics, notably the applicability of the market metaphor to labor issues and the potential for measurement and quantification (Teixeira 2007). It was also the role of education and its economic effects, with many authors believing that education was primarily a socializing force that instilled values of discipline, obedience and motivation that were rewarded by the labor market. Then there were those emphasizing the family background effect on earnings, suggesting that students with better opportunities would have much better possibilities of achieving and benefiting from higher levels of education.

However, the major challenge to human capital theory came in terms of the role of education against that of ability. Accordingly, education basically identified students with particular attributes, acquired either at birth or by virtue of family background, but did not produce or improve those attributes, thus reducing education's social role to its ability to select more productive individuals and provide that information to employers. This was in a sense part and parcel of increasing attention to the topic of imperfect information in the theory of markets, which gained momentum in the early 1970s. The problem with ability was that of being possibly correlated with schooling achievement, which made it extremely hard to disentangle the effects of the one and the other. This would lead to a very long debate on the real effects of schooling and extensive empirical research on the isolation of both effects.

Conclusion

The development of human capital theory owes much to the collective and articulated research efforts of a group of authors, of whom the pioneers were Schultz, Mincer and Becker. For Becker, human capital started as an analysis of lifetime patterns of income and decisions concerning investment on these activities (schooling and on-the-job training). However, already in the 1960s it became increasingly a framework for understanding several aspects of lifetime human behavior, providing an effective and powerful example of the ability of economics to deal with social issues. With time, Becker used human capital more and more as a building block for his 'economic approach' to social behavior (Becker 1976). The purpose was not to find what could distinguish economics from other social sciences, but to give economics the capacity to provide a unified perspective on human behavior in all its different contexts, through the basic assumptions of maximizing behavior, market equilibrium, and stable preferences. The role of human capital in Becker's 'economic approach' is illustrated by the chapters included in the third and last part of the book, consisting of previously published papers covering the inequality within and between families over generations (ch. IX), the division of labor and coordination costs (ch. X) and the interaction of human capital with fertility patterns and economic growth (ch. XI). These chapters point out both the wide applicability of the human capital approach and the loosening of its conceptual content.

The growing acceptance of the concept is the result of changes in other social sciences, namely through the increasing pervasiveness of rational choice theory in fields such as sociology and political science, and a tribute to the major impact that Becker has had beyond economics, being one of the most cited economists not only in economics, but also in many social sciences.

Notes

1. The third edition of *Human Capital* (Becker 1993) will be taken as our reference point, because it is the most readily available to the reader. The structure of the book, however, has not fundamentally changed since the first edition (1964); everything included in previous editions has been kept. In the second edition, Becker (1975) introduced three addenda: the first on the allocation of time and goods over time, taken from his monograph with Gilbert Ghez (1975, pp. 70–85); and two on income distribution – a portion of his paper with Barry Chiswick (1966), and his Woytinsky Lecture (1967). In the third edition Becker added a general overview of the achievements of human capital research, and a section consisting of three previously published papers on the relevance of human capital for family inequality, the division of labor and fertility behavior.
2. Becker picks up here the theme of trained labor as a quasi-fixed factor, first suggested by Walter Oi (1962).
3. Along these lines was his work with one of his students, Gilbert Ghez, on the allocation of resources by families over the lifetime of their members (Becker and Ghez 1975). Some initial work had been developed earlier by Yoram Ben-Porath (1967) in his doctoral dissertation at Harvard.
4. Initial attempts included his work with Barry Chiswick on a statistical formulation of income distribution that made explicit the relationship between earnings and the investment period, which they used to analyze regional differences within the US (Becker and Chiswick 1966, see Becker 1993, p. 102).

References

Becker, G.S. (1960), 'An economic analysis of fertility', in *Demographic and Economic Change in Developed Countries*, Princeton, NJ: Princeton University Press, pp. 209–31.

Becker, G.S. (1962), 'Investment in human capital: a theoretical analysis', *Journal of Political Economy*, **70** (5, part 2: Investment in human beings), 9–49.

Becker, G.S. (1964), *Human Capital: A Theoretical and Empirical Analysis, with Special Reference to Education*, New York: Columbia University Press.

Becker, G.S. (1965), 'A theory of the allocation of time', *Economic Journal*, **75** (299), 493–515.

Becker, G.S. (1967), *Human Capital and the Personal Distribution of Income: An Analytical Approach*, Ann Arbor, MI: University of Michigan, Institute of Public Administration.

Becker, G.S. (1975), *Human Capital: A Theoretical and Empirical Analysis, with Special Reference to Education*, 2nd edn, New York: Columbia University Press.

Becker, G.S. (1976), *The Economic Approach to Human Behavior*, Chicago, IL: University of Chicago Press.

Becker, G.S. (1993), *Human Capital: A Theoretical and Empirical Analysis, with Special Reference to Education*, 3rd edn, Chicago, IL: University of Chicago Press.

Becker, G.S. and B.R. Chiswick (1966), 'Education and the distribution of earnings', *American Economic Review*, **56** (1/2), 358–69.

Becker, G.S. and G. Ghez (1975), *The Allocation of Time and Goods over the Life Cycle*, New York: Columbia University Press.

Ben-Porath, Y. (1967), 'The production of human capital and the life cycle of earnings', *Journal of Political Economy*, **75** (4, Part 1), 352–65.
Gorseline, D.E. (1932), *The Effect of Schooling upon Income*, Bloomington, IN: University of Indiana Press.
Oi, W. (1962), 'Labor as a quasi-fixed factor', *Journal of Political Economy*, **70** (6), 538–55.
Schultz, T.W. (1961), 'Investment in human capital', *American Economic Review*, **51** (1), 1–17.
Teixeira, P.N. (2007), *Jacob Mincer: A Founding Father of Modern Labour Economics*, Oxford: Oxford University Press.

11 Chicago law and economics

*Steven G. Medema**

Introduction

The field of law and economics is arguably the most successful of economics' various imperialistic movements, and this success has been driven largely by scholars from the University of Chicago and their protégés. If one spends much time examining the current literature in the field, including 'surveys' of law and economics and its development, one comes away with the distinct impression that the field is a post-1960 phenomenon, one that dates roughly from the founding of the *Journal of Law & Economics* (*JL&E*) in the late 1950s and the publication of Ronald Coase's (1960) 'The problem of social cost'. In fact, of course, law and economics, conceived of as the study of the interrelations between legal and economic processes, is as old as economics itself. The ancient Greeks, the scholastics, Adam Smith, Karl Marx, Henry Sidgwick, the German Historical School, A.C. Pigou, and, *inter alia*, the early American institutionalists devoted significant attention to legal–economic relationships. Yet, the existence of this literature is noted only barely, if at all, in contemporary legal–economic scholarship, and, when taken note of, it is largely waved aside as something very different from (and irrelevant for) contemporary analysis.

The first four decades of the twentieth century witnessed a surge of interest in law and economics within both the legal and economics communities, and the vast majority of this scholarship was of a form very different from that of contemporary law and economics – not just in the techniques brought to bear, but in the general approach to and conception of the subject. The history of law and economics at the University of Chicago is a part of this, having begun well before the 1960s' birth of the 'new' law and economics, or 'economic analysis of law', that is now synonymous with the Chicago School. Indeed, the history is not only more extensive but more intertwined with phenomena outside of Chicago than is commonly understood or than many would care to believe. This broad-based past is not only important historically, but has a great deal to do with what is happening in law and economics today (see Mercuro and Medema 2006). That much having been said, it is the Chicago School that is primarily responsible for the mushrooming of the economic analysis of law in law schools, economics departments and courtrooms across the US and even around the world.

The legal–economic backdrop

The second half of the nineteenth century witnessed the attempt among certain social science disciplines to apply formalistic principles that would give them the status accorded to the natural sciences. In economics, this gave us the 'marginal revolution'; the legal manifestation was 'doctrinalism', a concern with the law as it is, apart from reference to the religious, metaphysical or socioeconomic principles evidenced in the jurisprudence of earlier eras. Law here is not a search for the principles of some natural or divine law, but rather a scientific enterprise which 'takes as its starting point a given legal order and distills from it by a predominantly inductive method certain fundamental notions, concepts, and distinctions' (Bodenheimer 1974, p. 95). It is, as Julius Stone (1950, p. 31) has said, primarily concerned with 'an analysis of legal terms, and an inquiry into the *logical* interrelations of legal propositions'.

These legal principles or doctrines were thought to be embedded in legal cases and revealed through the study of cases over time, making the judicial opinion preeminent in law (see, for example, Langdell 1871, Friedman 1973, pp. 530–36, Grey 1983). Judicial opinions embodied 'a handful of permanent, unchanging, and indispensable principles of law' (Posner 1990, p. 15) that revealed themselves in different guises in different cases. Law, under this approach, was self-referential, consisting of a set of objectively inferable rules and procedures logically applied. Law thus became both formal and insular. Jurisprudence consisted only in an established body of legal doctrine, a set of principles in which judicial discretion was minimized, and where ethics, social conditions, politics, ideologies and the insights of disciplines outside of the law had no proper place.

The reaction against doctrinalism had already begun to gain strength in the late nineteenth century. The first salvo, 'sociological jurisprudence', was a reaction against both the formalism of doctrinalism and the traditional concepts of natural or objectively determinable rights. Oliver Wendell Holmes, Jr., Benjamin Cardozo and Roscoe Pound, for example, claimed that law cannot be understood without reference to social conditions, and against the idea of the autonomy of law was posited the idea that insights from the other social sciences should be integrated into the law. Judges, they said, should be aware of the social and economic conditions which affect the path of law and which result from the legal decision-making process, and Cardozo, for one, believed that when precedent conflicted with the greater interests of justice or social welfare, the latter should carry the day (Bodenheimer 1974, pp. 120–21).

Holmes, too, emphasized the limits of doctrinalism and discounted both the positive and normative roles played by logical reasoning in jurisprudence: 'The felt necessities of the time, the prevalent moral and political theories, intuitions of public policy, avowed or unconscious, even the prejudices which judges share with their fellow men, have a good deal more to do than the syllogism in determining the rules by which men should be governed' (Holmes 1923, p. 1). Law, in Holmes's view, both expresses the will of the dominant interests in society and works as 'a tool for achieving social ends'. As such, 'to understand law requires an understanding of social conditions' (Posner 1987, p. 762), and judges need to have an acquaintance with law's historical, social and economic aspects (see also Bodenheimer 1974, p. 123).

These pragmatic and socially attuned conceptions of law set the stage for an even more pronounced move away from the past – legal realism.[1] The legal–realist movement, which reached its zenith in the 1930s, was the most influential of the challenges to doctrinalism (see Fisher et al. 1993, Duxbury 1995, ch. 2), and was part of a more general move away from formalism and logical reasoning in the early twentieth century. The realists, following on the work of Holmes, sought to turn law outward to make it more attuned to the social realities of the day, and the reverence for the traditions of the law, so central within doctrinalism, held little sway among them. They rejected the existence of objectively determinable rights; the use of rigid legal rules, categories and classifications; appeals to the authority of the past – citations, eminent jurists and classic treatises; and the logic of reasoning from precedent. The judge, rather than the logic of the law, was seen as the central factor in the resolution of legal cases. The human factor underlying precedential reasoning was apparent to the realists: it is essentially the determination whether the decision in an earlier case could be applied in straightforward fashion to the facts of the case at hand, and such decisions inevitably entail a choice as to the relation between the facts of one case and another, one that is necessarily determined by subjective value judgments rather than by logic (Mensch 1990, p. 22). Because decisions rest on the judge's conception of right and wrong, social, political, and economic considerations became important variables. Against the formalist view of law as a deductive science, then, came the realist emphasis on developing legal theory through inductive scientific principles (Duxbury 1995, p. 80).

Along with the idea that law cannot be a logical, self-contained discipline came the prescription that it should cease all pretensions of being so, and that law should become more overtly attuned to the social ends that it necessarily serves. The realists held a strong instrumentalist conception of law: for them, law was, and had to be seen as, a 'working tool' (Friedman 1973, p. 592). Every legal decision was understood to have social, ethical, political, and economic implications, and the realists maintained that these should be recognized and explicitly dealt with by judges, not hidden behind a veil of logical reasoning. Understanding these implications, of course, entailed the exploration of the interrelations between law and the other social sciences, including sociology, psychology, political science and economics.

Of particular import for present purposes is the realist interest in using economics to understand and to guide the development of law. The realists argued that the importance of the interrelations between law and economics can be seen in the twin facts that legal change is often a function of economic ideas and conditions, which necessitate and/or generate demands for legal change, and that economic change is often governed by legal change. Karl Llewellyn, a leading legal realist and professor at that hot-bed of legal realism, Columbia, and later at the University of Chicago Law School, pointed to a number of ways in which law influences economic conditions, including its role in providing a foundation for the economic order, its influence on the operation and outcomes of the competitive market process (particularly through the structure of law pertaining to property, contract and credit, and through restrictions placed by law on the competitive process), and the influence of taxation, social welfare legislation and public enterprise on production and distribution (Llewellyn 1925, pp. 678–81; see also the discussion in Samuels 1993, pp. 247–8).

Given the important interdependencies that they saw between law and economy, it is not surprising that realists such as Llewellyn considered economic analysis a useful tool for understanding law and legal change and for devising laws that would improve the social condition. While they found certain aspects of neoclassical economics, such as marginal analysis, useful, it was with institutional economics that the realists developed a close affinity.[2] Most significant here were Henry Carter Adams, Richard T. Ely, Walton H. Hamilton (1930), Robert Lee Hale (1927, 1952) and John R. Commons (1924 [1974]). Hamilton (Yale) and Hale (Columbia) were two of the first economists to serve on Law School faculties, and all of these individuals were dedicated to the exploration of the underpinnings of the legal–economic nexus. From this realist–institutionalist project came numerous studies that attempted to probe the linkages between law and economy, and, in the process to inform legal and economic thinking and decision making.

Early Chicago

While the realist–institutionalist interaction of the 1920s and 1930s did a great deal to bring law and economics together, a similar interaction, but with a distinctly different flavor, commenced in the 1930s at the University of Chicago (see Reder 1982, Kitch 1983, Coase 1993, Duxbury 1995, ch. 5, Hovenkamp 1995, Medema 1998). Within the Law School, the origins of Chicago law and economics can be traced back to the latter part of the 1930s, when the faculty, under the leadership of Dean Wilber Katz, instituted a four-year curriculum that included courses in economics, accounting and other subjects outside of the traditional realm of legal training (Katz 1937). This curriculum was overtly linked to the realist tradition in its strong emphasis on the social sciences, including economics. In 1939, the Law School appointed its first economist, Henry Simons, in order to staff the economics courses that were part of the new curriculum. Simons was neither the first economist on a Law School faculty (Hamilton and Hale both preceded him), nor the first non-lawyer on the Chicago Law School faculty. Mortimer Adler had the latter honor, having been appointed in 1930. Simons had been Frank Knight's student at Iowa State, and Knight brought him along when he came to Chicago. The ongoing political battle between Knight and Paul Douglas within the Department of Economics, combined with Simons's poor reputation as a teacher and very limited scholarly output, resulted in a departmental fight over his promotion and tenure. The matter was resolved with Simons's part-time appointment to the law faculty, where he taught a course entitled 'Economic analysis of public policy', and, in 1945, became the first economist granted tenure by the Law School.

In the pamphlet *A Positive Program for Laissez Faire*, Simons (1934) had set down a blueprint for a legal/regulatory regime that would ensure the maintenance of competitive conditions in the face of increasing concentration in corporate America. Simons's proposals here ranged from nationalization to legal limits on advertising to redefining the courts' criterion regarding the maximum firm size consistent with competition. If Simons's position qualified as 'market-oriented', it was only relative to the New Deal liberalism of the day. As Stigler (1988, p. 149) has noted, 'Much of [Simons's] program was almost as harmonious with socialism as with private-enterprise capitalism'. Apart from giving far more credence to the possibilities of government than one would expect from a 'founder' of the Chicago law and economics tradition, Simons provided no empirical underpinnings for his analysis, offered no evidence for the ability of the government to bring off such competition policy or for the effects of such policies to enhance the efficiency with which the economy operated. That is, even in a methodological sense, Simons's approach was 'the very antithesis of that which was to become dominant as a result of the emergence of that new subject, law and economics' (Coase 1993, p. 242).

Simons's work on tax law is also worthy of note in this context, and, like his *Positive Program*, is a bit different from what one might expect from someone so significant to the Chicago tradition (see Simons 1938, 1948, 1950, and the discussion by Groves 1974) . He was a strong supporter of progressive taxation, a derivative of his concern that equals be treated equally. Simons's basis here was not utilitarian; rather, he simply believed that there was a normative presumption in favor of greater equality, and he believed that this value outweighed the expense of some efficiency loss. Simons was a staunch opponent of corporate income taxes, sales taxes and the like, which he felt interfered with the allocation of resources via market mechanisms, and he believed that the tax system which would do the least amount of harm was one that relied almost exclusively on personal income taxation. He also felt that the national government should be the primary taxing authority, but that the revenues generated would be most efficiently employed if they were dispensed to the states in the form of block grants. Harold Groves (1974, p. 85), who by no means agreed with Simons's outlook on things, suggests that Simons's work 'may remain for a long time as the most penetrating and original American contribution in public finance', and Posner (2003) continues to cite it in his discussion of tax law in *Economic Analysis of Law*.

Of course, Simons was ultimately best known for his work in monetary theory, and, as Coase (1993, p. 242) has pointed out, 'played little or no part in the development of the ideas which make up the modern subject of law and economics'. However, his price-theoretic perspective had a significant influence on, for example, Aaron Director, Milton Friedman, George Stigler, Gordon Tullock, and Warren Nutter, and his view that law should be structured so as to promote competition reflected the perspective that became a cornerstone of Chicago law and economics. Even more important was the role that Simons played in the establishment of the law and economics program at Chicago. His most significant contribution here may well have been his role (together with Friedrich A. Hayek and financial backing from the Volker Fund) in bringing to the Law School the individual most responsible for firmly establishing the Chicago law and economics tradition – Aaron Director. Director, like Simons, was a student of Frank Knight and had been a member of the economics faculty in the early 1930s. In 1946, Director assumed the directorship of a university center (affiliated with the Law School) dedicated to undertaking 'a study of a suitable legal and institutional framework of an effective competitive system' (Coase 1993, p. 246) and, upon Simons's death, took over responsibility for teaching his course on 'Economic analysis of public policy'.

Director was eventually invited by Edward Levi to collaborate in the teaching of the antitrust course and, through his teaching, had a formidible influence on Chicago law students, including several individuals – for example, Robert Bork, John McGee, and Ward S. Bowman, Jr. – who went on to be prominent scholars. During his tenure at the Law School, Director formally established the nation's first law and economics program (derivative of the school's antitrust project), which maintained visiting fellowships for law and economics scholars, promoted the Economics Department's hard-nosed workshop attitude toward research evaluation and critique in the Law School, and, in 1958, founded *JL&E*. Director's published legacy is minimal, and his impact on Chicago law and economics is almost exclusively oral: throughout his tenure at Chicago, he imparted a persuasive message to the students – that markets, not government, tend to be the preferable coordinating and regulating mechanism. This message was one that often resulted in traditional legal reasoning losing out to economic analysis, and was, to the students of law, 'a message which was at once both unfamiliar and yet quite understandable' (Duxbury 1995, p. 344). As Bork has put it, 'There is a quality about the teaching at that time that doesn't come through. A lot of us who took the antitrust course or the economics course underwent what can only be called a religious conversion. It changed our view of the entire world' (Kitch 1983, p. 183).

Nowhere did early Chicago law and economics make a greater and more enduring impact than on the field of antitrust law, the goal of which, from the Chicago perspective, should be the promotion of efficiency (see Posner 2001a). As Hovenkamp (1986, p. 1020) has pointed out, 'the Chicago School has done more for antitrust policy than any other coherent economic theory since the New Deal. No one . . . can escape [its] influence on antitrust analysis'. Reflecting the emphasis within the Chicago tradition on the efficacy of the competitive system, monopoly was viewed as occasional, unstable and transitory – a potential outcome of the competitive process, but one that would soon be removed (in effect if not in existence) by competitive pressures. Given this, rigorous antitrust enforcement was thought to be unnecessary, and, even when monopolies were shown to generate long-term inefficiencies, the governmental cure was thought to be often worse than the disease, owing to the inefficiencies of government.

The third major figure in early Chicago law and economics is Ronald Coase. Coase was brought to the Law School from the University of Virginia in 1964 to succeed Director on the faculty and as editor of *JL&E*. The study of the relationship between law and economy came rather naturally for Coase, who, as a student, had himself taken several courses in law, and whose mentor, Arnold Plant (1974), had done pioneering work on the analysis of the economic implications of rules governing patents, copyrights and intellectual property generally. Coase believed that there were important lessons to be learned by examining the relationship between law and economy – by 'examining cases, examining business practices, and showing that there was some sense to them, but it wasn't the sense that people had given to them before' (quoted in Kitch 1983, p. 193). This perspective, initially applied at Chicago in the area of antitrust, was expanded to various aspects of legal and regulatory activity largely through the influence of Director and Coase as editors of *JL&E*, 'the aim of which was said to be the examination of public policy issues of interest to lawyers and economists' (Coase 1993, p. 251).

Coase himself was a regular contributor to *JL&E* prior to his arrival at Chicago. In an article entitled 'The Federal Communications Commission' (1959), he took issue with the fiat-based mechanism by which broadcasting licenses were issued in the US, arguing that frequencies being scarce and valuable resources, greater attention should be paid to the efficiency of their allocation. Coase showed how, under idealized conditions, a market in frequencies would allocate them to those who value them most highly, and more generally how, in any situation of well-defined rights and costless transacting, rights will be allocated efficiently, regardless of to whom they are initially assigned. But, recognizing that markets always function at least somewhat imperfectly, he went on to consider the various impediments to achieving the allocation implied by a perfectly functioning market – considerations relevant to the issue of how a market in broadcast frequencies might actually work in practice. The culmination of his discussion was what might best be described as a plea for comparative institutional analysis on the part of the policy makers, an analysis that took into consideration both the existence of alternative institutional structures for frequency allocation and the imperfections that attend each.

Coase wrote 'The problem of social cost' as a response to challenges raised by Chicago economists to his critique of the Pigovian system in 'The Federal Communications Commission'. To illustrate his point about the efficiency of smoothly functioning markets in resolving disputes over rights, Coase invoked several British common law cases to show, hypothetically, how rights would be rearranged among agents so as to end up in their highest-valued use, regardless of the legal rule in force. Because transaction costs will almost always preclude such efficient voluntary reallocations, Coase argued that the economic interests of society would be best served if externality policy was designed so as to promote the greatest possible value of output in society, which, given the inefficiencies associated with the operations of government (often overlooked in Pigovian public economics), may involve the use of markets, hierarchies, taxes, subsidies, regulations or simply doing nothing at all about the externality problem because the cure may be worse than the disease (see Medema 1994, 1996).[3]

A further 'early' contribution to Chicago law and economics, and one very much of a piece with Coase's analysis, came through the work of Armen Alchian (1959, 1961) and Harold Demsetz (1964, 1967) on the economics of property rights.[4] The property rights approach emerged as some economists began to once again appreciate that legal–institutional arrangements, such as the nature and form of property rights, that constrain the behavior of individuals and firms can have an important effect on the allocation of resources and the distribution of income in the economy, with the resulting implication that the study of alternative property right regimes can generate insights into economic performance. The argument here consisted of two parts, one reflecting the influence of law on economy and the other the influence of economy on law. First, it was argued that the value of resources is tied directly to the bundles of rights running with the resources; that is, the more complete and definite is the specification of property rights (the less attenuated is the rights structure), the more uncertainty is diminished, which, in turn, tends to promote a more efficient allocation of resources. Second, proponents of the property rights approach inquired whether the standard theory of production and exchange was capable of explaining the emergence of the institution of property rights over scarce resources. The associated empirical research suggested an affirmative answer to this question – that the emergence and development of new property rights can be explained as a consequence of value-seeking behavior brought on by new technologies and market opportunities. The property rights approach, although owing its origins to the work of many Chicago-oriented economists, occupies a central place in the new institutional economics and has moved well beyond orthodox Chicago thinking. Nonetheless, core elements of the property rights approach remain at the heart of Chicago law and economics.

The work of Alchian and Demsetz is reflective of the links between the legal and economics sides at Chicago. Of the several major figures associated with the Chicago Economics Department in the early years, Frank Knight and Jacob Viner had the most significant impact on what has come to be known as 'Chicago law and economics'. Henry Simons makes the nature of their contribution to a 'Chicago perspective' clear in a letter to Hayek: 'A distinctive feature of Chicago economics as represented recently by Knight and Viner, is its traditional liberal political philosophy, its emphasis on the dispersion of economic power, free markets, and a political decentralization', an 'intellectual tradition . . . now almost entirely unrepresented among the great universities save for Chicago' (quoted in Epstein et al. 1997, pp. 1132–3). This served to set the Chicago perspective, including the message imparted to students, apart from what was going on in much of the rest of the economics profession. Viner also brought the Marshallian approach that has come to be associated so closely with the Chicago price-theoretic tradition underlying the entire history of law and economics at Chicago.

The next generation of Chicago economists undertook to elaborate, extend and fortify this tradition, demonstrating, in formal terms, the detailed nexus between competitive markets and efficient outcomes. Led by Milton Friedman and George Stigler, post-war Chicago economists buttressed theory with empirical research to argue for less government intervention, fewer wealth redistribution policies, reliance on voluntary exchange and on the common law for mediating conflicts, and an across-the-board promotion of more private enterprise – which, based on the evidence provided by their empirical research, would facilitate a more efficient allocation of resources.

From law and economics to economic analysis of law

While 'The problem of social cost' meshed very nicely with the old Chicago law and economics tradition, it also (and unintentionally) triggered the development of something far more substantial. Coase applied his analysis to the courts, pointing to the economic questions at issue in a number of rather typical legal cases. He argued first, from a normative standpoint, that judges should, at minimum, take allocational considerations into account in making decisions over rights which impact economic performance. He further suggested that 'it is clear from a cursory study [of the case record] that the courts have often recognized the economic implications of their decisions and are aware (as many economists are not) of the reciprocal nature of the [externality] problem' (Coase 1960, p. 19). Moreover, while '[t]he courts do not always refer very clearly to the economic problems posed by the cases brought before them . . . it seems probable that in the interpretation of words and phrases like "reasonable" or "common or ordinary use" there is some recognition, perhaps largely unconscious and certainly not very explicit, of the economic aspects of the questions at issue (p. 22).[5] These suggestions regarding judges' applications of economic thinking later stimulated a number of scholars – Richard Posner in particular (see Kitch 1983, p. 226) – to examine whether there might be an efficiency logic underlying the development of legal rules across the common law. Doing so involved the application of individual decision-making calculus to agents faced with constraints imposed by common law rules, and the assessment of the resulting outcomes according to the dictates of wealth maximization. And of course, where extant rules were found to be inefficient, the determination of rules which would induce optimal behavior was a natural extension.

Coase was not alone in the use of economics to analyze tort cases; Guido Calabresi (1961) was doing so at the same time, and their work became the springboard for a new economic analysis of common law rules. Suddenly, the economic nature of many of the questions of legal analysis – that legal rules and decisions across many traditional fields of law beget both benefits and costs, and thus are amenable to analysis in efficiency terms – and the potential for the application of economic analysis to these questions became apparent and stimulated research in the areas of property, contract and tort law.

The 1960s saw the emergence of a second and equally important strand of the economic analysis of law. Gary Becker's (1957) *The Economics of Discrimination* had contributed to the early development of economics imperialism by showing how the model of *homo economicus* could be applied to areas beyond the norm. 'Crime and punishment: an economic approach' (Becker 1968) brought this perspective to the analysis of criminal behavior and criminal law. Criminals, he said, are essentially rational utility maximizers like everyone else, but the relevant constraints and opportunity sets they encounter generate maximizing outcomes that involve engaging in criminal activity. At least as important, though, is the associated implication that criminal activity, like any other labor–occupational–economic choice, is subject to alteration by scaling price incentives – that is, by altering legal rules – in one direction or the other. What some would consider an 'extreme' application of economic logic to the analysis of criminal behavior made the applications to property, torts and contracts – things that, to the lay mind, are more overtly 'economic' and less subject to the 'deviance' label – seem relatively tame and less inappropriate than they might have otherwise. This was Robbins (1932) on steroids, but the impact of Becker's pathbreaking work in attracting the attention of economists and legal scholars to the new economic analysis of law and in the spread of economics imperialism more generally (which itself helped the economic analysis of law gain acceptance) should not be underestimated (see also Becker 1976).[6]

By the early 1970s, the economic analysis of law had developed to the point that Richard Posner (1973) could write a substantial treatise on the subject, and the *Journal of Legal Studies* was established to handle the burgeoning output in the field. The field was running in every direction in which legal rules affect individual behavior through the adjustment of incentives, but it all revolved around three core elements. First, in contrast to the standard legal view of individuals as reasonable agents behaving according to the norms and customs of society as reflected in legal rules, the economic approach posits agents as rational maximizers of their satisfactions.[7] Second, legal rules are viewed as prices which are taken as given by individuals and used by them in the process of calculating their utility – or profit-maximizing response to these legal rules. Changes in legal rules thus function as changes in the constraints subject to which individuals maximize, with corresponding implications for individual behavior. One of the implications of these first two points is that, while the traditional approach to law considers law-breaking and law-breakers unreasonable, the economic approach sees both law-breakers and non-law-breakers as rational – their behavioral differences being accounted for by the different constraints under which they maximize utility. Finally, the assessment of legal rules proceeds on the basis of the efficiency of the outcomes generated by these rules, in contrast to the 'justice' or 'fairness' criterion underlying traditional legal reasoning (although Posner (1981) has defended efficiency as a reasonable definition of justice).

The Chicago School remained at the center of the meteoric rise of the economic analysis of law over the next twenty years, even while law and economics programs began to mushroom at elite law schools around the country. Fresh blood in the form of, among others, William Landes, Dennis Carlton, Alan Sykes, Douglas Baird and Daniel Fischel brought new ideas and specialties into the law and economics program at Chicago and facilitated both its development and entrenchment.[8] Richard Epstein evolved from vociferous natural-rights-based critic to fellow traveler. Baird and Fischel went on to become deans of the Law School. Students went out to spread the gospel literally around the world – most famously, Henry Manne, who founded or helped to develop multiple law and economics programs as well as a series of summer institutes, colloquially known as 'Pareto in the Pines', that taught economic analysis to judges. And, of course, there is the influence of Chicago law and economics on the bench, particularly in the form of Posner, Frank Easterbrook, Robert Bork and Antonin Scalia. The former and latter pairs are indicative of the non-homogeneity in the Chicago tradition, with Posner and Easterbrook being more activist along the lines implied by economic principles, and Bork and Scalia falling more heavily on the side of judicial restraint.[9]

Emperor, or just new clothes?

The fundamental differences in approach between the old and the new law and economics can be described at two different levels of sophistication. At a basic level, the old law and economics was concerned with analyzing the interaction between the law and the economy (as an important or even necessary component of the economic theorizing process), whereas the new law and economics is concerned with applying economic theory to analyze agent behavior within the legal arena and has little or nothing to do with understanding the legal bases of the economic system. At a more sophisticated level, the old and the new law and economics represent distinctive versions of social theory. The old law and economics reflected a multifaceted, pluralistic (as regards the method of economic theorizing), interdisciplinary approach to the analysis of the institutional structure of society – one in which law and economy are mutually determined and determining. The new law and economics, in contrast, is part of a larger imperialist movement within economics that, in effect, presents neoclassical microeconomics as social theory. Here, rational choice analysis becomes the key to understanding (and, in the hands of some, normatively prescribing) the behavior of agents in all manner of social contexts. That is, it consciously reaches beyond the boundaries of economics into other fields to influence the scholarship within those fields, rather than to bring back to economics insights that will enhance our understanding of the operation of the economic system. The economic analysis of law was one of the earliest applications of the tools of economic theory to the analysis of 'non-economic' or 'non-market' phenomena, reflecting a larger process in which economic analysis was coming to be viewed as an approach, method or toolkit applicable to all areas of life in which choices are made, rather than simply as the study of the economic system *per se*. The logic of extending this paradigm beyond things traditionally economic is simple: economics is the study of choice, and all of life involves making choices; should not economics, then, apply to all manner of human decisions and thus all areas of human life?[10]

Although there was some initial questioning of the appropriate boundaries for applying economic analysis, for many economists the application to legal theory seemed a natural extension of the economic paradigm – a precedent for which already existed in public choice analysis, which was well along the development path by this time. On the other hand, the growth of law and economics stirred up a great deal of controversy within the legal community (for example, academic turf wars, the applicability of the economic model of human behavior, and the 'efficiency as justice' issue), and certainly helped to fuel the critical legal studies movement and its vociferous opposition to the Chicago approach.[11]

Apart from questions about the applicability of the economic model to the legal realm, the Chicago School has come in for heavy criticism for the normative overtones that many believe go along with, or even drive, the economic analysis of law. There can be little question that the economic analysis of law has provided a sturdy intellectual foundation for a market-oriented approach to legal decision making. The Coase theorem – so named and formalized by Stigler (1966), it should be noted – opens the door to the analysis of rights allocation within a traditional market framework and to a relatively simple question: if rights over scarce resources are allocated through the market for all manner of goods, why not also for rights over pollution, the ability to breach contracts, tortious harms, and so on? To a mindset which finds market allocation most congenial, the Coase theorem opens up a vast new scope for the operation of markets. If market processes are able to work and are allowed to work, legal outcomes will be exactly those dictated by the laws governing competitive markets. The implications of this insight are straightforward and were quickly seized upon: (i) let the market work in allocating rights; (ii) facilitate the working of the market here by removing legal impediments to its operation; and (iii) when (i) and (ii) are not possible, assign rights or design legal rules so as to mimic the outcome of a competitive market – the outcome that would have obtained in any event had there not been impediments to the market's operation.

This argument is amazingly powerful, since it implies that the law should simply be structured so as to let people do that which they would naturally agree to do if transaction costs did not preclude them from doing so. In an era in which so-called 'activist judges' were making decisions which often seemed to conflict with the ideology of the market, the implications of the economic analysis of law were welcome ammunition for those who favored the market. As such, it is not surprising that the new law and economics movement was launched from within the Chicago School, even given its important place within law and economics of the old variety. In addition, the willingness of certain conservative-oriented organizations to provide financial support for the law and economics movement (such as the John M. Olin Foundation, which has provided substantial funding for a number of law and economics programs across the US) helped to facilitate both the program of research and the classroom dissemination of these ideas.

It bears emphasizing that none of these normative conclusions is inherent in the analysis of legal rules using the tools of neoclassical economic analysis, and it is both incorrect and irresponsible to equate the new law and economics with conservative ideology. Indeed, the scholars working in the field come from a wide variety of perspectives and draw many conclusions at odds with conservative ideology. However, it would be difficult to deny that law and economics has been used by some to promote normative agendas – not unlike, at times, institutionalist–realist law and economics. When combined with the goal of facilitating competitive market outcomes, the Pandora's Box opened by 'The problem of social cost' gave ample opportunity for individuals so inclined to design legal rules that would comport with the dictates of competitive markets.

Regardless of one's position on the ideological implications of Chicago law and economics, it would be erroneous to suggest that impetus for its development was anti-interventionism. Kitch perhaps best described the thrust of law and economics at Chicago and other law schools during the first half of the century when he said:

> My impression from what I've been able to find on Chicago is that the interest that law schools had in economics did not come out of any anti-interventionist thinking. It essentially came out of the idea that the legal system is going to be doing this [that is, overtly dealing with economic issues] now and that means we need to learn how to do it right and maybe economists know something about how to do it right. . . . There is a great legitimacy given to the idea that government is going to be doing these things and we in the law schools should try to help the government do it right. (1983, pp. 175–6)

And Gary Becker, recalling Stigler's (1959) discussion of economics training making people more conservative, has suggested:

> The appreciation of how markets function and how individuals choose gives one an orientation toward the belief that a decentralized system is typically going to operate better than a

> centralized system, whether coming from government or some other source. So this association of Law and Economics with 'conservative' or smaller government is not a happenstance of the particular economists who have been attracted to Law and Economics, but it is an implication of bringing economics into any discipline. (Epstein et al. 1997, p. 1149)

In fact, the diversity that characterized the Chicago Economics Department for so long and the relatively small place of economics within the Law School at Chicago in the early years would not have allowed for any large, concerted political agenda. As Stigler (1988, p. 148) has pointed out, 'There was no Chicago School of Economics . . . at the end of World War II'.[12]

Nor, indeed, of law and economics. Prior to the arrival of Coase in 1964, the law school never had more than one economist on the faculty, although there were some faculty with sympathies for examining antitrust cases, regulatory issues and so on through the lens of economic analysis – enough, in fact, that a small reading group of economics and legal faculty was formed. And the presence of scholars such as Llewellyn on the faculty managed to ensure that there was always strong resistance to expansion of the influence of neoclassical economics in the 1950s. Henry Manne has reported that the neoclassical economic analysis that was in the air 'infuriated' Llewellyn, particularly when students would use it in the attempt to refute positions that Llewellyn would take in the classroom (Kitch 1983, p. 184), and Llewellyn went so far as to question whether Chicago was doing a proper job of training lawyers (ibid., p. 191). Levi, as Dean, protected and encouraged law and economics, but, as Director has pointed out, on the whole there was neither 'any great resistance to' nor 'any great enthusiasm for' law and economics – at least until it was proposed that a second economist be hired (ibid. 1983, p. 186). The status of economics in the law school even then was such that Coase's initial appointment was partially in the Business School. But Chicago in that period *was* a fairly fertile and decentralized place, where doing new, different and non-traditional things was encouraged.

The history of law and economics at Chicago is by no means one of a narrow or homogeneous enterprise, and the idea that the march from Henry Simons to Richard Posner was a natural progression cannot sustain the weight of the facts. It was a Coasean accident that sent law and economics careening off in a very different (and no less interesting or illuminating) direction – to the economic analysis of law which now looms as so large a force in both economics and law. Nor is all of the causation here internal. The legal realism to which Chicago is so hostile[13] opened a door that could not be closed; law turned outward, and the ferment of legal realism was a big reason why law and economics could gain a foothold at Chicago and eventually sprout and spread in new form. Posner's repeated attempts to dismiss such a link miss the point:

> The 'crits' worry that the practitioners of law and economics will contest with them the mantle of legal realism. They needn't worry. We economic types have no desire to be pronounced the intellectual heirs of . . . William Douglas, Jerome Frank, or Karl Llewellyn. The law and economics movement owes little to legal realism – perhaps nothing beyond the fact that Donald Turner and Guido Calabresi, pioneering figures in the application of economics to law, graduated from Yale Law School and may have been influenced by the school's legal–realist tradition to examine law from the perspective of another discipline. Although the legal realist Robert Hale anticipated some of the discoveries (inventions?) of law and economics, most modern law and economics scholars were unware of his work until recently. It is difficult to measure and therefore treacherous to disclaim influence, but, speaking as one who received his legal education at the Harvard

> Law School between 1959 and 1962, I can attest that to a student [the school] seemed untouched by legal realism. And none of the legal and economic thinkers who since law school have most shaped my own academic and judicial thinking – Holmes, Coase, Stigler, Becker, Director, and others – was himself a product in whole or in part of legal realism. (Posner 1995, p. 3)

Indeed, they were not. But that Coase, Stigler, Becker, and Director *could* shape and influence the perspective, scholarship, and judicial opinions of one of the most influential legal scholars of the late twentieth century, and, by extension, stimulate the development of a new, externalist approach to legal inquiry is not only a legacy of realism but perhaps its foremost one.

Notes

* The author thanks Neil Duxbury, Richard Posner, and Warren Samuels for instructive comments on an earlier version of the chapter.

1. It should be noted that neither those scholars falling under the banner of sociological jurisprudence nor the realists who followed them were able to totally shed formalistic elements from their thought. Nor did they necessarily attempt to do so. Holmes, for example, saw an important role for logical analysis within legal thinking. See Duxbury (1995, pp. 10, 32–64).
2. For a discussion of the links between realism and institutionalism, as well as economics generally, see Samuels (1993), Duxbury (1995, pp. 97–111) and Fried (1998).
3. Frank Knight (1924 [1999]) had previously challenged Pigou's analysis, and the flavor of Coase's criticism is somewhat similar to that of Knight.
4. For a concise overview of the early economics of property rights literature, see Furubotn and Pejovich (1974); for a more up-to-date discussion, see Anderson and McChesney (2002).
5. One finds a similar line of argument already in Commons (1924 [1974]).
6. Posner's (2001b, ch. 1) linking of Becker's work on crime with Bentham's analysis is suggestive of historical precedent for the Chicago approach.
7. It is worth noting at this point that the last decade has witnessed an increasing attention to the potential limits of the strict rational maximization approach and the role that social norms may play in human behavior among law and economics scholars at Chicago and elsewhere. See, for example, McAdams (1997), Jolls et al. (1998), Eric Posner (2000) and Duxbury (2001). For an alternative perspective, see Posner (2001b, ch. 8).
8. Landes, Carlton and Sykes are all trained in economics, with Sykes holding a JD as well.
9. Bork has also criticized economic analysis of law, Chicago style.
10. Coase's stance on all of this is worth noting. He predicted the failure of economics imperialism specifically because economists lacked expertise in these 'outside' areas (Coase 1977); to date, his prediction has proven to be incorrect. He has also said that, in writing up 'The problem of social cost', he was not interested in offering a new perspective on jurisprudence but, rather, 'to improve our analysis of the working of the economic system. Law came into the article because, in a regime of positive transaction costs, the character of law becomes one of the main factors determining the performance of the economy' (Coase 1993, p. 251). Indeed, Coase consciously distances himself from Posner, whose 'main interest is in the legal system' (p. 251), noting that 'I have no interest in lawyers or legal education' (Coase, in Kitch 1983, p. 192), and acknowledging that 'In the development of the economic analysis of the law [that is, the "new" law and economics] . . . Posner has clearly played the major role' (Coase 1993, p. 251). Posner (1993a, 1993b) has taken Coase to task for this disavowal of his supposed progeny.
11. For a discussion as to why law and economics was so successful a movement in economics and in law, see Medema (1998) and Posner (1987), respectively. Mercuro and Medema (2006) discuss (without attempting to take sides) many of the criticisms that have been leveled at the Chicago approach.
12. There is perhaps no better evidence for this than Henry Simons's lumping of Henry Sidgwick and A.C. Pigou into a list of people whose work was squarely in the classical liberal tradition that Chicago embodied (Epstein et al. 1997, p. 1133).
13. See the discussion in Kitch (1983). The attitude toward institutionalism expressed there is very similar.

References

Alchian, A.A. (1959), 'Private property and the relative cost of tenure', in *The Public Stake in Union Power*, Bradley, P.D. (ed.), Charlottesville, VA: University of Virginia Press, pp. 350–71.

Alchian, A.A. (1961), *Some Economics of Property*, Santa Monica, CA: Rand Corporation.
Anderson, T.L. and F.S. McChesney (2002), *Property Rights: Cooperation, Conflict, and Law*, Princeton, NJ: Princeton University Press.
Becker, G.S. (1957), *The Economics of Discrimination*, Chicago, IL: University of Chicago Press.
Becker, G.S. (1968), 'Crime and punishment: an economic approach', *Journal of Political Economy*, **76** (2), 169–217.
Becker, G.S. (1976), *The Economic Approach to Human Behavior*, Chicago, IL: University of Chicago Press.
Bodenheimer, E. (1974), *Jurisprudence: The Philosophy and Method of the Law*, rev. edn, Cambridge, MA: Harvard University Press.
Calabresi, G. (1961), 'Some thoughts on risk distribution and the law of torts', *Yale Law Journal*, **70** (4), 499–553.
Coase, R.H. (1959), 'The Federal Communications Commission', *Journal of Law & Economics*, **2**, 1–40.
Coase, R.H. (1960), 'The problem of social cost', *Journal of Law & Economics*, **3**, 1–44.
Coase, R.H. (1977), 'Economics and contiguous disciplines', in *The Organization and Retrieval of Economic Knowledge*, Perlman, M. (ed.), Boulder, CO: Westview Press, pp. 481–91.
Coase, R.H. (1993), 'Law and economics at Chicago', *Journal of Law & Economics*, **36** (1, part 2), 239–54.
Commons, J.R. (1924 [1974]), *Legal Foundations of Capitalism*, Clifton, NJ: Augustus M. Kelley.
Demsetz, H. (1964), 'The exchange and enforcement of property rights', *Journal of Law & Economics*, **7**, 11–26.
Demsetz, H. (1967), 'Toward a theory of property rights', *American Economic Review*, **57** (2, Papers and proceedings), 347–59.
Duxbury, N. (1995), *Patterns of American Jurisprudence*, Oxford: Clarendon Press.
Duxbury, N. (2001), 'Signalling and social norms', *Oxford Journal of Legal Studies*, **21** (4), 719–36.
Epstein, R.A., G.S. Becker, R.H. Coase, M.H. Miller and R.A. Posner (1997), 'Roundtable: the future of law and economics', *University of Chicago Law Review*, **64** (4), 1129–65.
Fisher, W.W., M.J. Horwitz and T.A. Reed (1993), *American Legal Realism*, New York: Oxford University Press.
Fried, B.H. (1998), *The Progressive Assault on Laissez Faire: Robert Hale and the First Law and Economics Movement*, Cambridge, MA: Harvard University Press.
Friedman, L.M. (1973), *A History of American Law*, New York: Simon & Schuster.
Furubotn, E.G. and S. Pejovich (1974), *The Economics of Property Rights*, Cambridge, MA: Ballinger.
Grey, T.C. (1983), 'Langdell's orthodoxy', *University of Pittsburgh Law Review*, **45**, 1–53.
Groves, H.M. (1974), 'Henry Simons', in *The Tax Philosophers: Two Hundred Years of Thought in Great Britain and the United States*, Chicago, IL: University of Chicago Press, pp. 74–85.
Hale, R.L. (1927), 'Economics and the law', in *The Social Sciences and Their Interrelations*, Ogburn, W.F. and A.A. Goldenweiser (eds), Boston, MA: Houghton Mifflin, pp. 131–42.
Hale, R.L. (1952), *Freedom through Law*, New York: Columbia University Press.
Hamilton, W.H. (1930), 'Affectation with public interest', *Yale Law Journal*, **39** (8), 1089–112.
Holmes, O.W., Jr. (1923), *The Common Law*, Boston, MA: Little, Brown.
Hovenkamp, H. (1986), 'Chicago and its alternatives', *Duke Law Journal*, **6**, 1014–29.
Hovenkamp, H. (1995), 'Law and economics in the United States: a brief historical survey', *Cambridge Journal of Economics*, **19** (2), 331–52.
Jolls, C., C.R. Sunstein and R. Thaler (1998), 'A behavioral approach to law and economics', *Stanford Law Review*, **50** (5), 1471–550.
Katz, W. (1937), 'A four-year program for legal education', *University of Chicago Law Review*, **4** (4), 527–36.
Kitch, E.W. (1983), 'The fire of truth: a remembrance of law and economics at Chicago, 1932–1970', *Journal of Law & Economics*, **26** (1), 163–234.
Knight, F.H. (1924 [1999]), 'Some fallacies in the interpretation of social cost', in *Selected Essays by Frank H. Knight*, vol. 1: *'What Is truth' in Economics?*, Emmett, R.B. (ed.), Chicago, IL: University of Chicago Press, pp. 94–111.
Langdell, C.C. (1871), *A Selection of Cases on the Law of Contracts*, Boston, MA: Little, Brown.
Llewellyn, K.N. (1925), 'The effect of legal institutions upon economics', *American Economic Review*, **15** (4), 665–83.
McAdams, R.H. (1997), 'The origin, development, and regulation of norms', *Michigan Law Review*, **96** (2), 338–433.
Medema, S.G. (1994), *Ronald H. Coase*, London: Macmillan.
Medema, S.G. (1996), 'Of Pangloss, Pigouvians, and pragmatism: Ronald Coase on social cost analysis', *Journal of the History of Economic Thought*, **18** (1), 96–114.
Medema, S.G. (1998), 'Wandering the road from pluralism to Posner: the transformation of law and economics, 1920s–1970s', in *From Interwar Pluralism to Postwar Neoclassicism*, Morgan, M.S. and M. Rutherford (eds), Durham, NC: Duke University Press, pp. 202–24.

Mensch, E. (1990), 'The history of mainstream legal thought', in *The Politics of Law: A Progressive Critique*, Kairys, D. (ed.), New York: Pantheon Books, pp. 13–37.
Mercuro, N. and S.G. Medema (2006), *Economics and the Law: From Posner to Postmodernism and Beyond*, 2nd edn, Princeton, NJ: Princeton University Press.
Plant, A. (1974), *Selected Economic Essays and Addresses*, London: Routledge & Kegan Paul.
Posner, E. (2000), *Law and Social Norms*, Cambridge, MA: Harvard University Press.
Posner, R.A. (1973), *Economic Analysis of Law*, Boston, MA: Little, Brown.
Posner, R.A. (1981), *The Economics of Justice*, Cambridge, MA: Harvard University Press.
Posner, R.A. (1987), 'The decline of law as an autonomous discipline: 1962–1987', *Harvard Law Review*, **100** (4), 761–80.
Posner, R.A. (1990), *The Problems of Jurisprudence*, Cambridge, MA: Harvard University Press.
Posner, R.A. (1993a), 'The new institutional economics meets law and economics', *Journal of Institutional and Theoretical Economics*, **149** (1), 73–87.
Posner, R.A. (1993b), 'Ronald Coase and methodology', *Journal of Economic Perspectives*, **7** (4), 195–210.
Posner, R.A. (1995), *Overcoming Law*, Cambridge, MA: Harvard University Press.
Posner, R.A. (2001a), *Antitrust Law*, 2nd edn, Chicago, IL: University of Chicago Press.
Posner, R.A. (2001b), *Frontiers of Legal Theory*, Cambridge, MA: Harvard University Press.
Posner, R.A. (2003), *Economic Analysis of Law*, 6th edn, New York: Aspen.
Reder, M.W. (1982), 'Chicago economics: permanence and change', *Journal of Economic Literature*, **20** (1), 1–38.
Robbins, L. (1932), *An Essay on the Nature and Significance of Economic Science*, London: Macmillan.
Samuels, W.J. (1993), 'Law and economics: some early journal contributions', in *Economic Thought and Discourse in the Twentieth Century*, Samuels, W.J., J.E. Biddle and T.W. Patchak-Schuster (eds), Aldershot, UK and Brookfield, VT, USA: Edward Elgar, pp. 217–85.
Simons, H.C. (1934), *A Positive Program for Laissez Faire: Some Proposals for a Liberal Economic Policy*, Chicago, IL: University of Chicago Press.
Simons, H.C. (1938), *Personal Income Taxation*, Chicago, IL: University of Chicago Press.
Simons, H.C. (1948), *Economic Policy for a Free Society*, Chicago, IL: University of Chicago Press.
Simons, H.C. (1950), *Federal Tax Reform*, Chicago, IL: University of Chicago Press.
Stigler, G.J. (1959), 'The politics of political economists', *Quarterly Journal of Economics*, **73** (4), 522–32.
Stigler, G.J. (1966), *The Theory of Price*, 3rd edn, New York: Macmillan.
Stigler, G.J. (1988), *Memoirs of an Unregulated Economist*, New York: Basic Books.
Stone, J. (1950), *The Province and Function of Law*, Cambridge, MA: Harvard University Press.

12 Friedman, positive economics, and the Chicago Boys

*Eric Schliesser**

Introduction

> Experiences in controversies as these brings out the impossibility of learning anything from facts till they are examined and interpreted by reason; and teaches that the most reckless and treacherous of all theorists is he who professes to let facts and figures to speak for themselves, who keeps in the background the part he played, perhaps unconsciously, in selecting and grouping them, and in suggesting the argument *post hoc ergo propter hoc*.
>
> Alfred Marshall (1885 [1925], p. 168), epigraph in Friedman and Schwarz (1963)

Milton Friedman offers two denials in his 1976 Nobel lecture. The first (a) is the denial that 'Economics and its fellow social sciences' ought to be 'regarded more nearly as branches of philosophy'. The second (b) is the denial that economics is 'enmeshed with values at the outset because they deal with human behaviour' (Friedman 1976 [1992], p. 267). I call claim (b) Friedman's basic claim, or FBC. By exploring the details of Friedman's methodological commitments, I argue against FBC. It does not follow that the denial of FBC means commitment to (a). In fact, I show that by Friedman's own methodological lights as presented in 'The methodology of positive economics' (1953; hereafter F1953) he ought to be committed to the claim that positive science (all science) is enmeshed in values. However, along the way, by calling attention to the furore concerning Friedman's public entanglement with the so-called 'Chicago Boys', I also make the case that it still would be wiser and healthier for economists (not to say the rest of us) that it also be regarded as a branch of philosophy, even though, despite its being enmeshed in values, economics is 'scientific'.

The next section diagnoses a technical problem in Friedman's argument, leading to the conclusion that Friedman's appeal to his methodology in the Nobel lecture fails on conceptual grounds internal to his methodology. Moreover, I show that the failure is related to a broader systematic problem: when properly understood, Friedman's methodology shows that positive economics is (in a non-trivial sense) enmeshed in values. In order to account for Friedman's overreaching and to clarify the meaning and implications of my argument, the following section turns to the charged social context between the announcement of the Nobel award to Friedman and the Nobel lecture. I conclude by explaining why I re-open the old chestnut of values in positive science. The entire episode from the award of the Nobel to Friedman to his lecture provides the opportunity to raise a question of fundamental import about the relationship between expertise and society.

Can positive science be value-free?

> No observer of the social scene can remove himself from the observed, and personal and subjective attitudes necessarily color all activity, including the scientific.
>
> James M. Buchanan (1960 [1987], p. 324)

The Nobel lecture

In his Nobel lecture, 'Inflation and unemployment', Friedman offers an argument for his basic claim that economics is not enmeshed with values at the outset because it deals with human behavior. The argument is by way of a historical case study that is supposed to be illustrative of the scientific nature of the practice of economics. As Friedman explains:

> The relation between inflation and unemployment . . . is an admirable illustration [of FBC] because it has been a controversial political issue throughout the period, yet the drastic change that has occurred in accepted professional views was produced primarily by the scientific response to experience that contradicted a tentatively accepted hypothesis – precisely the classical process for the revision of a scientific hypothesis. (Friedman 1976 [1992], p. 268)

For the sake of argument, I do not dispute the details of Friedman's case study. I grant that professional economists changed their views on the relationship between inflation and unemployment in the way described by Friedman. Moreover, I allow that Friedman's example is significant for two reasons: it was a non-trivial issue *within* economics, touching on many fundamental theoretical commitments; it is an issue with large policy and political ramifications. It is also appropriate for the occasion of the Nobel lecture because Friedman's ability and enormous personal influence in connecting theory and policy had been singled out by the Award Committee.[1] All three reasons are also reflected in the quote by Friedman (that is, 'controversial political issue' and 'drastic change . . . in accepted professional views'). Thus, Friedman's argumentative strategy is to offer a case study that is a best-case scenario for the thesis that he challenges. This is why Friedman calls it 'admirable'. Fair enough.

Even if we accept the appropriateness of the case study and Friedman's description of it, there are at least four problems with Friedman's argument. First a willingness to change one's position in light of disconfirming evidence may be a necessary condition for being scientific,[2] but it is not a sufficient condition. After all, even some ideologies are characterized by their willingness to adjust to changing circumstances; this is a feature that can give them longevity. (For present purposes I use 'ideology' rather than 'philosophy' as the contrast to 'science'. To be sure, some ideologies, for example, Marxism or Intelligent Design, effectively employ the language or rhetoric of 'science', but this is why it is all the more important to clarify what science is.)

Friedman appeals to a methodological criterion to help distinguish science from ideology. (Recall, 'the scientific response to experience that contradicted a tentatively accepted hypothesis – precisely the classical process for the revision of a scientific hypothesis'.) This methodology accounts for theory change within science. Presumably ideologies are characterized by commitment to some doctrines, rather than tentatively accepted hypotheses.

Since Kuhn's *Structure of Scientific Revolutions* (1962), few philosophers and historians of science have been willing to accept what Friedman calls 'the classical process' as a factual description of many (if not most) theory changes.[3] History offers many examples of first-rate scientists (or whole scientific communities) who are extremely stubborn in the face of disconfirming evidence (and are sometimes vindicated for this). Accounting for the lunar orbit with inverse square gravity, for example, was a major problem for Isaac Newton and early Newtonians in the eighteenth century, but this did not lead to wholesale abandonment of the theory. If one accepts Kuhn's historical claims, then the 'classical process' is neither necessary nor sufficient to distinguish science from ideology. (It is well known that Kuhn deplored how Kuhnians appealed to his account to infer that science was, thus, ideology. The inference need not follow, of course.) Moreover, even if one is unmoved by Kuhnian historical evidence, some adherents to ideologies may well distinguish between, say, central dogmas (un-falsifiable) and tentative hypotheses (to be put to the test). Contemporary defenders of Intelligent Design may be morphing into such creatures.

So even if one shows that the 'classical process' does cover all theory changes within science, it can at best be said to be a necessary condition in order to distinguish science from some ideologies. Moreover, even if it achieved the status of a necessary condition of distinguishing science from ideology, it may still be too broad to do the work Friedman wants from it. For it is quite possible that the choice among maxims or rules of thumb embedded in what some call 'common sense' is also governed by the 'classical process'. If science is merely an extension, correction or refinement of the methods of common sense (as some philosophers from Thomas Reid to Willard Van Quine have thought and many economic educators/popularizers often claim), then, depending on how one wishes to distinguish between common sense and science, the methodological criterion may be overly broad.

Here the limits of argument by case study become immediately apparent. No single case study can show that science is necessarily characterized by the 'classical process' or that something is legitimately scientific if it contains the 'classical process'. This problem does not arise when what science is, is not contested. But this is not the case here. Of course, it would be unfair to suggest that Friedman is committed to the claim that his case study is meant to illustrate what science is. Rather the case study is meant to illustrate that economics is scientific.[4] Friedman's argument from the case study to his conclusion (FBC) also presupposes that something is scientific (as opposed to 'philosophy') if it is not 'enmeshed' in values. That is, Friedman assumes that scientific practice is in an important sense value free. The idea that 'positive' economics is a matter of value-free expertise is no surprise; it can be traced back in Friedman's writings (at least) to F1953: 'Positive economics is in principle independent of any particular ethical position or normative judgment' (1953, p. 4). That positive and ethical positions can and should be separated is often traced back to David Hume (often mentioned by Friedman when discussing the quantity theory of money) and more recently Max Weber (mentor, Frank Knight, and friend, George J. Stigler).[5]

Now if Friedman can get assent for his position – namely, that the claims of economics are tested in a value-free fashion – from economists that may disagree on values or politics then he has scored a non-trivial point. My initial concession not to dispute the facts of the case study may appear, thus, to concede the argument to Friedman. But here arises a second problem: one can grant that science appeals to 'experience' in evaluating the relative merits of competing hypotheses, yet still claim that it is enmeshed with values. Friedman should distinguish between the content of the theories and the observations (as well as the methods) that are supposed to make it true or false. Even if there is an unproblematic sense in which experience provides objective observation, the claims being vindicated by experience may still be shot through with values (here is a popular one: 'Liberal democracies never go to war with each other'[6]), even if they are re-formulated as the 'observation sentences' favored by my analytic ancestors.[7]

Friedman should distinguish between the possibility of reaching intersubjective agreement or even objectivity and the possibility of avoiding being enmeshed in values. This can build on an important point from F1953 ignored in the Nobel lecture. In F1953, Friedman emphasizes the importance of the public articulation of the 'rules for using the model'. Friedman (1953, p. 25) writes:

> In seeking to make a science as 'objective' as possible, our aim should be to formulate rules explicitly in so far as possible and continually to widen the range of phenomena for which it is possible to do so. But, no matter how successful we may be in this attempt, there inevitably will remain room for judgment in applying the rules.

Leaving aside the ironic fact that Friedman uses without justification what he calls 'normative language' ('our aim should be') to motivate a positive science, all Friedman would need for an argument that economics is in the appropriate way scientific, objective, or reasonable (and so on) is to divorce it from FBC. As Friedman's treatment of public rules to ensure objectivity suggests, it is the explicit and public availability of a standard or set of rules on how to use economic theories (or apply models, offer evidence, and so on) that makes it a candidate for being objective, not its value neutrality.

Thus, the case study cannot carry the weight of the argument. All it shows is that economists appeal to experience as a reason for adjudicating between competing hypotheses. (Of course, empirical verification need not be the same as confirmation.) Let us grant that this makes economists (potentially) reasonable. Let us even grant that this makes economics a candidate for being considered objective or scientific. It does not show that economics is either scientific or value free (or both). For an appeal to experience is entirely compatible with the claim that the axioms of economics are enmeshed in or presuppose non-arbitrary values, leaving aside problems of how to define 'arbitrary'. (My claim here is agnostic about whether or not science is or should be value free.)

On theory and experience

So far I have listed two problems with Friedman's argument in the Nobel lecture. Friedman's case study only provides evidence for a (potential) necessary condition for viewing economics as scientific, and Friedman mistakenly conflates objectivity with being value free. Now certainly there are ways around these problems, and a charitable reader of Friedman could introduce helpful distinctions without violating the spirit of Friedman's argument. But Friedman's appeal to experience proves problematic given his larger methodological commitments, many of which (by the way) I find quite congenial to my own.

Here I reflect on how the appeal to experience plays a non-trivial role in Friedman's Nobel lecture. Friedman concludes by offering the moral to be drawn from the case study: '*Brute experience* proved far more potent than the strongest of political or ideological experience' (1976 [1992], p. 285, my emphasis; in context, Friedman is talking about the experience with hyperinflation in Latin America in the 1970s). What follows is an *ad hominem* argument in my treatment of Friedman. I have no illusion that my argument works for all positions on these matters or that Friedman's position cannot be repaired, even if the problems I diagnose turn out to be very difficult to evade. I appeal to F1953 to attack Friedman because in the Nobel lecture itself Friedman (ibid., p. 268) appeals to F1953 to justify his claims.[8] While F1953 was written when Friedman and Stigler were debating the Cowles Commission, E.H. Chamberlin's monopolistic competition and

Walrasian economics more generally, by the time of the Nobel lecture the 1953 methodology piece had become iconic in the economics profession. Without doing justice to the rich context of F1953, one can still discern some important methodological principles that go beyond the crass instrumentalism with which F1953 is often associated.[9]

When we turn to F1953, it is clear that by Friedman's own lights the whole notion of 'brute experience' makes no sense. This is the third problem with Friedman's argument. Recall Friedman's understanding of what he calls 'positive economics' in the Nobel lecture and F1953. I ignore all the usual debates pertaining to F1953 (and the so-called 'F-Twist'), and call attention to some generally ignored features of Friedman's account of the nature of (economic/scientific) theories. According to Friedman, one should not offer a theory in an attempt to give a 'photographic reproduction' of the world, but only as a way to 'analyze' (1953, p. 35) it by offering a 'fundamental and relatively simple structure' (p. 33). 'A theory is the way we perceive "facts", and we cannot perceive "facts" without a theory' (p. 34). Thus, for Friedman, 'experience' is made possible by theory. This locution may strike those unfamiliar with the history of philosophy as somewhat strange, if not bizarre. But it is familiar sort of constructivism usually associated with Immanuel Kant, and has influenced all kinds of philosophers and social theorists since. As attention to Friedman's repeated use of scare-quotes within F1953 reveals ('explain', 'objective', 'real world', 'reality' (pp. 14, 4, 24, 41, respectively), he is consistent in calling attention to how facts, objectivity and even worlds are constructed. Notwithstanding the similarities with a Kuhnian perspective, which Friedman anticipates, Friedman's position (including the use of scare-quotes) has a respectable pedigree within philosophy. It can be identified – in a very wide sense – as a branch of neo-Kantianism. (It may reflect the influence of Max Weber or Talcott Parsons who were important to Frank Knight and George Stigler in this period;[10] it is also a presupposition of the philosophy of science of a group associated with the Vienna Circle, the so-called 'logical positivists/empiricists',[11] as well as their rivals the pragmatists. Kuhn, too, is committed to this outlook. To speak metaphorically, this view was 'in the air' at the start of the twentieth century.)

So, to be succinct and stark: there can be no such thing as 'brute experience' in Friedman's methodology. I regard this as a virtue of the discussion in F1953. A corollary of this view is that we can only perceive 'facts' that theory enables 'us' to perceive. A nice, unanticipated feature of this, is that it would allow the Friedman of F1953 to incorporate reference to 'framing-effects', the existence and importance of which became widely recognized due to the work of another Nobel laureate, Daniel Kahneman.

Friedman's methodology commits him to the view that 'experience' is, in a certain sense, generated (although not overdetermined) by theory in a non-trivial fashion. In Friedman's account 'experience' is not simply available to be inspected (or mythically 'given' as certain philosophers are wont to say; see Sellars 1965) but is rather itself the product of the collaborative or joint action of our theories (or conceptual apparatus), our faculties/senses and other information-gathering techniques, as well as the 'object' studied or the 'real world'.

The crucial point is this: if Friedman's case study is an accurate description of how two competing hypotheses of competing theories were indeed put to the test by appeal to 'experience', then on Friedman's methodology this implies some non-negligible facts about the nature of the competing theories. First, they share enough theoretical content to make possible more or less the same 'experience'. Friedman must grant this if he wants to claim that the 'drastic change that has occurred in accepted professional views' was produced by appeal to 'experience'. If he denies this then it follows from his methodology that other important considerations determined why this 'experience' is considered relevant or decisive at all, thus raising doubt about his position.[12] Incidentally, this is one reason why, post-Kuhn, historians and philosophers have recognized the rarity of so-called crucial experiments in deciding between major theoretical competitors; many theories gain strength from potentially disjunctive 'experience'.[13] (Of course, one can imagine that two distinct competing theories might give rise to overlapping 'experience', but this would be a marvellous coincidence.) This is why adherents to genuinely competitive theories have debates over what will count as 'data' as well as over what will serve as the appropriate methods to analyze it. As Deirdre McCloskey might say, 'of course on the frontiers of science the rhetoric is in dispute; *that is why they are the frontiers*'. It follows that 'experience' is more likely to be decisive (in an uncontroversial sense) when the competing hypotheses are generated by theories that share important family resemblances. In F1953, Friedman tacitly (and perhaps partially) recognizes this when he discusses how hard it would be for sociologists and economists to arrive at a 'satisfactory test' (1953, pp. 29–30).

Thus, given Friedman's own methodology, a more reasonable way to approach the case study is with the proviso that if one can genuinely and decisively adjudicate between two competing hypotheses on the basis of 'experience' one is almost certainly dealing with a debate within a theory, a debate between two versions of a theory or a debate between two closely related theories.[14] Once one recognizes this, one can see that the case study can only support a limited claim about the relationship between values and theories. For in general, the theoretical commitments that make possible (enough of) a shared 'experience' will track important values over core shared assumptions (and, as F1953 emphasizes, shared rules of application).

According to Friedman, a theory has several components: (a) a tautological 'language', which serves as a 'filing system for organizing empirical material and facilitating our understanding of it'. This filing system comes with (b) 'criteria by which it is to be judged . . . *appropriate* to a filing system. Are the categories clearly and precisely defined? Are they exhaustive?' [and so on]; and (c) a 'body of substantive hypotheses designed to abstract essential features of complex reality' (ibid., p. 7, emphasis added).

So, the fourth problem is this. It follows from Friedman's neo-Kantianism that one can accept Friedman's claims about methodology and still assert that science is enmeshed in values. Values can enter into theory at least at four levels:

1. at the level of the claims embedded within or among the tautologies that make up the basic (untestable) assumptions of theory (Kantians use the language of 'constitutive principles');
2. at the level of the criteria by which these are considered 'appropriate' to a filing system;
3. at the level of principles that guide the choice between, say, one particular theory/language system or another.

(I detail the fourth level below.) To adapt the language of Rudolf Carnap (a philosophical contemporary of Friedman's at The University of Chicago in the 1950s), the first two are questions *internal* and the third is *external* to a framework.[15] (It is convenient that there is a broad similarity between a Carnapian framework and Friedman's focus on the role of language in theories.) In the quote above, Friedman explicitly recognizes the importance of values in the second of these: he has entered the realm of normativity by using the language of 'appropriateness', and he even identifies the particular values with which to evaluate a filing system (that is, simplicity, fundamentality, completeness, consistency, exhaustiveness, and so on). So, there is a straightforward sense in which Friedman recognizes that science is enmeshed in values.

To be sure, Friedman may respond by granting that values enter into the criteria by which a language is considered 'appropriate' to a filing system (and by admitting that his rhetoric carried him away in the Nobel lecture), but these values are relatively innocent. They are internal, as it were, to the scientific enterprise and, in fact, make it possible for people with different substantial moral values to still get on with positive economics. (The same can be said for the central assumptions or constitutive principles that may never be put to the test.) I have some sympathy with this move, but note three things: (i) these criteria themselves are often in the eye of the beholder. Or to say this more kindly, they require good judgment (emphasized throughout F1953) which in turn may be a consequence of certain epistemic cultivation or intellectual virtues. This is why Friedman (again anticipating Kuhn) emphasizes the importance of cultivation and judgment (ibid., p. 25); (ii) they need not be stable or exhaustive;[16] (iii) Friedman's list may be incompatible with certain other competing criteria of appropriateness or competing intuitions about how to understand such criteria (this suggests that (i) and (iii) may not be distinct). For example, one may be committed to simplicity, by which one can mean avoiding needless multiplication of entities (that is, Occam's razor), or mean keeping the theory mathematically tractable. Neither of these will seem very controversial, even if they can occasionally conflict with each other and with common sense and scientific importance. But if one were to interpret simplicity to mean that ordinary people can understand one's arguments and results then it should be fairly evident that this can have a substantial impact on one's evaluation of appropriateness. In effect, it would change the nature of one's expertise.

But let us grant for the sake of argument that values embedded in the criteria of appropriateness of a filing system are relatively innocent and may have many virtues. They may be widely shared among many different frameworks that engage in science. (I am skeptical whether this is understood either as a historical/factual or as a conceptual claim, but so be it.) Friedman needs to show that the values that enter into the 'tautologies' (for example, the basic assumptions) of the theory and the external values that guide a choice of language (for Carnap these are 'optative') are innocent, too.

The values at play in these two levels are generally (albeit tacitly) connected at a fourth level where values can enter into a theory. Friedman recognizes that

4. the 'categories of the 'analytical filing system' have a meaningful empirical counterpart, that is, whether they are *useful* in analyzing a particular class of concrete problems' (ibid., p. 7, emphasis added).

For Friedman it is a matter of instrumental rationality that there must be a useful relationship between the external, optative values (whatever they may be) that guide language/framework choice and the categories that govern the basic assumptions of the framework. Now there may be a sense in which this notion of usefulness can be interpreted as a further, innocent value not unrelated to the criteria by which a language is considered 'appropriate' to a filing system. (This is why I am willing to use the language of instrumental rationality about this.) Yet, this concession is overly generous. While general (external) values that guide theory can be so vague as to be relatively innocent (commitment to truth, human flourishing, and so on), once they are translated either into concepts and categories that are operationalized within the theory (for example, 'the household;' 'the firm'; 'industry'; 'inflation'; 'unemployment'; 'the natural rate') or the pragmatic choice of concrete problems to analyze, then they tend to be highly contestable. What may be true in the abstract can become phoney at the level of scientific and practical detail.

A focus on increasing household income, say, may obscure relative movements of income within the household that are welfare reducing for some of its members.[17] In some contexts, one may increase political stability (compare Friedman 1976, p. 280 on the economic impact of political unrest) and investment in human capital if one favors policies that may reduce (increases) in overall household income but favor the formation of (human) capital by wives/mothers. Friedman's treatment of unemployment in the Nobel lecture shows how institutional/political priorities influence the supply and demand conditions that create the 'natural rate' on 'recorded unemployment'. A 'problem' may appear solvable if it is analyzed in terms of 'recorded unemployment', but not, say, in terms of the caloric intake of female infants. (In a patriarchal/hierarchical society in which 'recorded unemployment' is low, a baby girl can still suffer because her father devotes resources to his eldest son.) Measurement of inflation is tricky enough, but it may make a difference for real people if we take the weighted basket of goods to be representative of a mean or median household,[18] homeowners or renters, retirees or military personnel, and so on, even if for many classes of policy problems the differences iron out.[19]

Instead of multiplying examples, let me just state my conclusion about the phenomena based on Friedman's analysis of the structure of theories: whenever economists make conceptual or theoretical decisions about how to individuate and aggregate entities (or create index numbers, and so on) and how to represent these symbolically or mathematically they run the risk of introducing/disguising contested values.[20] In F1953, Friedman recognizes how tricky aggregation and individuation decisions are. In his discussion of how one analyzes the world with 'Marshall's apparatus' (p. 37) he recognizes how hard it is to group firms into 'industries' (p. 35); 'everything depends on the problem' (p. 36). This problem does not disappear even if these 'abstract models' (p. 35) track the causal structure of the 'world' (p. 35).[21]

Moreover, if for Friedman 'a theory is the way we perceive "facts", and we cannot perceive "facts" without a theory' (as shown earlier), then the concrete problems a theory is calibrated to focus on will make one miss 'facts' that may only be evident with a different theoretical framework which in turn may be designed to solve different problems. This connects to one important feature of Friedman's methodology that I admire: 'facts' (or data) are not available on the cheap, that is, 'facts' must be made amenable to theory-mediated perception. Of course, statistical agencies do not merely gather data (and analyze them, make them public, and so on) as a Baconian naturalist would. Given scarcity of resources and the political aims of government (and its internal factions), choices are made about what data are collected and measured. This is why changes in measurement practices of the consumer price index or unemployment statistics can generate political controversy. It follows from Friedman's methodology that there will be a tighter 'fit' (to echo Friedman's language of appropriateness) between the language of the theory and the practical application to particular concrete problems if our measures and our data-gathering devices themselves conform to concepts and categories in the theory. We would expect then that there will be trade-offs and interactions among the aims of the government or agencies in charge of data collection and the theoretical models that these agencies (and their constituents) employ. Values of all kinds will enter into the decision-making process to establish what 'facts' will be 'perceived' at all (see Rodenburg 2006). Of course, once 'facts' are around they can be used for all kinds of purposes, as Deirdre McCloskey (1998) taught us in her work on rhetoric.

A theory/language choice is a form of conceptual engineering (Carnap 1950 [1956]) all the way through the scientific supply chain. If theory is the basis of regime construction, then conceptual engineering is *social* engineering. The point is not that observation is theory laden (although Friedman is committed to that), or that some possible social 'happenings' may be unperceivable with a privileged conceptual apparatus (Friedman is committed to this, too), or that theories can be refuted (of course, they can), but, rather, that theories/languages/frameworks are normatively laden and that the choice of a framework (concepts, categories and so on) in the human sciences cannot escape 'our' commitments or interests. I agree with Friedman (1976 [1992], p. 268) that in principle, the social sciences are in no worse position than the so-called 'exact' sciences.[22] This is common sense: the enterprise of knowledge is, after all, valuable to 'us'. I use scare-quotes, because who is included in 'us' is contestable, too. Thus, FBC is incompatible with some of the most subtle elements of Friedman's methodology in F1953.

In this section, I argued at an abstract level that Friedman's methodological commitments in F1953 fatally undermine FBC. Even 'positive' economics is deeply enmeshed in values. Not being value free does not undermine the possibility of reasonable theory change or objectivity within 'positive' economics or its 'scientific' status. But without awareness of how values enter in, its practitioners are irrational – in the sense of lacking self-understanding about their activity. To quote Friedman (1953, p. 40): 'The importance of its subject matter to everyday life and to major issues of public policy impedes objectivity and promotes confusion between scientific analysis and normative judgment . . . More than other scientists, social scientists need to be self-conscious about their methodology'.

If the Chicago Boys (and many other economists) were taught a narrative which denied FBC, then they learned to think about their science in a way that did not reflect its reality.[23] They were (no doubt unintentionally) denied a reflexive understanding of 'positive' science. To state the end of the Nobel lecture back at Friedman (1976 [1992], p. 284, quoting Pierre S. DuPont): 'Bad logicians have committed more involuntary crimes than bad men have done intentionally'.

Yet, one may wonder why Friedman did not perceive the implications of his own methodology. I do not believe that this is due to lack of philosophic sophistication, bad logic (see Mäki 1986), or even the changed historical circumstances that the arguments of F1953 were meant to address. Rather, in the next section I speculate that the aims of the Nobel lecture can be best understood in the context of the furore over Friedman's association with the Chicago Boys' activity in Pinochet's Chile. I shall be able to make more concrete what is at stake in the seemingly abstract issues I have been engaged with thus far.

From Santiago to the award ceremony

> '[A]t all times sincere friends of freedom have been rare, and its triumphs have been due to minorities, that have prevailed by associating themselves with auxiliaries whose objects often differed from their own; and this association, which is always dangerous, has sometimes been disastrous'.
>
> (Lord Acton, quoted in Hayek 1956 [2007], p. 42)

In this section, I argue that Friedman's eagerness to prove FBC is a response to the public controversy arising from his association with the Chicago Boys. In the first subsection, I call attention to the importance of Orlando Letelier's attack on Friedman's media defence of the Chicago Boys. In the second, I argue that Friedman also used his Nobel lecture to defend the necessity of the economic policies of his Chilean admirers. Appendix 12A is provided at the end of the chapter to assist the reader with the timeline of events referred to in this section.

Letelier's attack

In March 1975, two University of Chicago professors, Friedman and Arnold Harberger, visited Chile for six days. On March 21, Friedman met Chile's strongman, Augusto Pinochet. A month after his visit, on April 25, Friedman wrote Pinochet to suggest shock therapy. A year later, Orlando Letelier, Salvador Allende's exiled foreign minister, published an article in the *Nation* that attacked Friedman for his role in the Pinochet regime.[24] He called Friedman the 'intellectual architect and unofficial adviser for the team of economists now running the Chilean economy' (Letelier 1976, p. 137). Shortly thereafter Letelier's Chilean citizenship was revoked by the junta, and on September 21 he was assassinated in Washington, DC by members of DINA, Chile's secret service. A few weeks later, on October 14, the Bank of Sweden announced its award of the Nobel Prize to Milton Friedman. On December 10, Friedman accepted the prize in Stockholm.

The following is Friedman's description of these events in his autobiography, *Two Lucky People*:

> That six-day visit [to Chile] plus my prior role as a professor *turned out to have consequences we never anticipated* and that we had to deal with for the next decade, including organized protests against me almost wherever I went, the largest being in Stockholm at the 1976 Nobel award ceremonies. . . . My crime was that I was allegedly 'the intellectual architect and unofficial adviser for the team of economists . . . running the Chilean economy'. (Friedman and Director Friedman 1998, p. 400, emphasis added)

Two Lucky People was published more than 20 years after the events described. Letelier's description of Friedman is quoted three times in the book (see also pp. 445 and 597). So it is fair to say that Letelier's charges and the public outcry they provoked and reflected stuck a nerve in Friedman. I claim that the content of the Nobel lecture reflects this.

Moreover, Letelier's piece was in large part devoted to attacking a claim Friedman made in *Newsweek* (Friedman 1976), which anticipates FBC:

> Milton Friedman . . . stated: '*In spite of my profound disagreement with the authoritarian political system of Chile, I do not consider it as evil for an economist to render technical economic advice to the Chilean Government, any more than I would regard it as evil for a physician to give technical medical advice to the Chilean Government to help end a medical plague.*' It is curious that the man who wrote a book, *Capitalism and Freedom*, to drive home the argument that only classical economic liberalism can support political democracy can now so easily disentangle economics from politics when the economic theories he advocates coincide with an absolute restriction of every type of democratic freedom. (Letelier 1976, p. 137; emphasis in original)

Letelier's focus of attack is Friedman's identification of economics as a form of technical expertise that is distinct from the politics required to implement its medicine. Of course, Letelier also charges that the Chilean case undercuts one of Friedman's fundamental claims about the relationship between economic and political freedoms.

While most of Letelier's article in the *Nation* describes the policies of the Chicago Boys and their economic and political impact on Chile, in his concluding lines he returns to an indictment of Friedman's claim that the policy advice offered by economists is best understood as a technical prescription, independent of the political context required to implement it:

> While the *Chicago boys* have provided an appearance of technical respectability to the *laissez-faire* dreams and political greed of the old landowning oligarchy and upper bourgeoisie of monopolists and financial speculators, the military has applied the brutal force required to achieve those goals. Repression for the majorities and *economic freedom* for small privileged groups are in Chile two sides of the same coin.
>
> There is, therefore, an inner harmony between the central priorities announced by the junta after the coup in 1973: the *destruction of the Marxist cancer* . . . the establishment of a free *private economy* and the control of inflation à la Friedman. It is nonsensical, consequently, that those who inspire, support or finance that economic policy should try to present their advocacy as restricted to *technical considerations*, while pretending to reject the system of terror it requires to succeed. (Letelier 1976, p. 142; emphasis in original)

It is clear that Letelier thinks that Friedman's appeal to an apolitical, technical expertise of economics is 'nonsensical' in the context of the Chilean experience.

Letelier further attacks the economist as doctor of (political/economic) society analogy in another way. The use of 'shock treatment' as the 'only medicine' for high inflation (Letelier is quoting a statement Friedman made to a Chilean newspaper) is identified with the junta's aim to remove the 'Marxist cancer', which leads to the torture and potential demise of most of the patients, that is, the 'majorities' of the Chilean people, while all benefits are for 'the old landowning oligarchy and upper bourgeoisie of monopolists and financial speculators'.

We can restate Letelier's diagnosis in terms closer to the argument made earlier. If the analogy with medicine holds then language/theory choice, the choice of basic assumptions and the particular concrete problems that are the focus of economists are all guided and made to cohere by the economic equivalent of a doctor aiming at good health or human flourishing. This kind of language goes back to Plato and was fiercely attacked by Karl Popper (1950; Popper is one of the few philosophers Friedman claimed to have read).[25] This would justify as innocent the interpretation of Friedman's use of the normative language of 'appropriateness' and would allow a charitable reading of the claim that 'positive economics is in principle independent of any particular ethical position'. Economic flourishing (or utility maximization) as the general good or fundamental value should do the job. Yet, according to Letelier's account, the example of Chile suggests two kinds of problems for the analogy. First, even if it were true (something that Letelier vigorously denies) that aggregate numbers vindicate the Chicago Boys' policies, they come with the cost of very regressive capital and income policies. Second, and more fundamental, the good that technical, economic experts promote can conflict with other potentially more fundamental values, for example, democratic participation, political freedom, the right to human dignity, justice, and so on. Even if one were willing to defend the Chicago Boys' particular choices, this point transcends the local circumstances of Chile. In the next section, I provide evidence of an assumption (held constant between F1953 and 1976) that prevented Friedman from grasping this point.

Now we are in position to better appreciate what is at stake in the argument of the Nobel lecture. Friedman and his students had become associated in the public with a defense of economics that in its self-understanding allows its expertise to be divorced from the political context in which policy advice is being implemented. This defense had been initiated by Friedman in his *Newsweek* article, but it follows naturally from the argument in F1953 that 'positive economics is in principle independent of any particular ethical position or normative judgment'. In the next section I show that in the Nobel lecture Friedman is also concerned to vindicate FBC in light of the Chilean circumstances.

The Nobel lecture

> 'If the idea is that Chicago-School economics has a bias in that direction [social engineering] I would say it is false. It is rather the *other* people who do. After all, we are the libertarians. Many of those people [that is, the Chicago Boys], I have mentioned, were *my* students, and they certainly didn't learn to love killing people in my classes'.
>
> Deirdre McCloskey, personal communication (see Hayek 1944, p. 24, 1942–44 [1979])

While the main point of the Nobel lecture does not focus on political applications of economics, Friedman soon explains the contemporary political relevance of the particulars of his case study:

> Many countries around the world are today experiencing socially destructive inflation, abnormally high unemployment, misuse of economic resources, and, in some cases, the suppression of human freedom not because evil men deliberately sought to achieve these results, nor because of differences in values among their citizens, but because of erroneous judgments about the consequences of government measures: errors that at least in principle are capable of being corrected by the progress of positive economic science. (1976 [1992], p. 268)

The main point of this passage is, of course, that high inflation is caused by preventable and correctable mistakes. Improved understanding of positive economics can cure this problem. Three elements of Friedman's statement are of concern here.

First there is an unmistakable nod to the situation in Chile, where the period before the coup (that is, the 'suppression of human freedom') was characterized by high inflation, and the time after by persistent inflation and abnormally high unemployment. Much later, reflecting back on the circumstances of his trip to Chile, Friedman said: 'I believe that the "Chicago Boys" had already reached the conclusion that a shock treatment was required to end the inflation and establish the basis for economic growth' (Friedman and Director Friedman 1998, p. 399). Of course, the description in the Nobel lecture captures the situation in Chile and many countries. In his lecture, Friedman is careful to mention the 'chronically high inflation' in 'many Latin American' countries (1976 [1992], p. 278). He speaks of the 'acute outbreak of super- or hyperinflation, as occurred recently in Chile and Argentina' (p. 279), and of 'forces [that] may render the political and economic system dynamically unstable and produce hyperinflation and radical political change – as in many defeated countries after World War I, or in Chile and Argentina more recently' (p. 281). Chile is not singled out. But the repeated references to it throughout the lecture show that it is never far from Friedman's mind.

Second, Friedman identifies 'radical political change' and 'suppression of freedom' not with the motives of individual agents, but with 'forces' that make economic systems very unstable and thus overwhelm political systems. While as a form of social explanation this treatment of historical change in terms of large impersonal 'forces' may be unobjectionable (provided that the mechanisms through which these forces cause their effects can be identified), it is surprising from an author normally associated with methodological individualism. But Friedman is driven into this awkward position because of a stance which reflects a deeper, more fundamental commitment.

For, third, Friedman wants to connect the 'suppression of freedom' with larger 'forces' because he wants to show it is not the result of 'evil men [that] deliberately sought to achieve these results, nor because of differences in values among their citizens'. Now, it is one thing to want to show that the Chicago Boys *qua* economic experts offering technical service are not 'evil' (recall Letelier's quote from Friedman's *Newsweek* article), but it is quite another thing to show that the agents of 'the suppression of freedom' are not 'evil'.[26] To my knowledge this is as close as Friedman has come to absolving Pinochet's junta (and other dictatorships). It is at odds with his condemnations of Pinochet's destruction of political freedoms and his 'authoritarian' policies (recall again the quote from the *Newsweek* article). He has written, for example, that Pinochet's adoption of free-market policies

> has given rise to the *myth* that only an authoritarian regime can successfully implement a free-market policy . . . Chile is an exception not the rule . . . But I predict that the free-market policy *will not last unless* the military government is replaced by a civilian government dedicated to political liberty – as the junta has announced is its intention. (Emphasis added)[27]

What causes Friedman's slip, however, is suggested by the rest of the claim. Friedman denies that there are 'differences in values among their citizens'. In order to treat this claim charitably I amend Friedman to mean that there are no differences in fundamental values or ultimate goods of the sort that guide theory choice or the concrete problems that economists ought to focus on. Thus, Friedman can be taken to mean that 'the suppression of freedoms' is a consequence of the forces of bad economic policy (itself caused by ignorance of positive economics), not of the actions of agents that may be pursuing aims incompatible with the values of those whose freedoms are suppressed. There is a remark in *Two Lucky People* that is in line with this. Friedman suggests that in the case of

Chile there was no 'other [responsible?] economic theory [sic!] that would have avoided the economic repression' (Friedman and Director Friedman 1998, p. 401), again implying that there is no responsibility on the part of the principal agents and policy makers of the Junta, and that there was no conflict over basic values.

I argued that Letelier's analysis of Chile had undermined Friedman's assumption of a fundamental unanimity about ultimate goods.[28] (Economists may recognize the assumption as positing the existence of a countrywide single welfare function.[29]) Friedman's Nobel lecture affirms this at a cost. Recall my claim that if theory is the basis of regime construction, then conceptual engineering becomes *social* engineering. Friedman's embrace of the crucial assumption of fundamental value unanimity removes the (logical) barrier between conceptual engineering and social engineering. Thus, Friedman tacitly endorses the benevolent dictator model of social engineering in the Nobel lecture.

To be clear: in earlier writings Friedman had never asserted that political freedom is a means toward economic freedom. Rather he argues, 'economic freedom is also an *indispensable* means toward the achievement of political freedom' (Friedman 1962, p. 8, see also Hayek 1944, p. 110). Moreover, he does not think that economic freedom must result in political freedom:

> Political freedom in this instance [that is, in the Western World] clearly came along with the free market and the development of the capitalist institutions. So also did political freedom in the golden age of Greece and in the early days of the Roman Era. History suggests only that capitalism is a necessary condition for political freedom. Clearly it is not a sufficient condition . . . It is . . . clearly possible to have economic arrangements that are fundamentally capitalist and political arrangements that are not free. (Friedman 1962, p. 10)[30]

Leaving aside Friedman's curious neglect of the role of slavery and the lack of enfranchised women in the economies of Ancient Greece and Rome, the position in the Nobel lecture is at least consistent with some of his earlier views. Nevertheless, it contradicts one of Friedman's fundamental claims:

> To deny that the end justifies the means is indirectly to assert that the end in question is not the ultimate end, that the ultimate end is itself the use of proper means. Desirable or not, any end that can be attained only by the use of bad means must give way to the more basic end of the use of acceptable means. To the liberal, the appropriate means are free discussion and voluntary co-operation, which implies that any form of coercion is inappropriate. (Ibid., p. 22)

With its tacit endorsement of the benevolent dictator model of social engineering, the Nobel lecture position violates the 'ultimate end' of 'the use of proper means', namely, 'free discussion and voluntary co-operation'. An ultimate end is not up for grabs even in the face of large social forces. (No doubt this is one reason why Friedman made such an attractive target for Letelier's ire.) Deirdre McCloskey has reported (in personal communication) evidence that suggests that even in the period under discussion Friedman was deeply committed to this ultimate end:

> When [in the early 1970s] the Shah of Iran proposed to give the University of Chicago a large amount of money for a chair in Economics and sending to Chicago good grad students, a la Chile and Brazil (which agreements were made, remember, with *democracies*) Milton Friedman killed it. I was at the meeting. The expert-believing people were behind it . . . Milton said, 'We can't make such an agreement with a despot', End of discussion.

Moreover, the position of the Nobel lecture is not overdetermined by his earlier views. In F1953, Friedman's denial of 'fundamental differences in basic values' had been relativized to the existence of 'disinterested citizens'[31] and the 'circumstances' prevailing in 'the Western World' and 'especially the United States' (1953, p. 5). Moreover, in the context of F1953 it is clear that Friedman offers the claim as a broad generalization not an exceptionless law. He also recognizes that differences in basic values can cause men to 'fight' (p. 5). So Friedman could have attempted a defense of FBC without treating 'the suppression of freedoms' as a strict consequence of the forces of bad economic policy. I suspect that Friedman's eagerness to defend FBC in the context of attacks on his integrity is what leads him to this disastrous position. He slides into an unintentional embrace of social engineering, one that is at odds (as Letelier recognized) with the position outlined in Friedman's other earlier writings. A defense of social engineering is a recurring temptation for economists and other experts.[32] Hayek, of course, noted it among those of socialist inclination. But the temptation has not been eradicated among prominent so-called mainstream economists today.[33]

Conclusion: the role of public intellectuals

> I conclude – and perhaps I am alone in concluding – that when the economist goes to Washington, he deserves no more credence, and no less, than any other political appointment, and it is mildly deceptive to address him as Doctor or Professor.
>
> George Stigler (1988, pp. 135–6)

In conclusion, I briefly reflect on why Friedman was chosen as the main target of Letelier's criticism and the public furore, especially because Al Harberger was more closely involved with the Chicago Boys as an intellectual and personal mentor.[34] All evidence suggests that Friedman had far less involvement with the Chicago Boys than, say, Harberger, Gregg Lewis and Larry Sjaastad. Friedman taught the basic course in economic theory and ran a workshop on money and banking, but had little involvement with the Chicago programs in South America or recruiting and advising Latin American students.[35] Nevertheless, in 1971, before the events of the Pinochet coup, a critic of the Chicago Boys claimed that 'The Chileans who returned from Chicago after 1960 are even more Friedmanite than Friedman himself'.[36] In *Two Lucky People* Friedman offers this explanation: 'The reason that I was chosen for special attention is obvious. My connection with Goldwater and Nixon, my *Newsweek* column, and my being awarded the Nobel prize made me better known to the *general public* and hence a more useful target' (Friedman and Director Friedman 1998, p. 403, emphasis added). So Friedman's own explanation is that he was more of a public intellectual than other possible targets. (Recall that this role is part of what landed him the Nobel Prize.) But Friedman also used his role as a public intellectual to offer intellectual cover to the policies of the Chicago Boys. As he clarifies: 'I believe that the "Chicago Boys" had already reached the conclusion that a shock treatment was required to end the inflation and establish the basis for economic growth . . . *Our role was to check their conclusion, give it, as it were, the stamp of approved, and help to sell it to the public and the military junta*' (ibid. pp. 399–400, emphasis added). So Friedman's public role and his embrace of it made him a natural target of criticism.

For Friedman, 'the really important thing about the Chilean business is that free markets did work their way in bringing about a free society' (Public Broadcasting Corporation 2000). It is disturbing that Friedman does not address how he balances this outcome with the 2,095 deaths and 1,102 'disappearances' (conservative estimate) recorded by the Chilean government's Rettig Commission. But my purpose here is not to re-fight the cold war or the events surrounding the Pinochet junta. As should be clear, I disagree with Friedman about what is really important about this topic.

It is worth reminding ourselves that Letelier was by no means the only notable critic of Friedman. He became the most prominent because – as Friedman realizes – Letelier's assassination made him a 'martyr' (Friedman and Director Friedman 1998, p. 402). In *Two Lucky People*, Friedman spends considerable space quoting from Anthony Lewis's column in the *New York Times* (21 September 1975). Lewis asks about the nature of the 'responsibility' of intellectual 'authors' of public policy. He is willing to grant that policy 'can be perverted from what its framers' intended'. Nevertheless, Lewis thinks that 'there are troubling questions here about the social role of academics' (quoted in Friedman and Director Friedman 1998, p. 401). Although he quotes Lewis at length, Friedman is not much troubled by these questions. In *Two Lucky People*, he responds to Lewis by suggesting that in Chile no responsible economic theory could have been implemented without repression (see the above quote). Thus, even though Friedman repeatedly denounced Pinochet elsewhere, in the Nobel lecture and in *Two Lucky People*, Friedman ends up in a position close to the 'the French writers who laid the foundations of modern socialism', in the sense that they 'had no doubt that their ideas could be put into practice only by strong dictatorial government' (Hayek 1944, p. 28).

Lewis raises one of the oldest questions that preoccupied philosophers since the trial of Socrates: what responsibility do philosophers have for the actions of their students? It turns out that this question is a species of the more fundamental question: how is rational and free thought possible in (a democratic) society?[37] Reflection on this question with help from Friedman's predecessors as public intellectuals and economists, Adam Smith and David Hume, should make good on my promissory note that philosophy can benefit economists and the public at large. But that should await another occasion.

Notes

* I am indebted to the comments of participants and audience members at 'Chicago Day' during the fifth edition of the Summer Institute for the Preservation of the History of Economics, at George Mason University, July 2005, especially David Levy, Sandy Peart, Ali Khan, Leon Montes, and Maria Paganelli; the Department of Economics, New York University, especially Mario Rizzo and Sandy Ikeda; the Department of Economics, University of Groningen, especially Menno Rol; Erasmus University's Institute for Philosophy and Economics Seminar at Erasmus University, especially, Uskali Mäki and Jack Vromen; and a session on 'Chicago' at the 2006 Allied Social Science Associations Meeting with Phil Morowski and Dan Hammond commenting. Special thanks are due to Mark Blaug, Warren Samuels, Ross Emmett and, in particular, Sarah Brouillette and Deirdre McCloskey for very helpful comments on an earlier draft. I also wish to thank Warren Samuels and Deirdre McCloskey for permission to use comments from personal communications with me.

1. Erik Lundberg's (1976) presentation speech states, 'It is rare indeed that an economist has gained such direct and indirect influence as Friedman has, not only on the course of scientific research, but also on actual policies'.
2. Friedman probably has Popperian falsification in mind. See, for example, 'there is no "certain" substantive knowledge; only tentative hypotheses that can never be "proved", but can only fail to be rejected, hypotheses in which we may have more or less confidence, depending on such features as the breadth of experience they encompass relative to their own complexity and relative to alternative hypotheses, and the number of occasions on which they have escaped possible rejection' (Friedman 1976 [1992], p. 267).

3. For some of the curious entanglement of Chicago economics, especially George Stigler, with Kuhn's philosophy of science, see Schliesser (forthcoming). Uskali Mäki (1986) appears to be the first to have called attention to the many similarities between Friedman and Kuhn.
4. The Bank of Sweden press release announcing the award to Friedman repeatedly calls attention to the 'scientific' nature of Friedman's achievements and invokes a 'scientific point of view' when it makes its claims about Friedman (Royal Swedish Academy of Sciences 1976).
5. See Emmett (2006) and Schliesser (2011).
6. The claim that liberal democracies don't war against each other is often offered up as a prediction, an observation, a justification, a moral injunction and propaganda (or all at once).
7. Even in Quine, no logical positivist, observation sentences play a very important role (see Quine 1993).
8. My situation is somewhat ironic because elsewhere I offer a sympathetic reading of F1953 (Schliesser 2005a).
9. See for useful corrective Hoover (2009).
10. See Emmett (2006) and Schliesser (2001).
11. The logical positivists should not be confused with those advocating positive economics or with the caricatures of logical positivism often found in descriptions of it (based on familiarity with Hempel's (1941 [1965]) little textbook).
12. An argument of this sort is exploited by adherents to the so-called 'Strong Program' (Barry Barnes, David Bloor, Harry Collins and others) to insist that values play a crucial role in science.
13. 'Observed facts are necessarily finite in number; possible hypotheses, infinite. If there is one hypothesis that is consistant [sic] with the available evidence, there are always an infinite number that are' (Friedman 1953, p. 9). Moreover, Friedman realizes that 'the choice among alternative hypotheses equally consistent with the available evidence must to some extent be arbitrary' (p. 10). For more discussion see my treatment of Friedman's identification of the Duhem–Quine thesis in Schliesser (2005a).
14. Here I leave aside how difficult it is in practice to make any empirical evidence bear directly on a theory or hypothesis of it. This is true in the experimental and non-experimental sciences. In F1953 Friedman makes wise comments about this. (Warren Samuels (personal communication) states that 'in the pre-Keynesian period both those who supported over-saving and those who supported under-consumption pointed to the *same* data, namely, unsold goods'.) One sign of the over-reliance on statistical and data-mining techniques in contemporary economics is that it has become entirely too easy to test or bring data to bear on theory: see my comments on Lucas (1973) in Schliesser (2005a). This is not the place to resolve the merely apparent paradox.
15. See Rudolf Carnap (1950 [1956]). My use of Carnap is strictly for purposes of clarification. While there are striking similarities between Carnap's approaches to frameworks and Friedman's understanding of structural features of theories, I do not claim that there was mutual influence without further evidence, if any, of (say) Savage's links to Carnap (who was very interested in developing probability theory).
16. I read Adam Smith's 'The history of astronomy' as offering an account of the changing character and number of such norms within science (Schliesser 2005b). See also McCloskey (1994).
17. This is especially the case in economies that transition from barter to markets, or from protected to liberalized policies. (Of course, legal arrangements concerning property and marriage, and so on have an impact, too.)
18. David M. Levy (1995) taught me how important it is to distinguish between mean and median utility.
19. Deirdre McCloskey has suggested to me in person that technical problems in index numbers are *on their very face* matters of conflicting values.
20. For an important, very sophisticated, technical treatment of how values can enter into decision sciences, see Tribe (1973). I thank Yitzhak Melamed for calling my attention to Tribe's piece. See also Putnam (2004) for a recent influential philosophical treatment of these issues.
21. See also Friedman's discussion of how in different kinds of markets, 'supply' and 'demand' factors can become very difficult to distinguish (Friedman 1953, p. 8). The assertion made here deflects the intuition that if one can show that positive economics accurately describes the causal structure of our (social) world then a version of FBC is back in business even if we may have to decouple FBC from Friedman's particular views about causation. Of course, if by causes we mean physical causes then the intuition is secure given the resources developed in this paper. But no *economist* should find this much solace.
22. It is no coincidence that Friedman quotes anecdotal evidence from the geneticist, R.A. Fisher, to this effect. Values are more difficult to disentangle from the bio-life sciences than certain obscure areas in physics and chemistry.
23. Of course, this claim requires substantial historical evidence that the Chicago Boys were committed to FBC.
24. Dan Hammond's presidential address to the History of Economics Society (2003), called attention to the importance of Letelier's essay and his subsequent assassination in order to understand the intensity and

nature of the public outcry over the award of the Nobel Prize to Friedman. However, Hammond does not explore how Friedman's lecture responds to Letelier's charges.

25. A possible source may be the sociologist Talcott Parsons, a correspondent of Knight and fellow translator of Max Weber who influenced 'new Chicago' methodology just as it was being developed (Stigler 1950, p. 23, see Parsons 1964, Buxton and Turner 1992).
26. Frank Knight (1939 [1999], pp. 42, 43) had no qualms about calling Marxists 'wicked' or 'evil'.
27. These comments appear in a 1982 issue of *Newsweek*, and are quoted in *Two Lucky People* (Friedman and Director Friedman 1998, pp. 406–7). See Hayek's (2007, p. 173) comment: 'This process of creating "myth" to justify his action need not be conscious'. In other contemporary contexts, Friedman was a fierce *critic* of some of the economic policies pursued by the 'Chicago Boys'. See his piece on the currency board that was run by Chile until the 'major recession' of the early 1980s (Friedman 1994, p. 236). It is a striking fact that post-Pinochet, democratic Chile has in many respects been more faithful and (on nearly all measures) successful in applying genuine market-based policies than the Chicago Boys who lurched from crisis to crisis (not surprising given Chile's then reliance on earnings from copper and the lack of automatic stabilizers in the system). For some reason this fact is overlooked by all sides of the debate!
28. Frank Knight may have been a (an unintentional) source for this claim. In his three-part article 'Ethics and economic reform', Knight's treatment of this matter evolves in fascinating and subtle fashion. First, Knight claims that 'society depends upon – we may almost say that it *is* – moral likemindedness' (1939 [1999], p. 1). His analysis does not offer evidence for this position. But a few pages later, he offers a weaker and more plausible claim, that 'every social order is . . . necessarily ethical' (p. 4). In the third article, however, Knight reverts to a more (legal) Positivist view: society is now 'properly defined as the legal order under which any group of people lives'. However, Knight is not a mere (legal) Positivist because he insists on the importance of the 'accepted rules' in defining the existence of a society (p. 54). Knight calls attention to the fact that 'social problems . . . root in the brute fact that all organised relationships, or relationships of any degree of permanence whatever, imply a common recognition of rules or an accepted pattern of action' (p. 54). When the common recognition is absent this should have disastrous consequences (as most civil wars and revolutions suggest, see p. 73, n. 40).
29. I ignore here the question why Friedman thought he could assume this given Arrow's impossibility theorem. As I show below, the statement in F1953 is so weak that Arrow's result need not impact it. But reflection on Arrow's result (especially given the assumptions of citizen sovereignty and of non-dictatorship) should have made Friedman more cautious in his claims in the Nobel lecture.
30. One wishes that contemporary commentators of China, Singapore, and Russia would reflect on this before they would pontificate on how economic reform will lead to political reform.
31. Of course, economists as experts find it difficult to be disinterested citizens when they enter the political realm given the opportunities for rent-seeking, status enhancement, visibility, power, riches, and so on.
32. Harberger transforms the temptation into an act of pioneering *courage*:

    > [You] can't say that these reforms are inevitably shackled to a military government.
    >
    > Now it can be said, however, that the first ones to do something, the pioneers, always have a harder time than those that follow them. And in the context of the middle and late 1970s in Latin America it took a great deal of courage to take those steps. Given that there was a military government, the idea that they were willing to cede economic authority to a group of technocrats made that transition easier than it would have been in a democratic context of the same time and place. (Levy 1999)

33. For example, writing in *Businessweek*, Professor Robert J. Barro (2002) stated,

    > China managed to liberalize slowly without losing control of the legal system and the political process. The often-condemned suppression of the Tiananmen Square student uprising in 1989 was a crucial part of this approach. Had the government yielded to the student protests, the likely result would have been political chaos and poorer economic performance. China has also advanced in legal rights . . . Even religious freedom is practiced – the suppression of the Falun Gong was not on religious grounds but out of fear that the group would facilitate anti-government protests.

    I cannot resist quoting my youthful rejoinder in a letter sent to the editor of *Business Week*, but not published:

    > Why is it that when otherwise sane academics visit China they lose their ability to think clearly and start pontificating on areas outside their competence? . . . For Adam Smith, a wiser economist, there was no doubt that stable, prosperity-producing political authority depended on the good-will of the citizens toward their government. It's sad that Barro is using his cosseted life of academic tenure to become a spokesperson for continued tyranny.

34. 'My only direct involvement in Chile came when Al Harberger asked me to accompany him to Chile under

the auspices of Banco Hipotecario . . . in a week of seminars and public talks. . . . One of our meetings was with General Pinochet – which gave an iota of substance to later charges that I was a personal adviser to the general. . . but he [Pinochet] did stress and urge that I write him my judgment after the end of my visit to Chile. This I did after we got back to Chicago' (Friedman and Director Friedman 1998, pp. 398–9). Banco Hipotecario was controlled by Manuel Cruzat, one of the initial Chicago Boys (Valdés 1995, p. 229).

35. This is, for example, Harberger's own view (Levy 1999).
36. Mario Zanartu, an economist trained at Columbia University, quoted in Valdés (1995, p. 206).
37. In work elsewhere, I call this the 'Socratic Problem'. I distinguish between five variants: (SP1) a philosopher claims that practical philosophy takes precedence (in some way) over theoretical philosophy (for example, because the right/duty to do theoretical philosophy must be deduced in practical philosophy); (SP2) a philosopher explains how statements of traditional religious texts (and so on) can be understood as expressions of his philosophical doctrines; (SP3) a philosopher appeals to non-philosophical (political, religious, social) sources as authoritative; (SP4) a philosopher is forced (or threatened) by outside authorities to adjust his views; (SP5) a philosopher is held accountable for the impact of his teachings on his students. My name ('Socratic Problem') for this is meant to suggest that the submission of philosophy's freedom to other political/moral/religious authority is a perennial issue for philosophy; the Galileo affair is a famous example from the seventeenth century. These five variants may occur simultaneously or be blended in various ways (Schliesser in press).

References

Barro, R.J. (2002), 'China's slow but steady march to reform', *Business Week*, September 30.

Buchanan, J.M. (1960 [1987]), 'La Scienza delle Finanze: the Italian tradition in fiscal theory', in *Economics: Between Predictive Science and Moral Philosophy*, College Station, TX: Texas A&M University Press, pp. 317–56.

Buxton, W. and S. Turner (1992), 'From education to expertise: sociology as "profession"', in *Sociology and Its Publics*, Halliday, T.C. and M. Janowitz (eds), Chicago, IL: University of Chicago Press, pp. 373–407.

Carnap, R. (1950 [1956]), 'Empiricism, semantics, and ontology', in *Meaning and Necessity: A Study in Semantics and Modal Logic*, 2nd edn, Chicago, IL: University of Chicago Press, pp. 205–21.

Emmett, Ross (2006), 'Frank Knight, Max Weber, Chicago Economics, and Institutionalism', *Max Weber Studien* (1), 101–19.

Friedman, M. (1953), 'The methodology of positive economics', in *Essays in Positive Economics*, Chicago, IL: University of Chicago Press, pp. 3–43.

Friedman, M. (1962), *Capitalism and Freedom*, Chicago, IL: University of Chicago Press.

Friedman, M. (1976), 'Reply to letter from the Citizen's' Committee on Human Rights and Foreign Policy', *Newsweek*, June 14.

Friedman, M. (1976 [1992]), 'Inflation and unemployment', in *Nobel Lectures, Economics 1969–1980*, Lindbeck, A. (ed.), Singapore: World Scientific, pp. 267–86.

Friedman, M. (1994), 'Chile and Israel: identical policies – opposite outcomes', in *Money Mischief: Episodes in Monetary History*, New York: Harcourt Brace Jovanovich, pp. 234–48.

Friedman, M. and R. Director Friedman (1998), *Two Lucky People: Memoirs*, Chicago, IL: University of Chicago Press.

Hammond, J.D. (2003), 'Remembering economics', *Journal of the History of Economic Thought*, **25**, 133–44.

Hayek, F.A. (1942–44 [1979]), 'Scientism and the study of society', in *The Counter-revolution of Science: Studies on the Abuse of Reason*, 2nd edn, Indianapolis, IN: Liberty Press, pp. 17–182.

Hayek, F.A. (1944), *The Road to Serfdom*, Chicago, IL: University of Chicago Press.

Hayek, F.A. (1956 [2007]), 'Foreword to the 1956 American paperback edition', in *The Road to Serfdom: Text and Documents: Definitive Edition*, Caldwell, B. (ed.), Chicago, IL: University of Chicago Press, pp. 39–52.

Hayek, F.A. (2007), *The Road to Serfdom: Text and Documents: Definitive Edition*, Caldwell, B. (ed.), Chicago, IL: University of Chicago Press.

Hempel, C.G. (1941 [1965]), 'The function of general laws in history', in *Aspects of Scientific Explanation and Other Essays in the Philosophy of Science*, New York: Free Press, pp. 231–43.

Hoover, Kevin D. (2009), 'Friedman's methodological stance: causal realism', in *The Methodology of Positive Economics: Reflections on the Milton Friedman Legacy*, Uskali Mäki (ed.), Cambridge: Cambridge University Press.

Knight, F.H. (1939 [1999]), 'Ethics and economic reform', in *Selected Essays by Frank H. Knight*, vol. 2: *Laissez-faire: Pro and Con*, Emmett, R.B. (ed.), Chicago, IL: University of Chicago Press, pp. 1–75.

Kuhn, T.S. (1962), *The Structure of Scientific Revolutions*, Chicago, IL: University of Chicago Press.

Letelier, O. (1976), 'The Chicago Boys in Chile: economic freedom's awful toll', *The Nation*, August 28 pp. 137–42.

Levy, D.M. (1995), 'The partial spectator in the *Wealth of Nations*: a robust utilitarianism', *European Journal of the History of Economic Thought*, **2** (2), 299–326.
Levy, D. (1999), 'Interview with Arnold Harberger', available at: minneapolisfed.org/pubs/region/99-03/harberger.cfm (accessed July 17, 2007).
Lucas, R.E., Jr. (1973), 'Some international evidence on output–inflation tradeoffs', *American Economic Review*, **63** (3), 326–34.
Lundberg, E., (1976), 'Presentation speech', available at: http://nobelprize.org/nobel_prizes/economics/laureates/1976/presentation-speech.html (accessed February 9, 2008).
Mäki, U. (1986), 'Rhetoric at the expense of coherence: a reinterpretation of Milton Friedman's methodology', in *Research in the History of Economic Thought and Methodology*, vol. 4, Samuels, W.J. (ed.), Greenwich, CT: JAI Press, pp. 127–43.
Marshall, A. (1885 [1925]), 'The present position in economics', in *Memorials of Alfred Marshall*, Pigou, A.C. (ed.), London: Macmillan, pp. 153–71.
McCloskey, D.N. (1994), *Knowledge and Persuasion in Economics*, Cambridge: Cambridge University Press.
McCloskey, D.N. (1998), *The Rhetoric of Economics*, 2nd rev. edn, Madison, WI: University of Wisconsin Press.
Parsons, T. (1964), 'Propaganda and social control', in *Essays in Sociological Theory*, Glencoe, IL: Free Press, pp. 142–76.
Popper, K. (1950), *The Open Society and Its Enemies*, Princeton, NJ: Princeton University Press.
Public Broadcasting Corporation (2000), 'Commanding heights: Milton Friedman', available at: http://www.pbs.org/wgbh/commandingheights/shared/minitextlo/int_miltonfriedman.html#10 (accessed September 15, 2008).
Putnam, H. (2004), *The Collapse of the Fact/Value Dichotomy and Other Essays*, Cambridge, MA: Harvard University Press.
Quine, W.V. (1993), 'In praise of observation sentences', *Journal of Philosophy*, **90** (3), 107–16.
Rodenburg, P. (2006), 'The construction of instruments for measuring unemployment', dissertation, Economics and Econometrics, University of Amsterdam.
Royal Swedish Academy of Sciences (1976), 'This year's economics prize to an American', available at: http://nobelprize.org/nobel_prizes/economics/laureates/1976/press.html (accessed February 9, 2008).
Schliesser, E. (2005a), 'Galilean reflections on Milton Friedman's "Methodology of positive economics": with thoughts on *Economics in the Laboratory*', *Philosophy of the Social Sciences*, **35** (1), 50–74.
Schliesser, E. (2005b), 'Wonder in the face of scientific revolutions: Adam Smith on Newton's "proof" of Copernicanism', *British Journal for the History of Philosophy*, **13** (4), 697–732.
Schliesser, E. (2011), 'The surprising Weberian roots to Milton Friedman's Methodology', in *Explanation, Prediction and Confirmation: New Trends and Old Ones Reconsidered*, Dieks, D. et al. (eds), Dordrecht: Springer.
Schliesser, E. (forthcoming), 'Inventing paradigms, monopoly and methodology at "Chicago" Economics: Nutter and Stigler' in *Building Chicago Economics: New Perspectives on the History of America's Most Powerful Economics Program*, Van Horn, R., P. Mirowski and T. Stapleford (eds), Cambridge: Cambridge University Press.
Schliesser, E. (in press), 'The Newtonian refutation of Spinoza' in *Interpreting Newton*, Janiak, A. and E. Schliesser (eds), Cambridge: Cambrdige University Press.
Sellars, W. (1965), 'Empiricism and the philosophy of mind', in *Minnesota Studies in the Philosophy of Science*, vol. 1, *The Foundations of Science and the Concepts of Psychology and Psychoanalysis*, Feigl, H. and M. Scriven (eds), Minneapolis, MN: University of Minnesota Press, pp. 253–329.
Stigler, G.J. (1950), *Five Lectures on Economic Problems*, New York: Macmillan.
Stigler, G.J. (1988), *Memoirs of an Unregulated Economist*, New York: Basic Books.
Tribe, L.H. (1973), 'Policy science: analysis or ideology?', *Philosophy and Public Affairs*, **2** (1), 66–110.
Valdés, J.G. (1995), *Pinochet's Economists: The Chicago School of Economics in Chile*, Cambridge: Cambridge University Press.

Appendix 12A Timeline of Chilean events

1955–64: USAID finances arrangement between University of Chicago and Catholic University, Santiago, Chile
1970: Salvador Allende elected president with 36.8 percent of vote
1970–71: expansionary policies, nationalizations, land-reform, etc.
1972–73: hyper-inflation (ca 800 percent/year) and recession
1973, September: Military coup under General Augusto Pinochet (CIA); President Allende dies (murder/suicide); installation of 'Chicago Boys', who had prepared 'El Ladrillo' (the Brick) in secret for the Navy
1974: 12.9 percent drop in GDP; 340 percent/yr inflation
1975: heavy recession (despite financial assistance from US and the International Monetary Fund: IMF)
1975, March: Friedman and Arnold Harberger visit Chile invited by a bank; Friedman gives two public talks at the Catholic University and the University of Chile
1975, March 21: Friedman meets Pinochet
1975, April 25: Friedman writes Pinochet to suggest shock therapy
1976, August: Orlando Letelier, exiled foreign/defense minister of Allende, publishes article in *The Nation*, attacking Friedman
1976, September 21: Letelier assassinated in Washington, DC, by members of DINA (Chile's secret service)
1976, October 14: announcement of Nobel Prize to Milton Friedman
1976, December 10: Milton Friedman accepts Nobel Prize
1975–1981: 7.2 percent annual growth in Chile (74–81: 2.6 percent); selective privatization favoring 'Chicago Boys' – connected insiders
1979: labor markets freed
1981: Pinochet wins plebiscite
1982–83: deep recession in Chile: (17 percent fall in GDP, 30 percent unemployment)
1983, January: banking system bail-out (re-nationalization)
1983–85: Chilean Central Bank compensates domestic debtors
1983–86: social protests
1983–87: IMF bail-out ($760 million/year) → 'Washington Consensus'
1984: Chile's GDP is back at 1968 levels (more unequal distribution and *persistent inflation*)
1986–89: Chile's economy starts growing again (7.7 percent/year), privatization more serious, but government spending overheats economy, yet again
1988, October 5: Pinochet loses plebiscite
1989, December: despite Chicago Boys' warnings, Patricio Aylwin elected president
1991: Rettig Commission: (conservative estimate) 2,095 deaths, 1,102 'disappearances'

13 Neoliberalism and Chicago

*Robert Van Horn and Philip Mirowski**

Introduction

'Neoliberalism' is a term of art in philosophy, history and political theory, although much less commonly used in economics. It refers to a pronounced change in the doctrines related to classical liberalism, dating from the middle of the twentieth century (George 1999, Burns 2004), occurring both in America and in Europe. Often confused or conflated with neo-conservatism and neo-libertarianism, it in fact a fairly coherent and elaborate doctrine, with a well-defined set of origins intimately related to many members of the Chicago School of Economics (Van Horn and Mirowski 2009). It was also invented and nurtured in its early stages by members of the Mont Pèlerin Society (MPS) (Hartwell 1995, Walpen 2004). Moreover, one of its main proponents, Milton Friedman, actually used the term to refer to the movement in its earliest stages (Friedman 1951), although he dropped the reference thereafter. Since the term tends to be used in divergent ways among historians (Denord 2001, Walpen 2004), philosophers influenced by Michel Foucault (Burchell et al. 1991, Barry et al. 1996, Lemke 2001, Foucault 2004), political scientists (Amadae 2003, Mirowski 2005), critics of globalization and a few economists (De Long 1990), we shall attempt here to provide a summary description that captures the salient points of each of their contributions.

Neoliberalism

The starting point of neoliberalism is the admission, contrary to classical liberalism, that their political program will triumph only if it becomes reconciled to the fact that the conditions for its success must be *constructed*, and will not come about 'naturally' in the absence of concerted effort. This had direct implications for the neoliberal attitude towards the state, as well as towards political parties and other corporate entities that were the result of conscious organization, and not simply unexplained 'organic' growths. In a phrase, 'The Market' would not naturally conjure up the conditions for its own continued flourishing. As Milton Friedman joked in a letter to Friedrich Hayek, 'our faith requires that we are skeptical of the efficacy, at least in the short run, of organized efforts to promulgate [the creed]' (quoted in Hartwell 1995, p. xiv). The ultimate purpose of institutions such as the MPS and the Chicago School was not so much to revive a dormant classical liberalism, as it was to forge a neoliberalism better suited to modern conditions.

The classical liberalism of the eighteenth-century philosophers was a theory of natural tendencies in human nature, which might have been stifled or misdirected by misguided understandings of the natural order. It took as its benchmark the 'obvious and simple system of natural liberty [which] establishes itself of its own accord', as Adam Smith (1776 [1976]) put it in Book IV of *The Wealth of Nations*. It was this conception of liberty which Friedman was citing as the prior 'creed': a political doctrine so transparent and robust that one did not need to organize special cadres to argue out its tenets, or forge cabals to spread its practice. The previous theorists of classical liberalism had exhibited a tendency to be either such inveterate optimists that they would perceive no need for concerted political and social organization in the interests of liberty, or else, curmudgeonly elitists who would feel their individuality soiled by participation in actual political activity. The building of political movements and the innovation of lasting institutions for the purpose of the spread of liberal doctrines was not a natural part of the heritage of either wing of the tradition.

The term 'neoliberalism' was first coined at the Colloque Walter Lippmann in Paris in 1938 (Denord 2001, p. 24, Lemke 2001) explicitly in order to herald the appearance of a new orientation towards the previous liberal tradition, as well as a different approach to state power.

> Neoliberalism replaces the naturalism of [classical] liberalism with a certain kind of constructivism. [It] differs from earlier forms of liberalism in that they do not regard the market as an existing quasi-natural reality situated in a kind of economic nature reserve space marked off, secured and supervised by the State. Rather, the market exists, and can only exist, under certain political, legal and institutional conditions that must be actively constructed by the government. (Barry et al. 1996, p. 10)

As Friedman wrote in his early prospectus (Friedman 1951, p. 91), 'a basic error in the 19th century individualist philosophy [is that it] assigned almost no role to the state other than the maintenance of order and enforcement of contracts. It was a negative philosophy'. The neoliberal project has found itself primarily concerned with overcoming the dualism of state and economy that had been inscribed at the heart of classical liberalism, and to conceptually blur the presumptive boundaries between state and market, while simultaneously openly co-opting the organs of the state to further the neoliberal project. It sought a 'positive program', or as Friedman put it, a 'substitute for the 19th century goal of laissez faire . . . the goal of the competitive order' (ibid., p. 92).

It is noteworthy that this program did not spring fully formed from the head of Athena, but took quite a long while to be argued out, mainly at the University of Chicago and at the international meetings of the MPS. It was not spelled out in Hayek's (1944) *The Road to Serfdom*, nor indeed in Friedman's (1951) manifesto. We (Van Horn and Mirowski 2009) have argued elsewhere that it was constructed in large part by Aaron Director, Friedrich Hayek, Milton Friedman (but *not* Frank Knight) and a host of other figures over the course of the 1950s in the 'Free Market Project', the 'Antitrust Project' and a number of other initiatives at the University of Chicago and at the meetings of the MPS, which have been the subject of some excellent recent histories (Raynor 2000, Amadae 2003, Walpen 2004, Plehwe and Walpen 2005).[1] By the time we get to *Capitalism and Freedom* (Friedman 1962), *Economic Analysis of Law* (Posner 1973), *The Antitrust Paradox* (Bork 1978 [1993]), *The Calculus of Consent* (Buchanan and Tullock 1962) and *In Defense of Industrial Concentration* (McGee 1971), its outlines become more clear. We might characterize its tenets in the following list:

1. The Market is an artifact, but it is an ideal processor of information. It knows more than any individual, and therefore cannot be surpassed as a mechanism of coordination.
2. Neoliberalism starts with a critique of state reason. The limits of government are related to intrinsic limitations on a state's power to know, and hence to supervise.

These limits are not fixed for all time, however. Nevertheless, The Market always surpasses the state's ability to process information.

3. Neoclassical economics is a good representation of the capacities of The Market as information processor. Here the Chicago Program tended to diverge from Hayek himself. This is related to a profound change in neoclassical economics located just after the Second World War (Mirowski 2002).
4. Politics *as if* it were a market, and an economic theory of 'democracy'. This supports the application of neoclassical models to previously political topics; but it also explains why the neoliberal movement must seek and consolidate political power by operating from within the state. The 'night-watchman' version of the state is repudiated. It also justifies alliances with the powerful in order to push the neoliberal agenda, and reconfigures a right-wing suspicion about the virtues of democracy.
5. Government structures predicated on the government of the self. Freedom is not the realization of any *telos*, but rather the positing of autonomous self-governed individuals, all naturally equipped with a neoclassical version of 'rationality' and motives of self-interest. Foucault is strongest on the role of these 'technologies of the self', which involve an elaborate revision in concepts of human freedom and morality. Here the story of the building of bridges with the Christian Right still awaits its historian.
6. Corporations can do no wrong. This is one of the strongest areas of divergence from classical liberalism, with its ingrained suspicion of joint stock companies and monopoly. It underwrites a 'degovernmentalization of the state' through privatization of education, health and even portions of the military.
7. Discipline of the nation-state through international initiatives. This was initially implemented through neoliberal takeover of the International Monetary Fund (IMF), the World Trade Organization (WTO), the World Bank and other previously classical liberal transnational institutions. It began as advocacy of 'free trade' and floating exchange rates, but rapidly became subordinate to the programs of transnational corporations, to whom it became attached.
8. The Market (suitably re-engineered and promoted) can always provide solutions to problems seemingly caused by The Market in the first place. Monopoly is eventually undone by 'competition'; pollution is abated by the trading of 'emissions permits'; McCarthyism is thwarted by competition between employers (Friedman 1962, p. 20); terrorism by disgruntled disenfranchised foreigners can be offset by a 'futures market in terrorist acts'.

Neoliberalism claims to value 'freedom' above all else: 'economic freedom is an end in itself' (ibid., p. 8). However, it will be indispensable to grasp that neoliberalism did *not* prescribe the abolition of all controls over human action – in this respect, it was most assuredly a divergence from previous anarchist or libertarian doctrines. In fact, controls were not to be banished so much as recoded and reconfigured into a new version of 'competitive order'. Chicago neoliberalism transcends the classical liberal tension between the self-interested agent and the patriotic duty of the citizen by reducing both state and market to the identical flat ontology of the neoclassical model of the economy.[2] 'Freedom' is thus recoded to mean the capacity for self-realization attained *solely* through individual striving for a set of necessarily unexplained (and usually interpersonally ineffable) prior wants and desires. Isaiah Berlin (1958 [1969]) captured this innovation with his distinction between 'negative' freedom, which was a state of immunity from encroachment by others upon the realization of given desires, and 'positive' freedom, which viewed the agent as being encouraged to engage in a process of finding those desires in an environment which actualized that quest; Berlin (and the neoliberals) linked positive freedom with totalitarian movements. Once this new lexicon was firmly set in place, it became essentially impossible within this discourse to regard any economic transaction whatsoever as coercive (Smith 1998, p. 80), which was a massive divergence from classical liberal discourse. Neoliberals then promoted two practical political innovations (here designated Λ, to distinguish them from the earlier list of doctrines) which would tend to set them apart:

- Λ1 explore the options to make pact with state structures in order to pursue nominally anti-statist (but in practice pro-corporate) policies and projects; and
- Λ2 explore the options to make pact with 'unified science' to nominally buttress the political legitimacy of selected state reforms (since the Cold War state leaned heavily upon science for expert legitimization), but in practice to justify neoliberal projects.

More concretely, neoliberals tended to subscribe to a more up-to-date naturalized 'human nature' (Λ2) in order to short-circuit appeals to 'positive' freedom, and therefore recast state activities as market-like in consequence (Λ1). The neoliberal citizen was no longer deemed responsible for his/her own 'freedom' – that became the province of the neoliberal expert – but was instead relegated to the roles of 'consumer' and 'entrepreneur of the self' (Rose 1999, pp. 164–5). Neoliberalism became a top-down project, well suited to be promoted by corporate public relations campaigns and 'detached' yet well-funded conclaves of cosseted academics. Hence neoliberalism was ideally suited to be nurtured and pursued through a structure of 'thinktanks' and other formations, which barely existed prior to the Second World War (Cockett 1995).

The Chicago School's notorious innovation was the idea that much of politics could be understood as if it were a market process, and therefore amenable to be formalized through neoclassical theory. Politicians, it was claimed, were just trying to maximize their own utility, as were voters. Unfortunately, this implied that the state was merely an inferior means of attaining outcomes that could be better and more efficiently provided directly by the market; and that in turn led to a rather jaundiced assessment of the virtues and benefits of democracy.[3] This doctrine was then linked with a rather unflattering assessment of the intellectual qualities of the populace; for instance, education was no longer understood as the price to be paid to build a competent democratic citizenry, but rather just another commodity that should go to the highest bidder. Since the vast mass of the poor were not in a position to buy very much of it, that in turn suggested that it was imperative that an elite cadre of experts should exert itself behind the scenes to shape and execute public policy. As indicated above, 'individualism' began to take on all sorts of collectivist overtones hitherto undreamt of in classical liberal doctrines; and of necessity, the very meaning of 'freedom' had to undergo profound revision.[4]

The reverse side of the flattening of the state/market distinction was a repression of considerations of power, both within economics and in neoliberal political theory.

Corporations, in particular, were inevitably characterized as passive responders to outside forces. In economics, the only market actor accused of misusing power was the trade union, which was uniformly treated as illegitimate; whereas any other instance of market power, as in the case of monopoly or oligopoly, were either treated as harmless and temporary, or else attributed to some nefarious policy of the state. The 'reform' of international rule structures in order to discipline the political economy of various states was another project that rapidly became a trademark Chicago method to circumvent direct analytical considerations of power. The unfocused character of power helped ratify their convenient notion that the neoliberals were bravely pitted against entrenched elites, little freshwater Davids to the coastal Goliath/Leviathan, appealing to their restive libertarian wing by making it seem that they were not, themselves, mouthpieces for certain powerful interests. American economics had become well and truly politicized, while spokesmen like Friedman and George Stigler would persist in claiming that it managed to exist outside of political discourse, partaking instead of the otherworldly virtues of science. It was a very effective strategy, deployed in popular outlets (Friedman 1983) as well as academic journals.

The emergence of neoliberalism at Chicago

While characterizing the political process as a market process and repressing considerations of power are attributed to Chicago elsewhere (Lemke 2001), a story of how neoliberalism emerged at Chicago is often untold. What follows is a brief version of that story. Of course, recounting the actual reformulation ranges beyond the feasible scope of this chapter. Nonetheless, what follows will sketch the initiative to reformulate the liberal doctrine and the confusion as to how to do so, and it will highlight some liberal doctrines that were reformulated in the areas of monopoly and antitrust and will emphasize the shift in attitude toward corporations. It concludes by pointing to other eventual areas that were reformulated.

Aaron Director headed a three-year project (1946–49), the Free Market Study, bankrolled by the Volker Fund – a Kansas City corporation heavily involved in right-wing funding in the post-war period. The project, organized by the sedulous, persistent efforts of Friedrick Hayek and the Volker Fund, entailed writing an *American Road to Serfdom* (see Van Horn and Mirowski 2009 for a detailed archival study). The project had the complementary aim to study and describe 'a suitable legal and institutional framework of an effective competitive system' (quoted in Coase 1998, p. 603). Besides Director, the Free Market Study comprised Friedman, Knight, T.W Schultz, Wilbur Katz, Edward Levi and Garfield Cox.

At the premier meeting, Director typed up a short essay entitled: 'A program of factual research into questions basic to the formulation of liberal economic policy', which proposed that the Free Market Study empirically investigate the facts taken for granted by liberals and their opponents in various policy areas, including: monopoly, economies of scale, unions and private investment. The aptly named Director and the Free Market Study members sought to reevaluate some of the fundamental premises of liberalism and reformulate the liberal doctrine based on this reevaluation.

In achieving this objective, Director organized monthly and sometimes bimonthly meetings. Most of the meetings' agendas and essays available from 1946 to 1949 focus on the fundamental liberal components, including industrial concentration, barriers to entry, corporate ownership and management and government restrictions, and aside from the premier meeting, none of the meetings examines the basic liberal premises of labor unions or tariffs. The essays and outlines from the meetings suggest that how to reformulate liberalism was unclear and indicate that the Free Market Study served as a venue to debate some of the possible trajectories of the reformulation of liberalism.

In 1946, at the second meeting, Director restated the generally accepted explanation for industrial concentration: 'It is widely held' that industrial concentration resulted from social economies of scale, which thus indicated 'an underlying tendency to monopoly in our economic organization'. As a result, such industries ought to be regulated by the government. Director, however, disagreed with this view. He offered two alternative possibilities:

> Of course we could start from the position that existing concentration has already reached a point which makes it objectionable from a political point of view, or again we may start from the position that the existing concentration results in the most efficient use of resources and does not eventuate in significant departures from competitive behavior. (Minutes, November 15, 1946, T.W. Schultz Papers, Box 39 (addenda), Folder: Free Market Study)

The former represented a contemporary liberal view, and the latter represented the eventual trademark position of the post-war Chicago School.

At a 1947 meeting, Friedman submitted a proposal to the Free Market Study group that addressed the problem of the divergence between ownership and control in corporations.

> It is hard to see any social function performed by [the separation of ownership from effective control]; on the contrary, separation of ownership from control has important social disadvantages. It encourages utilization of resources for purposes other than maximization of their return; greatly facilitates the securing of monopoly positions; and gives rise to private economies of scale that are not matched by social economies. (T.W. Schultz Papers, Box 39 (addenda), Folder: Free Market Study)

He proposed an investigation into the problem of reorganizing the structure of corporations. Friedman believed that 'by identifying ownership with control, the proposal would eliminate many of the present abuses of the corporate form. . . . These effects would themselves retard the tendency (if it exists) toward increasingly large and monopolistic organizations and stimulate the breakdown of existing giant corporations' (T.W. Schultz Papers, Box 39 (addenda), Folder: Free Market Study).

Another telling instance occurred when Roland McKean, a graduate student at Chicago at the time and an employee of the RAND Corporation in the 1950s, submitted a research proposal outline to the Free Market Study group about implementing monetary policy in the United States. Though the outline forgoes elaboration on most key points, McKean does evince his classical liberal sentiments with the following outline point and subpoint: 'Anti-monopoly campaigning a necessary complement to monetary policy': 'Maximum price flexibility, and also resource mobility, are necessary to the reduction of "structural" unemployment so that a monetary policy of stabilization will not be frustrated – in addition, of course, to other objectives of attacking monopoly' (undated, T.W. Schultz Papers, Box 39 (addenda), Folder: Free Market Study). The fact that the Free Market Study entertained the prospect of anti-monopoly campaigning is revealing.

As these three examples illustrate, the trademark post-war Chicago positions on corporations, industrial concentration and monopoly were opaque in the immediate post-war period. The Free Market Study played a crucial role in providing a venue to debate positions which would become part of the neoliberal doctrine at Chicago. In fact, just a year after the Free Market Study formally concluded, Director advanced an unprecedented Chicago position on monopoly.

In 1950, Director maintained, 'Enterprise monopoly cannot permanently rely on restrictions of its own supply. If it is to endure it must find means of preventing additions to supply by other sources' (Director 1950, p. 165). Why? Because the market system through the 'corroding influence of competition' has the 'effective tendency' to 'destroy *all* types of monopoly' (pp. 165–6, emphasis added). For Director, the invariant force behind this tendency is competition. Furthermore, Director maintains that, 'So far in the absence of governmental aid and encouragement the competitive tendencies have triumphed over the exclusive or restrictive tendencies' (p. 166). These claims of Director are especially striking when juxtaposed with his 1946 speculation that 'their faith in the inevitability of monopoly would be shaken if it were found that, government intervention aside, monopoly tends to disappear and competition to revive even where once dormant' because the 1950 claim suggests that sufficient research has been carried out in the past three years to dispel his 1946 curiosity. In short, Director's 1946 statement of possibility became Director's 1950 assertion of fact. Here is one important classical liberal and neoliberal watershed at Chicago.

Besides a confirmation of the effect of competition on monopoly, the attitude toward monopoly became relatively sanguine in the early 1950s when compared to McKean's 'anti-monopoly campaign' and Friedman's concern about the divergence between ownership and control facilitating monopoly formation. Friedman characterized the contemporary widespread notion that monopoly is ubiquitous and inevitable as a hyperbolic depiction. The reasons are twofold. First, 'Monopoly is much more prevalent in manufacturing than in other industries, and there is a general tendency to overrate the importance of manufacturing as whole' (Friedman 1951 [1952], p. 15). For the second, Friedman appeals to the 'invisible hand' metaphor: 'monopoly is highly 'visible', and draws attention to itself whereas the workings of competition are devious and hidden' (p. 15). He went on to say, 'The actions and methods whereby monopolies exercise their monopoly power are likely to be relatively dramatic and open; the means whereby competitive forces limit monopoly power are subtle, multifarious and hidden, involving expansion and contraction of numerous industries, minor changes in numerous prices, places, and so on' (p. 16). Friedman emphasized that 'Monopoly *is* less important in the United States than widely believed' (p. 16). After returning from a voyage to Europe, Friedman stated, 'I came back [from Europe] saying that I was going to tell my students . . . that America had perfect competition everywhere. I regard as the essentially outstanding feature of the American system the fact that it has so relatively little monopoly' (Friedman 1953, pp. 11–12). For Friedman, the antitrust laws have provided the US with an openly hostile climate to monopoly, and monopoly has only persisted where it has received open support from government (Friedman 1951 [1952], p. 17). Friedman's claims illustrate a shift in attitude toward monopoly at Chicago. No longer does an anti-monopoly campaign need to be considered for monopolies are not prevalent. Furthermore, and perhaps most importantly, monopoly is not a major problem that demands immediate attention – partly because when monopoly activity actually occurs, it is readily apparent.

Besides monopoly, the attitude toward corporations became relatively sanguine too in the early 1950s, and Friedman's worry about the divergence between ownership and control was no longer an issue. In 1951, Director claimed that the formation of a large or a larger corporation or of an augmented concentration of control does not necessarily alter the competitive character of the market. He claimed that 'it is evident that a horizontal combination of 100 firms in 100 markets, each of which accounted for say 1 percent of its market, might result in a very large firm indeed; but the competitive character of the market would not be affected' (Director 1951, p. 19). Furthermore, Director (p. 19) maintained, 'the vertical integration of firms each of which is competitive in its own market might result in very large firms without altering the competitive character of the market'.

With regard to whether the modern corporation contributes to monopoly, Director did not squarely address the issue. Instead, he addressed it with a hypothetical: 'If the corporate form of organization is conducive to the formation of monopoly, it is also conducive to undermining it. If it facilitates large-scale organization which can take advantage of size to reap the gains of monopoly, it also facilitates entry to reduce these gains' (ibid., pp. 20–21). For Director, 'The road to monopoly even with neutral rules is not a one-way road' (p. 20). In 1947, Friedman made no such assumption.

Furthermore, Director maintained that corporations are not conducive to monopoly because corporations approximate the ideal of the impersonal relations of the market and the ideal form of control: 'The ideal form of control is that which prevails in the modern mail order house or department store, where it is exercised not by bargaining – personal relations – but by choosing an alternative source of supply. The modern corporation approximates this ideal' (ibid., p. 22). On another score, Director also believed that 'the corporate form of organization is indeed ideal' (p. 22). Regarding Director's 1946 inquiry of whether concentrations of economic power should be politically objectionable or whether they should be regarded an approximation competition, clearly Director steadfastly adhered to the latter. In fact, Director curiously and tellingly confined his analysis to economic issues 'since in the view of history of the past thirty years *no one* is concerned with any undue influence exercised by property owners individually or collectively over political institutions' (p. 18, emphasis added).

With regard to the issue of the divergence between ownership and control, Director asserted, 'The discipline of a competitive capital market provides a more general and more effective instrument for preventing significant and continuous divergence of interest' (p. 23). For Director, the shares market was analogous to the product market. Like price adjustment occurs in the product market by the attraction of alternative sources of supply, 'the reduction in the price of shares occasioned by the divergence of interest will make it profitable for alternative sources of supply of control to purchase such shares for the very purpose of removing the divergence of interest' (p. 24). Director, however, readily conceded that instances where this has transpired cannot be frequently found, which, according to him, 'May show that the capital market is not sufficiently competitive' (p. 24). Yet, Director points out, 'It may also show that the existence of the mechanism is sufficient to keep within moderate limits any marked tendencies toward a divergence of interest between shareholders and those in control' (p. 24).

When considering monopoly, industrial concentration and corporations, salient differences appear when juxtaposing the claims and speculations of the Free Market Study and the assertions of Director and Friedman in the early 1950s. This marked a sharp shift in the liberal doctrine, a shift to a neoliberal doctrine. This doctrine regarded corporations as approximations of the impersonal ideal of the market, and not concentrations of economic power inimical to competition. Espousers of this doctrine have a relatively sanguine attitude toward monopoly. Competition will have a corroding influence on monopoly, and if monopoly practices transpire, such practices will be conspicuous and are likely to be condemned and ameliorated by antitrust law (the Chicago-based Antitrust Project will qualify the latter).

However, the reformulations highlighted in the aforementioned areas were not simply pigeonholed in fields of economic theory. Given the interdisciplinary proclivities of neoliberals and the perceived importance of law for establishing rules of the game, the reformulations in the areas of monopoly and corporations presently undergirded antitrust arguments at Chicago. The Volker Fund paid for fellowships for an Antitrust Project for Robert Bork, John McGee, Ward Bowman, William Letwin and others to come to Chicago and research antitrust issues. Under Director, the Antitrust Project produced a prodigious amount of antitrust scholarship on the issues of tying arrangements, predatory pricing, vertical integration, resale price maintenance, trade regulation and the Sherman Act. Generally, the project challenged the usefulness of efforts to control specific forms of conduct by which market power may make itself felt and challenged the commonly held perception that antitrust law is firmly grounded in a common law heritage. The most telling analysis of the application of the reformulation of liberalism to antitrust law is found in Bork (1954).

Bork's economic analysis of the vertical integration – where he argued that courts should not employ the concept of vertical integration as an analytical tool, but as a descriptive tool – contained some of the neoliberal premises espoused just a few years earlier by Director and Friedman. In fact, Bork treated these premises as if they are firmly grounded in economic theory, but in fact, as the analysis above indicates, such premises were relatively novel at Chicago. For instance, like Director and Friedman, Bork adopted a relatively sanguine attitude toward monopoly. Bork considered circumstances under which a combination between monopolies may prove beneficial to consumers.

Moreover, like Director, Bork argued that the economic domain is the proper ground to consider the issue of vertical integration, and Bork took the purpose of the Sherman Act for granted and performed his analysis in the economic domain. He stated, 'If it is accepted that the purpose of the antitrust law is the preservation of a competitive economy, an evaluation of the vertical-integration concept must run largely in terms of its value as an analytical tool' (Bork 1954, p. 194). Bork also evaluated the issues of barriers to entry solely in the economic domain, claiming that the only way vertical integration could influence entry is when the integrated firm monopolized both levels. For Bork, political and social influences were irrelevant.

Like Director, Bork assumed that competition could exist among corporations, however large or however few, and unlike Friedman in 1947, Bork assumed that the divergence between ownership and control was not an issue. Moreover, like Director, Bork claimed political power was irrelevant to his analysis. In fact, Bork dismissed political power as an 'amorphous concept', and he emphasized that the law's tests of vertical integration were 'in economic terms, in terms of market power' (ibid., p. 201).

Bork also echoed Director's assertion that vertical integration does not necessarily alter the competitive character of the market. Bork asserted that 'such integration can be said to add nothing to monopoly power' (p. 195). Furthermore, Bork claimed that vertical integration does not influence a firm's pricing policy, and that vertical integration does not transmit monopoly power from one level to another.

By adopting the premises of Director and Friedman in his analysis, Bork adopted a relatively pro-trust line when compared to the analysis of previous Chicago economists such as Henry Simons. In the end, Bork's economic analysis evinces the transition just recounted, the transition to neoliberalism. Moreover, Bork's work foreshadowed the later economic analysis at Chicago, which would form part of the Chicago School of Law and Economics (Van Horn 2007).

Conclusion

Though the analysis above traces neoliberal developments in the areas of monopoly, corporations and antitrust, such developments were by no means circumscribed to these areas. Such developments also extended into the area of intellectual property (ibid.), and they later extended into other legal fields, including tort law and property law. As the variegated fields cited at the outset of this chapter suggest, neoliberal themes and doctrines surfaced in numerous areas, and though Chicago was responsible for galvanizing and carrying out reformulations of the liberal doctrine in various areas and applying them in many more areas, Chicago was just one component of a larger neoliberal initiative.

Notes

* We wish to thank T. Paul Schultz and the University of Chicago Archives for permission to use material from the Theodore W. Schultz Papers in the Department of Economics Records, Special Collections Research Center, University of Chicago Library.

1. Hartwell (1995), on the other hand, is a relatively uninformative history of the Mont Pèlerin Society.
2. The situation at MPS, and particularly Hayek's relationship to it, was much more complex over time (Mirowski 2007).
3. This hostility to democratic processes is discussed at much greater length in Amadae (2003) and Mirowski (2005). Nominally 'left-wing' versions of neoclassical theory, such as that represented by Cowles, also tended to share this attribute (see Mirowski 2002, ch. 6).
4. Indeed, fierce battles over the relationship of freedom to ethics and religion, not to mention political participation in the life of the nation, were some of the most contested terrain in the early Mont Pèlerin Society.

References

T.W. Schultz Papers, Department of Economics Records, Special Collections Research Center, University of Chicago Library.

Amadae, S.M. (2003), *Rationalizing Capitalist Democracy: The Cold War Origins of Rational Choice Liberalism*, Chicago, IL: University of Chicago Press.

Barry, A., T. Osborne and N. Rose (eds) (1996), *Foucault and Political Reason – Liberalism, Neoliberalism and the Rationalities of Government*, London: UCL Press.

Berlin, I. (1958 [1969]), 'Two concepts of liberty', in *Four Essays on Liberty*, Oxford: Oxford University Press, pp. 118–72.

Bork, R.H. (1954), 'Vertical integration and the Sherman Act: the legal history of an economic misconception', *University of Chicago Law Review*, **22** (1), 157–201.

Bork, R.H. ([1978] 1993), *The Antitrust Paradox: A Policy at War with Itself*, New York: Free Press.

Buchanan, J.M. and G. Tullock (1962), *The Calculus of Consent: Logical Foundations of Constitutional Democracy*, Ann Arbor, MI: University of Michigan Press.

Burchell, G., C. Gordon and P. Miller (eds) (1991), *The Foucault Effect*, Chicago, IL: University of Chicago Press.

Burns, J. (2004), 'In retrospect: George Nash's *Conservative Intellectual Movement in America*', *Reviews in American History*, **32** (3), 447–62.

Coase, R.H. (1998), 'Aaron Director', in *The New Palgrave Dictionary of Economics and the Law*, Newman, P. (ed.), New York: Macmillan, pp. 601–5.

Cockett, R. (1995), *Thinking the Unthinkable*, New York: HarperCollins.

De Long, J.B. (1990), 'In defense of Henry Simons' standing as a classical liberal', *Cato Journal*, **9** (3), 601–18.

Denord, F. (2001), 'Aux Origines du néo-libéralism en France: Louis Rougier et le Colloque Walter Lippmann de 1938' (The origins of neo-liberalism in France: Louis Rougier and the Walter Lippman Colloque of 1938), *Le Mouvement Social* (195), 9–34.

Director, A. (1950), 'Review of *Unions and Capitalism*, by Charles E. Lindblom, *University of Chicago Law Review*, **18** (1), 164–7.

Director, A. (1951), *The Modern Corporation and the Control of Property*, paper presented at University of Chicago Law School conference on corporation law and finance 17.

Foucault, M. (2004), *Naissance de la biopolitique* (Birth of neoliberal governmentality), Paris: Éditions Galimard.

Friedman, M. (1951), 'Nyliberalismen Og Dens Muligheter' (Neoliberalism and its prospects), *Farmand*, February 17, pp. 89–93.

Friedman, M. (1951 [1952]), 'Free enterprise', *University of Chicago Roundtable*, no. 744.

Friedman, M. (1953), 'What is American capitalism?', *University of Chicago Roundtable*, no. 794.

Friedman, M. (1962), *Capitalism and Freedom*, Chicago, IL: University of Chicago Press.

Friedman, M. (1983), *Bright Promises, Dismal Performances*, Sun Lakes, AZ: Thomas Horton & Daughters.

George, S. (1999), 'A short history of neo-liberalism: twenty years of elite economics and emerging opportunities for structural change', paper presented at conference on economic sovereignty in a globalising world, Bangkok, Thailand, March.

Hartwell, R.M. (1995), *A History of the Mont Pèlerin Society*, Indianapolis, IN: Liberty Fund.

Hayek, F.A. (1944), *The Road to Serfdom*, Chicago, IL: University of Chicago Press.

Lemke, T. (2001), '"The birth of bio-politics": Michel Foucault's lecture at the Collège de France on neoliberal governmentality', *Economy and Society*, **30** (2), 190–207.

McGee, J.S. (1971), *In Defense of Industrial Concentration*, New York: Praeger.

Mirowski, P. (2002), *Machine Dreams: Economics Becomes a Cyborg Science*, Cambridge: Cambridge University Press.

Mirowski, P. (2005), Review essay: 'Sleights of the Invisible Hand: economists' postwar interventions in political theory', *Journal of the History of Economic Thought*, **27** (1), 87–99.

Mirowski, P. (2007), 'Naturalizing the market on the road to revisionism: Bruce Caldwell's *Hayek's Challenge* and the challenge of Hayek interpretation', *Journal of Institutional Economics*, **3** (3), 351–72.

Plehwe, D. and B. Walpen (2005), 'Between network and complex organization: the making of neoliberal knowledge and hegemony', in *Neoliberal Hegemony: A Global Critique*, Plehwe, D., B. Walpen and G. Nuenhoffer (eds), London: Routledge, pp. 27–50.

Posner, R.A. (1973), *Economic Analysis of Law*, Boston, MA: Little, Brown.

Raynor, G. (2000), 'Engineering social reform: the rise of the Ford Foundation and Cold War liberalism, 1908–59', PhD dissertation, New York University, New York.

Rose, N. (1999), *Powers of Freedom*, Cambridge: Cambridge University Press.

Smith, A. (1776 [1976]), *An Inquiry into the Nature and Causes of the Wealth of Nations*, Glasgow edn, Campbell, R.H. and A.S. Skinner (eds), Indianapolis, IN: Liberty Classics.

Smith, V.R. (1998), 'Friedman, liberalism, and the meaning of negative freedom', *Economics and Philosophy*, **14** (1), 75–94.

Van Horn, R. (2007), 'The origins of the Chicago School of law and economics', PhD dissertation, Department of Economics, Notre Dame University, South Bend, IN.

Van Horn, R. and P. Mirowski (2009), 'The rise of the Chicago School of economics and the birth of neoliberalism', in *The Road from Mont Pèlerin: The Making of the Neoliberal Thought Collective*, Mirowski, P. and D. Plehwe (eds), Cambridge, MA: Harvard University Press, pp. 139–78.

Walpen, B. (2004), *Die Offenen Feinde und Ihre Gesellschaft: Eine hegemonietheoretische Studie zur Mont Pèlerin Society* (The open enemies and their society: a hegemony theory study of the Mont Pèlerin Society), Hamburg: VSA Verlag.

14 Armen Alchian on evolution, information, and cost: the surprising implications of scarcity

*Daniel K. Benjamin**

Jobs are always easily available.
A. Alchian

Introduction

At first blush a paper on the work of Armen Alchian in a volume examining the Chicago School must seem anomalous. It is true that Alchian published famous papers in the *Journal of Political Economy* (*JPE*) and the *Journal of Law & Economics* (*JL&E*), gave the keynote address at the dedication of the new University of Chicago Law School building in 1957 and was Ford Foundation Visiting Professor at Chicago in 1968. But Alchian trained at Stanford and spent essentially his entire professional career at UCLA, and I expect any bemusement he felt at Paul Samuelson's (1970) claim that UCLA was a Chicago 'farm club' was mixed with irritation. Yet the linkages, both personal and intellectual, between Alchian and Chicago stretch throughout his career.

Alchian's first published professional paper, 'Uncertainty, evolution and economic theory' (1950 [1977]), which I discuss below, was written initially not for publication, but simply to help himself and his graduate students understand the issues more clearly. Only at the suggestion of Stephen Enke did Alchian consider submitting it for publication; even then, it took some strongly encouraging remarks by Milton Friedman (who had seen a copy) to induce Alchian to send the paper to the *JPE*. This paper dovetails extraordinarily nicely with Friedman's own work on 'positive economics' (Friedman 1953), so it is easy to see why he was interested in having Alchian publish it. And together with Friedman's work, Alchian's paper brought an entire line of inquiry (or mode of thinking) to a grinding halt. Economists had been struggling with the question 'how do people think?'. Alchian made it clear that this matters not. What is relevant is how they behave: this is all we can observe, and all that will determine the outcome of their decisions.[1]

Alchian's paper, 'Costs and outputs' (1959 [1977]), about which I also write below, has no such direct link to Chicago, as far as I know. Nevertheless, its origins lie in an institution – the RAND Corporation – where many Chicago economists have worked. Indeed, it was at RAND that Alchian first met Reuben Kessel, upon the latter's arrival there in the mid-1950s. Kessel had written his dissertation on the topic of inflation at Chicago (1954), and Alchian admired both Kessel's way of thinking and the data he had acquired. At Alchian's suggestion, Kessel successfully applied for funding to work further on the problem. The result was a long and productive partnership on some of the best work ever done on the microeconomic consequences of inflation, including their famous papers in the *JPE* and the then-fledgling *JL&E* (Kessel and Alchian 1959, 1960, 1962).

The third paper about which I write, 'Information costs, pricing and resource unemployment' (Alchian 1969 [1977]) was undertaken at a time when economists were re-examining the foundations of the literature that had grown up in the footsteps of John Maynard Keynes's *General Theory* (1936). One day while playing golf with George Stigler, Alchian complained that the existing literature simply could not explain unemployed resources.[2] Stigler said, 'Have you ever thought about information costs?'. Alchian replied, 'Yes, that's a good idea; that might be it'. Alchian's resulting contribution to this literature was notable in at least two respects. First, it demonstrated that it was possible to think about *macro*economic issues using *micro*economic tools. Just as importantly, this paper made it clear that 'unemployment' – whether of people or of non-human resources – was in fact productive activity, and could be thought of as the outcome of choices made by individuals in a world in which information is a scarce good.

The intellectual ties between Alchian and Chicago clearly extend well beyond the papers I write about here. For example, the theory of the firm has been considerably advanced by Alchian's work with two members of the Chicago School. The paper with Harold Demsetz, begun while the latter was on the faculty at Chicago, helped spark an enormous revival of interest in this topic (Alchian and Demsetz 1972). The *JL&E* paper on expropriable rents and vertical integration (Klein et al. 1978), has changed the way we think about both the firm and a host of other contracts.

At the same time, I think it is fair to say that during much of his career, Alchian worked on problems that his contemporary Chicago economists largely assumed did not exist. Notwithstanding Coase's (1960) famous paper, 'The problem of social cost' (written, I should note, while Coase was still at Virginia), Alchian's seminal work on property rights sought to answer questions that simply were not being asked at Chicago. Similarly, Stigler's important paper on the survivorship principle (1958) can be viewed (perhaps harshly) as saying that Alchian's work on 'Costs and outputs' is (like other efforts to understand firms' costs functions) simply irrelevant to much of what economists should be interested in. And finally, of course, Alchian's work on the measurement and consequences of inflation was almost perfectly complementary to that of Friedman and his many students – who already knew what it was and what it did.

Indeed, the complementarity between Alchian's research and much of the work done at Chicago during the height of his career may be the best reason of all for including a chapter about him in a volume such as this. Even as Chicago economists were demonstrating how much of the world we could understand using the paradigm of scarcity, Alchian was demonstrating how much more there was that we did not – as yet – understand. And so just as the 'conceptual boxes' were being filled in, so too were more being opened, both actions paving the way for a greater understanding of the world around us.

Alchian's themes

Three themes unify Armen Alchian's work on economics. Together, they outline both a coherent methodology for doing economics, and a view of the world that celebrates the importance of individual liberty. For Alchian, the unit of analysis is always the individual; hence, the theory must be consistent with each person acting as an individual utility – or wealth-maximizer. This view of the world compels us to recognize that the ultimate source of and responsibility for choices lies with the individual, who is thus the ultimate source of all human power – whether that power happens temporarily to reside in a set of democratic institutions or in the hands of a dictator.

In Alchian's view, economic theory must be as general as possible. It must apply to both sides of the market, to markets for all types of goods and services, and to the decisions of all economic agents. The economic theorist is not permitted the luxury of concocting Theory A for one setting and Theory B for another. In this sense, Alchian is unremitting in demanding that economics be ruled by theory rather than by theorist, thus insisting on the general applicability of any proposition that purports to be economic theory.

Finally, both theory and theorist are constrained, indeed governed, by the facts. Rather than the other way around, theory must always confront and conform to the facts. The theory must yield refutable implications, and if these are in fact refuted, it is the theory – not the facts – that must yield. The purpose of theory is never theory in and of itself; it is instead to help individuals understand the world around them. In this sense, the ultimate consumers of economic theory are the people whom it describes; and in Alchian's view, *noster patronis emptor est* – our boss is the consumer.[3]

In what follows I shall try to illustrate how these principles are developed and utilized in three papers which span roughly the first half of Alchian's career in economics. Apart from the fact that, together, they illustrate fully the themes that run through all of his work, these papers have several characteristics to recommend them. First, when given a choice to select his favorite papers, Alchian just happened to pick these (see Alchian 1996, McChesney 1996). Second, because these papers are solely authored by him, there is no question as to liability for errors; and speaking as someone who has seen him in action in the classroom, I assert (despite any possible demurral by him) that there is no question as to credit, either. If you like these papers, you like what Alchian does as an economist. His work over the years with Harold Demsetz, Reuben Kessel, Ben Klein and others has been magnificent; but these three papers are unmistakably Armen Alchian. Third, these papers reflect the full gamut of impacts that Alchian's articles have had (or not had) over the years. The information cost paper has been so completely absorbed into the existing literature that most well-trained freshmen have been exposed to considerable portions of it. His evolution paper has amazing staying power, having been cited and discussed widely over the nearly half a century since it was published, and even now serving as the foundation for research seeking unification of biology and economics (for example see De Vany 1996). And then there is the cost paper, as profound as any, and yet almost completely ignored – a potential treasure trove that is largely unexplored but suitable as the launch pad for a literature unto itself (for example, see Haddock and McChesney 1994). The final motive for selecting these papers is the sheer surprise factor in them, the amazement that economic theory in the hands of just one persistent, enquiring individual could reveal so much – about ourselves, our environment and our science. Few others, to my knowledge, have disclosed so much to their fellows about the surprising implications of scarcity.

Uncertainty, evolution, and economic theory

> Even in a world of stupid men there would still be profits.
> A. Alchian

Even a randomly selected biologist would tell us that the observed prevalence of any species is the product of two forces: mutation and natural selection. Alchian's objective in this paper is to inform us that the biologist's wisdom fruitfully may be applied to economics. Thus, he argues, the observed prevalence of any activity, or behavior, is the product of two prior probabilities: the probability that it will appear (mutation) and the probability of its survival or viability, once it has appeared (natural selection). An implicit feature of the economist's mode of thinking (constrained maximization) is the notion that these two probabilities are closely related – specifically, that those behaviors that have the best chance for survival will be the behaviors that are most likely to be tried. In fact, Alchian argues, this need not be – and probably is not – true. In a world of uncertainty (itself the result of both costly information and costly decision making) there is no guarantee that these two probabilities will in fact be strongly – or even positively – correlated. Nevertheless, he contends, the economist's modes of thought may still be useful as a means of scientific investigation, even if they are not useful descriptions of what people do or why they do it.[4]

As he notes elsewhere (Alchian 1996), the paper was written in response to his frustration that leading economists could so easily confuse their science with the objects of their scientific enquiry. Must economic agents use (or understand) economic principles in order to behave in ways that can be predicted using those principles? No more than apples must be schooled in Newtonian mechanics if they wish to fall down rather than up when departing a tree. In itself, this point surely was not original to Alchian, but he was the first (to my knowledge) to show the strength of the link between economics and important areas of biology. Although it took more than a quarter of a century for that link to be strengthened and significantly added to, the rapidly expanding overlap between economics and biology is testimony to the importance and fundamental insights of this paper (see Hirshleifer 1978, Samuelson 1985, Ridley 1997).

The importance of adoption

In the presence of uncertainty, two factors determine observed behavior: selection *by* the environment and adaptation *to* the environment. Alchian initially suspends consideration of the second to focus on the implications of the first. He will ultimately conclude that much of what appears to be adaptation may actually be adoption; yet this does not prevent the economist from usefully thinking about agents as *though* they adapt.

Alchian begins with the proposition that in a world of overlapping distributions of outcomes, there is no *maximum* distribution of profits, even though there may be an *optimum* (preferred) one. But to discern even this preferred outcome, one must have an agreed-upon objective function. When this paper was written, no such function existed; and with the co-existence of numerous (not always consistent) objective functions in the modern literature (including expected utility, expected profit, and mean-variance approaches), one cannot claim that an agreed-upon one exists even today. Hence, we have no basis as economists for selecting which actions are best.[5] Fortunately, even if we do not know which is best, we may still be able to discern, under some circumstances, which is better. This is the essence of the comparative statics method, and it is what Alchian claims that economic agents (and economists) are limited (at most!) to doing.

The economic system selects survivors on the basis of outcomes, not motives: those who realize positive profits survive, while those who suffer losses disappear. And note that it is realized positive profits, not maximum profits, that are both (i) observable and (ii) the criterion for success. Success accompanies relative, not absolute, superiority, and success does not require 'proper' motivation or reasoning, but may simply be the result of fortuitous circumstances. In the presence of varied, risk-taking individuals, changes in circumstances (the economic environment) will select in favor of some and against others, regardless of what motivates those individuals. And the greater the uncertainty, the greater the chance that profits will go to the lucky than to the logical.[6]

Through all of this, Alchian goes to great lengths to assure us that random behavior does not imply a lack of order (it is the constraints that imply the order), nor does consistent success imply the absence of random behavior (which he illustrates with the example from Borel of the coin-tossing Frenchmen). Randomness *can* lead to the 'best', or perfect foresight outcome, *if* the variety of actions is sufficiently large (although, of course, it need not).[7] Conversely, foresighted, motivated (maximizing) behavior in the presence of uncertainty does not imply outcomes that are necessarily different from what would be observed if all decisions were random.[8]

In a world of uncertainty – a world in which luck plays an important role – it is the constraints agents face that generate the systematic component of their behavior. This is fortuitous (lucky?), because in the economist's models of constrained maximization, it is the constraints that yield refutable propositions, not the objective functions (Alchian 1950 [1977], pp. 22, 25 and 27).[9] It matters not what people say about what they are doing, nor what the reasoning was that led them to do it; what matters is what they did and what effect (positive or negative profits) it had.

Because individual motivation and foresight are sufficient but not necessary for marginal analysis to be useful and valid, empirical questionnaires are incapable of evaluating the validity of marginal analysis. The validity of the economist's method relies instead on an entirely different footing: for the economist to be able to predict outcomes, all that is required is the existence of slight differences among economic agents, so that those who fortuitously happen to be closer to the 'new, but unknown, optimum' have a higher probability of survival and growth.[10] Thus, for our tools and concepts to be useful,

> all that is needed by economists is their own awareness of the survival conditions and criteria of the economic system and a group of participants who submit various combinations and organizations for the system's selection and adoption. Both these conditions are satisfied. (Ibid., p. 27)

The role of adaptation

Even once we allow for the purposive pursuit of profits,[11] the pervasive effects of uncertainty prevent agents from knowing what actions are 'optimal'; hence, two specific modes of conscious adaptive behavior are observed. First, because 'nothing succeeds like success', rough-and-ready imitative rules of behavior will be adopted: 'What would otherwise appear to be merely customary rules of behavior turn out to be codified imitations of observed success' (ibid., p. 29).[12] According to Alchian, the factors that account for this imitative behavior include: (i) the awareness that superiority to one's competitors is crucial (hikers in bear country will attest that one need not be faster than the grizzly, only faster than one of the people with whom one is hiking); and (ii) the non-availability of a trial-and-error process converging to equilibrium.

Despite – indeed, importantly because of – imitation, the result will be innovation.

Conditions change, and when they do, departures from the rules can enhance the chances of survival; thus, survival demands not only imitation, but also the willingness to depart from it at the 'right' time and under the 'correct' circumstances: 'Those who are different and successful "become" innovators, while those who fail "become" reckless violators of tried-and-true rules' (ibid., p. 30).[13] In addition, the urge to imitate *per se* generates its own innovation, in the form of *mistakes*. Imperfections in the imitation result in the unwitting acquisition of attributes that, under the prevailing circumstances, prove partly responsible for success. Others will imitate the one who successfully erred, and thus the cycle of imitation and innovation continues.

The second mode of conscious adaptive behavior that may be expected in the presence of pervasive uncertainty is trial and error, although Alchian argues that, for two reasons, the capacity of this to lead to some ultimate 'maximization' of profits is suspect: (i) it must be possible to classify a trial as a success or a failure, if one is going to determine whether or not one's trial has led to a local improvement; and (ii) there must be a continuous rising toward some '*optimum optimorum*' without intervening descents, if one is to determine if the trial resulted in a global improvement. He then goes on to assert:

> The above convergence conditions do not apply to a changing environment, for there can be no observable comparison of the result of an action with any other . . . the measure of goodness of actions in anything except a tolerable–intolerable sense is lost, and . . . [t]rial and error becomes survival or death. It cannot serve as a basis of the *individual's* method of convergence to a 'maximum' or optimum position. (Ibid., p. 31, emphasis in original)

We are thus back to the conclusion that while better is distinguishable from worse, the notion of 'best' is of little use to either economic agent or economist.[14]

Extensions and implications

Alchian's analysis could be pursued in many directions, only a few of which I shall touch upon here. First, both adoption and adaptation lead to uniformity of behavior among economic agents: adoption winnows the field and adaptation induces imitation. Indeed, imitation and uniformity, so often decried by social commentators, are the inevitable result of survival in the presence of uncertainty.[15] A corollary of this may be that what appears to be so easy that 'everyone' can figure it out, may in fact be too difficult for *anyone* to figure out – suggesting that claims for the 'obvious' superiority of expertise over market outcomes is even more suspect than usually suspected.

Second, as long as there is any randomness in individuals' choices, both adoption and adaption will yield innovation. Adoption produces it because the random deviations from the norm will, in the presence of changing circumstances, be selected for survival and thus will prosper. And adaptation yields it due to imperfect attempts to imitate, as well as to conscious attempts to respond to change.

Third, both adoption and adaptation will lead to 'cascades' of behavior, in which change is spread on the basis of publicly rather than privately available information. The existence of fads, fashions and the like are thus fundamentally no different from the proliferation of new species in response to successful genetic mutation or successfully adapting to environmental change. Much of the recent literature on information cascades thus has its antecedents, even if not its citations, in Alchian's insights (see Anderson and Holt 1997).

Fourth, innovation typically will be seen by observers to be 'reactionary' rather than 'forward looking': necessity will indeed be the mother of invention. The noble Thomas Edison, driven by a vision from which others are blocked, will be lamented as all too rare. But of course this lament is internally inconsistent. In a world of great uncertainty, there is no future into which one can look with any confidence for guidance as to where innovation is both necessary and desirable; conversely, in a world of certainty, there is no innovation, for everything is known by everyone, *ab ovo*. Hence, innovation *by definition* must either be a matter of luck, mistake or reaction.

Finally, Alchian's argument implies a clear value to *society* of allowing *individuals* to make choices and thus *mistakes*, because their mistakes produce two types of innovations – as exemplified by the hula hoop and the Edsel – that reveal to others where *to* go as well as where *not* to go:[16]

> The economic counterparts of genetic heredity, mutations, and natural selection are imitation, innovation, and positive profits. . . . Like the biologist, the economist predicts the effects of environmental changes on the surviving class of living organism; the economist need not assume that each participant is aware of, or acts according to, his cost and demand conditions. (Alchian 1950 [1977], pp. 32, 34)

Imagine, in such a world, attempting to run everything centrally – unless, of course, you are God . . . or perhaps the Chief Economist!

Costs and outputs

> The method of production is a function of the volume of output . . .
> A. Alchian

Given Alchian's insistence that theory conform to the facts, it is unsurprising that this paper arose from an inconsistency between economic theory and the facts – both those asserted by engineers populating the RAND Corporation, where Alchian was a consultant, and the facts arising from data on airframe production during the Second World War. It eventually became apparent to Alchian that the source of the inconsistency was twofold. First, when the engineers referred to 'output' they were talking about cumulated *volume* of production, while economists used 'output' to mean the *rate* at which some output was produced. Second, when the engineers estimated the 'cost' of some program, they were prone to focus solely on the initial year's flow of 'cost'. While economists rarely made this simple mistake, their narrow-minded focus on the flow of production all too often led to a failure to account for all of the elements of the contemplated present and future outlays – the appropriate capital value measure of cost. It was Alchian's effort to reconcile the seemingly inconsistent views of these two disciplines, as well as his insistence that the economics match the facts, that ultimately led to this paper.

Terminology

Costs are defined by Alchian as the change in equity caused by the performance of a specified action, where, for simplicity, any accompanying change in income is excluded from the computation of the change in equity. Thus, throughout the paper, the term 'cost' always means the capital value concept.

Alchian asserts that there are four characteristics of an output operation, beginning with: (i) the rate of output; (ii) total contemplated volume of output; and (iii) the programmed time schedule of availability of output. Combining these yields the following definition, which also defines a fourth characteristic, m, the total *length* of the programmed schedule of outputs:

$$V = \sum_{T}^{T+m} x(t)\,dt,$$

where V is the total contemplated volume of output; $x(t)$ is the output rate at moment t; T is the moment at which the first unit of output is to be completed; and m is the length of the interval over which the output is made available.[17] Only three of these are, of course, independently assignable; and in the discussion that follows, he always discusses changes in only one of x, T, and V, letting the full compensatory adjustment be made in m.[18]

Rate and volume

The distinction between rate of production ('rate') and total planned volume of output ('volume') is the *sine qua non* of this paper. Table 14.1 summarizes Alchian's propositions regarding the effects on costs of changes in each. The key elements are these:

1. increases in rate or volume increase total costs;
2. increases in rate increase marginal, incremental and average costs, while increases in volume *decrease* marginal, incremental and average costs;[19]
3. producing sooner rather than later increases total, marginal, incremental, and average costs, although the increases are not uniform across inputs; and
4. there is learning by doing, so that total costs of *future* output fall as a function of prior volume.

Having advanced these propositions, Alchian inquires, 'What must have been assumed in our present literature about the factors mentioned here?' (1959 [1977], p. 298). His reply is disconcerting:

> The answer could not be ascertained from an exhausting reading of the literature nor from analogically implied conditions. Certainly the standard cost curve analysis does not envisage a perpetuity output at some given rate, nor does it seem to specify the effects of shorter-length runs at any output. (p. 298)[20]

Elsewhere in the paper, he does consider the effects of simultaneous increases in rate and volume and – to me, at least – suggests that this might be the sort of exercise some textbooks have in mind. Unfortunately, as he notes, his propositions are silent on the net effect of simultaneous changes in both rate and volume. For example, he remarks:

> [O]ne possible path is to start from the origin and move out some ray [into the C, x, V space]. This gives costs as a function of proportional increases in both the rate and the total output for a fixed interval of production, m, but the behavior of the cost slope of this slice, except for the fact that it is positive, cannot be derived from these propositions. (p. 279)

Thus, 'what would be the net effect of increases in both [rate and volume on marginal cost] cannot be deduced from the present propositions' (p. 283), although he does admit

Table 14.1 Alchian's propositions on costs and outputs

Proposition	Comments	Notes
1. $\partial C/\partial x > 0$ $(T = T_0, V = V_0)$	The faster the rate at which a given volume of output is produced, the greater its cost*	The same total number of units is being produced, with the same start time, so m is being reduced to speed up the production process
2. $\partial^2 C/\partial x^2 > 0$ $(T = T_0, V = V_0)$	Marginal cost is an increasing function of the output rate*	Again, m is being reduced – the (average) location of production is being moved closer to the present
3. $\partial C/\partial V > 0$ $(x = x_0, T = T_0)$	More total output entails the use of more (scarce) inputs, so C increases with V	Because T and x are fixed, the program of production must last a longer length of time, that is, m increases
4. $\partial^2 C/\partial V^2 < 0$ $(x = x_0, T = T_0)$	As total planned output rises by uniform increments, cost will increase by diminishing increments*	The rise in V involves an increase in m, and each successive equal increment in V is farther into the future
5. $\partial(C/V)/\partial V < 0$ $(x = x_0, T = T_0)$	Average cost *per unit* decreases as total volume rises*	This is a direct implication of Proposition 4, but is stated as a separate proposition
6. $\partial^2 C/\partial V\partial x = \partial^2 C/\partial x\partial V < 0$ $(T = T_0)$	When volume increases, marginal cost in the rate dimension decreases; when rate increases, incremental cost in the volume dimension decreases	There is a family of marginal cost curves in the C–x plane, each lower one tied to a greater volume of output; and a family of incremental cost curves in the C–V plane, lower ones linked to higher rates of output
7. $\partial C/\partial T < 0$ $(x = x_0, V = V_0)$	The longer the time between the decision to produce and the initial delivery of output, the lower is cost*	A corollary of Proposition 2: the slower the rate at which inputs are purchased, the lower their price, because the lower are the costs to the seller, when Proposition 2 is applied to him
8. All the derivatives in Propositions 1–5 are diminishing functions of T, but not all diminish at the same rate	This asserts a difference in the extent to which inputs will be varied in the immediate, the short, and the longer period	There is not both a 'long-run' and a 'short-run' cost for any given output program. For any given output program there is only *one* pertinent cost (*not* two), and that is the *cheapest* cost of doing whatever the operation is specified to be. . . . There is a range of operations to be considered, but to each there is only *one* cost
9. As the total quantity of units produced increases, the cost of *future* output declines	This is the learning-by-doing postulate	This is not identical with Proposition 4, where the result is due to varying *techniques* of production. Here it is asserted that knowledge increases as a result of production – that the cost function is actually *lowered* for any subsequent V

Note: *Because cost is a present-value concept, at least Propositions 1, 2, 4, 5, 7, and 8 *could* be generated by invoking the existence of a positive interest rate, for each of these involves deferring a negative cash flow. But, as I discuss more fully in the text, Alchian clearly intends more than this: each of these propositions involves a change in the entire *technique* that is used throughout the length of the production process.

Table 14.2 Revised version of Alchian's Table 1 on costs, volume of output and rates of output

	Volume of output			
Die costs	1	2	3	4
Rate of output, x (per year)	85	170	250	322
1	100	180	255	325
2	120	195	265	330
3	145	215	280	340
4	175	240	300	355

the *possibility* 'that higher rates of production might be available at lower unit costs if they are associated with a larger volume of output, because this latter factor may be sufficient to overcome the effects of the higher output rate' (p. 283). And finally,

> Even returns to scale seem to have been confused with the effect of size of output. It is conjectured that a substantial portion of the alleged cases of increasing returns to scale in industries is the result of ignoring the relation of costs to volume (rather than to rate) of output. (p. 284)

It is probably worth emphasizing that because cost is a present-value concept, at least Propositions 1, 2, 4, 5, 7, and 8 *could* be generated simply by invoking a positive interest rate, for each of these involves deferring a negative cash flow. But Alchian clearly intends more than this. For example, 'it is total contemplated volume of output – not the longer duration of output – that is here asserted (maybe erroneously) to be the factor at work in Propositions 3 and 4' (p. 283). Similarly, 'it is cheaper to produce from a *plan* for a two-year output of two units at a rate of one a year than to produce two by repetition of methods which contemplate only one total unit of output at the same rate of one a year' (p. 281, emphasis in original), which makes it evident that (except for Proposition 9), this paper is about choices between *alternative production processes*. And finally, Alchian notes that 'a larger planned V is produced in a different way from that of a smaller planned V' (p. 282). Thus, each of these propositions involves a change in the entire *technique* that is used *throughout* the length of the production process. To make this even more explicit, I would propose a modification to his Table 1 (p. 280) to rectify the omission of one key piece of information – the 'die' cost of the production technique associated with each volume of output shown there. I have reproduced the modified version of this as Table 14.2, with my proposed revision emphasized.

Proposition 1 implies that for any given volume, the marginal cost of producing at a rate of 1 versus 0 must be less than the marginal cost of producing at a rate of 2 versus 1. This enables us to infer some limits as to the die costs that Alchian must have had in mind when he constructed his table. The ones I have inserted here were suggested to me by Alchian in correspondence, although they are merely sufficient rather than necessary to conform to his cost propositions (for volumes 1, 2, 3, and 4, die costs necessarily must be *greater than* 80, 165, 245, and 320, respectively, to satisfy Proposition 1).

I have not seriously investigated the implications of the existence of die costs for the results of empirical cost studies that ignore such costs, and for production function estimates that ignore the potential for different techniques that might be used to produce the same rate but with different contemplated volumes. Nevertheless, it seems as though one might usefully think of current, observed inputs (of whatever type) as comprising two components – planned and unplanned, that is, those whose current usage was contemplated when the original investment in production technique (or dies) was made, and those that have been added (or subtracted) since, in response to unanticipated changes in conditions. If so, then the estimated production function relationship between outputs and inputs (and hence any estimated cost functions) would depend on the mix of planned versus unplanned inputs.[21]

The short and long runs

Both Propositions 7 and 8 bear on issues related to the 'short run' and the 'long run'. Proposition 7 asserts that when Proposition 2 (rising marginal costs, that is, $\partial^2 C/\partial x^2 > 0$) is applied to input suppliers, deferring the time at which they must deliver will lower their marginal costs, thereby lowering the price that must be paid for inputs purchased from them. Hence, 'it is not merely . . . the price elasticity of supply that determines which inputs are going to be increased earliest. Rather it is the rate at which those price elasticities *change* with deferred purchase that is critical' (ibid., p. 287, emphasis in original). The argument implies, of course, that firms' choices of inputs will depend not merely on current prices but also expected future prices. This is standard fare regarding the importance of expectations, but it is worth noting that because this pattern is *predictable* (high current input prices are those most likely to have been rising in the past) it suggests that empirically, *past* input prices typically will contain information relevant to understanding *current* input choices, in much the same way that Becker et al. (1994) note that past cigarette prices are useful in understanding current cigarette consumption decisions. Here is one more implication of Alchian's analysis that, to my knowledge, has not been exploited in the literature.

On the matter of 'fixed' and 'variable' inputs, Alchian asserts that there is no fixed factor in any interval other than the immediate moment '*when all are fixed*' (1959 [1977], p. 287, emphasis in original). Instead, the rates at which inputs are varied will depend on the costs of doing so; these costs differ across inputs, and the ratios of these costs vary with the time interval within which the variation is to be made. Ultimately, he says, 'the purpose of the short run/long run distinction is to explain the path of prices or output . . . over time in response to some change in demand or supply' (p. 288). Hence, he proposes that the distinction be thought of in terms of 'near *T*' and 'distant *T*' (that is, in terms of how soon production is to be initiated) because this 'yields all the valid implications that the [fixed-variable distinction] did and more besides, while at the same time avoiding the empirically false implications' (p. 289). So again we see him insisting – even in the midst of a purely theoretical paper – that the standard by which the theory is to be judged lies in its conformity with the facts. Finally, and most importantly,

> Proposition 8 makes it clear that there is not both a 'long-run' and a 'short-run' cost for any given output program. For any given output program there is only *one* pertinent cost, *not* two. Unambiguous specification of the output or action to be costed makes the cost definition unambiguous and destroys the illusion that there are two costs to consider, a short-run and a long-run cost for any given output. There is only one cost for any given output and that is the *cheapest* cost of doing whatever the operation is specified to be. . . . There is a range of operations to be considered, but to each there is only *one* cost. The question is not, What are the long-run or

> short-run costs of some operation? but, instead, How do total, average, and marginal costs vary as the T increases, according to Propositions 7 and 8. (pp. 289–90, emphasis in original)[22]

Learning by doing

Except for Proposition 9, this paper is about choice of method or technique. In Proposition 9, however, Alchian asserts that knowledge increases as production takes place, and that as a result, costs are lowered. 'It is not simply a matter of a larger V, but rather a lower cost for any subsequent V, consequent to improved knowledge' (p. 291). Usually this proposition is known as the 'learning curve' or the 'progress curve'.[23]

Total volume of output thus affects costs in two conceptually distinct ways: first, because of changes in technique via Proposition 4, and, second, because the larger is the ultimately realized output, the greater is the accumulated experience and knowledge at any point in the future via Proposition 9. Thus, the average cost per unit of output will be lower, the greater is the planned and ultimately experienced output.[24]

Cost as a capital value measure

Alchian is emphatic in his insistence that if, and only if, *no* assets or liabilities are involved can money flows be identified with costs. Once assets and liabilities are admitted, money flows are no longer synonymous with costs; instead, the measure of costs becomes the change in present value of net equity consequent to some action (ignoring receipts). Given this, Alchian goes on to deconstruct some of the confusion that routinely attaches to the identification of costs when positive and negative cash flows are spread out over time. The example he uses is of a firm that commits itself to a series of actions over time. If the firm signs a contract that commits it to produce some quantity of output, then (ignoring receipts) the cost it incurs in signing the contract and obligating itself to produce the output is the resulting decrease in equity it suffers. The difference, $E_a - E_b$, between the equity (E_a) at the beginning and the *present* value (E_b) of the equity at the end of the operation (E_t), is the cost (C) of the operation. Thus,

> Ignoring the contractual liability for obligation to produce according to the contract, the equity declines along the [E_aE_t] line; but if one does regard the contract performance liability, the equity does not change as output is produced because there is an exactly offsetting reduction in the contractual liability as output is produced. The equity of the firm stays constant over the interval if the outlays and asset values initially forecast were forecast correctly. (p. 295)

This, of course, is precisely the methodology that has guided the enormous financial economics literature on 'event studies' over the past 20 years, but for many economists it was a radically different way of viewing the world when Alchian proposed it.[25]

Conclusions

The theory laid out here enables us to understand the lower average costs attendant on larger quantities of output – not rates of output. These lower costs are due both to choice of technique (the volume effect) and to the accumulation of knowledge due to prior output (the learning effect). Also, the identification of each program of output with a calendar date, together with the postulate that the more distant the date the smaller the cost, provides a way to escape the (unnecessary) bind imposed by the definition of short-run costs as that which result from fixed inputs. The ambiguous idea of two different costs, a short-run and a long-run cost for a given output, disappears and is replaced by one cost for each different program of output.

As Alchian (1996) notes, it is puzzling that this paper has not had a greater impact. He speculates on two possible causes – its publication in a festschrift, rather than in the *American Economic Review*, by which it had been accepted;[26] and the fact that while this paper successfully reconstructed the supply side of our paradigm, it left the complementary demand side untouched. I would add to these possible explanations a combination of two other factors. As Alchian (1963 [1977]) makes clear, the empirical implementation of this suggested approach seems to require cost data that are notoriously difficult to obtain and interpret. At about the same time that 'Costs and outputs' appeared, Stigler (1958) offered an alternative approach to studying some of the same issues (such as economies of scale) – an approach that did not require the acquisition and interpretation of slippery cost data. It seems plausible that some of the resources devoted to pursuing the agenda suggested by Stigler might have been drawn from the agenda suggested by Alchian. Whatever the real reason that Alchian's cost paper (temporarily?) failed to meet the 'survivorship' criteria laid down by either Alchian (1950) or Stigler (1958), there is a substantial body of empirical literature that has ignored the issues raised by Alchian, a literature that seems ripe for revision by incorporating the propositions contained in this paper.

Information costs, pricing, and resource unemployment

> It is curious that while we economists never formalize our analysis on the basis of an analytical ideal of . . . costless production . . . we have postulated costless information as a formal ideal for analysis. Why?
>
> A. Alchian

This paper (Alchian 1969 [1977]) was written at a time when a majority of the profession felt that the problem of unemployment had been solved, because the proper application of fiscal policy could maintain the economy at full employment. Moreover, should the policy maker decide that full employment meant either too little or too much unemployment, the Phillips curve seemed to provide the menu for selecting either more or less. Yet there was a small but growing band of economists who had begun to suspect that something was terribly wrong with this picture, in a variety of dimensions: is it monetary rather than fiscal policy that should be relied upon? Does the level of full employment itself depend on institutional, demographic and other factors? Does the Phillips curve really reflect a stable trade-off between inflation and unemployment? Into the midst of this discussion jumped Alchian, with one of his characteristically (and deceptively) simple questions: why does unemployment – of any resource – even exist? While many of the debates that emerged at this time have disappeared into the annals of the history of thought, Alchian's simple question and the equally simple answer he proposed have survived as part of our core learning.

Two propositions on information costs

The analysis begins here: '*collating information about potential exchange opportunities* is costly and can be performed in various ways' (Alchian 1969 [1977], p. 38, emphasis in original). Thus starts an inquiry into two separate questions. First, how do economic agents minimize the costs of collecting the information that must be collected? Second, what measures do they take to avoid having to incur those costs in the first place?

Two propositions about the costs of production of market opportunity information are critical in the ensuing analysis:

> 1) Dissemination and acquisition (that is, the production) of information conforms to the ordinary laws of costs of production – viz., faster dissemination or acquisition costs more. (p. 39, original emphasis removed)
> 2) Like any other production activity, specialization in information is efficient. Gathering and disseminating information about goods or about oneself is in some circumstances more efficiently done while the good or service is not employed, and thus able to specialize (that is, while specializing) in the production of information. (p. 40, original emphasis removed)

If there were not rising marginal costs with speed of acquisition (Proposition 1), then the second proposition would be rendered empirically moot: even if it were efficient to become unemployed to search for new information, the search would be infinitely fast and thus the unemployment would be empirically undetectable. Similarly, without the *differential* (lower) cost of acquiring information while 'unemployed' (Proposition 2) people would choose wage cuts rather than unemployment as they searched for new information.[27] Thus, without *both* propositions, unemployment of the type discussed here would not be observed.

We now come to two striking observations about the world and about our view of the world: 'Jobs are always easily available. Timely information about the pay, working conditions, and life expectancy of all available jobs is not cheap. . . . This applies to nonhuman resources as well' (pp. 41–2). Thus, contrary to what many new PhDs may believe, they do not spend the second-worst 3–4 months of their graduate careers searching for a job; they are merely looking for timely information regarding the pay, working conditions, and life expectancy of the host of 'easily available' jobs that are right in front of their faces. Moreover, 'we can now identify a "perfect" market – one in which all potential bids and offers are known at zero cost to every other person, and in which contract-enforcement costs are zero' (p. 42, n. 5). Hence, in a perfect market – at least according to economists – the costs of producing (i) information, (ii) exchanges, and (iii) contract fulfillment are zero, even though the costs of producing everything else are positive! It probably is not something we would want to *explicitly* try to sell our students, but it is something that we do *implicitly* all the time. Is it any wonder that people think economists are a bit odd?

The basic search model

Using Alchian's note 3 as a guide, with a slight change in notation (replacing W with P), we can illustrate the basic results of search costs in his model.[28] Consider someone seeking to sell a good at price P. The marginal benefit of search for a higher price is given by:

$$\text{MB} = \frac{\sigma}{t \cdot (2 \log \lambda t)^{0.5}} > 0,$$

where σ is the standard deviation of buyers' potential bid prices, t is time, and λ is the number of bids collected during each unit of time. Because t enters only the denominator, it is clear that the marginal benefit of search is a decreasing function of time.

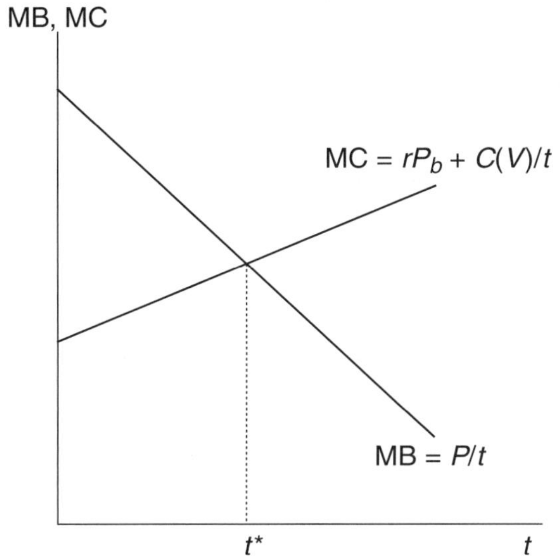

Figure 14.1 *Alchian's basic search model*

If we let the highest bid price actually received so far be designated P_b, and the interest rate is r, then the marginal costs of search are given by:

$$MC = r \cdot P_b + \partial C(V)/\partial t,$$

where $C(V)$ is out-of-pocket search costs, and V describes the search environment. It is evident that the marginal costs of search rise with t, both because P_b will increase as search proceeds, and because techniques entailing higher out-of-pocket costs (per unit of information gathered) will have to be relied upon as search proceeds. The optimal amount of search, t^*, is obtained by equating marginal costs and benefits.

Much of the rest of the paper focuses on the comparative statics predictions of this simple model, combined with a great deal of discussion of how to link the model to reality so as to generate propositions that are in fact refutable. Thus, it is useful to put the model though a few simple exercises, with Figure 14.1 as a guide.

Consider first a rise in the rate of interest. This increases the cost of forgoing the best extant offer, thereby making search more costly. The marginal cost curve shifts up and the optimal amount of search declines. Similarly, if the searcher happens upon a new offer that exceeds the best previously known, this increases P_b and thus the marginal costs of additional search; the result is to reduce the expected duration of additional search.

Changes in λ or σ obviously affect the marginal benefits of search. A rise in σ, reflecting higher variance in potential bid prices, will increase the marginal benefits of search and so induce more search. A higher variance might be the result of less knowledge on the part of buyers about the specific attributes of the particular item being sold; or it could be due to greater variation in the characteristics (and thus bid prices) of the potential buyers themselves. Either way, the optimal amount of search will be greater.

Changes in λ have clear implications for the length of the optimal search, but appear to have ambiguous implications for the amount of information collected, and thus upon the expected price of the good. Because λ enters only the denominator of the marginal benefits of search, it is clear that these marginal benefits decline when λ rises, and so the amount of time spent searching decreases. This has the partial effect of reducing the expected price received, P. But the higher λ means that more information is produced during each unit of time spent searching; this has the partial effect of increasing P. There seems to be no way a priori to determine which of these effects dominates.

Finally, note the theory implies that more search will be undertaken when selling (or buying) more valuable goods. Intuitively, this is because out-of-pocket costs (for example, time costs of the seller, shoe leather, advertising rates and so on) are independent of the value of the good.[29] Hence, when the value of the good is greater, the marginal benefits of search rise relative to marginal costs, implying that more time will be spent searching. This also implies that, when the search process is complete, the seller (or buyer, for the same model can be applied to a person seeking lower prices at which to purchase a good) will know much more about the market for a valuable good than about the market for a less expensive good.

In Alchian's notation, P_0 denotes the price received in the absence of search, P_1 denotes the (gross) value of the expected price, and t_1 is the expected duration of search necessary to obtain that price. If we let P_n be the expected price *net* of search costs, then $P^* = P_n e^{-rt}$ is the present value of P_n. This suggests two different components of the vector of elements contributing to the 'liquidity' of an asset: the ratio P_1/P^*, and the expected time to achieve that price, t_1. A perfectly liquid asset is then one for which $P^* = P_1 = P_n$. Money presumably comes closest to achieving this ideal.

The analysis also opens a role for broker-middlemen as specialists in the business of collecting and disseminating (producing) information. Note that, in the notation used here, the maximum price a broker would pay *now* for something expected to yield a net price of P_n in the future is P^*. The observed retail price at which the broker sells is P_1, so that the difference between P^* and P_1 is the wholesale–resale price spread, or the bid–ask spread of the middleman. Clearly, only lower search costs by the middleman (that is, a comparative advantage in the production of information) enable him to offer a price now (P^*) that exceeds the net present value that can be expected by sellers contemplating search on their own.

Price stability: economizing on information and market adjustment costs

There are three ways to adjust to unanticipated demand fluctuations: (i) output adjustment; (ii) price adjustment; and (iii) inventories and queues (including reservations). Alchian's point is this: each of these forms of adjustment entails costs; there is no reason why only *one* form (for example, price changes) should be utilized, regardless of the costs of the others. The cost of output adjustment stems from the fact that marginal costs rise with the rate of output, so that for a given total volume, production at an uneven rate will elevate average and thus total costs. The cost of price adjustment arises because uncertain prices induce (costly) search on the part of customers seeking the best price in a distribution of prices. The third method of adjustment entails obvious holding and queuing costs. Presumably, the objective of the seller will be to minimize the total of these costs. Much of the rest of the paper is an effort to explore some implications of this cost minimization.[30]

The many forms of commonly observed behavior that Alchian suggests may be explained by this theory include the following:

1. *manufacturer*-imposed fair trade laws, which eliminate price dispersion between stores, thereby reducing search and thus total purchase costs to consumers with high time costs;
2. shops that stay open even when no customers are in sight, when they could close and have customers ring the bell or make reservations for service;
3. apartment owners who build more units than they expect on the average to rent, knowing they face the choice between low vacancy and a lower, flexible price, always moving to clear the market, versus higher vacancy and a higher, stable price;[31] and
4. homes built with enough bathrooms and dining room capacity to accommodate more visitors than one ordinarily will have.

And thus Alchian concludes:

> To say that there is 'idle', 'wasted', or 'unemployed' . . . capacity is to consider only the cost of the extra capacity while ignoring its infrequent-use value and the *greater* costs of other ways of obtaining equally high convenience value. . . . [I]n a society with (a) costs of obtaining information about prices of all sellers, (b) costs of sellers' obtaining information about amounts of demand of customers, and (c) a tendency for unpredicted price changes to induce extra search by buyers and sellers, the 'ideal' market will *not* be characterized by prices that instantly fluctuate so as to always clear the market without queues by buyers or sellers . . . (Ibid. p. 49, emphasis in original)

Labor markets

When confronted with a proposed pay cut, an employee may sensibly reject it, reasoning that he can get approximately his old wage at some other job: 'after all, that is why he was getting what he did get at his current job' (p. 52). In general, a seller faced with decreased demand by *one* buyer may not regard that as a reliable indicator of similar changes in demand by all other demanders for that service: 'A decrease in price available from *a* buyer does not mean all other buyers have reduced their offer prices' (p. 53, n. 15, emphasis in original). This is particularly true in labor markets (as opposed to, say, securities markets), where information about the attributes on both sides of the market – employees and jobs – is much more costly.

While the theory seems to be applicable chiefly to quits by workers, Alchian argues that it applies to layoffs as well. When wage cuts sufficient to maintain profitability would also be sufficient to induce employees to look elsewhere, employers announce layoffs rather than undertaking 'fruitless wage renegotiations'.[32] If the decline in demand is temporary, and if there are costs of changing jobs, then the layoff is 'temporary'; and if the temporary demand decline is predictable, the result is what we refer to as normal working hours (say, 8–5, Monday–Friday). Note finally that '*differential* [between unemployed and employed] information costs are necessary for the incidence of unemployment' (p. 55, emphasis in original) due to unanticipated demand decreases; otherwise, employees would continue collecting paychecks while they searched for new job information.

Of course the search for information is not confined to employees: employers do it too, and job vacancies are the counterpart to unemployment. In effect, the employer has two different ways to generate information about prospective employees: the first is to leave the job vacant while interviewing, the second is to fill the job immediately and learn about the suitability of the new person while he or she is on the job. The choice will depend on a host of factors, including: (i) how much can be learned about an employee without having to watch the person in action; and (ii) the amount of damage the employee can do while on the job during the probationary period.[33]

Some implications for the business cycle

Although the principal focus of the exposition is the development of the microeconomic implications of the theory, Alchian presents a fair dose of macroeconomic implications as well. Almost offhandedly, for example, he offers one of the earliest explanations for two features of the Phillips curve that are routinely embodied in undergraduate texts today, but were then radical propositions. He notes first that unanticipated changes in demand will generate a short-run Phillips relation that is actually a series of loops, joined at the 'zero price-level-change' (natural) rate of unemployment. But for correctly *anticipated* changes in aggregate demand, the unemployment rate 'will be independent of the anticipated [inflation] rate' (p. 60), that is, the long-run Phillips curve will be a vertical line.

The theory also has implications for the behavior of real wages and for productivity over the business cycle. There is no reason, for example, for wages to lag behind prices (generating a rise in real wages during recessions and a fall in real wages during expansion): 'wage rates and all other prices can fall [or rise] at the *same* rate' (p. 60, emphasis in original). The only 'lag' that occurs is between the discernment of and the actual level of the new best prices of all goods, labor included. Hence, there is no reason to expect real wages to move in any predictable manner over the business cycle.[34]

One key point that Alchian is making in this discussion is that information costs are particularly high in labor markets compared to other markets, so that the behavioral responses to information costs are likely to be particularly pronounced there.[35] For example, he notes that employers will sometimes choose to keep employees (and other inputs) on the payroll even when their current marginal product is less than their factor prices, due to the costs of finding *new* workers when demand returns to its normal level. Here the driving force may be thought of as the desire to *avoid* having to produce information, rather than an effort to reduce the costs of producing a given amount of information.[36] Recognition of the high information costs in the labor market also suggests that there may be sensibility in Keynes's definition of 'involuntary unemployment' in which a seemingly bizarre distinction is made between workers' responses to a decline in the nominal wage and a rise in the price level:

> Men are involuntarily unemployed if, in the event of a small rise in the price of wage-goods relative to the money-wage, both the aggregate supply of labour willing to work for the current money wage and the aggregate demand for it at that wage would be greater than the existing volume of employment. (Keynes 1936, p. 15)

Alchian's contention is that the price-level rise conveys different information to workers. A higher price level means that there is a decline in money-wages everywhere relative to prices; a cut in one's own money wages does not imply that options elsewhere have fallen

– only that one is less valuable in one's current employment. The crucial distinction then, is the differential information revealed about prospects elsewhere (see Leijonhufvud 1968). The proposed nominal wage cut suggests that search for a higher wage elsewhere would be profitable; the rise in the price level does not.

Potential tests of the theory

A paper by Alchian would hardly be recognizable as such unless there were considerable effort directed to revealing ways in which the theory can be proved false. Hence, in addition to the numerous refutable implication sprinkled throughout the paper up to this point, Alchian closes with a section devoted to nothing else. I have summarized the bulk of them in Box 14.1.

BOX 14.1 POTENTIAL TESTS OF ALCHIAN'S THEORY OF INFORMATION COSTS AND RESOURCE UNEMPLOYMENT

1. The extent of recovery in employment from a downturn will be positively correlated with extent of the preceding decline, but there will be *zero* correlation between the magnitude of an expansion and the subsequent decline.[1]

2. Resources with less *differentiated* costs (while employed or unemployed) of obtaining or dispersing information will have lower incidence, as well as shorter periods, of unemployment.

   Employer knows more about own employees than those of other employers, so probability of job changes (in tasks and grades) should be greater within a firm than among firms.

   The excess probability should decrease in the higher paid tasks, because extra search is more economic the higher the marginal product of an employee's position.

3. Homogeneous goods, with low costs of information, should have low unemployment rates.

   Tract houses, built by one builder, should be 'easier' to sell (for a given cost of search, realized price should be closer to maximum).[2]

   Frequent, repeated purchases by buyers should be correlated with knowledge about the item and alternative sources of purchases, so the bid–ask spread should be lower, which also implies smaller ratio of inventories to sales for such goods.

   Formal markets reduced information costs, so bid–ask spreads should be lower there, for example, spreads on stocks on organized markets should be lower than for over-the-counter stocks.

Insofar as new goods involve higher information costs, there should be higher ratios of inventories to sales for such goods, and thus higher bid–ask spreads.[3]

New 'unseasoned' stocks and bonds should be markedly different (and presumably larger) in bid–ask spread from older, established stocks and bonds.

The highest and lowest priced variant of any class of goods will have longer inventory period and larger retail–wholesale price spread than typical or modal variety (this assumes that extremes are less familiar and hence have higher information costs).

Standard types of used (and new?) automobiles (and general-use 'X' compared to special-use 'X') should have shorter inventory interval and lower ratio of inventory to sales ratio than do unusual used (and new) cars because information about the standard type is more common among potential buyers.[4]

More dispersion among bid prices of potential buyers implies larger gross gain from search, due to larger *absolute* (not relative) increments of discerned maximum prices; hence, there will be longer search and larger markup for more expensive unusual items (such as works of art).

4. Information about employers is more readily available if there are fewer employers to search and to be told of one's talents.

Hence, the fewer the major employers in the community, the shorter will be the length and the lower the incidence of unemployment; wages should be adjusted more quickly in areas with only one (or a few?) employer(s).

Highly paid employees will resort more to employment agencies to economize on their (more valuable) search time.[5] And, higher-paid workers will be more likely to use private agencies rather than public agencies, because private agencies can change differential fees and thus have greater incentive to devote more resources to placement of higher-paid people.

Job vacancies for expensive, heterogeneous executives will be longer-lived than for lower productivity and standard-duty types of workers; this implies larger (absolute or relative?) employment agency fees for higher-paying jobs.

Discrimination solely according to eye shape, sex, skin color, and ethnic background is less profitable and thus less probable in higher-paying jobs, because the extra value of additional information about a person's abilities is higher for a higher-paid person. The same applies for long-term versus short-term employees. It also implies that cheaply observable characteristics should be more uniform among lower-paid individuals than among higher-paid individuals.

Notes

1. Friedman and Schwartz (1963, pp. 493–9) provide some evidence on this. Much of the macroeconomic literature on whether the economy is 'trend-stationary' or not has missed Alchian's original insight here. But see Diebold and Senhadji (1996) on this.
2. I infer that there should be lower real estate commissions on such houses, less time on the market and more turnover (because that turnover is cheaper). Analogously, apartments of standard design should have lower vacancy rates. (Recall the common 'Valley' design in San Fernando apartment houses in the early 1970s, where the population was very transient – driving by at the speed limit one knew *exactly* the product being offered for sale.)
3. This sheds some light on a host of features regarding women's versus men's clothes.
4. This suggests that new car spreads and inventory to sales ratios should be lower than for used cars, for the same reason.
5. This assumes that a higher-skilled worker has a higher ratio of wages per hour to value of self-generated income from extended search.

The discussion goes on for five pages, and one has the impression in reading it that Alchian could have gone on for five (or fifty) more – and probably would have delighted in doing so, except for a beckoning golf course. Where, no doubt, he amused himself by thinking of still more of those surprising implications of scarcity.

Concluding remarks

I once heard the late Karl Brunner say, 'If you want to be good you must be willing to be wrong'.[37] Brunner's meaning is aptly demonstrated in much the same terms that I began this chapter, by describing the threads that weave throughout Armen Alchian's work. Starting with his insistence that the individual is the appropriate unit of analysis, Alchian's work is always simple – not necessarily easy, but always simple in a way that is characteristic of an unstinting application of Occam's razor. There is no ambiguity, no excess baggage, no smoke or mirrors to disguise incoherent or imprecise thought. And although there are often many levels to his words, there is never any doubt about the precise meaning of each level.

Second, Alchian's propositions about the world are always general, applying across markets and goods and economic agents of all sorts. There is always the search for the 'unified' theory – for the proposition that will combine other propositions into one, and thus explain more with less.

And finally, these propositions – whether they be about the natural selection of the marketplace, or the choice of production technologies or the duration of unemployment – are fundamentally useful, in the sense that they generate testable implications, implications that when confronted with the facts are capable of being falsified – simply, clearly, unmistakably. Always there is an effort to put his ideas into the center of the arena where the most powerful evidence possible can be brought to bear upon them, revealing their weaknesses or falsehoods, wherever they might be. And so it is that in his unstinting efforts to give other people the opportunity to prove him wrong, Armen Alchian has taught us much that is correct about the world.

Notes

* An earlier version of this chapter was prepared for a Liberty Fund conference, and financial support from the Liberty Fund is gratefully acknowledged.

1. The paper also got Alchian's career off to a fast start. As Kenneth Arrow (who was a colleague of

Alchian's at RAND in the 1950s) has remarked, 'what made Armen really famous was his paper in 1950 on evolution' (personal communication).

2. Alchian's complaint to Stigler was a follow-up to a dinner conversation he had with Rose and Milton Friedman. As Alchian recounted the conversation, 'I started questioning Milton about unemployment. Milton kept saying wages are sticky. I said, "that doesn't explain anything". But Milton just kept saying that wages are sticky. Rose – she is very good – said "Come on Milton, that fails to explain *why* they are sticky", and he agreed and we started looking for an explanation' (personal communication).
3. Articulated in the English version by the then-president of Coca-Cola when consumer rejection of New Coke in 1985 forced the company to return Coke Classic to the market.
4. Although he notes that the economist's modes of thinking may be poor guides to *action* in the real world, because they assume to be true things that are not true. Similarly, what people have to say about what they are doing or why may be of little value in predicting their behavior, because what they say has little bearing on the success or failure of what they do.
5. An appalling thought, one must imagine, for the chief economists at many government agencies!
6. A corollary of this is that the 'expert' may be of little relevance in such a world; indeed, as the amount of uncertainty increases, the role for the expert diminishes and the importance of the individual decision maker (regardless of his/her knowledge or reasoning power) rises. An implication of this, it would seem, is that those times of greatest uncertainty, when the calls for expertise and centrally directed action are the greatest (times of 'crises'), are the very times when we should rely most heavily on decentralized, individual, non-directed decision making (see also Benjamin and Dougan 1997).
7. This certainly suggests that the chances of achieving the 'best' are enhanced if maximum freedom is given to the expression of action by individuals – hinting at the possibility that we live in a world in which we began the Cold War with a thousand Maxwell Smarts and have anointed the survivor James Bond.
8. When a small sailboat is caught by a severe storm in the open ocean, the greatest peril it faces is from large waves, whose size and behavior are subject to large random variation. There are two basic survival mechanisms: (1) keep steering the boat (with or without some scrap of sails up), or (2) lash the helm in place and either 'heave to' with small sails set to produce opposing and neutralizing forces, or let the boat 'lie a-hull' without sails, surviving as well as it can without any human intervention. Option 1 involves considerable (and highly motivated) maximizing behavior on the part of the crew. Either version of option 2 results in what amounts to a series of random 'decisions' (outcomes), based on which waves happen to strike in what manner. There are many survivors who swear by each option (and against the other). The opinions of those who have not survived are not known. See Coles (1975) for details.
9. Alchian's exposition on this issue is one of the earliest emphatic statements of a proposition that is today not merely well-understood, but is routinely drilled into our students in intermediate price theory – something that can be said about many other propositions in Alchian's work. Professor Eugene Silberberg of the University of Washington has brought to my attention an equally striking but much earlier discussion on this point from Henry George's *Progress and Poverty* (1933, p. 12):

   > [W]e safely base the reasoning and actions of daily life . . . on the metaphysical law . . . that men seek to gratify their desires with the least exertion. And although in the domain of political economy we cannot test our theories by artificially produced combinations or conditions, as may be done in some other sciences, yet we can apply tests no less conclusive, by comparing societies in which different conditions exist, or by, in imagination, separating, combining, adding or eliminating forces or factors of known direction.

10. As Alchian (1950 [1977], p. 26) notes, our predictions are not about individual firms, but about 'representative' firms, that is, about 'a set of statistics summarizing the various "modal" characteristics of the population'.
11. 'The pursuit of profits, and not some hypothetical and undefinable perfect situation, is the relevant objective whose *fulfillment* is rewarded with survival' (Alchian 1950 [1977], p. 28, emphasis in original).
12. Note the implications of this regarding psychologists and others who worry about heuristic behavior (see Kahneman et al. 1982).
13. The discussion appears to anticipate some recent significant developments in the theory of optimal strategies in repeated games (see Ridley 1997, ch. 4). If this seems to impute excess prescience to Alchian, note that he was one of the two participants in the original experiment involving a repeated prisoner's dilemma game (see ibid., pp. 58–9).
14. To return to the sailing analogy, the relevant (and achievable, one hopes) objective is the avoidance of being rolled over and sunk by the next wave, rather than the adherence to some rhumb line penciled on a chart.

15. If survival in the presence of uncertainty implicitly demands uniformity and imitation, and if the competitive market generates the same, does this suggest that the market may indeed be the ultimate survival-ensuring mechanism?
16. 'The modification suggested here incorporates this search for more knowledge as an essential foundation' (Alchian 1950 [1977], p. 33, n. 15). Note the clear link here between Hayek (1945) and Alchian (1969).
17. Note Alchian's repeated use of the words 'programmed' and 'contemplated', implying that advance planning is crucial, and that a *method of production* rather than a learning process is being discussed (except in Proposition 8, where learning is explicitly the essence). As a rule, the distinction between rate and volume, and thus any meaningful discussion of the *method* of production, is ignored in the standard graduate texts. See Varian (1992) and Silberberg and Suen (2000) for examples of the rule, and Layard and Walters (1977) and Stigler (1987) for exceptions – which are in fact almost token exceptions. Layard and Walters confine their discussion to a vestigial appendix, while Stigler's two-page discussion is at the end of a chapter and is not referred to elsewhere in the book. Moreover, although Stigler carefully and correctly distinguishes between the effects of planned future volume and actual past volume on pp. 174–5, he fails to do so on the very next page.
18. Except in Proposition 7, where there is no adjustment in *m*; the entire production schedule (unchanged in shape) is instead being moved (see Alchian 1959 [1977], p. 286).
19. I shall use *incremental* cost to refer to a change in cost due to a change in volume ($\partial C/\partial V$), thus distinguishing it from *marginal* costs, a term reserved for a change in cost due to a change in rate ($\partial C/\partial x$).
20. Although Stigler (1987, p. 174) claims that infinite production runs are the standard assumption, Layard and Walters (1977, p. 213) explicitly work with finite productions runs, and Stigler's claim is inconsistent with his own discussion of short-run cost curves (Stigler 1987, p. 141).
21. Obviously, the distinction I have in mind here parallels that made between permanent versus transitory income when estimating consumption functions (see Friedman 1957).
22. I have found that some of the commonplace confusions on this issue among first-year graduate students can be revealed with some variant of this exam question: '*True/False/Uncertain and Explain*: Because all costs can be avoided in the long run but not the short run, the long run marginal cost curve can never be above the short run marginal cost curve. (NOTE: Be sure to reconcile your answer with the standard method of drawing these curves.)'.
23. 'Sometimes the [learning or progress] curve is called an 80 percent progress curve, because it is sometimes asserted that the cost of the 2*n*th item is 80 percent of the cost of the *n*th item Thus the fortieth plane would involve only 80 percent of the direct man hours and materials that the twentieth plane did' (Alchian 1959 [1977], p. 292, n. 9). In a classic paper, Arrow (1962) formalized the arguments proposed here, and Alchian (1963 [1977]) subsequently attempted to empirically implement them.
24. Because Proposition 4 distinguishes between planned and unplanned changes in volume, even though Proposition 9 does not, such a distinction should be made in any empirical investigation of the implications of learning by doing.
25. And, as Alchian (1996) notes, he had actually done what may be the first-ever event study several years before writing this paper.
26. A lesson, perhaps, for junior faculty whose focus sometimes is not enough on the question of 'who will read what I have written?'.
27. There are two reasons for this inherent preference for input price cuts rather than unemployment: higher income, plus the implicit recommendation of being currently employed. Of course there are always costs associated with being employed: the forgone value of leisure for human resources and the wear and tear for human and non-human resources alike. But, as we shall see, Alchian clearly means something more than this when he speaks of the possibility that unemployment is cheaper than employment when producing information.
28. Assuming that bid prices are normally distributed with mean *m* and variance σ^2, the expected maximum bid price received after *n* observations is approximately:

$$P(n) = m + \sigma(2 \log n)^{0.5}.$$

Assuming that λ observations per unit time are obtained, then $n = \lambda t$, and we can write:

$$P(t) = m + \sigma(2 \log \lambda t)^{0.5}.$$

The rate of change of the maximum bid is given by:

$$\partial P/\partial t = \frac{\sigma}{t \cdot (2 \log \lambda t)^{0.5}} > 0,$$

which is clearly a decreasing function of time (t). I refer to $\partial P/\partial t$ as the marginal benefits of search.

29. Consider a more valuable good for which the distribution of prices differs from the first by the factor $\varphi > 1$. Then the expected price of this good is φm and the variance is $\varphi^2\sigma^2$. Hence the marginal benefits of search are given by:

$$\partial P/\partial t = \frac{\phi\sigma}{t \cdot (2 \log \lambda t)^{0.5}} > 0,$$

while the expected marginal costs are given by:

$$r{\cdot}\varphi P_b + \partial C(V)/\partial t.$$

A rise in φ clearly increases marginal benefits relative to marginal costs (because φ operates on all of marginal benefits but only on a portion of marginal costs), implying more search.

30. Of course, all of this discussion is directed at unpredictable demand fluctuations. Regarding predictable demand changes, he asserts that 'prices would vary – as they do for afternoon and evening restaurant and theater, for example' (Alchian 1969 [1977], p. 47).

But what about predictable demand shifts that are *predictably* accompanied by price changes insufficient to ration demand? Consider motels along the interstate over the year, where demand generally is highest in summer and lowest in winter. Prices should be highest in summer and lowest in winter, and would (according to Alchian) be expected to adjust enough to ration demand fully. But in fact, they do not seem to fully ration demand. Instead, vacancy rates are high in the winter when prices are low and low in the summer when prices are high.

Benjamin and Dougan (1997) argue that the demand shifts that cause the price changes also change the cost of holding inventories over the year: When prices are high, it is expensive to have empty rooms, but when prices are low, empty rooms are cheap. Hence, over the course of the year, the responsibility for holding inventories is shifted from supplier to demander. Thus, vacancies fall in the summer, at the same time that the percentage of rooms secured in advance by reservations rises.

Another factor in some regions is the cost to consumers of going without a room (or of searching longer for a room): this cost is higher in the winter (in cold climates) and lower in the summer (due to both better weather and added daylight). This suggests a predictable difference for off-peak behavior when temperature is not a threat: the value of inventories to consumers is lower and so vacancy rates should be lower than when weather is a threat, and prices should be lower.

31. Note that the apartment vacancies offer information services to prospective renters, stable prices for existing renters and spontaneous moves for all. The alternative is for renters to either adjust continuously to rental price changes (if prices were flexible), or make reservations in advance (if prices were stable and there were no vacancies).
32. But see Gordon (1974) for a more compelling discussion of the rationale for layoffs.
33. In recent years, a third method has spread, the use of temporary-employment agencies such as Kelly Services, which learn about and certify prospective employees, and then keep them on the agency's payroll until the prospective permanent employer decides to accept or reject them.
34. Of course Kessel and Alchian (1959, 1960, 1962) already had discovered this in a series of articles that overturned the then-prevailing conventional wisdom on this issue – so Alchian was hardly sticking his neck out in making this prediction!
35. This is an insight that was largely ignored until the mid-1980s, when the literature on tournaments and executive compensation began to appear.
36. Note also the implications of this 'labour hoarding' (as it is termed in Britain and elsewhere in Europe) for 'productivity' over the business cycle. During downturns, output falls more than employment, and so measured productivity declines. During the ensuing expansion, output rises more than employment, and so productivity increases. See Benjamin and Kochin (1979) for some additional implications.
37. Although spoken in his strong Germanic-Swiss accent, it actually sounded more like, 'If you *vant* to be good you must be *villing* to be *ronk*'.

References

Alchian, A.A. (1950), 'Uncertainty, evolution and economic theory', *Journal of Political Economy*, **58** (3), 211–21.

Alchian, A.A. (1950 [1977]), 'Uncertainty, evolution and economic theory', in *Economic Forces at Work: Selected Works by Armen A. Alchian*, Benjamin, D.K. (ed.), Indianapolis, IN: Liberty Press, pp. 15–35.

Alchian, A.A. (1959 [1977]), 'Costs and outputs', in *Economic Forces at Work: Selected Works by Armen A. Alchian*, Benjamin, D.K. (ed.), Indianapolis, IN: Liberty Press, pp. 273–99.

Alchian, A.A. (1963 [1977]), 'Reliability of progress curves in airframe production', in *Economic Forces at*

Work: Selected Works by Armen A. Alchian, Benjamin, D.K. (ed.), Indianapolis, IN: Liberty Press, pp. 335–60.
Alchian, A.A. (1969), 'Information costs, pricing and resource unemployment', *Economic Inquiry*, **7** (2), 109–28.
Alchian, A.A. (1969 [1977]), 'Information costs, pricing and resource unemployment', in *Economic Forces at Work: Selected Works of Armen A. Alchian*, Benjamin, D.K. (ed.), Indianapolis, IN: Liberty Press, pp. 37–71.
Alchian, A.A. (1996), 'Principles of professional advancement', *Economic Inquiry*, **34** (3), 520–26.
Alchian, A.A. and H. Demsetz (1972), 'Production, information costs, and economic organization', *American Economic Review*, **62** (5), 777–95.
Anderson, L.A. and C.A. Holt (1997), 'Information cascades in the laboratory', *American Economic Review*, **87** (5), 847–62.
Arrow, K.J. (1962), 'The economic implications of learning by doing', *Review of Economic Studies*, **29** (3), 155–73.
Becker, G.S., M. Grossman and K.M. Murphy (1994), 'An empirical analysis of cigarette addiction', *American Economic Review*, **84** (3), 396–418.
Benjamin, D.K. and W.R. Dougan (1997), 'Individuals' estimates of the risks of death: part I – a reassessment of previous evidence', *Journal of Risk and Uncertainty*, **15** (2), 115–33.
Benjamin, D.K. and L.A. Kochin (1979), 'Searching for an explanation of unemployment in interwar Britain', *Journal of Political Economy*, **87** (3), 441–78.
Coase, R.H. (1960), 'The problem of social cost', *Journal of Law and Economics*, **3**, 1–44.
Coles, K.A. (1975), *Heavy Weather Sailing*, rev. edn, Clinton Corners, NY: John de Graff.
De Vany, A. (1996), 'Information, chance, and evolution: Alchian and the economics of self-organization', *Economic Inquiry*, **34** (3), 427–43.
Diebold, F.X. and A.S. Senhadji (1996), 'The uncertain unit root in real GNP: comment', *American Economic Review*, **86** (5), 1291–8.
Friedman, M. (1953), 'The methodology of positive economics', in *Essays in Positive Economics*, Chicago, IL: University of Chicago Press, pp. 3–43.
Friedman, M. (1957), *A Theory of the Consumption Function*, Princeton, NJ: Princeton University Press.
Friedman, M. and A.J. Schwartz (1963), *A Monetary History of the United States, 1867–1960*, Princeton, NJ: Princeton University Press.
George, H. (1933), *Progress and Poverty*, 50th anniversary edn, New York: Robert Schalkenbach Foundation, Macmillan.
Gordon, D.F. (1974), 'A neo-classical theory of Keynesian unemployment', *Economic Inquiry*, **12** (4), 431–59.
Haddock, D.D. and F.S. McChesney (1994), 'Why do firms contrive shortages? The economics of intentional mispricing', *Economic Inquiry*, **32** (4), 562–81.
Hayek, F.A. (1945), 'The use of knowledge in society', *American Economic Review*, **35** (4), 519–30.
Hirshleifer, J. (1978), 'Competition, cooperation, and conflict in economics and biology', *American Economic Review*, **68** (2), 238–43.
Kahneman, D., P. Slovic and A. Tversky (eds) (1982), *Judgment under Uncertainty: Heuristics and Biases*, Cambridge: Cambridge University Press.
Kessel, R.A. (1954), 'Inflation and wealth redistribution: an empirical study', PhD dissertation, Economics, University of Chicago, Chicago.
Kessel, R.A. and A.A. Alchian (1959), 'Real wages in the North during the Civil War: Mitchell's data reinterpreted', *Journal of Law and Economics*, **2**, 95–113.
Kessel, R.A. and A.A. Alchian (1960), 'The meaning and validity of the inflation-induced lag of wages behind prices', *American Economic Review*, **50** (1), 43–66.
Kessel, R.A. and A.A. Alchian (1962), 'Effects of inflation', *Journal of Political Economy*, **70** (6), 521–37.
Keynes, J.M. (1936), *The General Theory of Employment, Interest and Money*, New York: Harcourt, Brace.
Klein, B., R.G. Crawford and A.A. Alchian (1978), 'Vertical integration, appropriable rents and the competitive contracting process', *Journal of Law & Economics*, **21** (2), 297–326.
Layard, R. and A.A. Walters (1977), *Microeconomic Theory*, New York: McGraw-Hill.
Leijonhufvud, A. (1968), *Keynesian Economics and the Economics of Keynes*, New York: Oxford University Press.
McChesney, F.S. (1996), 'An introduction to Alchian's "Principles of professional advancement"', *Economic Inquiry*, **34** (3), 519.
Ridley, M. (1997), *The Origins of Virtue: Human Instincts and the Evolution of Cooperation*, New York: Penguin.
Samuelson, P.A. (1970), 'Who's who in economics', *Newsweek*, January 19, p. 78.

Samuelson, P.A. (1985), 'Modes of thought in economics and biology', *American Economic Review*, **75** (2), 166–72.
Silberberg, E. and W. Suen (2000), *The Structure of Economics*, 3rd edn, New York: McGraw-Hill.
Stigler, G.J. (1958), 'The economies of scale', *Journal of Law & Economics*, **1**, 54–71.
Stigler, G.J. (1987), *The Theory of Price*, 4th edn, New York: Macmillan.
Varian, H. (1992), *Microeconomic Analysis*, 3rd edn, New York: Norton.

15 The Chicago roots of the Virginia School

*Gordon L. Brady**

Introduction

The story of the Virginia School of Political Economy is in large part the story of how graduates of the University of Chicago developed a new paradigm in a new location. As noted by Dennis C. Mueller in 1986, the founders were still working and imparting their insights some thirty years from the time James M. Buchanan and Gordon Tullock were first associated. Now, over twenty years later, this continues to be the case.

In order to better understand the origins of the Virginia School, this chapter seeks to answer two questions. First, what are the distinctive characteristics of the Virginia School? Second, which of these characteristics have roots in the Chicago School? The latter question is most effectively addressed by focusing on James Buchanan.

As an exercise in intellectual history, the chapter goes beyond economics to include the sociology of knowledge and an account of the strong-willed personalities at Chicago who had a major influence on Buchanan, the principal founder of the Virginia School. To some extent this process was replicated at UCLA where Armen A. Alchian (post-doctoral fellow, 1968) and Harold Demsetz (Chicago 1963–71), worked on the economics of property rights. An appropriate metaphor to describe these emissaries at UCLA and Virginia is that of spores. Those involved were characterized by a deep and abiding respect for the intellectual tradition of economics at the University of Chicago and through their achievements reflected well on their *alma mater*.[1]

From its roots in the late 1950s at the Thomas Jefferson Center for the Study of Political Economy at the University of Virginia, the Virginia School of Political Economy has challenged the supremacy of mainstream neoclassical economics and interventionist presumptions by providing a new vision of the market order and an economic explanation of government failure. Those associated with the Virginia School have been critical of abstract mathematical modeling and high-powered econometrics which does not take into account the complex institutional arrangements of advanced economies. Buchanan and Tullock founded the field of public choice and Ronald H. Coase was a founder of the new field of law and economics. In recognition of their contributions to economics, the Nobel Prize in Economic Science was awarded to Buchanan in 1986 and to Coase in 1991.

The leaders of the Virginia School were pioneers in the application of economic analysis to new topics such as, bureaucracy, voting, constitutions, and law and economics. Buchanan's early work on subjectivism was important in challenging the equilibrium focus of mainstream economists. Imbued with these subjectivist insights, Buchanan's approach recognized that individuals act according to their own perception of costs and benefits. From this it follows that politicians are self-regarding and not necessarily promoters of the public interest broadly conceived. It is not surprising that this view of politicians, which became associated with the Virginia School gave rise to charges that the school embraced an ideological point of view and this perception was used to criticize the Virginia School then and now. While the founders of the Virginia School have been recognized as major innovators in the development of economic analysis, the acceptance of their work has been slow.

Mueller (1986) describes the Virginia School as focusing on how self-interested individuals interact with political institutions, and how we can step outside the system and design institutions with incentives that would better achieve our ends. The Virginia School recognizes that, as actors constrained by a system of rules, individuals play two roles. First, they are the beneficiaries of the existing institutions and therefore may oppose changing the rules. Second, the rules will only get changed if they are persuaded to do so. As an example of changing the rules, if super majorities replace simple majorities, special interest group politics will be less important and will limit undesirable outcomes.

Congleton (2002) points out that there is no textbook treatment of the Virginia School and he notes the several ways in which it differs from the mainstream. Underlying this approach is the idea that self-regarding individuals learn to use the rules of a political system in ways to achieve their ends. Therefore, only by reforming the rules can we alter the outcomes. The Virginia School recognizes that both good and bad economic policies are the outcomes of rational individuals making choices within specific institutional arrangements. Undesirable public policies such as protective tariffs, costly and ineffective regulation, distortionary taxes, wasteful expenditures, and ill-conceived transfer programs are not accidents or mistakes waiting to be corrected, but the consequences of self-interested individuals choosing within particular institutional settings. In order to improve the outcomes of particular institutional arrangements, it is necessary to change the rules of the game, not simply to change the players or to give them better economic or policy advice. Institutional arrangements should then be compared to each other and relative to what is feasible Finally, in so far as we consider people's goals as given, the role of the Virginia School economist is to find the most efficacious means to achieve those goals. This approach therefore entails positive rather than normative prescriptions.

The essentials of the Virginia School may therefore be summarized in four points. First, the focus is on institutional arrangements as the reason for economic success or failure. Second, it recognizes that the only way to turn economic failure into success is by changing the institutional arrangements. Third, institutional arrangements are compared by reference to the outcomes they yield and with reference to their feasibility. Finally, the analyst is constrained to provide positive rather than normative recommendations.

What the Chicago School of Economics stands for

We begin with a brief description of the Chicago School and its early faculty, and then focus on how some of these people influenced James M. Buchanan (b. 1919), Gordon Tullock (b. 1922), G. Warren Nutter (1923–77), D. Rutledge Vining (1908–99) and Ronald H. Coase (b. 1910).

The main characteristics of the Chicago School are twofold: the belief in the power of neoclassical price theory to explain observed economic behavior; and the belief in the efficacy of free markets to coordinate individual actions, and to allocate resources and distribute income. The ideas associated with the Chicago School include Adam Smith's 'invisible hand' postulate, opposition to government intervention in general and Keynesianism in particular, monetarism, and, as a later development, the economic analysis of the law. The 'invisible hand' describes the phenomenon by which desirable outcomes are achieved without human design. It is used to explain some of the consequences of individual behavior and the evolution of institutions. The methodology associated with the Chicago School is that articulated by Milton Friedman (1953) in his renowned essay on positive economics, which has for decades been the dominant paradigm within the economics profession.

The founders of the Chicago School

Jacob Viner (at Chicago from 1919 to 1946), Frank H. Knight (from 1927 until his death; he retired in 1952), Henry C. Simons (1927–46), and Aaron Director (1946–65) are the more familiar names associated with the early years of the Chicago School (biographies of each appear elsewhere in this volume). Among the founders of the Chicago School we may wish to distinguish those with a crusade or mission (Simons's crusade for what he believed was freedom and equality), those with a passion (Knight and Director were puzzlers), and those who sought to develop a system (Viner's rigorous analytical framework). The approach and contributions of some of the founders and their successors fit more than one category. Simons's mission was to advance political freedom and some measure of income equality which he thought could be obtained by a progressive tax structure and restraints on monopolies.[2] He feared that government would expand dramatically during the 1930s and that this development would be difficult, if not impossible, to reverse.

Both Knight and Simons emphasized the need to be critical in evaluating scientific work and that the age or high office of the researcher was of no consequence. Along with Director, their inquiry left no stone unturned and considered no doctrine sacrosanct no matter the identity of its originator. Chicago economists in general have been problem oriented and advocates of the use of the simplest theoretical tools necessary to accomplish the task at hand. The causes determining a particular economic event are numerous and complex, but exponents of the Chicago School believe that economists should focus on the role of incentives in explaining human behavior. General equilibrium theorists, on the other hand, seek comprehensive and rigorous mathematical theories to show how the economic system can attain equilibrium under a set of rarefied assumptions.

Although the principal members of the Chicago School had similar leanings toward key elements of economic theory and policy, their personal approaches differed greatly and these differences affected the development and dissemination of their ideas, and hence the development of the Chicago School. The Chicago tradition of Viner, Knight, Simons, and Director was a crucial element in the Virginia School constructed by Buchanan, Nutter, Tullock, Vining and Coase.

Later, during the 1950s and early 1960s, the Chicago School became widely known for the work of Milton Friedman[3] in monetary economics and George J. Stigler[4] in industrial organization and regulation. Although Buchanan and Nutter, as students at Chicago, knew these men, they were not influenced by them.

Jacob Viner

Viner was a systematizer who held fewer of the ideas associated with the Chicago School than did Knight. However, he may be credited with the emphasis of the Chicago School on microeconomics and his view of the economy as a complex system which could be modeled. He was both economic theorist and historian of economic thought, and he possessed a strong empirical orientation. Viner worked primarily on problems in international trade and related issues in monetary theory. He not only had an analytical mind that held many original ideas but he combined this with an expansive understanding of the humanities and social sciences (Spiegel 1998, p. 813).

Although Viner did consulting and other work for the federal government, he was foremost an academic. His book *The Customs Union Issue* (1950) carefully distinguishing between trade creation and trade diversion, had a lasting influence on the policy debate in international trade. He jointly edited the *Journal of Political Economy* from 1929 to 1946 with Knight, although they were known to differ on many issues. Viner and Knight shared an interest in the development of economic thought, were both devotees of neoclassical price theory, and resisted the theoretical innovations of the 1930s, including the theories of E.H. Chamberlin (1933) and Joan Robinson (1933) on imperfect competition and J.M. Keynes's *General Theory* (1936). Further they opposed the interventionist aspects of the New Deal and the full employment policies of the latter part of the New Deal.

Viner's emphasis on rigorous analysis is likely to have influenced Buchanan and other students. According to Buchanan, Viner was 'the classically erudite scholar whose self-appointed task in life seemed to be that of destroying confidence in students', and 'he along with others were not the persons who encouraged students to believe that they too might eventually have ideas worthy of merit' (Breit and Spencer 1995, p. 174).[5] Viner's overbearing personal style explained his lack of acolytes (Buchanan 1992, p. 75) and his students never constituted a club but were dispersed in time and intellectual interest with little in common except their contact with Viner (Reder 1982).[6] However, despite his teaching style, Viner established successful research programs, enlisted graduate students as participants in his work, and supervised far more doctoral dissertations than Knight.

Having said that, Viner's influence on the Chicago School was not as great as that of Knight or Simons, perhaps owing to their personal charisma and ability to convert students to their way of thinking. According to Coase (1998, p. 603), although Director took courses from Paul H. Douglas, Knight, Theodore Yntema and Henry Schultz, the course which changed his way of looking at the world was one from Viner on Marshallian economics. Buchanan's and Knight's other students wrote well, networked widely, and became effective advocates of the ideas they held. In that they displayed rigorous analysis, Buchanan's methodological views were, ironically, more similar to Viner's than to Knight's.

In a 1970 letter to Patinkin, Viner elaborated on his peculiar niche in the Chicago School. While Viner's views on *laissez-faire* and government intervention were consistent with the views held by members of the Chicago School, 'on the whole he was a more pragmatic thinker and more aware of the need for qualification and consideration of circumstances of time and place'. For example, unlike Friedman and others at Chicago, Viner supported discretionary monetary management rather than a monetary rule (Spiegel 1998, p. 814).

Like Knight, Viner urged deficit spending during the Great Depression, and he went so far as to call the plea for an annual balanced budget a 'mouldy fallacy' (ibid. p. 814). He was critical of Hayek's libertarianism (Viner 1961, p. 232). However, in common with Knight, Viner denied that perfect competition was both a norm and normal. He further argued that monopoly was so prevalent in modern Western economies that competition seemed to him 'academic in the only pejorative sense of that adjective' (Viner 1960, p. 66). Like Knight and Simons, Viner was skeptical about received doctrine.

Frank Hyneman Knight (1885–1972)

Knight's work focused on the conceptual underpinnings of neoclassical price theory, and his main concerns were to clarify and improve its logical structure. Buchanan described Knight's qualities of mind as his willingness to question anything and anybody on any subject at any time. He categorically refused to accept anything as sacred and had a genuine openness to all ideas. Although Knight was sympathetic to the aspirations of those seeking to quantify economics, he was outspoken about his skepticism of their prospects for success. Buchanan describes Knight as having a basic conviction that most ideas peddled are nonsense or worse when examined critically (Buchanan 1992, p. 5). According to Buchanan, Knight recognized that the model of perfect competition is an idealization of reality, not a description. Buchanan argued that 'lesser theorists who followed Knight overlooked this essential point and erroneously expected real world institutions to match up descriptively with the idealized model' (Buchanan 1968, p. 424). It was their overly simplistic comparisons of theory and observed reality that are responsible for allowing the critics of a competitive economic order to undermine effectively much of its general social support, especially when comparisons failed to consider the flaws of alternative arrangements (Buchanan 1968).

According to Stigler and Buchanan (Breit and Spencer 1995, pp. 97 and 169), Knight's teaching style made him difficult to follow and his refusal to accept anything uncritically made him the source of endless ideas for student discussion and research. Buchanan further described him as a teacher who

> gave us who bothered to listen the abiding notion that all is up for intellectual grabs, that much of what paraded as truth was highly questionable, and that the hallmark of a scholar was his or her courage in cutting through the intellectual haze. The willingness to deny all gods, the courage to hold nothing as sacrosanct – these were the qualities of mind and character that best describe Frank Knight.
>
> Knight was an inveterate puzzler; but his thought process probed depths that the scholars about him could not realize even existed. To Knight, things were never so simple as they seemed, and he remained, at base, tolerant in the extreme because he sensed the elements of truth in all principles . . . Knight left us with the awful realization that if we did not have the simple courage to work out our own answers, we were vulnerable to victimization by false gods. (Buchanan 1992, p. 5)

Nutter, on the other hand, was said to have taken immediately to Knight's teaching style and found his ideas easy to absorb (Tullock 2001). Knight's views were highly idiosyncratic and his expository style made few concessions to listeners. Endless questions were spawned about what Knight really meant. Stigler described Knight as alternating between a great teacher and an absurd teacher, but communicating beyond any possible confusion the message that intellectual inquiry was a sacred calling, excruciatingly difficult for even the best of scholars to pursue with complete fidelity to truth and evidence (Breit and Spencer 1995, p. 96). The debates among students occasioned by Knight's lectures became a very important part of the Chicago tradition.

Knight viewed the aim of economic theory as to provide guidance on practical matters of economic policy. He believed that the basic principles of economics were derived from human motivation and were straightforward and obvious to most observers. Emphasizing that these simple principles were the most useful tools for understanding the real world, Knight sought to analyze the incentives generated by various institutional arrangements. In building his model, he distinguished between risk and uncertainty. He contrasted risk as a possible event, to which an objective probability calculus can be applied and which can be insured against, with uncertainty that described those possible events to which no such calculus can be applied. Profit (and loss) arose as the result of uncertainty, which was central to his theory of economic organization. Knight's monograph *The Economic Organization* (1933) was prepared in the mid-1920s while Knight was at the University of Iowa and was later duplicated for student use at Chicago (see the reading guide for *The Economic Organization*, ch. 4, this volume). It contains the elements of theory that helped to establish for Chicago its pre-eminence in neoclassical economics. While, according to Buchanan, there was little in the monograph that was wholly original, its value was in its emphasis on key points, its clarification of ambiguous concepts and notions, and its integrated approach to the economy as a social organization. According to Buchanan, several generations of undergraduate students at Chicago obtained their vision of the totality of the economic process only after encountering Knight (and Simons).

The Economic Organization did not circulate widely beyond Chicago, which explains why Knight's theoretical contributions became known primarily from his first work, *Risk, Uncertainty, and Profit* (1921), the book of his doctoral thesis, and from a series of important papers in the 1920s. Milton Friedman, Homer Jones, George Stigler, and Allen Wallis published a selection of these papers as *The Ethics of Competition* (Knight 1935). Their objective was to make available to students of the social sciences some of Knight's essays (primarily on social control and its implications) which they believed were particularly relevant to the social problems of the day. They noted that 'had the selection been made by the author, not only might the contents have been different, but some revisions might have been made' (ibid., p. 7).

The importance of Knight's influence was notable at the London School of Economics, where, largely at the urging of Lionel Robbins, *Risk, Uncertainty, and Profit* became required reading for an economics degree in addition to P.H. Wicksteed's *The Common Sense of Political Economy* (1910). These two books were thus important works for Coase and others. Coase notes that Knight was one of the most important influences in shaping his views (Kitch 1983). Coase got to know Knight personally during Knight's time at the Thomas Jefferson Center at the University of Virginia. He reflected that, although elderly and formally retired, Knight was still professionally involved and that one could still detect in him the 'fiery competitor' he once was (Demsetz 1999, p. 264).

Knight's contributions to economic theory went beyond his work in price theory. In *Risk, Uncertainty, and Profit,* he laid out his now familiar double dichotomy which distinguished between statics and dynamics and between the individual and the social economy. He described in detail his conception of an economic system, an approach that has become received doctrine in introductory textbooks. Knight's wheel of wealth emphasizes the circular flow of income in the economy as money is exchanged for factor services and final goods at successive stages in the production process. His emphasis on equalization of returns at the margin implicitly made his model an equilibrium one. And

Knight's approach contrasts with Carl Menger's emphasis on the demand for final goods determining the prices of factors of production. Knight stressed instead the importance of opportunity cost, a characteristic feature of both Chicago economics and the Virginia School of Political Economy.

Henry Calvert Simons (1899–1946)

While Knight questioned received doctrine and Viner emphasized rigorous theory, student attention tended to center around Simons, first when he was exclusively a member of the Economics Department and later when he had a joint appointment to teach economics in the Law School. Before moving to the Law School, Simons taught mainly undergraduates, including Gordon Tullock who was a candidate for the LLB. Tullock, who grew up in the Midwest as Republican and conservative found Simons to be of a different stripe in rejecting the gold standard, balanced budget, and protective tariffs. Simons's manner was cordial towards not only faculty but also students. W. Allen Wallis described Simons as a friendly man with brown hair, brown eyes, and warm manners, who demonstrated consideration toward others (apparently not always a hallmark of the academy). Simons lived at the Quad Club, where he had a fine Victrola and many good records. The Club had a rule about noise after 10 pm, but, at the request of many of the residents, had waived it for Simons's phonograph (Wallis 1992). Simons's copy of the Brandenberg concertos was very popular among the students. He became known for his *Positive Program for Laissez Faire* (1934), which was originally published as a pamphlet. Director's prefatory note to Simons's (1948) posthumous book *Economic Policy for a Free Society* provides an insight into Simons's influence on the Chicago School:

> Through his writings and more especially through his teaching at the University of Chicago, he was slowly establishing himself as the head of a 'school'. Just as Lord Keynes provided a respectable foundation for the adherents of collectivism, so Simons was providing a respectable foundation for the older faith of freedom and equality. (Director, in preface to Simons 1948, p. v)

One might argue that Simons versus Keynes is not an apposite contrast. Keynes considered himself in some respects to be a liberal in the older sense of that word. On the other hand, many of Simons's positions would not be considered those of a classical liberal. Although Simons, like other classical liberals, defended the market process (and this was not common in the 1930s), he made two departures. First, he insisted on government intervention to eliminate monopoly, and not just to remove the government-sponsored monopoly, by tackling its root causes. Second, he sought steeply progressive income taxes to reduce income inequality, not only to promote equality of opportunity but also because he found inequality to be 'unlovely'. Simons's use of the words 'positive' and 'laissez faire' set him apart from both non-interventionist conservatives and the interventionist liberals. Many would argue that Simons's use of the term 'laissez faire' was a misnomer. But his use reflects his view that there should be a division of responsibility between the government and the market. In Simons's model, the market would determine what gets produced, how it is produced, and for whom it is produced. On the other hand, the role of the government in his model was to maintain overall stability, to keep the market competitive, and to avoid extremes in the distribution of income (Simons 1948). He viewed an activist government as inevitable, but greatly feared it.

Simons was an avowed radical. He did not propose new policies as an overlay on the existing set of (ineffective) monetary rules, but insisted on a complete overhaul of the entire financial system. With regard to monopoly, Simons's aim was not to regulate it, as advocated by others, but to eliminate it. In his mind, the elimination of monopoly power would lead to greater price flexibility which in turn would lessen the impact of economic cycles. However, he recognized that these actions alone were not sufficient to guarantee stability.

Free markets and some equalization of income were the essential components of Simons's 'positive program for laissez faire'. He did not see the two as inconsistent.[7] Simons believed that taxes should be simple and direct and believed that tax policy should ensure that the true cost of government be levied equitably on the citizens. The primary virtue in his mind was liberty, which he defined as a condition which could be obtained only by preventing concentrations of economic power by removing the sources of monopoly. By 1934, Simons believed that the absence of widespread interference (which for Simons would permit the proliferation of monopoly power) and promiscuous political interference (which for Simons would strengthen such power) threatened 'disintegration and collapse' of the economic organization (ibid., p. vi). He saw that only the 'wisest measures by the state' could restore and maintain a free-market system. The Virginia School, on the other hand, sees the government as primarily responsible for the existence of monopolies and that removing its support would eliminate the problem. One may also compare Simons and Buchanan with regard to inheritance taxation. Buchanan (following Knight) has argued that the game would be more fair and exciting if inheritance were largely taxed away. Simons believed in steeply progressive income taxes but for the most part did not favor inheritance taxes.

Simons admired Knight, having served with him on the faculty at the University of Iowa prior to their simultaneous moves to Chicago in 1927. Their interests complemented each other well; Knight focused on theoretical issues while Simons concerned himself with policy. Their social philosophy stressed that the preservation of individual freedom was a goal far more important than the achievement of mere economic objectives. As a result of their reluctance to favor government over private actions in a market economy, each was branded a 'conservative'. For Simons the appellation of 'radical conservative' was awarded. As we have seen, Knight's work focused on the conceptual underpinnings of neoclassical price theory, and his main concerns were to clarify and improve its logical structure. No doubt their reluctance to support the New Deal stemmed in large part from their Midwestern mistrust of bureaucratic power. Simons was Knight's ally, but with a very independent mind.

Simons believed (to the extent of being a passion) that the world of the 1930s was facing a crisis of historic magnitude and that the survival of both freedom and prosperity in the West were at stake. Simons believed passionately that the crisis of the 1930s had to be handled well or the basic values of civilization would be lost, and he dedicated his life to that task. Knight, on the other hand, believed that the crisis was grave, and that it would be handled as badly as in the past, but that the West would survive.

Like members of the Virginia School, neither Simons nor Knight saw benefits from centralization in the hands of a few, whether it was government or any other group. This perspective became an important influence in shaping the framework of the Chicago School. Both Simons and Knight had their own following among the students, but their personal and teaching styles differed greatly. Simons had an outgoing personality and was held in high esteem by undergraduates. Although Simons was effective in stimulating intellectual inquiry, Buchanan does not consider him on a par with other teachers at Chicago. Knight, the dominant intellectual influence on the graduate students, was the person that graduate students talked about the most. Among the Chicago graduate students he had many admirers, including Friedman, Stigler, Wallis, and Buchanan.

Buchanan studied under Knight and Viner, but his exposure to Simons came from reading his work. Nutter took courses from Viner, Knight and Simons prior to being drafted in the Second World War. Resuming his studies after the war, Nutter began his dissertation under Simons. Tullock knew Henry Simons as a lecturer in the one economics class that he took before he was drafted into the US Army in 1941. Thus, Tullock experienced only the first six weeks of Simons's ten-week course (Brady 1999).

Aaron Director (1901–2004)

Aaron Director, whose impact is more difficult to discern because he did not publish, had a less outgoing personality and was not as popular with the students as Knight. The roots of law and economics may be traced to Director's work in the 1940s. With the help of Knight, he had been appointed after the death of Simons to the Law School where he taught the economic analysis of antitrust with Edward Levi. Director's contributions were mostly behind the scenes as colleague, teacher, and editor of the *Journal of Law & Economics* for the 1958–70 period.[8]

Director's views regarding industrial organization, for example, predatory pricing, tying arrangements, and resale price maintenance, became known through the writing of others at the University of Chicago. Simons indicates that Director had 'greatly influenced everything I have written and all my teaching', and Coase describes Director as a crusader (Coase 1998, p. 601). However, he probably best fits the category of puzzler since he raised contradictions and dilemmas. He was also a skeptic. According to Coase,

> Director was able to influence so many able people in such a profound way because of his command of economic theory, his wide reading and those personal qualities that Robbins described, all reinforced by his lucidity and persistence in argument. It is impossible to discover in what ways the views of all these people were changed. (Ibid., p. 604)

In 1958, Director and Coase founded the *Journal of Law & Economics*. Although Coase may have met Director when he first visited Chicago in 1930, we know that they met in 1937 when Director visited London to undertake work relating to his dissertation. The Bank of England was unwilling to allow Director access to their records and he spent much time at the London School of Economics. Coase introduced him to Lionel Robbins and Arnold Plant. Coase brought his distinctive approach to the Chicago School rather than the reverse when he arrived there in 1963 (Breit and Spencer 1995). Coase and Director were also instrumental in founding the *Journal of Legal Studies* in 1972 as an interdisciplinary journal of theoretical and empirical research.

Viner and Simons and economic policy

When he spoke before the Henry Simons Society, Allen Wallis (1992) noted that few of the faculty at Chicago were interested in formal participation in the economic policy debates of the day. While Viner served as a high-level advisor to US and foreign governments, and sought immediate impact on specific policy questions, Simons was an academic with little interest in direct participation in government and had little concern about what would happen even in the next decade. According to Director,

> He had a high standard of excellence, higher for his own work than for that of others. He was continuously in search of arrangements which would inhibit publication while fostering discussion. He had no illusions about the great obstacles to the re-creation of a free-market society, but he held that it was 'immoral' to accept as inevitable what is itself immoral. It was his contention that in a democracy the professional economists must hope that serious discussion will gradually and ultimately enlighten public policy and in the meanwhile will perpetuate the faith in discussion. (Simons 1948, p. vii)

In his 1934 pamphlet, Simons articulated his concern that the government might move toward collectivism in response to public opinion in the 1930s. His concerns had a major impact on the development of the Chicago School and, indirectly, the Virginia School. Unlike some of the more widely known faculty at Chicago, Simons's focus was on the long-term effects of government actions on freedom and equality. James Buchanan and members of the Virginia School are thus more similar to Simons in how they view public policy.

The intellectual environment at Chicago

The intellectual atmosphere at Chicago played an important role in the evolution of the Chicago School, its methodology, and the questions on which its members chose to focus. According to Allen Wallis (1992), the intellectual atmosphere at Chicago was much different from other graduate schools, then and today: 'The graduate students were treated as if they were colleagues and the faculty would act as if they thought they were going to get a good idea from you'. Wallis described many of the students of the 1930s (including himself and Friedman) as arriving at Chicago with an attitude about economic policy that he characterized as 'Norman Thomas socialist'.[9] Most of the graduate students read *The Nation* and *The New Republic*, which provided the ideological basis for the New Deal. They were soon disabused of the ideas in these publications through discussions with both students and faculty (Buchanan 1992, p. 22).

The post-war generation of students at Chicago also experienced a Chicago conversion. When Buchanan enrolled for the winter quarter of 1946, his knowledge of the University of Chicago was almost exclusively from his undergraduate teacher C.C. Sims, who had earned a doctorate in political science at Chicago in the late 1930s. Buchanan credits Sims as impressing upon him the importance of ideas and how the genuine life of the mind was present at the University of Chicago. Once there, Buchanan experienced an excitement that was 'unmatched anywhere else in the world'. Within a few short weeks, Buchanan had undergone a conversion in his understanding of markets and his views on socialism (Breit and Spencer 1995, p. 168).

Buchanan, and others entering graduate school in the immediate post-war years, were socialists of one sort or another. Some of the students, including Buchanan, considered themselves to be 'libertarian socialists' in that they placed a high value on individual liberty but, lacking an understanding of the principle of market coordination, were nevertheless socialists. Buchanan more precisely described them as 'libertarians first, socialists second' and viewed them as naive in their thinking about political alternatives. In

Buchanan's eyes they had an idealized view of populist democracy which was preferable to what they saw as the establishment-controlled economy (ibid., p. 170).

Buchanan's conversion from socialism came from understanding the role of markets in coordinating the activities of individuals and distinguishing this from the traditional view of markets as a means for distributing income. According to Buchanan, simply understanding the difference between 'allocation maximization' and 'catallactic coordination' liberated him.

From Knight, Buchanan got his grounding in the importance of the organizational structure of markets. It was this emphasis that elevated the coordination principle to center stage. By drawing attention toward a decision-making structure as a process, rather than the outcomes it generates, this approach allowed many of the notions of orthodox economic theory to fall away. In Buchanan's words:

> [T]o the allocationist the market is efficient if it works. His test of the market becomes the comparison with the abstract ideal defined in his logic. To the catallactic the market coordinates the separate activities of self-seeking persons without the necessity of detailed political direction. The test of the market is the comparison with its institutional alternative, politicized decision making. (Quoted in Breit and Spencer 1995, pp. 169–70)

Further to the point on the importance of this difference in perspective, Buchanan stated:

> Many modern economists remain firm supporters of the market order while at the same time remaining within the maximizing paradigm. I submit here, however, that there are relatively few economists whose vision is dominated by the catallactic perspective on market order who are predominantly critics of such an order. Once the relevant comparison becomes that between the workings of the market, however imperfect this may seem, and the workings of its political alternative, there must indeed be very strong offsetting sources of evaluation present. (Quoted in Breit and Spencer 1995, p. 170)

Buchanan argued that it was an understanding of this principle that enabled the young student socialists at Chicago to retain their long-held anti-establishment evaluative norms on politics and governance by recognizing that economic interaction need not embody the exercise of man's power over his fellows. Buchanan argued that, by their libertarian standards, politics appeared always to involve exploitation. Knight emphasized that markets, in contrast, need not involve exploitation.

Buchanan quickly appreciated the difference between these apparently similar, but in fact competing, paradigms. This realization had a major effect on his normative evaluation of institutions and, in particular, his advocacy of the market order (Breit and Spencer 1995, p. 171). Buchanan believed that his conversion stemmed from studying economics from Knight who led him to understand the importance of changing the rules of the game in order to change outcomes. The importance of Knight's insight became apparent to Buchanan when he examined rules that sought agreement by more than the simple majority which was viewed as the keystone of democratic institutions.

Buchanan's dissertation in public finance

Knight was an important intellectual and personal influence on Buchanan both during graduate school and later over the course of his career. A second major influence was

Knut Wicksell.[10] Buchanan's work in public finance was influenced by Knight and by his discovery of Wicksell's *Finanztheoretische Untersuchungen nebst Darstellung und Kritik des Steurewesens Schwedens* (Studies in the theory of public finance) (1896) which he came across by accident. Wicksell attempted to marry the principle of the sovereignty of the consumer with choices which are made through the political system when market failures require government provision. The use of this approach led him to advocate reform of the franchise, to delineate restrictions which should be placed on the power of the executive arm of the government and to devise parliamentary procedures regarding taxes and expenditure which reflected voters' choices. He sought methods for accurate reflection of voter preferences and speculated on the consequences of his proposed institutional changes for the future of public expenditure.

Buchanan's dissertation title was 'Fiscal equity in a federal state' (1948) which became the basis for his later work in that subject. Roy Blough[11] was his first reader because he was the principal figure in public finance at Chicago at that time. However, it was the second reader, Knight, whom Buchanan credits with having read his dissertation critically and having understood it. Public finance was not a major research interest at Chicago at that time and Buchanan was to pursue his research elsewhere.

The importance of Earl Hamilton in Buchanan's career

Earl J. Hamilton,[12] who studied Spanish monetary policy, impressed upon Buchanan the value of learning foreign languages, and his ability to read literature in foreign languages was clearly important to his intellectual development. We have just mentioned how Buchanan discovered Wicksell in German. Moreover, without a knowledge of Italian (gained during his Fulbright fellowship in Italy in 1955), the important insights of the Italian school of public finance would not have come to his attention. Buchanan also reads French.

Further, Buchanan credits Hamilton with recommending him to R. Tipton Snavely, chair of the Economics Department at the University of Virginia, and thus setting in motion a sequence of events that ultimately brought together Buchanan, Nutter and Tullock. Although Buchanan does not know if Hamilton was instrumental in Nutter's move from Yale to the University of Virginia in 1956, it would be plausible, given the Chicago connection (Buchanan 1999). In reading Hamilton's papers I learned that in 1967–68, Nutter sought to recruit him to the University of Virginia. There were several letters noting the beauty of Mrs. Hamilton's garden when they had been at Duke University and how Charlottesville had good soil and a pleasant climate. The time was not right for the Virginia department and the negotiations ended amicably although with great disappointment (and some personal embarrassment) for Nutter.

Building on the insights of Knight, Wicksell, and later the Italians, Buchanan laid the foundations for public choice and constitutional political economy, twin pillars of the Virginia School. The next phase was initiated with the arrival of Buchanan and Nutter at the University of Virginia in the fall of 1956.

The founding of the Thomas Jefferson Center

As Buchanan explains in his memoirs, the Virginia School of Political Economy originated from a conversation with Nutter in the foyer of the Social Sciences Building at the University of Chicago early in 1948 (Buchanan 1992, p. 95). Nearly ten years later, in

1957 in the University of Virginia's Rouse Hall, the Thomas Jefferson Center for Studies in Political Economy and Social Philosophy was established by Buchanan and Nutter, who were later joined by Tullock. Another key figure, however, had arrived at Virginia 11 years before Buchanan: D. Rutledge Vining.

Daniel Rutledge Vining (1908–99)

Vining was also a graduate of the Economics Department of the University of Chicago. Like Buchanan, he was much influenced by Frank H. Knight (see Vining 1950). And, like Buchanan, he taught at the University of Virginia, although he remained there until he retired. He was born in Birmingham, Alabama on August 12, 1908 and died in Charlottesville, Virginia on December 4, 1999. He arrived at Virginia in 1945 and remained on the faculty for more than 50 years, taking emeritus status in 1979. Vining is the least known of the Chicago-trained economists at the University of Virginia. Although Vining's research interests were in business cycles, spatial economics, and statistics, Buchanan credits him with emphasizing the importance of rules and institutions, a cornerstone of the Virginia School. He shared with Buchanan a southern upbringing, an interest in farming, and a PhD from the University of Chicago.[13]

Vining's doctoral thesis, 'An inquiry into the regional variation of short-run business fluctuations', does not identify his chair or committee, something not uncommon for University of Chicago dissertations. He wrote in the preface:

> Credit for any good that the study may contain must be attributed to the patient encouragement of Professors Oscar Lange, Jacob Marschak, and Lloyd Mints. Also, these acknowledgments must not fail to register the appreciation that the author profoundly feels for the background afforded by his association with Professor Frank Knight, although this influence was not direct and immediate. (Vining 1944)

His career at the University of Virginia began in 1945 and included service as director of the McIntire School of Business Administration at the University (1952–54). He remained at UVA until becoming emeritus professor in 1979. Vining was known as an independent mind who had limited association with other faculty members. He published in professional journals, contributed to books, and was author of several books and monographs, including *On Appraising the Performance of an Economic System* (Vining 1984), which took over twenty years to write (Personal communication with D.R. Vining, Jr., email, December 5, 2001).

Vining's and Knight's contributions to the Virginia School

On several occasions, Buchanan credits Vining with emphasizing the importance of rules and institutions in understanding alternative social regimes. For example, in their discussion on the 'Economic theory of constitutions' in *The Calculus of Consent*, Buchanan and Tullock (1962, pp. 79–80) express their debt to Vining for comparing the formation of a constitution to agreeing on the rules of a game, and for his emphasis on the essential differences between such rules and the appropriate individual strategies in playing a specific game. In this setting no player can anticipate which rules might benefit him during a particular play of the game, and it follows that the self-interest of each player will lead them to support rules that make the game rewarding for the average or representative player.

They further argue that agreement over initial rules minimizes the intense conflicts of interest that are expected to arise as the game is played.

In the appendix, 'Theoretical forerunners', Tullock further argues that the science of economics is rooted in the game analogy, and that early economists had discovered that the attempts of individual 'players' to adjust to the strategies chosen by other 'players' lead to a determinate result. Tullock noted that if a large number of people were engaged in buying and selling something and each attempted to adjust his strategy to the strategy (guessed or observed) of the others, then this would lead to an 'equilibrium' or 'saddle point', to use the term coined by game theorists. Tullock cites Vining as the source of this point (ibid., p. 339).

During the first half of 1958, Knight served as the center's first Inaugural Distinguished Visiting Scholar. He delivered six public lectures which were taped, transcribed, revised by the author, and edited for publication as *Intelligence and Democratic Action* (Knight 1960). In their introduction to the volume of Knight's lectures, Buchanan and Nutter (ibid., pp. v–vi) wrote that this book was not the one which Knight would have written in due course, but they wanted a publication to introduce Knight to the large group of scholars who have benefitted from the many contributions he has made during his long and distinguished scholarly career. To those others who might have been encountering Knight for the first time, the volume would serve as ample introduction.

Each lecture of Knight's series laid out the themes his work imparted to the Virginia School. 'The quest for rational norms' encouraged people to be aware of their natural romanticism and hence skeptical of quick diagnoses and remedies. Knight stressed the limitations of the knowledge existent in our society. 'The free society: historical background' argued that we can act intelligently only in so far as we can distinguish between what is inevitable and what is more or less subject to human control. Knight focused on the difficulty of learning history and of learning from history, reminding us that 'history as a whole is against the possibility of a free society; it looks like a strange accident under a very peculiar concourse of circumstances that would not be likely to last very long' (ibid., p. 38). 'The economic order: structure' focuses on the liberal market order and the role of entrepreneurship and competition. 'The economic order: general problems' returned to the themes of some of his earliest work (especially the first couple of chapters of Knight 1935), focusing on two problems which he defines as arising either because the system does not work in accordance with the theoretical description or because it does. He divided those problems into mechanistic problems (arising out of shortcomings of the system, such as monopolies and cyclical oscillations) and social philosophical issues like the morality of free enterprise. In 'The ethics of liberalism', Knight focused on what social ideals define progress and identified the direction of desirable change. He emphasized that there is no clear line between social necessity and the socially ideal. Finally, in 'Can the mind solve the problems raised by its liberation?', Knight concluded with a discussion of what goes on in society and measures for its improvement. He considered the question in two aspects, the problems raised and our capacity for dealing with them. As in his lectures at Chicago when Buchanan and Nutter were students, Knight raised more questions than he answered, thus setting the stage for fruitful discussion among faculty and students. No doubt Buchanan and Nutter believed that the presence of a senior figure from Chicago would enhance the stature of their enterprise at the University of Virginia.

Concluding comments

This chapter has discussed the Chicago influences on the development of the Virginia School. It examines the major figures at Chicago and what Buchanan and Vining brought to the Thomas Jefferson Center. In particular, it emphasizes the little-known contribution of Vining with regard to the crucial importance of rules and institutions in explaining how economic performance varies between economies. The key elements of the Virginia School owe much to the philosophical questions raised by Knight. The emphasis on analytical rigor came from Viner. Simons, like Knight, emphasized the need for evaluation of the fundamentals of a question without regard for the position or stature of its advocates. From this it was straightforward to question the fundamentals of democratic institutions with which the Virginia School of Political Economy would be associated in the years to come.

Notes

* The author wishes to thank Mark Brady for editorial guidance and research assistance, and James Buchanan and Gordon Tullock for permission to use material from the interviews he conducted with them. He also thanks James M. Buchanan, Royall Brandis, Ross Emmett, David Meiselman, and Gordon Tullock for comments on early drafts.

1. A more remote connection to the Chicago School is the New Institutional School associated with Douglass C. North of Washington University at St. Louis, who employs the insights of Armen Alchian and Harold Demsetz on property rights. North was a student of Frank H. Knight's brother Melvin M. Knight, who was an economic historian at Berkeley.
2. While Simons advocated steeply progressive income taxation, the Chicago School is associated with a proportional income tax or 'flat tax'. See Blum and Kalven (1952), Hayek (1960), and Friedman (1962).
3. Milton Friedman (b. 1912) was born in New York City and was educated at Rutgers (BA 1932), the University of Chicago (MA 1933), and Columbia University (PhD 1946). He was the recipient of the Nobel Prize in Economic Science in 1976.
4. George Joseph Stigler (1911–91) was born in Seattle, Washington and was educated at the University of Washington (BBA 1931), Northwestern University (MBA 1932), and the University of Chicago (PhD 1938). He was the recipient of the Nobel Prize in Economic Science in 1982.
5. Harry Johnson shared a similar opinion of Viner, but noted with admiration that J.M. Keynes tried (sometimes almost heroically), to find something of value in the views of graduate students (Skidelsky 2001). Keynes's (and Johnson's) desire to nurture independent thinking and development contrasts with Viner.
6. Apparently Viner's rigid approach was manifest in other ways. Coase (1998, p. 601) noted that students were seated alphabetically and this seating arrangement resulted in Rose Director (sister of Aaron) getting better acquainted with Milton Friedman whom she later married.
7. See Walter J. Blum and Harry Kalven's (1952, p. 505) discussion of Simons's views in which they note that 'whether the argument for redistributing income is put in terms of increasing general welfare or of redressing the injustice of the existing rewards, it is always precariously close to being rested simply on envy'.
8. Director's published work included one book, two jointly authored books, and six articles in economics and law journals.
9. Martin Bronfenbrenner (1997) expressed a similar view. When he arrived at Chicago, he considered himself a socialist, having read Marx and with the intention to vote for Norman Thomas in 1932 (had he been old enough). He thought the issue was not 'control versus the market' but simply 'control by whom?'. He viewed the faculty as 'quite balanced' including a conservative and later anti-Keynesian group (Knight, Simons, Lloyd Mints, and Viner) and a New Deal group (Paul H. Douglas, Henry Schultz, Harry Millis, Simeon Leland and John Nef).
10. John Gustav Knut Wicksell (1851–1926), journalist, pamphleteer and economist, was born in Stockholm, the youngest of six children. He studied at the University of Uppsala (BS cum laude 1871) and undertook graduate work over many years but did not receive an advanced degree. Having lived for many years on fellowships and stipends, in 1901 he was appointed associate professor at Lund where he remained until his retirement in 1916.

    The ideas in Wicksell's *Finanztheoretische Untersuchungen nebst Darstellung und Kritik des Steuerewesens Schwedens* (1896) had a lasting effect on Buchanan's views on public finance. Buchanan translated the first part of Wicksell's book (Wicksell 1896 [1958]), and that remains the only part available in English. The untranslated sections provide a historical sketch of the development of Sweden's system of taxation from the early sixteenth century up to the 1890s.

11. Jacob Roy Blough (1902–2000) was born in Pittsburgh, PA, received his undergraduate degree from Manchester College and received a master's degree and a doctorate from the University of Wisconsin. From 1938 to 1946, he was director of tax research at the US Treasury Department and assistant to the treasury secretary. From 1950 to 1952, he was a member of the President's Council of Economic Advisers. Later in the 1950s, he was principal director of the Economic Affairs Department at the United Nations. He also taught at several universities, including the University of Chicago from 1946 to 1952, and Columbia University from 1955 to 1970 when he retired.
12. Earl Jefferson Hamilton (1899–1989) was educated at the Mississippi State University (BS with honors, 1920), the University of Texas (MA 1924), and Harvard University (AM, 1925, PhD 1929). Hamilton helped to pioneer the field of quantitative economic history during a career that spanned 50 years. His publications include a classic series of books analyzing how American treasure affected price and wage structure in colonial Spain, a history of the Bank of Spain, and some three dozen articles or contributed chapters in the fields of economics and history. Hamilton held professorships in economics at Duke University (1927–44), Northwestern University (1944–47), and the University of Chicago (1947–67), and was Distinguished Professor of Economic History at the State University of New York, Binghamton (1966–69) after his retirement. He served as editor of the *Journal of Political Economy* and was President of the Economic History Association from 1951 to 1952 (Emmett 1999). His work on the indices of prices, wages, and money from primary sources was central to the development of the modern quantity theory.
13. Vining received a BBA (University of Texas, 1931), an MA (University of Chicago, 1935), and a PhD (University of Chicago, 1944). From 1935 to 1938 he was an instructor of economics and statistics at Westminster College in Fulton, Missouri. Subsequently, Vining was assistant professor of economics and statistics (1938–40) and associate professor (1941–43) at the University of Arkansas, before moving to Charlottesville. During his career he held various appointments including statistician at the Federal Reserve Bank in Atlanta (1941) and research assistant at the National Bureau of Economic Research (1948–49). He held visiting appointments at several universities including Columbia University (summer 1949), the University of California at Berkeley (summer 1956), and the University of Minnesota at Minneapolis (summer 1956). He was also a Ford Foundation Faculty Research Fellow at UVA (1956–57) and a Southern Regional Science Association Fellow, Atlanta (1987).

References

Blum, W.J. and H. Kalven, Jr. (1952), 'The uneasy case for progressive taxation', *University of Chicago Law Review*, **19** (3), 417–520.

Brady, G.L. (1999), 'Gordon Tullock: his development as an unconventional economist, 1947–1962', in *Public Choice Essays in Honor of a Maverick Scholar: Gordon Tullock*, Fishback, P.V., G.D. Libecap and E. Zajac (eds), Boston, MA: Kluwer Academic Publishers, pp. 151–67.

Breit, W. and R.W. Spencer (1995), *Lives of the Laureates: Thirteen Nobel Economists*, Cambridge, MA: MIT Press.

Bronfenbrenner, M. (1997), 'A conversation with Martin Bronfenbrenner', *Eastern Economic Journal*, **13** (1), 1–6.

Buchanan, J.M. (1948), 'Fiscal equity in a federal state', PhD dissertation, Economics, University of Chicago.

Buchanan, J.M. (1968), 'Frank H. Knight', in *The International Encyclopedia of the Social Sciences*, 3, Sills, D. (ed.), New York: Macmillan, pp. 424–8.

Buchanan, J.M. (1992), *Better than Plowing and Other Personal Essays*, Chicago, IL: University of Chicago Press.

Buchanan, J.M. (1999), Interview with Gordon L. Brady, Potsdam, Germany, October.

Buchanan, J.M. and G. Tullock (1962), *The Calculus of Consent: Logical Foundations of Constitutional Democracy*, Ann Arbor, MI: University of Michigan Press.

Chamberlin, E.H. (1933), *The Theory of Monopolistic Competition*, Cambridge, MA: Harvard University Press.

Coase, R.H. (1998), 'Aaron Director', in *The New Palgrave Dictionary of Economics and the Law*, Newman, P. (ed.), New York: Macmillan, pp. 601–5.

Congleton, R.D. (2002), 'Buchanan and the Virginia School', in *Method and Morals in Constitutional Economics: Essays in Honor of James M. Buchanan*, Brennan, H.G., H. Kliemt and R.D. Tollison (eds), Berlin: Springer, pp. 23–38.

Demsetz, H. (1999), 'Ronald H. Coase', in *The New Palgrave Dictionary of Law and Economics*, Newman, P. (ed.), New York: Palgrave Macmillan, pp. 262–70.

Emmett, R.B. (1999), 'Earl J. Hamilton', *American National Biography*, vol. 9, New York: Oxford University Press, pp. 917–18.
Friedman, M. (1953), 'The methodology of positive economics', in *Essays in Positive Economics*, Chicago, IL: University of Chicago Press, pp. 3–43.
Friedman, M. (1962), *Capitalism and Freedom*, Chicago, IL: University of Chicago Press.
Hayek, F.A. (1960), *The Constitution of Liberty*, Chicago, IL: University of Chicago Press.
Keynes, J.M. (1936), *The General Theory of Employment, Interest and Money*, New York: Harcourt, Brace.
Kitch, E.W. (1983), 'The fire of truth: a remembrance of law and economics at Chicago, 1932–1970', *Journal of Law & Economics*, **26** (1), 163–234.
Knight, F.H. (1921), *Risk, Uncertainty and Profit*, Boston, MA: Houghton Mifflin.
Knight, F.H. (1933), *The Economic Organization*, Chicago, IL: University of Chicago.
Knight, F.H. (1935), *The Ethics of Competition and Other Essays*, New York: Harper & Bros.
Knight, F.H. (1960), *Intelligence and Democratic Action*, Cambridge, MA: Harvard University Press.
Mueller, D.C. (1986), 'Rational egoism versus adaptive egoism as fundamental postulate for a descriptive theory of human behavior', *Public Choice*, **51** (1), 3–23.
Reder, M.W. (1982), 'Chicago economics: permanence and change', *Journal of Economic Literature*, **20** (1), 1–38.
Robinson, J. (1933), *The Economics of Imperfect Competition*, London: Macmillan.
Simons, H.C. (1934), *A Positive Program for Laissez Faire: Some Proposals for a Liberal Economic Policy*, Chicago, IL: University of Chicago Press.
Simons, H.C. (1948), *Economic Policy for a Free Society*, Chicago, IL: University of Chicago Press.
Skidelsky, R. (2001), *John Maynard Keynes*, vol. 3: *Fighting for Britain, 1937–1946*, New York: Penguin.
Spiegel, H.W. (1998), 'Jacob Viner', in Newman, P. (ed.), *The New Palgrave Dictionary of Economics and the Law*, New York: Palgrave Macmillan, pp. 812–14.
Tullock, G. (2001), Interview with Gordon L. Brady, Fairfax, VA, April.
Viner, J. (1950), *The Customs Union Issue*, New York: Carnegie Endowment for International Peace.
Viner, J. (1960), 'The intellectual history of laissez faire', *Journal of Law & Economics*, **3**, 45–69.
Viner, J. (1961), 'Hayek on freedom and coercion', review of *The Constitution of Liberty*, *Southern Economic Journal*, **27** (3), 230–36.
Vining, D.R. (1944), 'An inquiry into the regional variation of short-run business fluctuations', PhD dissertation, Economics, University of Chicago.
Vining, D.R. (1950), 'Methodological issues in quantitative economics: variations upon a theme by F.H. Knight', *American Economic Review*, **40** (3), 267–84.
Vining, D.R. (1984), *On Appraising the Performance of an Economic System*, Cambridge: Cambridge University Press.
Wallis, W.A. (1992), Paper presented at the Henry Simons Society, Washington, DC.
Wicksell, K. (1896), *Finanztheoretische Untersuchungen nebst Darstellung und Kritik des Steuerewesens Schwedens*, Jena: G. Fischer.
Wicksell, K. (1896 [1958]), 'A new principle of just taxation', in *Classics in the Theory of Public Finance*, Buchanan, J.M. (trans.), Musgrave, R.A. and A.T. Peacock (eds), London: Macmillan, pp. 72–118.
Wicksteed, P.H. (1910), *The Common Sense of Political Economy*, London: Macmillan.

PART II

SOME CHICAGO ECONOMISTS

16 Gary S. Becker

Pedro Nuno Teixeira

Despite becoming one of the most influential economists of the second half of the twentieth century, Gary Becker (1930–) was not immediately destined to study economics. In his first year in Princeton he accidentally took a course in economics, which attracted him by the combination of mathematical rigor and matters of social organization. He started to lose interest in economics when approaching the end of his studies, because it dealt less than he expected with relevant social problems; he even considered a change to sociology. Eventually, he decided to pursue graduate studies in economics at Chicago, which proved to be a turning point in his career (Becker 1993). Milton Friedman and the price theory course, Gregg Lewis and the analysis of labor markets using standard economic theory, and T.W. Schultz and the notion of human capital were three clear Chicago influences on Becker's developing research interests. All three increased his confidence in using economics to deal with relevant social issues.

After finishing his PhD in 1955, Becker started his academic career at Chicago. However, despite enjoying the academic environment there, the will to test new academic environments, and the attraction of working at the National Bureau of Economic Research (NBER), made him decide to move to New York in 1957. There he worked at Columbia University, where throughout the 1960s he developed one of his most important personal and academic partnerships, with Jacob Mincer through the Labor Workshop. Becker's activity at the NBER was also significant, because he increased the importance of social issues on the Bureau's research agenda.

Disappointed with student unrest, at the end of the 1960s he returned to Chicago, where he has remained since. During this second phase at Chicago he became very close to George Stigler. As a result of his enduring interest in the application of standard economics to social issues and of his influence beyond economics' boundaries, he was also appointed to the Sociology Department in 1983. Despite some heavy skepticism both inside and outside the discipline, his persistence was compensated with increasing attention and honors, such as the John Bates Clark Medal (American Economic Association, 1967), the Presidency of the American Economic Association (1987) and the Nobel Memorial Prize in Economics (1992). His recognition among the wider public as one of the most eminent, if controversial, contemporary economists was confirmed and enhanced by his regular contributions to *Business Week* from 1985 to 2004 (Becker and Nashat Becker 1997).

The fact that the application of economic theory to social issues was unusual in the mid-1950s did not discourage him from pursuing these themes at an early stage in his career.[1] His first major contribution came with his doctoral dissertation on discrimination in the marketplace (Becker 1955), a work that clearly indicates the mentoring of certain major figures in the Chicago Economics Department; in particular, Lewis, his supervisor, and Friedman, who nurtured Becker's confidence in addressing various social issues with standard economics. In his work Becker analyzed discrimination by using a neoclassical framework and produced quantified indications of its importance, measured by what he called the 'discrimination coefficient'. This attempt was regarded with skepticism, especially because his framework identified discrimination as a rational behavior. Not shying away from controversy, he pursued the attempt to show the explanatory power of economics in the social realm with an analysis of fertility (Becker 1960). With the growth of knowledge about contraception, Becker argued that the scope of family decision making had been enlarged; also, other environmental factors increased in importance. As a result, in his analysis children were regarded as consumption and durable goods, allowing him to use the theory of the demand for consumer durables in examining the social consequences of family decision making. Despite the controversial nature of these applications, which translated into either hostility or indifference from many economists and other social scientists, Becker got some support from the reviews of his *Economics of Discrimination* (Becker 1957), and especially from his colleagues at Chicago.

The major result of this early period came from his research on human capital. In the late 1950s, when Becker started working at the NBER, he decided to analyze the monetary rates of return to different levels of education, especially college education. Encouraged by T.W. Schultz, and by the discussions with Mincer and others at the Columbia Labor Workshop, Becker began to enlarge the scope of the project both theoretically and empirically. On the one hand, he began to develop a general theory of human capital investment, not merely focused on assessing the profitability of those investments. On the other hand, he enlarged the empirical analysis to cover a much wider set of different groups and time periods. The result of this research was the monograph *Human Capital* (Becker 1964), which provided an explanatory framework for the shape of age–earning profiles, the concentration of human capital investment at earlier ages, and the personal distribution of income, on the basis of the process of accumulation of human capital.[2] Becker expected to receive heavy criticism not only for the use of the label 'human capital', but also because he applied price theory to the explanation of educational decisions. He considered using another title due to the potential controversy, though he eventually decided to take his characteristic approach; that is, stick to his views and face the critics.

A further controversial application of economics to a social issue from this early period of research came in his work on the economics of crime (Becker 1968). Here he addressed the existence of legislation, the need of enforcement and the existence of a variety of penalties designed to both punish and prevent offences. Since the problem of crime is also a problem of the allocation of resources, Becker considered the usefulness of an economic analysis that focused on the measurement of the social loss from crime.

However, the more he developed these applications, the less satisfied he was with the consumption framework he had to use. Hence, in the following period of research he focused his energies in reformulating consumer theory, by adjusting it to the behavior of households (Becker 1965) and by giving attention to the increasing importance of non-working time. Building on the contributions of Mincer and the Labor Workshop at Columbia (Teixeira 2007), he proposed to adjust the traditional framework of choice between work and leisure, to the allocation of time and goods within the household, giving particular importance to the substitution effect between time and goods. The model was then extended to a framework of decisions over time and to investment in human capital. In this 'new' theory, all goods were inputs in the productive process of the non-market sector (Becker and Michael 1973). Accordingly, the household aimed to minimize costs and maximize utility, thus responding to variations in price and productivity of factors, to variations of relative shadow prices of commodities and to variations in full real income. Becker's analysis gave greater emphasis to income and price effects and less to the role of changing tastes. He urged the reformulation of the traditional theory of choice in order to produce testable hypotheses and to avoid too much reliance on appeals to variations among tastes and ad hoc reasoning (Stigler and Becker 1977).

Assisted by the reformulation of consumer theory, Becker moved increasingly into the analysis of individual behavior in a socially interactive context, giving rise to what can be considered a third phase of his research. As he recognized, one of the obvious applications of this social interactive framework was family behavior. For example, marriage could be regarded as a choice to which the economist could apply the standard tools of price theory. By assuming that mating behavior was mostly competitive, he analyzed a marriage market with competition for partners among men/women of different attributes. He explored the implications of this competitive mating in terms of demographic dynamics, labor force participation (especially of women), inequality in income, ability and other characteristics, and for the allocation of time in the household (Becker 1973, 1974a, 1974b).[3] Complementary to the analysis of marriage was the analysis of its instability or even collapse, by divorce (Becker et al. 1977). Becker maintained that bargaining within marriages took place in the shadow of competition in marriage markets, though competition was less effective when marriage contracts were not legally binding or when they allowed for only a fraction of possible contingencies.

Another important stream of the development of his economic approach to the family came with the analysis of fertility patterns. This stream started with his paper with H. Gregg Lewis (Becker and Lewis 1973) analyzing the interaction between quantity and quality in the demand of children. Attention to this interaction led Becker to play down his prior belief that contraceptive methods played a major role in fertility patterns; it also endogenized fertility choices because the interaction between quantity and quality sets the choices in terms of economic preferences.[4]

His work on the economics of the family was brought to a first synthesis in his *Treatise on the Family* (Becker 1981), in which he attempted a comprehensive presentation of the economic approach to family behavior. In Becker's work the family is portrayed as a highly interdependent organization, in which the head of the family transferred income to the other members, thus providing a sort of insurance for family members. These transfers tend to offset prior redistribution of income propelled by external forces, thus explaining the partial failure of public programs. The head of the family's behavior makes the other members act 'as if' they were altruistic, because they will then maximize their own income and the family income (this has an impact on intergenerational mobility as well), leading to the famous 'rotten kid theorem'.[5] He also insisted that the family mechanisms of transmission of wealth were based on utility maximization in behavior and in rational choices, something that again went against the usual perceptions about family behavior among social scientists and lay audiences alike. Families had become less close-knit and performed fewer functions in the modern economy – a result of the family's declining economic importance for individual behavior. The evolution of the modern family, then, paralleled the evolution of modern markets and government, which now provided commodities such as the education of youngsters and protection against illness or unemployment (previously functions of family networks), thus reducing the value of relying on families for any of these activities.

Becker's insistence on the stability of tastes and preferences has led him in more recent work to propose an economic explanation for habits and customs that emphasized the role of specific consumer knowledge and skills. Accordingly, Becker (1996) argued that individuals' decisions have little to do with basic needs, and are rather affected by two main types of capital – personal and social. The former included aspects such as past consumption and other personal experiences affecting consumption, and the latter included past actions by peers and attempts to capture elements of recognition, prestige and respect as influential forces of individual consumption. Although Becker assumed forward-looking behavior, he considered an expanded utility function that linked past and present utilities, though its formulation remained temporally stable.[6] Moreover, the consideration of changes in personal and social capital explained the apparent consistency of preferences. Accordingly, one's social relations are not given; the individual can influence them.

The thread that unites Becker's work is 'the economic approach to human behavior' (1976b), which he called a method of analysis rather than an assumption about human motivations. The economic approach is an attempt to explain various facets of human behavior through a set of simplified assumptions, regarding human behavior as a result of individual choices characterized by utility maximization, forward-looking stance, consistent rationality and stable and persistent preferences. The choices are constrained by income, time, imperfect memory and calculating capabilities, and the opportunities available. Although he often mentions that non-economic forces also play a role in terms of human behavior, Becker argues that rational choice theory provides a unifying approach to the analysis of multiple social issues, and not only market behavior. Moreover, the scope of non-economic factors seems to become increasingly diminished, since in his recent work rationality has been broadened to cover aspects such as habits, culture and social interactions. He sometimes suggests that people are not consciously rational but behave 'as if' they were, in a pattern consistent with an approach that models human behavior as rational.[7]

More than anyone else, Becker has come to epitomize the contemporary attempts to apply economic theory to new topics or areas of human behavior that are not normally analyzed with neoclassical price theory. Becker's economic approach came at a heavy price in terms of the initial acceptance of his work within and beyond economics. The problems faced by Becker's work are the result of a double challenge. On the one hand, Becker faces resistance from those who accept the neoclassical framework but consider him to be applying it to the wrong issues. On the other hand, he also faces criticism from those who find neoclassical economics to be a poor representation of human nature. Throughout most of his career, Becker has managed to infuriate and unite neoclassical economists, heterodox thinkers and many social scientists in criticisms to his work. The fact that the economic approach to human behavior has prospered and endured is a tribute to his persistence and creativity.

Notes

1. As a graduate student in the early 1950s, Becker submitted a paper to the *Journal of Political Economy* on what is now called the economics of politics. A very critical referee report by Frank Knight disappointed

Becker and delayed its publication a few years (Becker 1958). His interest in terms of an economic analysis of political structures and processes would be pursued several years later (Becker 1983).

2. A few years later, in his Woytinsky Lecture (Becker 1967), he developed a model of wealth maximization in order to explain the distribution of human capital investments, notably their concentration at earlier ages. This pattern was mainly due to a decline in benefits over time (due to a reduction in the number of years remaining), and a rise in investment costs (due to increasing forgone earnings).
3. One of the most controversial aspects of Becker's analysis has been his view that there were advantages to the division of labor between a couple that are not necessarily due to exploitation, but rather to sector-specific human capital. Becker maintains that small differences due to discrimination, biological or other forces, can create sizeable differences in wife/husband roles.
4. This reformulation was also linked with his analysis of altruism (Becker 1976a) and its role within the family, which he considered to be an important condition for the understanding of low fertility of Western countries since the 1950s (Becker and Barro 1988). The reformulation on fertility also led him to explore its implications for economic growth (Becker and Barro 1989).
5. A significant part of his work on altruism was in its role within the family, for example, exploring the determinants of unequal opportunity and its impact on intergenerational mobility (Becker and Tomes 1979).
6. The interdependence of past and present choices is closely related to Becker's work on rational addiction (Becker and Murphy 1988, Becker et al. 1991).
7. Although Becker has done increasingly less empirical work, he regards the economic approach's capacity to make predictions and its good performance in terms of empirical testing as one of its major strengths. Once again he pays tribute to his mentor, Milton Friedman.

References

Becker, G.S. (1955), 'Discrimination in the market place', PhD dissertation, Economics, University of Chicago, Chicago, IL.

Becker, G.S. (1957), *The Economics of Discrimination*, Chicago, IL: University of Chicago Press.

Becker, G.S. (1958), 'Competition and democracy', *Journal of Law & Economics*, **1**, 105–9.

Becker, G.S. (1960), 'An economic analysis of fertility', in *Demographic and Economic Change in Developed Countries*, Princeton, NJ: Princeton University Press, pp. 209–31.

Becker, G.S. (1964), *Human Capital: A Theoretical and Empirical Analysis, with Special Reference to Education*, New York: Columbia University Press.

Becker, G.S. (1965), 'A theory of the allocation of time', *Economic Journal*, **75** (299), 493–515.

Becker, G.S. (1967), *Human Capital and the Personal Distribution of Income: An Analytical Approach*, Ann Arbor, MI: University of Michigan, Institute of Public Administration.

Becker, G.S. (1968), 'Crime and punishment: an economic approach', *Journal of Political Economy*, **76** (2), 169–217.

Becker, G.S. (1973), 'A theory of marriage: part 1', *Journal of Political Economy*, **81** (4), 813–46.

Becker, G.S. (1974a), 'A theory of marriage: part 2', *Journal of Political Economy*, **82** (2, part 2: Marriage, family human capital, and fertility), S11–S26.

Becker, G.S. (1974b), 'A theory of social interactions', *Journal of Political Economy*, **82** (6), 1063–93.

Becker, G.S. (1976a), 'Altruism, egoism, and genetic fitness: economics and sociobiology', *Journal of Economic Literature*, **14** (3), 817–26.

Becker, G.S. (1976b), *The Economic Approach to Human Behavior*, Chicago, IL: University of Chicago Press.

Becker, G.S. (1981), *A Treatise on the Family*, Cambridge, MA: Harvard University Press.

Becker, G.S. (1983), 'A theory of competition among pressure groups for political influence', *Quarterly Journal of Economics*, **98** (3), 371–400.

Becker, G.S. (1993), 'Autobiography', in *Les Prix Nobel: The Nobel Prizes 1992*, Frängsmyr, T. (ed.), Stockholm: Nobel Foundation.

Becker, G.S. (1996), *Accounting for Tastes*, Cambridge, MA: Harvard University Press.

Becker, G.S. and R.J. Barro (1988), 'A reformulation of the economic theory of fertility', *Quarterly Journal of Economics*, **103** (1), 1–25.

Becker, G.S. and R.J. Barro (1989), 'Fertility choice in a model of economic growth', *Econometrica*, **57** (2), 481–501.

Becker, G.S., M. Grossman and K.M. Murphy (1991), 'Rational addiction and the effect of price on consumption', *American Economic Review*, **81** (2), 237–41.

Becker, G.S., E.M. Landes and R.T. Michael (1977), 'An economic analysis of marital instability', *Journal of Political Economy*, **85** (6), 1153–89.

Becker, G.S. and H.G. Lewis (1973), 'On the interaction between the quantity and quality of children', *Journal of Political Economy*, **82** (2, part 2), S279–88.

Becker, G.S. and R.T. Michael (1973), 'On the new theory of consumer behavior', *Swedish Journal of Economics*, **75** (4), 378–95.
Becker, G.S. and K.M. Murphy (1988), 'A theory of rational addiction', *Journal of Political Economy*, **96** (4), 675–700.
Becker, G.S. and G. Nashat Becker (1997), *The Economics of Life: From Baseball to Affirmative Action to Immigration, How Real-world Issues Affect Our Everyday Life*, New York: McGraw-Hill.
Becker, G.S. and N. Tomes (1979), 'An equilibrium theory of the distribution of income and intergenerational mobility', *Journal of Political Economy*, **87** (6), 1153–89.
Stigler, G.J. and G.S. Becker (1977), 'De gustibus non est disputandum', *American Economic Review*, **67** (2), 76–90.
Teixeira, P.N. (2007), *Jacob Mincer: A Founding Father of Modern Labour Economics*, Oxford: Oxford University Press.

17 Ronald Harry Coase
Steven G. Medema

Introduction

Ronald Harry Coase was born on December 29, 1910 in the London suburb of Willesden. An only child, Coase was educated at the Kilburn Grammar School and the London School of Economics (LSE), from which he graduated with a degree in commerce in 1932. Interestingly, Coase did not take a single economics course while he was at LSE, and he later suggested that this was to his benefit, in that it gave him 'a freedom in thinking about economic problems which [he] might not otherwise have had' (Coase 1990, p. 3). Coase is very quick to credit Arnold Plant's role in his intellectual development, and says that Plant's 'main influence was in bringing me to see that there were many problems concerning business practices to which we had no satisfactory answer' (Coase 1982a, p. 34, see also Coase 1986). Through Plant, he says, the students came to view the economic system as an essentially competitive one and to see many of the business practices attributed to the forces of monopoly as natural results of a competitive system (Kitch 1983, p. 214). As one moves through the pages of Coase's career, one can see clearly the profound impression that these ideas, along with Plant's approach of looking at real-world problems, made upon Coase.

Upon completing his studies at LSE, Coase taught at the Dundee School of Economics and Commerce from 1932 to 1934, at the University of Liverpool, 1934–35 and at LSE, 1935–51. His time at LSE was interrupted by the Second World War, during which he served as a statistician at the Forestry Commission (1940–41) and in the Central Statistical Office, Offices of the War Cabinet (1941–46). Coase left LSE for the USA and the University of Buffalo in 1951, remaining there until 1958. After spending a year at the Center for Advanced Study in the Behavioral Sciences at Stanford, he accepted an appointment at the University of Virginia in 1959.

Although Coase is most closely associated with the Chicago School, his two most influential works – 'The nature of the firm' (1937a) and 'The problem of social cost' (1960) – were written before he arrived at Chicago in 1964, to teach at the Law School and to join Aaron Director in editing the *Journal of Law & Economics* (*JL&E*).[1] Coase retired from the University of Chicago in 1981, and from the editorship of the *JL&E* in 1982. In 1991, at the age of 80, Coase was awarded the Alfred Nobel Memorial Prize in Economic Sciences.

Scholarly work

While most economists identify Coase with his two classic articles on the firm and social costs, the corpus of his writing is very broad, ranging across topics such as accounting, advertising, public goods, consumer surplus, public utility pricing, monopoly theory, blackmail, the economic role of government and the history of economic thought. Several themes appear throughout Coase's work: the importance of economic institutions, in particular the firm, the market and the law and the need to carefully assess the merits of alternative institutional structures; the role played by transaction costs in economic activity; the need for economists to engage in detailed and systematic studies of the real-world economic system; and the importance of building economic theory and policy analysis on a real-world base (see Coase 1988a, 1992, Medema 1994).

The lion's share of Coase's work during the first part of his career dealt, in one way or another, with firm behavior and organization. Coase's association with fellow Plant student Ronald Fowler bore fruit in an extensive analysis of the formation of producers' expectations (for example, Coase and Fowler 1935), an investigation undertaken in the 1930s with thc pig cycle as the case study. It was believed by many at that time that producers expected current prices and costs to continue into the future and that the adjustments in supply that resulted gave rise to disequilibrium cycles. Coase and Fowler found that this conventional, cobweb theorem explanation for the pig cycle was incorrect, that producers did in fact adjust their expectations of prices and costs very quickly and that the prediction errors arose from the difficulty of predicting variations in demand and in foreign supply. This work was later cited by J.F. Muth (1961, p. 334) in one of his classic papers on rational expectations. Coase also collaborated with Fowler and Ronald Edwards on a series of pieces dealing with the interrelations between accounting and economics (Coase 1938 [1952], Coase et al. 1938). These writings, which were very much in the LSE cost tradition (Buchanan and Thirlby 1973), demonstrated that traditional accounting practices do not adequately capture the true (opportunity) nature of costs and also pointed to the problematic nature of designing workable accounting methods to do so.

Coase wrote a number of articles dealing with monopoly and imperfect competition, a few of which bear mention of here. 'Some notes on monopoly price' (1937b) is of a piece with themes developed in Coase's contemporaneous work on accounting. Here, Coase undertook to refine and further develop Joan Robinson's (1933) theory of monopoly by recognizing that the limited information, especially regarding marginal revenue, marginal cost and demand, under which producers engage in their decision making, will often preclude monopolists from equating marginal revenue and marginal cost, and thus from producing the profit-maximizing level of output. A later foray into monopoly theory, 'Durability and monopoly' (1972a), demonstrated that a monopoly firm which produces a good that is infinitely durable will be forced to sell the good at the competitive price, unless it can decrease the durability of the good or make contractual arrangements through which it promises to limit its production – a result which has come to be known as 'the Coase conjecture'.

Coase's best-known work on monopoly deals with public utility pricing and regulation. Abba Lerner and others had claimed that marginal cost pricing accompanied by a government subsidy is the efficient pricing policy for public utilities. Coase offered his objections to this approach in 'The marginal cost controversy' (1946, see also, Coase 1970), arguing that marginal cost pricing is inferior to a system of multi-part pricing and may in fact be inferior to *average* cost pricing. This paper, and three related papers that followed it, are illustrative of one of the central themes in Coase's work – that in assessing the efficiency of economic outcomes, one must focus broadly, rather than narrowly, on benefits, costs and incentives. Coase also engaged in a series of historical studies of public utilities. His work on British broadcasting analyzes the development of wireless and wire radio broadcasting, as well as of television broadcasting and the rise of the BBC as the monopoly supplier of all of the above (Coase 1950, 1954). Articles on the British Post Office discuss the rise of the penny postage in Great Britain under Rowland Hill and the attempts by the Post Office to enforce its monopoly against incursions by private entrepreneurs, including the messenger companies (for example, 1955).

Without question, however, Coase's most influential work is contained in two papers – 'The nature of the firm' (1937a) and 'The problem of social cost' (1960) – the two works cited by the Royal Swedish Academy in awarding Coase the Nobel Prize. In the former, Coase set out to explain why firms exist and what determines the extent of a firm's activities. He found the answer in a concept to which most economists have until recently paid scant attention – transaction costs. Coase suggested that we tend to see firms emerge when the cost of internal organization is lower than the cost of transacting in the market, and that the limit of a firm's activities (or, the extent of internal organization) comes at the point where the cost of organizing another transaction internally exceeds the cost of transacting through the market. Although published in 1937, 'The nature of the firm' attracted little attention until the early 1970s (1972b), when these ideas served as a springboard for scholars such as Oliver Williamson (1975, 1985) Armen Alchian, Harold Demsetz and the legion of others who have built on or taken off from Coase's insights to further develop the theory of the firm and bring the importance of transaction costs and the contracting process to the fore in economic theory.

'The problem of social cost' took the transaction-cost paradigm in a different direction – the legal–economic arena and situations of conflicts over rights. Although this is one of the most-cited articles in all of the economics and legal literatures, it has also been widely misunderstood (Coase 1988a, Medema 1996). From this paper comes the now-famous Coase theorem,[2] which says that when transaction costs are zero and rights are fully specified, parties to a dispute will bargain to an efficient outcome, regardless of the initial assignment of rights. But Coase recognized that the transaction costs are pervasive and will generally preclude the working of this bargaining mechanism. Coase thus asserts that legal decision makers should assign rights in the way that maximizes the value of output in society – a concept that lies at the heart of the modern law and economics movement.

The crux of 'The problem of social cost', however, is Coase's attempt to dismantle the Pigovian tradition. The Coase theorem's purpose was to demonstrate that, under standard neoclassical assumptions, Pigovian remedies for externalities are unnecessary – costlessly functioning markets, like the costlessly functioning governments of Pigovian welfare theory, will generate efficient outcomes. The problem, as Coase pointed out, is that, neither markets nor government function costlessly. As such, neither will generate optimal solutions (in the traditional sense) and society thus faces a choice among a set of imperfect alternatives. Coase advocates a close examination of the benefits and costs of alternative policy options, in order to facilitate the adoption of policies (including possibly doing nothing at all) which maximize the value of output (Coase 1974a).

The foregoing reflects Coase's belief that government failure is at least as pervasive as market failure, and that economists are too quick to advocate tax, subsidy and regulatory solutions without a careful examination of the situation. His work on the US broadcasting system, and, especially, on the Federal Communications Commission (for example, 1959, 1966), as well as his article on the use of the lighthouse in public goods theory, namely the history of lighthouse provision in Great Britain (1974b), are classic examples of Coase's position here. When Coase looks at government, he sees agencies captured by special interests, making policies that usually make matters worse rather than better and operating in virtual ignorance of the virtues of the market. Yet, a careful reading of Coase suggests that he is not 'anti-government' but, rather, an advocate for economic theorizing and policy making which recognizes that policy choices are always between imperfect alternatives.

The foregoing is part of Coase's more general concern about the way that economists practice their trade (for example, 1975, 1982b). He is suspicious of consumer theory as a whole and of the way in which mathematical and quantitative techniques have been used in modern economics. Indeed, Coase's writings evidence some graphs and some technical intuitive analysis, but nary an equation, an approach which reflects Coase's lifelong distaste for using mathematics in his work. Reflecting the influence of Plant, he laments the failure of economists to engage in systematic analyses of the real-world economic system. Coase sees a profession wrapped up largely in what he calls 'blackboard economics', an economics where curves are shifted and equations are manipulated on the blackboard, with little attention to the correspondence (or lack thereof) between this work and the real-world economic system. This has manifested itself in economists' ignorance of transaction costs and economic institutions (especially the law), and in an approach to public policy that fails to examine in any kind of depth the consequences of alternative policy actions (1972a, 1988a).

Coase and Chicago

The relationship between Coase and the Chicago School could be considered a case study in the dangers of assuming some sort of Chicago homogeneity. That Coase 'fit' at Chicago – at least in the early years – is clear, both from his writings and from the impressions of his colleagues (see Kitch 1983). He acknowledges that he was 'greatly influenced' by the work of Frank Knight – 'although in what ways it is not easy to say' (Coase 1988b, p. 20), and especially by Knight's *Risk, Uncertainty and Profit* (1921), to which he was exposed during his time at LSE. He also admits that his experience at Chicago changed his views somewhat on a few things, such as advertising, antitrust and regulation, but he says that '[t]here were typical "Chicago" lessons that I didn't have to learn, and I got them through Plant' (Kitch 1983, p. 214). Chicago-style price theory, with its grounding in Alfred Marshall, was certainly consistent with Coase's way of thinking (1975), and while Coase would likely not be one to go all the way with, for example, the Friedmans' *Free to Choose* (1980), the limited government viewpoint so identified with the Chicago way of thinking is reasonably consistent with Coase's perception that the governmental cure is likely to be worse than the market disease.

On the other hand, we also see in Coase a degree of tension with certain aspects of the modern Chicago School. While the economic analysis of law and economics imperialism generally have loomed so large in the definition of Chicago economics over the past four decades, Coase has not attempted to hide his qualms about and lack of interest in these movements – flying in the face of the propensity to so closely identify Coase with this aspect of the Chicago tradition (for example, Coase 1977, 1993). Coase's interest is not the economic analysis of law, but rather the study of how the legal system impacts on the economic system – old-style Chicago law and economics of the sort being published in

JL&E in the 1950s, 1960s and 1970s. As such, his interest and intellectual commonalities lie much more with the new institutional economics (of which he is also regarded as a founding father) than with the modern economic analysis of law movement *à la* Posner (Posner 2007). In fact, he has been called in for criticism by Posner (1993) on this score, as well as for his methodological stance.

That Coase has a place among the venerated saints of the Chicago tradition goes without saying, but he has also remained his own man – dissenting from the received doctrine when it did not fit with his views. Coase did not transform economics; nor was he a pioneer of techniques. But, through his scholarship, he brought to the attention of economists certain fundamental issues previously neglected, and his efforts spawned several new lines of research.

Notes

1. Coase says that he would likely never have come to Chicago if it had not been for the existence of the *Journal of Law & Economics* (Kitch 1983, p. 192). Breit (1987, pp. 654–5), meanwhile, contends that the University of Virginia refused to make a serious effort to keep Coase from leaving for Chicago, apparently because of its dissatisfaction with the ideological make-up of the Economics Department.
2. The Coase theorem was actually coined and first named by George Stigler (1966, p. 113). See Medema (1999) and Medema and Zerbe (2000) for extensive analyses of the theorem.

References

Breit, W. (1987), 'Creating the "Virginia School": Charlottesville as an academic environment in the 1960s', *Economic Inquiry*, **25** (4), 645–57.

Buchanan, J.M. and G.F. Thirlby (1973), *L.S.E. Essays on Cost*, London: London School of Economics and Political Science.

Coase, R.H. (1937a), 'The nature of the firm', *Economica*, n.s. **4** (16), 386–405.

Coase, R.H. (1937b), 'Some notes on monopoly price', *Review of Economic Studies*, **5** (1), 17–31.

Coase, R.H. (1938 [1952]), 'Business organisation and the accountant', in *Studies in Costing*, Solomons, D. (ed.), London: Sweet & Maxwell, pp. 105–58.

Coase, R.H. (1946), 'The marginal cost controversy', *Economica*, n.s., **13** (51), 169–82.

Coase, R.H. (1950), *British Broadcasting: A Study in Monopoly*, London: Longmans, Green.

Coase, R.H. (1954), 'The development of the British television service', *Land Economics*, **30** (3), 207–22.

Coase, R.H. (1955), 'The postal monopoly in Great Britain: an historical survey', in *Economic Essays in Commemoration of the Dundee School of Economics, 1931–1955*, Eastham, J.K. (ed.), London: William Culcross & Sons, pp. 25–37.

Coase, R.H. (1959), 'The Federal Communications Commission', *Journal of Law & Economics*, **2**, 1–40.

Coase, R.H. (1960), 'The problem of social cost', *Journal of Law & Economics*, **3**, 1–44.

Coase, R.H. (1966), 'The economics of broadcasting and government policy', *American Economic Review*, **56** (2), 440–47.

Coase, R.H. (1970), 'The theory of public utility pricing and its application', *Bell Journal of Economics and Management Science*, **1** (1), 113–28.

Coase, R.H. (1972a), 'Durability and monopoly', *Journal of Law & Economics*, **15** (1), 143–9.

Coase, R.H. (1972b), 'Industrial organization: a proposal for research', in *Policy Issues and Research Opportunities in Industrial Organization*, Fuchs, V.R. (ed.), Cambridge, MA: National Bureau of Economic Research, pp. 59–73.

Coase, R.H. (1974a), 'Economists and public policy', in *Large Corporations in a Changing Society*, Weston, J.F. (ed.), New York: New York University Press, pp. 169–87.

Coase, R.H. (1974b), 'The lighthouse in economics', *Journal of Law & Economics*, **17** (2), 357–76.

Coase, R.H. (1975), 'Marshall on method', *Journal of Law & Economics*, **18** (1), 25–31.

Coase, R.H. (1977), 'Economics and contiguous disciplines', in *The Organization and Retrieval of Economic Knowledge*, Perlman, M. (ed.), Boulder, CO: Westview Press, pp. 481–91.

Coase, R.H. (1982a), 'Economics at LSE in the 1930's: a personal view', *Atlantic Economic Journal*, **10** (1), 31–4.

Coase, R.H. (1982b), *How Should Economists Choose? G. Warren Nutter Lecture in Political Economy*, Washington, DC: American Enterprise Institute for Public Policy Research.

Coase, R.H. (1986), 'Professor Sir Arnold Plant: his ideas and influence', in *The Unfinished Agenda: Essays on the Political Economy of Government Policy in Honour of Arthur Seldon*, Anderson, M.J. (ed.), London: Institute of Economic Affairs, pp. 81–90.
Coase, R.H. (1988a), *The Firm, the Market, and the Law*, Chicago, IL: University of Chicago Press.
Coase, R.H. (1988b), 'The nature of the firm: origin, meaning, influence', *Journal of Law, Economics, and Organization*, **4** (1), 3–17, 19–32, 33–47.
Coase, R.H. (1990), 'Accounting and the theory of the firm', *Journal of Accounting and Economics*, **12** (1–3), 3–13.
Coase, R.H. (1992), 'The institutional structure of production', *American Economic Review*, **82** (4), 713–19.
Coase, R.H. (1993), 'Law and economics at Chicago', *Journal of Law & Economics*, **36** (1, part 2), 239–54.
Coase, R.H., R.S. Edwards and R.F. Fowler (1938), *Published Balance Sheets as an Aid to Economic Investigation: Some Difficulties*, London: Accounting Research Association Publication no. 3.
Coase, R.H. and R.F. Fowler (1935), 'Bacon production and the pig-cycle in Great Britain', *Economica*, n.s., **2** (6), 142–67.
Friedman, M. and R. Director Friedman (1980), *Free to Choose: A Personal Statement*, New York: Harcourt Brace Jovanovich.
Kitch, E.W. (1983), 'The fire of truth: a remembrance of law and economics at Chicago, 1932–1970', *Journal of Law & Economics*, **26** (1), 163–234.
Knight, F.H. (1921), *Risk, Uncertainty and Profit*, Boston, MA: Houghton Mifflin.
Medema, S.G. (1994), *Ronald H. Coase*, London: Macmillan.
Medema, S.G. (1996), 'Of Pangloss, Pigouvians, and pragmatism: Ronald Coase on social cost analysis', *Journal of the History of Economic Thought*, **18** (1), 96–114.
Medema, S.G. (1999), 'Legal fiction: the place of the Coase theorem in law and economics', *Economics and Philosophy*, **15**, 209–33.
Medema, S.G. and R.O. Zerbe, Jr. (2000), 'The Coase theorem', in Bouckaert, B. and G. De Geest (eds), *The Encyclopedia of Law and Economics*, Cheltenham, UK and Northampton, MA, USA: Edward Elgar, pp. 836–92.
Muth, J.F. (1961), 'Rational expectations and the theory of price movements', *Econometrica*, **29** (6), 315–35.
Posner, R.A. (1993), 'Ronald Coase and methodology', *Journal of Economic Perspectives*, **7** (4), 195–210.
Posner, R.A. (2007), *Economic Analysis of Law*, 7th edn, New York: Wolters Kluwer.
Robinson, J. (1933), *The Economics of Imperfect Competition*, London: Macmillan.
Stigler, G.J. (1966), *The Theory of Price*, 3rd edn, New York: Macmillan.
Williamson, O.E. (1975), *Markets and Hierarchies: Analysis and Antitrust Implications*, New York: Free Press.
Williamson, O.E. (1985), *The Economic Institutions of Capitalism: Firms, Markets, Relational Contracting*, New York: Free Press.

18 Aaron Director

*Robert Van Horn**

Aaron Director (1901–2004) is often cited as a principal in establishing the post-war Chicago School (Samuelson 1998), the founder of a dominant school of jurisprudence, law and economics (Bork 2004), and key 'in reorienting antitrust policy along free-market lines' (Posner 2004). Through his extensive involvement in teaching and directing research at Chicago and Stanford, Director had a profound influence on later luminaries of the Chicago School such as Robert Bork, Lester Telser, Reuben Kessel, and Edward Levi. Although Director had a significant influence, he remains an opaque historical figure, partly because he seldom published. Only one biographical account currently exists (Coase 1998). What follows attempts to paint a fuller portrait of Director incorporating heretofore-unacknowledged archival sources (see Van Horn 2007 for a more extensive treatment).

Born in Charterisk, Ukraine (at that time a part of Russia), Harry A. Director was the son of a flour mill owner. He immigrated with his family in 1914 to Portland, Oregon, where his father worked as a laborer and then a retailer. In 1921, Director graduated from Lincoln High School in Portland and went to Yale on a scholarship. At Yale, Director, along with the painter Mark Rothko, helped produce the *Yale Saturday Evening Pest*, which wore a socialist cloak and a progressive cap. After a political survey at Yale revealed the presence of 225 Republicans, the *Pest* reported: 'We need not lose hope entirely. There were five Progressives and four Socialists' (quoted in Coase 1998, p. 601). After the *Pest* ceased publication in 1923, Director soon graduated and traversed the Midwest as a migrant laborer; he worked as a coal miner and a textile laborer. Then he taught at the Newark (NJ) Labor College. Thereafter he embarked on a cattle boat bound for England to study the education of adult workers. Finally he returned to Portland and taught at the Portland Labor College (run by the Oregon Federation of Labor).

In 1927, Director made his way to the University of Chicago to work with Paul Douglas, with whom he jointly authored *The Problem of Unemployment* (Douglas and Director 1931). A year prior to its publication, Director accepted a teaching position at Chicago. According to Paul Douglas, 'Beginning in 1932, Director increasingly fell under [Knight's] influence' (Douglas to Frank H. Knight, 5 January 1935, Jacob Viner Papers, Box 79, folder 'Chicago Dept. of Econ., Douglas & Knight'). After his conversion, Director gravitated towards Henry Simons, who became his 'best friend' and 'considerably influenced Director's views' (Coase 1998, p. 602). Subsequently, Director published a pamphlet, *The Economics of Technocracy*, which publicly demonstrates for the first time Director's affinity for price theory (1933).

In 1934, the Economics Department refused to renew Director's teaching contract:

> [I]n order to meet the views of the Administration that our teaching load was too light and should be stepped up, it was decided not to renew Director's appointment. There were also

> additional reasons for this, one of them being that in teaching Economics 240 (Labor Problems) he had come to the conclusion that there was nothing worth the while to talk about except monetary theory and policy and business cycles. (H.A. Millis to Viner, 31 January 1934, Viner Papers, Box 79, Folder 'Chicago University Department of Economics, Millis')

Consequently, Director went from the University of Chicago to the Treasury Department in Washington. In 1937, Director went to England to conduct research for a dissertation under Viner on the quantitative history of the Bank of England. However, because the Bank unexpectedly thwarted his efforts, Director stopped work on his thesis, which he never completed. While in England, he became more closely associated with Arnold Plant and Lionel Robbins, and befriended Friedrich Hayek who later would play a crucial role in bringing Director back to Chicago.

With the outbreak of the Second World War, Director returned to Washington where he worked at the American Youth Commission, joined the Brookings Institution where he assisted C.O. Hardy with *Wartime Control of Prices* (1940), and then worked at the War Department and the Alien Properties Bureau before ending his Washington stint at the Commerce Department. While in Washington, Director became one of Hayek's political allies in the United States, later persuading the University of Chicago Press to publish *The Road to Serfdom* (Hayek 1944) after numerous commercial publishers had turned it down. Not surprisingly, Director promptly wrote a laudatory book review for *The Road to Serfdom*: 'Professor Hayek is our most accomplished historian of the development of economic ideas' (Director 1945, p. 174).

Toward the end of the war in 1945, Hayek and Simons attempted to encourage Director to come to Chicago and undertake the leadership role of a project bankrolled by the Volker Fund – a Kansas City corporation heavily involved in right-wing funding in the post-war period. The project entailed writing an American *Road to Serfdom*. Harold Luhnow, the head of the Volker Fund, attempted to persuade Hayek to undertake this endeavor, but Hayek wished to organize an international project and felt disinclined toward burdening himself with the task of writing an American-centric manuscript. He convinced the Volker Fund to allow him to subcontract the project to Simons and Director. Immediately, Simons embraced the opportunity and subsequently drew up a memorandum. He stated that Director should head the project and direct research to advance the liberal doctrine. However, Director declined the opportunity in 1945.

When the war ended, Hayek and Simons again looked to Director to head the project. In the late spring of 1946, Director agreed to come to the Chicago Law School and head the Volker-funded Free Market Study project. The project had the prima facie objective to be 'a study of a suitable legal and institutional framework of an effective competitive system' (Coase 1998, p. 603). When the central administration of the Law School voted on the proposal of the Free Market Study, they refused to approve it because the proposal stipulated that after the five-year contractual term of the project ended, Director would receive permanent tenure. Within a week of the proposal's rejection by the central administration, Henry Simons committed suicide.

In the meantime, Wilber Katz, Dean of the Law School, and Robert Hutchins, President of the University of Chicago, had agreed on an emended proposal, which they submitted to Director. After the tragic news of his friend, Director turned to Hayek for advice. Hayek encouraged Director not to lose hope and to come to Chicago: '[After] your letter, I do want to say that in a sense it would seem to me even more important than before that you should accept. It seems to me the only chance that the tradition which Henry Simons created will be kept alive and continued in Chicago – and to me this seems tremendously important' (Hayek to Director, 10 July 1946, Hayek Papers, Box 58, Folder 'William Volker Fund 1939–1948'). After receiving Hayek's letter, Director enthusiastically agreed to head the project.

After arriving at Chicago in August of 1946, Director headed the Free Market Study, whose members included: Frank Knight, Theodore Schultz, Milton Friedman, Garfield Cox, Edward Levi and Wilber Katz. The project would investigate how to reformulate liberal doctrine, which in 1946 appeared in danger of extinction (Walpen 2005). Director conducted a meeting at least every two months, and with Volker money assigned investigations to Chicago graduate students like Warren Nutter (1951). Director also encouraged the undertaking of at least one Volker-funded project at UCLA conducted by J. Fred Weston – a Chicago Business School graduate – on *The Role of Mergers in the Growth of Large Firms* (Weston 1953).

During the Free Market Study Project, Director published a review on Charles Lindblom's *Unions and Capitalism*. He asserted that the market system through the 'corroding influence of competition', has the 'effective tendency' to 'destroy *all* types of monopoly'. Furthermore, Director maintained that, 'So far in the absence of governmental aid and encouragement the competitive tendencies have triumphed over the exclusive or restrictive tendencies' (Director 1950, pp. 165–6 passim; emphasis added). These claims of Director are especially striking when juxtaposed with his 1946 statement, which showed some relative ambivalence toward the power of competition: 'Of course we could start from the position that existing concentration has already reached a point which makes it objectionable from a political point of view, or again we may start from the position that the existing concentration results in the most efficient use of resources and does not eventuate in significant departures from competitive behavior' (Theodore W. Schultz Papers, November 1946, Memo, Box 39 (addenda), Folder 'Free Market Study'). His 1950 claim suggests that sufficient research has been carried out in the past three years to dispel his 1946 uncertainty – suggesting the importance of the Free Market Study for the development of Director's views.

In 1951, as the Free Market Study project wound down, Director participated in a Chicago Law School conference. Engaging Adolph Berle's view of the role of the modern corporation, he anticipated George Stigler's later argument against Berle and Gardiner Means's claims about the divergence between ownership and control: 'The discipline of a competitive capital market provides a more general and more effective instrument for preventing significant and continuous divergence of interest' (Director 1951, p. 23).

In 1953, Director headed the Volker-funded Antitrust Project, a project which Hayek also played a crucial role in facilitating (Van Horn 2007). The Volker Fund provided fellowships for Robert Bork, John McGee, Ward Bowman, William Letwin and others to come to Chicago and research antitrust issues. Under Director, the Antitrust Project produced a prodigious amount of antitrust scholarship on the issues of tying arrangements (Bowman 1957), predatory pricing (McGee 1958), resale price maintenance (Bowman 1952, Telser 1960), trade regulation (Director and Levi 1956) and the Sherman Act (Bork 1954). Generally, the project challenged the usefulness of efforts to control specific forms of conduct by which market power may make itself felt, and challenged the commonly held perception that antitrust law is firmly grounded in a common law heritage. Significantly, several of the articles attribute the central thesis or invaluable credit to Director.

Shortly before the Antitrust Project began, Director organized a conference funded by the Volker Fund concerning the regulation of military defense and mobilization. Director convened the conference because: 'at Chicago the advantages of the market as a method of organizing economic affairs are valued too highly to be laid aside during so-called emergency periods' (Director 1952, p. 158). The conference aim was to address the extent and nature of government controls, particularly with regard to the Korean War.

Two year later, in 1953, Director participated in the Law School's Conference on Freedom and the Law, Director (1964) sharply criticized those who would give priority to the free market of ideas over the free market economy. Favoring the former gave priority to political decision-making processes that undermined a market economy and, hence, freedom. Director argued that the free market economy should be given priority in order to maximize freedom.

Until he left the Chicago Law School in 1965, Director taught antitrust law and price theory in the Law School, engaged Law School faculty, and mentored graduate students of economics (Kitch 1983, Coase 1998). In 1965, Director moved to Los Altos, California, where he worked at the Hoover Institute and Stanford University, and from where he would retire from professional academic activity. Director died on September 11, 2004, at the age of 102.

Note

* All archival material quoted in the chapter is used with permission. The author gratefully acknowledges the permissions granted by T. Paul Schultz, the estate of F.A. Hayek, and the Princeton University Library.

References

Friedrich Hayek Papers, Hoover Institution Library and Archives, Stanford University.
Theodore W. Schultz Papers, Special Collections Research Center, University of Chicago Library.
Jacob Viner Papers, Mudd Manuscript Library, Princeton University.

Bork, R.H. (1954), 'Vertical integration and the Sherman Act: the legal history of an economic misconception', *University of Chicago Law Review*, **22** (1), 157–201.
Bork, R.H. (2004), 'Chicago's true godfather of law and economics', *Wall Street Journal* (May 3), A17.
Bowman, W.S., Jr (1952), 'Resale price maintenance – a monopoly problem', *Journal of Business*, **25** (3), 141–55.
Bowman, W.S., Jr (1957), 'Tying arrangements and the leverage problem', *Yale Law Journal*, **67** (1), 19–36.
Coase, R.H. (1998), 'Aaron Director', in *The New Palgrave Dictionary of Economics and the Law*, Newman, P. (ed.), New York: Macmillan, pp. 601–5.
Director, A. (1933), *The Economics of Technocracy*, Chicago, IL: University of Chicago Press.
Director, A. (1945), 'Review of *The Road to Serfdom*, by F.A. Hayek', *American Economic Review*, **35** (1), 173–5.
Director, A. (1950), 'Review of *Unions and Capitalism*, by Charles E. Lindblom', *University of Chicago Law Review*, **18** (1), 164–7.
Director, A. (1951), *The Modern Corporation and the Control of Property*, paper presented at University of Chicago Law School conference on corporation law and finance 17.
Director, A. (ed.) (1952), *Defense, Controls, and Inflation: A Conference Sponsored by the University of Chicago Law School*, Chicago, IL: University of Chicago Press.
Director, A. (1964), 'The parity of the economic market place', *Journal of Law & Economics*, **7**, 1–10.
Director, A. and E. Levi (1956), 'Trade regulation', *Northwestern University Law Review*, **51**, 281–96.
Douglas, P.H. and A. Director (1931), *The Problem of Unemployment*, New York: Macmillan.
Hardy, C.O. (1940), *Wartime Control of Prices*, Washington, DC: Brookings Institution.
Hayek, F.A. (1944), *The Road to Serfdom*, Chicago, IL: University of Chicago Press.

Kitch, E.W. (1983), 'The fire of truth: a remembrance of law and economics at Chicago, 1932–1970', *Journal of Law & Economics*, **26** (1), 163–234.
McGee, J.S. (1958), 'Predatory price cutting: the Standard Oil (N.J.) case', *Journal of Law & Economics*, **1**, 137–69.
Nutter, G.W. (1951), *The Extent of Enterprise Monopoly in the United States, 1899–1939*, Chicago, IL: University of Chicago Press.
Posner, R.A. (2004), 'Aaron Director dies at 102', *Washington Post* (September 13), B04.
Samuelson, P.A. (1998), 'How *Foundations* came to be', *Journal of Economic Literature*, **36** (3), 1375–86.
Telser, L.G. (1960), 'Why should manufacturers want fair trade?' *Journal of Law & Economics*, **3**, 86–105.
Van Horn, R. (2007), 'The origins of the Chicago School of law and economics', dissertation, Economics, Notre Dame University, South Bend, IN.
Walpen, B. (2005), 'The plan to end planning', paper presented at the How Neoliberalism Became a Transnational Movement, conference, International Center for Advanced Studies, New York University, April.
Weston, J.F. (1953), *The Role of Mergers in the Growth of Large Firms*, Berkeley, CA: University of California Press.

19 Paul H. Douglas

Glen G. Cain

Paul H. Douglas (1892–1976) was a member of the Economics Department at the University of Chicago from 1920 to 1948. He achieved fame in his profession for his enormous body of research in the field of labor economics. He pioneered in the application of statistical analysis to empirical research – an indispensable research method in modern economics and an area of strength in the university's Department of Economics that continues today. He will, however, be remembered mainly in the social and political history of the United States for his accomplishments in his 18 years from 1948 to1966 as the US Senator from Illinois.

The legislative record of Douglas in the Senate had for him more disappointments than successes, but, with the wisdom of hindsight, we can say that both his failed causes early in his Senate career and his later successes did him honor. He drew upon his scholarly background, his intellectual abilities and his basic humanitarianism to lead in passing laws that achieved civil rights for ethnic minorities, greater efficiency and equity in tax laws, environmental protection and safeguards for consumers by promoting price competition in markets and truth-in-lending laws in consumer finance. He personified and promoted political integrity, and he instructed the public at large about this aspect of governance with his book *Ethics in Government* (Douglas 1952).[1]

The economic research of Douglas, like that of virtually all applied economists of his generation, is no longer cited for its economic content. His name in economics, however, appears to be immortalized by a pervasive mathematical equation, namely the Cobb–Douglas production function, that he and Charles W. Cobb, a mathematician at Amherst College, used to express the relation between economic output (Y), and the assumed two inputs of production, labor (L) and capital (K). The Cobb–Douglas production function is $Y = AL^{\alpha}K^{\beta}$, where A, α and β are constants (Cobb and Douglas 1928). A modern econometrician, Murray Brown, called it

> the most ubiquitous form in economics, owing its popularity to the exceptional ease with which it can be manipulated and to the fact that it possesses the minimal properties that economists consider desirable. . . . It has been applied econometrically countless times, still surprising people that it can explain the data so well . . . (Brown 1987, p. 460)[2]

Douglas was born in Salem, Massachusetts on March 26, 1892, but he was raised and spent most of his childhood in 'a log cabin in the heart of the Maine woods' (Douglas 1971, p. 3) in hardship conditions, virtually an orphan, since his mother died of tuberculosis when he was four years old and his father was an unsuccessful traveling salesman. Douglas said, with regret, that his father was 'a prototype for the Willie Loman whom Arthur Miller commemorated in his *Death of a Salesman*' (ibid., p. 5). In growing up, he was effectively rescued by his stepmother. She divorced the mainly absent father and home-schooled Douglas and an elder brother during their elementary-school years. Both went on to attain college degrees. Douglas graduated from Bowdoin College in 1913 with scholastic honors and with the help of a scholarship entered the graduate program of economics at Columbia University (ibid., p. 27).

At Columbia Douglas became proficient in two major economic doctrines that influenced his academic career and were to become hallmarks of the Chicago School of Economics. One was Irving Fisher's monetary theory in macroeconomics. The second was neoclassical theory in microeconomics as taught by John Bates Clark. Fisher and Clark were his professors at Columbia. Neoclassical microeconomics was the basis for Douglas's subsequent research in the marginal productivity theory of labor and capital, testing the theory's validity by measuring the shares of national income and of industrial output earned by each of these two factors of production. Decades later, when Douglas served as the chairman of the US Senate Finance Committee in 1959, his sympathy with Fisher's monetary theory was a motive for inviting Milton Friedman, his former colleague at the University of Chicago, to testify on matters of macroeconomic policy.

This academic training, while certainly not strictly determinative of one's economic or political philosophy, has traditionally been associated with *laissez-faire*, or conservative, policies. Douglas, however, always had liberal leanings. Also, he was influenced at Columbia by Henry Seager, a prominent professor in the field of industrial relations and an advocate of labor unions and legislation to regulate wages, hours, and working conditions. Seager supervised Douglas's PhD dissertation, completed in 1921, on 'Apprenticeship and industrial education'. While at Columbia University, Douglas participated in street demonstrations to support workers' demands for labor reforms, and he worked briefly as a union organizer for the International Ladies Garment Workers Union. He was in New York at the time of the tragic fire at the Triangle Shirtwaist Company in 1914 that took the lives of some 200 workers, mostly young women – an iconic event in a period before workers' protective legislation and the rise of industrial unionism (Douglas 1971, pp. 28–34).

In 1915 Douglas married Dorothy Wolff, described by his biographer, Roger Biles, as 'a brilliant student from a prominent New York family [who] shared with him not only many scholarly interests but also a passion for progressive politics' (Biles 2002, p. 7). They had four children before their marriage ended in divorce in 1930. Douglas had brief academic employments at several colleges, beginning at the University of Illinois in 1915, before being hired at the University of Chicago in 1920. His wife earned a PhD in sociology and later joined the Sociology Department at Smith College, but she had not found employment in the Chicago area. At her urging, Douglas accepted a visiting position at Amherst College in 1927, where he teamed with Professor Cobb from the mathematics department in devising the Cobb–Douglas production function.

At the University of Chicago Douglas was prolific in his research and a popular teacher. His preeminence in labor economics was established by two major works. The first, *Real Wages in the United States, 1890–1926* (Douglas 1930), became a standard reference (with 326 tables and charts) for statistics of workers' wages and hours by industry and occupation, yearly cost-of-living measures, and supplemental measures of union membership and unemployment. The second, *The Theory of Wages* (Douglas 1934), was an ambitious attempt to analyze and measure the demand and supply functions of labor, based mainly on the neoclassical theory of marginal productivity but with sympathetic attention to criticisms of that theory.[3]

Soon after arriving in Chicago, Douglas began two additional parallel careers: first as a social reformer and then in politics. His existing dedication to various social reforms was further inspired by Jane Addams, a Chicagoan famous for her social work and peace activities. During the1920s Douglas's most famous venture in political reform was his decade-long contribution, eventually successful, to exposing the illegal monopoly and other corrupt practices of Samuel Insull, a utilities tycoon in Chicago. Closer to his profession as an economist were his efforts for consumer reforms involving advertising, labeling, and lending practices, and even closer to his expertise as a labor economist were his contributions to the wave of legislative programs at the state and federal levels for unemployment insurance and for what was to become social security. All the while he continued producing his large quantity of research in scholarly economics.

Douglas's entry into electoral politics began with his 1939 election for Alderman in the maverick Fifth Ward of Chicago, a ward long celebrated for its representation in the City Council by someone willing to oppose the dominant and corrupt political machine of the Mayor's office. Charles Merriam, a famous political scientist at the university, preceded Douglas in this office, and Leon Despres, a legendary lawyer from Hyde Park, held the office later. The ward included 10 neighborhoods of the university community but also 116 other neighborhoods, so Douglas's election showed he was able to appeal to a broad constituency (Biles 2002, p. 32).

He was aided in these political and reform activities by his second wife, Emily Taft, whom he married in 1931 and remained with until his death. Biles (ibid., p. 13) writes that she was 'the daughter of renowned sculptor Lorado Taft and an actress . . . a University of Chicago graduate and seasoned political activist'. She served as a US congresswoman from her Illinois district in 1944 to 1946, and authored three books: a historical novel (1948), a collection of biographical essays about 'great women who helped shape America' (1966) and a biography of Margaret Sanger (1970).

In 1942 Douglas attempted but failed to win the Democratic Party's nomination for the US Senate. With the United States at war, the 50-year old professor then made the astounding decision to volunteer for military service with the Marine Corps. More than just overcoming the barriers of his age and poor eyesight – the latter having kept him out of the First World War – he had to obtain a waiver of the Marine Corps' eligibility standards, as he had been a pacifist for years and was a Quaker (Society of Friends). He insisted upon combat duty, was wounded in action, and was awarded two Purple Heart medals and the Bronze Star. One combat injury permanently incapacitated the lower part of his left arm. When his military service ended in 1946, he had risen to the rank of lieutenant colonel (Biles 2002, pp. 39–42).

Douglas returned to his professorship at the University of Chicago, but his term there was brief. Of his colleagues he later wrote: 'the economic and political conservatives had acquired an almost complete dominance over my department', and 'I found myself increasingly out of tune with many of my faculty colleagues' (Douglas 1971, pp. 127–8). Also, academic economics had become increasingly theoretical in top departments like Chicago's, and this was not his strong suit. Even his econometric methods would have to be considered dated by the late 1940s.

It was no surprise that Douglas seized the opportunity to run for the Senate in 1948. But the political support this maverick Democrat received from the Chicago political machine, which was led by Jacob Arvey, and the fact that Douglas won the Senate election were surprising. The year 1948 was one of upset political victories. Of his 18-year

Senate career that followed, a seasoned commentator said: 'He won many of his struggles; others, he lost. Yet what is astonishing is how many of the so-called "lost causes" of yesterday have become in a few years the commonplaces of today' (Richard L. Strout, quoted in Biles 2002, p. 214).

Douglas lost the 1966 Senate race to Charles Percy. Douglas's strong defense of the Johnson administration's war in Vietnam divided voters in the Democratic Party, and the nation's voters were beginning their shift to Republican candidates. Douglas left Chicago and for several years maintained an active life in public service, writing, and teaching in the Economics Department of the New School of Social Research in New York. Ill health forced his retirement in 1971. He died on September 26, 1976.

Douglas's autobiography *In the Fullness of Time* (Douglas 1971), was reviewed in 1972 by Professor James Tobin, the 1981 Nobel laureate in economics. In reference to Douglas's 'four careers' as scholar, reformer, soldier and politician, Tobin stated: 'Any one alone would fill with distinction the lifetime of a man with unusually prodigious talent and energy. Men of Paul Douglas' range, intensity and dedication are not just unusual, they stride across the national scene only once or twice a generation' (Tobin 1972, p. 438).

Notes

1. For support of this favorable interpretation of Douglas's Senate career, see Biles (2002).
2. Two additional comments by Brown (1987, p. 461) deserve quotation. '[T]he Cobb–Douglas is at least a venerable form and, effectively, it and its putative inventor are regarded fondly'. Also: 'In sum, though it is restrictive and sometimes regarded as an economic toy, the Cobb–Douglas form is remarkably robust in a vast variety of applications and that it will endure is hardly in question'.
3. For tributes to and discussions of Douglas's contributions to economics, see 'In memoriam: Paul H. Douglas (1892–1976)' (1979), Rees (1979) and Samuelson (1979).

References

(1979), 'In memoriam: Paul H. Douglas (1892–1976)', *Journal of Political Economy*, **87** (5, part 1), 913–14.
Biles, R. (2002), *Crusading Liberal: Paul H. Douglas of Illinois*, DeKalb, IL: Northern Illinois University Press.
Brown, M. (1987), 'Cobb–Douglas functions', in *The New Palgrave: A Dictionary of Economics*, vol. 1, Eatwell, J., M. Milgate and P. Newman (eds), New York: Palgrave Macmillan, pp. 460–61.
Cobb, C.W. and P.H. Douglas (1928), 'A theory of production', *American Economic Review*, **18** (1 Supplement), 139–65.
Douglas, E.T. (1948), *Appleseed Farm*, New York: Abingdon-Cokesbury Press.
Douglas, E.T. (1966), *Remember the Ladies: The Story of Great Women Who Helped Shape America*, New York: G.P. Putnam's Sons.
Douglas, E.T. (1970), *Margaret Sanger: Pioneer of the Future*, New York: Holt, Rinehart, & Winston.
Douglas, P.H. (1930), *Real Wages in the United States, 1890–1926*, Boston, MA: Houghton Mifflin.
Douglas, P.H. (1934), *The Theory of Wages*, New York: Macmillan.
Douglas, P.H. (1952), *Ethics in Government*, Cambridge, MA: Harvard University Press.
Douglas, P.H. (1971), *In the Fullness of Time: The Memoirs of Paul H. Douglas*, New York: Harcourt, Brace, Jovanovich.
Rees, A. (1979), 'Douglas on wages and the supply of labor', *Journal of Political Economy*, **85** (5, part 1), 915–22.
Samuelson, P.A. (1979), 'Paul Douglas's measurement of production functions and marginal productivities', *Journal of Political Economy*, **87** (5, part 1), 923–39.
Tobin, J. (1972), 'The careers of Paul Douglas', *Yale Review*, **62**, 438–43.

20 Berthold Frank Hoselitz

*David Mitch**

Bert Hoselitz (1913–95) was affiliated with the University of Chicago's Department of Economics from 1945 until his retirement in 1978. In a University of Chicago (1963) press release he is described as 'one of the world's few "universal" social scientists'. He brought general social science and historical perspectives to bear on a broad range of topics including the economics of war and military occupation, long-run trends in urbanization, stage theories of economic growth and the role of entrepreneurship in economic development. He is especially known for his analysis of the role of cultural and sociological factors in explaining differences between underdeveloped and developed economies. His affiliation with the economics faculty underscores the broad range of social science perspectives that have been present in the intellectual milieu of the department. In the 1950s, Hoselitz was particularly influential in urging the value of an interdisciplinary but unified social science framework for addressing the problems of underdeveloped countries. He founded the Research Center in Economic Development and Cultural Change at Chicago in 1951 and continued as its director through 1974. As the Center's director, he played a key role in the development of the journal *Economic Development and Cultural Change*, initially founded in 1952; he was editor between 1953 and 1985. Among other honors, he was a Fellow of the Center for Advanced Studies in the Behavioral Sciences in Palo Alto in 1955–56 and a Guggenheim Fellow in 1961–62.

Hoselitz was born in Vienna in 1913 into a Jewish business family. He studied law and economics with an emphasis on economic history at the University of Vienna between 1932 and 1937, receiving a Doctor of Jurisprudence degree from there in 1936. Economics was integrated into the faculty of law at Vienna at this time and the study of law there commonly entailed broad exposure to the social sciences and history. Prominent leaders of the Austrian School of Economics such as Ludwig Mises and F.A. Hayek had departed Vienna by the time Hoselitz began his university studies. Between 1928 and 1938, Hoselitz belonged to the Austrian Social Democratic Labor Party. In 1938, the year of German annexation of Austria, Hoselitz left Vienna with a German passport and visa, bound for China with his father and younger brother. But after an uncle living in China warned them not to go there, they ended up in England. His mother died in 1942 in the Auschwitz concentration camp. Hoselitz left England for the United States in 1939 and became a US citizen in 1945. A US Quaker organization assisted in finding Hoselitz a teaching position and from 1940 to 1941, he was an instructor of economics at Manchester College in Indiana. In 1942–43, he attended the University of Chicago and received a Master's degree in economics in 1945. In 1943, he was a research assistant at the Institute of International Studies at Yale University, working with Jacob Viner. In 1945, he was appointed as an instructor in social sciences at the University of Chicago and in 1946, Assistant Professor of Economics. He was appointed as Associate Professor of Economics at the Carnegie Institute of Technology in 1947, but returned to Chicago in 1948 and was promoted to Professor of the Social Sciences in 1953. From

1963 onwards, he is listed in University *Announcements* as Professor of Economics and the Social Sciences (biographical details from Herdzina 1999).

The dual appointment reflected the multiple roles he came to play at the university. While he remained active in the department, he also chaired the Committee on International Relations in the early 1950s, led the Committee on Underdeveloped Areas, established and chaired the Divisional Master's program in the Social Sciences and taught in the College. His courses reflected his broad interests. In the Divisional Master's program he offered courses in 'Economic aspects of international politics' and 'Problems in international economic relations' as well as a course in economic development (Graduate Divisions *Announcements* 1954–55, p. 226; 1956–57, p. 234). In the College, he taught 'Theories of capitalism' and 'Economy and polity' (University of Chicago College *Announcements*, 1967–69, p. 147).

Between 1943 and 1951, Hoselitz published on a wide range of topics relating to both current economic policy and intellectual history. In 1944, he co-authored *The Economics of Military Occupation* (Bloch and Hoselitz 1944). A year later, he published a comment in the *American Economic Review* critical of Hayek's view that National Socialism and German Socialism shared similar intellectual origins (Hoselitz 1945). He was the translator and editor along with James Dingwall of the first English edition of the important Austrian economics text, Carl Menger's *Principles of Economics* (1950).

Starting in the early 1950s, Hoselitz published a series of articles on the contrast in social structures between economically developed and economically underdeveloped countries. His aim was to develop a general social science framework for analyzing economic growth. 'Social structure and economic growth' laid out his basic approach (Hoselitz 1953 [1960]). His measure of economic development was the common one of per capita real national income. However, Hoselitz sought to ascertain underlying differences in assignment of social roles and in social behaviors associated with the observed large differences in per capita income between developed and underdeveloped countries. For this purpose, he drew on Talcott Parsons's theory of social structure; in particular, his 'pattern variables of role-definition' (Parsons 1951, p. 66).

Hoselitz employed some of Parsons's pattern variables to construct a typology of developed versus underdeveloped economies. Although he considered non-economic barriers to development (Hoselitz 1952), his focus was on pattern variables which define the economic difference between developed and underdeveloped countries. First, he argued that developed economies assigned social position and rewards on the basis of objective measures of achievement such as educational attainment, while underdeveloped economies employed ascribed status based on factors such as kinship relationships or religion for this purpose. Second, he argued that developed economies employed universalistic value standards as embodied, for example, in general rules and laws while underdeveloped economies employed particularistic, personalized standards as reflected in caste systems or kinship relations. Henry Maine's notion of a shift in relationships 'from status to contract' (Maine 1920, p. 182) reflected the contrast between 'ascriptive norms in a highly particularistic context' that characterizes underdeveloped economies versus 'achievement norms in a wider, universalistic context' that characterizes developed economies (Hoselitz 1953 [1960], p. 33). Third, Hoselitz invokes Adam Smith's division of labor principle, arguing that underdeveloped economies are characterized by a very limited division of labor with little task or occupational specialization while developed economies have a very extensive division of labor. Interestingly, Hoselitz did not think that Parsons's distinction between the affective and the affective-neutral was relevant in the economic sphere. The view that the 'economic behavior of civilized man was . . . coldly rational; [that of] the primitive, naked savage was . . . as an irrational child', had been, he claimed, 'proved completely false' (ibid., p. 36). Here, Hoselitz appears to be arguing for the universality of maximizing behavior, a key tenet of many Chicago economists, as for example in T.W. Schultz's view that peasants in traditional agriculture were rational (Schultz 1964). Finally, Hoselitz argued that leaders in developed economies are more likely to be motivated by furthering collective goals, while in underdeveloped economies elites aim more at furthering their private interests. Hoselitz seems to have been one of the earliest and more influential writers to apply the Parsonian pentad of pattern variable dichotomies to the issue of economic development (Eisenstadt 1974).

In the last part of his 1953 article, Hoselitz considered the implications of his Parsonian framework for how an economy would make the transition from being underdeveloped to becoming developed. In his view, unlike the economic development of Western European capitalist economies, the governments of underdeveloped countries were likely to play a central role in the development process (1953 [1960], p. 43). Given this, he saw three basic issues arising from considering the 'social structural aspects of economic development' (ibid., pp. 46–7):

> 1) What types of deviant behavior could transform a given society from one with traditional cultural characteristics to one with modern characteristics?
> 2) Which group in a given culture would be most likely to affect such innovating activity?
> 3) Would such an innovating group be most likely to originate from within the culture it was to transform or would it arise from marginal cultural groups?

In addressing the first question, Hoselitz hypothesized that the 'major impetus to alter the significant social, structural pattern variables is likely to come from the plans for economic advancement already drawn up and partially in the course of implementation' (ibid., p. 47). He cites as examples 'the gradual dissolution of the caste system in Indian factories' (ibid., pp. 47–8) and the performance incentives established for Soviet industrialization (ibid., p. 48). In considering the second and third questions, Hoselitz hypothesizes that new leaders will be involved in the process of economic development and that they will tend to either originate from previously marginal groups in the existing traditional society or to be recent immigrants (ibid., p. 49).

One recurring theme emphasized by Hoselitz is the possibility of diverse routes to economic development. The existing social and institutional structure and cultural values and preceding historical course of change of currently developed countries should not be held up as the necessary paradigm for underdeveloped countries to emulate. In one of his landmark pieces, 'A sociological approach to economic development', Hoselitz (1955 [1960]) distinguishes three alternative models of social change associated with economic development: (a) the Marxist model driven by class conflict and class domination; (b) a social deviance model in which economic and social change was brought about by socially marginal groups whether immigrants or other social outsiders; and (c) a model in which existing ruling elites changed their objectives to embrace economic development without changing the social structure.

Hoselitz could be viewed as drawing on a Weberian tradition of distinguishing between traditional and rational motives, in his contrast between underdeveloped and developed societies. However, in Hoselitz (1961), he identified various types of traditions, with some types more beneficial for economic development than others. He distinguishes between tradition in (a) habits, (b) usages, (c) norms and (d) ideologies. Habits are far less limiting to development than traditional ideologies, which create what Hoselitz called 'traditionalistic societies'. These societies, defined by their formalized commitment to tradition, are most inimical to change. Hoselitz argued that tradition in and of itself often serves as a stabilizing factor in the presence of forces for substantial social change.

Hoselitz viewed the entrepreneur as a central agent for social and economic change. The emphasis on the role of the entrepreneur as an agent for economic development in the literature on the history of developed economies led Hoselitz (1956, 1952 [1960]) to examine the potential importance of entrepreneurship for developing countries. He considered both the psychological and sociological factors associated with the cultivation of entrepreneurship. In analyzing psychological factors, he employed David McClelland's theory of achievement motivation. He also utilized theories of social deviance, informed by the view that social outsiders were a particularly fertile source of creative new approaches required for effective entrepreneurship. Social deviance theories can be viewed as combining psychological and sociological elements. He then went on to consider how economic and political structure created an environment that influenced the nature of entrepreneurship. Thus, he viewed entrepreneurship, economic change, and economic structure as mutually interdependent rather than entailing one-directional causation. He distinguished between entrepreneurship in commercial, in financial and in industrial enterprises, designating the last as a critical factor in development but also as entailing especially complex psychological demands. He also considered the incentives societies offered to pursue different types of entrepreneurial activities depending on relative rewards in industry, commerce, finance or government. This can be seen as anticipating subsequent work by Baumol (1990) and Murphy et al. (1991) on incentive effects for productive versus destructive activity. He observed contrasts in the extent to which governments attempted to control entrepreneurial activity, and noted variations in the extent to which entrepreneurs either departed from the values and motivations of traditional elites or emulated their behavior.

Hoselitz (1953 [1960a]) also considered the role of the city in the process of economic development. His main theme was to emphasize the diversity and complexity of ways in which urbanization can function in the process of industrialization and economic growth. He distinguished various types of cities according to economic function whether commercial, administrative or industrial and according to whether they are generative (that is, growth promoting) or parasitic (draining resources away from the countryside). His examination also included the possible implications of urbanization for facilitating change in social and cultural values.

In his analysis of currently underdeveloped countries, Hoselitz made recurrent references to the social and economic history of Western developed countries, though as noted above he warned against presuming that the latter would provide paradigms for the former. In two articles, Hoselitz (1960, 1953 [1960b]) examined in considerable detail the historical literature on stage theories of economic growth with a particular focus on the German Historical School, including Friedrich List, Bruno Hildebrand, Karl Buecher, Gustav Schmoller and Werner Sombart. At the time he wrote these pieces, W.W. Rostow's

(1960) takeoff thesis was attracting attention to the notion of stages of economic growth. Hoselitz's objective was to call attention to previous stage theories of growth. According to Hoselitz (1953 [1960b], p. 16), the stages advanced by the German Historical School, 'were thought to represent generalized, but empirically determined, forms of economic life through which a people had to pass in order to experience economic growth'. But he also thought it important to dig beneath such descriptive generalizations to examine the strengths and weaknesses of the arguments advanced for particular classifications of stages and the justification for progression from one stage to another. He argued that an important achievement of Buecher and Sombart was that they emphasized 'the noneconomic and meta-economic factors which affect profoundly the conditions of economic progress', and noted that Sombart considered capitalism as 'a social rather than an economic system' and thus considered not only economic factors but also those from the political, sociological, and ideological realms (ibid., p. 20). In his own thinking, Hoselitz considered the contrast between underdevelopment and development as that between two 'stages'; one 'preceding' and the other 'following a period of rapid economic advance' (p. 21).

Subsequent work in economic development has been informed by neoclassical economic perspectives, and the tradition/modernity distinction often associated with the Parsonian approach has been largely abandoned by economists and sociologists (Tipps 1973, Eisenstadt 1974, Shiner 1975). Nevertheless, Hoselitz has had a continuing influence through the journal he helped establish, *Economic Development and Cultural Change.* By linking development and cultural change, the journal, and the research center which bore the same name, promoted the view that cooperative, interdisciplinary research along with work within traditional boundaries would be required to address the relevant issues. The faculty of the 'Committee on Underdeveloped Areas' that supervised the work of the center, itself came from a variety of disciplines and university affiliations. Prominent economists who participated in the seminars of the Center included Frank Knight, T.W. Schultz, Albert Rees, Lloyd Metzler, and D. Gale Johnson. Johnson was one of the founding participants of the Center and succeeded Hoselitz as editor of *Economic Development and Cultural Change*. Initially, the journal was significant for spotlighting the situation of developing countries in the midst of ongoing economic concerns with post-war reconstruction and emerging international tensions stemming from the Cold War. It was also distinctive for featuring an interdisciplinary but rigorous use of social science perspectives. *Economic Development and Cultural Change* has continued to be one of the leading journals in the field of economic development and is a legacy of Hoselitz's broadly informed approach to the process of economic change.

Note

* I gratefully acknowledge the assistance of Robert Dernberger in providing personal memoirs of Bert Hoselitz and of Harald Hagemann in sharing biographical information and making available Klaus Herdzina's biographical essay (1999). I am also grateful to Harald Hagemann, Hansjoerg Klausinger, and Peter Rosner for responding to specific queries.

References

Bert F. Hoselitz Papers, Special Collections Research Center, University of Chicago Library.

Baumol, W. (1990), 'Enterpreneurship: productive, unproductive, and destructive', *Journal of Political Economy*, **98** (5, part 1), 893–921.

Bloch, H.S. and B.F. Hoselitz (1944), *The Economics of Military Occupation*, Chicago, IL: University of Chicago Press.
Eisenstadt, S.N. (1974), 'Studies of modernization and sociological theory', *History and Theory*, **13** (3), 225–52.
Herdzina, K. (1999), 'Bert(hold) Frank Hoselitz', in *Biographisches Handbuch der deutschsprachigen wirtschaftswissenschaftlichen Emigration nach 1933*, 1, Hagemann, H. and C.-D. Krohn (eds), Munich: K.G. Saur.
Hoselitz, B.F. (1945), 'Professor Hayek on German socialism', *American Economic Review*, **35** (5), 929–34.
Hoselitz, B.F. (1952), 'Non-economic barriers to economic development', *Economic Development and Cultural Change*, **1** (1), 8–21.
Hoselitz, B.F. (1952 [1960]), 'Entrepreneurship and economic growth', in *Sociological Aspects of Economic Growth*, Glencoe, IL: Free Press, pp. 139–58.
Hoselitz, B.F. (1953, [1960]), 'Social structure and economic growth', in *Sociological Aspects of Economic Growth*, Glencoe, IL: Free Press, pp. 23–51.
Hoselitz, B.F. (1953 [1960a]), 'The role of cities in the economic growth of underdeveloped countries', in *Sociological Aspects of Economic Growth*, Glencoe, IL: Free Press, pp. 159–84.
Hoselitz, B.F. (1953 [1960b]), 'The scope and history of theories of economic growth', in *Sociological Aspects of Economic Growth*, Glencoe, IL: Free Press, pp. 1–22.
Hoselitz, B.F. (1955 [1960]), 'A sociological approach to economic development', in *Sociological Aspects of Economic Growth*, Glencoe, IL: Free Press, pp. 53–84.
Hoselitz, B. F. (1956), 'Entrepreneurship and capital formation in France and Britain since 1700', in *Capital Formation and Economic Growth*, National Bureau Committee of Economic Research (ed.), Princeton, NJ: National Bureau of Economic Research, pp. 291–338.
Hoselitz, B.F. (1960), 'Theories of stages of economic growth', in *Theories of Economic Growth*, Hoselitz, B.F., J.J. Spengler, J.M. Letiche, E. McKinley, J. Buttrick and H.J. Bruton (eds), Glencoe, IL: Free Press, pp. 193–238.
Hoselitz, B.F. (1961), 'Tradition and economic growth', in *Tradition, Values, and socio-economic Development*, Braibanti, R. and J.J. Spengler (eds), Durham, NC: Duke University Press, pp. 83–113.
Maine, H.S. (1920), *Ancient Law: Its Connection with the Early History of Society, and Its Relation to Modern Ideas*, Pollock, F. (ed.), London: J. Murray.
Menger, C. (1950), *Principles of Economics*, Dingwall, J. and B.F. Hoselitz (trans.), Glencoe, IL: Free Press.
Murphy, K.M., A. Shleifer and R.W. Vishny (1991), 'The allocation of talent: implications for growth', *Quarterly Journal of Economics*, **106** (2), 503–30.
Parsons, T. (1951), *The Social System*, New York: Free Press.
Rostow, W.W. (1960), *Stages of Economic Growth: A Non-communist Manifesto*, Cambridge: Cambridge University Press.
Schultz, T.W. (1964), *Transforming Traditional Agriculture*, New Haven, CT: Yale University Press.
Shiner, L.E. (1975), 'Tradition/modernity: an ideal type gone astray', *Comparative Studies in Society and History*, **17** (2), 245–52.
Tipps, D.C. (1973), 'Modernization theory and the comparative study of societies: a critical perspective', *Comparative Studies in Society and History*, **15** (2), 199–225.
University of Chicago (1963), 'Biography release on Bert F. Hoselitz,' Archival Biographical File, Special Collections Research Center, University of Chicago.

21 Frank H. Knight

Ross B. Emmett

Frank Hyneman Knight (1885–1972) was born in White Oak Township, McLean County, Illinois in November 1885. While the demands of farm life often took precedence over education, Knight and his siblings eventually were able to pursue university studies: three sons, including Frank, became economists. After graduating from Milligan College in 1911, Frank Knight completed a BSc and an MA (in German) at the University of Tennessee. He considered graduate study in Germany, but accepted instead a scholarship to study philosophy at Cornell University.

Knight transferred to economics during his first year at Cornell (1913–14) after his philosophy professor told him he was too skeptical to be a philosopher (Johnson 1952, p. 227). He completed his PhD in 1916, under the supervision of Allyn A. Young. Knight's dissertation is one of the most famous in the economics literature because it both provided closure to the version of neoclassical theory associated with John Bates Clark by providing a theory of profit and opened the door to a host of new questions with the introduction of a theory of uncertainty. The dissertation won second prize in the 1917 Hart, Schaffner and Marx essay competition, and was published in 1921 as *Risk, Uncertainty and Profit* (Knight 1921). A short stint as an instructor at Cornell (1916–17) was followed by two years at the University of Chicago (1917–19). But Chicago did not have a permanent position to offer Knight when the University of Iowa offered him the chance to replace Isaac A. Loos in 1919. Nine years later, he returned from Iowa City to Chicago permanently, intending to teach courses on the intersection of economics, institutionalism, comparative economic history and the history of economic thought – anything but economic theory, which was Jacob Viner's domain. While he did teach the history of economic thought, and a course on economics and the philosophy of democratic society, he inevitably ended up teaching price theory as well. The strong price-theoretic tradition that he and Viner laid in the interwar years set the stage for the central role that price theory played in the education of Chicago economists in the post-war period.

Knight's contribution to American economics was honored when, in 1957, the American Economic Association (AEA) awarded him the Francis A. Walker medal, given no more than once every five years to an economic theorist – the medal was discontinued in the 1970s after the establishment of the Nobel Prize. He had been named President of the AEA in 1950, and was awarded the prize for distinguished service to humanistic scholarship by the American Council of Learned Societies in 1961. Several European and American universities granted him honorary degrees, and Knight was also selected to be a member of the American Academy of Arts and Sciences and the Accademia Nazionale Dei Lincei in Italy. Knight officially retired from the University of Chicago in 1952, although he continued to teach until the early 1960s, and lectured frequently at other institutions. He continued to lecture and write until his death in April 1972.

Risk, Uncertainty and Profit (Knight 1921) placed uncertainty at the center of economic theorizing and the problem of knowledge in the social sciences. Uncertainty was a topic of concern to other economists at the time; in fact, John Maynard Keynes published his *Treatise on Probability* (Keynes 1921) in the same year. But where Keynes defined uncertainty in terms of the subjectivity of human knowledge, Knight located it in the subjectivity of human action (Greer 2001, Emmett 2009e). The difference is subtle, yet profound. Keynes argued that subjectivity allowed only probabilistic explanations of the complexities of both natural and social reality. Knight, on the other hand, argued that social reality presented an additional element – the voluntary and explorative nature of human conduct – that not only rendered our knowledge subjective in Keynes's sense, but also meant that even probabilistic explanations were insufficient. The real world of social interaction required us to assume not only that economic agents acted voluntarily, but also that they acted with the knowledge that others were capable of voluntary action. Agents, therefore, were forced to estimate (in a manner not captured by probabilistic reasoning) what course of action was best. The resulting uncertainty created the need for a social science that extends beyond the analytics of choice.

Knight's understanding of uncertainty also held wider implications for economics. The latter part of *Risk, Uncertainty and Profit* sketched out the argument that uncertainty would lead economic agents (especially firms) to create institutions by which they could reduce their exposure to uncertainty. Just as insurance allows firms to convert risks into costs, the organizational structure of firms allows them to convert the uncertainties of market transactions into internal firm transfers that will be more certain. The emergence of transaction cost and monitoring theories of the firm, which have played a major role in Chicago economics, have their roots in Knight's treatment of the firm (Demsetz and Alchian 1977, Coase 1988, Foss 1993, Langlois and Cosgel 1993).

The novel theoretical claims about the importance of uncertainty to human action developed in *Risk, Uncertainty and Profit* were overlaid on a relatively traditional methodological foundation. Following the standard logic that science involved the process of abstraction and analysis, Knight argued that uncertainty was simply the first assumption that needed to be removed in the process of moving from the theoretical world of perfect competition toward the reality of modern industrial capitalism – a method T.W. Hutchison called the 'optimistic' approach of successive approximation (Hutchison 1938, p. 73). Knight defended economic theorizing in these terms again in the early 1920s against the claim of some institutionalists that economic theory was simply unrealistic and irrelevant to social reality (Knight 1999g). His debates with the institutionalists over the course of the 1920s, however, provided him the occasion to articulate his philosophical and methodological approach to economics more fully. Although the notion of successive approximation continued to appear in his work (Knight 1999h), several other themes began to play a more important methodological role.

The first of these themes was the role of the *interests of the observer* in scientific activity. As early as 1925, Knight made the notion that scientists themselves have multiple interests a part of his argument that science does not occupy a privileged position within the realm of human action. 'Truth is an interest . . . and no human being does, or could, make the pursuit of truth . . . the sole content of his life' (Knight 1999d, pp. 115–16). Knight converted the notion of truth as an interest into a moral category in several essays in the 1940s. First, like any other interest, our quest for truth is inherently dynamic;

we want not simply to find truth, but to develop more and better truths. 'Truth is the supreme example of the principle that liberal idealism looks at the values of life in terms of pursuit as well as possession; they belong to the activity as much as to the result, to means as well as to ends' (Knight 1999j, p. 305). The human activity of searching for truth – the interaction of truth seeking with other interests, the process of framing better questions, the presence of constraints – were as much a part of science as were its discoveries. Knight used this idea later in his critique of Michael Polanyi's approach to the role of science in liberal society (Knight 1999l).

Knight also recognized that the moral nature of truth made it a 'social category; its only test is unanimous acceptance in some community of discussion' (Knight 1999j, p. 306). Knight's emphasis here is not on the relativist claim that truth is dependent on a discursive community (although he has been accused of relativism), but rather on the notion that no free community is ever completely in agreement about a truth claim, and hence that the commitment to free inquiry is essential. The great enemy of Truth is not competing truths or the threat of relativism, but authority figures that substitute *truth claims* for the community's commitment to the *pursuit of truth*. Knight retains his most vituperative language for religious and other authorities that try to subvert truth seeking: 'control of education is the first aim of the totalitarian' (Knight 1999i, p. 384, Emmett 2009c).

The second theme that emerged in Knight's later methodological work was the necessity of comparative historical and institutional research. During the late 1920s and early 1930s, Knight was involved in translating and studying the work of Max Weber (Emmett 2006). The first of Weber's works to appear in English (Weber 1927) was translated by Knight, and he taught a seminar on Weber's work during the 1930s. Translating *General Economic History* may appear an odd place to start acquainting the English world with Weber's work, but Knight had begun reading Weber because of his interest in economic history, and Weber's comparative historical approach attracted him. Although he disagreed with Weber on the role of religion in developing the spirit of capitalism – emphasizing with Lujo Brentano the similarity between capitalism and war – Knight appreciated Weber's notion of the 'ideal type' (Knight 1999e). After reading Weber, Knight seldom claimed that economics could move from the world of perfect competition to the reality of modern industrial society by successive approximation. Instead, he emphasized the idealized nature of perfect competition, and claimed that there was an impassable gulf between the worlds of equilibrium theorizing and that of history (Knight 1999k). No process of relaxing assumptions can bridge such a gulf. Thus, social science required more than just the analytics of equilibrium theory; it also required a mode of inquiry analogous to Weber's comparative historical approach. Knight's first major effort at such a study was 'Economic theory and nationalism' (Knight 1935).

Balancing his earlier emphasis on the independent scientific status of economic theory with his new concern for comparative historical study led Knight to develop a pluralistic approach to social scientific knowledge. In 'Social science' (Knight 1956), for example, Knight argued that economics was fine in so far as it went, but our understanding of human conduct and its social consequences operated at other levels as well. Prior to economics were explanations of human behavior that focused on physical or chemical aspects of our conduct. These explanations, Knight argued, were complete at their levels of explanation. No reference to human intentionality was needed for a physical or chemical description of human action. But human action is more than physical or chemical interactions; intentionality is undeniably present (Knight 1999d). Economics is a first step in the process of providing an explanation of human action that incorporates intentionality. Given stable wants and preferences, economics provides a complete explanation of conduct and its social consequences. However, Knight argued that other social sciences provide equally complete, and equally limited, explanations of human action that are independent of economics. If one wants to understand the totality of human action, then, one must incorporate all the social sciences and, ultimately, ethics: 'the social problem is not one of fact – except as values are also facts – nor is it one of means and end. It is a problem of values. And the content of social science must correspond with the problem of action in character and scope' (Knight 1956, p. 134).

Knight's pluralistic approach to social science brought him into direct conflict with the dominant trend of twentieth-century social science methodology, which emerged first in scientific naturalism and objectivism (Emmett 2009b), and became positivist in the post-war period. Indeed, despite Knight's influence on the price theory tradition and market orientation of Chicago economics, the inheritors of his tradition at Chicago departed significantly from him on methodology (Emmett 2009a). The standard reference for Knight's anti-positivism is the salvo (Knight 1999m) fired on the unsuspecting T.W. Hutchison in the context of a review of *The Significance and Basic Postulates of Economic Theory* (Hutchison 1938). Arguing against the positivist claim that we can separate our knowledge of reality from the process of learning what we know about reality, Knight reiterated his claims about the idealizing nature of perfect competition, and went on to argue that we know about economizing behavior better than we know 'the truth of any statement about any concrete physical fact' because we live 'in a world "with" other intelligent beings' (Knight 1999m, p. 383).

Knight's resistance to the positivism of much twentieth-century social science often led his work to be viewed as iconoclastic and outside the mainstream (Blaug 1997). But his impact on twentieth-century economic methodology is both more complex and somewhat ironic. Despite his change in methodological approach during the 1930s, one thing stayed constant: the claim that the basic postulates of economic theory were relevant to understanding economic activity even if they did not provide the basis for a strictly predictive science. At Chicago, this claim found expression in Knight's short book *The Economic Organization* (Knight 1933; see the reader's guide by Ross Emmett in this volume, ch. 4), and in his continued refinement of price theory over the 1930s and early 1940s. As an economist, Knight sought to clarify economic theory; his students picked up the challenge of showing that it was predictive in many situations. Thus, the prominence of the methodological essays by Milton Friedman (1953), George Stigler and Gary Becker (1977) among Chicago economists mask their connection to Knight's own work. It is a short step from Knight's clear delineation of an economics based on stable preferences (prefaced by the claim that preferences really were not stable and that values were the source of social conflict), to his students' position that assuming the stability of preferences is not unwarranted as long as the predictions yielded by the theory continue to hold up in practical application (Emmett 2009a, 2009d).

If Knight's pluralistic approach to social science was designed to ensure an independent place for economics in social inquiry, it was also designed to ensure an independent place for ethics. From the beginning of his career, Knight sought to keep ethical issues central to social inquiry. Separating economics from ethics kept an independent place in social inquiry for both. In the narrow world of perfect competition, the assumption of given tastes, preferences and values was appropriate in order to provide stability. But even in his earliest statements of economic methodology, he clearly states that these 'data' are not stable: 'Life is at bottom an exploration in the field of values, an attempt to discover values, rather than on the basis of knowledge of them to produce and enjoy them to the greatest possible extent. We strive to "know ourselves," to find out our real wants, more than to get what we want' (Knight 1999g, p. 1).

The exploratory nature of human action requires not only a broader social science, but also creates a place in social inquiry for an independent ethics. In an early essay, Knight challenged ethicists to stop trying to imitate economists, and to accept the 'creation of value' as something more than want satisfaction (Knight 1999b). A companion essay turned matters around and offered a critique of ethics, arguing that traditional approaches to ethics are insufficient for the modern world. In particular, he argued, ethics must come to terms with the games and sportsmanship of the business world. Such behavior fits neither a deontological ethic nor a virtue ethic. We search in vain, he argues, to find an ethics that provides justification for the competition that makes modern life efficient and wealthy. The essay leaves the reader unable to determine if this is the fault of ethics or modern life (Knight 1999c).

Knight's interest in ethics and social science broadened as he came to focus more attention on the problems of liberalism. In the early 1930s, his comparative historical studies led him to the conclusion that liberalism was passing, and a new form of social organization was going to emerge. Skepticism about the prospects of social control and a deep pessimism regarding the hopes for social progress often permeate his lectures and writings during the interwar period (Knight 1991). Central to his lament for the passing of liberalism is the claim that liberalism's strengths are also the source of its weaknesses. Liberal democracy is a form of government dedicated to the open-ended discussion of what we want to become, not simply the satisfaction of the wants we currently have. When people become satisfied with their existing wants, and close the conversation, liberalism is in danger. Liberalism's commitment to freedom of inquiry requires us to keep the pursuit of truth open, but social scientists often elevate their findings to the status of truth, and seek to use political power to implement policies constructed on an incomplete understanding of society (Knight 1935, 1999j).

The paradoxical relationship between ethics and social science continued in Knight's later work. He stands out from other post-war anti-Keynesian economists, including his students at Chicago, because he did not side with F.A. Hayek and the Austrian economists in the famous socialist calculation debate (Hayek 1948), who argued that the best case against socialism was the efficiency argument. Knight accepted the argument of Oskar Lange and Fred Taylor (1938) that a central planner could make all the necessary calculations to replace the market, and argued instead that ethics provided the only ground upon which to build a defense of liberal democratic capitalism (Knight 1936, 1999f). Yet every time he examined contemporary ethical theories, his analysis concluded that they were all insufficient for life in the modern world. His most far-reaching ethical analysis is in the three-part article 'Ethics and economic reform' (Knight 1999a). Focusing on the ethical possibilities for social reform imbedded in idealism, Marxism, and Christianity, Knight finds all wanting. The same themes regarding the tension between science and ethics came together at the end of his career in his joint attack on scientism and moralism as approaches to modern social problems (Knight 1999i, 1999j). And yet, in his last major work, the published text of a lecture series given at the University of Virginia in 1958, Knight concludes: 'the two things which we have especially to know in order to act intelligently are history . . . and ethics', the latter being 'the system of values that enables us to discriminate between the better and the worse in contemplating action with a view to changing the nature of society' (Knight 1960, p. 141). The difficulties, and possibilities, of combining history, social science, and ethics in confronting the issues of modern life is Knight's legacy.

References

Blaug, M. (1997), *Economic Theory in Retrospect*, 5th edn, Cambridge: Cambridge University Press.

Coase, R.H. (1988), 'The theory of the firm', in *The Firm, the Market and the Law*, Chicago, IL: University of Chicago Press, pp. 33–55.

Demsetz, H. and A.A. Alchian (1977), 'Production, information costs and economic organization', in *Economic Forces at Work*, Indianapolis, IN: Liberty Press, pp. 73–110.

Emmett, R.B. (2006), 'Frank H. Knight, Max Weber, Chicago economics, and institutionalism', *Max Weber Studies*, Beiheft 1: *Weber and Economics*, 101–19.

Emmett, R.B. (2009a), 'Did the Chicago School reject Frank Knight?: Assessing Frank Knight's place in the Chicago economics tradition', in *Frank Knight and the Chicago School in American Economics*, London: Routledge, pp. 145–55.

Emmett, R.B. (2009b), 'Frank Knight's dissent from Progressive social science', in *Frank Knight and the Chicago School in American Economics*, London: Routledge, pp. 63–72.

Emmett, R.B. (2009c), 'Frank Knight on the conflict of values in economic life', in *Frank Knight and the Chicago School in American Economics*, London: Routledge, pp. 98–108.

Emmett, R.B. (2009d), 'Realism and relevance in the economics of a free society', *Journal of Economic Methodology*, **16** (3), 341–50.

Emmett, R.B. (2009e), 'The therapeuetic quality of Frank Knight's *Risk, Uncertainty, and Profit*', in *Frank Knight and the Chicago School in American Economics*, London: Routledge, pp. 31–47.

Foss, N.J. (1993), 'More on Knight and the theory of the firm', *Managerial and Decision Economics*, **14** (3), 269–76.

Friedman, M. (1953), 'The methodology of positive economics', in *Essays in Positive Economics*, Chicago, IL: University of Chicago Press, pp. 3–43.

Greer, W.B. (2001), *Ethics and Uncertainty: The Economics of John Maynard Keynes and Frank H. Knight*, Cheltenham, UK, and Northampton, MA, USA: Edward Elgar.

Hayek, F.A. (1948), *Individualism and Economic Order*, Chicago, IL: University of Chicago Press.

Hutchison, T.W. (1938), *The Significance and Basic Postulates of Economic Theory*, London: Macmillan.

Johnson, A.S. (1952), *Pioneer's Progress*, New York: Viking Press.

Keynes, J.M. (1921), *A Treatise on Probability*, London: Macmillan.

Knight, F.H. (1921), *Risk, Uncertainty and Profit*, Boston, MA: Houghton Mifflin.

Knight, F.H. (1933), *The Economic Organization*, Chicago, IL: University of Chicago.

Knight, F.H. (1935), 'Economic theory and nationalism', in *The Ethics of Competition*, New York: Harper & Bros., pp. 277–359.

Knight, F.H. (1936), 'The place of marginal economics in a collectivist system', *American Economic Review (supplement)*, 26 (March), 255–66.

Knight, F.H. (1956), 'Social science', in *On the History and Method of Economics*, Chicago, IL: University of Chicago Press, pp. 121–34.

Knight, F.H. (1960), *Intelligence and Democratic Action*, Cambridge, MA: Harvard University Press.

Knight, F.H. (1991), 'The case for communism: from the standpoint of an ex-liberal', in *Research in the History of Economic Thought and Methodology*, Archival supplement, Samuels, W.J. (ed.), Stamford, CT: JAI Press, pp. 57–108.

Knight, F.H. (1999a), 'Ethics and economic reform', in *Selected Essays by Frank H. Knight*, vol. 2: *Laissez-faire: Pro and Con*, Emmett, R.B. (ed.), Chicago, IL: University of Chicago Press, pp. 1–75.

Knight, F.H. (1999b), 'Ethics and the economic interpretation', in *Selected Essays by Frank H. Knight*, vol. 1: *'What Is Truth' in Economics?*, Emmett, R.B. (ed.), Chicago, IL: University of Chicago Press, pp. 40–60.

Knight, F.H. (1999c), 'The ethics of competition', in *Selected Essays by Frank H. Knight*, vol. 1: *'What Is Truth' in Economics?*, Emmett, R.B. (ed.), Chicago, IL: University of Chicago Press, pp. 61–93.

Knight, F.H. (1999d), 'Fact and metaphysics in economic psychology', in *Selected Essays by Frank H. Knight*, vol. 1: *'What Is Truth' in Economics?*, Emmett, R.B. (ed.), Chicago, IL: University of Chicago Press, pp. 112–32.
Knight, F.H. (1999e), 'Historical and theoretical issues in the problem of modern capitalism', in *Selected Essays by Frank H. Knight*, vol. 1: *'What Is Truth' in Economics?*, Emmett, R.B. (ed.), Chicago, IL: University of Chicago Press, pp. 133–48.
Knight, F.H. (1999f), '*Laissez-faire*: pro and con', in *Selected Essays by Frank H. Knight*, vol. 2: *Laissez-faire: Pro and Con*, Emmett, R.B. (ed.), Chicago, IL: University of Chicago Press, pp. 435–53.
Knight, F.H. (1999g), 'The limitations of scientific method in economics', in *Selected Essays by Frank H. Knight*, vol. 1: *'What Is Truth' in Economics?*, Emmett, R.B. (ed.), Chicago, IL: University of Chicago Press, pp. 1–39.
Knight, F.H. (1999h), 'Realism and relevance in the theory of demand', in *Selected Essays by Frank H. Knight*, vol. 2: *Laissez-faire: Pro and Con*, Emmett, R.B. (ed.), Chicago, IL: University of Chicago Press, pp. 243–83.
Knight, F.H. (1999i), 'The role of principles in economics and politics', in *Selected Essays by Frank H. Knight*, vol. 2: *Laissez-faire: Pro and Con*, Emmett, R.B. (ed.), Chicago, IL: University of Chicago Press, pp. 361–91.
Knight, F.H. (1999j), 'The sickness of liberal society', in *Selected Essays by Frank H. Knight*, vol. 2: *Laissez-faire: Pro and Con*, Emmett, R.B. (ed.), Chicago, IL: University of Chicago Press, pp. 284–313.
Knight, F.H. (1999k), 'Statics and dynamics: some queries regarding the mechanical analogy in economics', in *Selected Essays by Frank H. Knight*, vol. 1: *'What Is Truth' in Economics?*, Emmett, R.B. (ed.), Chicago, IL: University of Chicago Press, pp. 149–71.
Knight, F.H. (1999l), 'Virtue and knowledge: the view of Professor Polanyi', in *Selected Essays by Frank H. Knight*, vol. 2: *Laissez-faire: Pro and Con*, Emmett, R.B. (ed.), Chicago, IL: University of Chicago Press, pp. 314–35.
Knight, F.H. (1999m), '"What is truth" in economics?', in *Selected Essays by Frank H. Knight*, vo. 1: *'What Is Truth' in Economics?*, Emmett, R.B. (ed,), Chicago, IL: University of Chicago Press, pp. 372–99.
Lange, O. and F.M. Taylor (1938), *On the Economic Theory of Socialism*, Minneapolis, MN: University of Minnesota Press.
Langlois, R.N. and M.M. Cosgel (1993), 'Frank Knight on risk, uncertainty, and the firm: a new interpretation', *Economic Inquiry*, **31** (3), 456–65.
Stigler, G.J. and G.S. Becker (1977), 'De gustibus non est disputandum', *American Economic Review*, **67** (2), 76–90.
Weber, M. (1927), *General Economic History*, Knight, F.H. (trans.), Chicago, IL: Greenberg.

22 J. Laurence Laughlin

William J. Barber

James Laurence Laughlin (1850–1933), the first Head Professor of Political Economy at the University of Chicago, was the principal mover and shaker of that department during the first quarter-century of its existence. He had been called to this post by William Rainey Harper, the university's first president, who was determined – with the aid of the John D. Rockefeller's checkbook – to build a world-class university virtually overnight. On its opening day in October 1892, the University of Chicago had a larger complement of students and faculty than any American institution of higher learning possessed before the Civil War.

Laughlin brought considerable academic credentials to this assignment. He had been awarded the AB and PhD degrees in history by Harvard University. He earned the latter qualification with a dissertation directed by Henry Adams on Anglo-Saxon legal procedures (Adams et al. 1876). Thereafter he turned attention to political economy and taught this subject at Harvard from 1878 to 1888. During this phase of his career, he prepared an abridged version of John Stuart Mill's *Principles of Political Economy*, with adaptations that he took to be suitable for American student audiences (Mill 1884). This meant that the illustrative material drew on the US (rather than British) experience; it also meant that Mill's comments on the virtues of free markets were emphasized and that his sympathetic references to the state as an agent for social amelioration were systematically purged. He also produced a volume on the history of bimetallism in the United States, a topic that was to be of sustained professional interest (Laughlin 1885a). In addition, he took the initiative in founding a Political Economy Club, the bulk of whose members – most notably Simon Newcomb (the mathematician–astronomer–economist) and William Graham Sumner (Yale's outspoken champion of Social Darwinism) – were voluble advocates of unbridled *laissez-faire*. This association set Laughlin unambiguously apart from those in his generation who set out in the mid-1880s to form an American Economic Association as a counterweight to the views of the 'Sumner–Newcomb crowd'. The lead promoter of that venture was Richard T. Ely (then of Johns Hopkins University) who was engaged in mobilizing younger economists – most of whom had received post-graduate training in German universities – who regarded governmental intervention as essential to social betterment. This set the scene for lively disputations between 'Old School' and 'New School' economists in the *Methodenstreit* of the 1880s and early 1890s (Coats 1961).

It is a matter for conjecture what the trajectory of the Chicago's Department of Political Economy would have been if Harper had made a different choice for its Head Professor. When first mulling over this matter, he had given thought to Ely as a possible candidate. Harper, an Old Testament scholar, had some intellectual affinity with Ely's brand of Christian Socialism and had come to know Ely as a colleague in a summer camp with a Christian orientation. Archival records of correspondence between the two men suggest that Harper reacted negatively to the tone of Ely's attempts to bargain on salary. Meanwhile Laughlin's possible availability had come to Harper's attention. This candidacy had a qualification that Ely lacked: Laughlin had spent the years 1888 through 1890 acquiring business experience as an officer in a mutual fire insurance company in Philadelphia. This interlude in the 'real world' was followed by a return to academic life with a professorship at Cornell. Laughlin agreed to accept Harper's invitation to move to Chicago on condition that he could bring along Thorstein Veblen, a maverick with an arrestingly original style, whom Laughlin had rescued from professional oblivion.

Laughlin's appointment as the Head Professor signaled a tilt in the direction of 'Old School' economics. Harper nonetheless hoped that views of the 'New School' would also be represented in the fledgling department and – with that objective in mind – negotiated with Edward W. Bemis, an Ely protégé with a doctorate from Johns Hopkins, about a junior appointment to the faculty. When Laughlin made clear that Bemis would not be welcome in his department, Harper assigned Bemis to the university's Extension Division (an entity charged to offer adult education and correspondence courses), but with a part-time affiliation with the Department of Political Economy. This arrangement was uneasy from the outset – and it fell apart completely in mid-1894. Passions in the city were then running high over the Pullman strike which had paralyzed Chicago's railway system. When Bemis criticized the behavior of railway management in a well-publicized speech before a church gathering, Laughlin called for his dismissal on grounds of incompetence. Not long thereafter, Bemis's employment at the university was terminated. This episode, it should be noted, was a special case (for more, see Barber 1988, pp. 249–55). As was underscored in memorial notices prepared by Chicago colleagues after his death, Laughlin had recruited and worked with other economists with views widely divergent from his own (Nef 1934). It is also worth recalling that he was responsible for keeping Veblen on the premises for a term longer than any other academic institution would employ him. When Veblen was ultimately fired at Chicago, it was Harper's doing, not Laughlin's.

Laughlin himself figured in public controversy in the mid-1890s. His public and professional writings had established him as a trenchant critic of the quantity theory of money as presented by the 'free silverites' (Laughlin 1884, 1885a, 1885b, 1887). (His critique was aimed primarily at the crude quantity theory, rather than at the more sophisticated statement in the equation of exchange.) The publication of the best-selling tract – entitled *Coin's Financial School* (Harvey 1894) – brought Laughlin's name before the general public. In Harvey's statement of the Populist position on free silver, a young boy is depicted as besting a learned 'Professor Laughlin' in debate. Laughlin was not amused by this caricature and wrote polemical rebuttals (Laughlin 1895a, 1895b). Indeed, his comments on 'unsound' money proposals were more intensely partisan than Bemis's remarks had been at the time of the Pullman strike. In his own view, Laughlin regarded his intervention in public controversy as a professional obligation to enlighten opinion on truths based on 'scientific' findings.

Laughlin's commitment to public enlightenment also found expression in his editorship of the *Journal of Political Economy* (*JPE*). Harper's vision of the University of Chicago's role in the larger society expected each of its departments to sponsor a learned journal. The Department of Political Economy led the way when its journal appeared in December 1892. In the opening article, Laughlin spoke to its larger purpose as follows: 'Never in our history have venerable fallacies and misinterpretations been more widely current. . . . We seem to be passing through an exceptional development of the heart without a corresponding development of the head'. Academic economists had a responsibility to correct this situation 'through new avenues of communication between the investigator and the public' (Laughlin 1892, pp. 2, 19). In the first issues of the *JPE*, much of the material was produced 'in-house'. But contributions from leading economists in the United States and abroad soon appeared. Nor was it necessary for authors to toe a particular party line. Despite Laughlin's strongly held views on sound money, material critical of his position was published.

Laughlin guarded jealously his prerogatives as Head Professor, a posture that at times put him at odds with the university's President. In 1902 – after interviewing two department members (Adolph Miller and Wesley C. Mitchell) who had decided to depart to the University of California – Harper wrote as follows to Laughlin: 'There is a strong feeling that the Department of Political Economy in our University is isolated from the work of Political Economy throughout the country; that the members of our staff do not come in contact with other men interested in the same subject, and with the work at large' (Harper to Laughlin, 15 August 1902, quoted in Barber 1988, p. 260). Laughlin vigorously protested this assessment. He allowed that there had been 'persistent attempts . . . to misrepresent the economic attitude of our department. . . . We have been represented as intolerant, rigid in our views, narrow, old-fashioned, and unwilling to take new departures'. But, he insisted, this was 'false, all through'. He attributed this negativity to jealousy on the part of officers in the American Economic Association (AEA) because he had refused 'to pool our publications with the Econ. Association'. This had 'excited a feeling that we propose to separate ourselves from the others' (Laughlin to Harper, 23 August 1902, quoted in Barber 1988, p. 260). But there was more to this than Laughlin was prepared to acknowledge. Well after the AEA had ceased to fly the 'New School' banner, he remained aloof. He finally joined the AEA in 1904 (Coats 1964, pp. 261–2).

In a memorial appraisal, Wesley C. Mitchell (who had known Laughlin both as a student and as a faculty colleague) observed that he 'was not an original thinker of great power', nor did he 'keep abreast of current developments in economic theory'. Despite the tenacity with which he clung to strongly held views, he maintained that his role as a teacher should be to instill 'the acquisition of independent power and methods of work, rather than specific beliefs' (Mitchell 1941, pp. 879–80). In this approach to pedagogy, he was eminently successful.

Laughlin remained the Head Professor of Chicago's Department of Political Economy until his retirement from the university in 1916. He took leave of absence from University work between 1911 and 1913, however, to serve as chairman of a committee of the National Citizens' League which had been organized to educate the public on the urgency of banking reforms, along lines that were ultimately imbedded in the Federal Reserve Act of 1913 (Laughlin 1912). In his final years, he continued to write on issues of money and banking, publishing a two-volume work, *A New Exposition of Money, Credit, and Prices*, in 1931 (Laughlin 1931).

References

Adams, H., H.C. Lodge, E. Young and J.L. Laughlin (1876), *Essays in Anglo-Saxon Law*, Boston, MA: Little, Brown.

Barber, W.J. (1988), 'Political economy in an atmosphere of academic entrepreneurship: the University of

Chicago', in *Breaking the Academic Mould: Economists and American Higher Learning in the Nineteenth Century*, Barber, W.J. (ed.), Middletown, CT: Wesleyan University Press, pp. 241–65.
Coats, A.W. (1961), 'The Political Economy Club: a neglected episode in American economic thought', *American Economic Review*, **51** (4), 624–37.
Coats, A.W. (1964), 'The American Economic Association, 1904–29', *American Economic Review*, **54** (4), 261–85.
Harvey, W.H. (1894), *Coin's Financial School*, Chicago, IL: Coin.
Laughlin, J.L. (1884), 'The silver danger', *Atlantic Monthly*, May, 667–81.
Laughlin, J.L. (1885a), *The History of Bimetallism in the United States*, New York: Appleton.
Laughlin, J.L. (1885b), 'Shall silver be demonitized?', *North American Review*, July, 492–97.
Laughlin, J.L. (1887), 'Gold and prices since 1873', *Quarterly Journal of Economics*, **1** (3), 319–55, 385–99.
Laughlin, J.L. (1892), 'The study of political economy in the United States', *Journal of Political Economy*, **1** (1), 1–19.
Laughlin, J.L. (1895a), 'Coin's food for the gullible', *Forum*, May, 573–85.
Laughlin, J.L. (1895b), *Facts about Money*, Chicago, IL: E.A. Weeks.
Laughlin, J.L. (ed.) (1912), *Banking Reform*, Chicago, IL: National Citizens' League.
Laughlin, J.L. (1931), *A New Exposition of Money, Credit and Prices*, 2 vols, Chicago, IL: University of Chicago Press.
Mill, J.S. (1884), *Principles of Political Economy*, abridged, Laughlin, J.L. (ed.), New York: Appleton.
Mitchell, W.C. (1941), 'J. Laurence Laughlin', *Journal of Political Economy*, **49** (6), 875–81.
Nef, J.U. (1934), 'James Laurence Laughlin (1850–1933)', *Journal of Political Economy*, **42** (1), 1–5.

23 Edward P. Lazear

Morley Gunderson

Edward Lazear (1948–) was born and grew up in Los Altos, California. At that time, the area was not part of Silicon Valley as it is today, but rather was predominantly fruit farming. As a youth, Eddie picked apricots and that early experience inspired him in two areas: piecerates as incentive compensation and university as an alternative to physical labor. Responding to these incentives, he received his AB and AM degrees from the University of California at Los Angeles in 1971 and his PhD in economics from Harvard University in 1974. Upon graduation he taught at the University of Chicago's Department of Economics and then at the Graduate School of Business, where he was the Brown Professor of Urban and Labor Economics from 1985 to 1992. In 1992, he accepted an appointment at the Stanford Graduate School of Business and in 1995 became the Jack Steele Parker Professor of Human Resources, Management and Economics. Currently at Stanford, he is also the Morris Arnold Cox Senior Fellow at the Hoover Institution as well as a Senior Fellow at the Stanford Institute for Economic Policy Research. He has been a Research Associate of the NBER since 1974; the Founding Editor of the *Journal of Labor Economics* from 1982 to 2001; Founder of the Society of Labor Economists in 1996 and its president in 1997–98; an elected Fellow of the American Academy of Arts and Science in 2000 as well as the Econometric Society in 1988; a member of the Board on Testing and Assessment of the National Academy of Sciences in 2001; a Research Fellow of the Institute for the Study of Labor (IZA) in Bonn since 2002, of the Centre for Economic Policy Research in London since 2004, and of the Centre for Corporate Performance in Denmark since 2004; member of the Research Board of the American Compensation Association 1996–99 and Chairman of its Academic Research Committee, 1999–2002; and a Member of the President's Panel on Federal Tax Reform in 2005.

Lazear has been a visiting professor and keynote speaker at universities and institutes throughout the world. At Stanford he has received numerous awards: Distinguished Teaching Award in 1994; Michael and Monica Spence Faculty Fellow 2000; and the Distinguished Service Award in 2000. He received the Leo Melamed Prize for Outstanding Research in 1998 and the Adam Smith Prize in 2003 from the European Association of Labor Economists, and the 2004 Prize in Labor Economics from IZA. Clearly, he not only writes about tournaments and contests, but he wins them.

Lazear excels in relating theory to practice as evidenced by his being an advisor to numerous presidents and governments: President Edvard Shevardnadze of the Republic of Georgia in 1994; the Supreme Economic Council of the Russian Republic from 1991 to 1993; the Prime Minister of Ukraine in 1993; the Vice Prime Minister of Romania in 1992; and the Ministry of Privatization in Czechoslovakia in 1991. Closer to home, and as a crowning achievement, he was the Chairman of the President's Council of Economic Advisors from 2006 to 2009. He is clearly on pace for winning another tournament: 'Most Air Miles Accumulated by an Academic'.

In between receiving his awards and advising throughout the world, Lazear managed to write numerous books and more than 100 articles in top journals. A sampling illustrates the range of topics: entrepreneurship (2005); promotions and the Peter Principle (2004b); the importance of the external labor market in wage setting within the internal labor markets of firms (Lazear and Oyer 2004); educational production (2001); performance pay and productivity (2000b); economic imperialism (2000a); variable pay, incentives and sorting (2000c); culture and language (1999a); incentives in basic research (1997); bait and switch tactics (1995a); peer pressure and partnerships (Kandel and Lazear 1992); labor economics and the psychology of organizations (1991); job security and employment (1990a); pay equality and industrial politics (1989); retail pricing and clearance sales (1986b); hours restrictions and productivity (1981); tournaments as optimum labor contracts (Lazear and Rosen 1981); and mandatory retirement (1979). While the topics are diverse, the methodology is in the best of the Chicago tradition: the insightful application of economic theory to explain behavioral phenomena and institutional arrangements and to understand their implications and (often) unintended consequences.

Most importantly, Lazear is regarded as the founder of the emerging field of the new economics of personnel. That field applies basic principles of economics to a variety of issues that were formerly dealt with in a more descriptive, institutional way in the areas of personnel and human resource management within the internal labor 'market' of firms. In the earlier literature, the emphasis was on internal rules, administrative procedures, custom, norms and tradition, idiosyncratic practices, or even irrational acts. Personnel economics, in contrast, seeks to explain such rules, regulations and practices as rational responses by the labor market actors to constraints such as asymmetric information, monitoring costs, incentive problems and difficulties in measuring output and performance. A *causal* understanding of such personnel practices facilitates understanding not only why they arise, but also how they are likely to change in the future when the causal determinants change, and how they may be affected by public policies or legislative initiatives (often with unintended consequences). Lazear's insights and contributions can be highlighted by some examples from his extensive publications.

Lazear (2004a, 2005) outlined a theory of entrepreneurship, deriving (and empirically confirming) the implication that entrepreneurs will tend to be jacks-of-all-trades with competency in a range of skills rather than masters of one.

After outlining the incentive effects of piecerate systems, Lazear (2000b) provided evidence indicating that a shift from hourly pay to piecerates increased productivity by about 44 percent. About half of the increase came from an increase in productivity per worker and half from the sorting effect, as high-ability workers remained with the firm while low-ability workers left.

Lazear (1990a) argued that expected termination costs (including legislative ones) can be anticipated by employers and hence factored in as quasi-fixed costs in their hiring decision. While protecting incumbent employees, such costs can deter the hiring of new employees, especially youths. His theoretical and empirical work in this area has spawned a wealth of studies indicating that such legislated termination costs reduce employment and foster the growth of non-standard employment, especially in Europe where termination costs are prominent.

Lazear (1979) highlighted that, at first glance, mandatory retirement appears to be an inefficient work rule or age discrimination. However, it may actually be an efficient rule in that it facilitates deferred compensation by providing a termination date to the 'overpayment' period, enabling the equilibrium condition whereby the present value of expected wages equal expected productivity over the contract period. Deferred compensation, in turn, can serve numerous positive purposes, such as deterring shirking. Pension benefit accruals can also be part of deferred compensation, embodying important incentive effects that can be used as a strategic tool by employers to encourage early retirement and discourage delayed retirement. This is especially the case when pensions are modeled as option values in that working an additional year preserves the option of further working additional years and being eligible for early retirement buyouts (1983, 1990b, Lazear and Moore 1988).

Lazear and Rosen (1981) analyzed executive compensation as a tournament prize in situations where it is difficult to judge the absolute performance of an individual, but it is feasible to rank the contestants and give the super-prize to the winner. Such a prize creates positive incentives for the holder of the prize to perform diligently to sustain the prize (for example, not be subject to a hostile take-over, or displaced by a decision of the board of directors) and it creates strong incentive effects for all vice presidents and even aspiring vice presidents to perform so as to be viable contestants for the prize.

Lazear (1989) argued that the optimal degree of pay inequality depends upon the type of behavior the firm wants to encourage and the ability to monitor performance. A more compressed, egalitarian pay structure may be merited if it is difficult to disentangle the individual's performance from that of the team, if the team members affect each other's performance in ways that are difficult to measure and reward, if team effort is important, and if risk-taking behavior is not important. Egalitarian pay structures that are based on the performance of the team, however, suffer from the problem that individual effort to the team yields a return of only $1/N$ so that peer pressure and peer rewards may be necessary to influence behavior (Kandel and Lazear 1992).

Lazear (1986a) analyzed the phenomenon of the winner's curse when applied to the raiding of personnel from other organizations. In a world of asymmetric information, the organization that was raided presumably had better 'inside' information on the employee and yet did not match the outside offer. As such, the raiding organization may be subject to the 'winner's curse' – successful in the raid only when they made a mistake in evaluating the employee, unless of course the individual were a better match for the raiding organization.

Personnel economics as developed by Lazear focuses on the *quality* dimension and the intensive *effort* margins associated with work. It also has a normative, prescriptive and practical bent. In the Chicago tradition, it relies on notions of efficiency and equilibrium whereby personnel practices are designed to exhaust any arbitrage opportunities or 'gains from trade'. Personnel practices that at first glance appear anomalous and even inefficient have survival value in competitive markets because they may well serve positive functions in terms of creating incentives that are in the joint interests of the parties.

In his presidential address to the Society of Labor Economists, Lazear (1999b, p. 201) argued that personnel economics 'is a field that is wide open to discovery'. He has endeavoured to open those doors by bringing the theoretical framework together in the prestigious Wicksell lectures. They resulted in the publication of his book *Personnel Economics* (1995b), which won the MIT Press Outstanding Book Award in 1996 and the Princeton award for one of the ten most important books in labor economics in 1996. That book, in turn, laid the more formal foundations for his textbook *Personnel Economics for Managers* (1998). The arrival of personnel economics as a discipline is evidenced in various ways: the subject matter of a special issue of the *Journal of Labor Economics* in October 1987; its content being summarized in journal syntheses and handbooks – Gibbons (1998), Gibbons and Waldman (1999), Malcomson (1999), Prendergast (1999); its incorporation into advanced-level economics textbooks (Milgrom and Roberts 1992, Part V); its being recognized as one of the three streams of labor economics in the Social Sciences Research Network; and the ultimate accolade: a summer camp. The first summer camp was at Stanford in 1998. A recent one was held in Styer, Austria in 2003, highlighting that Lazear has not only a superb production function, but also excellent tastes.

Lazear lives life to the fullest not only in his academic and policy pursuits, but also in his choice of activities – mogul skiing, wind surfing and motorcycle riding. He clearly operates on (and sometimes beyond) the production possibility frontier in all areas. His legacy will emanate not only from his individual contributions to academic scholarship in a range of areas, but also his bringing together his own work and that of others into the exciting new field of personnel economics. As well, he has synthesized that work into a scholarly book as well as a textbook, and bridged the gap between academic research and policy advising. In any tournament in this area, he is the clear winner.

References

Gibbons, R. (1998), 'Incentives in organizations', *Journal of Economic Perspectives*, **12** (4), 115–32.

Gibbons, R. and M. Waldman (1999), 'Careers in organizations: theory and evidence', in *Handbook of Labor Economics*, vol. 3B, Ashenfelter, O. and D. Card (eds), New York: North-Holland, pp. 2373–437.

Kandel, E. and E.P. Lazear (1992), 'Peer pressure and partnerships', *Journal of Political Economy*, **100** (4), 801–17.

Lazear, E.P. (1979), 'Why is there mandatory retirement?', *Journal of Political Economy*, **87** (6), 1261–84.

Lazear, E.P. (1981), 'Agency, earnings profiles, productivity and hours restrictions', *American Economic Review*, **71** (4), 606–20.

Lazear, E.P. (1983), 'Pensions as severance pay', in *Financial Aspects of the United States Pension System*, Bodie, Z. and J.B. Shoven (eds), Chicago, IL: University of Chicago Press, pp. 57–85.

Lazear, E.P. (1986a), 'Raids and offer-matching', *Research in Labor Economics*, **8**-A, 141–65.

Lazear, E.P. (1986b), 'Retail pricing and clearance sales', *American Economic Review*, **76** (1), 14–32.

Lazear, E.P. (1989), 'Pay equality and industrial politics', *Journal of Political Economy*, **97** (3), 561–80.

Lazear, E.P. (1990a), 'Job security provisions and employment', *Quarterly Journal of Economics*, **105** (3), 699–726.

Lazear, E.P. (1990b), 'Pensions and deferred benefits as strategic compensation', *Industrial Relations*, **28** (2), 263–80.

Lazear, E.P. (1991), 'Labor economics and the psychology of organizations', *Journal of Economic Perspectives*, **5** (2), 89–110.

Lazear, E.P. (1995a), 'Bait and switch', *Journal of Political Economy*, **103** (4), 813–30.

Lazear, E.P. (1995b), *Personnel Economics*, Cambridge, MA: MIT Press.

Lazear, E.P. (1997), 'Incentives in basic research', *Journal of Labor Economics*, **15** (1, part 2), S167–97.

Lazear, E.P. (1998), *Personnel Economics for Managers*, New York: Wiley.

Lazear, E. P. (1999a), 'Culture and language', *Journal of Political Economy*, **107** (6, part 2), S95–26.

Lazear, E.P. (1999b), 'Personnel economics: past lessons and future directions', *Journal of Labor Economics*, **17** (2), 199–236.

Lazear, E.P. (2000a), 'Economic imperialism', *Quarterly Journal of Economics*, **115** (1), 99–146.

Lazear, E.P. (2000b), 'Performance pay and productivity', *American Economic Review*, **90** (5), 1346–61.

Lazear, E.P. (2000c), 'The power of incentives', *American Economic Review*, **90** (2), 410–14.

Lazear, E.P. (2001), 'Educational production', *Quarterly Journal of Economics*, **116** (3), 777–803.

Lazear, E.P. (2004a), 'Balanced skills and entrepreneurship', *American Economic Review*, **94** (2), 208–11.

Lazear, E.P. (2004b), 'The Peter Principle: a theory of decline', *Journal of Political Economy*, **112** (1, part 2), S141–63.
Lazear, E.P. (2005), 'Entrepreneurship', *Journal of Labor Economics*, **23** (4), 649–80.
Lazear, E.P. and R.L. Moore (1988), 'Pensions and turnover', in *Pensions in the U.S. Economy*, Bodie, Z., J.B. Shoven and D.A. Wise (eds), National Bureau of Economic Research Project Report, Chicago, IL: University of Chicago Press, pp. 163–88.
Lazear, E.P. and P. Oyer (2004), 'The structure of wages and internal mobility', *American Economic Review*, **94** (2), 212–16.
Lazear, E.P. and S. Rosen (1981), 'Rank-order tournaments as optimal labor contracts', *Journal of Political Economy*, **89** (5), 841–64.
Malcomson, J.M. (1999), 'Individual employment contracts in labor markets', in *Handbook of Labor Economics*, vol. 3B, Ashenfelter, O. and D. Card (eds), New York: North-Holland, pp. 2291–372.
Milgrom, P. and J. Roberts (1992), *Economics, Organisations, and Management*, Englewood Cliffs, NJ: Prentice-Hall.
Prendergast, C. (1999), 'The provision of incentives in firms', *Journal of Economic Literature*, **37** (1), 1–63.

24 H. Gregg Lewis

Jeff E. Biddle

Harold Gregg Lewis (1914–92) was born in Homer, Michigan. He received both his AB and PhD degrees in economics from the University of Chicago, the former in 1936 and the latter in 1947. Lewis's abilities as an economist were recognized while he was an undergraduate, as he was permitted (along with Paul Samuelson and Herbert Simon) to enroll in graduate courses. Later in life, he mentioned Jacob Viner, Frank Knight, and Henry Simons as influential teachers. As a graduate student he served as a research assistant to both Henry Schultz and Paul Douglas, and worked with T.O. Yntema doing statistical research for US Steel.[1]

Lewis joined the Chicago faculty in 1939. The death of Henry Schultz in the previous year had left several departmental courses without a teacher, including advanced statistics. The department was divided over the question of a successor to Schultz, and Lewis, who had distinguished himself in Yntema's statistics class and in his work for Schultz, emerged as a compromise candidate who could satisfy both Paul Douglas and Henry Simons. He remained on the faculty for over 35 years, retiring in 1975 to accept a position at Duke University.

As Bruce Kaufman notes in his contribution to this volume (ch. 9), Lewis was one of the pioneers in the movement that reoriented the field of labor economics in the last third of the twentieth century. At the time Lewis was starting his career, 'labor economics' involved the study of a wide range of topics including wage and employment determination, but also the causes and consequences of low living standards of workers, the structure and behavior of labor unions, strategies for managing non-union employees, and the proximate and ultimate causes of worker discontent and strikes. Historical and institutional surveys or case studies and tabulations of data from questionnaires or government wage and employment statistics gave the field an empirical base, and this empirical material was interpreted using an eclectic mix of theoretical concepts and frameworks borrowed or adapted from those used in other social sciences. Few labor specialists believed that Marshallian or marginalist approaches to analyzing individual choice and market equilibrium could provide much insight into important theoretical questions and policy issues concerning labor.

Mathematical models of marginalist economics, however, provided the starting point for all Lewis's research. He began by conceptualizing a research problem in terms of such a model, then analyzed successively complex versions of his model with meticulous thoroughness. This theorizing was almost always designed to inform some proposed or actual empirical analysis, the goal of which was to measure, through the application of appropriate statistical techniques, the real-world manifestations of key relationships and parameters identified in the theoretical model. In this Lewis was following Henry Schultz, whose own research program (with which Lewis had assisted as a student) involved statistical estimation of the supply and demand elasticities of Walrasian models of multi-market equilibrium.

Lewis was also, like Schultz, a careful statistician. He was a capable user of multiple regression analysis at a time when few economists understood the technique (Biddle 1999). He was attentive to issues of data quality, such as whether the data satisfied the statistical conditions necessary for regression analysis to produce reliable estimates, and the extent to which a particular dataset could produce estimates that could be generalized to times or places other than those in which the data were collected. Possible shortcomings of the data or estimates were frankly discussed. Colleagues characterized Lewis's empirical work as 'craftsmanlike' (Freeman 1994).

Lewis did no research on labor topics prior to 1950; after 1950 almost all of his own work and most of the doctoral dissertations that he supervised dealt with topics today considered part of labor economics. There is reason to believe that this change is related to Lewis's relationship with Henry Simons. The two men's research styles could not have been more different: Simons was a polemicist, using verbal and sometimes loose neoclassical reasoning to develop and defend a broad libertarian policy agenda, while Lewis, following Yntema, pursued the ideal of the objective scientist, using precise mathematical and statistical techniques to attack narrowly defined questions of theory and estimation. However, in the years after Lewis joined the Chicago faculty, the two became close friends, and Lewis was very much affected when Simons took his own life in 1946. Lewis's work on labor unions probably grew out of a desire to carry on some of Simons's work in his own research. Lewis's first article on a labor topic, published in 1951, was entitled 'The labor-monopoly problem: a positive program' (Lewis 1951). With a title that echoed Simons's book *A Positive Program for Laissez-faire* (Simons 1934), the article had the stated purpose of filling a gap in that book, which had extensively described the problem of 'monopoly unionism', but had offered no policy to address it.

The article proved to be Lewis's only exercise in explicit policy advocacy, but also the beginning of a program of research into unionism that would occupy him for the rest of his life. For underlying Simons's lengthy indictment of labor unions was a question of positive economics: how much monopoly power do labor unions really have? And this question, Lewis realized, could be framed in terms of a neoclassical model of labor markets, and explored with econometrics. As he noted in a 1959 lecture:

> Many of the differences among economists in the positions they hold regarding public policy towards trade unions, as well as their assessments of the importance of unionism as a labor market factor, stem from disagreement on the answer to this question: What is the impact of unionism on relative real wages? If we knew the answer to this question, we would surely know much about the extent to which unionism is monopolistic, the conditions that strengthen or weaken monopoly unionism, and the consequences of unionism for the distribution of wage and salary income and for the allocation of labor and other resources among uses. (Lewis 1959, p. 181)

In the late 1940s and early 1950s, Lewis helped to direct several PhD theses investigating the impact of unions on wages in various labor markets. In 1956 he received funding from the American Enterprise Association for research on 'the relative wage effects of unions', a project in which he would synthesize and reconcile the results of these and other studies of the impact of unionism on wages and generate a nationwide estimate based on times series he constructed of average wages and the nationwide extent of unionism. The result was his best-known book, *Unionism and Relative Wages in the United States*

(Lewis 1963). His survey of the several studies, which often involved reworking the original authors' data and re-estimating their regressions, concluded that the pay gap between union workers and similar non-union workers was seldom more than 25 percent and often less than 5 percent, that it rose with deflation and fell with inflation, and that it averaged between 10 and 15 percent over the economy as a whole. As more data and richer datasets containing workers' wages and union affiliation became available to labor economists in the two decades following the publication of Lewis's book, the question of the impact of unions on labor markets, as framed by Lewis, was the subject of over 100 additional studies. In a second book published in 1986, Lewis reviewed and synthesized these studies as well (Lewis 1986).

As Reder (1982, p. 29) has noted, the work of Lewis and his students on the impact of unionism on wages, starting in the 1950s, was part of a shift in Chicago labor economics 'from normative condemnation to positive analysis' of labor unions. The touchstone of the research was not a view of unions as inimical to economic liberty and prosperity, but a model of the labor market in which unions appeared as a 'tax-like distortion'.[2] This model allowed the possibility that unions had many of the deleterious effects identified by Simons, but did not ensure it. Thus Lewis could conclude, without contradicting his neoclassical model, that concentration in the product market did not lead to concentration in the labor market, that unionism did not imply an absence of labor market competition and that any impact of unionism on wage inequality was likely to be small. At the same time, Lewis's influential strategy of exploring the economic impact of unionism exclusively within the confines of a neoclassical model precluded analysis of many aspects of union activity that had been research topics of the previous generation of labor specialists, such as the impact of unions on worker morale or managerial behavior.

Most of Lewis's relatively short record of published research after 1950 is related to his research program on the effect of unions on labor markets; an exception that bears mention is his 1956 article 'Hours of work and hours of leisure' (1956). In this paper, Lewis used a neoclassical model of the consumer's demand for leisure as a vehicle for understanding the secular decline in the average work week and other empirical patterns found in the time series describing hours worked by laborers. This model, although known to the profession in one form or another since the work of William S. Jevons in the 1870s, had not been taken seriously by most labor economists as a framework for understanding time-series or cross-sectional variation in average hours of work, under the assumption that it abstracted away from the institutional features of employer/employee relationships that played a crucial role in determining how many hours a laborer worked. Lewis applied the model unapologetically, however, in what turned out to be an early example of the methodological approach later made explicit by Stigler and Becker (1977): that of attempting to explain as wide a range of empirical phenomena as possible in terms of a model in which agents with stable preferences respond to changes in prices and incomes, properly defined. It was also the precursor of, if not the exemplar for, a large body of empirical research aimed at estimating the 'labor supply elasticities' implied by the neoclassical model of the demand for leisure, a research program which grew rapidly starting in the 1960s with the multiplication of large datasets recording the labor market experiences of individual workers.

All who have written about Lewis's career agree that he exerted his greatest influence on labor economics as a mentor and teacher of graduate students at the University of Chicago, an aspect of his career that is discussed in more detail by Rees (1976). In 1945 Lewis was appointed 'departmental counselor', with administrative responsibility for both undergraduate and graduate students and programs. In 1964 his position was upgraded to 'Director of the Graduate Program', and he held this position until his retirement in 1975. In this capacity, his office hours were 9 to 5, five days a week. Lewis served on the supervisory committee of over 70 successful doctoral candidates and was the chair of about a third of these committees. The list of students he advised in this capacity is peppered with the names of those who would become the prominent economists of the next generation, both in labor economics (Gary Becker, Albert Rees, Sherwin Rosen, Finis Welch) and other fields (Don Patinkin, Robert Lucas, Claudia Goldin, Zvi Griliches). When Lewis announced his retirement, George Stigler wrote to Lewis that 'the Chicago miracle of turning out innumerable well trained economists' was due to him more than any other person (George J. Stigler to H. Gregg Lewis, 3 January 1975, H. Gregg Lewis Papers, Box 10).[3]

Lewis's best-known student is Gary Becker, who completed his doctoral dissertation under Lewis's supervision in 1955. The subject of the dissertation was discrimination, particularly the economic consequences of discrimination in labor markets, and Becker's innovation was to take a phenomenon that had previously been regarded as a topic to be studied by sociologists and psychologists and explore it within the context of neoclassical models of individual optimization and market equilibrium. The thesis was published in 1957 under the title *The Economics of Discrimination* (Becker 1957), and in the 'acknowledgements' section Becker wrote that Lewis 'influenced every page' of the work. Becker and Lewis remained close, and in 1973 co-authored a paper 'On the interaction between the quantity and quality of children' (Becker and Lewis 1973) an early contribution to Becker's 'Economics of the family' research program, in which neoclassical models were used to analyze phenomena such as marriage and fertility decisions.

In the late 1960s, Lewis wrote a manuscript entitled 'Employer interests in employee hours of work' (Lewis 1969). The manuscript, which was eventually published in a Spanish language journal, outlined a model of competitive labor market equilibrium in which, because of heterogeneous tastes among workers and heterogeneous cost conditions across firms, workers could choose among jobs offering different combinations of hourly wages and weekly hours of work. In the early 1970s, Sherwin Rosen, a former Lewis student, generalized this approach to modeling markets in an extremely influential paper entitled 'Hedonic prices and implicit markets: product differentiation in pure competition' (Rosen 1974). Rosen cites the Spanish version of the Lewis manuscript, and in the acknowledgment footnote of the paper comments that 'The substance of this paper arose from conversations with H. Gregg Lewis several years ago'. In addition, the Lewis papers contain long letters between the two men on the theoretical issues later treated in Rosen's paper.[4]

Beyond these two examples of Lewis's indirect influence on economics via his students, one can point to the fact that work in the field of labor economics today typically bears a much closer resemblance to the work Lewis was doing in the 1950s than to what the institutionalist labor economists of the time were doing. Rees (1976, pp. S3–S4) claimed that 'No one can rival Lewis in being responsible' for the transformation of labor economics in the 1960s and 1970s. This is probably an overstatement, but considering the large number of Lewis's students whose names appear as authors of important journal articles on labor topics during that period, and as faculty members in PhD-granting Economics Departments training a subsequent generation of labor economists, it appears to be based on an important reality.

Notes

1. See Biddle (1996) for complete biographical information.
2. The statement comparing a union to a tax-like distortion in the labor market was made during a lecture to a graduate class attended by the author in 1983.
3. A list of the Chicago PhD dissertations for which Lewis served as a member of the faculty guidance committee can be found in Becker (1976).
4. It is difficult to exaggerate the impact of this paper on applied microeconomics; as of December 2006, Google Scholar reported that it had been cited over 900 times.

References

H. Gregg Lewis Papers, 1939–1990, Rare Book, Manuscript and Special Collections Library, Duke University Durham, North Carolina.

Becker, G.S. (1957), *The Economics of Discrimination*, Chicago, IL: University of Chicago Press.
Becker, G.S. (1976), 'Dissertations', *Journal of Political Economy*, **84** (4, part 2: Essays in labor economics in honor of H. Gregg Lewis), S249–54.
Becker, G.S. and H.G. Lewis (1973), 'On the interaction between the quantity and quality of children', *Journal of Political Economy*, **82** (2, part 2), S279–88.
Biddle, J.E. (1996), 'H. Gregg Lewis', in *American Economists of the Late 20th Century*, Samuels, W.J. (ed.), Cheltenham, UK and Brookfield, VT, USA: Edward Elgar, pp. 174–93.
Biddle, J.E. (1999), 'Statistical economics, 1900–1950', *History of Political Economy*, **31** (4), 607–51.
Freeman, R. (1994), 'H.G. Lewis and the study of union wage effects', *Journal of Labor Economics*, **12** (1), 143–9.
Lewis, H.G. (1951), 'The labor-monopoly problem: a positive program', *Journal of Political Economy*, **59** (4), 277–87.
Lewis, H.G. (1956), 'Hours of work and hours of leisure', in *Proceedings of the Ninth Annual Meetings*, Champaign, IL: Industrial Relations Research Association, pp. 196–206.
Lewis, H.G. (1959), 'Competitive and monopoly unionism', in *The Public Stake in Union Power*, Bradley, P. (ed.), Charlottesville, VA: University of Virginia Press, pp. 181–208.
Lewis, H.G. (1963), *Unionism and Relative Wages in the United States: An Empirical Inquiry*, Chicago, IL: University of Chicago Press.
Lewis, H.G. (1969), 'Interes del Empleador en las Horas de Trabajo del Empleado' (Employer interests in employee hours of work), *Cuadernos de Economia*, **18**, 38–54.
Lewis, H.G. (1986), *Union Relative Wage Effects: A Survey*, Chicago, IL: University of Chicago Press.
Reder, M.W. (1982), 'Chicago economics: permanence and change', *Journal of Economic Literature*, **20** (1), 1–38.
Rees, A. (1976), 'H. Gregg Lewis and the development of analytical labor economics', *Journal of Political Economy*, **84** (4, part 2: Essays in labor economics in honor of H. Gregg Lewis), S3–8.
Rosen, S. (1974), 'Hedonic prices and implicit markets: product differentiation in pure competition', *Journal of Political Economy*, **82** (1), 34–55.
Simons, H.C. (1934), *A Positive Program for Laissez Faire: Some Proposals for a Liberal Economic Policy*, Chicago, IL: University of Chicago Press.
Stigler, G.J. and G.S. Becker (1977), 'De gustibus non est disputandum', *American Economic Review*, **67** (2), 76–90.

25 Deirdre N. McCloskey

Stephen T. Ziliak

'I try to show that you don't have to be a barbarian to be a Chicago School economist.' That, in her own words, is Deirdre McCloskey's main – though she thinks 'failed' – contribution to Chicago School economics (McCloskey 2002).

Donald Nansen McCloskey (1942–) was born in Ann Arbor, Michigan and raised in Cambridge, Massachusetts. Donald changed gender in 1995, from male to female, becoming Deirdre (McCloskey 1999). She is the oldest of three children born to Helen Stueland McCloskey and the late Robert G. McCloskey. Her father, whose life was cut short by a heart attack, was in Deirdre's youth a tenured professor of government at Harvard University. He was fluent in the humanities as much as in law and social science; Joseph Schumpeter and the writer W.H. Auden were his personal friends and coffee break mates. Helen's passion was in poetry and opera. She did not deny the children the values and joys of intellectual and artistic life pursuits – 'burn always with a gem-like flame', she told Deirdre and the others. (Books were all over the McCloskey household: each child was supplied with a personal library.) Cambridge and family conspired to make Deirdre into a professor by, Deirdre figures, 'about age five' (McCloskey 2002). She read widely, but especially in history and literature. Yet like most professors, she stumbled in her early years. At age 10, for example, she understood that her father was the author of a fine new book but she was not sure if his book was *Make Way for Ducklings* or *Blueberries for Sal*; actually, the book was *American Conservatism in the Age of Enterprise*, by the *other* Robert McCloskey (1951).

In 1964 McCloskey earned a BA in economics from Harvard College; in 1970 she was awarded a PhD in economics from Harvard University. She was attracted to the engineering-style of inquiry she detected in the economics of John R. Meyer. If Chicago economist Frank Knight wanted mainly to know how idealized economies functioned in theory, then McCloskey wanted mainly to know how actual economies fit together, that is, by what magnitudes, in the real world. She apprenticed herself to Meyer, who was an assistant professor, and became his research assistant. Meyer was primarily a transportation economist and McCloskey first worked with his team of engineers and economists on a simulation of the Columbian transport system. Meyer then asked McCloskey to help him assemble some papers in economic history for his forthcoming book with A.H. Conrad, *The Economics of Slavery, and Other Studies in Econometric History* (Conrad and Meyer 1964). That experience proved to be fruitful – in fact, fateful. McCloskey was by temperament an analytic historian (a trait that had helped her to duck the campus Trotskyites she sympathized with). In the positivist era of economics the methodology of history seemed to McCloskey (1989) too soft, even meaningless. But in Meyer's seminal work on the economics of slavery she realized – still thinking like a positivist – that she could write history while being scientific. Soon thereafter she met Alexander Gerschenkron, the great economic historian and polyglot scholar, who at Harvard was helping to create, through his students, 'cliometrics' – the new economic history – quantitative, theoretical, humanistic and historical, all at once, the cliometrician promised. She took a course in economic history offered by Peter Temin at MIT, joined Gerschenkron's Economic History Workshop, and the second die was cast. Gerschenkron became her dissertation advisor (it would be fatuous to say that he *supervised* the dissertation) and a durable model for McCloskey's scholarly life (see McCloskey 1992, Dawidoff 2002).

McCloskey's attractions to Gerschenkron were many. Put simply, she was attracted to his example of the belief that knowledge is One. Gerschenkron – exiled from Bolshevik Odessa and Nazi Vienna – was foremost an expert on Russian and European economic history. Yet he had published technical papers on the index number problem, publicly shamed Nabokov's translation of Pushkin's *Eugene Onegin*, allegedly advised Ted Williams on baseball, built ships for the American war effort and could read in 20 different languages. 'Like Gerschenkron', McCloskey (2002) said, 'like my father, I see knowledge as One Thing'. To McCloskey theirs is not a transcendental idea. It is the pluralistic idea that if you are going to claim to know something you are obliged to examine all the ways of knowing it – in theory, mathematics, sciences, criticism, literature, art, poetry, statistics, history, language, philosophy, rhetoric and, no less importantly, through personal experience. It was of course the road less traveled. Testing hypotheses is what the herd did. 'But like Gerschenkron', she said, 'I wanted to be an economist [and econometrician] who knew and quoted Shakespeare effortlessly'. Her dissertation, 'Economic maturity and entrepreneurial decline: British iron and steel, 1870–1913', was not yet that, but it was awarded the David A. Wells Prize for best dissertation at Harvard (Robert Solow had won the prize years before) in 1970 and was published by Harvard University Press (McCloskey 1973).

McCloskey's work on iron and steel was strong enough to land a tenure-track job at the University of Chicago, in 1968. The work and its author survived the job interview, a grueling oral exam, really, which consisted of giving a lecture on iron and steel without melting in front of Milton Friedman, George Stigler, Robert Fogel and others. She had been persuaded by Chicago-style price theory – freed finally of Trotsky – as a student back in Peter Temin's seminar. But she became an economist during her tenure as a faculty member at the University of Chicago, 1968 to 1980. At 'The Quadrangle' the ritual of eating lunch supplied a regular excuse to theorize the world of price with Friedman, Stigler, Becker, Robert Gordon, Zvi Griliches, Steven Cheung and J. Richard Zecher (a student of Karl Brunner). In the Business School cafeteria she improved in econometric method and refined her financial mind with Henri Theil, Eugene Fama, Myron Scholes and Merton Miller. And most significantly, in Fogel's Workshop she applied statistics, price theory and Gerschenkronianism to the large questions of economic history. There, with the constant criticism of Fogel and of graduate students such as Claudia Goldin, Michael Mussa and Joseph Reid, she began to rewrite the economic history of Britain.

By the mid-1970s McCloskey had published articles establishing her as the leading quantitative historian of Britain. 'Did Victorian Britain fail?' (McCloskey 1970 [2001]) looked seriously at the idea that British businessmen had failed at home – had missed plump opportunities for a larger output. 'Statistical economists and literary historians, Englishmen and foreigners, late Victorians and moderns have accepted some version of it', she said (ibid., p. 3). Yet McCloskey supplied in a spare prose and muscular simulation the evidence that resources available to businessmen were not elastic in supply and that 'reallocation of them (capital abroad, for example) would have brought little or no additional growth' (ibid., p. 16). The article – an early piece of supply-side economics – had put the burden of alternative hypotheses to the test of economic significance, resulting in a cool dismissal of J.M. Keynes and David Landes. Victorian Britain did not fail.

But 'English open fields as behavior towards risk' (McCloskey 1976 [2001]) is probably the finest example of an economics that examines 'all the evidence'. The economic point was believable (though social and legal historians had scoffed at it): in twelfth- and thirteenth-century England, she argued, scattering one's plots of land was rational insurance against human or natural disaster. Yet the richness of the historical defense, its range and gravity of evidence, its graceful perspectivalism, the apt simulations and a steady rain of modern and medieval imagery had given the paper its distinction. The work on open fields was not her final contribution to empirical economics. Her study with J. Richard Zecher on the gold standard, using the monetary approach to the balance of payments, was seminal (McCloskey and Zecher 1976 [2001]). But 'English open fields' had secured McCloskey's reputation as a premier economist and historian, the learned one who, like Gerschenkron, was easy to read, difficult to imitate, and costly to refute.

McCloskey admires what she calls 'The Good Old Chicago School': that of Frank H. Knight, Theodore W. Schultz, Ronald H. Coase and Margaret Reid. She considers herself to be a member of the 'second wave' of The Good Old Chicago School (a long wave, in her reckoning, from Friedman to Griliches). A significant source of her influence on others sprang from her style of teaching in the second wave. She was the Director of Graduate Studies in Economics from 1976 to 1980 (in fact, the current description of the PhD program was written mostly by McCloskey in the late 1970s). From 1969 to 1979 she taught the course in price theory that was designed for first-year graduate students (ECON 300). The course was open to students from any discipline, and grew at peak enrollment to 120. Still, about three-fourths of all the regularly enrolled students in the Economics PhD program took her course. Her project was 'to deVarianize economic education'. She held in highest esteem George Stigler's *The Theory of Price* (Stigler 1966) but believed that Stigler's book could be improved upon. McCloskey wanted to show that price theory works in the real world, that it stands up to history and criticism, and illustrated how in *The Applied Theory of Price* (McCloskey 1985).

McCloskey could not be one of Friedman's groupies but neither could she stand to be a maverick or random Patinkin, shoved aside. She likes to be in the thick of things and yet she carries few banners besides the one that demands excellence in scholarship. These characteristics bubbled up to unrest in the late 1970s when she discovered her interest in the rhetoric of economics. Friedman was at the Hoover Institution, Fogel had moved to Harvard, and Stigler, no fan of McCloskey's, was getting the last word on departmental issues. McCloskey was reading philosophy of science again; an interest she developed in graduate school but only casually and up to Karl Popper's *Logic of Scientific Discovery*. She read Michael Polanyi and Paul Feyerabend. And she noticed that Stigler's rhetoric was indefensibly couched in a 1920s positivism applied with a 1950s, McCarthy-like ethic. She began saying so, earning no one's interest. Her friend Wayne Booth, the eminent rhetorician, had invited her to give a talk in the English Department concerning 'the rhetoric of economics'. Though grasping for a language of economic criticism that she would soon master, McCloskey was flummoxed to find that Stigler and Becker,

Chicago's leading economists, had no good arguments for believing what they believed, and lacked the desire to acquire any. In 1980 she resigned and moved to the University of Iowa.

Iowa named McCloskey the John F. Murray Professor of Economics and Professor of History. But her project was to grow in her understanding of the rhetoric of economics, the art of economic persuasion. She spoke less and less about Victorian failure and open fields but talked daily and excitedly about Aristotle, Kenneth Burke, warrants of assent and the tragic tropes of the *t*-test. Her colleagues grew anxious. But by 1982 she had lectured around the world on her new paper, 'The rhetoric of economics', and published it in 1983 in the *Journal of Economic Literature*. An instant *cause célèbre*, 'The rhetoric of economics' was a prelude to her classic book of that name and to six additional books, scores of papers and two book series. *The rhetoric of economics* (McCloskey 1998) is a permanent contribution to Chicago School economics. It changed the conversation of economic methodology and it opened a space for heterodox economics. It shows that best-practice economics is neither positivist nor monist; that Milton Friedman is neither the high priest nor the tiny demon of positivism (and was neither in 1953 when he published the 'Essay'); it shows that poets and economists do not differ in their methodologies; that Marxist professors of English and Chicago professors of economics should read each other's works; and it shows that an improved and pluralistic rhetoric will follow the examples of Ronald Coase and John Ruskin.

Since the early 1990s McCloskey has been concerned with reforming economics. She believes that economics, including Chicago economics, has developed a phony rhetoric of quantification. Half the profession does 'blackboard economics', she says, solving theoretical problems in game theory or in recursive dynamics, yet giving no indication of its relevance to real economies. The produce of blackboard economics, she believes, should fall to its analogous share in physics and chemistry, to less than 10 percent. Significance testing has become the master trope of empirical economics. Yet she shows in many papers and a book with Stephen T. Ziliak that economists – and other scientists – do not know what significance testing is (McCloskey and Ziliak 1996, Ziliak and McCloskey 2004, 2008). Worse, show McCloskey and Ziliak, most economists do not care to measure economic significance, the magnitudes that hold economies together.

Deirdre McCloskey is now the Distinguished Professor of Economics, History and English at the University of Illinois (Chicago). In 2008 she received two honorary doctoral degrees. Recently she held a five year-long visiting position as Tinbergen Distinguished Professor of Economics, Philosophy, Art and Cultural Studies at Erasmus University (Rotterdam). Her recent book *The Bourgeois Virtues* (2006) argues that bourgeois virtues – specifically, free market feminist virtues – are what's lacking in Samuelsonian economics and literature after Marx. Love comes first, she says, then utility. Putting love inside the utility function, as Becker has, creates only an ethical monster, Max U. A contribution to Chicago School economic philosophy, McCloskey's book on the bourgeois virtues will no doubt be judged against Knight's *The Ethics of Competition* (1935).

References

Conrad, A.H. and J.R. Meyer (1964), *The Economics of Slavery, and Other Studies in Econometric History*, Chicago, IL: Aldine.

Dawidoff, N. (2002), *The Fly Swatter: How My Grandfather Made His Way in the World*, New York: Pantheon.
Friedman, M. (1953), 'The methodology of positive economics', in *Essays in Positive Economics*, Chicago: University of Chicago Press, pp. 3–43.
Knight, F.H. (1935), *The Ethics of Competition*, New York: Harper & Bros.
McCloskey, D.N. (1970 [2001]), 'Did Victorian Britain fail?', in *Measurement and Meaning: The Essential Deirdre McCloskey*, Ziliak, S.T. (ed.), Cheltenham, UK and Northampton, MA, USA: Edward Elgar, pp. 3–16.
McCloskey, D.N. (1973), *Economic Maturity and Entrepreneurial Decline: British Iron and Steel, 1870–1913* Cambridge, MA: Harvard University Press.
McCloskey, D.N. (1976 [2001]), 'English open fields as behavior towards risk', in *Measurement and Meaning: The Essential Deirdre McCloskey*, Ziliak, S.T. (ed.), Cheltenham, UK and Northampton, MA, USA: Edward Elgar, pp. 17–63.
McCloskey, D.N. (1985), *The Applied Theory of Price*, 2nd edn, New York: Macmillan.
McCloskey, D.N. (1989), 'Why I am no longer a positivist', *Revew of Social Economy*, **47** (3), 225–38.
McCloskey, D.N. (1992), 'Alexander Gerschenkron: by a student', *American Scholar*, **61** (2), 241–6.
McCloskey, D.N. (1998), *The Rhetoric of Economics*, 2nd rev. edn, Madison, WI: University of Wisconsin Press.
McCloskey, D.N. (1999), *Crossing: A Memoir*, Chicago, IL: University of Chicago Press.
McCloskey, D.N. (2002), Interview with Stephen T. Ziliak, Chicago, August.
McCloskey, D.N. (2006), *The Bourgeois Virtues: Ethics for an Age of Commerce*, Chicago, IL: University of Chicago Press.
McCloskey, D.N. and J.R. Zecher (1976 [2001]), 'How the gold standard worked, 1880–1913', in *Measurement and Meaning: The Essential Deirdre McCloskey*, Ziliak, S.T. (ed.), Cheltenham, UK and Northampton, MA, USA: Edward Elgar, pp. 64–81.
McCloskey, D.N. and S.T. Ziliak (1996), 'The standard error of regressions', *Journal of Economic Literature*, **34** (1), 97–114.
McCloskey, R.G. (1951), *American Conservatism in the Age of Enterprise*, New York: Harper & Row.
Stigler, G.J. (1966), *The Theory of Price*, 3rd edn, New York: Macmillan.
Ziliak, S.T. and D.N. McCloskey (2004), 'Size matters: the standard error of regressions in the *American Economic Review*', *Journal of Socio-economics*, **33** (5), 527–46.
Ziliak, S.T. and D.N. McCloskey (2008), *The Cult of Statistical Significance: How the Standard Error Cost Us Jobs, Justice and Lives*, Ann Arbor, MI: University of Michigan Press.

26 Richard A. Posner

*Steven G. Medema**

Richard A. Posner (1939–) was born on January 11, 1939 in New York City. He received his BA from Yale College (1959) and his LLD from Harvard Law School (1962), where he served as President of the *Law Review*. The period following his graduation was spent in Washington, DC, first clerking for Supreme Court Justice William J. Brennan, Jr. and then working in the Kennedy and Johnson administrations. Posner was appointed Associate Professor of Law at Stanford in 1968 and it was there that he came into contact with Aaron Director, who exposed him to the economic approach to analyzing legal rules. Posner moved on to the University of Chicago law school in 1969. Since 1981, he has served as a Judge of the US Court of Appeals for the Seventh Circuit, including as Chief Judge from 1993 until 2000. During his tenure on the Court, Posner has continued both to teach regularly at Chicago and to publish at a prolific rate.

It would surely not be an overstatement to rank Posner among the foremost legal scholars of the second half of the twentieth century. For if, as both its advocates and critics acknowledge, the law and economics movement ranks as the most significant development in jurisprudential analysis during this period, Posner, as the leading presence in this movement in scholarship and on the bench, deserves much of the credit. His *Economic Analysis of Law*, now in its seventh edition, served both to develop the subject well beyond the classical applications to property, contract, tort and criminal law, and to present the subject matter in a way that facilitated its integration into the Law School curriculum. He has taken on issues as diverse as sex, aging and euthanasia, the AIDS epidemic, law and literature, sexually transmitted diseases, the Clinton impeachment proceedings, the Supreme Court's role in the 2000 Bush–Gore election, the current economic crisis, terrorism and the role of intelligence agencies, cloning, homosexuality, surrogate parenting, religious freedom, plagiarism and adoptions, as well as a vast array of more traditional topics spanning virtually every area of law and jurisprudence – all these analyses being infused, in some cases to a greater extent and in other cases to a lesser extent, with an underlying economic flavor. If Gary Becker opened the floodgates to an economic analysis that touches on all areas of life, it was Posner who took this approach and ran with it to the far corners of the legal arena.

Posner is a legal pragmatist in the tradition of Oliver Wendell Holmes (jurisprudentially) and John Dewey (philosophically), and to attempt to pigeonhole him as, for example, a 'conservative', would be overly simplistic. While Posner is a continual thorn in the side of the left, he can hardly be considered a fellow traveler of the right, as evidenced by his views on issues such as the adoption market, drug legalization and the rule of the law. 'Pragmatic Libertarian' may be an oxymoron, but it is probably as accurate a label as one can put on Posner. His pragmatism – a position to which he has evolved over the last decade or so – is accompanied by a propensity to hammer away at moral philosophy generally and, in particular, to recoil at the idea of a law infused with overarching ethical and moral principles embodied in concepts such as 'justice' and 'fairness'. This position has led him into no small amount of debate with other prominent legal scholars, including Ronald Dworkin and Martha Nussbaum (see Dworkin 1998, 2000, Nussbaum 1998, Posner 1998b, 1998c).[1]

One of the problems with analyzing Posner's scholarship is the tendency to look at the extremes rather than the mean. Posner has achieved tremendous notoriety for his supposed advocacy of a market for babies, infuriated feminists with his analysis in *Sex and Reason* (1992b), made literary critics apoplectic with the positions invoked in *Law and Literature: A Misunderstood Relation* (1998a) and earned the ire of those PhD-holders who pontificate for the media on all manner of public issues of the day in *Public Intellectuals* (2001d). That Posner enjoys tweaking the establishment, and especially the post-modern elites within academia and without, is unquestionable.[2] It is also not overreaching to suggest that doing so may well have cost him a Supreme Court appointment. But the simple fact of the matter is that Posner's signal contributions are, from this writer's perspective at least, in the more traditional areas of legal analysis: antitrust, property (and especially, of late, intellectual property), torts, contracts, privacy, criminal law, constitutional law, overarching issues in jurisprudence and the analysis of the judicial system.[3]

The success of the modern law and economics movement has hinged crucially on the effectiveness of two streams of argument. The first was the demonstration of how economic analysis can inform legal thinking – in particular, how the assumption of *homo economicus* responding to the incentives created by legal rules assists us in understanding the potential effects of alternative legal rules, and the assessment of these rules and associated outcomes based upon their efficiency properties. Posner's *Economic Analysis of Law* has been instrumental in the development and spread of this line of reasoning. First published in 1973, its pages, like the rings of a tree, mark the development of the field over the past three decades. Weighing in at roughly 170 000 words (400 pages) in its first edition, *Economic Analysis of Law* has grown to 580 000 words (780 pages of much finer print) – a threefold increase over the six subsequent editions.

Economic Analysis of Law uses basic price theory – rational maximization, the law of demand, opportunity costs, and the idea that voluntary exchange allows resources to gravitate toward their highest-valued uses – as the glass through which law is examined. The contents span virtually the entire range of law and, as Posner calls it, 'the legal regulation of non-market behavior' (2007, p. xxi) – property, contracts, torts, family, criminal, antitrust, employment, utility and common carrier regulation, regulation of financial markets, tax, inheritance, procedure, due process, federalism, discrimination, speech, search and seizure, and evidence. What is perhaps most surprising is the enormous percentage of this material already present in the first edition, thereby showing in the days of the field's infancy the tremendous possibilities of the application of economic theory to legal analysis and outlining a framework for a field of analysis that others were only too happy to begin to fill.

The second stream of argument central to the success of the law and economics movement was making the case for 'efficiency as justice', and this was done both historically and philosophically. The historical aspect was accomplished by arguing that common law rules tend to exhibit an underlying economic logic – that is, consciously or not, the decisions reached by judges over time have had a tendency to promote wealth maximization. This idea was first hinted at by Ronald Coase (1960) in 'The problem of social cost' but was more extensively developed by Posner and others in the 1970s and 1980s. Posner's position is that 'The logic of the common law is an economic logic' (Landes and Posner 1987, p. 312), and, in an extensive body of published analysis – particularly *The Economic Structure of Tort Law* (Landes and Posner 1987) – Posner has helped to build the case; in fact, he has been its primary architect. Like most collections of facts, the general sweep of common law case and doctrinal history shows consistency with multiple possible stories; nevertheless, the case made for the efficiency theory is a compelling one, whether the result of a conscious judicial logic or not. Posner has been much more reticent about claims regarding causation. The interest group theory – that inefficient rules will be litigated at a greater rate because of the net losses engendered and will inevitably be overturned – certainly has some plausibility, and Posner has also offered what many would argue are compelling grounds for the idea that judges take efficiency considerations into account. The argument is not that all common law rules are efficient or that the application of rules from common law precedents is always efficient; the point, for Posner, is that 'the law creates incentives for parties to behave efficiently', not that people actually do so (ibid., p. 312).

The philosophical component involved making the case for the use of the efficiency or wealth maximization criterion in legal decision making as against other principles that could inform judicial reasoning. Here, Posner has played a particularly interesting role over time. In *The Economics of Justice* (Posner 1981, pp. 48–115), he both distances wealth maximization from utilitarianism (see also Posner 2001c, pp. 96–8) and attempts to ground an ethical defense of wealth maximization, or efficiency, in the notion of consent, operating via the Pareto criterion. That is, a wealth-maximizing legal change is one where, with appropriate side-payments if necessary, one or more parties are made better off and no one is made worse off. Such a change would command unanimous consent among rational agents. Wealth maximization differs from the Pareto criterion in that it does not preclude losers. But, argues Posner, compensation comes *ex ante* or, at the very least, the wealth-maximizing set of rules is one that would command unanimous consent among rational agents *ex ante*.[4]

Needless to say, the ethical case for efficiency as justice has its controversial, and even problematic, aspects, as pointed out by numerous commentators (see the 'Symposium on efficiency as a legal concern' review 1980). And, in recent years, Posner has moved away from, even rejected, the ethical defense of wealth maximization – practically, because of the questions regarding the relationship between efficiency and the distribution of wealth,[5] and, philosophically, because his pragmatism now causes him to reject the idea of an underlying ethical basis for law. Posner nevertheless finds pragmatic justification for the wealth-maximization criterion on multiple fronts. First, political stability and average income in society tend to be positively correlated; that is, wealth maximization as a legal decision rule will tend to promote political stability (Posner 2001c, pp. 102ff). Beyond this, Posner argues that wealth maximization and the benefit–cost analysis that underlies it are operationally valid, tend to be more immune from political prejudices and pressures than are other decision rules, and can enhance the quality of government decision making (ibid., p. 123).[6] And while Posner no longer attempts to ground wealth maximization ethically in the idea of consent, he does continue to hold the view that a wealth-maximizing rule for common law decision making might command something like unanimous consent *ex ante* if some method existed for voting on the issue. And he continues to insist that efficiency 'is perhaps the most common' meaning of 'justice' (Posner 1992a, p. 27).

That having been said, Posner is not so dogmatic or narrow-minded as to think that economics is the be all and end all of legal thinking: 'an economic theory of law', he says, 'will not capture the full complexity, richness, and confusion of the phenomena . . . that it seeks to illuminate' (ibid., p. 17). Posner is also willing to allow that there is life beyond efficiency: 'there is more to justice than economics, a point the reader should keep in mind in evaluating the normative statements in this book. There may well be definite although wide boundaries on both the explanative and reformative power of economic analysis of law' (ibid., p. 27).[7] But ever the economist, he continues by noting, 'Always, however, economics can provide value clarification by showing the society what it must give up to achieve a noneconomic ideal of justice. The demand for justice is not independent of its price' (ibid., p. 27).

Notes

* The comments of Richard Posner and Warren Samuels on a previous draft of this chapter are gratefully acknowledged.

1. While much of this debate falls into the 'different views of the world' category, 'pragmatism' functions as Posner's moral philosophy just as atheism or agnosticism are, ultimately, 'religions'.
2. His criticisms of academics have led Dworkin (2000), for one, to label Posner 'anti-intellectual'.
3. Apart from his *Economic Analysis of Law* (Posner 2007), see Posner (1990, 2001a, 2001b) and Landes and Posner (1987).
4. The commonality with the Rawlsian veil of ignorance and with James Buchanan's constitutional economics should not be lost on the reader (on the former, see Posner 1981, pp. 99–101).
5. The distributional issues are two: first, wealth-maximization results based on an unjust underlying distribution of income may not themselves have credible claims to being just; second, there are issues regarding willingness/ability to pay and the resulting impact on valuation.
6. The operational validity claim is called into question by the circularity of efficiency-based reasoning – that is, the idea that efficiency is a function of rights, and not the other way around (see Samuels 1981, Veljanovski 1981, Bromley 1990).
7. Posner's pragmatism is as practical as it is philosophical, judging by his work on the bench (see Posner 1984, Samuels and Mercuro 1984, 1986).

References

Bromley, D.W. (1990), 'Ideology of efficiency: searching for a theory of policy', *Journal of Environmental Economics and Management*, **19** (1), 86–107.

Coase, R.H. (1960), 'The problem of social cost', *Journal of Law & Economics*, **3**, 1–44.

Dworkin, R. (1998), 'Darwin's new bulldog', *Harvard Law Review*, **111** (7), 1718–38.

Dworkin, R. (2000), 'Philosophy and Monica Lewinsky', review of *An Affair of State: The Investigation, Impeachment, and Trial of President Clinton* and *The Problematics of Moral and Legal Theory*, *New York Review of Books*, no. 4, 9 March.

Landes, W. and R.A. Posner (1987), *The Economic Structure of Tort Law*, Cambridge, MA: Harvard University Press.

Nussbaum, M.C. (1998), 'Still worthy of praise', *Harvard Law Review*, **111** (7), 1776–95.

Posner, R.A. (1981), *The Economics of Justice*, Cambridge, MA: Harvard University Press.

Posner, R.A. (1984), 'Wealth maximization and judicial decision-making', *International Journal of Law and Economics*, **4** (2), 131–5.

Posner, R.A. (1990), *The Problems of Jurisprudence*, Cambridge, MA: Harvard University Press.

Posner, R.A. (1992a), *Economic Analysis of Law*, 4th edn, Boston, MA: Little, Brown.

Posner, R.A. (1992b), *Sex and Reason*, Cambridge, MA: Harvard University Press.

Posner, R.A. (1998a), *Law and Literature*, rev. and enlarged edn, Cambridge, MA: Harvard University Press.

Posner, R.A. (1998b), 'The problematics of moral and legal theory', *Harvard Law Review*, **111** (7), 1637–717.

Posner, R.A. (1998c), 'Reply to critics of the problematics of moral and legal theory', *Harvard Law Review*, **111** (7), 1796–823.

Posner, R.A. (2001a), *Antitrust Law*, 2nd edn, Chicago, IL: University of Chicago Press.

Posner, R.A. (2001b), *The Economic Structure of Law: The Collected Economic Essays of Richard A. Posner*, 3 vols, Parisi, F. (ed.), Cheltenham, UK and Northampton, MA, USA: Edward Elgar.
Posner, R.A. (2001c), *Frontiers of Legal Theory*, Cambridge, MA: Harvard University Press.
Posner, R.A. (2001d), *Public Intellectuals: A Study of Decline*, Cambridge, MA: Harvard University Press.
Posner, R.A. (2007), *Economic Analysis of Law*, 7th edn, New York: Wolters Kluwer.
Samuels, W.J. (1981), 'Maximization of wealth as justice: an essay on Posnerian law and economics as policy analysis', *Texas Law Review*, **60** (1), 147–72.
Samuels, W.J. and N. Mercuro (1984), 'Posnerian law and economics on the bench', *International Review of Law and Economics*, **4** (2), 107–30.
Samuels, W.J. and N. Mercuro (1986), 'Wealth maximization and judicial decision-making: the issues further clarified', *International Journal of Ethics*, **6** (1), 133–7.
'Symposium on efficiency as a legal concern' (1980), *Hofstra Law Review*, **8** (3).
Veljanovski, C. (1981), 'Wealth maximization, law and ethics: on the limits of economic efficiency', *International Review of Law and Economics*, **1** (1), 5–28.

27 Albert Rees

Orley Ashenfelter and John Pencavel

Albert Rees (1921–92) was born in New York City and earned his BA degree at Oberlin College in 1943. His MA degree at the University of Chicago was followed by his appointment as an assistant professor in the Economics Department at Chicago. His PhD was awarded at Chicago in 1950. He remained at Chicago until 1966 when he assumed a position as Professor of Economics at Princeton University. His Princeton appointment lasted until 1979 (having been Provost between 1975 and 1977). During his tenure at Princeton, he spent several years in Washington, DC, involved in administrative efforts to restrain wage and price inflation. He served as President of the Alfred P. Sloan Foundation from 1979 to 1989.

Rees's scholarship centered on labor economics and his contributions ranged from theoretical modeling to resourceful empirical research to the careful construction of original data. The public policy ramifications of this work were never far from his research. He was a very conscientious and courteous adviser of many students. Teaching was important to him and in the 1970s he authored the major textbook at that time in labor economics (Rees 1973). His gracious manner made him a popular teacher and colleague. He served as editor of the *Journal of Political Economy* for a number of years.

A persistent social issue for Rees – as it was for many economists of his generation – concerned the effects and appropriate public policy role of labor unions. His years as an undergraduate and graduate student were a period when unionism in the United States expanded and became a major policy concern for the country. Unlike some economists, Rees was eager to apply the analytical tools of economics to the study of unionism. No doubt, this suited the climate of the Chicago Economics Department at the time. Perhaps the best example of his readiness to subject unionism to classical economic reasoning is Rees's (1963) well-known estimates of the resource misallocation costs of unionism. In this work, Rees applied to labor markets Arnold Harberger's (1954) methods of assessing the cost of product market monopolistic pricing. Ostensibly, the gap between the wages of workers in unionized and non-unionized markets is a source of resource misallocation because equally productive labor is being sold at different prices. Rees's calculations suggested that, in the United States in the late 1950s, the costs of this source of resource misallocation were approximately 0.14 percent of national output, an amount that did not seem to justify some of the alarmist views about labor union activities in the United States.

The study of unionism was Rees's lifelong interest and his fundamental views about American unionism appear to have changed little from his early scholastic days to his later years. He tended to regard the *economic* effects of unionism as largely undesirable. Thus, in the third edition of his text *The Economics of Trade Unions,* he wrote:

> If the union is viewed solely in terms of its effect on the economy, it must in my opinion be considered an obstacle to the optimum performance of our economic system. It alters the wage

> structure in a way that impedes the growth of employment in sectors of the economy where productivity and income are naturally high and that leaves too much labor in low-income sectors of the economy. (Rees 1989, p. 191)

Yet he immediately proceeds to describe this judgment as 'narrow' if offered as a complete assessment of unionism. He wrote in an early review of a wide-ranging denunciation of unions, 'The least that can be said for unions is that their noneconomic activities are, by and large, highly beneficial. Through grievance procedures, seniority, and control of the speed and conditions of work, unions have given the industrial worker a new sense of dignity, individual worth, and participation in the process of production' (Rees 1950, p. 257). Rees saw 'a strong union movement [as] the best guaranty against movements which might lead workers to demand the exchange of our democratic freedoms for the "security" of a police state' (ibid., pp. 261–2). In appraising unionism, Rees was ready to accept the basic framework of economic reasoning, but also recognized that a full evaluation required a broader perspective.

Rees was conscious of the problem posed by the public policy goals of full employment and price stability in a context in which labor unions may be a strong force on wage-setting. He pursued this concern both at a microeconomic level by examining wage determination in a single industry, steel (Rees 1951a), one of the subjects of his PhD thesis, and from a macroeconomic perspective by asking 'Do unions cause inflation?' (Rees 1959). He demonstrated (Rees 1952) that one measure of union activity, the incidence of industrial strikes, increases as the economy approaches full employment with the peak in strikes slightly preceding the peak in business activity. The general positive covariation of strikes and the business cycle suggests that union activity was an integral part of a structural interpretation of the movement of wages and prices. In 1967, after reviewing efforts to estimate Phillips curve relationships for the United States, he urged the authors of Phillips curves to label them conspicuously as 'Unstable. Apply with extreme care' (Rees and Hamilton 1967). Later he identified what he saw as the policy issues presented by the Phillips curve (Rees 1970b).

This deep scholastic interest in the junction of full employment, stable prices and labor union activity ultimately led to Rees assuming administrative positions in government in the early 1970s as part of an attack on what seemed like a relentless tendency for inflation to accelerate. In 1971–73, Rees was a member of the Construction Industry Stabilization Committee whose work was addressed to bringing public pressure to bear on wage and price inflation in the construction industry and, in 1974–75, he was Director of the Council on Wage and Price Stability where the anti-inflationary mission was wider. Though he was acutely aware of the limits of incomes policies, he did feel that some public pressure on relieving the wage–price spiral would be worthwhile if this reduced the need for deflationary measures that would diminish employment. In incomes policy, his preference was for gentle public suasion over a set of explicit rules and penalties (Rees 1965).

Rees's interest in the problems presented by full employment, price stability and unionism reflected his deeper interest in how labor markets function whether in the absence or in the presence of unionism. He tended to believe that, in the absence of unions, the conventional neoclassical model served as a useful device, and his original research into information networks in labor markets revealed his respect for market mechanisms (Rees 1966). This work drew on his detailed study of Chicago labor markets, a major research project whose results were published in an important monograph written jointly with George P. Schultz who had been Dean of the Graduate School of Business at Chicago (Rees and Schultz 1970). Rees's examination of the ways in which job seekers collect information about alternative jobs and how employers find workers emphasized the value of informal channels such as referrals from existing employees and other employers. The channels that economists often extolled – state employment services, employment agencies, newspaper advertisements, union hiring halls and school placement bureaus – tended to be used less by market participants.

However, Rees found the standard market-clearing model manifestly unsatisfactory when applied to the experience of labor markets during the 1930s' Depression. In one of his early papers (Rees 1951b), he conjectured that wage levels do not always clear labor markets and, in particular, wages may be at levels at which more people seek employment than firms choose to employ. This was most likely to occur when aggregate demand had fallen and when wages were slow to adjust to restore market-clearing. He provided a number of reasons for the absence of market-clearing in such situations. The implied presence of involuntary unemployment in these situations made him very skeptical of research that presumed market-clearing throughout the 1930s, and an exchange with Robert Lucas and Leonard Rapping in the early 1970s provides a clear and forceful statement of his beliefs. Lucas and Rapping (1969) proposed that unemployed workers may choose not to accept wage offers they consider temporarily low and, as a first approximation, movements in unemployment are to be understood as the consequence of misperceptions by the unemployed. But Rees asked,

> How long does it take workers to revise their expectations of normal wages in light of the facts? Unemployment was never below 14 percent of the labor force between 1931 and 1939 and was still about 17 percent of the labor force in 1939, a decade after the depression began. It is hard to imagine the long-term unemployed holding out for jobs comparable with their old jobs, at their old real compensation, over periods of up to ten years. (Rees 1970a, p. 308)

Finally, as a scholar, Rees was above all an empiricist. Even his papers that focused on theoretical models are infused with data. He constructed (1961) the definitive series on real wages in manufacturing industry in the 25 years before the First World War (Rees 1961), and, in committee reports with others, he advised on the government's methods of measuring prices, unemployment and productivity (President's Committee 1962; Panel to Review Productivity Statistics 1979; Price Statistics Research Committee 1961). With Schultz, he led a major empirical project examining Chicago's labor markets which involved the collection of large bodies of data on wages, employment and many other aspects of labor markets (Rees and Schultz 1970). Later, he was a principal investigator in the New Jersey/Pennsylvania Income Maintenance Experiment whose purpose was to determine the response of low-income people to different terms of welfare benefits (Rees 1974). He collaborated on a survey and analysis on faculty retirement behavior designed to anticipate the effects of the ending of mandatory retirement in universities (Rees and Smith 1991). This uninterrupted commitment to careful measurement informed by public policy issues and by the precepts of economic theory is the type of scholarship that has the hallmark of the best labor economics research, which is why so many of today's researchers think of Rees as their intellectual paragon.

References

Harberger, A.C. (1954), 'Monopoly and resource allocation', *American Economic Review*, **44** (2), 77–87.

Lucas, R.E., Jr. and L.A. Rapping (1969), 'Real wages, employment, and inflation', *Journal of Political Economy*, **77** (5), 721–54.

Panel to Review Productivity Statistics, Assembly of Behavioral and Social Sciences (1979), *Measurement and Interpretation of Productivity*, Washington, DC: National Academy of Sciences.

President's Committee to Appraise Employment and Unemployment Statistics (1962), *Measuring Employment and Unemployment*, Washington, DC: US Government Printing Office.

Price Statistics Research Committee (1961), *The Price Statistics of the Federal Government*, New York: National Bureau of Economic Research.

Rees, A. (1950), 'Labor unions and the price system', *Journal of Political Economy*, **58** (3), 254–63.

Rees, A. (1951a), 'Postwar wage determination in the basic steel industry', *American Economic Review*, **41** (3), 389–404.

Rees, A. (1951b), 'Wage determination and involuntary unemployment', *Journal of Political Economy*, **59** (2), 143–53.

Rees, A. (1952), 'Industrial conflict and business fluctuations', *Journal of Political Economy*, **60** (5), 371–82.

Rees, A. (1959), 'Do unions cause inflation?' *Journal of Law & Economics*, **2** (October), 84–94.

Rees, A. (1961), *Real Wages in Manufacturing, 1890–1914*, Princeton, NJ: Princeton University Press.

Rees, A. (1963), 'The effects of unions on resource allocation', *Journal of Law & Economics*, **6** (October), 69–78.

Rees, A. (1965), 'An incomes policy for the United States?' *Journal of Business*, **38** (4), 374–8.

Rees, A. (1966), 'Information networks in labor markets', *American Economic Review*, **56** (2), 559–66.

Rees, A. (1970a), 'On equilibrium in labor markets', *Journal of Political Economy*, **78** (2), 306–10.

Rees, A. (1970b), 'The Phillips curve as a menu for policy choice', *Economica*, n.s. **37** (147), 227–38.

Rees, A. (1973), *Economics of Work and Pay*, New York: Harper & Row.

Rees, A. (1974), 'An overview of the labor-supply results', *Journal of Human Resources*, **9** (2), 158–80.

Rees, A. (1989), *The Economics of Trade Unions*, 3rd edn, Chicago, IL: University of Chicago Press.

Rees, A. and M.T. Hamilton (1967), 'The wage–price–productivity perplex', *Journal of Political Economy*, **75** (1), 63–70.

Rees, A. and G.P. Schultz (1970), *Workers and Wages in an Urban Labor Market*, Chicago, IL: University of Chicago Press.

Rees, A. and S.P. Smith (1991), *Faculty Retirement in the Arts and Sciences*, Princeton, NJ: Princeton University Press.

28 Margaret Gilpin Reid

Evelyn Forget

Margaret Reid (1896–1991) was born on a farm near Carberry, Manitoba in 1896. After finishing high school, she supported herself by teaching in rural schools until 1916, when she took the opportunity offered by a new degree program in home economics offered by the Manitoba Agricultural College. After graduating in 1921, Reid went to the University of Chicago to work with Hazel Kyrk.

Reid earned a PhD in economics from the University of Chicago in 1931, submitting a dissertation entitled 'The economics of the household'. After expansion and revision, this was published as *The Economics of Household Production* (1934). She lectured in home economics at Connecticut College during the 1929–30 academic year, then took up a position in the departments of Economics and Home Economics at Iowa State College where she lectured on consumption economics. At Iowa State, Reid met and began to work with Elizabeth Hoyt who, along with Hazel Kyrk, would become her lifelong colleague and friend.

Reid was promoted to full professor in 1940. In 1943–44, she joined the Executive Office of the President, where she worked as an economist in the Division of Statistical Standards. From 1945 to 1948 she was Head of the Family Economics Division of the Department of Agriculture. In 1948, Reid was appointed Professor of Economics at the University of Illinois at Urbana-Champaign. In 1951, she returned to the University of Chicago as full professor of economics, a post she held until her retirement in 1961. After retirement from full-time academic duties, Reid continued working for more than 25 years on a book that she would never complete, examining the field of population health, with a particular emphasis on the relationship between income and health. A complete bibliography of her work is available in Forget (2000, pp. 360–61).

In 1980, Margaret Reid was the first woman to be designated Distinguished Fellow by the American Economic Association. The citation reads:

> [One] of the pioneers in several areas of research on consumer and household behavior, each of which has now burgeoned into a major field of study of its own. For example, she did some of the earliest work on the concept and measurement of permanent income. Again, she was one of the first to see that one could systematically study the economics of the household use of time. And, of course, she has been a major contributor to the statistical analysis of the demand for housing. The empirical tradition at the University of Chicago owes much to Margaret Reid's example and teaching. (American Economic Association 1980)

When Franco Modigliani accepted his Nobel Prize in 1985, he noted that a fundamental contribution to his own work on the life-cycle model, and to Milton Friedman's permanent income hypothesis, was Margaret Reid's 'highly imaginative analysis' that suggested a novel explanation for the association between the saving ratio and relative income, namely that consumption was related to normal or 'permanent' rather than current income (Modigliani 1986, p. 299). Milton Friedman acknowledged both the highly stimulating conversations among Rose Friedman, Margaret Reid, Dorothy Brady and himself, and the persistence with which Reid pressed him to write up the underlying theory so that she could refer to it in a paper citing her own results (Friedman 1957, p. ix).

These statistical underpinnings of work that would be honored by the economics profession as theoretical breakthroughs developed naturally out of Reid's earliest work even though it appears quite distinct. Reid, along with Kyrk and Hoyt, was instrumental in changing the nature of home economics education in America, shifting the focus to an analysis of the economic well-being of families. Reid's *Consumers and the Market* (1938) examined issues such as advertising, labeling, credit, legal protection and the responsibility of the state for consumer protection. Her statistical work on the demand for housing derives from these same preoccupations. By 1951, when Reid arrived back in Chicago, these interests in consumer economics became more consistent with mainstream economics. From that date, her publications appear consistently in economics, rather than home economics, journals.

Reid's most original contribution was in the field of consumption economics, especially household production. She recognized that unless we understand the family as a productive unit, and housework as productive work, we cannot make sense of women's labor market decisions, nor can we come to an accurate understanding of the contributions women make to the national economy. Household production, however, is very difficult to distinguish from consumption. It seems obvious that leisure is not production, but how does one value the time spent interacting with one's own children? That time, she noted, is either production or consumption, depending on the utility one derives from the activity. Reid therefore chose to define household production as the provision of goods and services that could substitute for market-produced goods and services.

Reid considered four methods of valuing household production: opportunity cost, retail price, hired worker cost, and boarding service cost (Reid 1934, pp. 160–69). All were in some ways inadequate. Opportunity cost measured the value of potential earnings forgone because of time spent on household production. This method is useful for understanding labor market decisions but it is inadequate as a measure of output because it attributes higher values to products produced by people who could earn more in alternative employment even when the output is inferior. This was the method Becker (1965) adopted in 'A theory of the allocation of time', although he makes no mention of Reid's earlier work in this area.

The retail price method attempts to estimate the value added by household production by deducting the cost of purchased inputs from the prices of market substitutes for household produced goods and services. This was the analysis Reid used in *Food for People* (1943, pp. 134–6).

The cost of hiring someone else to do the work provided by household producers, a common method of valuing housework in the legal system, assumes that the same quality of goods and services could and would be produced by hired labor as by a family member. The final method Reid examined, the boarding service cost, suffers from the same limitation.

In 1951, this earlier work in consumption economics began to take a less prominent role than her increasing involvement in the statistical analyses surrounding income, consumption and savings. She saw this as a continuation of her earlier attempts to explain household production as a function of income, geographical differences, education, race, tastes and stages of the life cycle (ibid., pp. 93–117). After her retirement in 1961, she attempted to bring all of these interests to bear on a new field of population health. The unfinished book included a detailed consideration of education levels, income security, changes in health-care techniques, changes in permanent income related to position in the life cycle and so on. That this ambitious undertaking was never completed is, perhaps, not surprising. The same issues continue to plague population health researchers today.

Reid never married. She died in 1991 after a long illness, leaving her papers and much of her estate to the University of Chicago with the intent of encouraging the study of consumption economics by young economists.

References

American Economic Association (1980), 'Margaret Reid: distinguished fellow 1980', *American Economic Review*, **70** (4).

Becker, G.S. (1965), 'A theory of the allocation of time', *Economic Journal*, **75** (299), 493–515.

Forget, E.L. (2000), 'Margaret Gilpin Reid (1896–1991)', in *A Biographical Dictionary of Women Economists*, Dimand, R.W., M.A. Dimand and E.L. Forget (eds), Cheltenham, UK and Northampton, MA, USA: Edward Elgar, pp. 357–61.

Friedman, M. (1957), *A Theory of the Consumption Function*, Princeton, NJ: Princeton University Press.

Modigliani, F. (1986), 'Life cycle, individual thrift and the wealth of nations', *American Economic Review*, **76** (3), 297–313.

Reid, M.G. (1934), *The Economics of Household Production*, New York: Wiley.

Reid, M.G. (1938), *Consumers and the Market*, New York: F.S. Crofts.

Reid, M.G. (1943), *Food for People*, New York: John Wiley.

29 Sherwin Rosen

Hao Li

Sherwin Rosen (1938–2001) was born in Chicago. His parents, Nell and Joe Rosen, met on a kosher dairy farm in Quebec, Canada. His mother was Canadian, and his father was from Illinois. Along with his uncle, Harry, Sherwin's father owned a hardware store, where Sherwin spent much of his youth. He was very close to his brother Eddie, who died when both men were only in their thirties.

Rosen completed his undergraduate education in engineering at Purdue in 1960. Despite his early exposure to building supplies and his engineering training, he decided to pursue graduate studies in economics at Chicago. It appeared at first that perhaps economics was not a good match; he failed the general core exam, and was advised by Milton Friedman to leave economics, perhaps for accounting. Rosen continued despite this advice, and completed his PhD in 1966 under the supervision of the labor economist Gregg Lewis.[1]

Rosen began his academic career at the University of Rochester in 1964. He was named Kenan Professor of Economics in 1975. While he certainly was productive at Rochester – he wrote his famous hedonic pricing paper there – he was most at home at Chicago and left Rochester for Chicago in 1977. He became the Edwin A. and Betty L. Bergman Distinguished Service Professor in 1983, and served as Department Chairman from 1988 to 1994. Although he did spend summers at the Hoover Institute at Stanford as the Peter and Helen Bing Senior Fellow, he turned down numerous offers to leave Chicago; the Chicago intellectual atmosphere was simply part of him.

Rosen was elected a fellow of the Econometric Society in 1986, and the American Academy of Arts and Sciences in 1984; he was also a member of the Mont Pèlerin Society. He became a member of the National Academy of Sciences at the age of 59, and was serving as president of the American Economic Association at the time of his death. Shortly after his death, the Society of Labor Economists honored his lifetime achievement by establishing 'The Sherwin Rosen Prize for Outstanding Contributions in the Field of Labor Economics'. It was first awarded in 2004 to Daron Acemoglu of MIT.

One of the great applied microeconomists of his time, Rosen made many contributions, publishing over 80 journal articles and book chapters; several of his articles were reprinted multiple times. A theme that ran through his work was understanding heterogeneity. His famous paper on hedonic prices (Rosen 1974) provides the basis for how to understand diversity. In the market, consumers have heterogeneous demands for characteristics by consumers due to different preferences and incomes, and firms have heterogeneous supply functions due to differences in terms of factor prices and technology. The price of these characteristics is determined by the matching of demands and supplies. Exactly what combinations of characteristics will form the final goods is determined by the distribution of consumer characteristics and of firm technologies. The key insight is that the final good is indivisible, and the price reflects the characteristics of the good. For example, two cars with 50 horsepower each is not equivalent to a single car with 100 horsepower.

The importance of indivisibility can be seen again in another famous paper on the economics of superstars (Rosen 1981). Here, a collection of mediocre performers will never add up to one really good one. Rosen presented a simple model, but one that is able to explain the existence of a very skewed wage distribution by the combination of indivisibility, and a product with attributes similar to a public good in that it can be reproduced or consumed by many at little marginal cost. For example, one musician, who may be only slightly better than many others, commands such a higher wage, because his/her performance can be enjoyed, either in concert or on a recording, at little marginal cost. The answer then becomes obvious as to why a few superstars can earn wages that are so much higher than performers who may be only slightly less good than themselves: why would anyone want to listen to a performance by the second best when it costs the same to hear the best?

A similar question, although one that led Rosen and Edward Lazear (Lazear and Rosen 1981) to a different modeling strategy, is why there are such large increases in salaries at the top end of the corporate hierarchy. Why does a vice president who is earning $500 000 command compensation of one million dollars when he/she becomes CEO? What is the purpose of a firm that sets such a skewed wage policy? Lazear and Rosen's answer to this question started the literature known as 'tournament theory'. The key insight of the tournament paper is that executive compensation schemes are based on relative, not absolute, performance. Since the contributions of effort and luck to a good result cannot be disentangled, the firm's information about performance is often limited to a rank ordering of output. In competing for a fixed prize, the winner takes all. The prize, or top salary is fixed in advance, and the person who wins doesn't do so because he/she is good, as all the competitors are great; the winner wins because he/she is the best. The salary the winner obtains is the one that goes with the job, not necessarily the one that matches his/her ability, and it serves not only to compensate the actual CEO, but also to motivate the vice presidents. The outcome of such a tournament is a skewed wage distribution, one that would be difficult to reconcile by appealing to differences in marginal productivity. We have seen a similar outcome with the superstars paper, but the mechanism is very different. In the superstar case, it is the technology allowing the best performance to be enjoyed by all that creates the great divide between the very good and the good; in the tournament case it is asymmetric information, or the non-observability of true ability that makes the winner-take-all wage structure optimal, as it elicits the most effort from those competing for the top prize. In his follow-up paper, Rosen (1986) generalized the model to a tournament with many rounds, with the same result: the biggest wage gain is made in the last round. In order to elicit effort from the competitors, it is necessary to make the prize the largest in the last round to compensate for the fact that there are no more rounds to be won, and for the fact that competition is fiercest at top levels as the competitors are all winners of the previous rounds.

In a discussion of Rosen's contributions it would be a mistake not to mention his landmark empirical study on self-selection in education with Robert Willis (Willis and Rosen 1979). Here they addressed the question of to what extent the positive correlation between earnings and education can be thought of as causal, or simply as a result of more able people attending school. Rosen demonstrated a desire to estimate structural parameters in this work. Applying a revealed preference analysis in a sorting context, the Roy model, Rosen and Willis showed that not only are those who go to college better at college-type jobs, but those who choose not to go to college are better at high-school-type jobs. The recognition that one needs to go beyond a bias correction due to not having a variable to control for ability, and the recognition that the schooling choice is made in a context of comparative advantage, make these estimates very rich. The paper brought out Rosen's view that heterogeneity is the rule, not the exception, his admiration for simple models that explain a lot and his desire to put economic models to rigorous empirical tests.

Although he was best known for his groundbreaking contributions in labor economics, Rosen was also an outstanding microeconomic theorist. His paper with Michael Mussa (Mussa and Rosen 1978) was the first to formalize the now familiar features of price discrimination based on self-selection. Today it is on the list of classical papers on asymmetric information and mechanism design. However, at the end of his career he became somewhat disillusioned with increasing generalization and abstraction at the cost of losing economic insights in some quarters of microeconomic theory, and was not altogether happy about his role in its early development.

While the papers discussed so far are arguably Rosen's most famous works, it should not be thought that his productivity or his influence on the discipline ended by the 1980s. He contributed chapters to both the *Handbook of Labor Economics* (1987) and, with Derek Neal, the *Handbook of Income Distribution* (Neal and Rosen 2000). In 1999 Rosen turned his attention to the 'Potato paradox', demonstrating how the simple, yet critical, insight that potatoes are an investment good (whole potatoes are needed to start next year's crop since they do not produce seeds) as well as a consumption good, provided a deeper understanding of the Irish potato famine and put a stake through the heart of the notion that they are 'Giffen goods' (Rosen 1999).

Rosen believed that people respond to incentives in a well-organized and predictable way, and that we can understand what we observe in the world by a careful examination of incentives and the environment in which economic agents are acting. I had the opportunity to collaborate with Sherwin near the end of his life. The two papers we published together are good examples of how an appreciation for heterogeneity and uncertainty, combined with a simple model, can provide a satisfying and convincing explanation for seemingly puzzling behavior of economic agents. In the first project we worked on, we asked why in some professions employment contracts are signed long before the job is to begin, when information about qualifications of the job candidates and about availability of job positions is scarce (Li and Rosen 1998). Examples of such 'unraveling' of labor contracting are easy to find in sports; the National Basketball Association draft is obvious, but unraveling also happens in other markets for entry-level professionals, such as those for medical interns and law students, where hiring can occur several years before professional certification of the job candidates takes place. We showed that unraveling is the result of risk aversion in an incomplete market where participants are unable to write employment contracts contingent on the realized conditions about the availability of qualified candidates and desirable positions and on the realized match qualities of individual participants. Unraveling relieves some of the uncertainty about available jobs for applicants, and some of the uncertainty about the qualified candidates for firms, at the cost of forming mismatches due to lack of information about good matches at the early contracting stage.

Our second project set out to understand how committees make decisions (Li et al. 2001). Committee members often have conflicting objectives but at the same time share a common interest in making a better decision, which in an uncertain world means bringing their diverse information to the decision. For example, a hiring committee member in an economics department may be biased toward a candidate in his own field, but could be dissuaded from making the offer if other members have good information suggesting that the candidate is unqualified. It is this contrast between conflicts and common interests in a committee that determines how the decision is made in the committee when each member's information is private and subject to misrepresentation. In particular, voting is shown to be the only incentive compatible mechanism of reaching a decision in such a committee. The reason is that voting limits the scope of manipulation of private information by sufficiently coarsening the information content of each member's position, while at the same time allowing some information of each member to impact the decision through their votes.

Rosen died shortly after our second paper was accepted for publication. His career was cut short while he was still writing insightful papers. He would have two posthumous publications: his AEA Presidential address, 'Markets and diversity' (Rosen 2002), and 'The engineering labor market' (Ryoo and Rosen 2004).

Note

1. Biographical information drawn from Hartog (2002) and Lazear (2003).

References

Hartog, J. (2002), 'Desperately seeking structure: Sherwin Rosen (1938–2001)', *Economic Journal*, **112** (483), F519–31.

Lazear, E.P. (2003), 'Sherwin Rosen, September 29, 1938–March 17, 2001', *National Academy of Sciences Biographical Memoirs*, **83**, 176–95.

Lazear, E.P. and S. Rosen (1981), 'Rank-order tournaments as optimal labor contracts', *Journal of Political Economy*, **89** (5), 841–64.

Li, H. and S. Rosen (1998), 'Unraveling in matching markets', *American Economic Review*, **88** (3), 371–87.

Li, H., S. Rosen and W. Suen (2001), 'Conflicts and common interests in committees', *American Economic Review*, **91** (5), 1478–97.

Mussa, M. and S. Rosen (1978), 'Monopoly and product quality', *Journal of Economic Theory*, **18** (2), 301–17.

Neal, D. and S. Rosen (2000), 'Theories of the distribution of earnings', in *Handbook on Income Distribution*, vol. 1, Atkinson, A.B. and F. Bourguignon (eds), Amsterdam: North-Holland, pp. 379–427.

Rosen, S. (1974), 'Hedonic prices and implicit markets: product differentiation in pure competition', *Journal of Political Economy*, **82** (1), 34–55.

Rosen, S. (1981), 'The economics of superstars', *American Economic Review*, **71** (5), 845–58.

Rosen, S. (1986), 'Prizes and incentives in elimination tournaments', *American Economic Review*, **76** (4), 701–15.

Rosen, S. (1987), 'The theory of equalizing differences', in *Handbook on Labor Economics*, vol. 1, Ashenfelter, O. and R. Layard (eds), Amsterdam: North-Holland, pp. 641–92.

Rosen, S. (1999), 'Potato paradoxes', *Journal of Political Economy*, **107** (6, part 2: Symposium on the economic analysis of social behavior in honor of Gary S. Becker), S294–313.

Rosen, S. (2002), 'Markets and diversity', *American Economic Review*, **92** (1), 1–15.

Ryoo, J. and S. Rosen (2004), 'The engineering labor market', *Journal of Political Economy*, **112** (1, part 2: Essays in honor of Sherwin Rosen), S110–40.

Willis, R.J. and S. Rosen (1979), 'Education and self-selection', *Journal of Political Economy*, **87** (5, part 2), S7–36.

30 Henry Schultz

D. Wade Hands

Henry Schultz (1893–1938) was a member of the Chicago Economics Department for only twelve years (1926–38). After completing his magnum opus *The Theory and Measurement of Demand* (1938), he took a semester's leave to teach at UCLA; where, on November 26, 1938 he was killed – along with his wife and two daughters – in a car accident on a mountain road near San Diego. Harold Hotelling reports that: 'He jestingly remarked after the completion of this book that it was a good time to die' (Hotelling 1939, p. 98). Despite the brevity of his professional career, Schultz had a profound impact on both the Chicago School and the economics profession more generally.

Schultz was born in Poland in 1893 and immigrated to the United States in 1907. In 1916 he received a Bachelor of Arts degree from City College of New York and entered Columbia University. His Columbia studies were interrupted by military service and later by an army scholarship to the London School of Economics and the Galton Laboratory of University College London. After he returned to the United States he was employed by a number of governmental agencies including the War Trade Board, the Bureau of the Census, and the Children's Bureau of the Department of Labor. He completed his Columbia PhD in 1925, and his dissertation research – 'The statistical law of demand as illustrated by the demand for sugar' – was published in the *Journal of Political Economy* the same year (Schultz 1925). His research on sugar was further expanded in his first book, *Statistical Laws of Demand and Supply: With Special Application to Sugar* (Schultz 1928).

It is often said that Schultz was a student of Henry Ludwell Moore (1869–1958); but the expression 'was a student of' significantly understates the strength of Schultz's expressed commitment to his mentor's research program. Schultz dedicated his entire professional life to estimating statistical demand curves for individual commodities and attempting to link those estimated curves to the theory of individual rational choice. In all of the various contributions he made to this field of research, he never missed an opportunity to give credit to Moore: 'Trail Blazer in the Statistical Study of Demand' (Schultz 1938, dedication).

Although Schultz's work consistently focused on the twin themes of estimating commodity demand functions and reconciling those estimates with rational choice theory, the details of how he characterized the relationship between these two aspects of the program evolved over the course of his research. Schultz consistently emphasized that his work was not merely empirical; he clearly wanted to obtain demand functions that could be used in the analysis of practical policy problems, but that was not the only, or perhaps even the main, purpose of his work. At least as important as empirical estimation was the desire to ground the resulting empirical relationships in the neoclassical theory of Léon Walras and Vilfredo Pareto (actually Schultz would say 'Lausanne' theory; he used the term 'neoclassical' exclusively for Marshallian partial equilibrium theory). He viewed his research program (and for that matter Moore's) as a '"statistical complement" to pure theory' (Schultz 1931, p. 661), a way for the solution of the problem of general equilibrium to be 'expressed in terms that admit of immediate practical application' (Schultz 1928, p. viii). As Theodore Yntema put it in Schultz's festschrift: 'Schultz undertook to bridge the gap between factless theory and theoryless fact' (Lange et al. 1942, p. 16). Although the goal of relating demand theory to empirical fact remained the same throughout his career, the way he characterized the relevant theory shifted significantly over the course of his research. His early work on the demand for sugar discussed Walrasian theory, but in actuality the only general equilibrium feature was that quantity demanded was allowed to depend on more than one independent price variable. In particular, there was no discussion of utility maximization or rational consumer choice; the relevant general equilibrium theory could just as well have been Gustav Cassel as Walras or Pareto.

By the 1933 paper 'Interrelations of demand', Schultz's theoretical framework had changed. He still focused on the 'interrelations' – substitutability and complementarity – of demand functions, but those functions were now based on utility-maximizing behavior. Although he did not explicitly discuss the consumer's budget constraint, he did take the 'fundamental equation of mathematical economics' (Schultz 1933, p. 474),

$$\varphi_m = \frac{\varphi_1}{p_1} = \frac{\varphi_2}{p_2} = \ldots,$$

as his starting point; where the φ_is are the partial derivatives (marginal utilities) of the consumer's utility function $\varphi = \varphi(x_1, x_2, \ldots, x_n)$, the p_is are the prices, and φ_m is the marginal utility of money income. Following Pareto, F.Y. Edgeworth and others, Schultz defined competing (substitute) and completing (complement) goods in terms of the signs of the second derivatives of the utility function:

$\varphi_{ij} > 0 \Leftrightarrow$ goods *i* and *j* are completing,
$\varphi_{ij} = 0 \Leftrightarrow$ goods *i* and *j* are independent,
$\varphi_{ij} < 0 \Leftrightarrow$ goods *i* and *j* are competing.

Under the assumption of the constancy of the marginal utility of money, these three definitions extend to the (cross-) partial derivatives of demand functions $\partial p_i/\partial x_j$. So that

$\frac{\partial p_i}{\partial x_j} > 0 \Leftrightarrow$ goods *i* and *j* are completing,

$\frac{\partial p_i}{\partial x_j} = 0 \Leftrightarrow$ goods *i* and *j* are independent,

$\frac{\partial p_i}{\partial x_j} < 0 \Leftrightarrow$ goods *i* and *j* are competing.

The constancy of the marginal utility of money also implies that the symmetry of the cross-partials of the utility function will transfer over to consumer demand functions, so the following 'integrability' conditions also hold:

$$\frac{\partial x_i}{\partial p_j} = \frac{\partial x_j}{\partial p_i} \quad \text{or} \quad \frac{\partial p_i}{\partial x_j} = \frac{\partial p_j}{\partial x_i} \qquad \text{for all} \quad i \neq j.$$

In Schultz's words, the integrability conditions guarantee that the 'consumer in question is consistent or rational' (Schultz 1933, p. 507). He correctly attributes these conditions to Hotelling (1932), who derived them from a different maximization problem: one without a budget constraint, and therefore without the marginal utility of money (constant or otherwise). Schultz then tested these various conditions for a number of different agricultural products including barley, corn, hay and oats. In general the empirical results did not turn out as expected – either with respect to complementarity-substitutability or integrability – but Schultz did not place the blame on the theory of consumer choice. The problems were rather 'the treacherous difficulties of inference from time series, or that important factors have been overlooked, or that the data are not reliable for the purpose in view' (Schultz 1933, p. 502).

In 'Interrelations of demand, price, and income' Schultz (1935) shifted the theoretical focus yet again. By this time he had become aware of Slutsky's famous 1915 paper, and used Slutsky's results to break the total change in demand $\partial p_i/\partial x_j$ down into substitution and income effects. Although there continues to be some debate about the exact role that Schultz played in the discovery of Slutsky's paper – for example, Mirowski and Hands (1998), Weber (1999), and Chipman and Lenfant (2002) – everyone does seem to agree that he played at least some role in the dissemination of this well-known result. The Slutsky symmetry conditions,

$$\frac{\partial x_i}{\partial p_j} + x_j \frac{\partial x_i}{\partial M} = \frac{\partial x_j}{\partial p_i} + x_i \frac{\partial x_j}{\partial M} \qquad \text{for all} \quad i \neq j,$$

where M is money income, provided Schultz with an additional testable implication of the theory of rational consumer choice. He also used the Slutsky terms to define substitutability and complementarity – what are now called net substitutability and net complementarity – definitions that do not require the additional assumption of the constancy of the marginal utility of money income. He then tested both of the symmetry conditions – the Hotelling integrability conditions on regular demand functions and the Slutsky symmetry conditions on compensated demand functions – using data on beef, pork and mutton. Although he found a number of interesting results, the statistical tests were again not very conclusive: 'Actually, the two conditions are satisfied only approximately, the more general Slutsky condition, which is free from the assumption of the measurability of utility and the constancy of the final utility of money, yielding approximately the same results as the simple Hotelling condition' (Schultz 1935, p. 477). Schultz concluded that 'the statistical evidence is conflicting' (p. 481), but he did not consider this sufficient reason to reject the Slutsky condition, 'essentially a test of a rational or consistent individual' (p. 480). Despite these rather unsatisfying empirical results, Schultz never lost faith in the research program; each paper, each set of less-than-perfect results, was yet another reason to continue his quest.

Schultz's final contribution *The Theory and Measurement of Demand* (1938) was clearly his most substantive work: most substantive in terms of the sheer bulk of the assembled material, as well as with respect to the nuances of his theoretical framework and empirical techniques. The book reproduced much of his earlier work – particularly the 1933 and 1935 papers – but it also extended both the analysis and the dataset in substantive ways. The book contained a separate chapter on each of the commodities tested – sugar, corn, cotton, hay, wheat, potatoes, and so forth – including not only all of the relevant empirical data, but also a detailed discussion of the history and economic uses of each of the specific goods. The amount of data and statistical analysis was massive (particularly given the available computational and statistical technology), but as in previous studies, the results turned out to be less than entirely satisfying. Schultz offered a number of reasons for the poor empirical performance, but the greatest problem remained the 'lack of accurate statistics on the consumption and prices of related goods'; although he also suggests the need for 'a better theory of choice' (Schultz 1938, p. 604).

In the end Schultz's work should not be judged by either the enduring quality of his specific empirical estimates or the sophistication of his theoretical framework – Schultz himself was never content with his empirical results and many others have criticized his theoretical assumptions (particularly his neglect of homogeneity) – but rather by the importance of his overall research program, and by the diligence and dedication with which he pursued it. Despite its difficulties, his research program remains one of the most important developments in twentieth-century economic theory. His project – 'the development and unification of the theoretical–quantitative and the empirical–quantitative approaches to economics' (ibid., p. 666) – became the main focus of economic research during the decades that followed. Schultz's questions conditioned the discourse in both microeconomics and macroeconomics, in Chicago and elsewhere, throughout the interwar and immediate post-war period. Even those who ultimately chose another path – that of Arrow–Debreu general equilibrium theory, for example – remain, in many ways, the offspring of Schultz's research program. When one adds the fact that Schultz was an extraordinary teacher who influenced the careers of many of the next generation's most important economists (including Milton Friedman), his importance looms even larger.

References

Chipman, J.S. and J.-S. Lenfant (2002), 'Slutsky's 1915 article: how it came to be found and interpreted', *History of Political Economy*, **34** (3), 553–97.

Hotelling, H. (1932), 'Edgeworth's taxation paradox and the nature of demand and supply functions', *Journal of Political Economy*, **40** (5), 577–616.

Hotelling, H. (1939), 'The work of Henry Schultz', *Econometrica*, **7** (2), 97–103.

Lange, O., F. McIntyre and T.O. Yntema (eds) (1942), *Studies in Mathematical Economics and Econometrics: In Memory of Henry Schultz*, Chicago, IL: University of Chicago Press.

Mirowski, P. and D.W. Hands (1998), 'A paradox of budgets: the post-war stabilization of American neoclassical demand theory', in *From Interwar Pluralism to Postwar Neoclassicism*, Morgan, M.S. and M. Rutherford (eds), Durham, NC: Duke University Press, pp. 260–92.

Schultz, H. (1925), 'The statistical law of demand as illustrated by the demand for sugar', *Journal of Political Economy*, **33** (5, 6), 481–504, 577–637.

Schultz, H. (1928), *Statistical Laws of Demand and Supply: With Special Application to Sugar*, Chicago, IL: University of Chicago Press.

Schultz, H. (1931), 'Henry L. Moore's contribution to the statistical law of demand', in *Methods in Social Science*, Rice, S.A. (ed.), Chicago, IL: University of Chicago Press, pp. 645–61.

Schultz, H. (1933), 'Interrelations of demand', *Journal of Political Economy*, **41** (4), 468–512.

Schultz, H. (1935), 'Interrelations of demand, price, and income', *Journal of Political Economy*, **43** (4), 433–81.

Schultz, H. (1938), *The Theory and Measurement of Demand*, Chicago, IL: University of Chicago Press.

Slutsky, E.E. (1915), 'Sulla teoria del bilancio del consumatore', *Giornale degli economisti*, **51** (July), 1–26.

Weber, C.E. (1999), 'Slutsky and additive utility functions, 1947–1972', *History of Political Economy*, **31** (2), 393–416.

31 Theodore William Schultz

Pedro Nuno Teixeira

T.W. Schultz's life (1902–98) spanned the twentieth century, and his career as economist not only reflected many of the changes that economics underwent during the period, but also contributed in no small amount to those transformations (Bowman 1980, Nerlove 1999, Gardner 2006).[1] Schultz used to blame several events that occurred during his youth for driving him towards economics, not least the difficulties faced by farmers during the first decades of the twentieth century, which instilled in him an enduring concern with the improvement of the productive and welfare conditions of agriculture. Those hard times made him interrupt his secondary education to start working full-time. He returned to formal education late in his teens (1921), entering a short course in agriculture at the South Dakota State College. Three years later he decided to continue his studies on agricultural economics at that institution and obtained a BA in 1927 and an MS in 1928. In 1928 he was accepted to undertake graduate studies in agricultural economics at the University of Wisconsin, where he was taught by some of the leading figures of institutionalism at the time, notably John R. Commons. Although this period nurtured in Schultz a deep respect for Commons and his work, as time went by he became increasingly critical of institutionalism as a general economic approach and aligned himself with neoclassical economics.

After finishing his PhD at Wisconsin in 1930, he was hired at Iowa State College (now University), where he was asked five years later to be department head (Wolff and Hayward n.d.), and started to show his impressive organizational talents.[2] He resigned his place in Iowa in 1943 after a huge row over what became known as 'the oleomargarine affair' (ibid.), and moved to the Department of Economics of the University of Chicago. At Chicago he would become Chairman of the Economics Department (1946–61), and in 1952 became Charles L. Hutchison Distinguished Service Professor. He remained at Chicago until his retirement, being active until a very advanced age. Later in his life, and among several honors, he was President of the American Economic Association (AEA) (1960), received the Francis Walker Medal (1972) of the AEA and was awarded the Nobel Memorial Prize in Economics (1979).

Trained as an agricultural economist, Schultz devoted most of his energies to the analysis of the problems of agriculture, especially during his first decades of research. At the time agriculture was regarded as a different type of economic activity, and agricultural economics was thus considered a separate subject, a view reinforced by the institutionalist dominance of the research field. Schultz, on the other hand, regarded agriculture as part and parcel of the economic system and insisted on linking agricultural research with the economic discipline through an integrated approach between theory and empirical research, since he believed that standard economics was relevant to the analysis of agriculture. The first paper he published (Schultz 1932) was a critique of the historic law of diminishing returns in agriculture, emphasizing the role of improvements in the ability and skill of farm people and technical developments as the major forces explaining the non-verification of that principle. During the following years he continued to publish on agricultural subjects (Schultz 1939, 1943).

Prior to the Second World War, Schultz was primarily concerned with agricultural research, especially on the impact of macroeconomic fluctuations on the welfare of farmers. According to him, the major problems affecting American agriculture in the mid-twentieth century were its underproductive employment of human resources and the instability of farming income (Schultz 1945). The employment problems were due to the slow pace of the industrial development and its difficulty in absorbing labor from agriculture. Thus, the migration of people from rural to industrial areas assumed crucial importance in redressing the maldistribution of the labor force and its negative impact on the earnings of labor employed in agriculture. In order to correct these distortions on the allocation of resources, Schultz believed that a strong case could be made for increased expenditure on services that rendered people more productive, namely education, since these would not only improve productivity, but would also stimulate mobility of the labor factor out of agricultural activities. Moreover, he regarded education also as an important mechanism of promoting intergenerational upward social mobility and as an instrument of improved farming practices (Schultz 1949, 1953).

By mid-century, the confluence of his personal interests and the paths of the discipline made him increasingly aware of the problems of economic growth and development, and the special role of agriculture in developing nations. In his writings on economic development he emphasized once again the role played by the quality of the labor force in improving the technical and allocative efficiency of a modernizing economy in general, and of agriculture in particular. For Schultz, poverty was primarily due to differences in productivity-enhancing self-investments; hence, the importance of factors such as the quality of the inputs to the improvement in national efficiency and the consideration of education as human investment. Accordingly, he criticized the overly narrow concept of capital used by most economists and urged increased attention to the quality of people as productive agents. Economic growth was for him not so much a matter of using more inputs, but rather improving their quality and using them more efficiently.

Alongside his research he became increasingly involved in development projects and policy design, notably in Latin American countries (Valdés 1995). These experiences, often supported by aid agencies or by private foundations, made him spend significant time visiting those countries and familiarizing himself with their economic and social situation. Through his academic duties at Chicago, he participated extensively in economic cooperation activities, reflecting his concerns for socially and politically relevant economic research, and his methodological appreciation for the complementary relationship between empirical and theoretical research.

By the early 1950s, Schultz's work on agriculture and development placed the idea of investment in human capacities at the core of his thinking. He may have been stimulated by his experience in the post-war period, when he was part of the Commission advising the reconstruction plans for West Germany. He had seen the evidence of the destruction of Germany's physical capital stock and the fact that it had been rebuilt rather quickly. That experience would solidify his previous view that education made economic agents more productive, providing significant help to overcoming productive constraints. His thinking on investment in human capital was consolidated during his year as Research Fellow of the Center for Advanced Study in Behavioral Sciences (Stanford) in 1956–57.

His publication record thereafter registers an increasing dominance of the economic role of education in his research interests, though he seemed to hesitate for a while between using 'human wealth' or 'human capital', due to the potentially controversial character of the latter usage. His first attempts to estimate the value of capital formation by education and of the returns to education also date from this period (Schultz 1960, 1963).

The climax of this increasing attention to human capital came with one of his most important interventions and certainly a crucial moment for human capital theory – his presidential address to the AEA in 1960 (Schultz 1961). Although for many this was the departure point for human capital research, for Schultz it represented the consolidation of a view that had been emerging in his work for many decades. In his address, Schultz blended the results of his own research on the importance of education to private and social development, with general statements of past economists such as Alfred Marshall and Johann von Thünen, and the emerging results of younger academics such as Jacob Mincer and Gary Becker. Schultz considered five main categories of human capital activities: health, on-the-job training, schooling, adult education, and migration. This broad concept of human capital, especially enhancing the role of health and migration, articulated, with his previous work on health and nutrition effects on development, and the problems of agriculture in terms of maldistribution of labor.

The impact of his address was such that many regard him as the 'father' of human capital. Although the paternity of human capital theory is a complicated issue, his role as the 'midwife' of this theory is incontrovertible. Schultz played a crucial role in coordinating the development of human capital research at its early stages. In the turn to the 1960s he stimulated many of his former and current students to explore the possibilities of this approach. He was also fundamental in coordinating and stimulating these efforts, especially through his skilled research stewardship. (In fact, he viewed research not as the product of a string of coincidences, but rather as the result of a favorable and efficient organizational context.) Some of the best examples of this capacity are exemplified by the set of volumes/conferences he organized on human capital themes, in particular the *Journal of Political Economy* supplement on 'Investment in human beings' (Schultz 1962). A landmark in human capital research, the supplement's articles have been influential and have served as a kind of manifesto, demonstrating the scope of human capital theory through application not only to schooling and training, but also in terms of migration, health, economic growth and social benefits.

The importance of Schultz's work was magnified by the fact that, whereas Mincer and Becker were young researchers, Schultz was a highly respected member of the discipline at that time, with strong connections with many public and private funding bodies (especially with the Rockefeller and Ford foundations). And he would use those connections to raise awareness of the importance of investments on human capital, getting them to place human capital high on their research and policy-making agenda. He also used that visibility to voice significant work that was being done by much less-known researchers in exploring human capital potential. Throughout the 1960s he found an increasingly wide and interested audience on his views on the importance of investments in human capital, and he grasped that opportunity with determination and effectiveness, multiplying his public and scholarly interventions (see Schultz 1971).

His work from the early 1960s onwards would be systematically at the crossroads of his two major research interests, the quality of labor force and the modernization of traditional agriculture. A major piece of research from this period, and probably one of his best-known works, was *Transforming Traditional Agriculture* (Schultz 1964). He argued that the achievement of high productive standards in farming required investment in both human and non-human capital, in particular by introducing the knowledge that made the transformation possible. However, he maintained that often in low-productive agriculture few incentives existed to encourage change; change simply cost too much. Investments required opportunities and efficiency incentives, but these were often neglected in agricultural research and policy. Schultz therefore came to emphasize farmers' rationality and responsiveness to incentives and the need to adjust those incentives in order to promote the modernization of agriculture. His views on the economic rationality of farmers in developing countries was received at the time with skepticism – even derision – similar to what he had faced when he put forth similar views on American agriculture twenty years earlier.

His work on low-income regions and traditional agriculture led him to emphasize progressively the idea of development as a succession of disequilibria, thus the need to improve the capacity to cope with that. These aspects, already present in some of his earlier work, had important implications for matters mostly overlooked by mainstream economics. On the one hand, it was important to consider an enlarged concept of entrepreneurship that was not restricted to business activities, but rather included household activities and production. Moreover, it was important to regard it as a scarce resource with impact on allocation abilities. On the other hand, it was important to recognize that the economic system was not always in equilibrium, nor was the equilibrating process instantaneous (Schultz 1975).

In his later work Schultz showed some dismay regarding the policy and theoretical developments of economics. He was very critical of the state of development economies, especially in terms of agriculture, where he considered that distortions had actually increased in magnitude, due to the persistence of what he considered to be an ideological bias. Some disenchantment also concerned the state of economic theory, especially in its higher concern with elegance rather than with relevance. Being exposed during his long academic career to very different methodological and philosophical economic approaches, he developed a complementary and inclusive research approach to theory, data and mathematics. Although he was very supportive of the attempts by many of his former students, notably Becker, to apply economic (neoclassical) theory to new areas of human and social behavior (for example, family and fertility), he was far less enamored with the contemporary economists' attachment to mathematical rigor and skill. Despite playing a prominent role in bringing agricultural and development economics under the neoclassical canopy, his economics consisted of a blend of various pieces of data aimed at helping to solve puzzles and improving people's lives. This started to sound like old-fashion economics, and though many prominent economists would read and profit from his work, the younger generations became unaccustomed to his type of economics, finding it too literary. Once again, and as in many moments before in his academic career, he was going against the tide.

Notes

1. Additional biographical information gleaned from Schultz (1992) and Johnson (2000).
2. This organizational capacity in terms of research was neatly illustrated by his role in the development

of human capital research. Moreover, he frequently showed interest in reflecting upon the institutional dimension of research, and its economic determinants.

References

Bowman, M.J. (1980), 'On Theodore W. Schultz's contributions to economics', *Scandinavian Journal of Economics*, **82** (1), 80–107.

Gardner, B.L. (2006), 'T.W. Schultz's contributions to the economic analysis of US agriculture', *Review of Agricultural Economics*, **28** (3), 326–31.

Johnson, D.G. (2000), 'Theodore William Schultz', *National Academy of Sciences Biographical Memoirs*, **77**, 302–9.

Nerlove, M. (1999), 'Transforming economics: Theodore W. Schultz, 1902–1998: In Memoriam', *Economic Journal*, **109** (459), F726–48.

Schultz, T.W. (1932), 'Diminishing returns in view of progress in agricultural production', *Journal of Farm Economics*, **14** (4), 640–49.

Schultz, T.W. (1939), 'Scope and method in agricultural economics research', *Journal of Political Economy*, **47** (5), 705–17.

Schultz, T.W. (1943), *Redirecting Farm Policy*, New York: Macmillan.

Schultz, T.W. (1945), *Agriculture in an Unstable Economy*, New York: McGraw-Hill.

Schultz, T.W. (1949), *Production and Welfare of Agriculture*, New York: Macmillan.

Schultz, T.W. (1953), *The Economic Organization of Agriculture*, New York: McGraw-Hill.

Schultz, T.W. (1960), 'Capital formation by education', *Journal of Political Economy*, **68** (6), 571–83.

Schultz, T.W. (1961), 'Investment in human capital', *American Economic Review*, **51** (1), 1–17.

Schultz, T.W. (ed.) (1962), 'Investment in human beings', *Journal of Political Economy*, **70** (5, part 2).

Schultz, T.W. (1963), *The Economic Value of Education*, New York: Columbia University Press.

Schultz, T.W. (1964), *Transforming Traditional Agriculture*, New Haven, CT: Yale University Press.

Schultz, T.W. (1971), *Investment in Human Capital: The Role of Education and Research*, New York: Free Press.

Schultz, T.W. (1975), 'The value of the ability to deal with disequilibria', *Journal of Economic Literature*, **13** (3), 827–45.

Schultz, T.W. (1992), 'Autobiography', in *Nobel Lectures, Economics, 1969–1980*, Lindbeck, A. (ed.), Singapore: World Scientific.

Valdés, J.G. (1995), *Pinochet's Economists: The Chicago School of Economics in Chile*, Cambridge: Cambridge University Press.

Wolff, N. and J. Hayward (n.d.), *The Historical Development of the Department of Economics at Iowa State, 1929–1985*, available from http://www.econ.iastate.edu/department/history/EconomicsHistory1929–1985.pdf (accessed July 22, 2007).

32 Henry Calvert Simons

Sherryl D. Kasper

Henry Simons (1899–1946) stands out as one of the leading figures of the Chicago School of the 1930s. His particular contribution was to provide what George Stigler (1988, p. 139) characterized as the 'lucid blueprint of the good society' of classical liberalism. This blueprint instilled in later generations of Chicago economists both the ideas and the assurance that sustained them during the years of the Keynesian consensus. The ideas first appeared in his essay *A Positive Program for Laissez Faire* (Simons 1934), a preliminary theoretical explanation of the Depression with an accompanying set of interrelated policies founded on the organizing principle of classical liberalism that were designed to save the devastated American economy. Simons would devote much of his professional life to expanding on the ideas presented in this essay, and some of them would go on to feature prominently in Chicago economics. The assurance Simons provided to subsequent generations of Chicago economists originated in his belief that it was his moral responsibility to foster discussions about ways to re-create a free-market society for the twentieth century. The exchanges he promoted extended across disciplines and in and out of the academy. Furthermore, they featured an idealistic quality that went on to permeate Chicago economics.

Simons was born on October 9, 1899 in Virden, Illinois, the son of Henry Calvert Simons, Sr., a moderately successful lawyer, and Mollie Willis Sims Simons, an extremely ambitious homemaker. He graduated second in his high-school class by the age of 16, but due to a decline in the family's financial situation, he could not follow his older sister to an eastern college (Ella Simons Siple had graduated from Wellesley College). Instead, in 1916 he enrolled at the University of Michigan with the aim of becoming a lawyer. He was soon captivated by economic theory, inspired by the teaching of Fred M. Taylor: 'Taylor gave me an ideal introduction to economics – what a tough old drill sergeant gives to neophytes in the army' (Henry Simons to Frank A. Fetter, Sr., 6 July 1942, Henry C. Simons Papers, Box 2, Folder 61, p. 1).[1]

Simons graduated with an AB in 1920 and immediately began graduate study in economics at the University of Michigan. In January 1921, upon receiving an offer of a part-time teaching position in principles and railroads, he moved to the University of Iowa. At this time, Simons became an early disciple of Frank Knight: 'Knight was nearly perfect as an influence at the next stage [of my professional career]' (Simons to Fetter, 6 July 1942, Henry C. Simons Papers, Box 2, Folder 61, p. 1). His new mentor encouraged Simons to continue with graduate study. First he attended Columbia University in the summer of 1922, taking classes with Knight's former teacher Herbert Davenport. Later during the summers of 1923, 1924, and the academic year of 1925–26, he attended classes at the University of Chicago. Even though the University of Iowa had promoted him to assistant professor in 1925, Simons followed Knight to the University of Chicago in 1927. At that time, he took more graduate classes and became a lecturer in the Department of Economics. In 1928, Simons spent six months in Germany, part of the time at the University of Berlin. The purpose of the trip was to learn German and to make progress on his dissertation about income taxation. Yet, despite these efforts, Simons never earned a PhD for two reasons. First, he did not submit his dissertation for formal review, even though he later published it as *Personal Income Taxation* (Simons 1938). Second, he did not take the necessary oral examinations. A childhood friend later conjectured that the oral exams represented the main obstacle, because 'he did not want to be examined by inferior minds' (quoted from the transcript of an interview with an unidentified friend of Simons's family, 16 November 1972, Henry C. Simons Papers, Box 10, Folder 11).

Up until the publication of the *Positive Program* in 1934, Simons was not an active participant in economic discourse. While at Iowa, he published one article on taxes, and, in 1926 and 1929, he published two rather dull book reviews about the economics of taxation. In 1933, his apparent indolence was replaced with intense activity. Simons published his 'Syllabus materials for Economics 201' (Simons 2002). He wrote two book reviews that displayed the urgency about contemporary economic events that went on to permeate the *Positive Program*. He also helped to write three memoranda about banking and monetary policy signed by a group of Chicago economists that were sent to academic economists and key policy makers in Washington, DC. In March 1934, Simons went to Washington to help Senator Bronson Cutting outline a bill that would bring the money supply and availability of credit under stronger federal control (Phillips 1995, pp. 81–93). This frenzy of activity culminated in the publication of the *Positive Program*, and with its publication, Simons moved from professional insignificance to 'slowly establishing himself as the head of a "school"' (Director 1948, p. v).

Simons was spurred to create the 'Positive program' for three reasons. First, like many of his contemporaries, he was alarmed about the 'economic chaos' of the Great Depression (Simons 1934, p. 56). Second, he was distressed about the 'chaos of political thought' underlying the early New Deal policies (p. 77). In particular, he was concerned that advocates of national planning and a managed economy had emerged as respected members of Franklin D. Roosevelt's Brains Trust and were working successfully to pass laws like the National Recovery Act that would spell doom for classical liberalism in America. Third, he felt the necessity to provide a document that could serve as a basis for discussion among fellow classical liberals and that could lead to 'a consensus of opinion' about the policy reforms necessary to preserve 'political and economic freedom' (pp. 76–7). It is interesting to note that Simons became quite disillusioned with Knight at this time, because he perceived that Knight had given up the fight for classical liberalism. He expressed these concerns in a letter to F.A. Hayek about the 'Positive program':

> If my proposals seem, as a whole, too drastic, let me explain that both the religion of freedom, and intellectual interests along liberal lines, seem deader here than in England. One must struggle as hard with friends as with enemies; the competent people are mainly, like Frank Knight, ready to abandon all their hope and faith, and to occupy themselves largely with explanations of why the deluge is both imminent and inevitable. (Henry C. Simons to F. A. Hayek, 18 December 1934, Henry C. Simons Papers, Box 3, Folder 40, p. 2)

Simons's theoretical analysis of reasons for the Depression was twofold: 'The depression is essentially a problem (1) of relative inflexibility in prices which largely determine costs and (2) of contraction in the volume and velocity of effective money' (Simons 1934,

p. 74). He used a cartel model later described by Don Patinkin to study the problem of price inflexibility (Patinkin 1947 [1981]). He adapted Irving Fisher's version of the quantity theory to study the problem of money. With that choice, he contributed to what Milton Friedman (1956, p. 3) termed the 'Chicago oral tradition throughout the 1930s and 1940s where students continued to study monetary theory and to write on monetary problems'.

Based on this analysis, Simons offered the 'Positive program' as an interrelated set of policy recommendations 'in a descending scale of relative importance' (Simons 1934, p. 57). Its essential elements were:

> 1. Elimination of monopoly in all its forms . . .
> 2. Establishment of more definite and adequate 'rules of the game' with respect to money . . .
> 3. Drastic change in our whole tax system, with regard primarily for effects of taxation upon the distribution of wealth and income . . .
> 4. Gradual withdrawal of the enormous differential subsidies implicit in our present tariff system . . .
> 5. Limitation upon the squandering of our resources in advertising and selling activities. (Simons 1934, p. 57)

At first glance, his policy recommendations appear to be vintage Chicago economics – the promotion of free competition, the adoption of rules for monetary policy and the support for free international trade. But the details of these recommendations reveal differences with later Chicago economists. For example, primarily and foremost, Simons recommended that the state reduce the power of organized groups. The means to this goal was for the state to abolish private monopoly, either through strong enforcement of antitrust or public ownership of natural monopolies. In this regard, he envisioned that 'the Federal Trade Commission should become perhaps the most powerful of government agencies' and considered limiting market share to 5 percent, believing that any loss in efficiency would be offset by the gain in dispersed power (ibid., p. 58). Second, in the realm of monetary policy, Simons counseled establishment of a 100 percent reserves policy to end the power of private institutions to influence the supply of money and to return currency control to the proper authority, the state. He also recommended a legislated rule for monetary policy to ensure that the state would use its monopoly control of the money supply in an unbiased and predictable manner. Interestingly, he never settled on one particular rule. Early on he recommended fixing the quantity of money in circulation or stabilizing some index of commodity prices; later he argued that, due to the presence of near-monies, it would be difficult to define money in a way that the Federal Reserve could fix its quantity, and he turned his attention to developing some type of price-index rule. Third, he suggested a radical alteration of the federal tax structure to make it more progressive so as to lessen the concentration of income and wealth that gave certain members of society more economic and political power. He also advocated defining income more broadly to include the taxpayer's consumption plus the addition to his net assets. Fourth, Simons offered that the gradual movement to free trade would diminish the power of protected domestic producers. And finally, he believed that applying revenues earned from taxing advertising to consumer education and the establishment of uniform commodity standards would arm consumers with additional information to offset the power of enterprises that used marketing to manipulate demand.

Simons expanded on these ideas for the academic community in later papers and monographs and with different degrees of emphasis throughout the rest of his career. Beginning in the mid-1930s, he extended his ideas about developing policies to re-create the free-market system in 'The requisites of free competition' (1936 [1948]), about monetary theory and policy in 'Rules versus authorities in monetary policy' (1936), and about taxation in *Personal Income Taxation* (1938). In the early 1940s, Simons turned his attention to the problem of industrial monopoly in 'For a free-market liberalism' (1941 [1948]) and to the growing influence of Keynesian economics in 'Hansen on fiscal policy' (1942 [1948]). By the mid-1940s, he became less concerned about industrial monopolies because he did not believe that they were sustainable in the long run, and turned his attention to the problem of labor monopolies discussed in a controversial article entitled 'Some reflections on syndicalism' (1944 [1948]). At this time, he also investigated ways to set up both the national and international post-war economies in a way that would preserve classical liberalism. These and other essays were collected in a volume entitled *Economic Policy for a Free Society* after his death (Simons 1948).

Always the idealistic advocate, in the early 1940s Simons also worked to broaden the discussion about preserving classical liberalism beyond the academy. He became interested in writing for the popular press in magazines such as *Harpers*, *Time*, *The New Republic*, *American Mercury*, and *Fortune*. He also sent numerous letters to editors of national newspapers including *The Washington Post*, *The New York Times*, and *The New York Herald Tribune*. When asked to provide a reason for this new interest, his childhood friend described her belief that once Simons had developed his ideas in economic theory and policy, he wanted to describe them to a wider audience because 'he might convince some people of his thinking' (quoted from the transcript of an interview with an unidentified friend of Simons's family, 16 November 1972, Henry C. Simons Papers, Box 10, Folder 11, p. 8). One measure of his success was an appreciative posthumous biography written by John Davenport (1946) that appeared in *Fortune* and the *University of Chicago Law Review*.

Simons's lack of success in the Chicago Economics Department created another opportunity for him to expand the discussion about the preservation of classical liberalism. In the mid-1930s, his absent PhD, minimal publications and poor teaching skills created frictions in the Chicago Economics Department. In fact, George Stigler (1988, pp. 180–90) reported that by 1934 Paul Douglas and Knight did not speak in part because of the issue of Simons taking up a position in the Economics Department at Chicago. Partly to deal with this problem, in 1939 Simons moved to the Chicago Law School in a half-time appointment as its first economics professor and taught one course. He met with greater success in this position. His law students found him a better teacher, and he had a substantial influence on Malcolm Sharp and Wilbur Katz in particular. It was with the Law School's support that in 1942, he was finally promoted to Associate Professor. His promotion to Professor was delayed until 1945 because a dean was angry about Simons's attack on organized labor in the 1944 'Syndicalism' article.

Simons also began the groundwork for an international organization that would keep alive the discussion about classical liberalism during the years of the Keynesian consensus. In the 1940s, he made a proposal to set up an 'Institute of Political Economy' at the University of Chicago that 'would preserve and promote the "traditional-liberal political philosophy" of "Chicago economics"' (Bowler 1974, p. 9). At the time of his death in 1946, Hayek carried Simons's idea forward. First, Hayek with financial backing from the Volker Fund organized the Free Market Study led by Aaron Director to write an *American Road to Serfdom* and to develop a description of an effective, liberal system (Van Horn and Mirowski 2009). Later Hayek founded the Mont Pèlerin Society as a sympathetic forum for individuals interested in the traditional-liberal political philosophy.

Simons spent much of his time at the University of Chicago living as a bachelor at the Quadrangle Club. He developed his interest in classical music, played tennis and billiards, and spent time at Handley's tavern talking with his students. On May 30, 1941, after many years as a bachelor, Simons married Marjorie Kimball Powell. They had one daughter, Mary Powell Simons, born on January 27, 1944. Beginning in 1945, Simons had problems with stomach ulcers and insomnia. He died on June 19, 1946, according to published reports the victim of an accidental overdose of sleeping pills.

When differentiating among the early Chicago economists, Stigler (1974 [1982], p. 170) characterized Simons as 'the utopian' of the group. Initially the 'Positive program' gave classical liberals both ideas and the rallying cry that Patinkin (1981, p. 4) later described combined 'the same qualities that made Marxism so appealing to many other people at the time: simplicity together with apparent logical completeness; idealism combined with radicalism'. Equally important, outside the classroom and on an individual basis, this groundwork joined with his gregarious nature had a profound influence on key members of the Chicago School. It seemed to imbue in them both a sense of purpose and a feeling of optimism as they set out to build a theoretical foundation for the reconstruction of a free-market economy.

Note

1. Basic biographical information on Simons drawn from Bowler (1973), Stigler (1974 [1982]), Elzinga (1999), Kitch (1983) and Stein (1987).

References

Henry C. Simons Papers, Special Collections Research Center, University of Chicago Library.

Bowler, C.A. (1973), 'Biographical data', in *The Henry C. Simons Papers: A Guide to the Collection*, Bowler, C.A. (ed.), Chicago, IL: University of Chicago Law School Library, pp. ix–x.

Bowler, C.A. (1974), 'The papers of Henry C. Simons', *Journal of Law & Economics*, **17** (1), 7–11.

Davenport, J. (1946), 'The testament of Henry Simons', *University of Chicago Law Review*, **14** (1), 5–14.

Director, A. (1948), 'Prefatory note', in *Economic Policy for a Free Society*, Simons, H.C. (ed.), Chicago, IL: University of Chicago Press, pp. v–viii.

Elzinga, K.G. (1999), 'Henry Calvert Simons', in Garraty, J.A. and M.C. Carnes (eds), *American National Biography*, New York: Oxford University Press, pp. 13–14.

Friedman, M. (1956), 'The quantity theory of money – a restatement', in *Studies in the Quantity Theory of Money*, Friedman, M. (ed.), Chicago, IL: University of Chicago Press, pp. 3–21.

Kitch, E.W. (1983), 'The fire of truth: a remembrance of law and economics at Chicago, 1932–1970', *Journal of Law & Economics*, **26** (1), 163–234.

Patinkin, D. (1947 [1981], 'Multiple-plant firms, cartels, and imperfect competition', in *Essays on and in the Chicago Tradition*, Durham, NC: Duke University Press, pp. 91–123.

Patinkin, D. (1981), 'Introduction: reminiscences of Chicago, 1941–47', in *Essays on and in the Chicago Tradition*, Durham, NC: Duke University Press, pp. 3–20.

Phillips, R.J. (1995), *The Chicago Plan and New Deal Banking Reform*, Armonk, NY: M.E. Sharpe.

Simons, H.C. (1934), *A Positive Program for Laissez Faire: Some Proposals for a Liberal Economic Policy*, Chicago, IL University of Chicago Press.

Simons, H.C. (1936), 'Rules versus authorities in monetary policy', *Journal of Political Economy*, **44** (1), 1–30.
Simons, H.C. (1936 [1948]), 'The requisites of free competition', in *Economic Policy for a Free Society*, Chicago, IL: University of Chicago Press, pp. 78–89.
Simons, H.C. (1938), *Personal Income Taxation: The Definition of Income as a Problem of Fiscal Policy*, Chicago, IL: University of Chicago Press.
Simons, H.C. (1941 [1948]), 'For a free-market liberalism', in *Economic Policy for a Free Society*, Chicago, IL: University of Chicago Press, pp. 90–106.
Simons, H.C. ([1942] 1948), 'Hansen on fiscal policy', in *Economic Policy for a Free Society*, Chicago, IL: University of Chicago Press, pp. 184–219.
Simons, H.C. (1944 [1948]), 'Some reflections on syndicalism', in *Economic Policy for a Free Society*, Chicago, IL: University of Chicago Press, pp. 121–59.
Simons, H.C. (1948), *Economic Policy for a Free Society*, Chicago, IL: University of Chicago Press.
Simons, H.C. (2002), 'The Simons' syllabus', in *The Chicago Tradition in Economics, 1892–1945*, vol. 8, Emmett, R.B. (ed.), London: Routledge, pp. 3–70.
Stein, H. (1987), 'Henry Christopher [sic] Simons', in Eatwell, J., M. Milgate and P. Newman (eds), *The New Palgrave Dictionary of Economics*,pp. 333–5, London: Macmillan.
Stigler, G.J. (1974 [1982]), 'Henry Calvert Simons', in *The Economist as Preacher, and Other Essays*, Chicago, IL: University of Chicago Press, pp. 166–70.
Stigler, G.J. (1988), *Memoirs of an Unregulated Economist*, New York: Basic Books.
Van Horn, R. and P. Mirowski (2009), 'The rise of the Chicago School of economics and the birth of neoliberalism', in *The Road from Mont Pèlerin: The Making of the Neoliberal Thought Collective*, Mirowski, P. and D. Plehwe (eds), Cambridge, MA: Harvard University Press, pp. 139–78.

33 George J. Stigler

Edward Nik-Khah

George Joseph Stigler was one of the most influential economists of the second half of the twentieth century. During a career that spanned seven decades, from the 1930s to the 1990s, Stigler won some of the highest accolades a scholar can receive, including election to the National Academy of Sciences (1973), a National Medal of Science (1987), and the Nobel Prize in Economics (1982). Whether due to his authorship of one of the primary textbook presentations of Chicago price theory or his extension of it to industrial organization, information, regulation, and politics, Stigler is universally regarded as a principal architect of the post-war Chicago School (Mincer 1983, Schmalensee 1983, Demsetz 1993, Peltzman 1993). Receiving less attention was Stigler's control of the Walgreen Foundation and the Center for the Study of the Economy and the State after his return to Chicago in 1958. The Foundation and Center became key institutions in the production and promulgation of post-war Chicago doctrine (Nik-Khah forthcoming).

George Stigler was born on January 17, 1911 into a German-speaking household in Renton, Washington, the only child to a father who had emigrated from Bavaria and a mother from Hungary (then, Austria-Hungary). Stigler attended school at the University of Washington, where he obtained a bachelor's degree in business administration, hoping to prepare for a career in business; he earned an MBA at Northwestern University in 1932. His professors failed to make much of an impression on the young Stigler, save for the Northwestern economist Coleman Woodbury, who drew his interest toward academic study of the subject. His interest in the field aroused, Stigler enrolled at the University of Chicago in 1933 to pursue a PhD in economics. Self-described as a 'tabula rasa' (Stigler 1986, p. 81), he quickly gravitated toward Frank Knight and Henry Simons, and his fellow students Milton Friedman and W. Allen Wallis. Knight became Stigler's dissertation supervisor; a study of production and distribution in the history of economic thought was completed in 1938 (Stigler 1941). Simons's *A Positive Program for Laissez Faire* (1934) deeply influenced Stigler's views on the appropriate economic role of the state, particularly on the need for robust anti-monopoly policies to safeguard competition (Stigler 1988).

Stigler's views underwent a profound transformation in the 1950s, largely as a result of his participation in the Mont Pèlerin Society (MPS). Organized by F.A. Hayek, the MPS was a group of economists, political theorists and other scholars that devoted itself to reformulating liberalism as a counterblast against social welfare liberalism and socialism. The MPS turned out to be an obligatory passageway for those most heavily involved in constructing the post-war Chicago School of Economics (Van Horn and Mirowski 2009), including Hayek (who came to the University of Chicago in 1950), Stigler's classmates and friends Friedman and Wallis, and Aaron Director. Director had been at Chicago during the 1930s, but he and Stigler only became friends after the initial MPS meeting. Director was an especially important influence on Stigler: 'If we had been in Greece', Stigler acknowledged, 'I'm sure I would have called him Socrates' (Stigler

1986, p. 85) – an apt comparison, since Director was a skilled interlocutor but rarely wrote. In the context of their shared participation in the MPS project, Stigler came to believe that monopoly behavior was 'outside the logic of the [market] system', now preferring instead to conceive firm behavior as efficiency enhancing (Stigler 1963, pp. 87–88, 1988, pp. 161–6). With respect to policy, Stigler revised his beliefs about the appropriate economic role of the state and now opposed an activist antitrust policy. The link between his academic work and his participation in the MPS project is especially evident in *The Citizen and the State* (Stigler 1975a), which places such pieces as 'What can regulators regulate?' alongside more conspicuously political tracts as 'Reflections on Liberty'. As Stigler has noted (1988, p. 148), there was no 'Chicago School' in the current sense of the term prior to the first meeting of the MPS, but in the context of that project Stigler, Director, Friedman, and others set to the task of constructing one. Stigler remained committed to the MPS throughout his career, serving as president from 1976 to 1978.

Upon his return to Chicago in 1958 (he spent the intervening years at Minnesota, Brown, and Columbia), Stigler was viewed as a leading member of the Chicago School. He was already associated with the School through his friendships with Friedman, Wallis and Director, and Chicago economists were quite familiar with the existing body of his work; by that time, *The Theory of Price* (Stigler 1952) had already gone into its second edition and Chicago economics graduate students were expected to familiarize themselves with it (McDonald 2009). But Stigler's stature at Chicago was bolstered by the Walgreen Foundation, which had been established by a grant from the drugstore magnate Charles Walgreen, relocated from political science to the Graduate School of Business (GSB), and placed under Stigler's control upon his arrival by Wallis (now dean of the GSB). Shortly thereafter, Stigler announced his intention to devote the Walgreen resources to a study of the 'causes and effects of governmental control over economic life' (Stigler to Walgreen, December 28, 1959, GSRL Box 13, File: Walgreen Correspondence). He hired a full-time research assistant (Claire Friedland), established the famous Industrial Organization Workshop, and funded research he deemed relevant to the study of governmental control. Stigler himself contributed studies of the regulation of electricity and securities and of the enforcement of antitrust laws, and financed several others (Stigler and Friedland 1962, Stigler 1964, 1966). As a result it became a shared creed at the GSB that government policies would never accomplish their publicly stated goals.

Stigler's famous article 'The economics of information' (1961) provided a theory of how information was acquired in markets through (costly) individual search, an approach which he then used to portray advertising as an 'extremely efficient' method of conveying information to the consumer, hereafter another GSB creed. Stigler also used an information-based approach to oligopoly to upbraid those who did not deduce firm behavior from the 'traditional theory of profit maximizing enterprises' (1968, p. 39). During this period, the GSB rejected the kind of behavioral theories of the firm produced at rival business programs such as Carnegie's Graduate School of Industrial Administration (Van Overtveldt 2007). Finally, Stigler financed studies that combined various elements of these approaches; for example, by attacking government regulation on the grounds that it was a poor substitute for privately produced information (see Landau 1973).

By the early 1970s, Stigler had begun to envision a much more ambitious project that would study the 'nature' and 'capacities' of the political process. It was an unapologetically imperialistic endeavor: 'Let us be candid: economists are beginning to apply their logic and analytical apparatus to the political process, and with luck will conquer much of political science!' (GSRL Box 21, File: A Research Institute in Economics). As a prelude to launching this imperialistic expedition, Stigler used his Walgreen funds to recruit to Chicago a handful of leading economists (Gary Becker from Columbia University, Sam Peltzman from UCLA, Robert Lucas from Carnegie) and to finance short stays for other economists sympathetic to his efforts. In 1977, he founded the Center for the Study of the Economy and the State (CSES) with an initial roster that included Becker, Richard Posner, Peltzman, Peter Linneman, and George Borjas, with Stigler assuming the directorship. Of course, maintaining such a roster required an operating budget in excess of what the Walgreen Foundation provided. Stigler met the Center's needs by courting large corporations (Amoco, Getty, Proctor & Gamble) and conservative foundations (Olin, Lilly, Scaife). Stigler had long believed that the success of an intellectual contribution could be measured by its ability to attract financial support in the 'marketplace of ideas' (1963, 1975b). The CSES has proven to be a hit at Chicago. Since 1980, its base of support has expanded (for example, the pharmaceutical giant Pfizer has become an important corporate contributor), attracting millions in contributions, and producing well over 200 papers. Persuading corporations and conservative foundations to finance imperialistic expeditions into political science and policy studies stands as one of Stigler's most significant unheralded accomplishments.

A primary motivation for Stigler's studies in politics was his belief that misguided views about the 'capacities' of democracy were driving public policy:

> The relevance of this work to public policy will be both indirect and decisive . . . [It] is intended to work its effects upon the appropriate disciplines (economics and political science) rather than directly on public opinion. The work will often shatter the fond hopes of the scholarly professions. (GSRL Box 21, File: A Research Institute in Economics)

That the 'fond hopes' Stigler hoped to 'shatter' were held by scholars suggested to him that scholarly studies of politics offered the best way to challenge or otherwise counteract them. Stigler attributed these hopes to political scientists and economists alike – including some with which one might normally expect him to agree:

> As I mentally review Milton [Friedman]'s work, I recall no important occasion on which he has told businessmen how to behave . . . Yet Milton has shown no comparable reticence in advising Congress and public on monetary policy, tariffs, schooling, minimum wages, the tax benefits of establishing a ménage without benefit of clergy, and several other subjects . . . Why should businessmen – and customers and lenders and other economic agents – know and foster their own interests, but voters and political coalitions be so much in need of his and our lucid and enlightened instruction? (1975b, p. 312)

In his work on the economics of politics, Stigler posited a symmetry between the 'political market' and the market for goods: people operating in both markets rationally gather information. Stigler therefore believed that efforts to popularize neoclassical economics (like Friedman's) were a waste of time. And yet despite the fact that voters are held to collect the individually rational amount of information, Stigler was dubious of democracy: 'The best econ[omics] in the US is not the one the public would elect' (GSRL

Box 26, File: Mont Pèlerin Society 10th Anniversary Meeting). Democracy would neither make the best use of social science, nor was it generally a good way to organize intellectual life:

> Affairs of science, and intellectual life generally, are not to be conducted on democratic procedures. One cannot establish a mathematical theorem by a vote, even a vote of mathematicians. [Therefore] an elite must emerge and instill higher standards than the public or the profession instinctively desire. (GSRL Box 26, File: Mont Pèlerin Society 10th Anniversary Meeting)

Democracy fails in politics and science alike because, according to Stigler, few people possess the right instincts. He denied that democratic results such as the public's willingness to countenance an expansion of government regulation were the outcome of reasoned reflection, holding instead that they were the inevitable outcome of the poor instincts possessed by the vast majority of people – public and professors alike. But rather than call for the public to rethink its views and eliminate regulation (a prospect Stigler believed to be unrealistic in most cases), Stigler sought to immunize government policy from the public, for example by developing for regulators a set of 'intelligent guides', and subjecting regulators to performance audits to be conducted by scientific bodies that had been purged of their public interest attitudes (see Stigler 1975a). Therefore, Stigler's program to study the 'capacities' of democracy was informed by a profoundly negative view of the instincts of the vast majority of people.

Stigler remained at Chicago, producing research on politics and serving as director of the CSES until his death on December 1, 1991. Soon thereafter the CSES was renamed the 'George J. Stigler Center for the Study of the Economy and the State', which serves today as a living monument not only to Stigler's intellectual accomplishments, but to his beliefs about the best way to promote them. Both stand as enduring contributions to the Chicago School of Economics.

References

(GSRL) George J. Stigler Papers, Regenstein Library, University of Chicago.

Demsetz, H. (1993), 'George J. Stigler: midcentury neoclassicist with a passion to quantify', *Journal of Political Economy*, **101** (5), 793–808.
Landau, R. (1973), *Regulating New Drugs*, Chicago, IL: University of Chicago Center for Policy Study.
McDonald, J. (2009), 'Graduate education in economics: microeconomics at Chicago and Yale in the 1960s', *Journal of the History of Economic Thought*, **31** (2), 161–80.
Mincer, J. (1983), 'George J. Stigler's contributions to economics', *Scandinavian Journal of Economics*, **85** (1), 65–75.
Nik-Khah, E. (forthcoming), 'George Stigler, the GSB, and the pillars of the Chicago School', in *Building Chicago Economics*, Van Horn, R., P. Mirowski and T. Stapleford (eds), Cambridge: Cambridge University Press.
Peltzman, S. (1993), 'George Stigler's contributions to the economic analysis of regulation', *Journal of Political Economy*, **101** (5), 818–32.
Schmalensee, R. (1983), 'George Stigler's contributions to economics', *Scandinavian Journal of Economics*, **85** (1), 77–86.
Simons, H.C. (1934), *A Positive Program for Laissez Faire: Some Proposals for a Liberal Economic Policy*, Chicago, IL: University of Chicago Press.
Stigler, G.J. (1941), *Production and Distribution Theories: The Formative Period*, New York: Macmillan.
Stigler, G.J. (1952), *The Theory of Price*, rev. edn, New York: Macmillan.
Stigler, G.J. (1961), 'The economics of information', *Journal of Political Economy*, **69** (3), 213–25.
Stigler, G.J. (1963), *The Intellectual and the Market Place, and Other Essays*, New York: Free Press.
Stigler, G.J. (1964), 'Public regulation of the securities markets', *Journal of Business*, **37** (2), 117–42.

Stigler, G.J. (1966), 'The economic effects of the anti-trust laws', *Journal of Law & Economics*, **9**, 225–58.
Stigler, G.J. (1968), *The Organization of Industry*, Homewood, IL: Irwin.
Stigler, G.J. (1975a), *The Citizen and the State*, Chicago, IL: University of Chicago Press.
Stigler, G.J. (1975b), 'The intellectual and his society', in *Capitalism and Freedom: Problems and Prospects*, Selden, R.T. (ed.), Charlottesville, VA: University of Virginia Press, pp. 311–21.
Stigler, G.J. (1986), 'George J. Stigler', in *Lives of the Laureates: Seven Nobel Economists*, Breit, W. and R.W. Spencer (eds), Cambridge, MA: MIT Press, pp. 79–93.
Stigler, G.J. (1988), *Memoirs of an Unregulated Economist*, New York: Basic Books.
Stigler, G.J. and C. Friedland (1962), 'What can regulators regulate? The case of electricity', *Journal of Law & Economics*, **5**, 1–16.
Van Horn, R. and P. Mirowski (2009), 'The rise of the Chicago School of Economics and the birth of neoliberalism', in *The Road from Mont Pèlerin: The Making of the Neoliberal Thought Collective*, Mirowski, P. and D. Plehwe (eds), Cambridge, MA: Harvard University Press, pp. 139–78.
Van Overtveldt, J. (2007), *The Chicago School: How the University of Chicago Assembled the Thinkers Who Revolutionized Economics and Business*, Chicago, IL: Agate.

34 Jacob Viner

William J. Barber

Jacob Viner (1892–1970), one of the most respected economists of his time, was born in Canada and received his early education there. After graduating from McGill University in 1914, he began graduate work at Harvard. In 1916, he was appointed to an instructorship in Chicago's Department of Political Economy as the last member to be recruited by J. Laurence Laughlin, the Department's Head Professor since its founding. Service with the United States Tariff Commission interrupted his teaching from 1917 to 1919. While in Washington, he worked under the supervision of his Harvard mentor, Frank W. Taussig.

Viner was awarded a Harvard PhD in 1922 with a dissertation on 'Canada's balance of international indebtedness, 1900–1913'. This study received the coveted David A. Wells Prize and soon thereafter appeared in book form (Viner 1924). The analysis Viner offered is still regarded as a classic in the pure theory of international adjustment. Meanwhile he progressed through the ranks at Chicago, achieving a full professorship in 1925. He became a naturalized US citizen in 1924.

Though Viner regarded international trade to be his primary professional specialism, he also made innovative contributions to price theory. In a brief essay entitled 'Price policies: the determination of market price', he set out the conceptual framework for the doctrines of monopolistic (and imperfect) competition that were to be elaborated a decade later by E.H. Chamberlin and Joan Robinson (Viner 1921 [1958]). In 1931, he produced a novel demonstration of the behavior of long-run cost curves which contained a technical error (Viner 1931). When this article was republished, he chose not to correct the mistake, but added a memorable comment. The error on one of the charts, he observed,

> is left uncorrected, so that future teachers and students may share the pleasure of many of their predecessors of pointing out that if I had known what an 'envelope' was I would not have given my excellent draftsman the technically impossible and economically inappropriate assignment of drawing an AC [long-run average cost] curve which would pass through the lowest cost points of all the AC [short-run average cost] curves and yet not rise above any AC curve at any point. (Viner 1950b [1953], p. 227)

Viner's towering scholarly achievement during his Chicago years was the preparation of *Studies in the Theory of International Trade* (Viner 1937). In this volume, he displayed an exhaustive command of the seventeenth- and eighteenth-century literature produced by the mercantilist pamphleteers that formed the backdrop to Adam Smith's formulation of the case for free trade. This volume included learned surveys as well as nineteenth-century British debates over monetary theory and policy, of historic treatments of the specie flow mechanism in balance-of-payments adjustments, and of formulations of the doctrine of comparative costs. This scholarship greatly enriched the theory of international trade and it also established Viner as a historian of economic thought of the first rank. In the judgment of one authority, Viner was 'quite simply the greatest historian of economic thought that ever lived' (Blaug 1985, p. 256).

Viner's scholarly output in the 1930s is all the more remarkable in view of the fact that he committed substantial blocks of time to public service. His interest in policies to cope with the Great Depression was exhibited when he joined a group of economists organized by the Chicago Department in January 1932 who petitioned President Herbert Hoover to call upon the Federal Reserve to mount expansionary open-market operations and to instruct the Treasury to fund an accelerated program of public-works spending as responses to the Great Depression. (He parted company with most of his Chicago colleagues, however, when he declined to endorse the '100 per cent reserves' scheme as a partial answer to the emergency.) In the administrations of President Franklin D. Roosevelt, he was active as an economic adviser, initially to the Treasury Department and subsequently to the State Department.

From 1929 to 1946, Viner's departmental duties at Chicago included co-editorship (with Frank H. Knight) of the *Journal of Political Economy*. And, of course, he carried his share of the teaching load. His courses were regarded as exceptionally demanding and, to the best students at least, they were inspiring. Paul Samuelson, who took Viner's graduate theory course as an undergraduate senior, reports that it was reputed to be the 'best course in economic theory being given in the America of those days' and that he believed that 'it probably deserved that accolade' (Samuelson 1972, p. 6). In his Chicago years, Viner was also active in the profession at large, serving as President of the American Economic Association in 1939.

In 1946, Viner resigned his post at Chicago and accepted a professorship at Princeton where he taught until his retirement in 1960. He reflected on his Chicago years in a letter to Don Patinkin written in the year before his death. Viner then wrote:

> It was not until after I left Chicago in 1946 that I began to hear rumors about a 'Chicago School' which was engaged in organized battle for *laissez-faire* and the 'quantity theory of money' and against 'imperfect competition' theorizing and 'Keynesianism'. I remained skeptical about this until I attended a conference sponsored by University of Chicago professors in 1951. . . . [T]he program for discussion, the selection of chairmen, and everything about the conference except for the unscheduled statements and protests from individual participants were so patently rigidly structured, so loaded, that I got more amusement from the conference than from any other I ever attended. . . . From then on, I was willing to consider the existence of a 'Chicago School' (but one not confined to the Economics Department and not embracing all of the department) and that this 'School' had been in operation, and had won many able disciples, for years before I left Chicago. But at no time was I consciously a member of it, and it is my vague impression that if there was such a school it did not regard me as a member, or at least as a loyal and qualified member. (Viner to Don Patinkin, 24 November 1969, quoted in Patinkin 1969 [1981], p. 266)

Viner's teaching at Princeton consisted of two graduate courses per year: one in the theory of international trade, the other in the history of economic doctrines. While there, he sustained a vigorous publishing program. Books produced in this phase of his career included *The Customs Union Issue* (1950), *International Trade and Economic Development* (1953), *Problems of Monetary Control* (1964) and an introduction to John Rae's *Life of Adam Smith* (Viner 1965). He also wrote a series of articles that were ornaments to the literature of the history of economics (collected in Viner 1991). Two works appeared posthumously, both dealing with historic linkages between religious thought and economic society (Viner 1972, 1978).

Viner's professional stature is well conveyed in the citation accompanying the American Economic Association's award of the Francis A. Walker Medal in 1962. This honor is bestowed only once in every five years to an economist who has made 'a contribution of the highest distinction'. The citation read:

> He represents the greatest combination of theoretical keenness (with no need for fancy techniques), alertness to policy issues, and historical scholarship in both economic institutions and economic ideas. In all the fields to which he has contributed, including his specialty, international economics, his name will survive brightly as a deflator of pretentious nonsense as well as an original creator. (Quoted in Machlup 1972, p. 4)

References

Blaug, M. (1985), *Great Economists since Keynes*, Cambridge: Cambridge University Press.
Machlup, F. (1972), 'What the world thought of Jacob Viner', *Journal of Political Economy*, **80** (1), 1–4.
Patinkin, D. (1969 [1981]), 'The Chicago tradition, the quantity theory, and Friedman', in *Essays on and in the Chicago Tradition*, Durham, NC: Duke University Press, pp. 241–74.
Samuelson, P.A. (1972), 'Jacob Viner, 1892–1970', *Journal of Political Economy*, **80** (1), 5–11.
Viner, J. (1921 [1958]), 'Price policies: the determination of market price', in *The Long View and the Short*, Glencoe, IL: Free Press, pp. 3–7.
Viner, J. (1924), *Canada's Balance of International Indebtedness, 1900–1913: An Inductive Study in the Theory of International Trade*, Cambridge, MA: Harvard University Press.
Viner, J. (1931), 'Cost curves and supply curves', *Zeitschrift für Nationalökonomie*, **3**, 23–46.
Viner, J. (1937), *Studies in the Theory of International Trade*, New York: Harper & Bros.
Viner, J. (1950a), *The Customs Union Issue*, New York: Carnegie Endowment for International Peace.
Viner, J. (1950b [1953]), 'Supplementary note', in *Readings in Price Theory*, Boulding, K.E. and G.J. Stigler (eds), London: George Allen & Unwin, pp. 227–32.
Viner, J. (1953), *International Trade and Economic Development*, Oxford: Clarendon Press.
Viner, J. (1964), *Problems of Monetary Control*, Princeton, NJ: International Finance Section, Department of Economics, Princeton University.
Viner, J. (1965), 'Guide to John Rae's *Life of Adam Smith*', in *Life of Adam Smith*, Rae, J. (ed.), New York: A.M. Kelley, pp. 5–145.
Viner, J. (1972), *The Role of Providence in the Social Order: An Essay in Intellectual History*, Philadelphia, PA: American Philosophical Society.
Viner, J. (1978), *Religious Thought and Economic Society: Four Chapters of an Unfinished Work*, Melitz, J. and D. Winch (eds), Durham, NC: Duke University Press.
Viner, J. (1991), *Essays on the Intellectual History of Economics*, Irwin, D.A. (ed.), Princeton, NJ: Princeton University Press.

Index